The Gospel According to
St. John

The Gospel According to
St. John

Alfred Plummer

BAKER BOOK HOUSE
Grand Rapids, Michigan 49506

Reprinted 1981 by
Baker Book House Company

First published in 1882 as part
of the Cambridge Greek Testament
for Schools and Colleges

ISBN: 0-8010-7068-6

PHOTOLITHOPRINTED BY CUSHING - MALLOY, INC.
ANN ARBOR, MICHIGAN, UNITED STATES OF AMERICA

ON THE GREEK TEXT

In undertaking an edition of the Greek text of the New Testament with English notes for the use of Schools, the Syndics of the Cambridge University Press have not thought it desirable to reprint the text in common use*. To have done this would have been to set aside all the materials that have since been accumulated towards the formation of a correct text, and to disregard the results of textual criticism in its application to MSS., Versions and Fathers. It was felt that a text more in accordance with the present state of our knowledge was desirable. On the other hand the Syndics were unable to adopt one of the more recent critical texts, and they were not disposed to make themselves responsible for the preparation of an

* The form of this text most used in England, and adopted in Dr Scrivener's edition, is that of the third edition of Robert Stephens (1550). The name "Received Text" is popularly given to the Elzevir edition of 1633, which is based on this edition of Stephens, and the name is borrowed from a phrase in the Preface, "Textum ergo habes nunc ab omnibus receptum '

entirely new and independent text: at the same time it would have been obviously impossible to leave it to the judgement of each individual contributor to frame his own text, as this would have been fatal to anything like uniformity or consistency. They believed however that a good text might be constructed by simply taking the consent of the two most recent critical editions, those of Tischendorf and Tregelles, as a basis. The same principle of consent could be applied to places where the two critical editions were at variance, by allowing a determining voice to the text of Stephens where it agreed with either of their readings, and to a third critical text, that of Lachmann, where the text of Stephens differed from both. In this manner readings peculiar to one or other of the two editions would be passed over as not being supported by sufficient critical consent; while readings having the double authority would be treated as possessing an adequate title to confidence.

A few words will suffice to explain the manner in which this design has been carried out.

In the *Acts*, the *Epistles*, and the *Revelation*, wherever the texts of Tischendorf and Tregelles agree, their joint readings are followed without any deviation. Where they differ from each other, but neither of them agrees with the text of Stephens as printed in Dr Scrivener's edition, the consensus of Lachmann with either is taken in preference to the text of Stephens. In all other cases the text of Stephens as represented in Dr Scrivener's edition has been followed.

In the *Gospels*, a single modification of this plan has been rendered necessary by the importance of the Sinai MS. (א), which was discovered too late to be used by Tregelles except in the last chapter of St John's Gospel and in the following books. Accordingly, if a reading which Tregelles has put in his margin agrees with א, it is considered as of the same authority as a reading which he has adopted in his text; and if any words which Tregelles has bracketed are omitted by א, these words are here dealt with as if rejected from his text.

In order to secure uniformity, the spelling and the accentuation of Tischendorf have been adopted where he differs from other Editors. His practice has likewise been followed as regards the insertion or omission of Iota subscript in infinitives (as ζῆν, ἐπιτιμᾶν), and adverbs (as κρυφῆ, λάθρα), and the mode of printing such composite forms as διαπαντός, διατί, τουτέστι, and the like.

The punctuation of Tischendorf in his eighth edition has usually been adopted: where it is departed from, the deviation, together with the reasons that have led to it, will be found mentioned in the Notes. Quotations are indicated by a capital letter at the beginning of the sentence. Where a whole verse is omitted, its omission is noted in the margin (*e.g.* Matt. xvii. 21; xxiii. 12).

The text is printed in paragraphs corresponding to those of the English Edition.

Although it was necessary that the text of all the portions of the New Testament should be uniformly constructed in accordance with these general rules, each editor has been left at perfect liberty to express his preference for other readings in the Notes.

It is hoped that a text formed on these principles will fairly represent the results of modern criticism, and will at least be accepted as preferable to "the Received Text" for use in Schools.

J. J. STEWART PEROWNE

CONTENTS

		PAGES
I.	INTRODUCTION	
	Chapter I The Life of S. John	xi—xx
	Chapter II. The Authenticity of the Gospel...	xx—xxxv
	Chapter III. The Place and Date	xxxv—xxxvii
	Chapter IV. The Object and Plan	xxxvii—xli
	Chapter V. The Characteristics of the Gospel	xli—xlix
	Chapter VI. Its Relation to the Synoptic Gospels	xlix—liii
	Chapter VII. Its Relation to the First Epistle	liv
	Chapter VIII. The Text of the Gospel	lv—lix
	Chapter IX. The Literature of the Gospel......	lix—lx
	Analysis of the Gospel in Detail	lx—lxiv
II.	TEXT AND NOTES	1—357
III.	APPENDICES	359—366
IV.	INDICES...	367—382

INTRODUCTION

CHAPTER I

THE LIFE OF S. JOHN

THE life of S. John falls naturally into two divisions, the limits of which correspond to the two main sources of information respecting him. (1) From his birth to the departure from Jerusalem after the Ascension; the sources for which are contained in N.T. (2) From the departure from Jerusalem to his death; the sources for which are the traditions of the primitive Church. In both cases the notices of S. John are fragmentary, and cannot be woven together into anything like a complete whole without a good deal of conjecture. But the fragments are in the main very harmonious, and contain definite traits and characteristics, enabling us to form a portrait, which though imperfect is unique.

(i) *Before the Departure from Jerusalem*

The date of S. John's birth cannot be determined. He was probably younger than his Master and than the other Apostles. He was the son of Zebedee and Salome, and brother of James, who was probably the older of the two. Zebedee was a fisherman of the lake of Galilee, who seems to have lived in or near Bethsaida (i. 44), and was well enough off to have hired servants (Mark i. 20). He appears only once in the Gospel-narrative (Matt. iv. 21, 22; Mark i. 19, 20), but is mentioned frequently as the father of S. James and S. John. Salome (see on xix. 25) was probably the sister of the Virgin, and in that case S. John was our Lord's first cousin. This relationship harmonizes well with the special intimacy granted to the beloved disciple by his Lord, with the fact of S. James also being among the chosen three, and with the final committal of the Virgin to S. John's care. Salome was one of those women who followed Christ and 'ministered to Him of their substance' (Mark xv. 40; comp. Matt. xxvii. 55; Luke viii. 3). This was probably after Zebedee's death. S. John's parents, therefore, would seem to have been people of means; and it is likely from xix. 27 that the Apostle himself was fairly well off, a conclusion to which his acquaintance with the high-priest (xviii. 15) also points.

S. John, therefore, like all the Apostles, excepting the traitor, was a Galilean; and this fact may be taken as in some degree accounting for that fieriness of temper which earned for him and his brother the name of 'sons of thunder' (Mark iii. 17). The inhabitants of Galilee, while they had remained to a large extent untouched by the culture of the rest of the nation, remained also untouched by the enervation both in belief and habits which culture commonly brings. Ignorant of the glosses of tradition, they kept the old simple faith in the letter of the Law. Uninterested alike in politics and philosophy, they preferred the sword to intrigue, and industry to speculation. Thus, while the hierarchy jealously scrutinise all the circumstances of Jesus' position, the Galileans on the strength of a single miracle would 'take Him by force' (vi. 14, 15) and make Him king. Population was dense and mixed, and between the Syrians and Jews there were often fierce disputes. To this industrious, hardy, and warlike race S. John belonged by birth and residence, sharing its characteristic energy and its impatience of indecision and intrigue. Hence, when the Baptist proclaimed the kingdom of the Messiah, the young fisherman at once became a follower, and pressed steadily onwards until the goal was reached.

Christian art has so familiarised us with a form of almost feminine sweetness as representing the beloved disciple, that the strong energy and even vehemence of his character is almost lost sight of. In his writings as well as in what is recorded of him both in N.T. and elsewhere we find both sides of his character appearing. And indeed though apparently opposed they are not really so; the one may beget the other, and did so in him. The calmness of suppressed emotion leads naturally to passionate utterance, when the fire kindles and at last the tongue speaks.

In yet another way his Galilean origin might influence S. John. The population of the country, as has been said, was mixed. From a boy he would have the opportunity of coming in contact with Greek life and language. Hence that union of Jewish and Greek characteristics which are found in him, and which have led some to the conclusion that the author of the Fourth Gospel was a Greek. We shall find as we go along that the enormous preponderance of Jewish modes of thought and expression, and of Jewish points of view, renders this conclusion absolutely untenable.

The young son of Zebedee was perhaps never at one of the rabbinical schools, which after the fall of Jerusalem made Tiberias a great centre of education, and probably existed in some shape before that. Hence he can be contemptuously spoken of by the hierarchy as an 'illiterate and common' person (Acts iv. 13). No doubt he paid the usual visits to Jerusalem at the proper seasons, and became acquainted with the grand liturgy of the Temple; a worship which while it kindled his deep spiritual emotions and gave him material for reverent meditation, would insensibly prepare the way for that intense hatred of the hierarchy, who had made the worship there worse than a mockery, which breathes through all the pages of his Gospel.

While he was still a lad, and perhaps already learning to admire and love the impetuosity of his older friend S. Peter, the rising of 'Judas of Galilee in the days of the taxing' (see on Acts v. 37) took place. Judas, like our own Wat Tyler, raised a revolt against a tax which he held to be tyrannical, and proclaimed that the people had 'no lord or master but God.' Whether the boy and his future friend sympathized with the movement we have no means of knowing. But the honest though ill-advised cry of the leaders of this revolt may easily have been remembered by S. John when he heard the false and renegade priests declare to Pilate, 'We have no king but Caesar' (xix. 15).

There was another movement of a very different kind, with which we know that he did sympathize heartily. After centuries of dreary silence, in which it seemed as if Jehovah had deserted His chosen people, a thrill went through the land that God had again visited them, and that a Prophet had once more appeared. His was a call, not to resist foreign taxation or to throw off the yoke of Rome, but to withstand their own temptations and to break the heavy bondage of their own crying sins: 'Repent ye, for the Kingdom of Heaven is at hand!' S. John heard and followed, and from the Baptist learnt to know and at once to follow 'the Lamb of God' that was to do what the lambs provided by man in the Temple could never do—'take away the sin of the world.' In the Baptist's teaching, as in that of Christ, S. John gives us a profounder element than that set forth by the Synoptists. They give *repentance* as the substance of his preaching. S. John insists rather on his *heralding the Messiah.* Assuming that the unnamed disciple (i. 40) is S. John, we infer (i. 41) that he proceeded to bring his brother S. James to Jesus as S. Andrew had brought S. Peter. But from 'that day' (i. 39), that never to be forgotten day, the whole tenour of the young man's life was changed. The disciple of the Baptist had become the disciple of Christ.

After remaining with Jesus for a time he seems to have gone back to his old employment; from which he was again called, and possibly more than once (Matt. iv. 18; Luke v. 1—11), to become an Apostle and fisher of men. Then the group of the chosen three is formed. At the raising of Jairus' daughter, at the Transfiguration, and in the Garden of Gethsemane, 'Peter, James, and John' are admitted to nearer relationship with their Lord than the rest; and on one other solemn occasion, when He foretold the destruction of Jerusalem (Mark xiii. 3), S. Andrew also is with them. In this group, although S. Peter takes the lead, it is S. John who is nearest and dearest to the Lord, 'the disciple whom Jesus loved.'

On three different occasions the burning temper of the 'sons of thunder' displayed itself. (1) 'And John answered Him, saying, Master, we saw one casting out devils in Thy name, and he followeth not us: and we forbad him, because he followeth not us' (Mark ix. 38; Luke ix. 49); a touch of zealous intolerance which reminds us of Joshua's zeal against Eldad and Medad (Numb. xi. 28), as Christ's reply recalls the reply of Moses. Probably his brother S. James is included in the '*we* forbad him.' (2) When the Samaritan villagers refused to receive Him, 'because His face was as though He would go to Jerusalem,' His disciples James and John said, 'Lord, wilt Thou that we command fire to come down from heaven and consume them?' (Luke ix. 54). Once again their zeal for their Master makes them forget the spirit of their Master. (3) On the last journey to Jerusalem Salome, as the mouthpiece of her two sons (Matt. xx. 20; Mark x. 35), begs that they may sit, the one on the Messiah's right hand, and the other on His left, in His kingdom. This is their bold ambition, shewing that in spite of their close intimacy with Him, they are still grossly ignorant of the nature of His kingdom. And in their reply to His challenge the same bold temper and burning zeal are manifest. They are willing to go through the furnace in order to be near the Son of God. When S. John and his mother stood beside the Cross, and when S. James won the crown of martyrdom, Christ's challenge was taken up and their aspiration fulfilled.

It will not be necessary to recount at length the history of the last Passover, in which S. John is a prominent figure. As he gives us so much more than the Synoptists about the family at Bethany, we may infer that he was a more intimate friend of Lazarus and His sisters. He and S. Peter prepare the Last Supper (Luke xxii. 8), at which S. Peter prompts him to ask who is the traitor; and after the betrayal S. John gets his friend introduced into the high-priest's palace. He followed his Master to judgment and death, was the one Apostle who dared to stand beside the Cross, and received His Mother as a farewell charge (xviii. 15, xix. 26, 27). His friend's fall does not break their friendship, and they visit the sepulchre together on Easter morning. (On the characteristics of the two as shewn in this incident see notes on xx. 4—6.) We find them still together in Galilee, seeking refreshment in their suspense by resuming their old calling (xxi. 2); and here again their different characters shew themselves (see notes on xxi. 7). S. Peter's thought is ever 'What must *I* do?' S. John's is rather 'What will *He* do?' The one acts; the other watches and waits. S. Peter cries, 'Let us make three tabernacles!' 'Shall we smite with the sword. S. John sees and believes. And the Gospel closes with Christ gentle rebuke to S. Peter's natural curiosity about his friend.

In the Acts S. John appears but seldom, always in connexion with, and always playing a second part to his friend (Acts iii., iv., viii. 14—25). We lose sight of him at Jerusalem (viii. 25) after the return from Samaria; but he was not there at the time of S. Paul's first visit (Gal. i. 18, 19). Some twelve or fifteen years later (c. A.D. 50) he seems to have been at Jerusalem again (Acts xv. 6), but for how long we cannot tell. Nor do we know why he left. Excepting his own notice of himself, as being 'in the island called Patmos for the word and testimony of Jesus' (Rev. i. 9), the N. T. tells us nothing further respecting him.

(ii) *From the Departure from Jerusalem to his Death*

For this period, with the exception of the notice in the Apocalypse just quoted, we are entirely dependent upon traditions of very different value. The conjecture that S. John lived at Jerusalem until the death of the Virgin, and that this set him free, is unsupported by evidence. Some think that she accompanied him to Ephesus. The persecution which followed the martyrdom of S. Stephen would loosen S. John's attachment to Jerusalem. From that time it became less and less the heart of Christendom. It would be during this prolonged residence at Jerusalem that he acquired that minute knowledge of the topography of the city which marks the Fourth Gospel.

It is quite uncertain whether the Apostle went direct from Jerusalem to Ephesus; but of two things we may be confident: (1) that wherever he was he was not idle, (2) that he was not at Ephesus when S. Paul bade farewell to that Church (Acts xx.), nor when he wrote the Epistle to the Ephesians, nor when he wrote the Pastoral Epistles. That S. John did work at Ephesus during the latter part of his life may be accepted as certain, unless the whole history of the subapostolic age is to be pronounced doubtful; but neither the date of his arrival nor of his death can be fixed. He is described (Polycrates in Eus. *H. E.* III. xxxi. 3, V. xxiv. 3) as a priest wearing the sacerdotal plate or mitre (πέταλον) which was a special badge of the high-priest (Exod. xxxix. 30); and we learn from the Apocalypse that from Ephesus as a centre he directed the churches of Asia Minor, which, after the fall of Jerusalem, became the most living portion of Christendom. What persecution drove him to Patmos or caused him to be banished thither is uncertain, as also is the date of his death, which may be placed somewhere near A.D. 100.

Of the traditions which cluster round this latter part of his life three deserve more than a passing mention. (1) John, the disciple of the Lord, going to bathe at Ephesus, and perceiving Cerinthus within, rushed out of the bath-house without bathing, crying out, 'Let us fly, lest even the bath-house fall on us, because Cerinthus, the enemy of the truth, is within' (Iren. III. iii. 4). Epiphanius (*Haer.* XXX. 24) substitutes Ebion for Cerinthus. Both Cerinthus and the Ebionites denied the reality of the Incarnation. This tradition, like the incidents recorded, Luke ix. 49, 54, shews that in later life also the spirit of the 'son of thunder' was still alive within him.

(2) After his return from Patmos he made a tour to appoint bishops or presbyters in the cities. In one place a lad of noble bearing attracted his attention, and he specially commended him to the bishop, who instructed and at last baptized him. Then he took less care of him, and the young man went from bad to worse, and at last became chief of a set of bandits. The Apostle revisiting the place remembered him and said, 'Come, bishop, restore to me my deposit,' which confounded the bishop, who knew that he had received no money from S. John. 'I demand the young man, the soul of a brother;' and then the sad story had to be told. The Apostle called for a horse, and rode at once to the place infested by the bandits and was soon taken by them. When the chief recognised him he turned to

fly. But the aged Apostle went after him and entreated him to stay, and by his loving tears and exhortations induced him to return with him to the church, to which in due time he restored him (Eus. *H.E.* III. xxxiii. from Clement of Alexandria).

(3) Towards the very end of his life, when he was so infirm that he had to be carried to church and was too weak to preach, he used often to say no more than this, 'Little children, love one another.' His hearers at last wearied of this, and said, 'Master, why dost thou always say this?' 'It is the Lord's command,' he replied, 'and if this alone is done, it is enough' (Jerome, *Comm. in Ep. ad Gal.* VI. 10).

Other traditions may be dismissed more briefly; but the first rests on respectable authority: that he was thrown into a cauldron of boiling oil at Rome and was none the worse (Tertullian, *Praescr. Haer.* xxxvi.); that he drank hemlock without being harmed by it; that in his old age he amused himself with a partridge, and pleaded that a bow could not always be bent, but needed relaxation; that after he was buried the earth above him heaved with his breathing, shewing that he was only asleep, tarrying till Christ came. This last strange story S. Augustine is disposed to believe: those who know the place must know whether the soil does move or not; and he has heard it from no untrustworthy people. The belief bears testimony to the unique position held by the last surviving Apostle. Even when he was in his grave Christians refused to believe that they had lost him.

These fragments form a picture, which (as was said at the outset) although very incomplete is harmonious, and so far as it goes distinct. The two sides of his character, tender love and stern intolerance, are the one the complement of the other; and both form part of the intensity of his nature. Intensity of action, intensity of thought and word, intensity of love and hate—these are the characteristics of the beloved disciple. In the best sense of the phrase S. John was 'a good hater,' for his hatred was part of his love. It was because he so loved the truth, that he so hated all lukewarmness, unreality, insincerity, and falsehood, and was so stern towards 'whosoever loveth and maketh a lie.' It is because he so loved his Lord, that he shews such uncompromising abhorrence of the national blindness that rejected Him and the sacerdotal bigotry that hounded Him to death. Intolerance of evil and of opposition to the truth was sometimes expressed in a way that called for rebuke; but this would become less and less so, as his own knowledge of the Lord and of the spirit of the Gospel deepened. With his eagle gaze more and more fixed on the Sun of Righteousness, he became more and more keenly alive to the awful case of those who 'loved the darkness rather than the light, because their works were evil' (iii. 19). With all such men compromise was impossible; and to S. John's character compromises of all kinds were foreign. To others sin may seem weakness; to him it is simply evil. Eternity for him was a thing not of the future but of the present (iii. 36, v. 24, vi. 47, 54); and whereas the world tries to make time the measure of eternity, he knows that eternity is the measure of time. Only from the point of view of eternal life, only from its divine side, can this life, both in its nothingness and in its infinite consequences, be rightly estimated: for 'the world passeth away and the lust thereof, but he that doeth the will of God abideth for ever' (1 John ii. 17).

We thus see how at the end of a long life he was specially fitted to write what has been well called 'the Gospel of Eternity' and 'the Gospel of Love.' It is at the end of life, and when the other side of the grave is in sight, that men can best form an estimate both of this world and of the world to come. If that is true of all men of ordinary seriousness, much more true must it have been of him, who from his youth upwards had been an Apostle, whose head had rested on the Lord's breast, who had stood beside the Cross, had witnessed the Ascension, had cherished till her death the Mother of the Lord, had seen the Jewish dispensation closed and the Holy City overthrown, and to whom the beatific visions of the Apocalypse had been granted. No wonder therefore if his Gospel seems to be raised above this world and to belong to eternity rather than to time. And hence its other aspect of being also 'the Gospel of Love:' for Love is eternal. Faith and Hope are for this world, but can have no place when 'we shall see Him as He is' and 'know even as we are known.' Love is both for time and for eternity.

"They sin who tell us Love can die,
With life all other passions fly,
All others are but vanity.
In heaven ambition cannot dwell,
Nor avarice in the vaults of hell;
Earthly, these passions of the earth
They perish where they had their birth.
But love is indestructible,
Its holy flame for ever burneth,
From heaven it came, to heaven returneth.
Too oft on earth a troubled guest,
At times deceived, at times oppressed,
It here is tried, and purified,
Then hath in heaven its perfect rest:
It soweth here with toil and care,
But the harvest-time of Love is there."

SOUTHEY

CHAPTER II

THE AUTHENTICITY OF THE GOSPEL

The Fourth Gospel is the battle-field of the New Testament, as the Book of Daniel is of the Old: the genuineness of both will probably always remain a matter of controversy. With regard to the Gospel, suspicion respecting it was aroused in some quarters at the outset, but very quickly died out; to rise again, however, with immensely increased force in the eighteenth century, since which time to the present day the question has scarcely ever been allowed to rest. The scope of the present work admits of no more than an outline of the argument being presented.

i. *The External Evidence*

In this section of the argument two objections are made to the Fourth Gospel: (1) the *silence* of the Apostolic Fathers;

(2) its *rejection* by Marcion, the Alogi, and perhaps another sect.

(1) *The silence of the Apostolic Fathers,* if it were a fact, would not be an insuperable difficulty. It is admitted on all sides that the Fourth Gospel was published long after the others, and when they were in possession of the field. There was nothing to lead men to suppose that yet another Gospel would be forthcoming; this alone would make people jealous of its claims. And when, as we shall see, it was found that certain portions of it might be made to assume a Gnostic appearance, jealousy in some quarters became suspicion. The silence, therefore, of the first circle of Christian writers is no more than we might reasonably expect; and when taken in connexion with the universal recognition of the Gospel by the next circle of writers (A.D. 170 onwards), who had far more evidence than has reached us, may be considered as telling for, rather than against the authenticity.

But the silence of the Apostolic Fathers is by no means certain. The EPISTLE OF BARNABAS (c. A.D. 120—130) probably refers to it: Keim is convinced of the fact, although he denies that S. John wrote the Gospel. The shorter Greek form of the IGNATIAN EPISTLES (c. A.D. 150) contains allusions to it, and adaptations of it, which cannot seriously be considered doubtful. Bishop Lightfoot[1] says of the expression ὕδωρ ζῶν (*Rom.* vii.) "Doubtless a reference to John iv. 10, 11, as indeed the whole passage is inspired by the Fourth Gospel," and of the words οἶδεν πόθεν ἔρχεται καὶ ποῦ ὑπάγει (*Philad.* vii.), "The coincidence (with John iii. 8) is quite too strong to be accidental;" and "the Gospel is prior to the passage in Ignatius;" for "the application in the Gospel is natural: the application in Ignatius is strained and secondary." Again, on the words αὐτὸς ὢν θύρα τοῦ πατρός (*Philad.* ix.) he says, "Doubtless an allusion to John x. 9." Comp. ὁ κύριος ἄνευ τοῦ πατρὸς οὐδὲν ἐποίησεν (*Magn.* vii.) with John viii. 28, *Magn.* viii. with John viii. 29, *Trall.* viii.

[1] I am enabled to make these quotations from the great work of his life (unhappily still unfinished and unpublished) through the great kindness of the Bishop of Durham.

with John vi. 51. The Epistle of Polycarp (c. a.d. 150) contains almost certain references to the First Epistle of S. John: and as it is admitted that the First Epistle and the Fourth Gospel are by the same hand, evidence in favour of the one may be used as evidence in favour of the other.

Besides these, Papias (martyred about the same time as Polycarp) certainly knew the First Epistle (Eus. *H. E.* iii. xxxix.). Basilides (c. a.d. 125) seems to have made use of the Fourth Gospel. Justin Martyr (c. a.d. 150) knew the Fourth Gospel. This may now be considered as beyond reasonable doubt. Not only does he exhibit types of language and doctrine closely akin to S. John's (e.g. ὕδωρ ζῶν, λόγος τοῦ θεοῦ, μονογενής, σαρκοποιηθῆναι), but in the *Dialogue with Trypho*, lxxxviii. (c. a.d. 146) he quotes the Baptist's reply, οὐκ εἰμὶ ὁ Χριστὸς ἀλλὰ φωνὴ βοῶντος (comp. John i. 20, 23) and in the *First Apology*, lxi., he paraphrases Christ's words on the new birth (John iii. 3—5). Moreover Justin teaches the great doctrine of S. John's Prologue, that Jesus Christ is the Word. Keim regards it as certain that Justin knew the Fourth Gospel.

When we pass beyond a.d. 170 the evidence becomes full and clear: Tatian, the Epistle to the Churches of Vienne and Lyons, Celsus, the Muratorian Fragment, the Clementine Homilies, Theophilus of Antioch (the earliest writer who mentions S. John by name as the author of the Gospel—c. a.d. 175), Athenagoras, Irenaeus, Clement of Alexandria, and Tertullian. Of these none perhaps is more important than Irenaeus, the pupil of Polycarp, who was the friend of S. John. It never occurs to him to maintain that the Fourth Gospel is the work of S. John; he treats it as a universally acknowledged fact. He not only knows of no time when there were not four Gospels, but with the help of certain quaint arguments he persuades himself that there *must* be four Gospels, neither more nor less (*Haer.* iii. i. 1, xi. 8: comp. v. xxxvi. 2). So firmly established had the Fourth Gospel become considerably before the end of the second century.

(2) The *rejection* of the Fourth Gospel by Marcion and some obscure sects is of no serious importance. There is no evidence to shew that the Gospel was rejected on critical grounds; rather because the doctrines which it contained were disliked. This is almost certain in the case of Marcion, and probable enough in the other cases.

Whether the obscure sect mentioned by Irenaeus (*Haer.* III. xi. 9) as rejecting the Fourth Gospel and the promises of the Paraclete which it contains are the same as those whom Epiphanius with a contemptuous *double entendre* calls Ἄλογοι ('devoid of [the doctrine of] the Logos' or 'devoid of reason'), is uncertain. But we can easily understand how a party might arise, who in perfectly good faith and with good but mistaken motives might reject the Fourth Gospel both for the doctrine of the Logos and for other peculiarities which *seemed* to favour the Gnosticism of Cerinthus. None of the Synoptists, none of the Apostles, had thus far used the term Λόγος; and the fact that Cerinthus made use of it must have made its prominence in the Prologue to the Fourth Gospel doubly suspicious. Cerinthus maintained that Jesus was a mere man on whom the Logos or Christ descended in the form of a dove at his baptism: and the Fourth Gospel says nothing about the miraculous conception of Christ, or about the wonders that attended and attested His birth, but begins with the Baptism and the descent of the Spirit. The Evangelist pointedly remarks that the miracle at Cana was the first miracle: perhaps this was to insinuate that previous to the Baptism Jesus (being a mere man) *could* do no miracle. This Gospel omits the Transfiguration, an incident from which a participation of His Human Body in the glory of the Godhead might be inferred. The 'prince' or 'ruler of this world,' an expression not used previously by any Evangelist or Apostle, might possibly be understood to mean the *Demiurgus* of the Cerinthian system, the Creator of the world, and the God of the Jews, but inferior to and ignorant of the Supreme God. Again, the Fourth Gospel is silent about the wonders which attended Christ's death; and this also harmonizes with the system of Cerinthus, who taught that the Logos or Christ departed when

Jesus was arrested, and that a mere man suffered on the Cross; for what meaning would there be in the sympathy of nature with the death of a mere man[1]? All this tends to shew that if the Fourth Gospel was rejected in certain quarters for a time, this tells little or nothing against its genuineness. Indeed it may fairly be said to tell the other way; for it shews that the universal recognition of the Gospel, which we find existing from A.D. 170 onwards, was no mere blind enthusiasm, but a victory of truth over baseless though not unnatural suspicion. Moreover, the fact that these over-wary Christians assigned the Gospel to Cerinthus is evidence that the Gospel was in their opinion written by a contemporary of S. John. To concede this is to concede the whole question.

ii. *The Internal Evidence*

We have seen already that there are some features of this Gospel which would seem to harmonize with a Gnostic system, and that it need not surprise us if some persons in the second century hastily concluded that it savoured of Cerinthus. It is more surprising that modern critics, after a minute study of the Gospel, should think it possible to assign it to a Greek Gnostic of the second century. To say nothing of the general tone of the Gospel, there are two texts which may almost be said to sum up the theology of the Evangelist and which no Gnostic would even have tolerated, much less have written: 'The Word became flesh' (i. 14); 'Salvation is of the Jews' (iv. 22). That the Infinite should limit itself and become finite, that the ineffable purity of the Godhead should be united with impure matter, was to a Gnostic a monstrous supposition; and this was what was implied in the Word becoming flesh. Again, that the longed-for salvation of mankind should come from the Jews was a flat contradiction of one of the main principles of Gnosticism, viz. that man's perfection is to be looked for in the attainment of a higher knowledge of God and the universe, to which the Jew as such had no special claim; on the contrary (as some Gnostics

[1] See Döllinger's *Hippolytus and Callistus*, Chap. v.

held), the Jews had all along mistaken an inferior being for the Supreme God. While much is promised in the Fourth Gospel to faith in Jesus Christ and union with Him, no rewards are offered to knowledge. On the contrary, knowledge is the fruit of loving obedience (vii. 17). Other passages in the Gospel which are strongly adverse to the theory of a Gnostic authorship will be pointed out in the notes (see on iii. 14, vi. 21, x. 35, xix. 35, xx. 31). And here the Gnostics themselves are our witnesses, and that in the second century. Although the Fourth Gospel was frequently used against them, they never denied its genuineness. They tried to explain away what told against them, but they never attempted to question the Apostolic authority of the Gospel.

But the Gospel not only contains both direct and indirect evidence which contradicts this particular hypothesis; it also supplies both direct and indirect evidence of the true hypothesis.

(1) There is *direct evidence* that the author was an *eye-witness* of what he relates. In two places (according to far the most reasonable, if not the only reasonable interpretation of the words) the Evangelist claims for himself the authority of an eyewitness: in a third he either claims it for himself or others claim it for him. 'We beheld His glory' (i. 14), especially when taken in conjunction with 'which we beheld and our hands handled' (1 John i. 1), cannot well mean anything else. Scarcely less doubtful is 'He that hath seen hath borne witness, and his witness is true, &c.' (xix. 35). 'This is the disciple who witnesseth concerning these things, and who wrote these things; and we know that his witness is true' (xxi. 24), even if it be the addition of another hand, is direct testimony to the fact that the Evangelist gives us not second-hand information, but what he himself has heard and seen. (See notes in all three places.)

Of course it would be easy for a forger to make such a claim; and accomplices or dupes might support him. But it would also be easy in so wide a field of narrative to test the validity of the claim, and this we will proceed to do by examining the *indirect* evidence. First, however, it will be well to state the enormous difficulties which would confront a writer who proposed in the second century to forge a Gospel.

The condition of Palestine during the life of Jesus Christ was unique. The three great civilisations of the world were intermingled there; Rome, the representative of law and conquest; Greece, the representative of philosophical speculation and commerce; Judaism, the representative of religion. The relations of these three elements to one another were both intricate and varied. In some particulars there was a combination between two or more of them; as in the mode of conducting the census (Luke ii. 3) and of celebrating the Passover (see on xiii. 23); in others there was the sharpest opposition, as in very many ceremonial observances. Moreover, of these three factors it was exceedingly difficult for the two that were Gentile to comprehend the third. The Jew always remained an enigma to his neighbours, especially to those from the West. This was owing partly to proud reserve on his part and contempt on theirs, partly to the inability of each side to express itself in terms that would be intelligible to the other, so utterly different were and still are Eastern and Western modes of thought. Again, if a Greek or Roman of the first century had taken the pains to study Jewish literature with a view to becoming thoroughly acquainted with this strange people, his knowledge of them would still have remained both defective and misleading, so much had been added or changed by tradition and custom. To a Gentile of the *second* century this difficulty would be very greatly increased; for Jerusalem had been destroyed and the Jewish nation had been once more scattered abroad on the face of the earth. With the destruction of the Temple the keeping of the Mosaic Law had become a physical impossibility; and the Jews who had lost their language in the Captivity had now to a large extent lost the ceremonial law. Even a Jew of the second century might easily be mistaken as to the usages of his nation in the early part of the first. How much more, then, would a Gentile be likely to go astray! We may say, therefore, that the intricate combination of Jewish and Gentile elements in Palestine between A.D. 1 and A.D. 50 was such that no one but a Jew living in the country at the time would be able to master them; and that the almost total destruction of the Jewish element in the latter part of the century would render a proper appreciation of the circumstances a matter of the utmost difficulty even to a careful antiquarian. Finally, we must remember that antiquarian research in those days was almost unknown; and that to undertake it in order to give an accurate setting to a historical fiction was an idea that was not born until long after the second century. We may safely say that no Greek of that age would ever have dreamed of going through the course of archæological study necessary for attempting the Fourth Gospel; and even if he had, the attempt would still have been a manifest failure. He would have fallen into far more numerous and far more serious errors than those which critics (with what success we shall see hereafter) have tried to bring home to the Fourth Evangelist (see on xi. 49).

(2) There is abundant *indirect evidence* to shew that the writer of the Fourth Gospel was a Jew, and a Jew of Palestine, who was an eyewitness of most of the events which he relates. If this can be made out with something like certainty, the circle of possible authors will be very much reduced. But in this circle of possible authors we are not left to conjecture. There is further evidence to shew that he was an Apostle, and the Apostle S. John. (See Sanday, *Authorship of the Fourth Gospel*, Chap. xix.)

The Evangelist was a Jew

He is perfectly at home in **Jewish opinions and points of view.** Conspicuous among these are *the ideas respecting the Messiah* current at the time (i. 19—28, 45—49, 51; iv. 25; vi. 14, 15; vii. 26, 27, 31, 40—42, 52; xii. 13, 34; xix. 15, 21). Besides these we have the *hostility between Jews and Samaritans* (iv. 9, 20, 22; viii. 48); estimate of *women* (iv. 27), of the *national schools* (vii. 15), of the *uneducated* (vii. 49), of the '*Dispersion*' (vii. 35), of *Abraham and the Prophets* (viii. 52, 53), &c. &c.

He is quite familiar also with **Jewish usages and observances.** Among these we may notice *baptism* (i. 25, iii. 22, 23, iv. 2), *purification* (ii. 6, iii. 25, xi. 55, xviii. 28, xix. 31), the Jewish

Feasts, especially the *F. of Dedication* which is mentioned neither in O.T. nor in the Synoptics (ii. 13, 23, v. 1, vi. 4, vii. 2, 37, x. 22, xiii. 1, xviii. 28, xix. 31, 42), *circumcision* and the *Sabbath* (vii. 22, 23), law of *evidence* (viii. 17, 18), *embalming* (xix. 40).

The **form of the Gospel**, especially the style of the narrative, is **essentially Jewish.** The language is Greek, but the arrangement of the thoughts, to some extent the structure of the sentences, and a great deal of the vocabulary are Hebrew. And the source of this Hebrew form is the O.T. This is shewn not only by frequent quotations but by the imagery employed;—the lamb, the brazen serpent, the living water, the manna, the shepherd, the vine, &c. And not only so, but the Christian theology of the Evangelist is based upon the theology of the O T. 'Salvation is of the Jews' (iv. 22); Moses wrote of Christ (v. 46; i. 45); Abraham saw His day (viii. 56); He was typified in the brazen serpent (iii. 14), the manna (vi. 32), the paschal lamb (xix. 36); perhaps also in the water from the rock (vii. 37) and the pillar of fire (viii. 12). Much that He did was done 'that the Scripture might be fulfilled' (xiii. 18, xvii. 12, xix. 24, 28, 36, 37; comp. ii. 22, xx. 9): and these fulfilments of Scripture are noticed not as interesting coincidences, but 'that ye may believe' (xix. 35). Judaism is the foundation of the Christian faith. No one but a Jew could have handled the O.T. Scriptures in this way.

The Evangelist was a Jew of Palestine

This is shewn chiefly by his **topographical knowledge**, which he uses both with ease and precision. In mentioning a fresh place he commonly throws in some fact respecting it, adding clearness or interest to the narrative. A forger would avoid such gratuitous statements, as being unnecessary and likely by being wrong to lead to detection. Thus, one *Bethany* is 'nigh unto Jerusalem, about fifteen furlongs off' (xi. 18), the other is 'beyond Jordan,' (i. 28); *Bethsaida* is 'the city of Andrew and Peter' (i. 44); 'Can any good thing come out of *Nazareth*' (i. 46); *Cana* is 'of Galilee' (ii. 1, xxi. 2), and one 'goes *down*' from Cana to Capernaum (iv. 47); *Aenon* is 'near to Salim,' and there are 'many waters' there (iii. 23); *Sychar* is 'a city of Samaria, near to the parcel of ground that Jacob gave to his son Joseph. Now Jacob's well was there' (iv. 5); *Ephraim* is a city 'near to the wilderness' (xi. 54). Comp. the minute local knowledge implied in vi. 22—24, iv. 11, 12, 20, ii. 12.

This familiarity with topography is the more remarkable in the case of Jerusalem, which (as all are agreed) was destroyed before the Fourth Gospel was written. He knows of the traffic in the Temple and of what it consisted (ii. 6); *Bethesda* is 'a pool by the sheep-gate, having five porches' (v. 2); *Siloam* is 'a pool, which is by interpretation Sent' (ix. 7); *Solomon's porch* is 'in the Temple' (x. 23). Comp. the minute knowledge of the city and suburbs implied in viii. 20, xi. 18, xviii. 1, 28, xix. 13, 17—20, 41, 42.

The way in which the author quotes the O. T. points to the same conclusion. He is not dependent on the LXX. for his knowledge of the Scriptures, as a Greek-speaking Jew born out of Palestine would very likely have been: he appears to know the original Hebrew, which had become a dead language, and was not much studied outside Palestine. Out of fourteen quotations three agree with the Hebrew against the LXX. (vi. 45, xiii. 18, xix. 37); not one agrees with the LXX. against the Hebrew. The majority are neutral, either agreeing with both, or differing from both, or being free adaptations rather than citations. (See also on xii. 13, 15.)

The Evangelist's **doctrine of the Logos** or Word confirms us in the belief that he is a Jew of Palestine. The form which this doctrine assumes in the Prologue is Palestinian rather than Alexandrian. (See note on 'the Word,' i. 1.)

The Evangelist was an Eyewitness of most of the events which he relates

The narrative is crowded with figures, which are no mere nonentities to fill up space, but which live and move. Where they appear on the scene more than once, their action throughout is harmonious, and their characteristics are indicated with a simplicity and distinctness which would be the most consummate art if it were not taken from real life. And where in the literature of the second century can we find such skilful delineation of fictitious characters as is shewn in the portraits given to us of the Baptist, the beloved disciple, Peter, Andrew, Philip, Thomas, Judas Iscariot, Pilate, Nicodemus, Martha and Mary, the Samaritan woman, the man born blind? Even the less prominent persons are thoroughly lifelike and real; Nathanael, Judas not Iscariot, Caiaphas, Annas, Mary Magdalene, Joseph.

Exact notes of time are frequent; not only *seasons*, as the Jewish Feasts noticed above, but *days* (i. 29, 35, 43, ii. 1, iv. 40, 43, vi. 22, vii. 14, 37, xi. 6, 17, 39, xii. 1, 12, xix. 31, xx. 1, 26) and *hours* (i. 39, iv. 6, 52, xix. 14; comp. iii. 2, vi. 16, xiii. 30, xviii. 28, xx. 1, 19, xxi. 4).

The Evangelist sometimes knows the exact or approximate number of persons (i. 35, iv. 18, vi. 10, xix. 23) and objects (ii. 6, vi. 9, 19, xix. 39, xxi. 8, 11) mentioned in his narrative.

Throughout the Gospel we have examples of graphic and vivid description, which would be astounding if they were not the result of personal observation. Strong instances of this would be the accounts of the cleansing of the Temple (ii. 14—16), the feeding of the 5000 (vi. 5—14), the healing of the man born blind (ix. 6, 7), the feet-washing (xiii. 4, 5, 12), the betrayal (xviii. 1—13), almost all the details of the Passion (xviii., xix.), the visit to the sepulchre (xx. 3—8).

To this it must be added that the state of the text of the Gospel, as we find it quoted by early writers. shews that before the end of the second century there were already a great many variations of readings in existence. Such things take time to arise and multiply. This consideration compels us to believe that the original document must have been made at a time when eyewitnesses of the Gospel history were still living. See notes on i. 13, 18, vii. 8 and ix. 35.

The Evangelist was an Apostle

He knows the thoughts of the disciples on certain occasions, thoughts which sometimes surprise us, and *which no writer of fiction would have attributed to them* (ii. 11, 17, 22, iv. 27, vi. 19, 60, xii. 16, xiii. 22, 28, xx. 9, xxi. 12). He knows also words that were spoken by the disciples in private to Christ or among themselves (iv. 31, 33, ix. 2, xi. 8, 12, 16, xvi. 17, 29). He is familiar with the haunts of the disciples (xi. 54, xviii. 2, xx. 19). Above all, he is one who was very intimate with the Lord; for he knows His motives (ii. 24, 25, iv. 1—3, v. 6, vi. 6, 15, vii. 1, xiii. 1, 3, 11, xvi. 19, xviii. 4, xix. 28) and can bear witness to His feelings (xi. 33, 38, xiii. 21).

The Evangelist was the Apostle S. John

The contents of the two previous sections are almost sufficient to prove this last point. We know from the Synoptists that three disciples were specially intimate with Jesus, Peter, James, and his brother John. S. Peter cannot be our Evangelist: he was put to death long before the very earliest date to which the Fourth Gospel can be assigned. Moreover the style of the Gospel is quite unlike the undoubted First Epistle of S. Peter. Still less can S. James be the author, for he was martyred long before S. Peter. Only S. John remains, and he not only entirely fits in with the details already noticed, but also having long outlived the rest of the Apostles he is the one person who could have written a Gospel considerably later in date than the other three.

But we have not yet exhausted the evidence. The concluding note (xxi. 24) declares that the Gospel was written by 'the disciple whom Jesus loved' (ἠγάπα, xxi. 20). This disciple is mentioned in three other places under the same title (xiii. 23, xix. 26, xxi. 7;—xx. 2 is different). He is some one who is intimate with S. Peter (xiii. 24, xxi. 7; comp. xviii. 15, xx. 2), and this we already know from the Synoptists that S. John was, and we learn from the Acts that he remained so (iii. 1, 3, 11, iv. 13, 19, viii. 14). He is one of those enumerated in xxi. 1, and unless he is one of the two unnamed disciples he must be S. John.

One more point, a small one, but of very great significance, remains. The Fourth Evangelist carefully distinguishes places and persons. He distinguishes Cana 'of Galilee' (ii. 1, xxi. 2) from Cana of Asher; Bethany 'beyond Jordan' (i. 28) from Bethany 'nigh unto Jerusalem' (xi. 18); Bethsaida, 'the city of Andrew and Peter' (i. 44), from Bethsaida Julias. He distinguishes also Simon Peter after his call from others named Simon by *invariably* adding the new name Peter, whereas the Synoptists often call him simply Simon. The traitor Judas is distinguished as the 'son of Simon' (vi. 71, xii. 4, xiii. 2, 26) from the other Judas, who is expressly said to be 'not Iscariot' (xiv. 22), while the Synoptists take no notice of the traitor's parentage. S. Thomas is thrice for the sake of additional clearness pointed out as the same who was called Didymus (xi. 16, xx. 24, xxi. 2), a name not given by the Synoptists. Comp. the careful identification of Nicodemus (xix. 39) and of Caiaphas (xi. 49, xviii. 13). And yet the Fourth Evangelist altogether neglects to make a distinction which the Synoptists do make. They distinguish John the son of Zebedee from his namesake by frequently calling the latter 'the Baptist' (more than a dozen times in all). The Fourth Evangelist never does so; to him the Baptist is simply 'John.' He himself being the other John, there is for him no chance of confusion, and it does not occur to him to mark the distinction.

iii. *Answers to objections*

We are now on too firm ground to be shaken by isolated difficulties. It would take a great many difficulties of detail to counterbalance the difficulty of believing that the Fourth Gospel was written by some one who was neither an Apostle nor even a contemporary. But there are certain difficulties supposed to be involved in the theory that the Evangelist is S. John the Apostle, some of which are important and deserve a separate answer. They are mainly these;—

(1) The marked dissimilarity between the Fourth Gospel and the three others.

(2) The marked dissimilarity between the Fourth Gospel and the Revelation.

(3) The difficulty of believing that S. John (*a*) would have "studiously elevated himself in every way above the Apostle Peter;" (*b*) would have magnified himself above all as 'the disciple whom Jesus loved.'

(4) The use made by S. Polycarp of S. John's authority in the Paschal controversy.

(1) The answer to the first of these objections will be found below in Chapter VI. of the *Introduction*, and in the introductory note to Chapter iii. of the Gospel.

(2) The answer to the second belongs rather to the Introduction to the Apocalypse. The answer to it is to a large extent a further answer to the first objection; for "the Apocalypse is doctrinally the uniting link between the Synoptists and the Fourth Gospel" (Westcott). The Gospel is a summary of Christian Theology; the Apocalypse is a summary of Christian Politics. The one exhibits the ideal life in God in the perfect Man, the other exhibits it in the perfect community. Great as are the differences between the two, the leading ideas of both are the same. The one gives us in a magnificent vision, the other in a great historic drama, the supreme conflict between good and evil and its issue. In both Jesus Christ is the central figure, whose victory through defeat is the issue of the conflict. In both the Jewish dispensation is the preparation for the Gospel, and the warfare and triumph of the Christ is described in language saturated with the O. T. Some remarkable similarities of detail will be pointed out in the notes (see on i. 14; iv. 6; vii. 30; xi. 44; xiii. 8; xv. 20; xix. 13, 17, 20, 37). Difference of date will go a long way towards explaining the great difference of style. And there are good reasons for believing that the Apocalypse was written early in S. John's life, before he had mastered the Greek language, and the Gospel and Epistle late in his life, after he had done so.

(3 *a*) The question, 'How could S. John have studiously elevated himself in every way above the Apostle Peter?' reminds

us of the famous question of Charles II. to the Royal Society. The answer to it is that S. John does nothing of the kind. In his whole narrative he speaks only thrice, and then very briefly; 'Rabbi, where abidest Thou?' (i. 38); 'Lord, who is it?' (xiii. 25); 'It is the Lord!' (xxi. 7). S. Peter takes the lead in the Fourth Gospel as in the other three. His introduction to Christ and significant naming stand at the very opening of the Gospel (i. 41, 42); he answers in the name of the Twelve (vi. 68); he is prominent if not first at the feet-washing (xiii. 6); he directs S. John to find out who is the traitor (xiii. 24); he takes the lead in defending his Master at the betrayal (xviii. 10); the news of the Resurrection is brought to him first (xx. 2); his companion does not venture to enter the sepulchre until he has done so (xx. 6—8); he is mentioned first in the list of disciples given xxi. 2, and there takes the lead (xxi. 3); he continues to take the lead when Jesus appears to them (xxi. 7, 11); he receives the last great charge, with which the Gospel concludes (xxi. 15—22).

(*b*) To suppose that the phrase 'the disciple whom Jesus loved' implies self-glorification at the expense of others is altogether to misunderstand it. It is not impossible that the designation was given to him by others before he used it of himself. At any rate the affection of the Lord for him was so well known that such a title would be well suited for an oblique indication of the author's personality. Besides thus gently placing us behind the scenes the phrase serves two purposes: (1) it is a permanent expression of gratitude on the part of the Evangelist for the transcendent benefit bestowed upon him; (2) it is a modest explanation of the prominent part which he was called upon to play on certain occasions. Why was he singled out (xiii. 23) to be told who was the traitor? Why was the care of the Lord's Mother (xix. 26) entrusted to him? Why was he allowed to recognise the Lord at the sea of Tiberias (xxi. 7) before any of the rest did so? The recipient of these honours has only one explanation to give: Jesus loved him.

(4) In the controversy as to the right time of keeping Easter S. Polycarp defended the Asiatic custom of keeping the

Christian Passover at the same time as the Jewish Passover, viz. the evening of the 14th Nisan, "because he had always (so) observed it *with John the disciple of our Lord*, and the rest of the Apostles, with whom he associated" (Eus. *H. E.* v. xxiv. 16). On this ground he refused to yield to Anicetus, Bishop of Rome, though he did not require Anicetus to give way to him. But, as we shall see (Appendix A), the Fourth Gospel clearly represents the Crucifixion as taking place on the 14th Nisan, and the Last Supper as taking place the evening before. Therefore, either Polycarp falsely appeals to S. John's authority (which is most improbable), or the Fourth Gospel is not by S. John. But this objection confuses two things, the Christian Passover or Easter, and the Last Supper or institution of the Eucharist. The latter point was not in dispute at all. The question debated was whether the Christian Churches in fixing the time of Easter were to follow the Jewish Calendar exactly or a Christian modification of it. S. Polycarp claimed S. John as sanctioning the former plan, and nothing in the Fourth Gospel is inconsistent with such a view. Schürer, who denies the authenticity of the Gospel, has shewn that no argument against the authenticity can be drawn from the Paschal controversy.

CHAPTER III

THE PLACE AND DATE

Tradition is unanimous in giving Ephesus as the place where S. John resided during the latter part of his life, and where the Fourth Gospel was written. There is no sufficient reason for doubting this strong testimony, which may be accepted as practically certain.

There is also strong evidence to shew that the Gospel was written at the request of the elders and disciples of the Christian Churches of Asia. We have this on the early and independent authority of the Muratorian Fragment (c. A.D. 170) and of Clement of Alexandria (c. A.D. 190); and it is confirmed by Jerome. No doubt S. John had often delivered the contents of his Gospel orally; and the elders wished before he died to preserve it in a permanent form. Moreover, difficulties had arisen in the Church which called for a recasting of Apostolic doctrine. The destruction of Jerusalem had given altogether a new turn to Christianity: it had severed the lingering and hampering connexion with Judaism; it had involved a readjustment of the interpretations of Christ's promises about His return. Again, the rise of a Christian philosophy, shading off by strange compromises and foreign colouring into mere pagan speculation, called for a fresh statement, in terms adequate to the emergency, and by a voice sufficient in authority, of Christian truth. There is both external and internal evidence to shew that a crisis of this kind was the occasion of the Fourth Gospel.

The precise date cannot be determined with certainty. There are indications in the Gospel itself that it was written late in the author's life-time. In his narrative he seems to be looking back after a long lapse of time (vii. 39, xxi. 19). And as we study it, we feel that it is the result of a larger experience of God's Providence and of a wider comprehension of the meaning of His Kingdom than was possible at the time when the other Evangelists, especially the first two of them, wrote their Gospels. As compared with them, it exhibits a marked development of doctrine. All this induces us to place the date of the Fourth Gospel as late as possible; and tradition (as we have seen pp. xvii, xviii) represents S. John as living to extreme old age. S. John would not begin to teach at Ephesus until some time after S. Paul left it, i.e. not much before A.D. 70. If Irenaeus is right in saying that S. Luke's Gospel was not written till after the death of S. Peter and S. Paul (*Haer.* III. i. 1), this would again place the writing of the Fourth Gospel considerably later than A.D. 70. It is not improbable that the first twenty chapters were written a considerable time before the Gospel was published, that the last chapter was added some years later, and then the whole given to the Church (see introductory note to chap. xxi.). S. John may have lived almost if not quite to the end of the century;

therefore from A.D. 80 to 95 would seem to be the period within which it is probable that the Gospel was published.

Those who deny that S. John is the author have tried almost every date from A.D. 110 to 165. Dividing this period into two, we have this dilemma:—If the Gospel was published between 110 and 140, why did not the *hundreds* of Christians, who had known S. John during his later years, denounce it as a forgery? If it was not published till between 140 and 165, how did it become universally accepted by 170?

CHAPTER IV

THE OBJECT AND PLAN

i *The Object*

These two subjects, the object and the plan, naturally go together, for the one to a large extent determines the other: the purpose with which the Evangelist wrote his Gospel greatly influences the form which it assumes. What that purpose was he tells us plainly himself: 'These have been written *that ye may believe that Jesus is the Christ, the Son of God, and that believing ye may have life in His name*' (xx. 31). His object is not to write the life of Christ; if it were, we might wonder that out of his immense stores of personal knowledge he has not given us a great deal more than he has done. Rather, out of these abundant stores he has made a careful and self-denying selection with a view to producing a particular effect upon his readers, and by means of that effect to open to them an inestimable benefit. In this way his object manifestly influences his plan. He might have given himself the delight of pouring forth streams of information, which he alone possessed, to a community ardently thirsting for it. But such prodigality would have obscured rather than strengthened his argument: he therefore rigidly limits himself in order to produce the desired effect. His narrative, most fragmentary as a biography, is complete as a Gospel.

The effect is twofold: (1) to create a belief that Jesus is the Christ; (2) to create a belief that Jesus is the Son of God. The first truth is primarily for the Jew; the second is primarily for the Gentile; then both are for all united. The first truth leads the Jew to become a Christian; the second raises the Gentile above the barriers of Jewish exclusiveness; the two together bring eternal life to both.

To the Jews the Evangelist would prove that Jesus, the Man who had been known to them personally or historically by that name, is the Christ, the Messiah for whom they had been looking, in whom all types and prophecies have been fulfilled, to whom therefore the fullest allegiance is due. To the Gentiles the Evangelist would prove that this same Jesus, of whom they also have heard, is the Son of God, the Only God, theirs as well as His, the Universal Father, their Father as well as His; whose Son's mission, therefore, must be coextensive with His Father's family and kingdom. Long before the promise was made to Abraham 'all things came into being through Him' (i. 3): if therefore the Jews had a claim on the Christ, the Gentiles had a still older claim on the Son of God.

These two great truths, that Jesus is the Christ, and that Jesus is the Son of God, being recognised and believed, the blessed result follows that believers have life in His name, i.e. in Him as revealed to them in the character which His name implies. There is neither Gentile nor Jew, circumcision nor uncircumcision, barbarian, Scythian, bond nor free; but Christ is all and in all; all are one in Christ Jesus (Col. iii. 11; Gal. iii. 28).

There is no need to look for any additional object over and above that which the Evangelist himself states; although this is frequently done. Thus from the time of Irenaeus (*Haer.* III. xi.) it has been common to say that S. John wrote his Gospel against Cerinthus and other heretics. By clearly teaching the main truths of the Gospel S. John necessarily refutes errors; and it is possible that here and there some particular form of error was in his mind when he wrote: but the refutation of error is not his object in writing. If his Gospel is not a life of Christ, still less is it a polemical treatise.

Again, from the time of Eusebius (*H. E.* III. xxiv. 11) and earlier it has been maintained that S. John wrote to supplement the Synoptists, recording what had not been recorded by them. No doubt he does supplement them to a large extent, especially as regards the ministry in Judaea: but it does not follow from this that he wrote in order to supplement them. Where something not recorded by them would suit his purpose equally well he would naturally prefer it; but he has no hesitation in retelling what has already been told by one, two, or even all three of them, if he requires it for the object which he has in view (see introductory note to chap. vi.).

ii. *The Plan*

In no Gospel is the plan so manifest as in the Fourth. Perhaps we may say of the others that they scarcely have a plan. We may divide and subdivide them for our own convenience; but there is no clear evidence that the three Evangelists had any definite scheme before them in putting together the fragments of Gospel history which they have preserved for us. It is quite otherwise with the Fourth Evangelist. The different scenes from the life of Jesus Christ which he puts before us, are not only carefully selected but carefully arranged, leading up step by step to the conclusion expressed in the confession of S. Thomas, 'My Lord and my God.' But if there is a development of faith and love on the one side in those who accept and follow Jesus, so also there is a development of unbelief and hatred on the other in those who reject and persecute Him. 'The Word became flesh;' but, inasmuch as He was not generally recognised and welcomed, His presence in the world necessarily involved a separation and a conflict; a separation of light from darkness, truth from falsehood, good from evil, life from death, and a conflict between the two. It is the critical episodes in that conflict round the person of the Incarnate Word that the Evangelist places before us one by one.

These various episodes taken one by one go far to shew,—taken altogether and combined with the issue of the conflict irrefragably prove,—'that Jesus is the Christ, the Son of God.'

The main outlines of the plan are these:—

I. THE PROLOGUE OR INTRODUCTION (i. 1—18).

1. The Word in His own Nature (i. 1—5).
2. His revelation to men and rejection by them (i. 6—13).
3. His revelation of the Father (i. 14—18).

II. FIRST MAIN DIVISION. CHRIST'S MINISTRY, OR HIS REVELATION OF HIMSELF TO THE WORLD (i. 19—xii. 50).

a. **The Testimony** (i. 19—51)

1. of John the Baptist (i. 19—37),
2. of the disciples (i. 38—51),
3. of the first sign (ii. 1—11).

b. **The Work** (ii. 13—xi. 57)

1. among Jews (ii. 13—iii. 36),
2. among Samaritans (iv. 1—42),
3. among Galileans (iv. 43—54),

(*The work has become a Conflict*) 4. among mixed multitudes (v.—xi.).

c. **The Judgment** (xii.)

1. of men (1—36),
2. of the Evangelist (37—43),
3. of Christ (44—50).

Close of Christ's public ministry.

III. SECOND MAIN DIVISION. THE ISSUES OF CHRIST'S MINISTRY, OR HIS REVELATION OF HIMSELF TO HIS DISCIPLES (xiii.—xx.).

d. **The inner Glorification of Christ in His last Discourses** (xiii.—xvii.).

1. His love in humiliation (xiii. 1—30).
2. His love in keeping His own (xiii. 31—xv. 27).
3. The promise of the Comforter and of His return (xvi.).
4. The prayer of the High-Priest (xvii.).

e. **The outer Glorification of Christ in His Passion** (xviii., xix.).

1. The betrayal (xviii. 1—11).
2. The ecclesiastical trial (xviii. 12—27).
3. The civil trial (xviii. 28—xix. 16).
4. The crucifixion and burial (xix. 17—42).

f. **The Resurrection** (xx.).

1. The manifestation to Mary Magdalene (1—18).
2. The manifestation to the ten (19—23).
3. The manifestation to S. Thomas with the ten (24—29).
4. The conclusion (30, 31).

IV. The Epilogue or Appendix (xxi.).

It is worth noting that, unlike the Synoptists, S. John begins and ends his narrative with *personal* experiences; the first great crisis in his life, when from the Baptist he passed to the Christ, and the second, when 'he saw and believed;' or, if we include the Appendix, when he received the commission to wait for his Lord.

CHAPTER V

THE CHARACTERISTICS OF THE GOSPEL

Here again, only a few leading points can be noticed: the subject is capable of almost indefinite expansion.

1. From the time of Clement of Alexandria (c. A.D. 190) this Gospel has been distinguished as a 'SPIRITUAL GOSPEL' (Eus. *H. E.* VI. xiv. 7). The Synoptists give us mainly the external acts of Jesus Christ: S. John lays before us glimpses of the inner life and spirit of the Son of God. Their narrative is chiefly composed of His manifold and ceaseless dealings with men: in S. John we have rather his tranquil and unbroken union with His Father. The heavenly element which forms

the background of the first three Gospels is the atmosphere of the Fourth.

It is quite in harmony with this characteristic of the Gospel that it should contain such a much larger proportion of Christ's words than we find in the others: discourses here form the principal part, especially in the latter half of the Gospel. Not even in the Sermon on the Mount do we learn so much of 'the spirit of Christ' as in the discourses recorded by S. John. And what is true of the central figure is true also of the numerous characters which give such life and definiteness to S. John's narrative: they also make themselves known to us by what they say rather than by what they do. And this suggests to us a second characteristic.

2. No Gospel is so rich in TYPICAL but thoroughly REAL AND LIFELIKE GROUPS AND INDIVIDUALS as the Fourth. They are sketched, or rather by their words are made to sketch themselves, with a vividness and precision which, as already observed, is almost proof that the Evangelist was an eyewitness of what he records, and an eyewitness of immense receptive power.

Among the groups we have *the disciples* strangely misunderstanding Christ (iv. 33, xi. 12) yet firmly believing on Him (xvi. 30); *His brethren*, dictating a policy to him and not believing on Him (vii. 3—5); *John's disciples*, with their jealousy for the honour of their master (iii. 26); *the Samaritans*, proud to believe from their own experience rather than on the testimony of a woman (iv. 42); *the multitude*, sometimes thinking Jesus possessed, sometimes thinking Him the Christ (vii. 20, 26, 41); *the Jews*, claiming to be Abraham's seed and seeking to kill the Messiah (viii. 33, 37, 40); *the Pharisees*, haughtily asking, 'Hath any one of the rulers or of the Pharisees believed on Him?' (vii. 48) and 'Are we also blind?' (ix. 40); *the chief priests*, professing to fear that Christ's success will be fatal to the national existence (xi. 48), and declaring to Pilate that they have no king but Caesar (xix. 15). In the sketching of these groups nothing is more conclusive evidence of the Evangelist being contemporary with his narrative than the way in which the conflict and fluctuations between belief and unbelief among the multitude and 'the Jews' is indicated.

The types of individual character are still more varied, and as in the case of the groups they exemplify both sides in the great conflict, as well as those who wavered between the two. On the one hand we have the Mother of the Lord (ii. 3—5, xix. 25—27), the beloved disciple and his master the Baptist (i. 6—37, iii. 23—36), S. Andrew and Mary of Bethany, all unfailing in their allegiance; S. Peter falling and rising again to deeper love (xviii. 27, xxi. 17); S. Philip rising from eager to firm faith (xiv. 8), S. Thomas from desponding and despairing love (xi. 16, xx. 25) to faith, hope, and love (xx. 28). There is the sober but uninformed faith of Martha (xi. 21, 24, 27), the passionate affection of Mary Magdalene (xx. 1—18). Among conversions we have the instantaneous but deliberate conviction of Nathanael (i. 49), the gradual but courageous progress in belief of the schismatical Samaritan woman (see on iv. 19) and of the uninstructed man born blind (see on xi. 21), and in contrast with both the timid, hesitating confessions of Nicodemus, the learned Rabbi (iii. 1, vii. 50, xix. 39). On the other side we have the cowardly wavering of Pilate (xviii. 38, 39, xix. 1—4, 8, 12, 16), the unscrupulous resoluteness of Caiaphas (xi. 49, 50), and the blank treachery of Judas (xiii. 27, xviii. 2—5). Among the minor characters there are the 'ruler of the feast' (ii. 9, 10), the 'nobleman' (iv. 49), the man healed at Bethesda (v. 7, 11, 14, 15).

If these groups and individuals are creations of the imagination, it is no exaggeration to say that the author of the Fourth Gospel is a genius superior to Shakspere.

3. From typical characters we pass on to typical or symbolical events. SYMBOLISM is a third characteristic of this Gospel. Not merely does it contain the three great allegories of the Sheep-fold, the Good Shepherd, and the Vine, from which Christian art has drawn its symbolism from the very earliest times; but the whole Gospel from end to end is penetrated with the spirit of symbolical representation. In nothing is this more apparent than in the eight miracles which the Evangelist

has selected for the illustration of his Divine Epic. His own word for them leads us to expect this: to him they are not so much miracles as 'signs.' The first two are introductory, and seem to be pointed out as such by S. John (ii. 11, iv. 54). The turning of the water into wine exhibits the Messiah's sovereign power over inanimate matter, the healing of the official's son His power over the noblest of living bodies. Moreover they teach two great lessons which lie at the very root of Christianity; (1) that Christ's Presence hallows the commonest events and turns the meanest elements into the richest; (2) that the way to win blessings is to trust the Bestower of them. The third sign, healing the paralytic, shews the Messiah as the great Restorer, repairing the physical as well as the spiritual ravages of sin (v. 14). In the feeding of the 5000 the Christ appears as the Support of life, in the walking on the sea as the Guardian and Guide of His followers. The giving of sight to the man born blind and the raising of Lazarus shew that He is the source of Light and of Life to men. The last sign, wrought by the Risen Christ, sums up and concludes the whole series (xxi. 1—12). Fallen man, restored, fed, guided, enlightened, delivered from the terrors of death, passes to the everlasting shore of peace, where the Lord is waiting to receive him.

In Nicodemus coming by night (iii. 2), in Judas going out into the night (xiii. 30), in the stormy weather at the Feast of the Dedication (x. 22), in the dusky ravine through which the Messiah goes to meet His Passion (xviii. 1), in the dividing of Christ's garments, and the blood and water from His side (xix. 24, 34), &c. &c., we seem to have instances of the same love of symbolism. These historical details are singled out for notice *because* of the lesson which lies behind them. And if we ask for the source of this mode of teaching, there cannot be a doubt about the answer: it is the form in which almost all the lessons of the Old Testament are conveyed. This leads us to another characteristic.

4. Though written in Greek, S. John's Gospel is in thought and tone, and sometimes in the form of expression also, thoroughly HEBREW, AND BASED ON THE HEBREW SCRIPTURES. Much has been already said on this point in Chapter II. ii. (2) in shewing

that the Evangelist must have been a Jew. The Gospel sets forth two facts in tragic contrast: (1) that the Jewish Scriptures in endless ways, by commands, types, and prophecies, pointed and led up to the Christ; (2) that precisely the people who possessed these Scriptures, and studied them most diligently, failed to recognise the Christ or refused to believe in Him. In this aspect the Gospel is a long comment on the mournful text, 'Ye search the Scriptures; because in them ye think ye have eternal life: and they are they which testify of Me. And ye will not come to Me, that ye may have life' (v. 39, 40). To shew, therefore, the way out of this tragical contradiction between a superstitious reverence for the letter of the law and a scornful rejection of its true meaning, S. John writes his Gospel. He points out to his fellow-countrymen that they are right in taking the Scriptures for their guide, ruinously wrong in the use they make of them: Abraham, Moses and the Prophets, rightly understood, will lead them to adore Him whom they have crucified. This he does, not merely in *general statements* (i. 45, iv. 22, v. 39, 46), but in detail, both by *allusions;* e.g. to Jacob (i. 47, 51) and to the rock in the wilderness (vii. 37), and by *direct references;* e.g. to Abraham (vii. 56), to the brazen serpent (iii. 14), to the Bridegroom (iii. 29), to the manna (vi. 49), to the paschal lamb (xix. 36), to the Psalms (ii. 17, x. 34, xiii. 18, xix. 24, 37), to the Prophets generally (vi. 45, [vii. 38]), to Isaiah (xii. 38, 40), to Zechariah (xii. 15), to Micah (vii. 42).

All these passages (and more might easily be added) tend to shew that the Fourth Gospel is saturated with the thoughts, imagery, and language of the O. T. "Without the basis of the Old Testament, without the fullest acceptance of the unchanging divinity of the Old Testament, the Gospel of S. John is an insoluble riddle" (Westcott, *Introduction*, p. lxix.).

5. Yet another characteristic of this Gospel has been mentioned by anticipation in discussing the plan of it (chap. IV. ii.); —its SYSTEMATIC ARRANGEMENT. It is the only Gospel which clearly has a plan. What has been given above as an outline of the plan (IV. ii.), and also the arrangement of the miracles in section 3 of this chapter, illustrate this feature of the Gospel.

Further examples in detail will be pointed out pp. lxi.—lxiv. and in the subdivisions of the Gospel given in the notes.

6. The last characteristic which our space will allow us to notice is its STYLE. The style of the Gospel and of the First Epistle of S. John is unique. But it is a thing to be felt rather than to be defined. The most illiterate reader is conscious of it; the ablest critic cannot analyse it satisfactorily. A few main features, however, may be pointed out; the rest being left to the student's own powers of observation.

Ever since Dionysius of Alexandria (c. A.D. 250) wrote his masterly criticism of the differences between the Fourth Gospel and the Apocalypse (Eus. *H. E.* VII. XXV.), it has been not uncommon to say that the Gospel is written in very pure Greek, free from all barbarous, irregular, or uncouth expressions. This is true in a sense; but it is somewhat misleading. The Greek of the Fourth Gospel is pure, as that of a Greek Primer is pure, because of its extreme simplicity. And it is faultless for the same reason; blemishes being avoided because idioms and intricate constructions are avoided. Elegant, idiomatic, classical Greek it is not.

(*a*) This, therefore, is one element in the style,—*extreme simplicity*. The clauses and sentences are connected together by simple conjunctions co-ordinately; they are not made to depend one upon another; ἐν αὐτῷ ζωὴ ἦν, **καὶ ἡ** ζωὴ ἦν τὸ φῶς τ. ἀνθρώπων, not **ἣ** ἦν τ. φῶς. Even where there is strong contrast indicated a simple *καί* is preferred to ἀλλά, καίτοι or ὅμως; εἰς τὰ ἴδια ἦλθεν, **καὶ** οἱ ἴδιοι οὐ παρέλαβον (i. 11). In passages of great solemnity the sentences are placed side by side without even a conjunction; ἀπεκρίθη Ἰησοῦς...ἀπεκρίθη ὁ Πιλάτος...ἀπεκρίθη Ἰησοῦς (xviii. 34—36). The words of others are given in direct not in oblique oration. The first chapter (19—51), and indeed the first half of the Gospel, abounds in illustrations.

(*b*) This simple co-ordination of sentences and avoidance of relatives and dependent clauses involves a good deal of repetition; and even when repetition is not necessary we find it employed for the sake of close connexion and emphasis. This *constant repetition* is very impressive. A good example of it is where the predicate (or part of the predicate) of one sentence becomes the subject (or part of the subject) of the next; or where the subject is repeated; Ἐγώ εἰμι **ὁ ποιμὴν ὁ καλός· ὁ ποιμὴν ὁ καλὸς** τ. ψυχὴν αὐτοῦ τίθησιν ὑπὲρ τ. προβάτων (x. 11); τὸ φῶς ἐν **τῇ σκοτίᾳ** φαίνει, καὶ **ἡ σκοτία** αὐτὸ οὐ κατέλαβεν (i. 5); ἐν ἀρχῇ ἦν **ὁ λόγος**, καὶ **ὁ λόγος** ἦν πρὸς τὸν θεόν, καὶ θεὸς ἦν **ὁ λόγος** (i. 1). Comp. xiii. 20, xv. 19, xvii. 9, 16, &c. Sometimes instead of repeating the subject S. John introduces an apparently superfluous demonstrative pronoun; ὁ ὢν εἰς τὸν κόλπον τοῦ πατρὸς **ἐκεῖνος** ἐξηγήσατο (i. 18); ὁ δὲ ζητῶν τὴν δόξαν τοῦ πέμψαντος αὐτὸν **οὗτος** ἀληθής ἐστιν (vii. 18). Comp. v. 11, 39, xiv. 21, 26, xv. 5, &c. The personal pronouns are frequently inserted for emphasis and repeated for the same reason. This is specially true of Ἐγώ in the discourses of Christ.

(*c*) Although S. John connects his sentences so simply, and sometimes merely places them side by side without conjunctions, yet he very frequently *points out a sequence in fact or in thought.* His two most characteristic particles are οὖν and ἵνα. Οὖν occurs almost exclusively in narrative, and points out that one fact is a consequence of another, sometimes in cases where this would not have been obvious; ἦλθεν **οὖν** πάλιν εἰς τὴν Κανά (iv. 46), because of the welcome He had received there before; ἐζήτουν **οὖν** αὐτὸν πιάσαι (vii. 30), because of His claim to be sent from God. Comp. vii. 40, 45, viii. 12, 21, &c. &c.—While the frequent use of οὖν points to the conviction that nothing happens without a cause, the frequent use of ἵνα points to the belief that nothing happens without a purpose. S. John uses ἵνα not only where some other construction would have been suitable, but also where another construction would seem to be much more suitable; οὐκ εἰμὶ ἄξιος **ἵνα** λύσω (i. 27); ἐμὸν βρῶμά ἐστιν **ἵνα** ποιήσω τὸ θέλημα (iv. 34); τοῦτό ἐστιν τὸ ἔργον τοῦ θεοῦ **ἵνα** πιστεύητε (vi. 29); τίς ἥμαρτεν...**ἵνα** τυφλὸς γεννηθῇ; (ix. 2). S. John is specially fond of this construction to point out the working of the Divine purpose, as in some of the instances just given (comp. v. 23, vi. 40, 50, x. 10, xi. 42, xiv. 16, &c. &c.) and in particular of the fulfilment of prophecy (xviii. 9, xix. 24, 28, 36). In this connexion an elliptical expression ἀλλ' ἵνα (=but *this was done* in order that) is not uncommon; οὔτε οὗτος ἥμαρτεν οὔτε οἱ γονεῖς αὐτοῦ, **ἀλλ' ἵνα** φανερωθῇ κ.τ.λ. (ix.

3; comp. xi. 52, xiv. 31, xv. 25, xviii. 28). Of the other very numerous Greek particles he uses but few; chiefly *καί* (very frequent), *δέ*, *ὡς* and *καθώς* (frequent), *μέν* (rather rare).

(*d*) S. John, full of the spirit of Hebrew poetry, frequently employs that *parallelism* which to a large extent is the very form of Hebrew poetry: 'A servant is not greater than his lord; neither one that is sent greater than he that sent him' (xiii. 16); 'Peace I leave with you, My peace I give unto you... Let not your heart be troubled, neither let it be fearful' (xiv. 27). Sometimes the parallelism is antithetic, and the second clause denies the opposite of the first; 'He confessed, and denied not' (i. 20); 'I give unto them eternal life, and they shall never perish' (x. 28). Comp. iii. 11, v. 37, vi. 35, 55, 56, xv. 20, xvi. 20.

(*e*) Another peculiarity, also of Hebrew origin, is *minuteness of detail*. Instead of one word summing up the whole action, S. John uses two or three stating the details of the action; **ἠρώτησαν** *αὐτὸν καὶ* **εἶπαν** *αὐτῷ* (i. 25); **ἐμαρτύρησεν** *Ἰωάννης* **λέγων** (i. 32); **ἔκραξεν** *οὖν ἐν τῷ ἱερῷ* **διδάσκων** *καὶ* **λέγων** (vii. 28). The frequent phrase *ἀπεκρίθη καὶ εἶπεν* illustrates both this particularity and also the preference for co-ordinate sentences (*a*). *Ἀπεκρίθη καὶ εἶπεν* occurs thirty-four times in S. John, and only two or three times in the Synoptists, who commonly write *ἀποκριθεὶς εἶπεν* or *ἀπεκρίθη λέγων*.

(*f*) In conclusion we may notice a few of S. John's favourite words and phrases; *μένειν* especially in the phrases expressing abiding in one another; *πιστεύειν εἴς τινα*, *ἀληθής*, *ἀληθινός*, *ἀληθῶς*, *ἀλήθεια*, *σκοτία* of moral darkness, *τὸ φῶς* of spiritual light, *ζωή*, *ἀγάπη*, *ἀγαπᾷν*, *φανεροῦν*, *μαρτυρία*, *μαρτυρεῖν*, *ζωὴ αἰώνιος*, *παρρησίᾳ*, *τὸν λόγον τὸν ἐμὸν τηρεῖν*, *οἱ Ἰουδαῖοι* of the opponents of Christ; *ὁ κόσμος*, of those alienated from Christ. The following words and phrases are used by S. John only; *ὁ παράκλητος* of the Holy Spirit, *ὁ λόγος* of the Son, *μονογενής* of the Son, *ἐξελθεῖν ἐκ τοῦ θεοῦ* or *παρὰ τοῦ θεοῦ* or *ἀπὸ θεοῦ* of the Son, *τιθέναι τὴν ψυχὴν αὐτοῦ* of Jesus Christ, *ὁ ἄρχων τοῦ κόσμου τούτου* of Satan, *ἡ ἐσχάτη ἡμέρα*, *ἀμὴν ἀμήν*.

These characteristics combined form a book which stands

alone in Christian literature, as its author stands alone among Christian teachers; the work of one who for threescore years and ten laboured as an Apostle. Called to follow the Baptist when only a lad, and by him soon transferred to the Christ, he may be said to have been the first who from his youth up was a Christian. Who, therefore, could so fitly grasp and state in their true proportions and with fitting impressiveness the great verities of the Christian faith? He had had no deep-seated prejudices to uproot, like his friend S. Peter and others who were called late in life. He had had no sudden wrench to make from the past, like S. Paul. He had not had the trying excitement of wandering abroad over the face of the earth, like most of the Twelve. He had remained at his post at Ephesus, directing, teaching, meditating; until at last when the fruit was ripe it was given to the Church in the fulness of beauty which it is still our privilege to possess and learn to love.

CHAPTER VI

ITS RELATION TO THE SYNOPTIC GOSPELS

The Fourth Gospel presupposes the other three; the Evangelist assumes that the contents of his predecessors' Gospels are known to his readers. The details of Christ's birth are summed up in 'the Word became flesh.' His subjection to His parents is implied by contrast in His reply to His mother at Cana. The Baptism is involved in the Baptist's declaration, 'I have seen (the Spirit descending and abiding on Him) and have borne witness' (i. 34). The Ascension is promised through Mary Magdalene to the Apostles (xx. 17), but left unrecorded. Christian Baptism is assumed in the discourse with Nicodemus, and the Eucharist in that on the Bread of Life; but the reference in each case is left to speak for itself to Christians familiar with both those rites. S. John passes over their institution in silence.

The differences between the Fourth Gospel and the three first are real and very marked: but it is easy to exaggerate them. They are conveniently grouped under two heads; (1) differences as to the scene and extent of Christ's ministry; (2) differences as to the view given of His Person.

(1) With regard to the first, it is urged that the Synoptists represent our Lord's ministry as lasting for one year only, including only one Passover and one visit to Jerusalem, with which the ministry closes. S. John, however, describes the ministry as extending over three or possibly more years, including at least three Passovers and several visits to Jerusalem.

In considering this difficulty, if it be one, we must remember two things: (*a*) that all four Gospels are very incomplete and contain only a series of fragments; (*b*) that the date and duration of Christ's ministry remain and are likely to remain uncertain. (*a*) In the gaps in the Synoptic narrative there is plenty of room for all that is peculiar to S. John. In the spaces deliberately left by S. John between his carefully-arranged scenes there is plenty of room for all that is peculiar to the Synoptists. When all have been pieced together there still remain large interstices which it would require at least four more Gospels to fill (xxi. 25). Therefore it can be no serious difficulty that so much of the Fourth Gospel has nothing parallel to it in the other three. (*b*) The additional fact of the uncertainty as to the date and duration of the Lord's public ministry is a further explanation of the apparent difference in the amount of time covered by the Synoptic narrative and that covered by the narrative of S. John. There is no contradiction between the two. The Synoptists nowhere say that the ministry lasted for only one year, although some commentators from very early times have proposed to understand 'the acceptable year of the Lord' (Luke iv. 19) literally. The three Passovers of S. John (ii. 13, vi. 4, xi. 55; v. 1 being omitted as very doubtful) compel us to give at least a little over two years to Christ's ministry. But S. John also nowhere implies that he has mentioned all the Passovers within the period; and the startling statement of Irenaeus (*Haer.* II. xxii. 5) must be borne in mind, that our

Lord fulfilled the office of a Teacher until He was over forty years old, "even as the Gospel and all the elders bear witness, who consorted with John the disciple of the Lord in Asia, (stating) that John had handed this down to them." Irenaeus makes the ministry begin when Christ was nearly thirty years of age (Luke iii. 23); so that he gives it a duration of more than ten years on what seems to be very high authority. All that can be affirmed with certainty is that the ministry cannot have begun earlier than A.D. 28 (the earlier alternative for the fifteenth year of Tiberius; Luke iii. 1) and cannot have ended later than A.D. 37, when Pilate was recalled by Tiberius shortly before his death. Indeed as Tiberius died in March, and Pilate found him already dead when he reached Rome, the recall probably took place in A.D. 36; and the Passover of A.D. 36 is the latest date possible for the Crucifixion. Chronology is not what the Evangelists aimed at giving us; and the fact that S. John spreads his narrative over a longer period than the Synoptists will cause a difficulty to those only who have mistaken the purpose of the Gospels.

(2) As to the second great difference between S. John and the Synoptists, it is said that, while they represent Jesus as a great Teacher and Reformer, with the powers and authority of a Prophet, who exasperates His countrymen by denouncing their immoral traditions, S. John gives us instead a mysterious Personage, invested with Divine attributes, who infuriates the hierarchy by claiming to be one with the Supreme God. It is urged, moreover, that there is a corresponding difference in the teaching attributed to Jesus in each case. The discourses in the Synoptic Gospels are simple, direct, and easily intelligible, inculcating for the most part high moral principles, which are enforced and illustrated by numerous parables and proverbs. Whereas the discourses in the Fourth Gospel are many and intricate, inculcating for the most part deep mystical truths, which are enforced by a ceaseless reiteration tending to obscure the exact line of the argument, and illustrated by not a single parable properly so called.

These important differences may be to a very great extent

explained by two considerations: (*a*) the peculiarities of S. John's own temperament; (*b*) the circumstances under which he wrote. (*a*) The main features of S. John's character, so far as we can gather them from history and tradition, have been stated above (chapter I. ii.), and we cannot doubt that they have affected not only his choice of the incidents and discourses selected for narration, but also his mode of narrating them. No doubt in both he was under the guidance of the Holy Spirit (xiv. 26): but we have every reason for supposing that such guidance would work with, rather than against, the mental endowments of the person guided. To what extent the substance and form of his Gospel has been influenced by the intensity of his own nature we cannot tell; but the intensity is there, both in thought and language, both in its devotion and in its sternness; and the difference from the Synoptists shews that *some* influence has been at work. (*b*) The circumstances under which S. John wrote will carry us still further. They are very different from those under which the first Gospels were written. Christianity had grown from infancy to manhood and believed itself to be near the great consummation of the Lord's return. It was 'the last time.' Antichrist, who, as Jesus had foretold, was to precede His return, was already present in manifold shapes in the world (1 John ii. 18). In the bold speculations which had mingled themselves with Christianity, the Divine Government of the Father and the Incarnation of the Son were being explained away or denied (1 John ii. 22, iv. 3). The opposition, shewn from the first by 'the Jews' to the disciples of the Teacher whom they had crucified, had settled down into a relentless hostility. And while the gulf between Christianity and Judaism had thus widened, that between the Church and the world had also become more evident. The more the Christian realised the meaning of being 'born of God,' the more manifest became the truth, that 'the whole world lieth in the evil one' (1 John v. 18, 19). A Gospel that was to meet the needs of a society so changed both in its internal and external relations must obviously be very different from those which had suited its infancy. And a reverent mind will here trace the

Providence of God, in that an Apostle, and he the Apostle S. John, was preserved for this crisis. It is scarcely too much to say that, had a Gospel, claiming to have been written by him near the close of the first century, greatly resembled the other three in matter and form, we should have had reasonable grounds for doubting its authenticity. (The special difficulty with regard to the discourses as reported by the Synoptists and by S. John is discussed in the introductory note to chap. iii.)

It must be remarked on the other side that, along with these important differences as regards the things narrated and the mode of narrating them, there are *coincidences* less conspicuous, but not less real or important.

Among the most remarkable of these are the characters of the Lord, of S. Peter, of Mary and Martha, and of Judas. The similarity in most cases is too subtle for the picture in the Fourth Gospel to have been drawn from that in the Synoptic account. It is very much easier to believe that the two pictures agree because both are taken from life.

The invariable use by the Synoptists of the expression 'Son of Man' is rigidly observed by S. John. It is always used by Christ of Himself; never by, or of, any one else. See notes on i. 51; and also on ii. 19 and xviii. 11 for two other striking coincidences.

The student will find tabulated lists of minor coincidences in Dr Westcott's *Introduction*, pp. lxxxii., lxxxiii. He sums up thus: "The general conclusion stands firm. The Synoptists offer not only historical but also spiritual points of connexion between the teaching which they record and the teaching in the Fourth Gospel; and S. John himself in the Apocalypse completes the passage from the one to the other."

CHAPTER VII

ITS RELATION TO THE FIRST EPISTLE

The chronological relation of the Gospel to the First Epistle of S. John cannot be determined with certainty. The Epistle presupposes the Gospel in some shape or other: but as the Gospel was given orally for many years before it was written, it is possible that the Epistle may have been written first. Probably they were written within a few years of one another. whichever was written first of the two. The Epistle is a philosophical companion to the Gospel; either an introduction or a supplement to it. The Gospel is a summary of Christian Theology, the Epistle is a summary of Christian Ethics. The one shews the Divine Life in the Person of Christ, the other shews it in the Christian.

In comparing the Fourth Gospel with the Synoptists we found great and obvious differences, accompanied by real but less obvious correspondences. Here the opposite is rather the case. The coincidences both in thought and expression between the Gospel and the First Epistle of S. John are many and conspicuous; but closer inspection shews some important differences.

The object of the Gospel, as we have seen, is to create a conviction 'that Jesus is the Christ, the Son of God.' The object of the Epistle is rather to insist that the Son of God is Jesus. The Gospel starts from the historical human Teacher and proves that He is Divine; the Epistle starts rather from the Son of God and contends that He has come in the flesh. Again, the Gospel is not polemical; the truth is stated rather than error attacked. In the Epistle definite errors, especially those of Cerinthus, are attacked.

The lesson of both is one and the same; faith in Jesus Christ leading to fellowship with Him, and through fellowship with Him to fellowship with the Father and with one another: or, to sum up all in one word, Love.

CHAPTER VIII

THE TEXT OF THE GOSPEL

The authorities are abundant and various. It will suffice to mention twelve of the most important; six Greek MSS. and six Ancient Versions.

Greek Manuscripts

Codex Sinaiticus (א). 4th century. Discovered by Tischendorf in 1859 at the monastery of S. Catherine on Mount Sinai, and now at St Petersburg. The whole Gospel.

Codex Alexandrinus (A). 5th century. Brought by Cyril Lucar, Patriarch of Constantinople, from Alexandria, and afterwards presented by him to Charles I. in 1628. In the British Museum. The whole Gospel, excepting vi. 50—viii. 52.

Codex Vaticanus (B). 4th century, but perhaps later than the Sinaiticus. In the Vatican Library. The whole Gospel.

Codex Ephraemi (C). 5th century. A palimpsest: the original writing has been partially rubbed out and the works of Ephraem the Syrian have been written over it. In the National Library at Paris. Eight fragments; i. 1—41; iii. 33—v. 16; vi. 38—vii. 3; viii. 34—ix. 11; xi. 8—46; xiii. 8—xiv. 7; xvi. 21—xviii. 36; xx. 26—xxi. 25.

Codex Bezae (D). 6th or 7th century. Given by Beza to the University Library at Cambridge in 1581. Remarkable for its interpolations and various readings. The whole Gospel, excepting i. 16—iii. 26: but xviii. 13—xx. 13 is by a later hand, possibly from the original MS.

Codex Regius Parisiensis (L). 8th or 9th century. Nearly related to the Vaticanus. At Tours. The whole Gospel, excepting xxi. 15—xxi. 25.

Ancient Versions

Old Syriac (Curetonian). 2nd century. Four fragments; i.—42; iii. 5—vii. 35; vii. 37—viii. 53, *omitting* vii. 53—viii. 11; xiv. 11—29.

VULGATE SYRIAC (Peschito = 'simple' meaning perhaps 'faithful'). 3rd century. The whole Gospel.

HARCLEAN SYRIAC (a revision of the Philoxenian Syriac, which is a servile translation of the 6th century). 7th century. The whole Gospel.

OLD LATIN (Vetus Latina). 2nd century. The whole Gospel in several distinct forms.

VULGATE LATIN (mainly a revision of the Old Latin by Jerome, A.D. 383—5). 4th century. The whole Gospel.

MEMPHITIC (Coptic, in the dialect of Lower Egypt). 3rd century. The whole Gospel.

Besides many other MSS. of every degree of excellence, and some other Ancient Versions, there is also the evidence of the *Fathers.* We have considerable fragments of the commentaries of Origen and Theodore of Mopsuestia, nearly the whole of that of Cyril of Alexandria, and the Homilies of Chrysostom and Augustine. In addition to these must be mentioned valuable quotations from the Gospel in various Greek and Latin writers in the second, third and fourth centuries. Quotations by writers later than the fourth century are of little or no value. By that time the corruption of the text was complete. The Diocletian persecution had swept away a large majority of the ancient copies, and a composite text emanating mainly from Constantinople gradually took their place.

Our main authorities, therefore, are the most ancient MSS., Versions, and Fathers. How are these authorities to be used? Our object in each disputed case will be to ascertain *the oldes reading;* and unless strong arguments against the authenticity of the earliest reading exist, its antiquity will be decisive in its favour. But the date of a MS. is not the same thing as the date of the text which it represents. Some MSS., as ℵBD, contain a text which can be traced back to the end of the second century. Others, as A, contain a text which is very little older than the MS. itself. Very few readings in the Gospels which are not supported by either B or ℵ or D are likely to be the true reading. Of these three very ancient authorities, B is the purest, D very much the most corrupt.

But in a very large number of disputed passages B and ℵ will be found to agree. In that case our choice is not difficult: it is where these two separate, and where neither of them has a very decided preponderance of support from other ancient authorities, that serious doubt arises. As between Bℵ on the one hand and A with its common supporters on the other we need not hesitate. It is easy in most cases to see how the reading of Bℵ has been softened or amplified into the reading of A; very difficult to see what could have induced copyists to alter the smooth readings of A into the harsher readings of Bℵ, or why when A makes the Evangelists agree the scribes of Bℵ should make them differ. All the probabilities shew that the text of A has been developed out of a text very similar to that of Bℵ, not the text of Bℵ manufactured by the mutilation of one similar to A. A few simple examples will illustrate this.

In i. 26, 27 the text of Bℵ stands thus;—

Ἐγὼ βαπτίζω ἐν ὕδατι· μέσος ὑμῶν στήκει ὃν ὑμεῖς οὐκ οἴδατε, ὀπίσω μου ἐρχόμενος, οὗ οὐκ εἰμὶ [ἐγὼ] ἄξιος ἵνα λύσω κ.τ.λ.

The text of A stands thus;—

Ἐγὼ βαπτίζω ἐν ὕδατι· μέσος **δὲ** *ὑμῶν* **ἕστηκεν** *ὃν ὑμεῖς οὐκ οἴδατε.* **αὐτός ἐστιν** *ὁ ὀπίσω μου ἐρχόμενος,* **ὃς ἔμπροσθέν μου γέγονεν,** *οὗ* **ἐγὼ οὐκ εἰμὶ** *ἄξιος ἵνα λύσω κ.τ.λ.*

(1) The insertion of *δέ* certainly makes the sentence less harsh. (2) *ἕστηκεν* is a very common form, *στήκει* a rare one. (3) *αὐτός ἐστιν ὁ* fills up the construction and assimilates the passage to *v.* 30: and other MSS. shew the assimilation in another form; *οὗτός ἐστιν*, or *αὐτός ἐστιν ὃν εἶπον.* (4) The insertion *ὃς ἔμπροσθέν μου γέγονεν* assimilates the passage to *vv.* 15, 30. (5) The transposition of *ἐγώ* (omitted by ℵ) gives emphasis to the Baptist's self-humiliation. In all these cases the change from Bℵ to A is much more intelligible than the change from A to Bℵ. What could induce a copyist to omit *δέ*, to change *ἕστηκεν* into *στήκει*, to create differences between this passage and *vv.* 15, 30, to weaken the Baptist's humility? The inference is that Bℵ have the earlier reading and A the derived or corrupted reading. The following table contains evidence pointing in the same direction:—

Reference.	*Reading of* Bא.	*Reading of* A.	*Probable cause of corruption.*
i. 39.	ὄψεσθε	ἴδετε	Assimilation to i. 47.
iv. 46, vi. 14.	omit	ὁ Ἰησοῦς	Insertion for clearness.
iv. 42.	omit	ὁ Χριστός	Explanatory gloss.
vi. 40	τοῦ πατρός μου	τοῦ πέμψαντός με	Assimilation to vi. 39.
ix. 6	omit	τοῦ τυφλοῦ	Insertion for clearness.
ix. 14	ἐν ᾗ ἡμέρᾳ	ὅτε	Simplification.
x. 27	ἀκούουσιν	ἀκούει	Grammatical correction.
xii. 7	ἄφες αὐτὴν ἵνα ...τηρήσῃ	ἄφες αὐτήν... ...τετήρηκεν	To avoid a difficulty of meaning.

Similarly in i. 43, xxi. 15, 16, 17, Bא give *John* as the father of S. Peter, while A gives *Jonas* in harmony with Matt. xvi. 17.

From the notes on the text at the head of the notes on each chapter the student may collect many other instances; all tending to shew that the change from Bא to A is much more probable than the converse change, and that therefore A is a corruption of Bא rather than Bא of A. His attention is specially directed to i. 16, 18, iii. 15, 34, iv. 51, v. 3, 4, 16, 37, viii. 59, ix. 4, 11, x. 12, 29, 38, xi. 19, xii. 1, 7, 13, xiii. 2, xiv. 4, 10, 23, xvii. 22, xviii. 10, 29, 30, xix. 7, 26, 27, 29, xx. 16, xxi. 6.

It is admitted on all hands that the history of the text in the second, third and fourth centuries is that of a gradual corruption. It is sometimes assumed that about the fourth century a process of purification began, and that later texts are consequently less corrupt than earlier ones. *Of this supposed process of purification there is absolutely no evidence whatever.* The process which shews itself with ever-increasing vigour in the fourth century is that of *eclecticism;* a picking-out from various sources of those readings which reduced differences and difficulties to a minimum. Whereas it is a recognised principle of textual criticism that *the more difficult reading is the more likely to be the true one.*

It is easy to get a very exaggerated idea of the amount of uncertainty which exists respecting the text of N.T. "If comparative trivialities, such as changes of order, the insertion or omission of the article with proper names, and the like, are set aside, the words in our opinion still subject to doubt can hardly amount to more than *a thousandth part* of the N.T." (Westcott and Hort, *The N.T. in Greek*, I. p. 561). Every reader of the Greek Testament who can afford the time should study the work just quoted. Those who cannot, should read Hammond's *Out-*

lines of Textual Criticism, a short, clear, and interesting statement of the main facts in a very inexpensive manual. Here, or in Scrivener's *Introduction to the Criticism of N.T.*, or in Vol. I. of Alford's Greek Testament, will be found information respecting the less important MSS. sometimes cited in this volume.

CHAPTER IX

THE LITERATURE OF THE GOSPEL

It would be impossible to give even a sketch of this within a small compass, so numerous are the works on S. John and his writings. All that will be attempted here will be to give more advanced students some information as to where they may look for greater help than can be given in a handbook for the use of schools.

Of the earliest known commentary, that of Heracleon (c. A.D. 150), only quotations preserved by Origen remain. Of Origen's own commentary (c. A.D. 225—235) only portions remain. Of the Greek commentators of the fourth century, Theodorus of Heraclea and Didymus of Alexandria, very little has come down to us. But we have S. Chrysostom's 88 *Homilies* on the Gospel, which have been translated in the Oxford 'Library of the Fathers.' S. Augustine's 124 *Lectures* (*Tractatus*) on S. John may be read in the 'Library of the Fathers,' or in the new translation by Gibb, published by T. & T. Clark, Edinburgh. But no translation can fairly represent the epigrammatic fulness of the original. The *Commentary* of Cyril of Alexandria has been translated by P. E. Pusey, Oxford, 1875. With Cyril the line of great patristic interpreters of S. John ends.

The *Catena Aurea* of Thomas Aquinas (c. A.D. 1250) was published in an English form at Oxford, 1841—45. It consists of a 'chain' of comments selected from Greek and Latin authors. Unfortunately Thomas Aquinas was the victim of previous forgers, and a considerable number of the quotations from early authorities are taken from spurious works.

Of modern commentaries those of Cornelius à Lapide (Van der Steen) and Maldonatus in the sixteenth century and of Lampe in the eighteenth must be mentioned. The last has been a treasury of information for many more recent writers.

The following foreign commentaries have all been published in an English form by T. & T. Clark, Edinburgh; Bengel, Godet, Luthardt, Meyer, Olshausen, Tholuck. Of these the works of Godet and Meyer may be specially commended. The high authority of Dr Westcott pronounces the commentary of Godet, "except on questions of textual criticism," to be "unsurpassed"—we may add, except by Dr Westcott's own.

Among original English commentaries those of Alford, Dunwell, McClellan, Milligan, Watkins, and Wordsworth are or are becoming well known to all students. But immensely superior to all preceding works is that by Dr Westcott, Murray, 1882.

Other works which give very valuable assistance are Ellicott's *Historical Lectures on the Life of our Lord*, Field's *Otium Norvicense*, Pars III, Liddon's *Bampton Lectures*, 1866, Lightfoot *On a Fresh Revision of the N.T.*, F. D. Maurice's *Gospel of St John*, Moulton's edition of Winer's *Grammar**, Sanday's *Authorship and Historical Character of the Fourth Gospel*, and *The Gospels in the Second Century*, and Westcott's *Introduction to the Study of the Gospels*, and *Characteristics of the Gospel Miracles*, and *The Gospel of the Risen Lord*.

The present writer is bound to express his obligations, in some cases very great, to most of the works mentioned above, as well as to many others. It was originally intended that Dr Sanday should undertake the present commentary, but press of other work induced him to ask leave to withdraw after having written notes on the greater part of the first chapter. His successor has had the advantage of these notes and has made large use of them, and throughout has in some measure remedied the loss caused by Dr Sanday's retirement by frequently quoting from his work on the Fourth Gospel, now unfortunately out of print.

* References to Winer in this volume are to Moulton's edition, 1877.

ANALYSIS OF THE GOSPEL IN DETAIL

I. 1—18. THE PROLOGUE.

1. The Word in His own nature (1—5).
2. His revelation to men and rejection by them (6—13).
3. His revelation of the Father (14—18).

I 19—XII. 50. THE MINISTRY.

a. I. 19—II. 11. **The Testimony.**

1. The Testimony of the Baptist (i. 19—37)

    to the deputation from Jerusalem (19—28),

    to the people (29—34),

    to Andrew and John (35—37).

2. The Testimony of Disciples (i. 38—51).
3. The Testimony of the First Sign (ii. 1—11).

b. II. 13—XI. 57. **The Work.**

1. The Work among Jews (ii. 13—iii. 36).

    First cleansing of the Temple (13—22).

    Belief without devotion (23—25).

    The discourse with Nicodemus (iii. 1 -21).

    The baptism and final testimony of John (22—36).

2. The Work among Samaritans (iv. 1—42).
3. The Work among Galileans (iv. 43—54).
4. The Work and conflict among mixed multitudes (v.—ix.).

(*a*) CHRIST THE SOURCE OF LIFE (v.).

The sign at the pool of Bethesda (1—9).

The sequel of the sign (10—16).

The discourse on the Son as the Source of Life (17—47).

(β) Christ the Support of Life (vi.).

The sign on the land; feeding the 5000 (1—15).
The sign on the lake; walking on the water (16—21).
The sequel of the two signs (22—25).
The discourse on the Son as the Support of Life (26—59).
Opposite results of the discourse (60—71).

(γ) Christ the Source of Truth and Light (vii. viii.).

The controversy with His brethren (vii. 1—9).
The discourse at the F. of Tabernacles (10—39).
Opposite results of the discourse (40—52).
[*The woman taken in adultery* (vii. 53—viii. 11)].
Christ's true witness to Himself and against the Jews (viii. 12—59).

Christ the Source of Truth and Life illustrated by a Sign (ix.).

The prelude to the sign (1—5).
The sign (6—12).
Opposite results of the sign (13—41).

(δ) Christ is Love (x.).

Allegory of the Door of the Fold (1—9).
Allegory of the Good Shepherd (11—18).
Opposite results of the teaching (19—21).
The discourse at the F. of the Dedication (22—38).
Opposite results of the discourse (39—42).

Christ is Love illustrated by a Sign (xi.).

The prelude to the sign (1—33).
The sign (33—44).
Opposite results of the sign (45—57).

c. XII. **The Judgment.**

1. The Judgment of men (1—36).

The devotion of Mary (1—8).
The hostility of the priests (9—11).
The enthusiasm of the people (12—18).
The discomfiture of the Pharisees (19).
The desire of the Gentiles (20—33).
The perplexity of the multitude (34—36).

2. The Judgment of the Evangelist (37—43).

3. The Judgment of Christ (44—50).

XIII.—XX. THE ISSUES OF THE MINISTRY.

d. XIII.—XVII. **The inner Glorification of Christ in His last Discourses.**

1. His love in Humiliation (xiii. 1—30).

2. His love in keeping His own (xiii. 31—xv. 27).
   Their union with Him illustrated by the allegory of the Vine (xv. 1—11).
   Their union with one another (12—17).
   The hatred of the world to both Him and them (18—25).

3. The Promise of the Paraclete and of Christ's Return (xvi.).
   The World and the Paraclete (xvi. 1—11).
   The disciples and the Paraclete (12—15).
   The sorrow turned into joy (16—24).
   Summary and conclusion (25—33).

4. The Prayer of the Great High Priest (xvii.).
   The prayer for Himself (xvii. 1—5),
   for the Disciples (6—19),
   for the whole Church (20—26).

e. XVIII. XIX. **The outer Glorification of Christ in His Passion.**

1. The Betrayal (xviii. 1—11).

2. The Jewish or Ecclesiastical Trial (12—27).

3. The Roman or Civil Trial (xviii. 28—xix. 16).

4. The Death and Burial (xix. 17—42).
   The crucifixion and the title on the cross (17—22).
   The four enemies and the four friends (23—27).
   The two words, 'I thirst,' 'It is finished' (28—30).
   The hostile and the friendly petitions (31—42).

f. XX. **The Resurrection and threefold Manifestation of Christ.**

1. The first Evidence of the Resurrection (1—10).

2. The Manifestation to Mary Magdalene (11—18).

3. The Manifestation to the Ten and others (19—23).

4. The Manifestation to S. Thomas and others (24—29).

5. The Conclusion and Purpose of the Gospel (30, 31).

XXI. THE EPILOGUE OR APPENDIX.

1. The Manifestation to the Seven and the Miraculous Draught of Fishes (1—14).

2. The Commission to S. Peter and Prediction as to his Death (15—19).

3. The misunderstood Saying as to the Evangelist (20—23).

4. Concluding Notes (24, 25).

ΕΥΑΓΓΕΛΙΟΝ ΚΑΤΑ ΙΩΑΝΝΗΝ

1 1 Ἐν ἀρχῇ ἦν ὁ λόγος, καὶ ὁ λόγος ἦν πρὸς τὸν
θεόν, καὶ θεὸς ἦν ὁ λόγος. 2 Οὗτος ἦν ἐν ἀρχῇ πρὸς
τὸν θεόν. 3 πάντα δι' αὐτοῦ ἐγένετο, καὶ χωρὶς αὐτοῦ
ἐγένετο οὐδὲ ἓν ὃ γέγονεν. 4 ἐν αὐτῷ ζωὴ ἦν, καὶ ἡ
ζωὴ ἦν τὸ φῶς τῶν ἀνθρώπων. 5 καὶ τὸ φῶς ἐν τῇ σκοτίᾳ
φαίνει, καὶ ἡ σκοτία αὐτὸ οὐ κατέλαβεν.

6 Ἐγένετο ἄνθρωπος, ἀπεσταλμένος παρὰ θεοῦ, ὄνομα αὐτῷ Ἰωάννης· 7 οὗτος ἦλθεν εἰς μαρτυρίαν, ἵνα
μαρτυρήσῃ περὶ τοῦ φωτός, ἵνα πάντες πιστεύσωσιν
δι' αὐτοῦ. 8 οὐκ ἦν ἐκεῖνος τὸ φῶς, ἀλλ' ἵνα μαρτυρήσῃ
περὶ τοῦ φωτός. 9 ἦν τὸ φῶς τὸ ἀληθινόν ὃ φωτίζει
πάντα ἄνθρωπον ἐρχόμενον εἰς τὸν κόσμον. 10 ἐν τῷ
κόσμῳ ἦν, καὶ ὁ κόσμος δι' αὐτοῦ ἐγένετο, καὶ ὁ κόσμος
αὐτὸν οὐκ ἔγνω. 11 εἰς τὰ ἴδια ἦλθεν, καὶ οἱ ἴδιοι αὐτὸν
οὐ παρέλαβον. 12 ὅσοι δὲ ἔλαβον αὐτόν, ἔδωκεν αὐτοῖς
ἐξουσίαν τέκνα θεοῦ γενέσθαι, τοῖς πιστεύουσιν εἰς τὸ
ὄνομα αὐτοῦ, 13 οἳ οὐκ ἐξ αἱμάτων οὐδὲ ἐκ θελήματος
σαρκὸς οὐδὲ ἐκ θελήματος ἀνδρὸς ἀλλ' ἐκ θεοῦ ἐγεννήθησαν.

14 Καὶ ὁ λόγος σὰρξ ἐγένετο καὶ ἐσκήνωσεν ἐν ἡμῖν,
καὶ ἐθεασάμεθα τὴν δόξαν αὐτοῦ, δόξαν ὡς μονογενοῦς
παρὰ πατρός, πλήρης χάριτος καὶ ἀληθείας. 15 Ἰωάννης

μαρτυρεῖ περὶ αὐτοῦ καὶ κέκραγεν λέγων· Οὗτος ἦν ὃν
εἶπον, Ὁ ὀπίσω μου ἐρχόμενος ἔμπροσθέν μου γέγονεν, ὅτι πρῶτός μου ἦν. 16 ὅτι ἐκ τοῦ πληρώματος αὐτοῦ ἡμεῖς πάντες ἐλάβομεν, καὶ χάριν ἀντὶ χάριτος·
17 ὅτι ὁ νόμος διὰ Μωυσέως ἐδόθη, ἡ χάρις καὶ ἡ ἀλήθεια
διὰ Ἰησοῦ Χριστοῦ ἐγένετο. 18 θεὸν οὐδεὶς ἑώρακεν πώ-
ποτε· μονογενὴς θεὸς ὁ ὢν εἰς τὸν κόλπον τοῦ πατρὸς
ἐκεῖνος ἐξηγήσατο.

19 Καὶ αὕτη ἐστὶν ἡ μαρτυρία τοῦ Ἰωάννου, ὅτε ἀπέστειλαν πρὸς αὐτὸν οἱ Ἰουδαῖοι ἐξ Ἱεροσολύμων ἱερεῖς
καὶ Λευείτας ἵνα ἐρωτήσωσιν αὐτόν, Σὺ τίς εἶ; 20 καὶ
ὡμολόγησεν καὶ οὐκ ἠρνήσατο, καὶ ὡμολόγησεν ὅτι
Ἐγὼ οὐκ εἰμὶ ὁ Χριστός. 21 καὶ ἠρώτησαν αὐτόν, Τί
οὖν; Ἠλίας εἶ σύ; καὶ λέγει, Οὐκ εἰμί. Ὁ προφήτης εἶ σύ; καὶ ἀπεκρίθη, Οὔ. 22 εἶπαν οὖν αὐτῷ,
Τίς εἶ; ἵνα ἀπόκρισιν δῶμεν τοῖς πέμψασιν ἡμᾶς· τί
λέγεις περὶ σεαυτοῦ; 23 ἔφη, Ἐγὼ φωνὴ βοῶντος ἐν τῇ
ἐρήμῳ, Εὐθύνατε τὴν ὁδὸν κυρίου, καθὼς εἶπεν Ἠσαΐας
ὁ προφήτης. 24 καὶ ἀπεσταλμένοι ἦσαν ἐκ τῶν Φαρι-
σαίων· 25 καὶ ἠρώτησαν αὐτὸν καὶ εἶπαν αὐτῷ, Τί οὖν
βαπτίζεις, εἰ σὺ οὐκ εἶ ὁ Χριστὸς οὐδὲ Ἠλίας οὐδὲ ὁ
προφήτης; 26 ἀπεκρίθη αὐτοῖς ὁ Ἰωάννης λέγων, Ἐγὼ
βαπτίζω ἐν ὕδατι· μέσος ὑμῶν στήκει, ὃν ὑμεῖς οὐκ οἴδατε, 27 ὁ ὀπίσω μου ἐρχόμενος, οὗ οὐκ εἰμὶ [ἐγὼ] ἄξιος
ἵνα λύσω αὐτοῦ τὸν ἱμάντα τοῦ ὑποδήματος. 28 ταῦτα
ἐν Βηθανίᾳ ἐγένετο πέραν τοῦ Ἰορδάνου, ὅπου ἦν ὁ
Ἰωάννης βαπτίζων.

29 Τῇ ἐπαύριον βλέπει τὸν Ἰησοῦν ἐρχόμενον πρὸς
αὐτόν, καὶ λέγει, Ἴδε ὁ ἀμνὸς τοῦ θεοῦ ὁ αἴρων τὴν
ἁμαρτίαν τοῦ κόσμου. 30 οὗτός ἐστιν ὑπὲρ οὗ ἐγὼ εἶπον,
Ὀπίσω μου ἔρχεται ἀνὴρ ὃς ἔμπροσθέν μου γέγονεν,

ὅτι πρῶτός μου ἦν. 31 κἀγὼ οὐκ ᾔδειν αὐτόν, ἀλλ' ἵνα
φανερωθῇ τῷ Ἰσραήλ, διὰ τοῦτο ἦλθον ἐγὼ ἐν ὕδατι
βαπτίζων. 32 καὶ ἐμαρτύρησεν Ἰωάννης λέγων ὅτι
Τεθέαμαι τὸ πνεῦμα καταβαῖνον ὡς περιστερὰν ἐξ οὐρανοῦ, καὶ ἔμεινεν ἐπ' αὐτόν. 33 κἀγὼ οὐκ ᾔδειν αὐτόν,
ἀλλ' ὁ πέμψας με βαπτίζειν ἐν ὕδατι, ἐκεῖνός μοι εἶπεν,
Ἐφ' ὃν ἂν ἴδῃς τὸ πνεῦμα καταβαῖνον καὶ μένον ἐπ'
αὐτόν, οὗτός ἐστιν ὁ βαπτίζων ἐν πνεύματι ἁγίῳ. 34 κἀγὼ ἑώρακα, καὶ μεμαρτύρηκα ὅτι οὗτός ἐστιν ὁ υἱὸς τοῦ
θεοῦ.

35 Τῇ ἐπαύριον πάλιν εἱστήκει Ἰωάννης καὶ ἐκ τῶν
μαθητῶν αὐτοῦ δύο. 36 καὶ ἐμβλέψας τῷ Ἰησοῦ περιπα-
τοῦντι λέγει, Ἴδε ὁ ἀμνὸς τοῦ θεοῦ.

37 Καὶ ἤκουσαν οἱ δύο μαθηταὶ αὐτοῦ λαλοῦντος, καὶ
ἠκολούθησαν τῷ Ἰησοῦ. 38 στραφεὶς δὲ ὁ Ἰησοῦς καὶ
θεασάμενος αὐτοὺς ἀκολουθοῦντας λέγει αὐτοῖς, 39 Τί
ζητεῖτε; οἱ δὲ εἶπαν αὐτῷ, Ῥαββί, (ὃ λέγεται μεθερμηνευόμενον Διδάσκαλε,) ποῦ μένεις; 40 λέγει αὐτοῖς,
Ἔρχεσθε καὶ ὄψεσθε. ἦλθαν οὖν καὶ εἶδαν ποῦ μένει,
καὶ παρ' αὐτῷ ἔμειναν τὴν ἡμέραν ἐκείνην· ὥρα ἦν ὡς
δεκάτη. 41 ἦν Ἀνδρέας ὁ ἀδελφὸς Σίμωνος Πέτρου εἷς
ἐκ τῶν δύο τῶν ἀκουσάντων παρὰ Ἰωάννου καὶ ἀκολου-
θησάντων αὐτῷ. 42 εὑρίσκει οὗτος πρῶτον τὸν ἀδελφὸν
τὸν ἴδιον Σίμωνα καὶ λέγει αὐτῷ, Εὑρήκαμεν τὸν
Μεσσίαν (ὅ ἐστι μεθερμηνευόμενον Χριστός). 43 ἤγαγεν
αὐτὸν πρὸς τὸν Ἰησοῦν. ἐμβλέψας αὐτῷ ὁ Ἰησοῦς
εἶπεν, Σὺ εἶ Σίμων ὁ υἱὸς Ἰωάννου· σὺ κληθήσῃ Κηφᾶς (ὃ ἑρμηνεύεται Πέτρος).

44 Τῇ ἐπαύριον ἠθέλησεν ἐξελθεῖν εἰς τὴν Γαλιλαίαν.
καὶ εὑρίσκει Φίλιππον καὶ λέγει αὐτῷ ὁ Ἰησοῦς, Ἀκολούθει μοι. 45 ἦν δὲ ὁ Φίλιππος ἀπὸ Βηθσαϊδά, ἐκ τῆς

πόλεως Ἀνδρέου καὶ Πέτρου. 46 εὑρίσκει Φίλιππος τὸν
Ναθαναὴλ καὶ λέγει αὐτῷ, Ὃν ἔγραψεν Μωυσῆς ἐν
τῷ νόμῳ καὶ οἱ προφῆται εὑρήκαμεν, Ἰησοῦν υἱὸν τοῦ
Ἰωσὴφ τὸν ἀπὸ Ναζαρέτ. 47 καὶ εἶπεν αὐτῷ Ναθαναήλ, Ἐκ Ναζαρὲτ δύναταί τι ἀγαθὸν εἶναι; λέγει
αὐτῷ ὁ Φίλιππος, Ἔρχου καὶ ἴδε. 48 εἶδεν Ἰησοῦς
τὸν Ναθαναὴλ ἐρχόμενον πρὸς αὐτὸν καὶ λέγει περὶ
αὐτοῦ, Ἴδε ἀληθῶς Ἰσραηλείτης ἐν ᾧ δόλος οὐκ ἔστιν.
49 λέγει αὐτῷ Ναθαναήλ, Πόθεν με γινώσκεις; ἀπεκρίθη Ἰησοῦς καὶ εἶπεν αὐτῷ, Πρὸ τοῦ σε Φίλιππον
φωνῆσαι ὄντα ὑπὸ τὴν συκῆν εἶδόν σε. 50 ἀπεκρίθη
αὐτῷ Ναθαναήλ, Ῥαββί, σὺ εἶ ὁ υἱὸς τοῦ θεοῦ, σὺ
βασιλεὺς εἶ τοῦ Ἰσραήλ. 51 ἀπεκρίθη Ἰησοῦς καὶ εἶπεν
αὐτῷ, Ὅτι εἶπόν σοι ὅτι εἶδόν σε ὑποκάτω τῆς συκῆς,
πιστεύεις; μείζω τούτων ὄψῃ. 52 καὶ λέγει αὐτῷ, Ἀμὴν
ἀμὴν λέγω ὑμῖν, ὄψεσθε τὸν οὐρανὸν ἀνεῳγότα καὶ
τοὺς ἀγγέλους τοῦ θεοῦ ἀναβαίνοντας καὶ καταβαίνον-
τας ἐπὶ τὸν υἱὸν τοῦ ἀνθρώπου.

2 1 Καὶ τῇ ἡμέρᾳ τῇ τρίτῃ γάμος ἐγένετο ἐν Κανᾶ
τῆς Γαλιλαίας, καὶ ἦν ἡ μήτηρ τοῦ Ἰησοῦ ἐκεῖ. 2 ἐ-
κλήθη δὲ καὶ ὁ Ἰησοῦς καὶ οἱ μαθηταὶ αὐτοῦ εἰς τὸν γά-
μον. 3 καὶ ὑστερήσαντος οἴνου λέγει ἡ μήτηρ τοῦ Ἰησοῦ
πρὸς αὐτόν, Οἶνον οὐκ ἔχουσιν. 4 λέγει αὐτῇ ὁ Ἰησοῦς,
Τί ἐμοὶ καὶ σοί, γύναι; οὔπω ἥκει ἡ ὥρα μου. 5 λέγει
ἡ μήτηρ αὐτοῦ τοῖς διακόνοις, Ὅ τι ἂν λέγῃ ὑμῖν,
ποιήσατε. 6 ἦσαν δὲ ἐκεῖ λίθιναι ὑδρίαι ἓξ κατὰ τὸν
καθαρισμὸν τῶν Ἰουδαίων κείμεναι, χωροῦσαι ἀνὰ με-
τρητὰς δύο ἢ τρεῖς. 7 λέγει αὐτοῖς ὁ Ἰησοῦς, Γεμίσατε
τὰς ὑδρίας ὕδατος. καὶ ἐγέμισαν αὐτὰς ἕως ἄνω. 8 καὶ
λέγει αὐτοῖς, Ἀντλήσατε νῦν καὶ φέρετε τῷ ἀρχιτρι-
κλίνῳ. οἱ δὲ ἤνεγκαν. 9 ὡς δὲ ἐγεύσατο ὁ ἀρχιτρίκλι-

νος τὸ ὕδωρ οἶνον γεγενημένον, καὶ οὐκ ᾔδει πόθεν ἐστίν,
οἱ δὲ διάκονοι ᾔδεισαν οἱ ἠντληκότες τὸ ὕδωρ, φωνεῖ
τὸν νυμφίον ὁ ἀρχιτρίκλινος, [10]καὶ λέγει αὐτῷ, Πᾶς
ἄνθρωπος πρῶτον τὸν καλὸν οἶνον τίθησιν, καὶ ὅταν μεθυσθῶσιν τὸν ἐλάσσω· σὺ τετήρηκας τὸν καλὸν οἶνον
ἕως ἄρτι. [11]ταύτην ἐποίησεν ἀρχὴν τῶν σημείων ὁ
Ἰησοῦς ἐν Κανᾶ τῆς Γαλιλαίας καὶ ἐφανέρωσεν τὴν
δόξαν αὐτοῦ· καὶ ἐπίστευσαν εἰς αὐτὸν οἱ μαθηταὶ
αὐτοῦ.

[12]Μετὰ τοῦτο κατέβη εἰς Καφαρναοὺμ αὐτὸς καὶ
ἡ μήτηρ αὐτοῦ καὶ οἱ ἀδελφοὶ καὶ οἱ μαθηταὶ αὐτοῦ,
καὶ ἐκεῖ ἔμειναν οὐ πολλὰς ἡμέρας.

[13]Καὶ ἐγγὺς ἦν τὸ πάσχα τῶν Ἰουδαίων, καὶ ἀνέβη
εἰς Ἱεροσόλυμα ὁ Ἰησοῦς.

[14]Καὶ εὗρεν ἐν τῷ ἱερῷ τοὺς πωλοῦντας βόας καὶ
πρόβατα καὶ περιστερὰς καὶ τοὺς κερματιστὰς καθημένους. [15]καὶ ποιήσας φραγέλλιον ἐκ σχοινίων πάντας
ἐξέβαλεν ἐκ τοῦ ἱεροῦ, τά τε πρόβατα καὶ τοὺς βόας,
καὶ τῶν κολλυβιστῶν ἐξέχεεν τὰ κέρματα καὶ τὰς τρα-
πέζας ἀνέστρεψεν, [16]καὶ τοῖς τὰς περιστερὰς πωλοῦσιν
εἶπεν, Ἄρατε ταῦτα ἐντεῦθεν, μὴ ποιεῖτε τὸν οἶκον τοῦ
πατρός μου οἶκον ἐμπορίου. [17]ἐμνήσθησαν οἱ μαθηταὶ
αὐτοῦ ὅτι γεγραμμένον ἐστίν, Ὁ ζῆλος τοῦ οἴκου σου
καταφάγεταί με.

[18]Ἀπεκρίθησαν οὖν οἱ Ἰουδαῖοι καὶ εἶπαν αὐτῷ,
Τί σημεῖον δεικνύεις ἡμῖν, ὅτι ταῦτα ποιεῖς; [19]ἀπε-
κρίθη Ἰησοῦς καὶ εἶπεν αὐτοῖς, Λύσατε τὸν ναὸν
τοῦτον, καὶ ἐν τρισὶν ἡμέραις ἐγερῶ αὐτόν. [20]εἶπαν
οὖν οἱ Ἰουδαῖοι, Τεσσεράκοντα καὶ ἓξ ἔτεσιν ᾠκο-
δομήθη ὁ ναὸς οὗτος, καὶ σὺ ἐν τρισὶν ἡμέραις ἐγερεῖς
αὐτόν; [21]ἐκεῖνος δὲ ἔλεγεν περὶ τοῦ ναοῦ τοῦ σώμα-

τος αὐτοῦ. 22 ὅτε οὖν ἠγέρθη ἐκ νεκρῶν, ἐμνήσθησαν οἱ
μαθηταὶ αὐτοῦ ὅτι τοῦτο ἔλεγεν· καὶ ἐπίστευσαν τῇ
γραφῇ καὶ τῷ λόγῳ ὃν εἶπεν ὁ Ἰησοῦς.
23 Ὡς δὲ ἦν ἐν τοῖς Ἱεροσολύμοις ἐν τῷ πάσχα ἐν
τῇ ἑορτῇ, πολλοὶ ἐπίστευσαν εἰς τὸ ὄνομα αὐτοῦ, θεωροῦντες αὐτοῦ τὰ σημεῖα ἃ ἐποίει. 24 αὐτὸς δὲ Ἰησοῦς
οὐκ ἐπίστευεν αὐτὸν αὐτοῖς, διὰ τὸ αὐτὸν γινώσκειν
πάντας· 25 καὶ ὅτι οὐ χρείαν εἶχεν ἵνα τις μαρτυρήσῃ
περὶ τοῦ ἀνθρώπου· αὐτὸς γὰρ ἐγίνωσκεν τί ἦν ἐν τῷ
ἀνθρώπῳ.
3 1 Ἦν δὲ ἄνθρωπος ἐκ τῶν Φαρισαίων, Νικόδημος
ὄνομα αὐτῷ, ἄρχων τῶν Ἰουδαίων. 2 οὗτος ἦλθεν πρὸς
αὐτὸν νυκτὸς καὶ εἶπεν αὐτῷ, Ῥαββί, οἴδαμεν ὅτι ἀπὸ
θεοῦ ἐλήλυθας διδάσκαλος· οὐδεὶς γὰρ δύναται ταῦτα
τὰ σημεῖα ποιεῖν ἃ σὺ ποιεῖς, ἐὰν μὴ ᾖ ὁ θεὸς μετ' αὐτοῦ. 3 ἀπεκρίθη Ἰησοῦς καὶ εἶπεν αὐτῷ, Ἀμὴν ἀμὴν
λέγω σοι, ἐὰν μή τις γεννηθῇ ἄνωθεν, οὐ δύναται ἰδεῖν
τὴν βασιλείαν τοῦ θεοῦ. 4 λέγει πρὸς αὐτὸν ὁ Νικόδημος, Πῶς δύναται ἄνθρωπος γεννηθῆναι γέρων ὤν; μὴ
δύναται εἰς τὴν κοιλίαν τῆς μητρὸς αὐτοῦ δεύτερον
εἰσελθεῖν καὶ γεννηθῆναι; 5 ἀπεκρίθη Ἰησοῦς, Ἀμὴν
ἀμὴν λέγω σοι, ἐὰν μή τις γεννηθῇ ἐξ ὕδατος καὶ πνεύματος, οὐ δύναται εἰσελθεῖν εἰς τὴν βασιλείαν τοῦ
θεοῦ. 6 τὸ γεγεννημένον ἐκ τῆς σαρκὸς σάρξ ἐστιν,
καὶ τὸ γεγεννημένον ἐκ τοῦ πνεύματος πνεῦμά ἐστιν.
7 μὴ θαυμάσῃς ὅτι εἶπόν σοι, Δεῖ ὑμᾶς γεννηθῆναι
ἄνωθεν. 8 τὸ πνεῦμα ὅπου θέλει πνεῖ, καὶ τὴν φωνὴν
αὐτοῦ ἀκούεις, ἀλλ' οὐκ οἶδας πόθεν ἔρχεται καὶ ποῦ
ὑπάγει· οὕτως ἐστὶν πᾶς ὁ γεγεννημένος ἐκ τοῦ πνεύματος. 9 ἀπεκρίθη Νικόδημος καὶ εἶπεν αὐτῷ, Πῶς δύναται ταῦτα γενέσθαι; 10 ἀπεκρίθη Ἰησοῦς καὶ εἶπεν

αὐτῷ, Σὺ εἶ ὁ διδάσκαλος τοῦ Ἰσραὴλ καὶ ταῦτα οὐ
γινώσκεις; 11 ἀμὴν ἀμὴν λέγω σοι ὅτι ὃ οἴδαμεν λαλοῦ-
μεν καὶ ὃ ἑωράκαμεν μαρτυροῦμεν, καὶ τὴν μαρτυρίαν
ἡμῶν οὐ λαμβάνετε. 12 εἰ τὰ ἐπίγεια εἶπον ὑμῖν καὶ οὐ
πιστεύετε, πῶς ἐὰν εἴπω ὑμῖν τὰ ἐπουράνια πιστεύσετε; 13 καὶ οὐδεὶς ἀναβέβηκεν εἰς τὸν οὐρανὸν εἰ μὴ ὁ ἐκ
τοῦ οὐρανοῦ καταβάς, ὁ υἱὸς τοῦ ἀνθρώπου ὁ ὢν ἐν τῷ
οὐρανῷ. 14 καὶ καθὼς Μωυσῆς ὕψωσεν τὸν ὄφιν ἐν τῇ
ἐρήμῳ, οὕτως ὑψωθῆναι δεῖ τὸν υἱὸν τοῦ ἀνθρώπου, 15 ἵνα
πᾶς ὁ πιστεύων ἐν αὐτῷ ἔχῃ ζωὴν αἰώνιον. 16 οὕτως γὰρ
ἠγάπησεν ὁ θεὸς τὸν κόσμον, ὥστε τὸν υἱὸν τὸν μονογενῆ ἔδωκεν, ἵνα πᾶς ὁ πιστεύων εἰς αὐτὸν μὴ ἀπόληται
ἀλλ' ἔχῃ ζωὴν αἰώνιον. 17 οὐ γὰρ ἀπέστειλεν ὁ θεὸς τὸν
υἱὸν εἰς τὸν κόσμον ἵνα κρίνῃ τὸν κόσμον, ἀλλ' ἵνα
σωθῇ ὁ κόσμος δι' αὐτοῦ. 18 ὁ πιστεύων εἰς αὐτὸν οὐ
κρίνεται· ὁ μὴ πιστεύων ἤδη κέκριται, ὅτι μὴ πεπίσ-
τευκεν εἰς τὸ ὄνομα τοῦ μονογενοῦς υἱοῦ τοῦ θεοῦ.
19 αὕτη δέ ἐστιν ἡ κρίσις, ὅτι τὸ φῶς ἐλήλυθεν εἰς τὸν
κόσμον καὶ ἠγάπησαν οἱ ἄνθρωποι μᾶλλον τὸ σκότος,
ἢ τὸ φῶς· ἦν γὰρ αὐτῶν πονηρὰ τὰ ἔργα. 20 πᾶς γὰρ ὁ
φαῦλα πράσσων μισεῖ τὸ φῶς καὶ οὐκ ἔρχεται πρὸς τὸ
φῶς, ἵνα μὴ ἐλεγχθῇ τὰ ἔργα αὐτοῦ· 21 ὁ δὲ ποιῶν τὴν
ἀλήθειαν ἔρχεται πρὸς τὸ φῶς, ἵνα φανερωθῇ αὐτοῦ τὰ
ἔργα, ὅτι ἐν θεῷ ἐστιν εἰργασμένα.

22 Μετὰ ταῦτα ἦλθεν ὁ Ἰησοῦς καὶ οἱ μαθηταὶ αὐτοῦ
εἰς τὴν Ἰουδαίαν γῆν, καὶ ἐκεῖ διέτριβεν μετ' αὐτῶν καὶ
ἐβάπτιζεν. 23 ἦν δὲ καὶ Ἰωάννης βαπτίζων ἐν Αἰνὼν
ἐγγὺς τοῦ Σαλείμ, ὅτι ὕδατα πολλὰ ἦν ἐκεῖ, καὶ παρε-
γίνοντο καὶ ἐβαπτίζοντο· 24 οὔπω γὰρ ἦν βεβλημένος
εἰς τὴν φυλακὴν Ἰωάννης. 25 ἐγένετο οὖν ζήτησις ἐκ
τῶν μαθητῶν Ἰωάννου μετὰ Ἰουδαίου περὶ καθαρισμοῦ.

26 καὶ ἦλθον πρὸς τὸν Ἰωάννην καὶ εἶπον αὐτῷ, Ῥαββί,
ὃς ἦν μετὰ σοῦ πέραν τοῦ Ἰορδάνου, ᾧ σὺ μεμαρτύρη-
κας, ἴδε οὗτος βαπτίζει καὶ πάντες ἔρχονται πρὸς αὐτόν. 27 ἀπεκρίθη Ἰωάννης καὶ εἶπεν, Οὐ δύναται ἄνθρωπος λαμβάνειν οὐδέν, ἐὰν μὴ ᾖ διδομένον αὐτῷ ἐκ
τοῦ οὐρανοῦ. 28 αὐτοὶ ὑμεῖς μοι μαρτυρεῖτε ὅτι εἶπον,
Οὐκ εἰμὶ ἐγὼ ὁ Χριστός, ἀλλ' ὅτι ἀπεσταλμένος εἰμὶ
ἔμπροσθεν ἐκείνου. 29 ὁ ἔχων τὴν νύμφην νυμφίος ἐσ-
τίν· ὁ δὲ φίλος τοῦ νυμφίου, ὁ ἑστηκὼς καὶ ἀκούων
αὐτοῦ, χαρᾷ χαίρει διὰ τὴν φωνὴν τοῦ νυμφίου. αὕτη
οὖν ἡ χαρὰ ἡ ἐμὴ πεπλήρωται. 30 ἐκεῖνον δεῖ αὐξάνειν,
ἐμὲ δὲ ἐλαττοῦσθαι. 31 ὁ ἄνωθεν ἐρχόμενος ἐπάνω πάντων ἐστίν. ὁ ὢν ἐκ τῆς γῆς ἐκ τῆς γῆς ἐστιν καὶ ἐκ τῆς
γῆς λαλεῖ. ὁ ἐκ τοῦ οὐρανοῦ ἐρχόμενος ἐπάνω πάντων
ἐστίν· 32 ὃ ἑώρακεν καὶ ἤκουσεν τοῦτο μαρτυρεῖ, καὶ τὴν
μαρτυρίαν αὐτοῦ οὐδεὶς λαμβάνει. 33 ὁ λαβὼν αὐτοῦ
τὴν μαρτυρίαν ἐσφράγισεν ὅτι ὁ θεὸς ἀληθής ἐστιν.
34 ὃν γὰρ ἀπέστειλεν ὁ θεός, τὰ ῥήματα τοῦ θεοῦ λαλεῖ·
οὐ γὰρ ἐκ μέτρου δίδωσιν τὸ πνεῦμα. 35 ὁ πατὴρ ἀγαπᾷ
τὸν υἱόν, καὶ πάντα δέδωκεν ἐν τῇ χειρὶ αὐτοῦ. 36 ὁ πιστεύων εἰς τὸν υἱὸν ἔχει ζωὴν αἰώνιον· ὁ δὲ ἀπειθῶν τῷ
υἱῷ οὐκ ὄψεται ζωήν, ἀλλ' ἡ ὀργὴ τοῦ θεοῦ μένει ἐπ'
αὐτόν.

4 1 Ὡς οὖν ἔγνω ὁ κύριος ὅτι ἤκουσαν οἱ Φαρισαῖοι ὅτι Ἰησοῦς πλείονας μαθητὰς ποιεῖ καὶ βαπτίζει ἢ
Ἰωάννης, 2 (καίτοιγε Ἰησοῦς αὐτὸς οὐκ ἐβάπτιζεν ἀλλ'
οἱ μαθηταὶ αὐτοῦ,) 3 ἀφῆκεν τὴν Ἰουδαίαν καὶ ἀπῆλθεν
πάλιν εἰς τὴν Γαλιλαίαν. 4 ἔδει δὲ αὐτὸν διέρχεσθαι
διὰ τῆς Σαμαρείας. 5 ἔρχεται οὖν εἰς πόλιν τῆς Σαμαρείας λεγομένην Συχάρ, πλησίον τοῦ χωρίου ὃ ἔδωκεν
Ἰακὼβ Ἰωσὴφ τῷ υἱῷ αὐτοῦ. 6 ἦν δὲ ἐκεῖ πηγὴ τοῦ

Ἰακώβ. ὁ οὖν Ἰησοῦς κεκοπιακὼς ἐκ τῆς ὁδοιπορίας
ἐκαθέζετο οὕτως ἐπὶ τῇ πηγῇ· ὥρα ἦν ὡς ἕκτη. 7 ἔρχεται γυνὴ ἐκ τῆς Σαμαρείας ἀντλῆσαι ὕδωρ. λέγει
αὐτῇ ὁ Ἰησοῦς, Δός μοι πεῖν. 8 οἱ γὰρ μαθηταὶ αὐτοῦ
ἀπεληλύθεισαν εἰς τὴν πόλιν, ἵνα τροφὰς ἀγοράσωσιν.
9 λέγει οὖν αὐτῷ ἡ γυνὴ ἡ Σαμαρεῖτις, Πῶς σὺ Ἰου-
δαῖος ὢν παρ' ἐμοῦ πεῖν αἰτεῖς γυναικὸς Σαμαρείτιδος
οὔσης; [οὐ γὰρ συγχρῶνται Ἰουδαῖοι Σαμαρείταις.] 10 ἀ-
πεκρίθη Ἰησοῦς καὶ εἶπεν αὐτῇ, Εἰ ᾔδεις τὴν δωρεὰν
τοῦ θεοῦ, καὶ τίς ἐστιν ὁ λέγων σοι, Δός μοι πεῖν, σὺ
ἂν ᾔτησας αὐτὸν καὶ ἔδωκεν ἄν σοι ὕδωρ ζῶν. 11 λέγει
αὐτῷ ἡ γυνή, Κύριε, οὔτε ἄντλημα ἔχεις, καὶ τὸ φρέαρ
ἐστὶ βαθύ· πόθεν οὖν ἔχεις τὸ ὕδωρ τὸ ζῶν; 12 μὴ σὺ
μείζων εἶ τοῦ πατρὸς ἡμῶν Ἰακώβ, ὃς ἔδωκεν ἡμῖν τὸ
φρέαρ, καὶ αὐτὸς ἐξ αὐτοῦ ἔπιεν καὶ οἱ υἱοὶ αὐτοῦ καὶ
τὰ θρέμματα αὐτοῦ; 13 ἀπεκρίθη Ἰησοῦς καὶ εἶπεν
αὐτῇ, Πᾶς ὁ πίνων ἐκ τοῦ ὕδατος τούτου διψήσει
πάλιν· 14 ὃς δ' ἂν πίῃ ἐκ τοῦ ὕδατος οὗ ἐγὼ δώσω αὐτῷ,
οὐ μὴ διψήσει εἰς τὸν αἰῶνα, ἀλλὰ τὸ ὕδωρ ὃ δώσω
αὐτῷ γενήσεται ἐν αὐτῷ πηγὴ ὕδατος ἁλλομένου εἰς
ζωὴν αἰώνιον. 15 λέγει πρὸς αὐτὸν ἡ γυνή, Κύριε, δός
μοι τοῦτο τὸ ὕδωρ, ἵνα μὴ διψῶ μηδὲ διέρχωμαι ἐνθάδε
ἀντλεῖν. 16 λέγει αὐτῇ, Ὕπαγε φώνησον τὸν ἄνδρα
σοῦ καὶ ἐλθὲ ἐνθάδε. 17 ἀπεκρίθη ἡ γυνὴ καὶ εἶπεν,
Οὐκ ἔχω ἄνδρα. λέγει αὐτῇ ὁ Ἰησοῦς, Καλῶς εἶπας
ὅτι Ἄνδρα οὐκ ἔχω· 18 πέντε γὰρ ἄνδρας ἔσχες, καὶ
νῦν ὃν ἔχεις οὐκ ἔστιν σου ἀνήρ· τοῦτο ἀληθὲς εἴρηκας.
19 λέγει αὐτῷ ἡ γυνή, Κύριε, θεωρῶ ὅτι προφήτης εἶ σύ.
20 οἱ πατέρες ἡμῶν ἐν τῷ ὄρει τούτῳ προσεκύνησαν· καὶ
ὑμεῖς λέγετε ὅτι ἐν Ἱεροσολύμοις ἐστὶν ὁ τόπος, ὅπου
προσκυνεῖν δεῖ. 21 λέγει αὐτῇ ὁ Ἰησοῦς, Πίστευέ μοι,

γύναι, ὅτι ἔρχεται ὥρα ὅτε οὔτε ἐν τῷ ὄρει τούτῳ οὔτε
ἐν Ἱεροσολύμοις προσκυνήσετε τῷ πατρί. 22 ὑμεῖς προσ-
κυνεῖτε ὃ οὐκ οἴδατε, ἡμεῖς προσκυνοῦμεν ὃ οἴδαμεν,
ὅτι ἡ σωτηρία ἐκ τῶν Ἰουδαίων ἐστίν· 23 ἀλλὰ ἔρχεται
ὥρα καὶ νῦν ἐστίν, ὅτε οἱ ἀληθινοὶ προσκυνηταὶ προσ-
κυνήσουσιν τῷ πατρὶ ἐν πνεύματι καὶ ἀληθείᾳ· καὶ γὰρ
ὁ πατὴρ τοιούτους ζητεῖ τοὺς προσκυνοῦντας αὐτόν.
24 πνεῦμα ὁ θεός· καὶ τοὺς προσκυνοῦντας αὐτὸν ἐν
πνεύματι καὶ ἀληθείᾳ δεῖ προσκυνεῖν. 25 λέγει αὐτῷ ἡ
γυνή, Οἶδα ὅτι Μεσσίας ἔρχεται, ὁ λεγόμενος Χριστός·
ὅταν ἔλθῃ ἐκεῖνος, ἀναγγελεῖ ἡμῖν ἅπαντα. 26 λέγει αὐτῇ
ὁ Ἰησοῦς, Ἐγώ εἰμι, ὁ λαλῶν σοι.

27 Καὶ ἐπὶ τούτῳ ἦλθαν οἱ μαθηταὶ αὐτοῦ, καὶ ἐθαύμαζον ὅτι μετὰ γυναικὸς ἐλάλει· οὐδεὶς μέντοι εἶπεν,
Τί ζητεῖς; ἤ Τί λαλεῖς μετ᾽ αὐτῆς; 28 ἀφῆκεν οὖν τὴν
ὑδρίαν αὐτῆς ἡ γυνὴ καὶ ἀπῆλθεν εἰς τὴν πόλιν, καὶ
λέγει τοῖς ἀνθρώποις, 29 Δεῦτε ἴδετε ἄνθρωπον ὃς εἶπέν
μοι πάντα ἃ ἐποίησα· μήτι οὗτός ἐστιν ὁ Χριστός;
30 ἐξῆλθον ἐκ τῆς πόλεως, καὶ ἤρχοντο πρὸς αὐτόν.

31 Ἐν τῷ μεταξὺ ἠρώτων αὐτὸν οἱ μαθηταὶ λέγοντες, Ῥαββί, φάγε. 32 ὁ δὲ εἶπεν αὐτοῖς, Ἐγὼ βρῶσιν
ἔχω φαγεῖν ἣν ὑμεῖς οὐκ οἴδατε. 33 ἔλεγον οὖν οἱ μαθηταὶ πρὸς ἀλλήλους, Μήτις ἤνεγκεν αὐτῷ φαγεῖν;
34 λέγει αὐτοῖς ὁ Ἰησοῦς, Ἐμὸν βρῶμά ἐστιν ἵνα ποιήσω τὸ θέλημα τοῦ πέμψαντός με καὶ τελειώσω αὐτοῦ
τὸ ἔργον. 35 οὐχ ὑμεῖς λέγετε ὅτι ἔτι τετράμηνός ἐστιν
καὶ ὁ θερισμὸς ἔρχεται; ἰδοὺ λέγω ὑμῖν, Ἐπάρατε τοὺς
ὀφθαλμοὺς ὑμῶν καὶ θεάσασθε τὰς χώρας, ὅτι λευκαί
εἰσιν πρὸς θερισμὸν ἤδη. 36 ὁ θερίζων μισθὸν λαμβάνει
καὶ συνάγει καρπὸν εἰς ζωὴν αἰώνιον, ἵνα καὶ ὁ σπείρων
ὁμοῦ χαίρῃ καὶ ὁ θερίζων. 37 ἐν γὰρ τούτῳ ὁ λόγος

ἐστὶν ἀληθινός, ὅτι ἄλλος ἐστὶν ὁ σπείρων καὶ ἄλλος ὁ
θερίζων. 38 ἐγὼ ἀπέστειλα ὑμᾶς θερίζειν ὃ οὐχ ὑμεῖς
κεκοπιάκατε· ἄλλοι κεκοπιάκασιν, καὶ ὑμεῖς εἰς τὸν κό-
πον αὐτῶν εἰσεληλύθατε. 39 ἐκ δὲ τῆς πόλεως ἐκείνης
πολλοὶ ἐπίστευσαν εἰς αὐτὸν τῶν Σαμαρειτῶν διὰ τὸν
λόγον τῆς γυναικὸς μαρτυρούσης ὅτι Εἶπέν μοι πάντα
ἃ ἐποίησα. 40 ὡς οὖν ἦλθον πρὸς αὐτὸν οἱ Σαμαρεῖται,
ἠρώτων αὐτὸν μεῖναι παρ' αὐτοῖς· καὶ ἔμεινεν ἐκεῖ δύο
ἡμέρας. 41 καὶ πολλῷ πλείους ἐπίστευσαν διὰ τὸν λόγον αὐτοῦ, 42 τῇ τε γυναικὶ ἔλεγον ὅτι Οὐκέτι διὰ τὴν
σὴν λαλιὰν πιστεύομεν· αὐτοὶ γὰρ ἀκηκόαμεν, καὶ οἴδαμεν ὅτι οὗτός ἐστιν ἀληθῶς ὁ σωτὴρ τοῦ κόσμου.

43 Μετὰ δὲ τὰς δύο ἡμέρας ἐξῆλθεν ἐκεῖθεν εἰς τὴν
Γαλιλαίαν. 44 αὐτὸς γὰρ Ἰησοῦς ἐμαρτύρησεν, ὅτι προφήτης ἐν τῇ ἰδίᾳ πατρίδι τιμὴν οὐκ ἔχει. 45 ὅτε οὖν
ἦλθεν εἰς τὴν Γαλιλαίαν, ἐδέξαντο αὐτὸν οἱ Γαλιλαῖοι,
πάντα ἑωρακότες ὅσα ἐποίησεν ἐν Ἱεροσολύμοις ἐν τῇ
ἑορτῇ· καὶ αὐτοὶ γὰρ ἦλθον εἰς τὴν ἑορτήν. 46 Ἦλθεν οὖν
πάλιν εἰς τὴν Κανᾶ τῆς Γαλιλαίας, ὅπου ἐποίησεν τὸ
ὕδωρ οἶνον. καὶ ἦν τις βασιλικὸς οὗ ὁ υἱὸς ἠσθένει ἐν
Καφαρναούμ. 47 οὗτος ἀκούσας ὅτι Ἰησοῦς ἥκει ἐκ τῆς
Ἰουδαίας εἰς τὴν Γαλιλαίαν, ἀπῆλθεν πρὸς αὐτόν, καὶ
ἠρώτα ἵνα καταβῇ καὶ ἰάσηται αὐτοῦ τὸν υἱόν· ἤμελλεν
γὰρ ἀποθνήσκειν. 48 εἶπεν οὖν ὁ Ἰησοῦς πρὸς αὐτόν, Ἐὰν
μὴ σημεῖα καὶ τέρατα ἴδητε, οὐ μὴ πιστεύσητε. 49 λέγει πρὸς αὐτὸν ὁ βασιλικός, Κύριε, κατάβηθι πρὶν
ἀποθανεῖν τὸ παιδίον μου. 50 λέγει αὐτῷ ὁ Ἰησοῦς,
Πορεύου· ὁ υἱός σου ζῇ. ἐπίστευσεν ὁ ἄνθρωπος τῷ
λόγῳ ὃν εἶπεν αὐτῷ Ἰησοῦς, καὶ ἐπορεύετο. 51 ἤδη δὲ
αὐτοῦ καταβαίνοντος οἱ δοῦλοι αὐτοῦ ὑπήντησαν αὐτῷ [καὶ ἀπήγγειλαν] λέγοντες ὅτι Ὁ παῖς αὐτοῦ ζῇ.

52 ἐπύθετο οὖν τὴν ὥραν παρ' αὐτῶν ἐν ᾗ κομψότερον
ἔσχεν. εἶπον οὖν αὐτῷ ὅτι Ἐχθὲς ὥραν ἑβδόμην ἀφῆκεν αὐτὸν ὁ πυρετός. 53 ἔγνω οὖν ὁ πατὴρ ὅτι ἐκείνῃ
τῇ ὥρᾳ ἐν ᾗ εἶπεν αὐτῷ ὁ Ἰησοῦς, ὁ υἱός σου ζῇ. καὶ
ἐπίστευσεν αὐτὸς καὶ ἡ οἰκία αὐτοῦ ὅλη. 54 τοῦτο πάλιν
δεύτερον σημεῖον ἐποίησεν ὁ Ἰησοῦς ἐλθὼν ἐκ τῆς Ἰουδαίας εἰς τὴν Γαλιλαίαν.

5 1 Μετὰ ταῦτα ἦν ἑορτὴ τῶν Ἰουδαίων, καὶ ἀνέβη
Ἰησοῦς εἰς Ἱεροσόλυμα. 2 ἔστιν δὲ ἐν τοῖς Ἱεροσολύμοις ἐπὶ τῇ προβατικῇ κολυμβήθρα ἡ ἐπιλεγομένη
Ἑβραϊστὶ Βηθεσδά, πέντε στοὰς ἔχουσα. 3 ἐν ταύταις
κατέκειτο πλῆθος τῶν ἀσθενούντων, τυφλῶν, χωλῶν, ξηρῶν.* 5 ἦν δέ τις ἄνθρωπος ἐκεῖ τριάκοντα καὶ ὀκτὼ
ἔτη ἔχων ἐν τῇ ἀσθενείᾳ αὐτοῦ· 6 τοῦτον ἰδὼν ὁ Ἰησοῦς
κατακείμενον, καὶ γνοὺς ὅτι πολὺν ἤδη χρόνον ἔχει,
λέγει αὐτῷ, Θέλεις ὑγιὴς γενέσθαι; 7 ἀπεκρίθη αὐτῷ
ὁ ἀσθενῶν, Κύριε, ἄνθρωπον οὐκ ἔχω ἵνα ὅταν ταραχθῇ τὸ ὕδωρ βάλῃ με εἰς τὴν κολυμβήθραν· ἐν ᾧ δὲ
ἔρχομαι ἐγώ, ἄλλος πρὸ ἐμοῦ καταβαίνει. 8 λέγει αὐτῷ ὁ Ἰησοῦς, Ἔγειρε, ἆρον τὸν κράβαττόν σου καὶ
περιπάτει. 9 καὶ εὐθέως ἐγένετο ὑγιὴς ὁ ἄνθρωπος,
καὶ ἦρεν τὸν κράβαττον αὐτοῦ, καὶ περιεπάτει.

Ἦν δὲ σάββατον ἐν ἐκείνῃ τῇ ἡμέρᾳ. 10 ἔλεγον
οὖν οἱ Ἰουδαῖοι τῷ τεθεραπευμένῳ, Σάββατόν ἐστιν,
καὶ οὐκ ἔξεστίν σοι ἆραι τὸν κράβαττον. 11 ἀπεκρίθη
αὐτοῖς, Ὁ ποιήσας με ὑγιῆ, ἐκεῖνός μοι εἶπεν, Ἆρον
τὸν κράβαττον σου καὶ περιπάτει. 12 ἠρώτησαν οὖν
αὐτόν, Τίς ἐστιν ὁ ἄνθρωπος ὁ εἰπών σοι, Ἆρον
καὶ περιπάτει; 13 ὁ δὲ ἰαθεὶς οὐκ ᾔδει τίς ἐστιν· ὁ
γὰρ Ἰησοῦς ἐξένευσεν ὄχλου ὄντος ἐν τῷ τόπῳ. 14 μετὰ

* Verse 4 omitted on the best MS. authority.

ταῦτα εὑρίσκει αὐτὸν ὁ Ἰησοῦς ἐν τῷ ἱερῷ καὶ εἶπεν
αὐτῷ, Ἴδε ὑγιὴς γέγονας· μηκέτι ἁμάρτανε, ἵνα μὴ
χεῖρόν σοί τι γένηται. 15 ἀπῆλθεν ὁ ἄνθρωπος καὶ
ἀνήγγειλεν τοῖς Ἰουδαίοις ὅτι Ἰησοῦς ἐστιν ὁ ποιήσας
αὐτὸν ὑγιῆ.

16 Καὶ διὰ τοῦτο ἐδίωκον οἱ Ἰουδαῖοι τὸν Ἰησοῦν, ὅτι
ταῦτα ἐποίει ἐν σαββάτῳ.

17 Ὁ δὲ Ἰησοῦς ἀπεκρίνατο αὐτοῖς, Ὁ πατήρ μου
ἕως ἄρτι ἐργάζεται, κἀγὼ ἐργάζομαι. 18 διὰ τοῦτο οὖν
μᾶλλον ἐζήτουν αὐτὸν οἱ Ἰουδαῖοι ἀποκτεῖναι, ὅτι οὐ
μόνον ἔλυεν τὸ σάββατον, ἀλλὰ καὶ πατέρα ἴδιον ἔλεγεν
τὸν θεόν, ἴσον ἑαυτὸν ποιῶν τῷ θεῷ. 19 ἀπεκρίνατο οὖν
ὁ Ἰησοῦς καὶ ἔλεγεν αὐτοῖς, Ἀμὴν ἀμὴν λέγω ὑμῖν, οὐ
δύναται ὁ υἱὸς ποιεῖν ἀφ᾽ ἑαυτοῦ οὐδέν, ἐὰν μή τι βλέπῃ
τὸν πατέρα ποιοῦντα· ἃ γὰρ ἂν ἐκεῖνος ποιῇ, ταῦτα καὶ
ὁ υἱὸς ὁμοίως ποιεῖ. 20 ὁ γὰρ πατὴρ φιλεῖ τὸν υἱὸν καὶ
πάντα δείκνυσιν αὐτῷ ἃ αὐτὸς ποιεῖ, καὶ μείζονα τούτων δείξει αὐτῷ ἔργα, ἵνα ὑμεῖς θαυμάζητε. 21 ὥσπερ
γὰρ ὁ πατὴρ ἐγείρει τοὺς νεκροὺς καὶ ζωοποιεῖ, οὕτω καὶ
ὁ υἱὸς οὓς θέλει ζωοποιεῖ. 22 οὐδὲ γὰρ ὁ πατὴρ κρίνει
οὐδένα, ἀλλὰ τὴν κρίσιν πᾶσαν δέδωκεν τῷ υἱῷ, 23 ἵνα
πάντες τιμῶσιν τὸν υἱὸν καθὼς τιμῶσιν τὸν πατέρα. ὁ
μὴ τιμῶν τὸν υἱὸν οὐ τιμᾷ τὸν πατέρα τὸν πέμψαντα
αὐτόν. 24 ἀμὴν ἀμὴν λέγω ὑμῖν ὅτι ὁ τὸν λόγον μου
ἀκούων καὶ πιστεύων τῷ πέμψαντί με ἔχει ζωὴν αἰώνιον, καὶ εἰς κρίσιν οὐκ ἔρχεται ἀλλὰ μεταβέβηκεν ἐκ
τοῦ θανάτου εἰς τὴν ζωήν. 25 ἀμὴν ἀμὴν λέγω ὑμῖν ὅτι
ἔρχεται ὥρα καὶ νῦν ἐστίν, ὅτε οἱ νεκροὶ ἀκούσουσιν
τῆς φωνῆς τοῦ υἱοῦ τοῦ θεοῦ καὶ οἱ ἀκούσαντες ζήσουσιν. 26 ὥσπερ γὰρ ὁ πατὴρ ἔχει ζωὴν ἐν ἑαυτῷ, οὕτως
καὶ τῷ υἱῷ ἔδωκεν ζωὴν ἔχειν ἐν ἑαυτῷ· 27 καὶ ἐξουσίαν

ἔδωκεν αὐτῷ κρίσιν ποιεῖν, ὅτι υἱὸς ἀνθρώπου ἐστίν.
28 μὴ θαυμάζετε τοῦτο, ὅτι ἔρχεται ὥρα, ἐν ᾗ πάντες οἱ
ἐν τοῖς μνημείοις ἀκούσουσιν τῆς φωνῆς αὐτοῦ, 29 καὶ
ἐκπορεύσονται οἱ τὰ ἀγαθὰ ποιήσαντες εἰς ἀνάστασιν
ζωῆς, οἱ τὰ φαῦλα πράξαντες εἰς ἀνάστασιν κρίσεως.
30 οὐ δύναμαι ἐγὼ ποιεῖν ἀπ' ἐμαυτοῦ οὐδέν. καθὼς
ἀκούω κρίνω, καὶ ἡ κρίσις ἡ ἐμὴ δικαία ἐστίν, ὅτι οὐ
ζητῶ τὸ θέλημα τὸ ἐμὸν ἀλλὰ τὸ θέλημα τοῦ πέμψαντός με.

31 Ἐὰν ἐγὼ μαρτυρῶ περὶ ἐμαυτοῦ, ἡ μαρτυρία μου
οὐκ ἔστιν ἀληθής· 32 ἄλλος ἐστὶν ὁ μαρτυρῶν περὶ ἐμοῦ,
καὶ οἶδα ὅτι ἀληθής ἐστιν ἡ μαρτυρία ἣν μαρτυρεῖ περὶ
ἐμοῦ.

33 Ὑμεῖς ἀπεστάλκατε πρὸς Ἰωάννην, καὶ μεμαρτύρηκεν τῇ ἀληθείᾳ· 34 ἐγὼ δὲ οὐ παρὰ ἀνθρώπου τὴν μαρτυρίαν λαμβάνω, ἀλλὰ ταῦτα λέγω ἵνα ὑμεῖς σωθῆτε.
35 ἐκεῖνος ἦν ὁ λύχνος ὁ καιόμενος καὶ φαίνων, ὑμεῖς δὲ
ἠθελήσατε ἀγαλλιαθῆναι πρὸς ὥραν ἐν τῷ φωτὶ αὐτοῦ.
36 ἐγὼ δὲ ἔχω τὴν μαρτυρίαν μείζων τοῦ Ἰωάννου· τὰ
γὰρ ἔργα ἃ δέδωκέν μοι ὁ πατὴρ ἵνα τελειώσω αὐτά,
αὐτὰ τὰ ἔργα ἃ ποιῶ, μαρτυρεῖ περὶ ἐμοῦ ὅτι ὁ πατήρ
με ἀπέσταλκεν· 37 καὶ ὁ πέμψας με πατήρ, ἐκεῖνος μεμαρτύρηκεν περὶ ἐμοῦ. οὔτε φωνὴν αὐτοῦ πώποτε ἀκη-
κόατε, οὔτε εἶδος αὐτοῦ ἑωράκατε, 38 καὶ τὸν λόγον
αὐτοῦ οὐκ ἔχετε ἐν ὑμῖν μένοντα, ὅτι ὃν ἀπέστειλεν
ἐκεῖνος, τούτῳ ὑμεῖς οὐ πιστεύετε. 39 ἐραυνᾶτε τὰς γρα-
φάς, ὅτι ὑμεῖς δοκεῖτε ἐν αὐταῖς ζωὴν αἰώνιον ἔχειν, καὶ
ἐκεῖναί εἰσιν αἱ μαρτυροῦσαι περὶ ἐμοῦ· 40 καὶ οὐ θέλετε
ἐλθεῖν πρός με ἵνα ζωὴν ἔχητε. 41 δόξαν παρὰ ἀνθρώπων οὐ λαμβάνω, 42 ἀλλὰ ἔγνωκα ὑμᾶς ὅτι τὴν ἀγάπην
τοῦ θεοῦ οὐκ ἔχετε ἐν ἑαυτοῖς. 43 ἐγὼ ἐλήλυθα ἐν τῷ

ὀνόματι τοῦ πατρός μου, καὶ οὐ λαμβάνετέ με· ἐὰν
ἄλλος ἔλθῃ ἐν τῷ ὀνόματι τῷ ἰδίῳ, ἐκεῖνον λήμψεσθε.
44πῶς δύνασθε ὑμεῖς πιστεῦσαι, δόξαν παρὰ ἀλλήλων
λαμβάνοντες, καὶ τὴν δόξαν τὴν παρὰ τοῦ μόνου θεοῦ
οὐ ζητεῖτε; 45μὴ δοκεῖτε ὅτι ἐγὼ κατηγορήσω ὑμῶν
πρὸς τὸν πατέρα· ἔστιν ὁ κατηγορῶν ὑμῶν Μωυσῆς,
εἰς ὃν ὑμεῖς ἠλπίκατε. 46εἰ γὰρ ἐπιστεύετε Μωυσῇ,
ἐπιστεύετε ἂν ἐμοί· περὶ γὰρ ἐμοῦ ἐκεῖνος ἔγραψεν.
47εἰ δὲ τοῖς ἐκείνου γράμμασιν οὐ πιστεύετε, πῶς τοῖς
ἐμοῖς ῥήμασιν πιστεύσετε;

6 1Μετὰ ταῦτα ἀπῆλθεν ὁ Ἰησοῦς πέραν τῆς θαλάσσης τῆς Γαλιλαίας τῆς Τιβεριάδος· 2ἠκολούθει δὲ
αὐτῷ ὄχλος πολύς, ὅτι ἐθεώρουν τὰ σημεῖα ἃ ἐποίει ἐπὶ
τῶν ἀσθενούντων. 3ἀνῆλθεν δὲ εἰς τὸ ὄρος Ἰησοῦς, καὶ
ἐκεῖ ἐκάθητο μετὰ τῶν μαθητῶν αὐτοῦ. 4ἦν δὲ ἐγγὺς
τὸ πάσχα ἡ ἑορτὴ τῶν Ἰουδαίων. 5ἐπάρας οὖν τοὺς
ὀφθαλμοὺς ὁ Ἰησοῦς καὶ θεασάμενος ὅτι πολὺς ὄχλος
ἔρχεται πρὸς αὐτόν, λέγει πρὸς Φίλιππον, Πόθεν ἀγοράσωμεν ἄρτους ἵνα φάγωσιν οὗτοι; 6τοῦτο δὲ ἔλεγεν
πειράζων αὐτόν· αὐτὸς γὰρ ᾔδει τί ἔμελλεν ποιεῖν.
7ἀπεκρίθη αὐτῷ Φίλιππος, Διακοσίων δηναρίων ἄρ-
τοι οὐκ ἀρκοῦσιν αὐτοῖς ἵνα ἕκαστος βραχύ τι λάβῃ.
8λέγει αὐτῷ εἷς ἐκ τῶν μαθητῶν αὐτοῦ, Ἀνδρέας ὁ
ἀδελφὸς Σίμωνος Πέτρου, 9Ἔστιν παιδάριον ὧδε ὃς
ἔχει πέντε ἄρτους κριθίνους καὶ δύο ὀψάρια· ἀλλὰ
ταῦτα τί ἐστιν εἰς τοσούτους; 10εἶπεν ὁ Ἰησοῦς, Ποιήσατε τοὺς ἀνθρώπους ἀναπεσεῖν. ἦν δὲ χόρτος πολὺς
ἐν τῷ τόπῳ. ἀνέπεσαν οὖν οἱ ἄνδρες τὸν ἀριθμὸν ὡς
πεντακισχίλιοι. 11ἔλαβεν οὖν τοὺς ἄρτους ὁ Ἰησοῦς καὶ
εὐχαριστήσας διέδωκεν τοῖς ἀνακειμένοις· ὁμοίως καὶ
ἐκ τῶν ὀψαρίων ὅσον ἤθελον. 12ὡς δὲ ἐνεπλήσθησαν,

λέγει τοῖς μαθηταῖς αὐτοῦ, Συναγάγετε τὰ περισσεύ-
σαντα κλάσματα, ἵνα μή τι ἀπόληται. 13 συνήγαγον
οὖν, καὶ ἐγέμισαν δώδεκα κοφίνους κλασμάτων ἐκ τῶν
πέντε ἄρτων τῶν κριθίνων, ἃ ἐπερίσσευσαν τοῖς βεβρω-
κόσιν. 14 οἱ οὖν ἄνθρωποι ἰδόντες ὃ ἐποίησεν σημεῖον
ἔλεγον ὅτι Οὗτός ἐστιν ἀληθῶς ὁ προφήτης ὁ ἐρχόμενος εἰς τὸν κόσμον. 15 Ἰησοῦς οὖν γνοὺς ὅτι μέλλουσιν ἔρχεσθαι καὶ ἁρπάζειν αὐτὸν ἵνα ποιήσωσιν
βασιλέα, ἀνεχώρησεν πάλιν εἰς τὸ ὄρος αὐτὸς μόνος.

16 Ὡς δὲ ὀψία ἐγένετο, κατέβησαν οἱ μαθηταὶ αὐτοῦ
ἐπὶ τὴν θάλασσαν, 17 καὶ ἐμβάντες εἰς πλοῖον ἤρχοντο
πέραν τῆς θαλάσσης εἰς Καφαρναούμ. καὶ σκοτία ἤδη
ἐγεγόνει καὶ οὔπω ἐληλύθει πρὸς αὐτοὺς ὁ Ἰησοῦς, 18 ἥ
τε θάλασσα ἀνέμου μεγάλου πνέοντος διηγείρετο. 19 ἐλη-
λακότες οὖν ὡς σταδίους εἴκοσι πέντε ἢ τριάκοντα
θεωροῦσιν τὸν Ἰησοῦν περιπατοῦντα ἐπὶ τῆς θαλάσσης
καὶ ἐγγὺς τοῦ πλοίου γινόμενον, καὶ ἐφοβήθησαν. 20 ὁ
δὲ λέγει αὐτοῖς, Ἐγώ εἰμι· μὴ φοβεῖσθε. 21 ἤθελον οὖν
λαβεῖν αὐτὸν εἰς τὸ πλοῖον, καὶ εὐθέως ἐγένετο τὸ πλοῖον
ἐπὶ τῆς γῆς εἰς ἣν ὑπῆγον.

22 Τῇ ἐπαύριον ὁ ὄχλος ὁ ἑστηκὼς πέραν τῆς θαλάσσης εἶδον ὅτι πλοιάριον ἄλλο οὐκ ἦν ἐκεῖ εἰ μὴ ἕν, καὶ
ὅτι οὐ συνεισῆλθεν τοῖς μαθηταῖς αὐτοῦ ὁ Ἰησοῦς εἰς τὸ
πλοῖον ἀλλὰ μόνοι οἱ μαθηταὶ αὐτοῦ ἀπῆλθον· 23 ἀλλὰ
ἦλθεν πλοιάρια ἐκ Τιβεριάδος ἐγγὺς τοῦ τόπου ὅπου
ἔφαγον τὸν ἄρτον εὐχαριστήσαντος τοῦ κυρίου. 24 ὅτε
οὖν εἶδεν ὁ ὄχλος ὅτι Ἰησοῦς οὐκ ἔστιν ἐκεῖ οὐδὲ οἱ
μαθηταὶ αὐτοῦ, ἐνέβησαν αὐτοὶ εἰς τὰ πλοιάρια, καὶ
ἦλθον εἰς Καφαρναοὺμ ζητοῦντες τὸν Ἰησοῦν. 25 καὶ
εὑρόντες αὐτὸν πέραν τῆς θαλάσσης εἶπον αὐτῷ,
Ῥαββί, πότε ὧδε γέγονας;

26 Ἀπεκρίθη αὐτοῖς ὁ Ἰησοῦς καὶ εἶπεν, Ἀμὴν ἀμὴν
λέγω ὑμῖν, ζητεῖτέ με, οὐχ ὅτι εἴδετε σημεῖα, ἀλλ' ὅτι
ἐφάγετε ἐκ τῶν ἄρτων καὶ ἐχορτάσθητε. 27 ἐργάζεσθε
μὴ τὴν βρῶσιν τὴν ἀπολλυμένην, ἀλλὰ τὴν βρῶσιν τὴν
μένουσαν εἰς ζωὴν αἰώνιον, ἣν ὁ υἱὸς τοῦ ἀνθρώπου ὑμῖν
δώσει· τοῦτον γὰρ ὁ πατὴρ ἐσφράγισεν ὁ θεός. 28 εἶπον οὖν πρὸς αὐτόν, Τί ποιῶμεν, ἵνα ἐργαζώμεθα τὰ
ἔργα τοῦ θεοῦ; 29 ἀπεκρίθη ὁ Ἰησοῦς καὶ εἶπεν αὐτοῖς,
Τοῦτό ἐστιν τὸ ἔργον τοῦ θεοῦ, ἵνα πιστεύητε εἰς ὃν
ἀπέστειλεν ἐκεῖνος. 30 εἶπον οὖν αὐτῷ, Τί οὖν ποιεῖς
σὺ σημεῖον, ἵνα ἴδωμεν καὶ πιστεύσωμέν σοι; τί ἐργάζῃ;
31 οἱ πατέρες ἡμῶν τὸ μάννα ἔφαγον ἐν τῇ ἐρήμῳ, καθώς
ἐστιν γεγραμμένον, Ἄρτον ἐκ τοῦ οὐρανοῦ ἔδωκεν αὐτοῖς
φαγεῖν. 32 εἶπεν οὖν αὐτοῖς ὁ Ἰησοῦς, Ἀμὴν ἀμὴν
λέγω ὑμῖν, Οὐ Μωυσῆς ἔδωκεν ὑμῖν τὸν ἄρτον ἐκ τοῦ
οὐρανοῦ· ἀλλ' ὁ πατήρ μου δίδωσιν ὑμῖν τὸν ἄρτον ἐκ
τοῦ οὐρανοῦ τὸν ἀληθινόν. 33 ὁ γὰρ ἄρτος τοῦ θεοῦ
ἐστιν ὁ καταβαίνων ἐκ τοῦ οὐρανοῦ καὶ ζωὴν διδοὺς τῷ
κόσμῳ. 34 εἶπον οὖν πρὸς αὐτόν, Κύριε, πάντοτε δὸς
ἡμῖν τὸν ἄρτον τοῦτον. 35 εἶπεν δὲ αὐτοῖς ὁ Ἰησοῦς,
Ἐγώ εἰμι ὁ ἄρτος τῆς ζωῆς· ὁ ἐρχόμενος πρὸς ἐμὲ οὐ
μὴ πεινάσῃ· καὶ ὁ πιστεύων εἰς ἐμὲ οὐ μὴ διψήσει
πώποτε. 36 ἀλλ' εἶπον ὑμῖν ὅτι καὶ ἑωράκατέ με καὶ οὐ
πιστεύετε. 37 πᾶν ὃ δίδωσίν μοι ὁ πατὴρ πρὸς ἐμὲ ἥξει·
καὶ τὸν ἐρχόμενον πρός με οὐ μὴ ἐκβάλω ἔξω· 38 ὅτι
καταβέβηκα ἀπὸ τοῦ οὐρανοῦ, οὐχ ἵνα ποιῶ τὸ θέλημα
τὸ ἐμόν, ἀλλὰ τὸ θέλημα τοῦ πέμψαντός με. 39 τοῦτο
δέ ἐστιν τὸ θέλημα τοῦ πέμψαντός με, ἵνα πᾶν ὃ δέδωκέν
μοι μὴ ἀπολέσω ἐξ αὐτοῦ, ἀλλὰ ἀναστήσω αὐτὸ ἐν τῇ
ἐσχάτῃ ἡμέρᾳ. 40 τοῦτο γάρ ἐστιν τὸ θέλημα τοῦ πατρός
μου, ἵνα πᾶς ὁ θεωρῶν τὸν υἱὸν καὶ πιστεύων εἰς αὐτὸν

ἔχῃ ζωὴν αἰώνιον καὶ ἀναστήσω αὐτὸν ἐγὼ ἐν τῇ ἐσχάτῃ ἡμέρᾳ.
41 Ἐγόγγυζον οὖν οἱ Ἰουδαῖοι περὶ αὐτοῦ, ὅτι εἶπεν,
Ἐγώ εἰμι ὁ ἄρτος ὁ καταβὰς ἐκ τοῦ οὐρανοῦ. 42 καὶ
ἔλεγον, Οὐχ οὗτός ἐστιν Ἰησοῦς ὁ υἱὸς Ἰωσήφ, οὗ
ἡμεῖς οἴδαμεν τὸν πατέρα καὶ τὴν μητέρα; πῶς νῦν
λέγει, Ὅτι ἐκ τοῦ οὐρανοῦ καταβέβηκα; 43 ἀπεκρίθη
Ἰησοῦς καὶ εἶπεν αὐτοῖς, Μὴ γογγύζετε μετ᾽ ἀλλήλων.
44 οὐδεὶς δύναται ἐλθεῖν πρός με, ἐὰν μὴ ὁ πατὴρ ὁ
πέμψας με ἑλκύσῃ αὐτόν, κἀγὼ ἀναστήσω αὐτὸν ἐν
τῇ ἐσχάτῃ ἡμέρᾳ· 45 ἔστιν γεγραμμένον ἐν τοῖς προφήταις,
Καὶ ἔσονται πάντες διδακτοὶ θεοῦ. πᾶς ὁ ἀκούσας
παρὰ τοῦ πατρὸς καὶ μαθὼν ἔρχεται πρὸς ἐμέ· 46 οὐχ ὅτι
τὸν πατέρα ἑώρακέν τις, εἰ μὴ ὁ ὢν παρὰ τοῦ θεοῦ,
οὗτος ἑώρακεν τὸν πατέρα. 47 ἀμὴν ἀμὴν λέγω ὑμῖν, ὁ
πιστεύων ἔχει ζωὴν αἰώνιον. 48 ἐγώ εἰμι ὁ ἄρτος τῆς
ζωῆς. 49 οἱ πατέρες ὑμῶν ἔφαγον ἐν τῇ ἐρήμῳ τὸ μάννα
καὶ ἀπέθανον· 50 οὗτός ἐστιν ὁ ἄρτος ὁ ἐκ τοῦ οὐρανοῦ
καταβαίνων, ἵνα τις ἐξ αὐτοῦ φάγῃ καὶ μὴ ἀποθάνῃ.
51 ἐγώ εἰμι ὁ ἄρτος ὁ ζῶν ὁ ἐκ τοῦ οὐρανοῦ καταβάς·
ἐάν τις φάγῃ ἐκ τούτου τοῦ ἄρτου, ζήσεται εἰς τὸν
αἰῶνα. καὶ ὁ ἄρτος δὲ ὃν ἐγὼ δώσω, ἡ σάρξ μου
ἐστίν, ὑπὲρ τῆς τοῦ κόσμου ζωῆς. 52 ἐμάχοντο οὖν πρὸς
ἀλλήλους οἱ Ἰουδαῖοι λέγοντες, Πῶς δύναται οὗτος
ἡμῖν δοῦναι τὴν σάρκα φαγεῖν; 53 εἶπεν οὖν αὐτοῖς ὁ
Ἰησοῦς, Ἀμὴν ἀμὴν λέγω ὑμῖν, ἐὰν μὴ φάγητε τὴν
σάρκα τοῦ υἱοῦ τοῦ ἀνθρώπου, καὶ πίητε αὐτοῦ τὸ αἷμα,
οὐκ ἔχετε ζωὴν ἐν ἑαυτοῖς. 54 ὁ τρώγων μου τὴν σάρκα
καὶ πίνων μου τὸ αἷμα ἔχει ζωὴν αἰώνιον, κἀγὼ ἀναστήσω αὐτὸν τῇ ἐσχάτῃ ἡμέρᾳ. 55 ἡ γὰρ σάρξ μου ἀληθής
ἐστιν βρῶσις, καὶ τὸ αἷμά μου ἀληθής ἐστιν πόσις. 56 ὁ

τρώγων μου τὴν σάρκα καὶ πίνων μου τὸ αἷμα ἐν ἐμοὶ
μένει κἀγὼ ἐν αὐτῷ. [57]καθὼς ἀπέστειλέν με ὁ ζῶν πατὴρ
κἀγὼ ζῶ διὰ τὸν πατέρα, καὶ ὁ τρώγων με κἀκεῖνος
ζήσει δι' ἐμέ. [58]οὗτός ἐστιν ὁ ἄρτος ὁ ἐξ οὐρανοῦ κατα-
βάς· οὐ καθὼς ἔφαγον οἱ πατέρες καὶ ἀπέθανον· ὁ τρώγων τοῦτον τὸν ἄρτον ζήσει εἰς τὸν αἰῶνα.

[59]Ταῦτα εἶπεν ἐν συναγωγῇ διδάσκων ἐν Καφαρναούμ.

[60]Πολλοὶ οὖν ἀκούσαντες ἐκ τῶν μαθητῶν αὐτοῦ
εἶπον, Σκληρός ἐστιν ὁ λόγος οὗτος· τίς δύναται αὐτοῦ
ἀκούειν; [61]εἰδὼς δὲ ὁ Ἰησοῦς ἐν ἑαυτῷ ὅτι γογγύζουσιν
περὶ τούτου οἱ μαθηταὶ αὐτοῦ, εἶπεν αὐτοῖς Τοῦτο ὑμᾶς
σκανδαλίζει; [62]ἐὰν οὖν θεωρῆτε τὸν υἱὸν τοῦ ἀνθρώπου ἀναβαίνοντα ὅπου ἦν τὸ πρότερον; [63]τὸ πνεῦμά
ἐστιν τὸ ζωοποιοῦν, ἡ σὰρξ οὐκ ὠφελεῖ οὐδέν· τὰ ῥήματα
ἃ ἐγὼ λελάληκα ὑμῖν πνεῦμά ἐστιν καὶ ζωή ἐστιν.
[64]ἀλλ' εἰσὶν ἐξ ὑμῶν τινες οἳ οὐ πιστεύουσιν. ᾔδει
γὰρ ἐξ ἀρχῆς ὁ Ἰησοῦς τίνες εἰσὶν οἱ μὴ πιστεύοντες
καὶ τίς ἐστιν ὁ παραδώσων αὐτόν. [65]καὶ ἔλεγεν, Διὰ
τοῦτο εἴρηκα ὑμῖν, ὅτι οὐδεὶς δύναται ἐλθεῖν πρός με
ἐὰν μὴ ᾖ δεδομένον αὐτῷ ἐκ τοῦ πατρός.

[66]Ἐκ τούτου πολλοὶ τῶν μαθητῶν αὐτοῦ ἀπῆλθον
εἰς τὰ ὀπίσω καὶ οὐκέτι μετ' αὐτοῦ περιεπάτουν. [67]εἶ-
πεν οὖν ὁ Ἰησοῦς τοῖς δώδεκα, Μὴ καὶ ὑμεῖς θέλετε
ὑπάγειν; [68]ἀπεκρίθη αὐτῷ Σίμων Πέτρος, Κύριε, πρὸς
τίνα ἀπελευσόμεθα; ῥήματα ζωῆς αἰωνίου ἔχεις· [69]καὶ
ἡμεῖς πεπιστεύκαμεν καὶ ἐγνώκαμεν ὅτι σὺ εἶ ὁ ἅγιος
τοῦ θεοῦ. [70]ἀπεκρίθη αὐτοῖς ὁ Ἰησοῦς, Οὐκ ἐγὼ ὑμᾶς
τοὺς δώδεκα ἐξελεξάμην; καὶ ἐξ ὑμῶν εἷς διάβολός
ἐστιν. [71]ἔλεγεν δὲ τὸν Ἰούδαν Σίμωνος Ἰσκαριώτου·
οὗτος γὰρ ἔμελλεν παραδιδόναι αὐτὸν, εἷς ἐκ τῶν
δώδεκα.

7 [1]Καὶ περιεπάτει ὁ Ἰησοῦς μετὰ ταῦτα ἐν τῇ
Γαλιλαίᾳ· οὐ γὰρ ἤθελεν ἐν τῇ Ἰουδαίᾳ περιπατεῖν, ὅτι
ἐζήτουν αὐτὸν οἱ Ἰουδαῖοι ἀποκτεῖναι. [2]ἦν δὲ ἐγγὺς
ἡ ἑορτὴ τῶν Ἰουδαίων ἡ σκηνοπηγία. [3]εἶπον οὖν πρὸς
αὐτὸν οἱ ἀδελφοὶ αὐτοῦ, Μετάβηθι ἐντεῦθεν καὶ ὕπαγε
εἰς τὴν Ἰουδαίαν, ἵνα καὶ οἱ μαθηταί σου θεωρήσουσιν
τὰ ἔργα σου ἃ ποιεῖς· [4]οὐδεὶς γάρ τι ἐν κρυπτῷ ποιεῖ
καὶ ζητεῖ αὐτὸς ἐν παρρησίᾳ εἶναι. εἰ ταῦτα ποιεῖς,
φανέρωσον σεαυτὸν τῷ κόσμῳ. [5]οὐδὲ γὰρ οἱ ἀδελφοὶ
αὐτοῦ ἐπίστευον εἰς αὐτόν. [6]λέγει οὖν αὐτοῖς ὁ Ἰησοῦς,
Ὁ καιρὸς ὁ ἐμὸς οὔπω πάρεστιν, ὁ δὲ καιρὸς ὁ ὑμέτερος
πάντοτέ ἐστιν ἕτοιμος. [7]οὐ δύναται ὁ κόσμος μισεῖν
ὑμᾶς, ἐμὲ δὲ μισεῖ, ὅτι ἐγὼ μαρτυρῶ περὶ αὐτοῦ ὅτι τὰ
ἔργα αὐτοῦ πονηρά ἐστιν. [8]ὑμεῖς ἀνάβητε εἰς τὴν
ἑορτήν· ἐγὼ οὐκ ἀναβαίνω εἰς τὴν ἑορτὴν ταύτην, ὅτι ὁ
ἐμὸς καιρὸς οὔπω πεπλήρωται. [9]ταῦτα εἰπὼν αὐτοῖς
ἔμεινεν ἐν τῇ Γαλιλαίᾳ.

[10]Ὡς δὲ ἀνέβησαν οἱ ἀδελφοὶ αὐτοῦ εἰς τὴν ἑορτήν,
τότε καὶ αὐτὸς ἀνέβη, οὐ φανερῶς ἀλλὰ ὡς ἐν κρυπτῷ.
[11]οἱ οὖν Ἰουδαῖοι ἐζήτουν αὐτὸν ἐν τῇ ἑορτῇ, καὶ ἔλεγον,
Ποῦ ἐστιν ἐκεῖνος; [12]καὶ γογγυσμὸς περὶ αὐτοῦ ἦν
πολὺς ἐν τοῖς ὄχλοις. οἱ μὲν ἔλεγον ὅτι Ἀγαθός
ἐστιν· ἄλλοι ἔλεγον, Οὔ· ἀλλὰ πλανᾷ τὸν ὄχλον.
[13]οὐδεὶς μέντοι παρρησίᾳ ἐλάλει περὶ αὐτοῦ διὰ τὸν
φόβον τῶν Ἰουδαίων.

[14]Ἤδη δὲ τῆς ἑορτῆς μεσούσης ἀνέβη Ἰησοῦς εἰς τὸ
ἱερὸν καὶ ἐδίδασκεν. [15]ἐθαύμαζον οὖν οἱ Ἰουδαῖοι λέγοντες, Πῶς οὗτος γράμματα οἶδεν μὴ μεμαθηκώς;
[16]ἀπεκρίθη οὖν αὐτοῖς Ἰησοῦς καὶ εἶπεν, Ἡ ἐμὴ δι-
δαχὴ οὐκ ἔστιν ἐμὴ ἀλλὰ τοῦ πέμψαντός με· [17]ἐάν τις
θέλῃ τὸ θέλημα αὐτοῦ ποιεῖν, γνώσεται περὶ τῆς δι-

δαχῆς, πότερον ἐκ τοῦ θεοῦ ἐστὶν ἢ ἐγὼ ἀπ' ἐμαυτοῦ
λαλῶ. 18 ὁ ἀφ' ἑαυτοῦ λαλῶν τὴν δόξαν τὴν ἰδίαν ζητεῖ·
ὁ δὲ ζητῶν τὴν δόξαν τοῦ πέμψαντος αὐτόν, οὗτος
ἀληθής ἐστιν καὶ ἀδικία ἐν αὐτῷ οὐκ ἔστιν. 19 οὐ
Μωυσῆς ἔδωκεν ὑμῖν τὸν νόμον; καὶ οὐδεὶς ἐξ ὑμῶν
ποιεῖ τὸν νόμον. τί με ζητεῖτε ἀποκτεῖναι; 20 ἀπεκρίθη
ὁ ὄχλος, Δαιμόνιον ἔχεις· τίς σε ζητεῖ ἀποκτεῖναι;
21 ἀπεκρίθη Ἰησοῦς καὶ εἶπεν αὐτοῖς, Ἓν ἔργον ἐποίησα καὶ πάντες θαυμάζετε. 22 διὰ τοῦτο Μωυσῆς δέδωκεν ὑμῖν τὴν περιτομήν, οὐχ ὅτι ἐκ τοῦ Μωυσέως ἐστίν,
ἀλλ' ἐκ τῶν πατέρων, καὶ ἐν σαββάτῳ περιτέμνετε ἄνθρωπον. 23 εἰ περιτομὴν λαμβάνει ἄνθρωπος ἐν σαββάτῳ ἵνα μὴ λυθῇ ὁ νόμος Μωυσέως, ἐμοὶ χολᾶτε ὅτι
ὅλον ἄνθρωπον ὑγιῆ ἐποίησα ἐν σαββάτῳ; 24 μὴ κρίνετε
κατ' ὄψιν, ἀλλὰ τὴν δικαίαν κρίσιν κρίνετε. 25 ἔλεγον
οὖν τινες ἐκ τῶν Ἱεροσολυμιτῶν, Οὐχ οὗτός ἐστιν ὃν
ζητοῦσιν ἀποκτεῖναι; 26 καὶ ἴδε παρρησίᾳ λαλεῖ, καὶ
οὐδὲν αὐτῷ λέγουσιν. μήποτε ἀληθῶς ἔγνωσαν οἱ ἄρχοντες ὅτι οὗτός ἐστιν ὁ Χριστός; 27 ἀλλὰ τοῦτον οἴδαμεν πόθεν ἐστίν· ὁ δὲ Χριστὸς ὅταν ἔρχηται, οὐδεὶς
γινώσκει πόθεν ἐστίν. 28 ἔκραξεν οὖν ἐν τῷ ἱερῷ διδάσκων ὁ Ἰησοῦς καὶ λέγων, Κἀμὲ οἴδατε καὶ οἴδατε
πόθεν εἰμί· καὶ ἀπ' ἐμαυτοῦ οὐκ ἐλήλυθα, ἀλλ' ἔστιν
ἀληθινὸς ὁ πέμψας με, ὃν ὑμεῖς οὐκ οἴδατε· 29 ἐγὼ οἶδα
αὐτόν, ὅτι παρ' αὐτοῦ εἰμι κἀκεῖνός με ἀπέστειλεν.
30 ἐζήτουν οὖν αὐτὸν πιάσαι· καὶ οὐδεὶς ἐπέβαλεν ἐπ'
αὐτὸν τὴν χεῖρα, ὅτι οὔπω ἐληλύθει ἡ ὥρα αὐτοῦ. 31 ἐκ
τοῦ ὄχλου δὲ πολλοὶ ἐπίστευσαν εἰς αὐτόν, καὶ ἔλεγον,
ὁ Χριστὸς ὅταν ἔλθῃ μὴ πλείονα σημεῖα ποιήσει ὧν
οὗτος ἐποίησεν; 32 ἤκουσαν οἱ Φαρισαῖοι τοῦ ὄχλου
γογγύζοντος περὶ αὐτοῦ ταῦτα. καὶ ἀπέστειλαν οἱ

ἀρχιερεῖς καὶ οἱ Φαρισαῖοι ὑπηρέτας, ἵνα πιάσωσιν
αὐτόν. 33 εἶπεν οὖν ὁ Ἰησοῦς, Ἔτι χρόνον μικρὸν μεθ'
ὑμῶν εἰμὶ καὶ ὑπάγω πρὸς τὸν πέμψαντά με. 34 ζητήσετέ με καὶ οὐχ εὑρήσετέ με· καὶ ὅπου εἰμὶ ἐγὼ ὑμεῖς
οὐ δύνασθε ἐλθεῖν. 35 εἶπον οὖν οἱ Ἰουδαῖοι πρὸς ἑαυτούς, Ποῦ οὗτος μέλλει πορεύεσθαι, ὅτι ἡμεῖς οὐχ
εὑρήσομεν αὐτόν; μὴ εἰς τὴν διασπορὰν τῶν Ἑλλήνων
μέλλει πορεύεσθαι καὶ διδάσκειν τοὺς Ἕλληνας; 36 τίς
ἐστιν ὁ λόγος οὗτος ὃν εἶπεν, Ζητήσετέ με, καὶ οὐχ εὑρήσετέ με· καί, Ὅπου εἰμὶ ἐγὼ ὑμεῖς οὐ δύνασθε ἐλθεῖν;

37 Ἐν δὲ τῇ ἐσχάτῃ ἡμέρᾳ τῇ μεγάλῃ τῆς ἑορτῆς
εἱστήκει ὁ Ἰησοῦς καὶ ἔκραξεν λέγων, Ἐάν τις διψᾷ,
ἐρχέσθω πρός με καὶ πινέτω· 38 ὁ πιστεύων εἰς ἐμέ,
καθὼς εἶπεν ἡ γραφή, ποταμοὶ ἐκ τῆς κοιλίας αὐτοῦ
ῥεύσουσιν ὕδατος ζῶντος. 39 τοῦτο δὲ εἶπεν περὶ τοῦ
πνεύματος οὗ ἔμελλον λαμβάνειν οἱ πιστεύσαντες εἰς
αὐτόν· οὔπω γὰρ ἦν πνεῦμα, ὅτι Ἰησοῦς οὔπω ἐδοξάσθη.

40 Ἐκ τοῦ ὄχλου οὖν ἀκούσαντες τῶν λόγων τούτων
ἔλεγον, Οὗτός ἐστιν ἀληθῶς ὁ προφήτης. 41 ἄλλοι
ἔλεγον, Οὗτός ἐστιν ὁ Χριστός. οἱ δὲ ἔλεγον, Μὴ γὰρ
ἐκ τῆς Γαλιλαίας ὁ Χριστὸς ἔρχεται; 42 οὐχ ἡ γραφὴ
εἶπεν, ὅτι ἐκ τοῦ σπέρματος Δαυείδ, καὶ ἀπὸ Βηθλεὲμ
τῆς κώμης ὅπου ἦν Δαυείδ, ἔρχεται ὁ Χριστός; 43 σχίσμα οὖν ἐγένετο ἐν τῷ ὄχλῳ δι' αὐτόν. 44 τινὲς δὲ ἤθελον
ἐξ αὐτῶν πιάσαι αὐτόν, ἀλλ' οὐδεὶς ἔβαλεν ἐπ' αὐτὸν
τὰς χεῖρας.

45 Ἦλθον οὖν οἱ ὑπηρέται πρὸς τοὺς ἀρχιερεῖς καὶ
Φαρισαίους, καὶ εἶπον αὐτοῖς ἐκεῖνοι, Διατί οὐκ ἠγάγετε
αὐτόν; 46 ἀπεκρίθησαν οἱ ὑπηρέται, Οὐδέποτε ἐλάλησεν
οὕτως ἄνθρωπος. 47 ἀπεκρίθησαν οὖν αὐτοῖς οἱ Φαρι-

σαῖοι, Μὴ καὶ ὑμεῖς πεπλάνησθε; 48 μή τις ἐκ τῶν
ἀρχόντων ἐπίστευσεν εἰς αὐτὸν ἢ ἐκ τῶν Φαρισαίων;
49 ἀλλὰ ὁ ὄχλος οὗτος ὁ μὴ γινώσκων τὸν νόμον ἐπά-
ρατοί εἰσιν. 50 λέγει Νικόδημος πρὸς αὐτούς, ὁ ἐλθὼν
πρὸς αὐτὸν πρότερον, εἷς ὢν ἐξ αὐτῶν, 51 Μὴ ὁ νόμος
ἡμῶν κρίνει τὸν ἄνθρωπον ἐὰν μὴ ἀκούσῃ πρῶτον παρ'
αὐτοῦ καὶ γνῷ τί ποιεῖ; 52 ἀπεκρίθησαν καὶ εἶπαν αὐ-
τῷ, Μὴ καὶ σὺ ἐκ τῆς Γαλιλαίας εἶ; ἐραύνησον καὶ ἴδε
ὅτι ἐκ τῆς Γαλιλαίας προφήτης οὐκ ἐγείρεται. 53 [Καὶ
ἐπορεύθησαν ἕκαστος εἰς τὸν οἶκον αὐτοῦ.

8 1 Ἰησοῦς δὲ ἐπορεύθη εἰς τὸ ὄρος τῶν Ἐλαιῶν. 2 ὄρθρου
δὲ πάλιν παρεγένετο εἰς τὸ ἱερόν, [καὶ πᾶς ὁ λαὸς ἤρχετο πρὸς
αὐτόν· καὶ καθίσας ἐδίδασκεν αὐτούς.] 3 ἄγουσιν δὲ οἱ γραμματεῖς
καὶ οἱ Φαρισαῖοι γυναῖκα ἐπὶ μοιχείᾳ κατειλημμένην, καὶ στήσαντες
αὐτὴν ἐν μέσῳ 4 λέγουσιν αὐτῷ, Διδάσκαλε, αὕτη ἡ γυνὴ κατείληπται ἐπαυτοφώρῳ μοιχευομένη. 5 ἐν δὲ τῷ νόμῳ Μωυσῆς ἡμῖν
ἐνετείλατο τὰς τοιαύτας λιθάζειν· σὺ οὖν τί λέγεις; 6 [τοῦτο δὲ ἔλεγον
πειράζοντες αὐτόν, ἵνα ἔχωσιν κατηγορεῖν αὐτοῦ.] ὁ δὲ Ἰησοῦς
κάτω κύψας τῷ δακτύλῳ κατέγραφεν εἰς τὴν γῆν. 7 ὡς δὲ ἐπέμενον
ἐρωτῶντες αὐτόν, ἀνέκυψεν καὶ εἶπεν αὐτοῖς, Ὁ ἀναμάρτητος ὑμῶν
πρῶτος ἐπ' αὐτὴν βαλέτω λίθον. 8 καὶ πάλιν κατακύψας ἔγραφεν
εἰς τὴν γῆν. 9 οἱ δὲ ἀκούσαντες ἐξήρχοντο εἷς καθ' εἷς, ἀρξάμενοι
ἀπὸ τῶν πρεσβυτέρων· καὶ κατελείφθη μόνος καὶ ἡ γυνὴ ἐν μέσῳ
οὖσα. 10 ἀνακύψας δὲ ὁ Ἰησοῦς εἶπεν αὐτῇ, Γύναι ποῦ εἰσιν;
οὐδείς σε κατέκρινεν; ἡ δὲ εἶπεν, Οὐδείς, κύριε. 11 εἶπεν δὲ ὁ
Ἰησοῦς, Οὐδὲ ἐγώ σε κατακρίνω· πορεύου, ἀπὸ τοῦ νῦν μηκέτι
ἁμάρτανε.]

12 Πάλιν οὖν αὐτοῖς ἐλάλησεν ὁ Ἰησοῦς λέγων, Ἐγώ
εἰμι τὸ φῶς τοῦ κόσμου· ὁ ἀκολουθῶν μοι οὐ μὴ περι-
πατήσῃ ἐν τῇ σκοτίᾳ, ἀλλ' ἕξει τὸ φῶς τῆς ζωῆς.
13 εἶπον οὖν αὐτῷ οἱ Φαρισαῖοι, Σὺ περὶ σεαυτοῦ μαρτυ-

ρεῖς· ἡ μαρτυρία σου οὐκ ἔστιν ἀληθής. 14 ἀπεκρίθη
Ἰησοῦς καὶ εἶπεν αὐτοῖς, Κἂν ἐγὼ μαρτυρῶ περὶ ἐμαυτοῦ, ἀληθής ἐστιν ἡ μαρτυρία μου· ὅτι οἶδα πόθεν
ἦλθον καὶ ποῦ ὑπάγω· ὑμεῖς δὲ οὐκ οἴδατε πόθεν ἔρχομαι ἢ ποῦ ὑπάγω. 15 ὑμεῖς κατὰ τὴν σάρκα κρίνετε·
ἐγὼ οὐ κρίνω οὐδένα. 16 καὶ ἐὰν κρίνω δὲ ἐγώ, ἡ κρίσις
ἡ ἐμὴ ἀληθινή ἐστιν· ὅτι μόνος οὐκ εἰμί, ἀλλ' ἐγὼ καὶ ὁ
πέμψας με πατήρ. 17 καὶ ἐν τῷ νόμῳ δὲ τῷ ὑμετέρῳ
γέγραπται ὅτι δύο ἀνθρώπων ἡ μαρτυρία ἀληθής ἐστιν.
18 ἐγώ εἰμι ὁ μαρτυρῶν περὶ ἐμαυτοῦ, καὶ μαρτυρεῖ περὶ
ἐμοῦ ὁ πέμψας με πατήρ. 19 ἔλεγον οὖν αὐτῷ, Ποῦ
ἐστὶν ὁ πατήρ σου; ἀπεκρίθη Ἰησοῦς, Οὔτε ἐμὲ οἴδατε
οὔτε τὸν πατέρα μου· εἰ ἐμὲ ᾔδειτε, καὶ τὸν πατέρα μου
ἂν ᾔδειτε. 20 ταῦτα τὰ ῥήματα ἐλάλησεν ἐν τῷ γαζοφυ-
λακίῳ διδάσκων ἐν τῷ ἱερῷ· καὶ οὐδεὶς ἐπίασεν αὐτόν,
ὅτι οὔπω ἐληλύθει ἡ ὥρα αὐτοῦ.

21 Εἶπεν οὖν πάλιν αὐτοῖς, Ἐγὼ ὑπάγω καὶ ζητήσετέ
με, καὶ ἐν τῇ ἁμαρτίᾳ ὑμῶν ἀποθανεῖσθε· ὅπου ἐγὼ
ὑπάγω ὑμεῖς οὐ δύνασθε ἐλθεῖν. 22 ἔλεγον οὖν οἱ Ἰουδαῖοι, Μήτι ἀποκτενεῖ ἑαυτόν, ὅτι λέγει, Ὅπου ἐγὼ
ὑπάγω ὑμεῖς οὐ δύνασθε ἐλθεῖν; 23 καὶ ἔλεγεν αὐτοῖς,
Ὑμεῖς ἐκ τῶν κάτω ἐστέ, ἐγὼ ἐκ τῶν ἄνω εἰμί· ὑμεῖς ἐκ
τούτου τοῦ κόσμου ἐστέ, ἐγὼ οὐκ εἰμὶ ἐκ τοῦ κόσμου
τούτου. 24 εἶπον οὖν ὑμῖν ὅτι ἀποθανεῖσθε ἐν ταῖς ἁμαρτίαις ὑμῶν· ἐὰν γὰρ μὴ πιστεύσητε ὅτι ἐγώ εἰμι, ἀποθανεῖσθε ἐν ταῖς ἁμαρτίαις ὑμῶν. 25 ἔλεγον οὖν αὐτῷ,
Σὺ τίς εἶ; εἶπεν αὐτοῖς ὁ Ἰησοῦς, Τὴν ἀρχὴν ὅ τι καὶ
λαλῶ ὑμῖν. 26 πολλὰ ἔχω περὶ ὑμῶν λαλεῖν καὶ κρίνειν·
ἀλλ' ὁ πέμψας με ἀληθής ἐστιν, κἀγὼ ἃ ἤκουσα παρ'
αὐτοῦ, ταῦτα λαλῶ εἰς τὸν κόσμον. 27 οὐκ ἔγνωσαν ὅτι
τὸν πατέρα αὐτοῖς ἔλεγεν. 28 εἶπεν οὖν ὁ Ἰησοῦς, Ὅταν

ὑψώσητε τὸν υἱὸν τοῦ ἀνθρώπου, τότε γνώσεσθε ὅτι ἐγώ
εἰμι, καὶ ἀπ' ἐμαυτοῦ ποιῶ οὐδέν, ἀλλὰ καθὼς ἐδίδαξέν
με ὁ πατήρ, ταῦτα λαλῶ. 29 καὶ ὁ πέμψας με μετ' ἐμοῦ
ἐστίν· οὐκ ἀφῆκέν με μόνον, ὅτι ἐγὼ τὰ ἀρεστὰ αὐτῷ
ποιῶ πάντοτε. 30 ταῦτα αὐτοῦ λαλοῦντος πολλοὶ ἐπίστευσαν εἰς αὐτόν.

31 Ἔλεγεν οὖν ὁ Ἰησοῦς πρὸς τοὺς πεπιστευκότας
αὐτῷ Ἰουδαίους, Ἐὰν ὑμεῖς μείνητε ἐν τῷ λόγῳ τῷ
ἐμῷ, ἀληθῶς μαθηταί μου ἐστέ, 32 καὶ γνώσεσθε τὴν
ἀλήθειαν, καὶ ἡ ἀλήθεια ἐλευθερώσει ὑμᾶς. 33 ἀπεκρίθησαν πρὸς αὐτόν, Σπέρμα Ἀβραάμ ἐσμεν, καὶ οὐδενὶ
δεδουλεύκαμεν πώποτε· πῶς σὺ λέγεις ὅτι Ἐλεύθεροι
γενήσεσθε; 34 ἀπεκρίθη αὐτοῖς ὁ Ἰησοῦς, ἀμὴν ἀμὴν
λέγω ὑμῖν, ὅτι πᾶς ὁ ποιῶν τὴν ἁμαρτίαν δοῦλός ἐστιν
τῆς ἁμαρτίας. 35 ὁ δὲ δοῦλος οὐ μένει ἐν τῇ οἰκίᾳ εἰς τὸν
αἰῶνα· ὁ υἱὸς μένει εἰς τὸν αἰῶνα. 36 ἐὰν οὖν ὁ υἱὸς ὑμᾶς
ἐλευθερώσῃ, ὄντως ἐλεύθεροι ἔσεσθε. 37 οἶδα ὅτι σπέρμα Ἀβραάμ ἐστε· ἀλλὰ ζητεῖτέ με ἀποκτεῖναι, ὅτι
ὁ λόγος ὁ ἐμὸς οὐ χωρεῖ ἐν ὑμῖν. 38 ἃ ἐγὼ ἑώρακα
παρὰ τῷ πατρὶ λαλῶ· καὶ ὑμεῖς οὖν ἃ ἠκούσατε παρὰ
τοῦ πατρὸς ποιεῖτε. 39 ἀπεκρίθησαν καὶ εἶπαν αὐτῷ,
Ὁ πατὴρ ἡμῶν Ἀβραάμ ἐστιν. λέγει αὐτοῖς ὁ Ἰησοῦς,
Εἰ τέκνα τοῦ Ἀβραάμ ἐστε, τὰ ἔργα τοῦ Ἀβραὰμ
ἐποιεῖτε. 40 νῦν δὲ ζητεῖτέ με ἀποκτεῖναι, ἄνθρωπον ὃς
τὴν ἀλήθειαν ὑμῖν λελάληκα, ἣν ἤκουσα παρὰ τοῦ θεοῦ·
τοῦτο Ἀβραὰμ οὐκ ἐποίησεν. 41 ὑμεῖς ποιεῖτε τὰ ἔργα
τοῦ πατρὸς ὑμῶν. εἶπον αὐτῷ, Ἡμεῖς ἐκ πορνείας οὐκ
ἐγεννήθημεν· ἕνα πατέρα ἔχομεν τὸν θεόν. 42 εἶπεν
αὐτοῖς ὁ Ἰησοῦς, Εἰ ὁ θεὸς πατὴρ ὑμῶν ἦν, ἠγαπᾶτε ἂν
ἐμέ· ἐγὼ γὰρ ἐκ τοῦ θεοῦ ἐξῆλθον καὶ ἥκω· οὐδὲ γὰρ
ἀπ' ἐμαυτοῦ ἐλήλυθα, ἀλλ' ἐκεῖνός με ἀπέστειλεν. 43 διατί

τὴν λαλιὰν τὴν ἐμὴν οὐ γινώσκετε; ὅτι οὐ δύνασθε
ἀκούειν τὸν λόγον τὸν ἐμόν. 44 ὑμεῖς ἐκ τοῦ πατρὸς τοῦ
διαβόλου ἐστὲ καὶ τὰς ἐπιθυμίας τοῦ πατρὸς ὑμῶν
θέλετε ποιεῖν. ἐκεῖνος ἀνθρωποκτόνος ἦν ἀπ᾽ ἀρχῆς καὶ ἐν
τῇ ἀληθείᾳ οὐχ ἕστηκεν, ὅτι οὐκ ἔστιν ἀλήθεια ἐν αὐτῷ.
ὅταν λαλῇ τὸ ψεῦδος, ἐκ τῶν ἰδίων λαλεῖ, ὅτι ψεύστης
ἐστὶν καὶ ὁ πατὴρ αὐτοῦ. 45 ἐγὼ δὲ ὅτι τὴν ἀλήθειαν
λέγω, οὐ πιστεύετέ μοι. 46 τίς ἐξ ὑμῶν ἐλέγχει με περὶ
ἁμαρτίας; εἰ ἀλήθειαν λέγω, διατί ὑμεῖς οὐ πιστεύετέ
μοι; 47 ὁ ὢν ἐκ τοῦ θεοῦ τὰ ῥήματα τοῦ θεοῦ ἀκούει· διὰ
τοῦτο ὑμεῖς οὐκ ἀκούετε ὅτι ἐκ τοῦ θεοῦ οὐκ ἐστέ.
48 ἀπεκρίθησαν οἱ Ἰουδαῖοι καὶ εἶπαν αὐτῷ, Οὐ καλῶς
λέγομεν ἡμεῖς ὅτι Σαμαρείτης εἶ σὺ καὶ δαιμόνιον
ἔχεις; 49 ἀπεκρίθη Ἰησοῦς, Ἐγὼ δαιμόνιον οὐκ ἔχω,
ἀλλὰ τιμῶ τὸν πατέρα μου, καὶ ὑμεῖς ἀτιμάζετέ με.
50 ἐγὼ δὲ οὐ ζητῶ τὴν δόξαν μου· ἔστιν ὁ ζητῶν καὶ
κρίνων. 51 ἀμὴν ἀμὴν λέγω ὑμῖν, ἐάν τις τὸν ἐμὸν λόγον
τηρήσῃ, θάνατον οὐ μὴ θεωρήσῃ εἰς τὸν αἰῶνα. 52 εἶπον
αὐτῷ οἱ Ἰουδαῖοι, Νῦν ἐγνώκαμεν ὅτι δαιμόνιον ἔχεις.
Ἀβραὰμ ἀπέθανεν καὶ οἱ προφῆται, καὶ σὺ λέγεις, Ἐάν
τις τὸν λόγον μου τηρήσῃ, οὐ μὴ γεύσηται θανάτου εἰς
τὸν αἰῶνα. 53 μὴ σὺ μείζων εἶ τοῦ πατρὸς ἡμῶν Ἀβραάμ,
ὅστις ἀπέθανεν; καὶ οἱ προφῆται ἀπέθανον· τίνα σεαυτὸν
ποιεῖς; 54 ἀπεκρίθη Ἰησοῦς, Ἐὰν ἐγὼ δοξάσω ἐμαυτόν,
ἡ δόξα μου οὐδέν ἐστιν· ἔστιν ὁ πατήρ μου ὁ δοξάζων
με, ὃν ὑμεῖς λέγετε ὅτι θεὸς ἡμῶν ἐστιν, 55 καὶ οὐκ ἐγνώκατε αὐτόν, ἐγὼ δὲ οἶδα αὐτόν· κἂν εἴπω ὅτι οὐκ οἶδα
αὐτόν, ἔσομαι ὅμοιος ὑμῖν ψεύστης· ἀλλὰ οἶδα αὐτὸν
καὶ τὸν λόγον αὐτοῦ τηρῶ. 56 Ἀβραὰμ ὁ πατὴρ ὑμῶν
ἠγαλλιάσατο ἵνα ἴδῃ τὴν ἡμέραν τὴν ἐμήν, καὶ εἶδεν καὶ
ἐχάρη. 57 εἶπον οὖν οἱ Ἰουδαῖοι πρὸς αὐτόν, Πεντήκοντα

ἔτη οὔπω ἔχεις καὶ Ἀβραὰμ ἑώρακας; [58]εἶπεν αὐτοῖς
Ἰησοῦς, Ἀμὴν ἀμὴν λέγω ὑμῖν, πρὶν Ἀβραὰμ γενέσθαι
ἐγώ εἰμι. [59]ἦραν οὖν λίθους ἵνα βάλωσιν ἐπ' αὐτόν·
Ἰησοῦς δὲ ἐκρύβη καὶ ἐξῆλθεν ἐκ τοῦ ἱεροῦ.

9 [1]Καὶ παράγων εἶδεν ἄνθρωπον τυφλὸν ἐκ γενετῆς.
[2]καὶ ἠρώτησαν αὐτὸν οἱ μαθηταὶ αὐτοῦ λέγοντες, Ῥαββί, τίς ἥμαρτεν, οὗτος ἢ οἱ γονεῖς αὐτοῦ, ἵνα τυφλὸς
γεννηθῇ; [3]ἀπεκρίθη Ἰησοῦς, Οὔτε οὗτος ἥμαρτεν οὔτε
οἱ γονεῖς αὐτοῦ, ἀλλ' ἵνα φανερωθῇ τὰ ἔργα τοῦ θεοῦ ἐν
αὐτῷ. [4]ἡμᾶς δεῖ ἐργάζεσθαι τὰ ἔργα τοῦ πέμψαντός
με ἕως ἡμέρα ἐστίν· ἔρχεται νὺξ ὅτε οὐδεὶς δύναται
ἐργάζεσθαι. [5]ὅταν ἐν τῷ κόσμῳ ὦ, φῶς εἰμι τοῦ κόσμου.

[6]Ταῦτα εἰπὼν ἔπτυσεν χαμαὶ καὶ ἐποίησεν πηλὸν ἐκ
τοῦ πτύσματος, καὶ ἐπέχρισεν αὐτοῦ τὸν πηλὸν ἐπὶ
τοὺς ὀφθαλμούς, [7]καὶ εἶπεν αὐτῷ, Ὕπαγε νίψαι εἰς τὴν
κολυμβήθραν τοῦ Σιλωάμ, ὃ ἑρμηνεύεται ἀπεσταλμένος.
ἀπῆλθεν οὖν καὶ ἐνίψατο, καὶ ἦλθεν βλέπων.

[8]Οἱ οὖν γείτονες καὶ οἱ θεωροῦντες αὐτὸν τὸ πρότερον ὅτι προσαίτης ἦν ἔλεγον, Οὐχ οὗτός ἐστιν ὁ
καθήμενος καὶ προσαιτῶν; [9]ἄλλοι ἔλεγον ὅτι Οὗτός
ἐστιν· ἄλλοι ἔλεγον, Οὐχί, ἀλλ' ὅμοιος αὐτῷ ἐστίν.
ἐκεῖνος ἔλεγεν ὅτι Ἐγώ εἰμι. [10]ἔλεγον οὖν αὐτῷ, Πῶς
ἠνεῴχθησάν σου οἱ ὀφθαλμοί; [11]ἀπεκρίθη ἐκεῖνος, Ὁ
ἄνθρωπος ὁ λεγόμενος Ἰησοῦς πηλὸν ἐποίησεν καὶ
ἐπέχρισέν μου τοὺς ὀφθαλμοὺς καὶ εἶπέν μοι ὅτι Ὕπαγε
εἰς τὸν Σιλωὰμ καὶ νίψαι. ἀπελθὼν οὖν καὶ νιψάμενος
ἀνέβλεψα. [12]εἶπαν αὐτῷ, Ποῦ ἐστιν ἐκεῖνος; λέγει, Οὐκ
οἶδα.

[13]Ἄγουσιν αὐτὸν πρὸς τοὺς Φαρισαίους, τόν ποτε
τυφλόν. [14]ἦν δὲ σάββατον ἐν ᾗ ἡμέρᾳ τὸν πηλὸν ἐποί-

ησεν ὁ Ἰησοῦς καὶ ἀνέῳξεν αὐτοῦ τοὺς ὀφθαλμούς.
15 πάλιν οὖν ἠρώτων αὐτὸν καὶ οἱ Φαρισαῖοι πῶς ἀνέβλεψεν. ὁ δὲ εἶπεν αὐτοῖς, Πηλὸν ἐπέθηκέν μου ἐπὶ
τοὺς ὀφθαλμούς, καὶ ἐνιψάμην, καὶ βλέπω. 16 ἔλεγον
οὖν ἐκ τῶν Φαρισαίων τινές, Οὐκ ἔστιν οὗτος παρὰ
θεοῦ ὁ ἄνθρωπος, ὅτι τὸ σάββατον οὐ τηρεῖ. ἄλλοι
ἔλεγον, Πῶς δύναται ἄνθρωπος ἁμαρτωλὸς τοιαῦτα σημεῖα ποιεῖν; καὶ σχίσμα ἦν ἐν αὐτοῖς. 17 λέγουσιν οὖν
τῷ τυφλῷ πάλιν, Σὺ τί λέγεις περὶ αὐτοῦ, ὅτι ἤνοιξέ σου
τοὺς ὀφθαλμούς; ὁ δὲ εἶπεν ὅτι Προφήτης ἐστίν.
18 οὐκ ἐπίστευσαν οὖν οἱ Ἰουδαῖοι περὶ αὐτοῦ, ὅτι ἦν
τυφλὸς καὶ ἀνέβλεψεν, ἕως ὅτου ἐφώνησαν τοὺς γονεῖς
αὐτοῦ τοῦ ἀναβλέψαντος, 19 καὶ ἠρώτησαν αὐτοὺς λέγοντες, Οὗτός ἐστιν ὁ υἱὸς ὑμῶν, ὃν ὑμεῖς λέγετε ὅτι
τυφλὸς ἐγεννήθη; πῶς οὖν βλέπει ἄρτι; 20 ἀπεκρίθησαν
οὖν οἱ γονεῖς αὐτοῦ καὶ εἶπαν, Οἴδαμεν ὅτι οὗτός ἐστιν
ὁ υἱὸς ἡμῶν καὶ ὅτι τυφλὸς ἐγεννήθη· 21 πῶς δὲ νῦν
βλέπει οὐκ οἴδαμεν· ἢ τίς ἤνοιξεν αὐτοῦ τοὺς ὀφθαλμοὺς ἡμεῖς οὐκ οἴδαμεν· αὐτὸν ἐρωτήσατε, ἡλικίαν ἔχει·
αὐτὸς περὶ ἑαυτοῦ λαλήσει. 22 ταῦτα εἶπαν οἱ γονεῖς
αὐτοῦ ὅτι ἐφοβοῦντο τοὺς Ἰουδαίους· ἤδη γὰρ συνετέθειντο οἱ Ἰουδαῖοι ἵνα ἐάν τις αὐτὸν ὁμολογήσῃ Χριστόν, ἀποσυνάγωγος γένηται. 23 διὰ τοῦτο οἱ γονεῖς
αὐτοῦ εἶπαν ὅτι Ἡλικίαν ἔχει, αὐτὸν ἐρωτήσατε.
24 ἐφώνησαν οὖν τὸν ἄνθρωπον ἐκ δευτέρου ὃς ἦν τυφλὸς
καὶ εἶπαν αὐτῷ, Δὸς δόξαν τῷ θεῷ· ἡμεῖς οἴδαμεν ὅτι
οὗτος ὁ ἄνθρωπος ἁμαρτωλός ἐστιν. 25 ἀπεκρίθη οὖν
ἐκεῖνος, Εἰ ἁμαρτωλός ἐστιν οὐκ οἶδα· ἓν οἶδα ὅτι
τυφλὸς ὢν ἄρτι βλέπω. 26 εἶπον οὖν αὐτῷ, Τί ἐποίησέν
σοι; πῶς ἤνοιξέν σου τοὺς ὀφθαλμούς; 27 ἀπεκρίθη αὐτοῖς, Εἶπον ὑμῖν ἤδη καὶ οὐκ ἠκούσατε· τί πάλιν

θέλετε ἀκούειν; μὴ καὶ ὑμεῖς θέλετε αὐτοῦ μαθηταὶ
γενέσθαι; 28ἐλοιδόρησαν αὐτὸν καὶ εἶπον, Σὺ μαθητὴς
εἶ ἐκείνου· ἡμεῖς δὲ τοῦ Μωυσέως ἐσμὲν μαθηταί. 29ἡ-
μεῖς οἴδαμεν ὅτι Μωυσεῖ λελάληκεν ὁ θεός, τοῦτον δὲ
οὐκ οἴδαμεν πόθεν ἐστίν. 30ἀπεκρίθη ὁ ἄνθρωπος καὶ εἶπεν αὐτοῖς, Ἐν τούτῳ γὰρ τὸ θαυμαστόν ἐστιν ὅτι ὑμεῖς
οὐκ οἴδατε πόθεν ἐστίν, καὶ ἤνοιξέν μου τοὺς ὀφθαλμούς.
31οἴδαμεν ὅτι ὁ θεὸς ἁμαρτωλῶν οὐκ ἀκούει, ἀλλ' ἐάν τις
θεοσεβὴς ᾖ καὶ τὸ θέλημα αὐτοῦ ποιῇ τούτου ἀκούει.
32ἐκ τοῦ αἰῶνος οὐκ ἠκούσθη ὅτι ἠνοιξέν τις ὀφθαλμοὺς
τυφλοῦ γεγεννημένου. 33εἰ μὴ ἦν οὗτος παρὰ θεοῦ, οὐκ
ἠδύνατο ποιεῖν οὐδέν. 34ἀπεκρίθησαν καὶ εἶπαν αὐτῷ,
Ἐν ἁμαρτίαις σὺ ἐγεννήθης ὅλος, καὶ σὺ διδάσκεις
ἡμᾶς; καὶ ἐξέβαλον αὐτὸν ἔξω. 35Ἤκουσεν Ἰησοῦς ὅτι
ἐξέβαλον αὐτὸν ἔξω, καὶ εὑρὼν αὐτὸν εἶπεν, Σὺ πιστεύεις εἰς τὸν υἱὸν τοῦ θεοῦ; 36ἀπεκρίθη ἐκεῖνος, Καὶ τίς
ἐστιν, κύριε, ἵνα πιστεύσω εἰς αὐτόν; 37εἶπεν δὲ αὐτῷ
ὁ Ἰησοῦς, Καὶ ἑώρακας αὐτόν, καὶ ὁ λαλῶν μετὰ σοῦ
ἐκεῖνός ἐστιν. 38ὁ δὲ ἔφη, Πιστεύω, κύριε· καὶ προσεκύνησεν αὐτῷ.

39Καὶ εἶπεν ὁ Ἰησοῦς, Εἰς κρίμα ἐγὼ εἰς τὸν κόσμον
τοῦτον ἦλθον, ἵνα οἱ μὴ βλέποντες βλέπωσιν καὶ οἱ
βλέποντες τυφλοὶ γένωνται. 40ἤκουσαν ἐκ τῶν Φαρισαίων ταῦτα οἱ μετ' αὐτοῦ ὄντες, καὶ εἶπον αὐτῷ, Μὴ
καὶ ἡμεῖς τυφλοί ἐσμεν; 41εἶπεν αὐτοῖς ὁ Ἰησοῦς, Εἰ
τυφλοὶ ἦτε, οὐκ ἂν εἴχετε ἁμαρτίαν· νῦν δὲ λέγετε ὅτι
Βλέπομεν· ἡ ἁμαρτία ὑμῶν μένει.

10 1Ἀμὴν ἀμὴν λέγω ὑμῖν, ὁ μὴ εἰσερχόμενος διὰ
τῆς θύρας εἰς τὴν αὐλὴν τῶν προβάτων ἀλλὰ ἀναβαί-
νων ἀλλαχόθεν ἐκεῖνος κλέπτης ἐστὶν καὶ λῃστής· 2ὁ δὲ
εἰσερχόμενος διὰ τῆς θύρας ποιμήν ἐστιν τῶν προβάτων.

[3]τούτῳ ὁ θυρωρὸς ἀνοίγει, καὶ τὰ πρόβατα τῆς φωνῆς
αὐτοῦ ἀκούει, καὶ τὰ ἴδια πρόβατα φωνεῖ κατ' ὄνομα
καὶ ἐξάγει αὐτά. [4]ὅταν τὰ ἴδια πάντα ἐκβάλῃ, ἔμπροσθεν αὐτῶν πορεύεται, καὶ τὰ πρόβατα αὐτῷ ἀκολουθεῖ,
ὅτι οἴδασιν τὴν φωνὴν αὐτοῦ· [5]ἀλλοτρίῳ δὲ οὐ μὴ ἀκολουθήσουσιν ἀλλὰ φεύξονται ἀπ' αὐτοῦ, ὅτι οὐκ οἴδασιν
τῶν ἀλλοτρίων τὴν φωνήν. [6]ταύτην τὴν παροιμίαν
εἶπεν αὐτοῖς ὁ Ἰησοῦς· ἐκεῖνοι δὲ οὐκ ἔγνωσαν τίνα ἦν ἃ
ἐλάλει αὐτοῖς.

[7]Εἶπεν οὖν πάλιν αὐτοῖς ὁ Ἰησοῦς, Ἀμὴν ἀμὴν λέγω
ὑμῖν, ἐγώ εἰμι ἡ θύρα τῶν προβάτων. [8]πάντες ὅσοι
ἦλθον πρὸ ἐμοῦ κλέπται εἰσὶν καὶ λῃσταί, ἀλλ' οὐκ
ἤκουσαν αὐτῶν τὰ πρόβατα. [9]ἐγώ εἰμι ἡ θύρα· δι' ἐμοῦ
ἐάν τις εἰσέλθῃ σωθήσεται καὶ εἰσελεύσεται καὶ ἐξε-
λεύσεται καὶ νομὴν εὑρήσει. [10]ὁ κλέπτης οὐκ ἔρχεται
εἰ μὴ ἵνα κλέψῃ καὶ θύσῃ καὶ ἀπολέσῃ· ἐγὼ ἦλθον ἵνα
ζωὴν ἔχωσιν καὶ περισσὸν ἔχωσιν.

[11]Ἐγώ εἰμι ὁ ποιμὴν ὁ καλός· ὁ ποιμὴν ὁ καλὸς τὴν
ψυχὴν αὐτοῦ τίθησιν ὑπὲρ τῶν προβάτων· [12]ὁ μισθωτὸς καὶ οὐκ ὢν ποιμήν, οὗ οὐκ ἔστιν τὰ πρόβατα ἴδια,
θεωρεῖ τὸν λύκον ἐρχόμενον καὶ ἀφίησιν τὰ πρόβατα
καὶ φεύγει· καὶ ὁ λύκος ἁρπάζει αὐτά, καὶ σκορπίζει·
[13]ὅτι μισθωτός ἐστιν, καὶ οὐ μέλει αὐτῷ περὶ τῶν προβάτων. [14]ἐγώ εἰμι ὁ ποιμὴν ὁ καλός, καὶ γινώσκω τὰ ἐμὰ
καὶ γινώσκουσί με τὰ ἐμά. [15]καθὼς γινώσκει με ὁ πατὴρ κἀγὼ γινώσκω τὸν πατέρα, καὶ τὴν ψυχήν μου
τίθημι ὑπὲρ τῶν προβάτων. [16]καὶ ἄλλα πρόβατα ἔχω,
ἃ οὐκ ἔστιν ἐκ τῆς αὐλῆς ταύτης· κἀκεῖνά δεῖ με ἀγα-
γεῖν, καὶ τῆς φωνῆς μου ἀκούσουσιν, καὶ γενήσεται μία
ποίμνη, εἷς ποιμήν. [17]διὰ τοῦτό με ὁ πατὴρ ἀγαπᾷ ὅτι
ἐγὼ τίθημι τὴν ψυχήν μου, ἵνα πάλιν λάβω αὐτήν.

18 οὐδεὶς αἴρει αὐτὴν ἀπ᾽ ἐμοῦ, ἀλλ᾽ ἐγὼ τίθημι αὐτὴν
ἀπ᾽ ἐμαυτοῦ. ἐξουσίαν ἔχω θεῖναι αὐτήν, καὶ ἐξουσίαν
ἔχω πάλιν λαβεῖν αὐτήν· ταύτην τὴν ἐντολὴν ἔλαβον
παρὰ τοῦ πατρός μου.

19 Σχίσμα πάλιν ἐγένετο ἐν τοῖς Ἰουδαίοις διὰ τοὺς
λόγους τούτους. 20 ἔλεγον δὲ πολλοὶ ἐξ αὐτῶν, Δαιμόνιον ἔχει καὶ μαίνεται· τί αὐτοῦ ἀκούετε; 21 ἄλλοι
ἔλεγον, Ταῦτα τὰ ῥήματα οὐκ ἔστιν δαιμονιζομένου· μὴ
δαιμόνιον δύναται τυφλῶν ὀφθαλμοὺς ἀνοῖξαι;

22 Ἐγένετο δὲ τὰ ἐγκαίνια ἐν τοῖς Ἱεροσολύμοις.
χειμὼν ἦν· 23 καὶ περιεπάτει ὁ Ἰησοῦς ἐν τῷ ἱερῷ ἐν τῇ
στοᾷ τοῦ Σολομῶνος. 24 ἐκύκλωσαν οὖν αὐτὸν οἱ Ἰουδαῖοι καὶ ἔλεγον αὐτῷ, Ἕως πότε τὴν ψυχὴν ἡμῶν
αἴρεις; εἰ σὺ εἶ ὁ Χριστός, εἰπὲ ἡμῖν παρρησίᾳ. 25 ἀπεκρίθη αὐτοῖς ὁ Ἰησοῦς, Εἶπον ὑμῖν, καὶ οὐ πιστεύετε.
τὰ ἔργα ἃ ἐγὼ ποιῶ ἐν τῷ ὀνόματι τοῦ πατρός μου
ταῦτα μαρτυρεῖ περὶ ἐμοῦ· 26 ἀλλὰ ὑμεῖς οὐ πιστεύετε,
ὅτι οὐκ ἐστὲ ἐκ τῶν προβάτων τῶν ἐμῶν. 27 τὰ πρόβατα τὰ ἐμὰ τῆς φωνῆς μου ἀκούουσιν, κἀγὼ γινώσκω
αὐτά, καὶ ἀκολουθοῦσίν μοι, 28 κἀγὼ δίδωμι αὐτοῖς ζωὴν
αἰώνιον, καὶ οὐ μὴ ἀπόλωνται εἰς τὸν αἰῶνα, καὶ οὐχ
ἁρπάσει τις αὐτὰ ἐκ τῆς χειρός μου. 29 ὁ πατήρ μου ὃ
δέδωκέν μοι πάντων μεῖζον ἐστίν· καὶ οὐδεὶς δύναται
ἁρπάζειν ἐκ τῆς χειρὸς τοῦ πατρός. 30 ἐγὼ καὶ ὁ πατὴρ
ἕν ἐσμεν. 31 ἐβάστασαν πάλιν λίθους οἱ Ἰουδαῖοι ἵνα
λιθάσωσιν αὐτόν. 32 ἀπεκρίθη αὐτοῖς ὁ Ἰησοῦς, Πολλὰ
ἔργα καλὰ ἔδειξα ὑμῖν ἐκ τοῦ πατρός· διὰ ποῖον αὐτῶν
ἔργον ἐμὲ λιθάζετε; 33 ἀπεκρίθησαν αὐτῷ οἱ Ἰουδαῖοι,
Περὶ καλοῦ ἔργου οὐ λιθάζομέν σε ἀλλὰ περὶ βλασφη-
μίας, καὶ ὅτι σὺ ἄνθρωπος ὢν ποιεῖς σεαυτὸν θεόν.
34 ἀπεκρίθη αὐτοῖς ὁ Ἰησοῦς, Οὐκ ἔστιν γεγραμμένον ἐν

τῷ νόμῳ ὑμῶν ὅτι ἐγὼ εἶπα, θεοί ἐστε; 35 εἰ ἐκείνους
εἶπεν θεούς, πρὸς οὓς ὁ λόγος τοῦ θεοῦ ἐγένετο, καὶ οὐ
δύναται λυθῆναι ἡ γραφή· 36 ὃν ὁ πατὴρ ἡγίασεν καὶ ἀπέστειλεν εἰς τὸν κόσμον, ὑμεῖς λέγετε ὅτι Βλασφημεῖς,
ὅτι εἶπον, Υἱὸς τοῦ θεοῦ εἰμι; 37 εἰ οὐ ποιῶ τὰ ἔργα τοῦ
πατρός μου, μὴ πιστεύετέ μοι· 38 εἰ δὲ ποιῶ, κἂν ἐμοὶ μὴ
πιστεύητε, τοῖς ἔργοις πιστεύετε· ἵνα γνῶτε καὶ γινώσκητε ὅτι ἐν ἐμοὶ ὁ πατὴρ, κἀγὼ ἐν τῷ πατρί.

39 Ἐζήτουν οὖν πάλιν αὐτὸν πιάσαι, καὶ ἐξῆλθεν ἐκ
τῆς χειρὸς αὐτῶν. 40 καὶ ἀπῆλθεν πάλιν πέραν τοῦ Ἰορδάνου εἰς τὸν τόπον ὅπου ἦν Ἰωάννης τὸ πρῶτον
βαπτίζων, καὶ ἔμεινεν ἐκεῖ. 41 καὶ πολλοὶ ἦλθον πρὸς
αὐτὸν καὶ ἔλεγον ὅτι Ἰωάννης μὲν σημεῖον ἐποίησεν
οὐδέν, πάντα δὲ ὅσα εἶπεν Ἰωάννης περὶ τούτου ἀληθῆ
ἦν. 42 καὶ πολλοὶ ἐπίστευσαν εἰς αὐτὸν ἐκεῖ.

11 1 Ἦν δέ τις ἀσθενῶν Λάζαρος ἀπὸ Βηθανίας, ἐκ
τῆς κώμης Μαρίας καὶ Μάρθας τῆς ἀδελφῆς αὐτῆς.
2 ἦν δὲ Μαρία ἡ ἀλείψασα τὸν κύριον μύρῳ καὶ ἐκμά-
ξασα τοὺς πόδας αὐτοῦ ταῖς θριξὶν αὐτῆς, ἧς ὁ ἀδελφὸς
Λάζαρος ἠσθένει. 3 ἀπέστειλαν οὖν αἱ ἀδελφαὶ πρὸς
αὐτὸν λέγουσαι, Κύριε, ἴδε ὃν φιλεῖς ἀσθενεῖ. 4 ἀκούσας
δὲ ὁ Ἰησοῦς εἶπεν, Αὕτη ἡ ἀσθένεια οὐκ ἔστιν πρὸς
θάνατον ἀλλ' ὑπὲρ τῆς δόξης τοῦ θεοῦ, ἵνα δοξασθῇ ὁ
υἱὸς τοῦ θεοῦ δι' αὐτῆς. 5 ἠγάπα δὲ ὁ Ἰησοῦς τὴν
Μάρθαν καὶ τὴν ἀδελφὴν αὐτῆς καὶ τὸν Λάζαρον. 6 ὡς
οὖν ἤκουσεν ὅτι ἀσθενεῖ, τότε μὲν ἔμεινεν ἐν ᾧ ἦν τόπῳ
δύο ἡμέρας. 7 ἔπειτα μετὰ τοῦτο λέγει τοῖς μαθηταῖς,
Ἄγωμεν εἰς τὴν Ἰουδαίαν πάλιν. 8 λέγουσιν αὐτῷ οἱ
μαθηταί, Ῥαββί, νῦν ἐζήτουν σε λιθάσαι οἱ Ἰουδαῖοι,
καὶ πάλιν ὑπάγεις ἐκεῖ; 9 ἀπεκρίθη Ἰησοῦς, Οὐχὶ δώδεκα
ὧραί εἰσιν τῆς ἡμέρας; ἐάν τις περιπατῇ ἐν τῇ ἡμέρᾳ,

οὐ προσκόπτει, ὅτι τὸ φῶς τοῦ κόσμου τούτου βλέπει·
10 ἐὰν δέ τις περιπατῇ ἐν τῇ νυκτί, προσκόπτει, ὅτι τὸ
φῶς οὐκ ἔστιν ἐν αὐτῷ. 11 ταῦτα εἶπεν, καὶ μετὰ τοῦτο
λέγει αὐτοῖς, Λάζαρος ὁ φίλος ἡμῶν κεκοίμηται· ἀλλὰ
πορεύομαι ἵνα ἐξυπνίσω αὐτόν. 12 εἶπον οὖν αὐτῷ οἱ
μαθηταί, Κύριε, εἰ κεκοίμηται, σωθήσεται. 13 εἰρήκει δὲ
ὁ Ἰησοῦς περὶ τοῦ θανάτου αὐτοῦ· ἐκεῖνοι δὲ ἔδοξαν ὅτι
περὶ τῆς κοιμήσεως τοῦ ὕπνου λέγει. 14 τότε οὖν εἶπεν
αὐτοῖς ὁ Ἰησοῦς παρρησίᾳ, Λάζαρος ἀπέθανεν, 15 καὶ
χαίρω δι' ὑμᾶς, ἵνα πιστεύσητε, ὅτι οὐκ ἤμην ἐκεῖ· ἀλλὰ
ἄγωμεν πρὸς αὐτόν. 16 εἶπεν οὖν Θωμᾶς ὁ λεγόμενος
Δίδυμος τοῖς συμμαθηταῖς, Ἄγωμεν καὶ ἡμεῖς ἵνα
ἀποθάνωμεν μετ' αὐτοῦ.

17 Ἐλθὼν οὖν ὁ Ἰησοῦς εὗρεν αὐτὸν τέσσαρας ἤδη
ἡμέρας ἔχοντα ἐν τῷ μνημείῳ. 18 ἦν δὲ ἡ Βηθανία ἐγγὺς
τῶν Ἱεροσολύμων ὡς ἀπὸ σταδίων δεκαπέντε· 19 πολλοὶ
δὲ ἐκ τῶν Ἰουδαίων ἐληλύθεισαν πρὸς τὴν Μάρθαν καὶ
Μαριάμ, ἵνα παραμυθήσωνται αὐτὰς περὶ τοῦ ἀδελφοῦ.
20 ἡ οὖν Μάρθα ὡς ἤκουσεν ὅτι Ἰησοῦς ἔρχεται, ὑπήντησεν αὐτῷ· Μαρία δὲ ἐν τῷ οἴκῳ ἐκαθέζετο. 21 εἶπεν
οὖν ἡ Μάρθα πρὸς Ἰησοῦν, Κύριε, εἰ ἦς ὧδε, οὐκ ἂν
ἀπέθανεν ὁ ἀδελφός μου. 22 καὶ νῦν οἶδα ὅτι ὅσα ἂν
αἰτήσῃ τὸν θεόν, δώσει σοι ὁ θεός. 23 λέγει αὐτῇ ὁ
Ἰησοῦς, Ἀναστήσεται ὁ ἀδελφός σου. 24 λέγει αὐτῷ ἡ
Μάρθα, Οἶδα ὅτι ἀναστήσεται ἐν τῇ ἀναστάσει ἐν τῇ
ἐσχάτῃ ἡμέρᾳ. 25 εἶπεν αὐτῇ ὁ Ἰησοῦς, Ἐγώ εἰμι ἡ
ἀνάστασις καὶ ἡ ζωή· ὁ πιστεύων εἰς ἐμὲ κἂν ἀποθάνῃ
ζήσεται, 26 καὶ πᾶς ὁ ζῶν καὶ πιστεύων εἰς ἐμὲ οὐ μὴ
ἀποθάνῃ εἰς τὸν αἰῶνα· 27 πιστεύεις τοῦτο; λέγει αὐτῷ,
Ναί, κύριε· ἐγὼ πεπίστευκα ὅτι σὺ εἶ ὁ Χριστὸς ὁ υἱὸς
τοῦ θεοῦ ὁ εἰς τὸν κόσμον ἐρχόμενος. 28 καὶ τοῦτο εἰποῦσα

ἀπῆλθεν καὶ ἐφώνησεν Μαριὰμ τὴν ἀδελφὴν αὐτῆς λάθρα
εἰποῦσα, Ὁ διδάσκαλος πάρεστιν καὶ φωνεῖ σε. 29 ἐκείνη
ὡς ἤκουσεν, ἠγέρθη ταχὺ καὶ ἤρχετο πρὸς αὐτόν. 30 οὔπω
δὲ ἐληλύθει ὁ Ἰησοῦς εἰς τὴν κώμην, ἀλλ' ἦν ἔτι ἐν τῷ
τόπῳ ὅπου ὑπήντησεν αὐτῷ ἡ Μάρθα. 31 οἱ οὖν Ἰουδαῖοι
οἱ ὄντες μετ' αὐτῆς ἐν τῇ οἰκίᾳ καὶ παραμυθούμενοι
αὐτήν, ἰδόντες τὴν Μαριὰμ ὅτι ταχέως ἀνέστη καὶ
ἐξῆλθεν, ἠκολούθησαν αὐτῇ, δόξαντες ὅτι ὑπάγει εἰς τὸ
μνημεῖον ἵνα κλαύσῃ ἐκεῖ. 32 ἡ οὖν Μαριὰμ ὡς ἦλθεν
ὅπου ἦν Ἰησοῦς ἰδοῦσα αὐτὸν ἔπεσεν αὐτοῦ πρὸς τοὺς
πόδας, λέγουσα αὐτῷ, Κύριε, εἰ ἦς ὧδε, οὐκ ἄν μου
ἀπέθανεν ὁ ἀδελφός.

33 Ἰησοῦς οὖν ὡς εἶδεν αὐτὴν κλαίουσαν καὶ τοὺς
συνελθόντας αὐτῇ Ἰουδαίους κλαίοντας, ἐνεβριμήσατο
τῷ πνεύματι καὶ ἐτάραξεν ἑαυτόν, 34 καὶ εἶπεν, Ποῦ
τεθείκατε αὐτόν; λέγουσιν αὐτῷ, Κύριε, ἔρχου καὶ ἴδε.
35 ἐδάκρυσεν ὁ Ἰησοῦς. 36 ἔλεγον οὖν οἱ Ἰουδαῖοι, Ἴδε
πῶς ἐφίλει αὐτόν. 37 τινὲς δὲ ἐξ αὐτῶν εἶπον, Οὐκ
ἐδύνατο οὗτος ὁ ἀνοίξας τοὺς ὀφθαλμοὺς τοῦ τυφλοῦ
ποιῆσαι ἵνα καὶ οὗτος μὴ ἀποθάνῃ; 38 Ἰησοῦς οὖν πάλιν
ἐμβριμώμενος ἐν ἑαυτῷ ἔρχεται εἰς τὸ μνημεῖον. ἦν δὲ
σπήλαιον, καὶ λίθος ἐπέκειτο ἐπ' αὐτῷ. 39 λέγει ὁ Ἰησοῦς,
Ἄρατε τὸν λίθον. λέγει αὐτῷ ἡ ἀδελφὴ τοῦ τετελευτηκότος Μάρθα, Κύριε, ἤδη ὄζει· τεταρταῖος γάρ ἐστιν.
40 λέγει αὐτῇ ὁ Ἰησοῦς, Οὐκ εἶπόν σοι ὅτι ἐὰν πιστεύσῃς
ὄψῃ τὴν δόξαν τοῦ θεοῦ; 41 ἦραν οὖν τὸν λίθον. ὁ δὲ
Ἰησοῦς ἦρεν τοὺς ὀφθαλμοὺς ἄνω καὶ εἶπεν, Πάτερ, εὐ-
χαριστῶ σοι ὅτι ἤκουσάς μου. 42 ἐγὼ δὲ ᾔδειν ὅτι πάντοτέ μου ἀκούεις· ἀλλὰ διὰ τὸν ὄχλον τὸν περιεστῶτα
εἶπον, ἵνα πιστεύσωσιν ὅτι σύ με ἀπέστειλας. 43 καὶ
ταῦτα εἰπὼν φωνῇ μεγάλῃ ἐκραύγασεν, Λάζαρε, δεῦρο

ἔξω. [44]ἐξῆλθεν ὁ τεθνηκὼς δεδεμένος τοὺς πόδας καὶ
τὰς χεῖρας κειρίαις, καὶ ἡ ὄψις αὐτοῦ σουδαρίῳ περιε-
δέδετο. λέγει αὐτοῖς ὁ Ἰησοῦς, Λύσατε αὐτὸν καὶ ἄφετε
αὐτὸν ὑπάγειν.

[45]Πολλοὶ οὖν ἐκ τῶν Ἰουδαίων, οἱ ἐλθόντες πρὸς
τὴν Μαριὰμ καὶ θεασάμενοι ἃ ἐποίησεν, ἐπίστευσαν εἰς
αὐτόν· [46]τινὲς δὲ ἐξ αὐτῶν ἀπῆλθον πρὸς τοὺς Φαρισαίους καὶ εἶπον αὐτοῖς ἃ ἐποίησεν Ἰησοῦς. [47]συνή-
γαγον οὖν οἱ ἀρχιερεῖς καὶ οἱ Φαρισαῖοι συνέδριον, καὶ
ἔλεγον, Τί ποιοῦμεν; ὅτι οὗτος ὁ ἄνθρωπος πολλὰ ποιεῖ
σημεῖα. [48]ἐὰν ἀφῶμεν αὐτὸν οὕτως, πάντες πιστεύσουσιν
εἰς αὐτόν, καὶ ἐλεύσονται οἱ Ῥωμαῖοι καὶ ἀροῦσιν ἡμῶν
καὶ τὸν τόπον καὶ τὸ ἔθνος. [49]εἷς δέ τις ἐξ αὐτῶν
Καϊάφας, ἀρχιερεὺς ὢν τοῦ ἐνιαυτοῦ ἐκείνου, εἶπεν αὐτοῖς,
Ὑμεῖς οὐκ οἴδατε οὐδέν, [50]οὐδὲ λογίζεσθε ὅτι συμφέρει
ὑμῖν ἵνα εἷς ἄνθρωπος ἀποθάνῃ ὑπὲρ τοῦ λαοῦ καὶ μὴ
ὅλον τὸ ἔθνος ἀπόληται. [51]τοῦτο δὲ ἀφ' ἑαυτοῦ οὐκ
εἶπεν, ἀλλὰ ἀρχιερεὺς ὢν τοῦ ἐνιαυτοῦ ἐκείνου ἐπροφήτευσεν ὅτι ἤμελλεν Ἰησοῦς ἀποθνήσκειν ὑπὲρ τοῦ
ἔθνους, [52]καὶ οὐχ ὑπὲρ τοῦ ἔθνους μόνον, ἀλλ' ἵνα καὶ τὰ
τέκνα τοῦ θεοῦ τὰ διεσκορπισμένα συναγάγῃ εἰς ἕν.
[53]ἀπ' ἐκείνης οὖν τῆς ἡμέρας ἐβουλεύσαντο ἵνα ἀποκτείνωσιν αὐτόν. [54]Ἰησοῦς οὖν οὐκέτι παρρησίᾳ περιεπάτει
ἐν τοῖς Ἰουδαίοις, ἀλλὰ ἀπῆλθεν ἐκεῖθεν εἰς τὴν χώραν
ἐγγὺς τῆς ἐρήμου, εἰς Ἐφραὶμ λεγομένην πόλιν, κἀκεῖ
διέτριβεν μετὰ τῶν μαθητῶν. [55]ἦν δὲ ἐγγὺς τὸ πάσχα
τῶν Ἰουδαίων· καὶ ἀνέβησαν πολλοὶ εἰς Ἱεροσόλυμα ἐκ
τῆς χώρας πρὸ τοῦ πάσχα, ἵνα ἁγνίσωσιν ἑαυτούς.
[56]ἐζήτουν οὖν τὸν Ἰησοῦν καὶ ἔλεγον μετ' ἀλλήλων ἐν
τῷ ἱερῷ ἑστηκότες, Τί δοκεῖ ὑμῖν; ὅτι οὐ μὴ ἔλθῃ εἰς τὴν
ἑορτήν; [57]δεδώκεισαν δὲ οἱ ἀρχιερεῖς καὶ οἱ Φαρισαῖοι

*ἐντολὰς ἵνα ἐάν τις γνῷ ποῦ ἐστὶν μηνύσῃ, ὅπως πιάσω-
σιν αὐτόν.*

12 1 Ὁ οὖν Ἰησοῦς πρὸ ἓξ ἡμερῶν τοῦ πάσχα ἦλθεν
εἰς Βηθανίαν, ὅπου ἦν Λάζαρος, ὃν ἤγειρεν ἐκ νεκρῶν
Ἰησοῦς.

2 Ἐποίησαν οὖν αὐτῷ δεῖπνον ἐκεῖ, καὶ ἡ Μάρθα διη-
κόνει, ὁ δὲ Λάζαρος εἷς ἦν τῶν ἀνακειμένων σὺν αὐτῷ.
3 ἡ οὖν Μαρία λαβοῦσα λίτραν μύρου νάρδου πιστικῆς
πολυτίμου ἤλειψεν τοὺς πόδας τοῦ Ἰησοῦ καὶ ἐξέμαξεν
ταῖς θριξὶν αὐτῆς τοὺς πόδας αὐτοῦ. ἡ δὲ οἰκία ἐπλη-
ρώθη ἐκ τῆς ὀσμῆς τοῦ μύρου. 4 λέγει οὖν Ἰούδας ὁ
Ἰσκαριώτης, εἷς ἐκ τῶν μαθητῶν αὐτοῦ, ὁ μέλλων αὐτὸν
παραδιδόναι, 5 Διατί τοῦτο τὸ μύρον οὐκ ἐπράθη τριακοσίων δηναρίων καὶ ἐδόθη πτωχοῖς; 6 εἶπεν δὲ τοῦτο
οὐχ ὅτι περὶ τῶν πτωχῶν ἔμελεν αὐτῷ, ἀλλ' ὅτι κλέπτης
ἦν καὶ τὸ γλωσσόκομον ἔχων τὰ βαλλόμενα ἐβάσταζεν.
7 εἶπεν οὖν ὁ Ἰησοῦς, Ἄφες αὐτήν, ἵνα εἰς τὴν ἡμέραν
τοῦ ἐνταφιασμοῦ μου τηρήσῃ αὐτό. 8 τοὺς πτωχοὺς γὰρ
πάντοτε ἔχετε μεθ' ἑαυτῶν, ἐμὲ δὲ οὐ πάντοτε ἔχετε.

9 Ἔγνω οὖν ὁ ὄχλος πολὺς ἐκ τῶν Ἰουδαίων ὅτι ἐκεῖ
ἐστίν, καὶ ἦλθον οὐ διὰ τὸν Ἰησοῦν μόνον, ἀλλ' ἵνα καὶ
τὸν Λάζαρον ἴδωσιν, ὃν ἤγειρεν ἐκ νεκρῶν. 10 ἐβουλεύσαντο δὲ οἱ ἀρχιερεῖς ἵνα καὶ τὸν Λάζαρον ἀποκτείνωσιν,
11 ὅτι πολλοὶ δι' αὐτὸν ὑπῆγον τῶν Ἰουδαίων καὶ ἐπίστευον εἰς τὸν Ἰησοῦν.

12 Τῇ ἐπαύριον ὄχλος πολὺς ὁ ἐλθὼν εἰς τὴν ἑορτήν,
ἀκούσαντες ὅτι ἔρχεται Ἰησοῦς εἰς Ἱεροσόλυμα, 13 ἔλαβον τὰ βαΐα τῶν φοινίκων καὶ ἐξῆλθον εἰς ὑπάντησιν
αὐτῷ, καὶ ἐκραύγαζον, Ὡσαννά, εὐλογημένος ὁ ἐρχόμενος
ἐν ὀνόματι Κυρίου, καὶ ὁ βασιλεὺς τοῦ Ἰσραήλ. 14 εὑρὼν
δὲ ὁ Ἰησοῦς ὀνάριον ἐκάθισεν ἐπ' αὐτό, καθώς ἐστιν

γεγραμμένον, 15 Μὴ φοβοῦ, θυγάτηρ Σιών· ἰδού, ὁ βασιλεύς
σου ἔρχεται καθήμενος ἐπὶ πῶλον ὄνου. 16 ταῦτα οὐκ
ἔγνωσαν οἱ μαθηταὶ αὐτοῦ τὸ πρῶτον, ἀλλ᾽ ὅτε ἐδοξάσθη
Ἰησοῦς, τότε ἐμνήσθησαν ὅτι ταῦτα ἦν ἐπ᾽ αὐτῷ γεγραμμένα καὶ ταῦτα ἐποίησαν αὐτῷ. 17 ἐμαρτύρει οὖν ὁ
ὄχλος ὁ ὢν μετ᾽ αὐτοῦ, ὅτε τὸν Λάζαρον ἐφώνησεν
ἐκ τοῦ μνημείου καὶ ἤγειρεν αὐτὸν ἐκ νεκρῶν· 18 διὰ
τοῦτο καὶ ὑπήντησεν αὐτῷ ὁ ὄχλος, ὅτι ἤκουσαν τοῦτο
αὐτὸν πεποιηκέναι τὸ σημεῖον.

19 Οἱ οὖν Φαρισαῖοι εἶπαν πρὸς ἑαυτούς, Θεωρεῖτε ὅτι
οὐκ ὠφελεῖτε οὐδέν· ἴδε ὁ κόσμος ὀπίσω αὐτοῦ ἀπῆλθεν.

20 Ἦσαν δὲ Ἕλληνές τινες ἐκ τῶν ἀναβαινόντων
ἵνα προσκυνήσωσιν ἐν τῇ ἑορτῇ· 21 οὗτοι οὖν προσῆλθον
Φιλίππῳ τῷ ἀπὸ Βηθσαϊδὰ τῆς Γαλιλαίας, καὶ ἠρώτων
αὐτὸν λέγοντες, Κύριε, θέλομεν τὸν Ἰησοῦν ἰδεῖν. 22 ἔρχεται Φίλιππος καὶ λέγει τῷ Ἀνδρέᾳ· ἔρχεται Ἀνδρέας
καὶ Φίλιππος καὶ λέγουσιν τῷ Ἰησοῦ. 23 ὁ δὲ Ἰησοῦς
ἀποκρίνεται αὐτοῖς λέγων, Ἐλήλυθεν ἡ ὥρα ἵνα δοξασθῇ ὁ υἱὸς τοῦ ἀνθρώπου. 24 ἀμὴν ἀμὴν λέγω ὑμῖν, ἐὰν μὴ
ὁ κόκκος τοῦ σίτου πεσὼν εἰς τὴν γῆν ἀποθάνῃ, αὐτὸς
μόνος μένει· ἐὰν δὲ ἀποθάνῃ, πολὺν καρπὸν φέρει. 25 ὁ
φιλῶν τὴν ψυχὴν αὐτοῦ ἀπολλύει αὐτήν· καὶ ὁ μισῶν
τὴν ψυχὴν αὐτοῦ ἐν τῷ κόσμῳ τούτῳ, εἰς ζωὴν αἰώνιον
φυλάξει αὐτήν. 26 ἐὰν ἐμοί τις διακονῇ, ἐμοὶ ἀκολου-
θείτω· καὶ ὅπου εἰμὶ ἐγώ, ἐκεῖ καὶ ὁ διάκονος ὁ ἐμὸς
ἔσται· ἐάν τις ἐμοὶ διακονῇ, τιμήσει αὐτὸν ὁ πατήρ.
27 νῦν ἡ ψυχή μου τετάρακται, καὶ τί εἴπω; Πάτερ,
σῶσόν με ἐκ τῆς ὥρας ταύτης. ἀλλὰ διὰ τοῦτο ἦλθον
εἰς τὴν ὥραν ταύτην. 28 Πάτερ δόξασόν σου τὸ ὄνομα.
ἦλθεν οὖν φωνὴ ἐκ τοῦ οὐρανοῦ, Καὶ ἐδόξασα καὶ
πάλιν δοξάσω. 29 ὁ οὖν ὄχλος ὁ ἑστὼς καὶ ἀκούσας

ἔλεγεν βροντὴν γεγονέναι. ἄλλοι ἔλεγον, Ἄγγελος *αὐτῷ*
λελάληκεν. 30 *ἀπεκρίθη* Ἰησοῦς *καὶ εἶπεν,* Οὐ *δι' ἐμὲ*
ἡ φωνὴ αὕτη γέγονεν ἀλλὰ δι' ὑμᾶς. 31 *νῦν κρίσις ἐστὶν*
τοῦ κόσμου τούτου, νῦν ὁ ἄρχων τοῦ κόσμου τούτου
ἐκβληθήσεται ἔξω· 32 *κἀγὼ ἐὰν ὑψωθῶ ἐκ τῆς γῆς, πάν-*
τας ἑλκύσω πρὸς ἐμαυτόν. 33 *τοῦτο δὲ ἔλεγεν σημαίνων*
ποίῳ θανάτῳ ἤμελλεν ἀποθνήσκειν.

34 Ἀπεκρίθη *οὖν αὐτῷ ὁ ὄχλος,* Ἡμεῖς *ἠκούσαμεν ἐκ*
τοῦ νόμου ὅτι ὁ Χριστὸς *μένει εἰς τὸν αἰῶνα, καὶ πῶς*
λέγεις σὺ ὅτι Δεῖ *ὑψωθῆναι τὸν υἱὸν τοῦ ἀνθρώπου;*
τίς ἐστιν οὗτος ὁ υἱὸς τοῦ ἀνθρώπου; 35 *εἶπεν οὖν αὐτοῖς*
ὁ Ἰησοῦς, Ἔτι *μικρὸν χρόνον τὸ φῶς ἐν ὑμῖν ἐστίν.*
περιπατεῖτε ὡς τὸ φῶς ἔχετε, ἵνα μὴ σκοτία ὑμᾶς κατα-
λάβῃ· καὶ ὁ περιπατῶν ἐν τῇ σκοτίᾳ οὐκ οἶδεν ποῦ
ὑπάγει. 36 *ὡς τὸ φῶς ἔχετε, πιστεύετε εἰς τὸ φῶς, ἵνα*
υἱοὶ φωτὸς γένησθε. ταῦτα ἐλάλησεν Ἰησοῦς, *καὶ*
ἀπελθὼν ἐκρύβη ἀπ' αὐτῶν.

37 Τοσαῦτα *δὲ αὐτοῦ σημεῖα πεποιηκότος ἔμπροσθεν*
αὐτῶν οὐκ ἐπίστευον εἰς αὐτόν· 38 *ἵνα ὁ λόγος* Ἠσαΐου
τοῦ προφήτου πληρωθῇ, ὃν εἶπεν, Κύριε, *τίς ἐπίστευσεν*
τῇ ἀκοῇ ἡμῶν; καὶ ὁ βραχίων Κυρίου *τίνι ἀπεκαλύφθη;*
39 *διὰ τοῦτο οὐκ ἠδύναντο πιστεύειν, ὅτι πάλιν εἶπεν*
Ἠσαΐας, 40 Τετύφλωκεν *αὐτῶν τοὺς ὀφθαλμοὺς καὶ*
ἐπώρωσεν αὐτῶν τὴν καρδίαν, ἵνα μὴ ἴδωσιν τοῖς ὀφθαλ-
μοῖς καὶ νοήσωσιν τῇ καρδίᾳ καὶ στραφῶσιν, καὶ ἰάσομαι
αὐτούς. 41 *ταῦτα εἶπεν* Ἠσαΐας *ὅτι εἶδεν τὴν δόξαν*
αὐτοῦ, καὶ ἐλάλησεν περὶ αὐτοῦ· 42 *ὅμως μέντοι καὶ ἐκ*
τῶν ἀρχόντων πολλοὶ ἐπίστευσαν εἰς αὐτόν, ἀλλὰ διὰ
τοὺς Φαρισαίους *οὐχ ὡμολόγουν, ἵνα μὴ ἀποσυνάγωγοι*
γένωνται. 43 *ἠγάπησαν γὰρ τὴν δόξαν τῶν ἀνθρώπων*
μᾶλλον ἤπερ τὴν δόξαν τοῦ θεοῦ.

44 Ἰησοῦς δὲ ἔκραξεν καὶ εἶπεν, Ὁ πιστεύων εἰς ἐμέ,
οὐ πιστεύει εἰς ἐμέ, ἀλλὰ εἰς τὸν πέμψαντά με· 45 καὶ ὁ
θεωρῶν ἐμὲ θεωρεῖ τὸν πέμψαντά με. 46 ἐγὼ φῶς εἰς
τὸν κόσμον ἐλήλυθα, ἵνα πᾶς ὁ πιστεύων εἰς ἐμὲ ἐν τῇ
σκοτίᾳ μὴ μείνῃ. 47 καὶ ἐάν τις μου ἀκούσῃ τῶν ῥημά-
των καὶ μὴ φυλάξῃ, ἐγὼ οὐ κρίνω αὐτόν· οὐ γὰρ ἦλθον
ἵνα κρίνω τὸν κόσμον, ἀλλ' ἵνα σώσω τὸν κόσμον. 48 ὁ
ἀθετῶν ἐμὲ καὶ μὴ λαμβάνων τὰ ῥήματά μου ἔχει τὸν
κρίνοντα αὐτόν· ὁ λόγος ὃν ἐλάλησα, ἐκεῖνος κρινεῖ αὐτὸν ἐν τῇ ἐσχάτῃ ἡμέρᾳ. 49 ὅτι ἐγὼ ἐξ ἐμαυτοῦ οὐκ
ἐλάλησα, ἀλλ' ὁ πέμψας με πατὴρ αὐτός μοι ἐντολὴν
δέδωκεν τί εἴπω καὶ τί λαλήσω· 50 καὶ οἶδα ὅτι ἡ ἐντολὴ
αὐτοῦ ζωὴ αἰώνιός ἐστιν. ἃ οὖν ἐγὼ λαλῶ, καθὼς εἴ-
ρηκέν μοι ὁ πατήρ, οὕτως λαλῶ.

13 1 Πρὸ δὲ τῆς ἑορτῆς τοῦ πάσχα εἰδὼς ὁ Ἰησοῦς
ὅτι ἦλθεν αὐτοῦ ἡ ὥρα ἵνα μεταβῇ ἐκ τοῦ κόσμου
τούτου πρὸς τὸν πατέρα, ἀγαπήσας τοὺς ἰδίους τοὺς ἐν
τῷ κόσμῳ, εἰς τέλος ἠγάπησεν αὐτούς· 2 καὶ δείπνου
γινομένου, τοῦ διαβόλου ἤδη βεβληκότος εἰς τὴν καρδίαν ἵνα παραδοῖ αὐτὸν Ἰούδας Σίμωνος Ἰσκαριώτης,
εἰδὼς 3 ὅτι πάντα ἔδωκεν αὐτῷ ὁ πατὴρ εἰς τὰς χεῖρας,
καὶ ὅτι ἀπὸ θεοῦ ἐξῆλθεν καὶ πρὸς τὸν θεὸν ὑπάγει,
ἐγείρεται ἐκ τοῦ δείπνου 4 καὶ τίθησιν τὰ ἱμάτια, καὶ
λαβὼν λέντιον διέζωσεν ἑαυτόν· 5 εἶτα βάλλει ὕδωρ εἰς
τὸν νιπτῆρα, καὶ ἤρξατο νίπτειν τοὺς πόδας τῶν μαθητῶν καὶ ἐκμάσσειν τῷ λεντίῳ ᾧ ἦν διεζωσμένος. 6 ἔρχεται οὖν πρὸς Σίμωνα Πέτρον· λέγει αὐτῷ, Κύριε, σύ
μου νίπτεις τοὺς πόδας; 7 ἀπεκρίθη Ἰησοῦς καὶ εἶπεν
αὐτῷ, Ὃ ἐγὼ ποιῶ σὺ οὐκ οἶδας ἄρτι, γνώσῃ δὲ μετὰ
ταῦτα. 8 λέγει αὐτῷ Πέτρος, Οὐ μὴ νίψῃς μου τοὺς
πόδας εἰς τὸν αἰῶνα. ἀπεκρίθη Ἰησοῦς αὐτῷ, Ἐὰν μὴ

νίψω σε, οὐκ ἔχεις μέρος μετ᾿ ἐμοῦ. 9λέγει αὐτῷ Σίμων Πέτρος, Κύριε, μὴ τοὺς πόδας μου μόνον ἀλλὰ καὶ
τὰς χεῖρας καὶ τὴν κεφαλήν. 10λέγει αὐτῷ Ἰησοῦς, Ὁ
λελουμένος οὐκ ἔχει χρείαν εἰ μὴ τοὺς πόδας νίψασθαι,
ἀλλ᾿ ἔστιν καθαρὸς ὅλος· καὶ ὑμεῖς καθαροί ἐστε, ἀλλ᾿
οὐχὶ πάντες. 11ᾔδει γὰρ τὸν παραδιδόντα αὐτόν· διὰ
τοῦτο εἶπεν ὅτι Οὐχὶ πάντες καθαροί ἐστε.

12Ὅτε οὖν ἔνιψεν τοὺς πόδας αὐτῶν καὶ ἔλαβεν τὰ
ἱμάτια αὐτοῦ καὶ ἀνέπεσεν πάλιν, εἶπεν αὐτοῖς, Γινώσκετε τί πεποίηκα ὑμῖν; 13ὑμεῖς φωνεῖτέ με, Ὁ διδάσκαλος, καὶ ὁ κύριος· καὶ καλῶς λέγετε, εἰμὶ γάρ. 14εἰ
οὖν ἐγὼ ἔνιψα ὑμῶν τοὺς πόδας ὁ κύριος καὶ ὁ διδάσκαλος, καὶ ὑμεῖς ὀφείλετε ἀλλήλων νίπτειν τοὺς πόδας.
15ὑπόδειγμα γὰρ ἔδωκα ὑμῖν, ἵνα καθὼς ἐγὼ ἐποίησα
ὑμῖν καὶ ὑμεῖς ποιῆτε. 16ἀμὴν ἀμὴν λέγω ὑμῖν, οὐκ
ἔστιν δοῦλος μείζων τοῦ κυρίου αὐτοῦ, οὐδὲ ἀπόστολος
μείζων τοῦ πέμψαντος αὐτόν. 17εἰ ταῦτα οἴδατε, μακάριοί ἐστε ἐὰν ποιῆτε αὐτά. 18οὐ περὶ πάντων ὑμῶν λέγω·
ἐγὼ οἶδα τίνας ἐξελεξάμην· ἀλλ᾿ ἵνα ἡ γραφὴ πληρωθῇ,
Ὁ τρώγων μετ᾿ ἐμοῦ τὸν ἄρτον ἐπῆρεν ἐπ᾿ ἐμὲ τὴν
πτέρναν αὐτοῦ. 19ἀπ᾿ ἄρτι λέγω ὑμῖν πρὸ τοῦ γενέσθαι, ἵνα πιστεύσητε ὅταν γένηται ὅτι ἐγώ εἰμι. 20ἀμὴν
ἀμὴν λέγω ὑμῖν, ὁ λαμβάνων ἄν τινα πέμψω ἐμὲ λαμ-
βάνει· ὁ δὲ ἐμὲ λαμβάνων λαμβάνει τὸν πέμψαντά με.

21Ταῦτα εἰπὼν Ἰησοῦς ἐταράχθη τῷ πνεύματι καὶ
ἐμαρτύρησεν καὶ εἶπεν, Ἀμὴν ἀμὴν λέγω ὑμῖν ὅτι εἷς ἐξ
ὑμῶν παραδώσει με. 22ἔβλεπον οὖν εἰς ἀλλήλους οἱ
μαθηταί, ἀπορούμενοι περὶ τίνος λέγει. 23ἦν ἀνακείμενος εἷς ἐκ τῶν μαθητῶν αὐτοῦ ἐν τῷ κόλπῳ τοῦ
Ἰησοῦ, ὃν ἠγάπα ὁ Ἰησοῦς· 24νεύει οὖν τούτῳ Σίμων
Πέτρος καὶ λέγει αὐτῷ, Εἰπὲ τίς ἐστιν περὶ οὗ λέγει.

25 ἀναπεσὼν ἐκεῖνος οὕτως ἐπὶ τὸ στῆθος τοῦ Ἰησοῦ
λέγει αὐτῷ, Κύριε, τίς ἐστιν; 26 ἀποκρίνεται ὁ Ἰησοῦς,
Ἐκεῖνός ἐστιν ᾧ ἐγὼ βάψω τὸ ψωμίον καὶ δώσω αὐτῷ.
βάψας οὖν τὸ ψωμίον λαμβάνει καὶ δίδωσιν Ἰούδᾳ
Σίμωνος Ἰσκαριώτου. 27 καὶ μετὰ τὸ ψωμίον, τότε
εἰσῆλθεν εἰς ἐκεῖνον ὁ Σατανᾶς. λέγει οὖν αὐτῷ
Ἰησοῦς, Ὃ ποιεῖς ποίησον τάχιον. 28 τοῦτο δὲ οὐδεὶς
ἔγνω τῶν ἀνακειμένων πρὸς τί εἶπεν αὐτῷ· τινὲς γὰρ
ἐδόκουν, 29 ἐπεὶ τὸ γλωσσόκομον εἶχεν Ἰούδας, ὅτι λέγει
αὐτῷ Ἰησοῦς, Ἀγόρασον ὧν χρείαν ἔχομεν εἰς τὴν
ἑορτήν, ἢ τοῖς πτωχοῖς ἵνα τι δῷ. 30 λαβὼν οὖν τὸ
ψωμίον ἐκεῖνος ἐξῆλθεν εὐθύς· ἦν δὲ νύξ.

31 Ὅτε οὖν ἐξῆλθεν, λέγει ὁ Ἰησοῦς, Νῦν ἐδοξάσθη ὁ
υἱὸς τοῦ ἀνθρώπου, καὶ ὁ θεὸς ἐδοξάσθη ἐν αὐτῷ. 32 [εἰ
ὁ θεὸς ἐδοξάσθη ἐν αὐτῷ,] καὶ ὁ θεὸς δοξάσει αὐτὸν ἐν
αὐτῷ, καὶ εὐθὺς δοξάσει αὐτόν. 33 Τεκνία, ἔτι μικρὸν
μεθ' ὑμῶν εἰμί. ζητήσετέ με, καὶ καθὼς εἶπον τοῖς
Ἰουδαίοις ὅτι Ὅπου ἐγὼ ὑπάγω ὑμεῖς οὐ δύνασθε
ἐλθεῖν, καὶ ὑμῖν λέγω ἄρτι. 34 ἐντολὴν καινὴν δίδωμι
ὑμῖν, ἵνα ἀγαπᾶτε ἀλλήλους, καθὼς ἠγάπησα ὑμᾶς
ἵνα καὶ ὑμεῖς ἀγαπᾶτε ἀλλήλους. 35 ἐν τούτῳ γνώσονται
πάντες ὅτι ἐμοὶ μαθηταί ἐστε, ἐὰν ἀγάπην ἔχητε ἐν
ἀλλήλοις. 36 Λέγει αὐτῷ Σίμων Πέτρος, Κύριε, ποῦ
ὑπάγεις; ἀπεκρίθη Ἰησοῦς, Ὅπου ὑπάγω, οὐ δύνασαί
μοι νῦν ἀκολουθῆσαι, ἀκολουθήσεις δὲ ὕστερον. 37 λέγει
αὐτῷ Πέτρος, Κύριε, διατί οὐ δύναμαί σοι ἀκολουθῆσαι
ἄρτι; τὴν ψυχήν μου ὑπὲρ σοῦ θήσω. 38 ἀποκρίνεται
Ἰησοῦς, Τὴν ψυχήν σου ὑπὲρ ἐμοῦ θήσεις; ἀμὴν ἀμὴν
λέγω σοι, οὐ μὴ ἀλέκτωρ φωνήσῃ ἕως οὗ ἀρνήσῃ με
τρίς.

14 1 Μὴ ταρασσέσθω ὑμῶν ἡ καρδία· πιστεύετε εἰς

τὸν θεόν, καὶ εἰς ἐμὲ πιστεύετε. 2ἐν τῇ οἰκίᾳ τοῦ
πατρός μου μοναὶ πολλαί εἰσιν· εἰ δὲ μή, εἶπον ἂν ὑμῖν·
ὅτι πορεύομαι ἑτοιμάσαι τόπον ὑμῖν· 3καὶ ἐὰν πορευθῶ καὶ ἑτοιμάσω τόπον ὑμῖν, πάλιν ἔρχομαι καὶ
παραλήμψομαι ὑμᾶς πρὸς ἐμαυτόν, ἵνα ὅπου εἰμὶ ἐγὼ
καὶ ὑμεῖς ἦτε. 4καὶ ὅπου ἐγὼ ὑπάγω οἴδατε τὴν ὁδόν.
5λέγει αὐτῷ Θωμᾶς, Κύριε, οὐκ οἴδαμεν ποῦ ὑπάγεις·
πῶς οἴδαμεν τὴν ὁδόν; 6λέγει αὐτῷ ὁ Ἰησοῦς, Ἐγώ εἰμι
ἡ ὁδὸς καὶ ἡ ἀλήθεια καὶ ἡ ζωή· οὐδεὶς ἔρχεται πρὸς
τὸν πατέρα εἰ μὴ δι' ἐμοῦ. 7εἰ ἐγνώκειτέ με, καὶ τὸν
πατέρα μου ἐγνώκειτε ἄν· καὶ ἀπ' ἄρτι γινώσκετε
αὐτὸν καὶ ἑωράκατε αὐτόν. 8λέγει αὐτῷ Φίλιππος,
Κύριε, δεῖξον ἡμῖν τὸν πατέρα, καὶ ἀρκεῖ ἡμῖν. 9λέγει
αὐτῷ ὁ Ἰησοῦς, Τοσούτῳ χρόνῳ μεθ' ὑμῶν εἰμί, καὶ οὐκ
ἔγνωκάς με Φίλιππε; ὁ ἑωρακὼς ἐμὲ ἑώρακε τὸν πα-
τέρα· πῶς σὺ λέγεις, Δεῖξον ἡμῖν τὸν πατέρα; 10οὐ
πιστεύεις ὅτι ἐγὼ ἐν τῷ πατρὶ καὶ ὁ πατὴρ ἐν ἐμοί
ἐστιν; τὰ ῥήματα ἃ ἐγὼ λέγω ὑμῖν ἀπ' ἐμαυτοῦ οὐ
λαλῶ· ὁ δὲ πατὴρ ὁ ἐν ἐμοὶ μένων ποιεῖ τὰ ἔργα αὐτοῦ.
11πιστεύετέ μοι ὅτι ἐγὼ ἐν τῷ πατρὶ καὶ ὁ πατὴρ ἐν
ἐμοί· εἰ δὲ μή, διὰ τὰ ἔργα αὐτὰ πιστεύετέ μοι. 12ἀμὴν
ἀμὴν λέγω ὑμῖν, ὁ πιστεύων εἰς ἐμέ, τὰ ἔργα ἃ ἐγὼ
ποιῶ, κἀκεῖνος ποιήσει, καὶ μείζονα τούτων ποιήσει·
ὅτι ἐγὼ πρὸς τὸν πατέρα πορεύομαι. 13καὶ ὅ τι ἂν
αἰτήσητε ἐν τῷ ὀνόματί μου, τοῦτο ποιήσω, ἵνα δοξασθῇ ὁ πατὴρ ἐν τῷ υἱῷ· 14ἐάν τι αἰτήσητέ [με] ἐν τῷ
ὀνόματί μου, ἐγὼ ποιήσω.

15Ἐὰν ἀγαπᾶτέ με, τὰς ἐντολὰς τὰς ἐμὰς τηρήσετε.
16κἀγὼ ἐρωτήσω τὸν πατέρα καὶ ἄλλον παράκλητον
δώσει ὑμῖν, ἵνα ᾖ μεθ' ὑμῶν εἰς τὸν αἰῶνα, 17τὸ πνεῦμα
τῆς ἀληθείας, ὃ ὁ κόσμος οὐ δύναται λαβεῖν, ὅτι οὐ

θεωρεῖ αὐτὸ οὐδὲ γινώσκει αὐτό. ὑμεῖς γινώσκετε αὐτό,
ὅτι παρ' ὑμῖν μένει καὶ ἐν ὑμῖν ἐστίν. 18 *οὐκ ἀφήσω*
ὑμᾶς ὀρφανούς· ἔρχομαι πρὸς ὑμᾶς. 19 *ἔτι μικρὸν καὶ*
ὁ κόσμος με οὐκέτι θεωρεῖ, ὑμεῖς δὲ θεωρεῖτέ με, ὅτι
ἐγὼ ζῶ καὶ ὑμεῖς ζήσετε. 20 *ἐν ἐκείνῃ τῇ ἡμέρᾳ γνώ-*
σεσθε ὑμεῖς ὅτι ἐγὼ ἐν τῷ πατρί μου καὶ ὑμεῖς ἐν ἐμοὶ
κἀγὼ ἐν ὑμῖν. 21 *ὁ ἔχων τὰς ἐντολάς μου καὶ τηρῶν*
αὐτάς, ἐκεῖνός ἐστιν ὁ ἀγαπῶν με· ὁ δὲ ἀγαπῶν με
ἀγαπηθήσεται ὑπὸ τοῦ πατρός μου· κἀγὼ ἀγαπήσω
αὐτὸν καὶ ἐμφανίσω αὐτῷ ἐμαυτόν. 22 *λέγει αὐτῷ*
Ἰούδας, οὐχ ὁ Ἰσκαριώτης, Κύριε, τί γέγονεν ὅτι ἡμῖν
μέλλεις ἐμφανίζειν σεαυτὸν καὶ οὐχὶ τῷ κόσμῳ; 23 *ἀπε-*
κρίθη Ἰησοῦς καὶ εἶπεν αὐτῷ, Ἐάν τις ἀγαπᾷ με, τὸν
λόγον μου τηρήσει, καὶ ὁ πατήρ μου ἀγαπήσει αὐτόν,
καὶ πρὸς αὐτὸν ἐλευσόμεθα καὶ μονὴν παρ' αὐτῷ ποιη-
σόμεθα. 24 *ὁ μὴ ἀγαπῶν με τοὺς λόγους μου οὐ τηρεῖ·*
καὶ ὁ λόγος ὃν ἀκούετε οὐκ ἔστιν ἐμὸς ἀλλὰ τοῦ
πέμψαντός με πατρός.

25 *Ταῦτα λελάληκα ὑμῖν παρ' ὑμῖν μένων·* 26 *ὁ δὲ*
παράκλητος, τὸ πνεῦμα τὸ ἅγιον ὃ πέμψει ὁ πατὴρ ἐν
τῷ ὀνόματί μου, ἐκεῖνος ὑμᾶς διδάξει πάντα καὶ ὑπο-
μνήσει ὑμᾶς πάντα ἃ εἶπον ὑμῖν. 27 *εἰρήνην ἀφίημι ὑμῖν,*
εἰρήνην τὴν ἐμὴν δίδωμι ὑμῖν· οὐ καθὼς ὁ κόσμος
δίδωσιν ἐγὼ δίδωμι ὑμῖν. μὴ ταρασσέσθω ὑμῶν ἡ
καρδία, μηδὲ δειλιάτω. 28 *ἠκούσατε ὅτι ἐγὼ εἶπον ὑμῖν,*
Ὑπάγω καὶ ἔρχομαι πρὸς ὑμᾶς. εἰ ἠγαπᾶτέ με, ἐχάρητε
ἂν ὅτι πορεύομαι πρὸς τὸν πατέρα, ὅτι ὁ πατὴρ μείζων
μου ἐστίν. 29 *καὶ νῦν εἴρηκα ὑμῖν πρὶν γενέσθαι, ἵνα*
ὅταν γένηται πιστεύσητε. 30 *οὐκέτι πολλὰ λαλήσω μεθ'*
ὑμῶν· ἔρχεται γὰρ ὁ τοῦ κόσμου ἄρχων, καὶ ἐν ἐμοὶ
οὐκ ἔχει οὐδέν, 31 *ἀλλ' ἵνα γνῷ ὁ κόσμος ὅτι ἀγαπῶ*

τὸν πατέρα, καὶ καθὼς ἐντολὴν ἔδωκέν μοι ὁ πατήρ,
οὕτως ποιῶ. ἐγείρεσθε, ἄγωμεν ἐντεῦθεν.

15 1 Ἐγώ εἰμι ἡ ἄμπελος ἡ ἀληθινή, καὶ ὁ πατήρ
μου ὁ γεωργός ἐστιν. 2 πᾶν κλῆμα ἐν ἐμοὶ μὴ φέρον
καρπόν, αἴρει αὐτό, καὶ πᾶν τὸ καρπὸν φέρον, καθαίρει
αὐτὸ ἵνα καρπὸν πλείονα φέρῃ. 3 ἤδη ὑμεῖς καθαροί
ἐστε διὰ τὸν λόγον ὃν λελάληκα ὑμῖν. 4 μείνατε ἐν
ἐμοί, κἀγὼ ἐν ὑμῖν. καθὼς τὸ κλῆμα οὐ δύναται καρπὸν
φέρειν ἀφ᾽ ἑαυτοῦ ἐὰν μὴ μένῃ ἐν τῇ ἀμπέλῳ, οὕτως
οὐδὲ ὑμεῖς ἐὰν μὴ ἐν ἐμοὶ μένητε. 5 ἐγώ εἰμι ἡ ἄμπελος,
ὑμεῖς τὰ κλήματα. ὁ μένων ἐν ἐμοὶ κἀγὼ ἐν αὐτῷ,
οὗτος φέρει καρπὸν πολύν, ὅτι χωρὶς ἐμοῦ οὐ δύνασθε
ποιεῖν οὐδέν. 6 ἐὰν μή τις μένῃ ἐν ἐμοί, ἐβλήθη ἔξω ὡς
τὸ κλῆμα καὶ ἐξηράνθη, καὶ συνάγουσιν αὐτὰ καὶ εἰς
πῦρ βάλλουσιν, καὶ καίεται. 7 ἐὰν μείνητε ἐν ἐμοὶ καὶ
τὰ ῥήματά μου ἐν ὑμῖν μείνῃ, ὃ ἐὰν θέλητε αἰτήσασθε,
καὶ γενήσεται ὑμῖν. 8 ἐν τούτῳ ἐδοξάσθη ὁ πατήρ μου,
ἵνα καρπὸν πολὺν φέρητε καὶ γένησθε ἐμοὶ μαθηταί.
9 καθὼς ἠγάπησέ με ὁ πατήρ, κἀγὼ ὑμᾶς ἠγάπησα·
10 μείνατε ἐν τῇ ἀγάπῃ τῇ ἐμῇ. ἐὰν τὰς ἐντολάς μου
τηρήσητε, μενεῖτε ἐν τῇ ἀγάπῃ μου· καθὼς ἐγὼ τοῦ
πατρὸς τὰς ἐντολὰς τετήρηκα καὶ μένω αὐτοῦ ἐν τῇ
ἀγάπῃ.

11 Ταῦτα λελάληκα ὑμῖν ἵνα ἡ χαρὰ ἡ ἐμὴ ἐν ὑμῖν ᾖ
καὶ ἡ χαρὰ ὑμῶν πληρωθῇ.

12 Αὕτη ἐστὶν ἡ ἐντολὴ ἡ ἐμή, ἵνα ἀγαπᾶτε ἀλλήλους
καθὼς ἠγάπησα ὑμᾶς. 13 μείζονα ταύτης ἀγάπην οὐδεὶς
ἔχει ἵνα τις τὴν ψυχὴν αὐτοῦ θῇ ὑπὲρ τῶν φίλων
αὐτοῦ. 14 ὑμεῖς φίλοι μου ἐστέ, ἐὰν ποιῆτε ἃ ἐγὼ ἐντέλλομαι ὑμῖν. 15 οὐκέτι λέγω ὑμᾶς δούλους, ὅτι ὁ δοῦλος
οὐκ οἶδεν τί ποιεῖ αὐτοῦ ὁ κύριος· ὑμᾶς δὲ εἴρηκα

φίλους, ὅτι πάντα ἃ ἤκουσα παρὰ τοῦ πατρός μου
ἐγνώρισα ὑμῖν. 16 οὐχ ὑμεῖς με ἐξελέξασθε, ἀλλ' ἐγὼ
ἐξελεξάμην ὑμᾶς, καὶ ἔθηκα ὑμᾶς ἵνα ὑμεῖς ὑπάγητε
καὶ καρπὸν φέρητε καὶ ὁ καρπὸς ὑμῶν μένῃ· ἵνα ὅ τι
ἂν αἰτήσητε τὸν πατέρα ἐν τῷ ὀνόματί μου δῷ ὑμῖν.
17 ταῦτα ἐντέλλομαι ὑμῖν, ἵνα ἀγαπᾶτε ἀλλήλους.

18 Εἰ ὁ κόσμος ὑμᾶς μισεῖ, γινώσκετε ὅτι ἐμὲ πρῶτον
ὑμῶν μεμίσηκεν. 19 εἰ ἐκ τοῦ κόσμου ἦτε, ὁ κόσμος ἂν
τὸ ἴδιον ἐφίλει· ὅτι δὲ ἐκ τοῦ κόσμου οὐκ ἐστέ, ἀλλ'
ἐγὼ ἐξελεξάμην ὑμᾶς ἐκ τοῦ κόσμου, διὰ τοῦτο μισεῖ
ὑμᾶς ὁ κόσμος. 20 μνημονεύετε τοῦ λόγου οὗ ἐγὼ εἶπον
ὑμῖν, Οὐκ ἔστιν δοῦλος μείζων τοῦ κυρίου αὐτοῦ. εἰ ἐμὲ
ἐδίωξαν, καὶ ὑμᾶς διώξουσιν· εἰ τὸν λόγον μου ἐτήρη-
σαν, καὶ τὸν ὑμέτερον τηρήσουσιν. 21 ἀλλὰ ταῦτα πάντα
ποιήσουσιν εἰς ὑμᾶς διὰ τὸ ὄνομά μου, ὅτι οὐκ οἴδασιν
τὸν πέμψαντά με. 22 εἰ μὴ ἦλθον καὶ ἐλάλησα αὐτοῖς,
ἁμαρτίαν οὐκ εἴχοσαν· νῦν δὲ πρόφασιν οὐκ ἔχουσιν
περὶ τῆς ἁμαρτίας αὐτῶν. 23 ὁ ἐμὲ μισῶν καὶ τὸν
πατέρα μου μισεῖ. 24 εἰ τὰ ἔργα μὴ ἐποίησα ἐν αὐτοῖς ἃ
οὐδεὶς ἄλλος ἐποίησεν, ἁμαρτίαν οὐκ εἴχοσαν. νῦν δὲ
καὶ ἑωράκασιν καὶ μεμισήκασιν καὶ ἐμὲ καὶ τὸν πατέρα
μου· 25 ἀλλ' ἵνα πληρωθῇ ὁ λόγος ὁ ἐν τῷ νόμῳ αὐτῶν
γεγραμμένος ὅτι ἐμίσησάν με δωρεάν. 26 ὅταν δὲ ἔλθῃ
ὁ παράκλητος ὃν ἐγὼ πέμψω ὑμῖν παρὰ τοῦ πατρός,
τὸ πνεῦμα τῆς ἀληθείας ὃ παρὰ τοῦ πατρὸς ἐκπορεύεται, ἐκεῖνος μαρτυρήσει περὶ ἐμοῦ· 27 καὶ ὑμεῖς δὲ μαρτυρεῖτε, ὅτι ἀπ' ἀρχῆς μετ' ἐμοῦ ἐστέ.

16 1 Ταῦτα λελάληκα ὑμῖν ἵνα μὴ σκανδαλισθῆτε.
2 ἀποσυναγώγους ποιήσουσιν ὑμᾶς· ἀλλ' ἔρχεται ὥρα
ἵνα πᾶς ὁ ἀποκτείνας ὑμᾶς δόξῃ λατρείαν προσφέρειν
τῷ θεῷ. 3 καὶ ταῦτα ποιήσουσιν ὅτι οὐκ ἔγνωσαν τὸν

πατέρα οὐδὲ ἐμέ. 4 ἀλλὰ ταῦτα λελάληκα ὑμῖν ἵνα ὅταν
ἔλθῃ ἡ ὥρα αὐτῶν μνημονεύητε αὐτῶν, ὅτι ἐγὼ εἶπον
ὑμῖν. ταῦτα δὲ ὑμῖν ἐξ ἀρχῆς οὐκ εἶπον, ὅτι μεθ' ὑμῶν
ἤμην. 5 νῦν δὲ ὑπάγω πρὸς τὸν πέμψαντά με, καὶ οὐδεὶς
ἐξ ὑμῶν ἐρωτᾷ με, Ποῦ ὑπάγεις; 6 ἀλλ' ὅτι ταῦτα λελάληκα ὑμῖν, ἡ λύπη πεπλήρωκεν ὑμῶν τὴν καρδίαν.
7 ἀλλ' ἐγὼ τὴν ἀλήθειαν λέγω ὑμῖν, συμφέρει ὑμῖν ἵνα
ἐγὼ ἀπέλθω. ἐὰν γὰρ μὴ ἀπέλθω, ὁ παράκλητος οὐκ
ἐλεύσεται πρὸς ὑμᾶς· ἐὰν δὲ πορευθῶ, πέμψω αὐτὸν
πρὸς ὑμᾶς. 8 καὶ ἐλθὼν ἐκεῖνος ἐλέγξει τὸν κόσμον
περὶ ἁμαρτίας καὶ περὶ δικαιοσύνης καὶ περὶ κρίσεως.
9 περὶ ἁμαρτίας μέν, ὅτι οὐ πιστεύουσιν εἰς ἐμέ· 10 περὶ
δικαιοσύνης δέ, ὅτι πρὸς τὸν πατέρα ὑπάγω καὶ οὐκέτι
θεωρεῖτέ με· 11 περὶ δὲ κρίσεως, ὅτι ὁ ἄρχων τοῦ κόσμου
τούτου κέκριται.

12 Ἔτι πολλὰ ἔχω ὑμῖν λέγειν, ἀλλ' οὐ δύνασθε
βαστάζειν ἄρτι· 13 ὅταν δὲ ἔλθῃ ἐκεῖνος, τὸ πνεῦμα τῆς
ἀληθείας, ὁδηγήσει ὑμᾶς εἰς τὴν ἀλήθειαν πᾶσαν. οὐ
γὰρ λαλήσει ἀφ' ἑαυτοῦ, ἀλλ' ὅσα ἀκούσει λαλήσει, καὶ
τὰ ἐρχόμενα ἀναγγελεῖ ὑμῖν. 14 ἐκεῖνος ἐμὲ δοξάσει, ὅτι
ἐκ τοῦ ἐμοῦ λήμψεται, καὶ ἀναγγελεῖ ὑμῖν. 15 πάντα ὅσα
ἔχει ὁ πατὴρ ἐμά ἐστιν· διὰ τοῦτο εἶπον ὅτι ἐκ τοῦ
ἐμοῦ λαμβάνει καὶ ἀναγγελεῖ ὑμῖν.

16 Μικρὸν καὶ οὐκέτι θεωρεῖτέ με, καὶ πάλιν μικρὸν
καὶ ὄψεσθέ με. 17 εἶπον οὖν ἐκ τῶν μαθητῶν αὐτοῦ
πρὸς ἀλλήλους, Τί ἐστιν τοῦτο ὃ λέγει ἡμῖν, Μικρὸν καὶ
οὐ θεωρεῖτέ με, καὶ πάλιν μικρὸν καὶ ὄψεσθέ με; καὶ
ὅτι Ὑπάγω πρὸς τὸν πατέρα; 18 ἔλεγον οὖν, Τί ἐστιν
τοῦτο ὃ λέγει τὸ μικρόν; οὐκ οἴδαμεν τί λαλεῖ. 19 ἔγνω
Ἰησοῦς ὅτι ἤθελον αὐτὸν ἐρωτᾷν, καὶ εἶπεν αὐτοῖς, Περὶ
τούτου ζητεῖτε μετ' ἀλλήλων ὅτι εἶπον, Μικρὸν καὶ οὐ

θεωρεῖτέ με, καὶ πάλιν μικρὸν καὶ ὄψεσθέ με; 20 ἀμὴν
ἀμὴν λέγω ὑμῖν ὅτι κλαύσετε καὶ θρηνήσετε ὑμεῖς, ὁ δὲ
κόσμος χαρήσεται· ὑμεῖς λυπηθήσεσθε, ἀλλ' ἡ λύπη
ὑμῶν εἰς χαρὰν γενήσεται. 21 ἡ γυνὴ ὅταν τίκτῃ λύπην
ἔχει, ὅτι ἦλθεν ἡ ὥρα αὐτῆς· ὅταν δὲ γεννήσῃ τὸ παιδίον, οὐκέτι μνημονεύει τῆς θλίψεως διὰ τὴν χαρὰν ὅτι
ἐγεννήθη ἄνθρωπος εἰς τὸν κόσμον. 22 καὶ ὑμεῖς οὖν νῦν
μὲν λύπην ἔχετε· πάλιν δὲ ὄψομαι ὑμᾶς, καὶ χαρήσεται
ὑμῶν ἡ καρδία, καὶ τὴν χαρὰν ὑμῶν οὐδεὶς ἀρεῖ ἀφ'
ὑμῶν. 23 καὶ ἐν ἐκείνῃ τῇ ἡμέρᾳ ἐμὲ οὐκ ἐρωτήσετε
οὐδέν. ἀμὴν ἀμὴν λέγω ὑμῖν, ἄν τι αἰτήσητε τὸν πατέρα
δώσει ὑμῖν ἐν τῷ ὀνόματί μου. 24 ἕως ἄρτι οὐκ ᾐτήσατε
οὐδὲν ἐν τῷ ὀνόματί μου· αἰτεῖτε, καὶ λήμψεσθε, ἵνα ἡ
χαρὰ ὑμῶν ᾖ πεπληρωμένη.

25 Ταῦτα ἐν παροιμίαις λελάληκα ὑμῖν· ἔρχεται ὥρα
ὅτε οὐκέτι ἐν παροιμίαις λαλήσω ὑμῖν, ἀλλὰ παρρησίᾳ
περὶ τοῦ πατρὸς ἀπαγγελῶ ὑμῖν. 26 ἐν ἐκείνῃ τῇ ἡμέρᾳ
ἐν τῷ ὀνόματί μου αἰτήσεσθε, καὶ οὐ λέγω ὑμῖν ὅτι ἐγὼ
ἐρωτήσω τὸν πατέρα περὶ ὑμῶν· 27 αὐτὸς γὰρ ὁ πατὴρ
φιλεῖ ὑμᾶς, ὅτι ὑμεῖς ἐμὲ πεφιλήκατε καὶ πεπιστεύκατε
ὅτι ἐγὼ παρὰ τοῦ θεοῦ ἐξῆλθον. 28 ἐξῆλθον ἐκ τοῦ πατρὸς
καὶ ἐλήλυθα εἰς τὸν κόσμον· πάλιν ἀφίημι τὸν κόσμον
καὶ πορεύομαι πρὸς τὸν πατέρα.

29 Λέγουσιν οἱ μαθηταὶ αὐτοῦ, Ἴδε νῦν ἐν παρρησίᾳ
λαλεῖς, καὶ παροιμίαν οὐδεμίαν λέγεις. 30 νῦν οἴδαμεν
ὅτι οἶδας πάντα καὶ οὐ χρείαν ἔχεις ἵνα τίς σε ἐρωτᾷ·
ἐν τούτῳ πιστεύομεν ὅτι ἀπὸ θεοῦ ἐξῆλθες. 31 ἀπεκρίθη αὐτοῖς Ἰησοῦς, Ἄρτι πιστεύετε; 32 ἰδοὺ ἔρχεται
ὥρα καὶ ἐλήλυθεν ἵνα σκορπισθῆτε ἕκαστος εἰς τὰ
ἴδια κἀμὲ μόνον ἀφῆτε· καὶ οὐκ εἰμὶ μόνος, ὅτι ὁ
πατὴρ μετ' ἐμοῦ ἐστίν. 33 ταῦτα λελάληκα ὑμῖν ἵνα ἐν

ἐμοὶ εἰρήνην ἔχητε. ἐν τῷ κόσμῳ θλῖψιν ἔχετε· ἀλλὰ
θαρσεῖτε, ἐγὼ νενίκηκα τὸν κόσμον.

17 [1]Ταῦτα ἐλάλησεν ὁ Ἰησοῦς, καὶ ἐπάρας τοὺς
ὀφθαλμοὺς αὐτοῦ εἰς τὸν οὐρανὸν εἶπεν, Πάτερ, ἐλήλυθεν ἡ ὥρα· δόξασόν σου τὸν υἱόν, ἵνα ὁ υἱὸς δοξάσῃ
σε, [2]καθὼς ἔδωκας αὐτῷ ἐξουσίαν πάσης σαρκός, ἵνα
πᾶν ὃ δέδωκας αὐτῷ δώσῃ αὐτοῖς ζωὴν αἰώνιον. [3]αὕτη
δέ ἐστιν ἡ αἰώνιος ζωή, ἵνα γινώσκουσίν σε τὸν μόνον
ἀληθινὸν θεὸν καὶ ὃν ἀπέστειλας Ἰησοῦν Χριστόν.
[4]ἐγώ σε ἐδόξασα ἐπὶ τῆς γῆς, τελειώσας τὸ ἔργον ὃ
δέδωκάς μοι ἵνα ποιήσω· [5]καὶ νῦν δόξασόν με σύ, πάτερ,
παρὰ σεαυτῷ τῇ δόξῃ ᾗ εἶχον πρὸ τοῦ τὸν κόσμον εἶναι
παρὰ σοί.

[6]Ἐφανέρωσά σου τὸ ὄνομα τοῖς ἀνθρώποις οὓς ἔδωκάς μοι ἐκ τοῦ κόσμου. σοὶ ἦσαν καὶ ἐμοὶ αὐτοὺς
ἔδωκας, καὶ τὸν λόγον σου τετήρηκαν· [7]νῦν ἔγνωκαν
ὅτι πάντα ὅσα δέδωκάς μοι παρὰ σοῦ εἰσίν· [8]ὅτι τὰ
ῥήματα ἃ ἔδωκάς μοι δέδωκα αὐτοῖς, καὶ αὐτοὶ ἔλαβον,
καὶ ἔγνωσαν ἀληθῶς ὅτι παρὰ σοῦ ἐξῆλθον, καὶ ἐπίστευσαν ὅτι σύ με ἀπέστειλας. ἐγὼ περὶ αὐτῶν ἐρωτῶ·
[9]οὐ περὶ τοῦ κόσμου ἐρωτῶ, ἀλλὰ περὶ ὧν δέδωκάς μοι,
ὅτι σοί εἰσιν, [10]καὶ τὰ ἐμὰ πάντα σά ἐστιν καὶ τὰ σὰ
ἐμά, καὶ δεδόξασμαι ἐν αὐτοῖς. [11]καὶ οὐκέτι εἰμὶ ἐν τῷ
κόσμῳ, καὶ οὗτοι ἐν τῷ κόσμῳ εἰσίν, κἀγὼ πρός σε
ἔρχομαι. πάτερ ἅγιε, τήρησον αὐτοὺς ἐν τῷ ὀνόματί
σου ᾧ δέδωκάς μοι, ἵνα ὦσιν ἓν καθὼς ἡμεῖς. [12]ὅτε
ἤμην μετ' αὐτῶν, ἐγὼ ἐτήρουν αὐτοὺς ἐν τῷ ὀνόματί σου
ᾧ δέδωκάς μοι, καὶ ἐφύλαξα, καὶ οὐδεὶς ἐξ αὐτῶν ἀπώλετο εἰ μὴ ὁ υἱὸς τῆς ἀπωλείας, ἵνα ἡ γραφὴ πληρωθῇ.
[13]νῦν δὲ πρός σε ἔρχομαι, καὶ ταῦτα λαλῶ ἐν τῷ κόσμῳ,
ἵνα ἔχωσιν τὴν χαρὰν τὴν ἐμὴν πεπληρωμένην ἐν ἑαυ-

τοῖς. 14ἐγὼ δέδωκα αὐτοῖς τὸν λόγον σου, καὶ ὁ κόσμος
ἐμίσησεν αὐτούς, ὅτι οὐκ εἰσὶν ἐκ τοῦ κόσμου καθὼς
ἐγὼ οὐκ εἰμὶ ἐκ τοῦ κόσμου. 15οὐκ ἐρωτῶ ἵνα ἄρῃς
αὐτοὺς ἐκ τοῦ κόσμου, ἀλλ᾽ ἵνα τηρήσῃς αὐτοὺς ἐκ τοῦ
πονηροῦ. 16ἐκ τοῦ κόσμου οὐκ εἰσὶν καθὼς ἐγὼ οὐκ
εἰμὶ ἐκ τοῦ κόσμου. 17ἁγίασον αὐτοὺς ἐν τῇ ἀληθείᾳ·
ὁ λόγος ὁ σὸς ἀλήθειά ἐστιν. 18καθὼς ἐμὲ ἀπέστειλας
εἰς τὸν κόσμον, κἀγὼ ἀπέστειλα αὐτοὺς εἰς τὸν κόσμον·
19καὶ ὑπὲρ αὐτῶν ἐγὼ ἁγιάζω ἐμαυτόν, ἵνα ὦσιν καὶ
αὐτοὶ ἡγιασμένοι ἐν ἀληθείᾳ.

20Οὐ περὶ τούτων δὲ ἐρωτῶ μόνον, ἀλλὰ καὶ περὶ
τῶν πιστευόντων διὰ τοῦ λόγου αὐτῶν εἰς ἐμέ· 21ἵνα
πάντες ἓν ὦσιν, καθὼς σύ, πατήρ, ἐν ἐμοὶ κἀγὼ ἐν σοί,
ἵνα καὶ αὐτοὶ ἐν ἡμῖν ὦσιν, ἵνα ὁ κόσμος πιστεύῃ ὅτι
σύ με ἀπέστειλας. 22κἀγὼ τὴν δόξαν ἣν δέδωκάς μοι,
δέδωκα αὐτοῖς, ἵνα ὦσιν ἕν, καθὼς ἡμεῖς ἕν· 23ἐγὼ ἐν
αὐτοῖς, καὶ σὺ ἐν ἐμοί, ἵνα ὦσιν τετελειωμένοι εἰς ἕν, ἵνα
γινώσκῃ ὁ κόσμος ὅτι σύ με ἀπέστειλας καὶ ἠγάπησας
αὐτοὺς καθὼς ἐμὲ ἠγάπησας. 24Πατήρ, ὃ δέδωκάς μοι,
θέλω ἵνα ὅπου εἰμὶ ἐγώ, κἀκεῖνοι ὦσιν μετ᾽ ἐμοῦ· ἵνα
θεωρῶσιν τὴν δόξαν τὴν ἐμήν, ἣν δέδωκάς μοι ὅτι ἠγάπησάς με πρὸ καταβολῆς κόσμου.

25Πατὴρ δίκαιε, καὶ ὁ κόσμος σε οὐκ ἔγνω, ἐγὼ δέ σε
ἔγνων, καὶ οὗτοι ἔγνωσαν ὅτι σύ με ἀπέστειλας· 26καὶ
ἐγνώρισα αὐτοῖς τὸ ὄνομά σου καὶ γνωρίσω, ἵνα ἡ
ἀγάπη ἣν ἠγάπησάς με ἐν αὐτοῖς ᾖ κἀγὼ ἐν αὐτοῖς.

18 1Ταῦτα εἰπὼν Ἰησοῦς ἐξῆλθεν σὺν τοῖς μαθηταῖς
αὐτοῦ πέραν τοῦ χειμάρρου τῶν Κέδρων, ὅπου ἦν κῆπος,
εἰς ὃν εἰσῆλθεν αὐτὸς καὶ οἱ μαθηταὶ αὐτοῦ. 2ᾔδει δὲ
καὶ Ἰούδας ὁ παραδιδοὺς αὐτὸν τὸν τόπον, ὅτι πολλά-
κις συνήχθη Ἰησοῦς ἐκεῖ μετὰ τῶν μαθητῶν αὐτοῦ. 3ὁ

οὖν Ἰούδας λαβὼν τὴν σπεῖραν καὶ ἐκ τῶν ἀρχιερέων
καὶ τῶν Φαρισαίων ὑπηρέτας ἔρχεται ἐκεῖ μετὰ φανῶν
καὶ λαμπάδων καὶ ὅπλων. 4 Ἰησοῦς οὖν εἰδὼς πάντα τὰ
ἐρχόμενα ἐπ' αὐτόν, ἐξῆλθεν καὶ λέγει αὐτοῖς, Τίνα
ζητεῖτε; 5 ἀπεκρίθησαν αὐτῷ, Ἰησοῦν τὸν Ναζωραῖον.
λέγει αὐτοῖς Ἰησοῦς, Ἐγώ εἰμι. εἱστήκει δὲ καὶ Ἰούδας
ὁ παραδιδοὺς αὐτὸν μετ' αὐτῶν. 6 ὡς οὖν εἶπεν αὐτοῖς,
Ἐγώ εἰμι, ἀπῆλθαν εἰς τὰ ὀπίσω καὶ ἔπεσαν χαμαί.
7 πάλιν οὖν ἐπηρώτησεν αὐτούς, Τίνα ζητεῖτε; οἱ δὲ
εἶπον, Ἰησοῦν τὸν Ναζωραῖον. 8 ἀπεκρίθη Ἰησοῦς, Εἶπον ὑμῖν ὅτι ἐγώ εἰμι· εἰ οὖν ἐμὲ ζητεῖτε, ἄφετε
τούτους ὑπάγειν. 9 ἵνα πληρωθῇ ὁ λόγος ὃν εἶπεν ὅτι
Οὓς δέδωκάς μοι, οὐκ ἀπώλεσα ἐξ αὐτῶν οὐδένα. 10 Σίμων οὖν Πέτρος ἔχων μάχαιραν εἵλκυσεν αὐτὴν καὶ
ἔπαισεν τὸν τοῦ ἀρχιερέως δοῦλον καὶ ἀπέκοψεν αὐτοῦ
τὸ ὠτάριον τὸ δεξιόν. ἦν δὲ ὄνομα τῷ δούλῳ Μάλχος.
11 εἶπεν οὖν ὁ Ἰησοῦς τῷ Πέτρῳ, Βάλε τὴν μάχαιραν εἰς
τὴν θήκην. τὸ ποτήριον ὃ δέδωκέν μοι ὁ πατήρ, οὐ μὴ
πίω αὐτό;

12 Ἡ οὖν σπεῖρα καὶ ὁ χιλίαρχος καὶ οἱ ὑπηρέται
τῶν Ἰουδαίων συνέλαβον τὸν Ἰησοῦν καὶ ἔδησαν αὐτόν, 13 καὶ ἤγαγον πρὸς Ἄνναν πρῶτον· ἦν γὰρ πενθερὸς
τοῦ Καϊάφα, ὃς ἦν ἀρχιερεὺς τοῦ ἐνιαυτοῦ ἐκείνου.
14 ἦν δὲ Καϊάφας ὁ συμβουλεύσας τοῖς Ἰουδαίοις ὅτι
συμφέρει ἕνα ἄνθρωπον ἀποθανεῖν ὑπὲρ τοῦ λαοῦ.
15 Ἠκολούθει δὲ τῷ Ἰησοῦ Σίμων Πέτρος καὶ ἄλλος
μαθητής. ὁ δὲ μαθητὴς ἐκεῖνος ἦν γνωστὸς τῷ ἀρχιερεῖ καὶ συνεισῆλθεν τῷ Ἰησοῦ εἰς τὴν αὐλὴν τοῦ
ἀρχιερέως, 16 ὁ δὲ Πέτρος εἱστήκει πρὸς τῇ θύρᾳ ἔξω.
ἐξῆλθεν οὖν ὁ μαθητὴς ὁ ἄλλος ὁ γνωστὸς τοῦ ἀρχιερέως καὶ εἶπεν τῇ θυρωρῷ, καὶ εἰσήγαγεν τὸν Πέτρον.

17 λέγει οὖν τῷ Πέτρῳ ἡ παιδίσκη ἡ θυρωρός, Μὴ καὶ σὺ
ἐκ τῶν μαθητῶν εἶ τοῦ ἀνθρώπου τούτου; λέγει ἐκεῖνος,
Οὐκ εἰμί. 18 εἱστήκεισαν δὲ οἱ δοῦλοι καὶ οἱ ὑπηρέται
ἀνθρακιὰν πεποιηκότες, ὅτι ψῦχος ἦν, καὶ ἐθερμαίνοντο·
ἦν δὲ καὶ ὁ Πέτρος μετ' αὐτῶν ἑστὼς καὶ θερμαινόμενος.
19 Ὁ οὖν ἀρχιερεὺς ἠρώτησεν τὸν Ἰησοῦν περὶ τῶν μαθητῶν αὐτοῦ, καὶ περὶ τῆς διδαχῆς αὐτοῦ. 20 ἀπεκρίθη
αὐτῷ Ἰησοῦς, Ἐγὼ παρρησίᾳ λελάληκα τῷ κόσμῳ· ἐγὼ
πάντοτε ἐδίδαξα ἐν συναγωγῇ καὶ ἐν τῷ ἱερῷ, ὅπου
πάντες οἱ Ἰουδαῖοι συνέρχονται, καὶ ἐν κρυπτῷ ἐλάλησα οὐδέν. 21 τί με ἐρωτᾷς; ἐρώτησον τοὺς ἀκηκοότας,
τί ἐλάλησα αὐτοῖς· ἴδε οὗτοι οἴδασιν ἃ εἶπον ἐγώ.
22 ταῦτα δὲ αὐτοῦ εἰπόντος, εἷς παρεστηκὼς τῶν ὑπηρε-
τῶν ἔδωκεν ῥάπισμα τῷ Ἰησοῦ εἰπών, Οὕτως ἀποκρίνῃ
τῷ ἀρχιερεῖ; 23 ἀπεκρίθη αὐτῷ Ἰησοῦς, Εἰ κακῶς ἐλάλησα, μαρτύρησον περὶ τοῦ κακοῦ· 24 εἰ δὲ καλῶς, τί με
δέρεις; ἀπέστειλεν οὖν αὐτὸν ὁ Ἅννας δεδεμένον πρὸς
Καϊάφαν τὸν ἀρχιερέα.

25 Ἦν δὲ Σίμων Πέτρος ἑστὼς καὶ θερμαινόμενος.
εἶπον οὖν αὐτῷ, Μὴ καὶ σὺ ἐκ τῶν μαθητῶν αὐτοῦ εἶ;
ἠρνήσατο ἐκεῖνος καὶ εἶπεν, Οὐκ εἰμί. 26 λέγει εἷς ἐκ
τῶν δούλων τοῦ ἀρχιερέως, συγγενὴς ὢν οὗ ἀπέκοψεν
Πέτρος τὸ ὠτίον, Οὐκ ἐγώ σε εἶδον ἐν τῷ κήπῳ μετ'
αὐτοῦ; 27 πάλιν οὖν ἠρνήσατο Πέτρος, καὶ εὐθέως ἀλέκτωρ ἐφώνησεν.

28 Ἄγουσιν οὖν τὸν Ἰησοῦν ἀπὸ τοῦ Καϊάφα εἰς τὸ
πραιτώριον· ἦν δὲ πρωΐ· καὶ αὐτοὶ οὐκ εἰσῆλθον εἰς τὸ
πραιτώριον, ἵνα μὴ μιανθῶσιν ἀλλ' ἵνα φάγωσιν τὸ
πάσχα. 29 ἐξῆλθεν οὖν ὁ Πιλᾶτος ἔξω πρὸς αὐτούς, καί
φησιν, Τίνα κατηγορίαν φέρετε κατὰ τοῦ ἀνθρώπου
τούτου; 30 ἀπεκρίθησαν καὶ εἶπαν αὐτῷ, Εἰ μὴ ἦν οὗτος

κακὸν ποιῶν, οὐκ ἄν σοι παρεδώκαμεν αὐτόν. 31εἶπεν
οὖν αὐτοῖς ὁ Πιλάτος, Λάβετε αὐτὸν ὑμεῖς καὶ κατὰ τὸν
νόμον ὑμῶν κρίνατε αὐτόν. εἶπον αὐτῷ οἱ Ἰουδαῖοι,
Ἡμῖν οὐκ ἔξεστιν ἀποκτεῖναι οὐδένα· 32ἵνα ὁ λόγος τοῦ
Ἰησοῦ πληρωθῇ, ὃν εἶπεν σημαίνων ποίῳ θανάτῳ ἤμελλεν ἀποθνήσκειν. 33Εἰσῆλθεν οὖν πάλιν εἰς τὸ πραιτώριον ὁ Πιλάτος, καὶ ἐφώνησεν τὸν Ἰησοῦν καὶ εἶπεν
αὐτῷ, Σὺ εἶ ὁ βασιλεὺς τῶν Ἰουδαίων; 34ἀπεκρίθη
Ἰησοῦς, Ἀπὸ σεαυτοῦ σὺ τοῦτο λέγεις, ἢ ἄλλοι σοι
εἶπον περὶ ἐμοῦ; 35ἀπεκρίθη ὁ Πιλάτος, Μήτι ἐγὼ
Ἰουδαῖός εἰμι; τὸ ἔθνος τὸ σὸν καὶ οἱ ἀρχιερεῖς παρέ-
δωκάν σε ἐμοί· τί ἐποίησας; 36ἀπεκρίθη Ἰησοῦς, Ἡ
βασιλεία ἡ ἐμὴ οὐκ ἔστιν ἐκ τοῦ κόσμου τούτου· εἰ ἐκ
τοῦ κόσμου τούτου ἦν ἡ βασιλεία ἡ ἐμή, οἱ ὑπηρέται ἂν
οἱ ἐμοὶ ἠγωνίζοντο, ἵνα μὴ παραδοθῶ τοῖς Ἰουδαίοις·
νῦν δὲ ἡ βασιλεία ἡ ἐμὴ οὐκ ἔστιν ἐντεῦθεν. 37εἶπεν
οὖν αὐτῷ ὁ Πιλάτος, Οὐκοῦν βασιλεὺς εἶ σύ; ἀπεκρίθη
ὁ Ἰησοῦς, Σὺ λέγεις ὅτι βασιλεύς εἰμι. ἐγὼ εἰς τοῦτο
γεγέννημαι καὶ εἰς τοῦτο ἐλήλυθα εἰς τὸν κόσμον, ἵνα
μαρτυρήσω τῇ ἀληθείᾳ· πᾶς ὁ ὢν ἐκ τῆς ἀληθείας,
ἀκούει μου τῆς φωνῆς. 38λέγει αὐτῷ ὁ Πιλάτος, Τί
ἐστιν ἀλήθεια; Καὶ τοῦτο εἰπὼν πάλιν ἐξῆλθεν πρὸς
τοὺς Ἰουδαίους, καὶ λέγει αὐτοῖς, Ἐγὼ οὐδεμίαν εὑρίσκω ἐν αὐτῷ αἰτίαν. 39ἔστιν δὲ συνήθεια ὑμῖν, ἵνα ἕνα
ὑμῖν ἀπολύσω ἐν τῷ πάσχα· βούλεσθε οὖν ἀπολύσω
ὑμῖν τὸν βασιλέα τῶν Ἰουδαίων; 40ἐκραύγασαν οὖν
πάλιν πάντες, λέγοντες, Μὴ τοῦτον, ἀλλὰ τὸν Βαραββᾶν. ἦν δὲ ὁ Βαραββᾶς λῃστής.

19 1Τότε οὖν ἔλαβεν ὁ Πιλάτος τὸν Ἰησοῦν, καὶ
ἐμαστίγωσεν. 2καὶ οἱ στρατιῶται πλέξαντες στέφανον
ἐξ ἀκανθῶν ἐπέθηκαν αὐτοῦ τῇ κεφαλῇ, καὶ ἱμάτιον

πορφυροῦν περιέβαλον αὐτόν, καὶ ἤρχοντο πρὸς αὐτὸν
3 καὶ ἔλεγον, Χαῖρε, ὁ βασιλεὺς τῶν Ἰουδαίων· καὶ ἐδί-
δοσαν αὐτῷ ῥαπίσματα. 4 καὶ ἐξῆλθεν πάλιν ἔξω ὁ
Πιλάτος καὶ λέγει αὐτοῖς, Ἴδε ἄγω ὑμῖν αὐτὸν ἔξω, ἵνα
γνῶτε ὅτι οὐδεμίαν αἰτίαν εὑρίσκω ἐν αὐτῷ. 5 ἐξῆλθεν
οὖν ὁ Ἰησοῦς ἔξω, φορῶν τὸν ἀκάνθινον στέφανον καὶ
τὸ πορφυροῦν ἱμάτιον. καὶ λέγει αὐτοῖς, Ἰδοὺ ὁ ἄνθρωπος. 6 ὅτε οὖν εἶδον αὐτὸν οἱ ἀρχιερεῖς καὶ οἱ ὑπηρέται, ἐκραύγασαν λέγοντες, Σταύρωσον, σταύρωσον. λέγει
αὐτοῖς ὁ Πιλάτος, Λάβετε αὐτὸν ὑμεῖς καὶ σταυρώσατε·
ἐγὼ γὰρ οὐχ εὑρίσκω ἐν αὐτῷ αἰτίαν. 7 ἀπεκρίθησαν
αὐτῷ οἱ Ἰουδαῖοι, Ἡμεῖς νόμον ἔχομεν, καὶ κατὰ τὸν
νόμον ὀφείλει ἀποθανεῖν, ὅτι υἱὸν θεοῦ ἑαυτὸν ἐποίησεν.
8 Ὅτε οὖν ἤκουσεν ὁ Πιλάτος τοῦτον τὸν λόγον, μᾶλλον
ἐφοβήθη, 9 καὶ εἰσῆλθεν εἰς τὸ πραιτώριον πάλιν καὶ
λέγει τῷ Ἰησοῦ, Πόθεν εἶ σύ; ὁ δὲ Ἰησοῦς ἀπόκρισιν
οὐκ ἔδωκεν αὐτῷ. 10 λέγει οὖν αὐτῷ ὁ Πιλάτος, Ἐμοὶ
οὐ λαλεῖς; οὐκ οἶδας ὅτι ἐξουσίαν ἔχω ἀπολῦσαί σε,
καὶ ἐξουσίαν ἔχω σταυρῶσαί σε; 11 ἀπεκρίθη αὐτῷ Ἰησοῦς, Οὐκ εἶχες ἐξουσίαν κατ᾽ ἐμοῦ οὐδεμίαν εἰ μὴ ἦν
δεδομένον σοι ἄνωθεν· διὰ τοῦτο ὁ παραδούς μέ σοι
μείζονα ἁμαρτίαν ἔχει. 12 ἐκ τούτου ὁ Πιλάτος ἐζήτει
ἀπολῦσαι αὐτόν· οἱ δὲ Ἰουδαῖοι ἐκραύγαζον λέγοντες,
Ἐὰν τοῦτον ἀπολύσῃς, οὐκ εἶ φίλος τοῦ Καίσαρος·
πᾶς ὁ βασιλέα ἑαυτὸν ποιῶν ἀντιλέγει τῷ Καίσαρι.
13 ὁ οὖν Πιλᾶτος ἀκούσας τῶν λόγων τούτων ἤγαγεν
ἔξω τὸν Ἰησοῦν, καὶ ἐκάθισεν ἐπὶ βήματος εἰς τόπον
λεγόμενον Λιθόστρωτον, Ἑβραϊστὶ δὲ Γαββαθᾶ. 14 ἦν
δὲ παρασκευὴ τοῦ πάσχα, ὥρα ἦν ὡς ἕκτη. καὶ λέγει
τοῖς Ἰουδαίοις, Ἴδε ὁ βασιλεὺς ὑμῶν. 15 ἐκραύγασαν
οὖν ἐκεῖνοι, Ἆρον, ἆρον, σταύρωσον αὐτόν. λέγει αὐτοῖς

ὁ Πιλάτος, Τὸν βασιλέα ὑμῶν σταυρώσω; ἀπεκρίθησαν
οἱ ἀρχιερεῖς, Οὐκ ἔχομεν βασιλέα εἰ μὴ Καίσαρα. 16 τότε
οὖν παρέδωκεν αὐτὸν αὐτοῖς ἵνα σταυρωθῇ.

17 Παρέλαβον οὖν τὸν Ἰησοῦν, καὶ βαστάζων αὐτῷ
τὸν σταυρὸν ἐξῆλθεν εἰς τὸν λεγόμενον Κρανίου τόπον,
ὃ λέγεται Ἑβραϊστὶ Γολγοθᾶ, 18 ὅπου αὐτὸν ἐσταύρωσαν,
καὶ μετ᾽ αὐτοῦ ἄλλους δύο ἐντεῦθεν καὶ ἐντεῦθεν, μέσον
δὲ τὸν Ἰησοῦν. 19 ἔγραψεν δὲ καὶ τίτλον ὁ Πιλάτος καὶ
ἔθηκεν ἐπὶ τοῦ σταυροῦ· ἦν δὲ γεγραμμένον, Ἰησοῦς ὁ
Ναζωραῖος ὁ βασιλεὺς τῶν Ἰουδαίων. 20 τοῦτον οὖν τὸν
τίτλον πολλοὶ ἀνέγνωσαν τῶν Ἰουδαίων, ὅτι ἐγγὺς ἦν
ὁ τόπος τῆς πόλεως ὅπου ἐσταυρώθη ὁ Ἰησοῦς· καὶ ἦν
γεγραμμένον Ἑβραϊστί, Ῥωμαϊστί, Ἑλληνιστί. 21 ἔλεγον
οὖν τῷ Πιλάτῳ οἱ ἀρχιερεῖς τῶν Ἰουδαίων, Μὴ γράφε,
ὁ βασιλεὺς τῶν Ἰουδαίων· ἀλλ᾽ ὅτι ἐκεῖνος εἶπεν, βασιλεύς εἰμι τῶν Ἰουδαίων. 22 ἀπεκρίθη ὁ Πιλάτος, Ὃ γέγραφα, γέγραφα.

23 Οἱ οὖν στρατιῶται, ὅτε ἐσταύρωσαν τὸν Ἰησοῦν,
ἔλαβον τὰ ἱμάτια αὐτοῦ, καὶ ἐποίησαν τέσσερα μέρη,
ἑκάστῳ στρατιώτῃ μέρος, καὶ τὸν χιτῶνα. ἦν δὲ ὁ
χιτὼν ἄραφος, ἐκ τῶν ἄνωθεν ὑφαντὸς δι᾽ ὅλου. 24 εἶπον
οὖν πρὸς ἀλλήλους, Μὴ σχίσωμεν αὐτόν, ἀλλὰ λάχωμεν περὶ αὐτοῦ, τίνος ἔσται· ἵνα ἡ γραφὴ πληρωθῇ,
Διεμερίσαντο τὰ ἱμάτιά μου ἑαυτοῖς, καὶ ἐπὶ τὸν ἱματισ-
μόν μου ἔβαλον κλῆρον. οἱ μὲν οὖν στρατιῶται ταῦτα
ἐποίησαν.

25 Εἱστήκεισαν δὲ παρὰ τῷ σταυρῷ τοῦ Ἰησοῦ ἡ
μήτηρ αὐτοῦ καὶ ἡ ἀδελφὴ τῆς μητρὸς αὐτοῦ, Μαρία ἡ
τοῦ Κλωπᾶ καὶ Μαρία ἡ Μαγδαληνή. 26 Ἰησοῦς οὖν
ἰδὼν τὴν μητέρα καὶ τὸν μαθητὴν παρεστῶτα ὃν ἠγάπα,
λέγει τῇ μητρί, Γύναι, ἴδε ὁ υἱός σου. 27 εἶτα λέγει τῷ

μαθητῇ, Ἴδε ἡ μήτηρ σου. καὶ ἀπ' ἐκείνης τῆς ὥρας
ἔλαβεν αὐτὴν ὁ μαθητὴς εἰς τὰ ἴδια.

28 Μετὰ τοῦτο εἰδὼς ὁ Ἰησοῦς ὅτι ἤδη πάντα τετέλεσται, ἵνα τελειωθῇ ἡ γραφή, λέγει, Διψῶ. 29 σκεῦος
ἔκειτο ὄξους μεστόν· σπόγγον οὖν μεστὸν τοῦ ὄξους
ὑσσώπῳ περιθέντες προσήνεγκαν αὐτοῦ τῷ στόματι.
30 ὅτε οὖν ἔλαβεν τὸ ὄξος ὁ Ἰησοῦς, εἶπεν, Τετέλεσται, καὶ
κλίνας τὴν κεφαλὴν παρέδωκεν τὸ πνεῦμα.

31 Οἱ οὖν Ἰουδαῖοι, ἐπεὶ παρασκευὴ ἦν, ἵνα μὴ μείνῃ
ἐπὶ τοῦ σταυροῦ τὰ σώματα ἐν τῷ σαββάτῳ, ἦν γὰρ
μεγάλη ἡ ἡμέρα ἐκείνου τοῦ σαββάτου, ἠρώτησαν τὸν
Πιλάτον ἵνα κατεαγῶσιν αὐτῶν τὰ σκέλη καὶ ἀρθῶσιν.
32 ἦλθον οὖν οἱ στρατιῶται, καὶ τοῦ μὲν πρώτου κατέαξαν
τὰ σκέλη καὶ τοῦ ἄλλου τοῦ συνσταυρωθέντος αὐτῷ·
33 ἐπὶ δὲ τὸν Ἰησοῦν ἐλθόντες ὡς εἶδον ἤδη αὐτὸν τεθνη-
κότα, οὐ κατέαξαν αὐτοῦ τὰ σκέλη, 34 ἀλλ' εἷς τῶν στρα-
τιωτῶν λόγχῃ αὐτοῦ τὴν πλευρὰν ἔνυξεν, καὶ ἐξῆλθεν
εὐθὺς αἷμα καὶ ὕδωρ. 35 καὶ ὁ ἑωρακὼς μεμαρτύρηκεν,
καὶ ἀληθινὴ αὐτοῦ ἐστὶν ἡ μαρτυρία, καὶ ἐκεῖνος οἶδεν
ὅτι ἀληθῆ λέγει, ἵνα καὶ ὑμεῖς πιστεύσητε. 36 ἐγένετο
γὰρ ταῦτα, ἵνα ἡ γραφὴ πληρωθῇ, Ὀστοῦν οὐ συντρι-
βήσεται αὐτοῦ. 37 καὶ πάλιν ἑτέρα γραφὴ λέγει, Ὄψονται εἰς ὃν ἐξεκέντησαν.

38 Μετὰ δὲ ταῦτα ἠρώτησεν τὸν Πιλάτον Ἰωσὴφ ἀπὸ
Ἀριμαθαίας, ὢν μαθητὴς τοῦ Ἰησοῦ κεκρυμμένος δὲ διὰ
τὸν φόβον τῶν Ἰουδαίων, ἵνα ἄρῃ τὸ σῶμα τοῦ Ἰησοῦ·
καὶ ἐπέτρεψεν ὁ Πιλάτος· ἦλθεν οὖν καὶ ἦρεν τὸ σῶμα
αὐτοῦ. 39 ἦλθεν δὲ καὶ Νικόδημος ὁ ἐλθὼν πρὸς αὐτὸν
νυκτὸς τὸ πρῶτον, φέρων μίγμα σμύρνης καὶ ἀλόης ὡς
λίτρας ἑκατόν. 40 ἔλαβον οὖν τὸ σῶμα τοῦ Ἰησοῦ, καὶ
ἔδησαν αὐτὸ ὀθονίοις μετὰ τῶν ἀρωμάτων, καθὼς ἔθος

ἐστὶν τοῖς Ἰουδαίοις ἐνταφιάζειν. 41ἦν δὲ ἐν τῷ τόπῳ
ὅπου ἐσταυρώθη κῆπος, καὶ ἐν τῷ κήπῳ μνημεῖον
καινόν, ἐν ᾧ οὐδέπω οὐδεὶς ἐτέθη· 42ἐκεῖ οὖν διὰ τὴν
παρασκευὴν τῶν Ἰουδαίων, ὅτι ἐγγὺς ἦν τὸ μνημεῖον,
ἔθηκαν τὸν Ἰησοῦν.

20 1Τῇ δὲ μιᾷ τῶν σαββάτων Μαρία ἡ Μαγδαληνὴ
ἔρχεται πρωῒ σκοτίας ἔτι οὔσης εἰς τὸ μνημεῖον, καὶ
βλέπει τὸν λίθον ἠρμένον ἐκ τοῦ μνημείου. 2τρέχει οὖν
καὶ ἔρχεται πρὸς Σίμωνα Πέτρον καὶ πρὸς τὸν ἄλλον
μαθητὴν ὃν ἐφίλει ὁ Ἰησοῦς, καὶ λέγει αὐτοῖς, Ἦραν
τὸν κύριον ἐκ τοῦ μνημείου, καὶ οὐκ οἴδαμεν ποῦ
ἔθηκαν αὐτόν. 3Ἐξῆλθεν οὖν ὁ Πέτρος καὶ ὁ ἄλλος
μαθητής, καὶ ἤρχοντο εἰς τὸ μνημεῖον. 4ἔτρεχον δὲ οἱ
δύο ὁμοῦ· καὶ ὁ ἄλλος μαθητὴς προέδραμεν τάχιον τοῦ
Πέτρου καὶ ἦλθεν πρῶτος εἰς τὸ μνημεῖον, 5καὶ παρακύψας βλέπει κείμενα τὰ ὀθόνια, οὐ μέντοι εἰσῆλθεν.
6ἔρχεται οὖν Σίμων Πέτρος ἀκολουθῶν αὐτῷ, καὶ
εἰσῆλθεν εἰς τὸ μνημεῖον, καὶ θεωρεῖ τὰ ὀθόνια κείμενα,
7καὶ τὸ σουδάριον, ὃ ἦν ἐπὶ τῆς κεφαλῆς αὐτοῦ, οὐ μετὰ
τῶν ὀθονίων κείμενον ἀλλὰ χωρὶς ἐντετυλιγμένον εἰς
ἕνα τόπον. 8τότε οὖν εἰσῆλθεν καὶ ὁ ἄλλος μαθητὴς ὁ
ἐλθὼν πρῶτος εἰς τὸ μνημεῖον, καὶ εἶδεν καὶ ἐπίστευσεν·
9οὐδέπω γὰρ ᾔδεισαν τὴν γραφήν, ὅτι δεῖ αὐτὸν ἐκ
νεκρῶν ἀναστῆναι. 10ἀπῆλθον οὖν πάλιν πρὸς αὐτοὺς
οἱ μαθηταί.

11Μαρία δὲ εἱστήκει πρὸς τῷ μνημείῳ ἔξω κλαίουσα.
ὡς οὖν ἔκλαιεν, παρέκυψεν εἰς τὸ μνημεῖον, 12καὶ θεωρεῖ
δύο ἀγγέλους ἐν λευκοῖς καθεζομένους, ἕνα πρὸς τῇ
κεφαλῇ, καὶ ἕνα πρὸς τοῖς ποσίν, ὅπου ἔκειτο τὸ σῶμα
τοῦ Ἰησοῦ, 13καὶ λέγουσιν αὐτῇ ἐκεῖνοι, Γύναι, τί κλαίεις;
λέγει αὐτοῖς ὅτι Ἦραν τὸν κύριόν μου, καὶ οὐκ οἶδα

ποῦ ἔθηκαν αὐτόν. 14 *ταῦτα εἰποῦσα ἐστράφη εἰς τὰ*
ὀπίσω, καὶ θεωρεῖ τὸν Ἰησοῦν *ἑστῶτα, καὶ οὐκ ᾔδει*
ὅτι ὁ Ἰησοῦς *ἐστίν.* 15 *λέγει αὐτῇ* Ἰησοῦς, Γύναι, *τί*
κλαίεις; τίνα ζητεῖς; ἐκείνη δοκοῦσα ὅτι ὁ κηπουρός
ἐστιν, λέγει αὐτῷ, Κύριε, *εἰ σὺ ἐβάστασας αὐτόν, εἰπέ*
μοι ποῦ ἔθηκας αὐτόν, κἀγὼ αὐτὸν ἀρῶ. 16 *λέγει αὐτῇ*
Ἰησοῦς, Μαριάμ. *στραφεῖσα ἐκείνη λέγει αὐτῷ* Ἑβρα-
ϊστί, Ῥαββουνί· *ὃ λέγεται, διδάσκαλε.* 17 *λέγει αὐτῇ ὁ*
Ἰησοῦς, Μή *μου ἅπτου, οὔπω γὰρ ἀναβέβηκα πρὸς τὸν*
πατέρα· πορεύου δὲ πρὸς τοὺς ἀδελφούς μου καὶ εἰπὲ
αὐτοῖς, Ἀναβαίνω *πρὸς τὸν πατέρα μου καὶ πατέρα*
ὑμῶν καὶ θεόν μου καὶ θεὸν ὑμῶν. 18 *ἔρχεται* Μαριὰμ
ἡ Μαγδαληνὴ *ἀγγέλλουσα τοῖς μαθηταῖς, ὅτι ἑώρακα*
τὸν κύριον, καὶ ταῦτα εἶπεν αὐτῇ.

19 Οὔσης *οὖν ὀψίας τῇ ἡμέρᾳ ἐκείνῃ τῇ μιᾷ σαβ-*
βάτων, καὶ τῶν θυρῶν κεκλεισμένων ὅπου ἦσαν οἱ
μαθηταὶ διὰ τὸν φόβον τῶν Ἰουδαίων, *ἦλθεν ὁ* Ἰησοῦς
καὶ ἔστη εἰς τὸ μέσον, καὶ λέγει αὐτοῖς, Εἰρήνη *ὑμῖν.*
20 *καὶ τοῦτο εἰπὼν ἔδειξεν καὶ τὰς χεῖρας καὶ τὴν*
πλευρὰν αὐτοῖς. ἐχάρησαν οὖν οἱ μαθηταὶ ἰδόντες τὸν
κύριον. 21 *εἶπεν οὖν αὐτοῖς πάλιν,* Εἰρήνη *ὑμῖν· καθὼς*
ἀπέσταλκέν με ὁ πατήρ, κἀγὼ πέμπω ὑμᾶς. 22 *καὶ τοῦτο*
εἰπὼν ἐνεφύσησεν καὶ λέγει αὐτοῖς, Λάβετε *πνεῦμα*
ἅγιον. 23 *ἄν τινων ἀφῆτε τὰς ἁμαρτίας, ἀφέωνται αὐτοῖς·*
ἄν τινων κρατῆτε, κεκράτηνται.

24 Θωμᾶς *δὲ εἷς ἐκ τῶν δώδεκα, ὁ λεγόμενος* Δίδυμος,
οὐκ ἦν μετ' αὐτῶν ὅτε ἦλθεν Ἰησοῦς. 25 *ἔλεγον οὖν*
αὐτῷ οἱ ἄλλοι μαθηταί, Ἑωράκαμεν *τὸν κύριον. ὁ δὲ*
εἶπεν αὐτοῖς, Ἐὰν *μὴ ἴδω ἐν ταῖς χερσὶν αὐτοῦ τὸν*
τύπον τῶν ἥλων καὶ βάλω τὸν δάκτυλόν μου εἰς τὸν
τύπον τῶν ἥλων καὶ βάλω μου τὴν χεῖρα εἰς τὴν

πλευρὰν αὐτοῦ, οὐ μὴ πιστεύσω. 26 καὶ μεθ᾽ ἡμέρας
ὀκτὼ πάλιν ἦσαν ἔσω οἱ μαθηταὶ αὐτοῦ, καὶ Θωμᾶς
μετ᾽ αὐτῶν. ἔρχεται ὁ Ἰησοῦς τῶν θυρῶν κεκλεισμένων, καὶ ἔστη εἰς τὸ μέσον καὶ εἶπεν, Εἰρήνη ὑμῖν.
27 εἶτα λέγει τῷ Θωμᾷ, Φέρε τὸν δάκτυλόν σου ὧδε καὶ
ἴδε τὰς χεῖράς μου, καὶ φέρε τὴν χεῖρά σου καὶ βάλε
εἰς τὴν πλευράν μου, καὶ μὴ γίνου ἄπιστος ἀλλὰ
πιστός. 28 ἀπεκρίθη Θωμᾶς καὶ εἶπεν αὐτῷ, Ὁ κύριός
μου καὶ ὁ θεός μου. 29 λέγει αὐτῷ ὁ Ἰησοῦς, Ὅτι
ἑώρακάς με, πεπίστευκας· μακάριοι οἱ μὴ ἰδόντες καὶ
πιστεύσαντες.

30 Πολλὰ μὲν οὖν καὶ ἄλλα σημεῖα ἐποίησεν ὁ Ἰησοῦς
ἐνώπιον τῶν μαθητῶν, ἃ οὐκ ἔστιν γεγραμμένα ἐν τῷ
βιβλίῳ τούτῳ. 31 ταῦτα δὲ γέγραπται ἵνα πιστεύητε
ὅτι Ἰησοῦς ἐστὶν ὁ Χριστὸς ὁ υἱὸς τοῦ θεοῦ, καὶ ἵνα
πιστεύοντες ζωὴν ἔχητε ἐν τῷ ὀνόματι αὐτοῦ.

21 1 Μετὰ ταῦτα ἐφανέρωσεν ἑαυτὸν πάλιν Ἰησοῦς
τοῖς μαθηταῖς ἐπὶ τῆς θαλάσσης τῆς Τιβεριάδος·
ἐφανέρωσεν δὲ οὕτως. 2 ἦσαν ὁμοῦ Σίμων Πέτρος καὶ
Θωμᾶς ὁ λεγόμενος Δίδυμος καὶ Ναθαναὴλ ὁ ἀπὸ
Κανᾶ τῆς Γαλιλαίας καὶ οἱ τοῦ Ζεβεδαίου καὶ ἄλλοι
ἐκ τῶν μαθητῶν αὐτοῦ δύο. 3 λέγει αὐτοῖς Σίμων
Πέτρος, Ὑπάγω ἁλιεύειν. λέγουσιν αὐτῷ, Ἐρχόμεθα
καὶ ἡμεῖς σὺν σοί. ἐξῆλθον καὶ ἐνέβησαν εἰς τὸ πλοῖον,
καὶ ἐν ἐκείνῃ τῇ νυκτὶ ἐπίασαν οὐδέν. 4 πρωΐας δὲ ἤδη
γινομένης ἔστη Ἰησοῦς ἐπὶ τὸν αἰγιαλόν· οὐ μέντοι
ᾔδεισαν οἱ μαθηταὶ ὅτι Ἰησοῦς ἐστίν. 5 λέγει οὖν αὐτοῖς
Ἰησοῦς, Παιδία, μή τι προσφάγιον ἔχετε; ἀπεκρίθησαν αὐτῷ, Οὔ. 6 ὁ δὲ εἶπεν αὐτοῖς, Βάλετε εἰς τὰ δεξιὰ
μέρη τοῦ πλοίου τὸ δίκτυον, καὶ εὑρήσετε. ἔβαλον οὖν,
καὶ οὐκέτι αὐτὸ ἑλκύσαι ἴσχυον ἀπὸ τοῦ πλήθους τῶν

ἰχθύων. 7λέγει οὖν ὁ μαθητὴς ἐκεῖνος ὃν ἠγάπα ὁ
Ἰησοῦς τῷ Πέτρῳ, Ὁ κύριός ἐστιν. Σίμων οὖν Πέτρος,
ἀκούσας ὅτι ὁ κύριός ἐστιν, τὸν ἐπενδύτην διεζώσατο,
ἦν γὰρ γυμνός, καὶ ἔβαλεν ἑαυτὸν εἰς τὴν θάλασσαν·
8οἱ δὲ ἄλλοι μαθηταὶ τῷ πλοιαρίῳ ἦλθον. οὐ γὰρ ἦσαν
μακρὰν ἀπὸ τῆς γῆς ἀλλὰ ὡς ἀπὸ πηχῶν διακοσίων,
σύροντες τὸ δίκτυον τῶν ἰχθύων. 9ὡς οὖν ἀπέβησαν
εἰς τὴν γῆν, βλέπουσιν ἀνθρακιὰν κειμένην καὶ ὀψάριον
ἐπικείμενον καὶ ἄρτον. 10λέγει αὐτοῖς ὁ Ἰησοῦς, Ἐνέγ-
κατε ἀπὸ τῶν ὀψαρίων ὧν ἐπιάσατε νῦν. 11ἀνέβη
Σίμων Πέτρος καὶ εἵλκυσεν τὸ δίκτυον εἰς τὴν γῆν
μεστὸν ἰχθύων μεγάλων ἑκατὸν πεντήκοντα τριῶν· καὶ
τοσούτων ὄντων οὐκ ἐσχίσθη τὸ δίκτυον. 12λέγει
αὐτοῖς Ἰησοῦς, Δεῦτε ἀριστήσατε. οὐδεὶς δὲ ἐτόλμα
τῶν μαθητῶν ἐξετασαι αὐτόν, Σὺ τίς εἶ; εἰδότες ὅτι ὁ
κύριός ἐστιν· 13ἔρχεται Ἰησοῦς καὶ λαμβάνει τὸν
ἄρτον καὶ δίδωσιν αὐτοῖς, καὶ τὸ ὀψάριον ὁμοίως.
14τοῦτο ἤδη τρίτον ἐφανερώθη Ἰησοῦς τοῖς μαθηταῖς
ἐγερθεὶς ἐκ νεκρῶν.

15Ὅτε οὖν ἠρίστησαν, λέγει τῷ Σίμωνι Πέτρῳ ὁ
Ἰησοῦς, Σίμων Ἰωάνου, ἀγαπᾷς με πλέον τούτων;
λέγει αὐτῷ Ναὶ κύριε, σὺ οἶδας ὅτι φιλῶ σε. λέγει
αὐτῷ, Βόσκε τὰ ἀρνία μου. 16λέγει αὐτῷ πάλιν δεύτερον, Σίμων Ἰωάνου, ἀγαπᾷς με; λέγει αὐτῷ, Ναὶ
κύριε· σὺ οἶδας ὅτι φιλῶ σε. λέγει αὐτῷ, Ποίμαινε
τὰ προβάτιά μου. 17λέγει αὐτῷ τὸ τρίτον, Σίμων Ἰωάνου,
φιλεῖς με; ἐλυπήθη ὁ Πέτρος, ὅτι εἶπεν αὐτῷ τὸ
τρίτον, φιλεῖς με; καὶ εἶπεν αὐτῷ, Κύριε, πάντα σὺ οἶδας·
σὺ γινώσκεις ὅτι φιλῶ σε. λέγει αὐτῷ Ἰησοῦς, Βόσκε
τὰ προβάτιά μου. 18ἀμὴν ἀμὴν λέγω σοι, ὅτε ἦς
νεώτερος, ἐζώννυες σεαυτὸν καὶ περιεπάτεις ὅπου ἤθελες·

ὅταν δὲ γηράσῃς, ἐκτενεῖς τὰς χεῖράς σου, καὶ ἄλλος σε
ζώσει καὶ οἴσει ὅπου οὐ θέλεις. [19]τοῦτο δὲ εἶπεν σημαίνων ποίῳ θανάτῳ δοξάσει τὸν θεόν. καὶ τοῦτο εἰπὼν
λέγει αὐτῷ, Ἀκολούθει μοι.

[20]Ἐπιστραφεὶς ὁ Πέτρος βλέπει τὸν μαθητὴν ὃν
ἠγάπα ὁ Ἰησοῦς ἀκολουθοῦντα, ὃς καὶ ἀνέπεσεν ἐν τῷ
δείπνῳ ἐπὶ τὸ στῆθος αὐτοῦ καὶ εἶπεν, Κύριε, τίς ἐστιν ὁ
παραδιδούς σε; [21]τοῦτον οὖν ἰδὼν ὁ Πέτρος λέγει τῷ
Ἰησοῦ, Κύριε, οὗτος δὲ τί; [22]λέγει αὐτῷ ὁ Ἰησοῦς, Ἐὰν
αὐτὸν θέλω μένειν ἕως ἔρχομαι, τί πρός σε; σύ μοι ἀκολούθει. [23]ἐξῆλθεν οὖν οὗτος ὁ λόγος εἰς τοὺς ἀδελφοὺς
ὅτι Ὁ μαθητὴς ἐκεῖνος οὐκ ἀποθνήσκει· καὶ οὐκ εἶπεν
αὐτῷ ὁ Ἰησοῦς ὅτι οὐκ ἀποθνήσκει· ἀλλ', Ἐὰν αὐτὸν
θέλω μένειν ἕως ἔρχομαι, τί πρός σε;

[24]Οὗτός ἐστιν ὁ μαθητὴς ὁ μαρτυρῶν περὶ τούτων
καὶ ὁ γράψας ταῦτα, καὶ οἴδαμεν ὅτι ἀληθὴς αὐτοῦ ἡ
μαρτυρία ἐστίν.

[25]Ἔστιν δὲ καὶ ἄλλα πολλὰ ἃ ἐποίησεν ὁ Ἰησοῦς,
ἅτινα ἐὰν γράφηται καθ' ἕν, οὐδ' αὐτὸν οἶμαι τὸν κόσμον
χωρήσειν τὰ γραφόμενα βιβλία.

NOTES

CHAPTER I

In the remarks on the results of textual revision prefixed to the Notes on each Chapter, it is not intended to enter minutely into each point, but to indicate generally the principal corrections, and occasionally to state the grounds on which a reading is preferred.

Ἰωάνην is preferred by the best recent editors to Ἰωάννην. The title of the Gospel is found in very different forms in ancient authorities, the earliest being the simplest; *κατὰ Ἰωάννην* or *-άνην* (ℵBD). **εὐαγγ.** *κ.* Ἰ. (ACLX); later MSS. have **τὸ** *κ.* Ἰ *εὐαγγ.*; and very many have *τὸ κ.* Ἰ. **ἅγιον** *εὐαγγ.* On **Εὐαγγ. κατά** see notes on S. Matthew, p. 80.

7. **πιστεύσωσιν.** Following the uncial MSS., the best editors add *ν ἐφελκυστικόν* before consonants and vowels alike: *πᾶσι* and *δυσί* are occasional exceptions, and perhaps *γιγνώσκουσι* (x. 14). Winer, 43.

16. **ὅτι** with ℵBC^{1}DLX for *καί* of T. R. with AC^{3}, perhaps to avoid *ὅτι* thrice in three lines.

18. **μον. Θεός** (ℵBC^{1}L) for *ὁ μον. υἱὸς* (AX, the secondary uncials, and all cursives except 33). Thus *no* ancient Greek authority supports *ὁ μον. υἱος*, while *μον. Θεὸς* is supported by three great types, B, ℵ, CL. The earliest authorities for *ὁ μ. υἱός*, *Lat. vet.* and *Syr. vet.*, are somewhat given to insert interpretations as readings. The evidence of the Fathers is divided and complicated.

27. *αὐτός ἐστιν* is an addition to fill out the construction, and *ὃς ἔμπ. μ. γ.* has been inserted (AC^{3}) from *vv.* 15, 30: ℵBC^{1}L omit both.

28. **Βηθανίᾳ**, with ℵ^{1}ABC^{1}, for *Βηθαβαρᾷ* of T. R., supported (in spite of Origen's defence of it) by only a small minority.

43. **Ἰωάννου** or **Ἰωάνου** (ℵBL, *Lat. vet.*, *Memph.*) for Ἰωνᾶ (AB^{2}), which is a correction from Matt. xvi. 17.

52. Before **ὄψεσθε** omit *ἀπ' ἄρτι* (Matt. xxvi. 64).

1—18. The Prologue or Introduction in three parts. **1—5**: The Word in His own nature. 6—13: His Revelation to men and rejection by them. 14—18: His Revelation of the Father. The three great characteristics of this Gospel, simplicity, subtlety, sublimity, are conspicuous in the prologue: the majesty of the first words is marvellous. The Gospel of the Son of Thunder opens with a peal.

1—5. The Word in His own Nature

ἐν ἀρχῇ. *In the beginning.* The meaning must depend on the context. In Gen. i. 1 it is an act done *ἐν ἀρχῇ;* here it is a Being existing *ἐν ἀρχῇ,* and therefore prior to all beginning. That was the first moment of time; this is eternity, transcending time. S. John insists on this and repeats it in *v.* 2; the Λόγος in Gnostic systems was produced in time. Thus we have an intimation that the later dispensation is the confirmation and infinite extension of the first. Ἐν ἀρχῇ here equals πρὸ τοῦ τὸν κόσμον εἶναι xvii. 5. Cf. xvii. 24; Eph. i. 4; and especially ὃ ἦν ἀπ' ἀρχῆς in 1 John i. 1, which seems clearly to refer to this opening of the Gospel. Contrast ἀρχὴ τοῦ εὐαγγελίου Ἰ. Χρ. Mark i. 1, which is the historical beginning of the public ministry of the Messiah. Cf. John vi. 64. The ἀρχή here is prior to all history. The context shews that ἀρχή cannot mean God, the Origin of all.

ἦν. Note the difference between ἦν and ἐγένετο. Εἶναι is 'to be' absolutely: γίγνεσθαι is 'to come into being.' The Word did not come into existence, but before the creation of the world was already in existence. The generation of the Word or Son of God is thus thrown back into eternity. Hence St Paul speaks of Him as πρωτότοκος πάσης κτίσεως (Col. i. 15), 'born *prior to*' (not 'first of') 'all creation.' Cf. Heb. i. 8, vii. 3; Rev. i. 8. On these passages is based the doctrine of the eternal generation of the Son: see Articles I. and II. The Arians maintained that there was a period when the Son was not (ἦν ὅτε οὐκ ἦν); but S. John says distinctly that the Son, or Word, was existing *before time began,* i.e. from all eternity.

ὁ λόγος. As early as the second century *Sermo* and *Verbum* were rival translations of this term. Tertullian (fl. A.D. 198—210) gives us both, but seems himself to prefer *Ratio. Sermo* first became unusual and finally was disallowed in the Latin Church. The Latin versions without exception adopted *Verbum,* and from it comes our translation 'the Word,' translations which have greatly affected Western theology. None of these translations are at all adequate; but neither Latin nor any modern language supplies anything really satisfactory. *Verbum* and 'the Word' do not give even the whole of *one* of the two sides of ὁ λόγος. The other side, which Tertullian tried to express by *Ratio,* is not touched at all. For ὁ λόγος means not only 'the spoken word,' but 'the *thought*' expressed by the spoken word; it is *the spoken word as expressive of thought.* Λόγος in the sense of 'reason' does not occur anywhere in the N.T.

The word is a remarkable one; all the more so because S. John assumes that his readers will at once understand it. This points to the fact that his Gospel was written in the first instance for his own disciples, who would be familiar with his teaching, in which the doctrine of the Logos was conspicuous.

But on what was this doctrine based? whence did S. John derive the expression? There can be little doubt that it has its origin in the Targums, or paraphrases of the Hebrew Scriptures, in use in Palestine, rather than in the mixture of Jewish and Greek philosophy prevalent at Alexandria and Ephesus. (1) In the *Old Testament* we find the Word or Wisdom of God personified, generally as an instrument for executing the Divine Will, as if it were itself distinct from that Will. We have the first faint traces of it in the 'God *said*' of Gen. i. 3, 6, 9, 11, 14, &c. The personification of the Word of God begins to appear in the Psalms; xxxiii. 6, cvii. 20, cxix. 89, cxlvii. 15. In Prov. viii. and ix. the Wisdom of God is personified in very striking terms. This Wisdom is manifested in the *power* and *mighty works* of God; that God is *love* is a revelation yet to come. (2) In the *Apocrypha* the personification is more complete than in the O.T. In Ecclesiasticus (B.C. 150—100) i. 1—20; xxiv. 1—22; and in the Book of Wisdom (B.C. 100) vi. 22 to ix. 18 we have Wisdom personified. In Wisd. xviii. 15 the 'Almighty Word' of God (ὁ παντοδύναμός σου λόγος) appears as an agent of vengeance. (3) In the *Targums*, or Aramaic paraphrases of the O.T., the development is carried still further. These, though not yet written down, were in common use among the Jews in our Lord's time; and they were strongly influenced by the growing tendency to separate the Divine Essence from immediate contact with the material world. Where Scripture speaks of a direct communication from God to man, the Targums substituted the *Memra*, or 'Word of God.' Thus in Gen. iii. 8, 9, instead of 'they heard the voice of the Lord God,' the Targums read 'they heard the voice of the *Word* of the Lord God;' and instead of 'God called unto Adam' they put 'the Word of the Lord called unto Adam,' and so on. It is said that this phrase 'the Word of the Lord' occurs 150 times in a single Targum of the Pentateuch. And *Memra* is not a mere utterance or ῥῆμα; for this the Targums use *pithgama*: e.g. 'The word (*pithgama*) of the Lord came to Abram in prophecy, saying, Fear not, Abram, My Word (*Memra*) shall be thy strength' (Gen. xv. 1); 'I stood between the Word (*Memra*) of the Lord and you, to announce to you at that time the word (*pithgama*) of the Lord' (Deut. v. 5). In what is called the *theosophy of the Alexandrine Jews*, which was a compound of Judaism with Platonic philosophy and Oriental mysticism, we seem to come nearer to a strictly *personal* view of the Divine Word or Wisdom, but really move farther away from it. Philo, the leading representative of this school (fl. A.D. 40—50), summed up the Platonic ἰδέαι, or Divine archetypes of things, in the single term λόγος. His philosophy contained various, and not always harmonious elements; and therefore his conception of the λόγος is not fixed or clear. On the whole his λόγος means that intermediate agency, by means of which God created material things and communicated with them. But whether this agency is one Being or more, whether it is personal or not, we cannot be sure, and perhaps Philo himself was undecided. Certainly his λόγος is very different from that of S. John; for it is scarcely a Person, and it is not the Messiah.

To sum up, the personification of the Divine Word in the O.T. is poetical, in Philo metaphysical, in S. John historical. The Apocrypha and the Targums serve to bridge the chasm between the O.T. and Philo: history fills the chasm which separates all from S. John. Between Jewish poetry and Alexandrine speculation on the one hand, and the Fourth Gospel on the other, lies the historical fact of the life of Jesus Christ, the Incarnation of the Logos.

The Logos of S. John, therefore, is not 'the thing uttered' (ῥῆμα); nor 'the One spoken of' or promised (ὁ λεγόμενος); nor 'He who speaks the word' (ὁ λέγων); nor a mere attribute of God (as σοφία or νοῦς). But the Logos is the Son of God, existing from all eternity, and manifested in space and time in the Person of Jesus Christ, in whom had been hidden from eternity all that God had to say to man, and who was the living expression of the Nature and Will of God. (Cf. the impersonal designation of Christ in 1 John i. 1.) Human thought had been searching in vain for some means of connecting the finite with the Infinite, of making God intelligible to man and leading man up to God. S. John knew that he possessed the key to the hitherto insoluble enigma. Just as S. Paul declared to the Athenians the 'Unknown God' whom they worshipped, though they knew Him not, so S. John declares to all the Divine Word, who had been so imperfectly understood. He therefore took the phrase which human reason had lighted on in its gropings, stripped it of its philosophical and mythological clothing, fixed it by identifying it with the Person of Christ, and filled it with that fulness of meaning which he himself had derived from Christ's own teaching.

πρὸς τὸν θεόν. Πρός = '*apud*' or the French '*chez*'; it expresses the distinct Personality of the Λόγος, which ἐν would have obscured. We might render 'face to face with God,' or 'at home with God.' So, 'His sisters, are they not all *with* us (πρὸς ἡμᾶς)?' Matt. xiii. 56. Cf. 1 Cor. xvi. 7; Gal. i. 18; 1 Thess. iii. 4; Philem. 13. Τὸν θεόν having the article, means the Father.

θεὸς ἦν ὁ λόγος. Ὁ λόγος is the subject in all three clauses. The absence of the article with θεός shews that θεός is the predicate (though this rule is not without exceptions); and the meaning is that the Logos partook of the Divine *Nature*, not that the Logos was identical with the Divine *Person*. In the latter case θεός would have had the article. The verse may be thus paraphrased; the Logos existed from all eternity, distinct from the Father, and equal to the Father.' 'Neither confounding the Persons, nor dividing the Substance.'

2. **οὗτος ἦν κ.τ.λ.** Takes up the first two clauses and combines them. Such recapitulations are characteristic of S. John. Οὗτος, **He or This** (Word), illustrates S. John's habit of using a demonstrative pronoun to sum up what has preceded, or to recall a previous subject, with emphasis. Comp. *v.* 7, iii. 2, vi. 46, vii. 18.

3. πάντα. Less definite and more comprehensive than *τὰ πάντα*, which we find 1 Cor. viii. 6; Col. i. 16; Rom. xi. 36; Heb. ii. 10; texts which should all be compared. See Lightfoot on Col. i. 16.

δι' αὐτοῦ. The Universe is created *ὑπὸ τοῦ πατρὸς διὰ τοῦ υἱοῦ*, by the Father through the agency of the Son. See the texts just quoted.

ἐγένετο. Comp. the frequent *ἐγένετο* in Gen. i. Note the climax: the sphere contracts as the blessing enlarges: existence for everything, life for the vegetable and animal world, light for men.

χωρὶς αὐτοῦ κ.τ.λ. Emphatic repetition by contradicting the opposite of what has been stated: frequent in Hebrew. Cf. v. 20, iii. 16, x. 5, 18, xviii. 20, xx. 27; 1 John i. 5, 6, ii. 4, 10, 11, 27, 28; Rev. ii. 13, iii. 9; Ps. lxxxix. 30, 31, 48, &c. &c. One of many instances of the Hebrew cast of S. John's style. The technical name is 'antithetic parallelism.'

οὐδὲ ἕν. *No, not one; not even one:* stronger than *οὐδέν*. Every single thing, however great, however small, throughout all the realms of space, came into being through Him. No event in the Universe takes place *without Him*,—apart from His presence and power. Matt. x. 29; Luke xii. 6. "Such a belief undoubtedly carries us into great depths and heights...It gives solemnity and awfulness to the investigations of science. It forbids trifling in them. It stimulates courage and hope in them. It makes all superstitious dread of them sinful" (Maurice).

ὃ γέγονεν. *That* **hath been made.** The A. V. makes no distinction between the aorist and the perfect: *ἐγένετο* refers to the moment and fact of creation; *γέγονεν* to the permanent result of that fact. Everything that has reached existence must have passed through the Will of the *Λόγος*: He is the Way to life. We find the same thought in the Vedas; 'the Word of Brahm has begotten all.'

Contrast both *ἐγένετο* and *γέγονεν* with *ἦν* in *vv.* 1, 2. The former denote the springing into life of what had once been non-existent; the latter denotes the perpetual pre-existence of the Eternal Word.

Most early Christian writers and some modern critics put a full stop at *οὐδὲ ἕν*, and join *ὃ γέγονεν* to what follows, thus; *That which hath been made in Him was life;* i.e. those who were born again by union with the Word felt His influence as life within them. This seems harsh and not quite in harmony with the context; but it has an overwhelming amount of support from the oldest versions and MSS. Tatian (*Orat. ad Graecos* XIX.) has *πάντα ὑπ' αὐτοῦ καὶ χωρὶς αὐτοῦ γέγονεν οὐδὲ ἕν*. See last note on *v.* 5.

4. ἐν αὐτῷ ζωή. He was the well-spring of life, from which every form of life—physical, intellectual, moral, spiritual, eternal,—flows.

Observe how frequently S. John's thoughts overlap and run into one another. Creation leads on to life, and life leads on to light. Without life creation would be unintelligible; without light all but the lowest forms of life would be impossible.

ἦν. Two important MSS. (ℵD. with old Latin and old Syriac Versions) have *ἐστίν*; but the weight of authority is against this reading, which would not be in harmony with the context. The Apostle is not contemplating the Christian dispensation, but a period long previous to it. The group of authorities which supports *ἐστίν* has a tendency to insert interpretations as readings.

καὶ ἡ ζωὴ ἦν τὸ φῶς. Not *φῶς*, but *τὸ Φῶς*, the one true Light, absolute Truth both intellectual and moral, free from ignorance and free from stain. The Source of Life is the Source of Light: He gives the power to *know* what is morally good.

τὸ φῶς τ. ἀν. Man shares life with all organic creatures: light, or Revelation, is for him alone; but for the whole race, male and female, Jew and Gentile (*τῶν ἀνθρώπων*). Luke ii. 32. What is specially meant is the communication of Divine Truth before the Fall.

5. **φαίνει.** The elementary distinction between *φαίνειν*, 'to shine,' and *φαίνεσθαι*, 'to appear,' is not always observed by our translators. In Acts xxvii. 20 *φαίνειν* is translated like *φαίνεσθαι*; in Matt. xxiv. 27 and Phil. ii. 15 the converse mistake is made. Here note the present tense, the only one in the section. It brings us down to the Apostle's own day: comp. *ἤδη φαίνει* (1 John ii. 8). Now, as of old, the Light shines, and shines in vain. In *vv.* 1, 2 we have the period preceding Creation; in *v.* 3 the Creation; *v.* 4 man before the Fall; *v.* 5 man after the Fall.

καὶ ἡ σκοτία. Note the strong connexion between *vv.* 4 and 5, as between the two halves of *v.* 5, resulting in both cases from a portion of the predicate in one clause becoming the subject of the next clause. Such strong connexions are very frequent in S. John.

ἡ σκοτία. All that the Divine Revelation does not reach, whether by God's appointment or their own stubbornness, ignorant Gentile and unbelieving Jew. *Σκοτία* in a metaphorical sense for moral and spiritual darkness is peculiar to S. John; viii. 12, xii. 35, 46; 1 John i. 5, ii. 8, 9, 11.

οὐ κατέλαβεν. *Did not* **apprehend**: very appropriate of that which requires mental and moral effort. Cf. Eph. iii. 18. The darkness remained apart, unyielding and unpenetrated. The words 'the darkness apprehendeth not the light' (*ἡ σκοτία τὸ φῶς οὐ καταλαμβάνει*) are given by Tatian as a quotation (*Orat. ad Graecos*, XIII.). As he flourished c. A.D. 150—170, this is early testimony to the existence of the Gospel. We have here an instance of what has been called the "tragic tone" in S. John: he frequently states a gracious fact, and in immediate connexion with it the very opposite of what might have been expected to result from it. 'The Light shines in darkness, and (instead of yielding and dispersing) the darkness shut it out.' Cf. *vv.* 10 and 11; iii. 11, 19, 32, v. 39, 40, vi. 36, 43, &c. *Καταλαμβάνειν* sometimes = 'to overcome,' which makes good sense here, as in xii. 35.

6—13. The Word revealed to Men and rejected by them

6. ἐγένετο ἄν. The contrast between *ἐγένετο* and *ἦν* is carefully maintained and should be preserved in translation: not 'there *was* a man' but 'there *arose* a man;' *ἄνθρωπος*, 'a human being,' in contrast to the Logos and also as an instance of that race which was illuminated by the Logos (*v.* 4); comp. iii. 1. Note (as in *v.* 1) the noble simplicity of language, and also the marked *asyndeton* between *vv.* 5 and 6. Greek is so rich in particles that asyndeton is generally remarkable.

ἀπεσταλμένος παρὰ θεοῦ. A Prophet. Cf. 'I will *send* my messenger,' Mal. iii. 1; 'I will *send* you Elijah the prophet,' iv. 5. John's mission proceeded, as it were, *from the presence of God*, the literal meaning of *παρά* with the genitive.

ὄνομα αὐτῷ Ἰωάννης. The clause is a kind of parenthesis, like *Νικόδημος ὄνομα αὐτῷ*, iii. 1. In the Fourth Gospel John is mentioned twenty times and is never once distinguished as 'the Baptist.' The other three Evangelists carefully distinguish 'the Baptist' from the son of Zebedee: to the writer of the Fourth Gospel there is only one John. This in itself is strong incidental evidence that he himself is the other John.

7. οὗτος sums up the preceding verse as in *v.* 2. **ἦλθεν** refers to the beginning of his public teaching: *ἐγένετο* in *v.* 6 refers to his birth.

εἰς μαρτυρίαν. *For witness*, not 'for *a* witness;' *to bear witness*, not 'to be a witness.' What follows, *ἵνα μ. π. τ. φ.*, is the expansion of *εἰς μαρτυρίαν*. The words *μαρτυρία* and *μαρτυρεῖν* are very frequent in S. John's writings (see on *v.* 34). Testimony to the truth is one of his favourite thoughts; it is inseparable from the idea of belief in the truth. Testimony and belief are correlatives.

ἵνα μαρτυρήσῃ. The subjunctive with *ἵνα* after a past tense, where in classical Greek we should have the optative, prevails throughout the N.T. The optative gradually became less and less used until it almost disappeared. When the pronunciation of *οι* became very similar to that of *η*, it was found that a distinction not discernible in speaking was not needed at all. On *ἵνα* see next verse.

πιστεύσωσιν. Used absolutely without an object expressed: comp. *v.* 51, iv. 41, 42, 48, 53, v. 44, vi. 36, 64, xi. 15, 40, xii. 39, xiv. 29, xix. 35, xx. 8, 29, 31.

δι' αὐτοῦ. Through the Baptist, the Herald of the Truth. Cf. v. 33; Acts x. 37, xiii. 24.

8. ἐκεῖνος. A favourite pronoun with S. John, often used merely to emphasize the main subject instead of denoting some one more remote, which is its ordinary use. 'It was not *he* who was the Light, but &c.' Comp. ii. 21, v. 19, 35, 46, 47, vi. 29, viii. 42, 44, ix. 9, 11, 25, 36, &c. As in *v.* 3, though not quite in the same way, S. John adds a negation to his statement to give clearness and incisiveness.

τὸ φῶς. The Baptist was not *τὸ φῶς* but *ὁ λύχνος ὁ καιόμενος καὶ φαίνων* (v. 35); he was *lumen illuminatum*, not *lumen illuminans*. At the close of the first century it was still necessary for S. John to insist on this. At Ephesus, where this Gospel was written, S. Paul in his third missionary journey had found disciples still resting in 'John's Baptism;' Acts xix. 1—6. And we learn from the *Clementine Recognitions* (I. LIV, LX) that some of John's disciples, perhaps the Hemerobaptists, proclaimed their own master as the Christ, for Jesus had declared John to be greater than all the Prophets. Translate '*the* Light,' not '*that* Light,' as A.V.

ἀλλ' ἵνα. No need to supply anything: *ἵνα* may depend on *ἦν*. 'John was in order to bear witness.' If anything is supplied, it should be 'came' rather than 'was sent.' *Ἵνα* is one of the particles of which S. John is specially fond, not only in cases where another particle or construction would have done equally well, but also where *ἵνα* is apparently awkward. This is frequently the case where the Divine purpose is indicated, as here. Cf. iv. 34, 47, vi. 29, xi. 50, xii. 23, xiii. 1, xv. 8, 12, 13, 17, and Winer, p. 425. For the elliptical *ἀλλ' ἵνα* comp. *v.* 31, ix. 3, xiii. 18, xiv. 31, xv. 25; 1 John ii. 19.

9. ἦν τὸ φῶς κ.τ.λ. Most Ancient Versions, Fathers, and Reformers take *ἐρχόμενον* with *ἄνθρωπον*, *every man that cometh into the world;* a solemn fulness of expression and not a weak addition. A number of modern commentators take *ἐρχ.* with *ἦν*; *the true Light, which lighteth every man, was coming into the world.* But *ἦν* and *ἐρχ.* are somewhat far apart for this. There is yet a third way; **There was the true Light, which lighteth every man, by coming into the world.** Observe the emphatic position of *ἦν*. 'There *was* the true Light,' even while the Baptist was preparing the way for Him.

τὸ ἀληθινόν. *Ἀληθής*=*verax*, 'true' as opposed to 'lying:' *ἀληθινός* =*verus*, 'true' as opposed to 'spurious.' *Ἀληθινός* is just the old English 'very;' e.g. in the Creed, 'Very God of very God' is a translation of *θεὸν ἀληθινὸν ἐκ θεοῦ ἀληθινοῦ*. *Ἀληθινός*='genuine,' 'that which comes up to its idea,' and hence 'perfect.' Christ is 'the perfect Light,' just as He is 'the perfect Bread' (vi. 32) and 'the perfect Vine' (xv. 1); not that He is the *only* Light, and Bread, and Vine, but that others are types and shadows, and therefore inferior. All words about truth are characteristic of S. John. *Ἀληθινός* occurs 9 times in the Gospel, 4 times in the First Epistle, 10 times in the Apocalypse; elsewhere only 6 times: *ἀληθής*, 14 times in the Gospel, twice in the First Epistle, once in the Second; elsewhere 9 times. *Ἀλήθεια* and *ἀληθῶς* are also very frequent.

πάντα ἄνθρωπον. The Light illumines every man, but not every man is the better for it; that depends on himself. Moreover it illumines 'each one singly,' not 'all collectively' (*πάντα* not *πάντας*). God deals with men separately as individuals, not in masses.

10. καὶ ὁ κόσμος. Close connexion obtained by repetition, as in *vv.* 4 and 5; also the tragic tone, as in *v.* 5. Moreover, there is a climax: 'He was in the world;' (therefore it should have known Him;) 'and the world was His creature;' (therefore it should have known Him;) 'and (yet) the world knew Him not.' Καί=καίτοι is very frequent in S. John, but it is best to translate simply 'and,' not 'and yet:' cf. *vv.* 5 and 11. It is erroneous to suppose that καί ever means 'but' either in S. John or elsewhere. Ὁ κόσμος is another of the expressions characteristic of S. John: it occurs nearly 80 times in the Gospel, and 22 times in the First Epistle.

Observe that ὁ κόσμος has not exactly the same meaning *vv.* 9 and 10: throughout the New Testament it is most important to distinguish the various meanings of κόσμος. Connected with κομεῖν and *comere*, it means (1) 'ornament;' 1 Pet. iii. 3: (2) 'the ordered universe,' *mundus;* Rom. i. 20: (3) 'the earth;' *v.* 9 ; Matt. iv. 8: (4) 'the inhabitants of the earth;' *v.* 29; iv. 42: (5) 'the world outside the Church,' those alienated from God; xii. 31, xiv. 17 and frequently. In this verse the meaning slips from (3) to (5).

αὐτόν. The masculine shews that S. John is again speaking of Christ as ὁ Λόγος, not (as in *v.* 9) as τὸ Φῶς.

οὐκ ἔγνω. 'Did not *acquire* knowledge' of its Creator. Γιγνώσκειν is 'to get to know, recognise, acknowledge.' Cf. Acts xix. 15.

11. εἰς τὰ ἴδια. The difference between neuter and masculine must be preserved: *He came to His own* **inheritance**; *and His own* **people** *received Him not.* In the parable of the Wicked Husbandmen (Matt. xxi. 33—41) τὰ ἴδια is the vineyard; οἱ ἴδιοι are the husbandmen, the Chosen people, the Jews. Or, as in xix. 27, we may render εἰς τὰ ἴδια *unto His own* **home**: cf. xvi. 32, xix. 27; Acts xxi. 6; Esth. v. 10, vi. 12. The tragic tone is very strong here, as in *vv.* 5 and 10.

παρέλαβον. A stronger word than ἔγνω. Παραλαμβάνειν is 'to take from the hand of another, accept what is *offered*.' Mankind in general did not recognise the Messiah; the Jews, to whom He was specially sent, did not *welcome* Him. There is a climax again in 9, 10, 11;—ἦν—ἐν τῷ κόσμῳ ἦν—εἰς τὰ ἴδια ἦλθε.

12. ἔλαβον. As distinguished from παρέλαβον, denotes the *spontaneous* acceptance of *individuals*, Jews or Gentiles. The Messiah was not specially *offered* to any individuals as He was to the Jewish nation: παρέλαβον would have been less appropriate here.

ἐξουσίαν. This word (from ἔξεστι) means '**right**, liberty, authority' to do anything; *potestas.* Δύναμις, which is sometimes coupled with it, is rather 'capability, faculty' for doing anything; *potentia.* Δύναμις is innate, an absence of internal obstacles; ἐξουσία comes from without, a removal of external restraints. We are born with a *capacity* for becoming the sons of God: that we have as men. He gives us the *right* to become such: that we receive as Christians.

τέκνα θεοῦ. Both S. John and S. Paul insist on this fundamental fact; that the relation of believers to God is a *filial* one. S. John gives us the human side, the 'new birth' (iii. 3); S. Paul the Divine side, 'adoption' (Rom. viii. 23; Gal. iv. 5). But *τέκνα θεοῦ* expresses a closer relationship than *υἱοθεσία*: the one is natural, the other is legal. Both place the universal character of Christianity in opposition to the exclusiveness of Judaism. Note **γένεσθαι.** Christ *is* from all eternity the Son of God; men are enabled to *become* sons of God.

τοῖς πιστ. εἰς. Epexegetic of *αὐτοῖς*; 'namely, *to those who believe on*.' Such epexegetic clauses are common in S. John; comp. iii. 13, v. 18. vii. 50. The test of a child of God is no longer descent from Abraham, but belief in His Son. The construction *πιστεύειν εἰς* is characteristic of S. John; it occurs about 35 times in the Gospel and 3 times in the First Epistle; elsewhere in N. T. about 10 times. It expresses the very strongest belief; motion to and repose upon the object of belief. It corresponds to S. Paul's *πίστις*, a word which S. John uses only once (1 John v. 4), and S. Paul about 140 times. On the other hand S. Paul very rarely uses *πιστεύειν εἰς*. *Πιστεύειν τινί* without a preposition has a weaker meaning, 'to give credence to,' or 'accept the statements of.'

τὸ ὄνομα αὐτοῦ. This is a frequent phrase in Jewish writings, both in the O. and N. T. It is not a mere periphrasis. Names were so often significant, given sometimes by God Himself, that a man's name served not merely to tell *who* he was, but *what* he was: it was an index of character. So also of the Divine Name: *τὸ ὄνομα τοῦ Κυρίου* is not a mere periphrasis for *ὁ Κύριος*; it suggests His attributes and His relations to us as Lord. The 'name' specially meant here is perhaps that of *Logos;* and the full meaning would be to give entire adhesion to Him as the Incarnate Son, the expression of the Will and Nature of God.

13. S. John denies thrice most emphatically that human generation has anything to do with Divine regeneration. Man cannot become a child of God in right of human parentage: the new Creation is far more excellent than the first Creation; its forces and products are spiritual not physical.

αἱμάτων. The blood was regarded as the seat of physical life. Gen. ix. 4; Lev. xvii. 11, 14. The plural is idiomatic (cf. *τὰ ὕδατα*, 'the waters,' *τὰ γάλακτα*), and does not refer to the two sexes. In Eur. *Ion*, 693 we have *ἄλλων τραφεὶς ἀφ' αἱμάτων*. Winer, p. 220.

οὐδὲ ἐκ θ. σαρκός. Nor yet from will of flesh, i. e. from any fleshly impulse. A second denial of any natural process.

οὐδὲ ἐκ θ. ἀνδρός. Nor yet from will of man, i.e. from the volition of any human father. Ἀνήρ is not here put for *ἄνθρωπος*, the human race generally; it means the male sex, human fathers in contrast to the Heavenly Father. A third denial of any natural process.

ἐγεννήθησαν. *Were* **begotten.** There is an interesting false reading here. Tertullian (circ. A.D. 200) read the singular, *ἐγεννήθη*, which he referred to Christ; and he accused the Valentinians of falsifying the text in reading *ἐγεννήθησαν*, which is undoubtedly right. These differences are most important: they shew that as early as A.D. 200 there were corruptions in the text, the origin of which had been lost. Such corruptions take some time to grow: by comparing them and tracing their ramifications we arrive with certainty at the conclusion that this Gospel cannot have been written later than towards the end of the first century, A.D. 85—100. See on *v.* 18, iii. 6, 13, ix. 35.

14—18. The Incarnate Word's revelation of the Father

14. καὶ ὁ λόγος σὰρξ ἐγένετο. This is the gulf which separates S. John from Philo. Philo would have assented to what precedes; but from this he would have shrunk. From *v.* 9 to 13 we have the *subjective* side; the inward result of the Word's coming to those who receive Him. Here we have the *objective;* the coming of the Word as a historical fact. The Logos, existing from all eternity with the Father (*vv.* 1, 2), not only manifested His power in Creation (*v.* 3), and in influence on the minds of men (*vv.* 9, 12, 13), but manifested Himself in the form of a man of flesh.—The *καί* is resumptive, taking us back to the opening verses.

σάρξ. Not *σῶμα*, nor *ἄνθρωπος*. There might have been a *σῶμα* without *σάρξ* (1 Cor. xv. 40, 44), and there might have been the form of a man, and yet no *σάρξ* (Matt. xiv. 26; Luke xxiv. 37—39). Docetism is by implication excluded: vi. 21, vii. 10, xix. 35. The important point is that the Logos became terrestrial and material; the creative Word Himself became a creature. The inferior part of man is mentioned, to mark His humiliation: He took the whole nature of man, including its frailty; all that nature in which He could grow, learn, struggle, be tempted, suffer, and die.

ἐσκήνωσεν. Tabernacled *among us.* The *σκηνή*, or Tabernacle, had been the seat of the Divine Presence in the wilderness. When God became incarnate, to dwell among the Chosen People, *σκηνοῦν* 'to tabernacle' was a natural word to use. We have here another link (see above on *ἀληθινός v.* 9) between this Gospel and the Apocalypse. *Σκηνοῦν* occurs here, four times in the Apocalypse, and nowhere else. Rev. vii. 15, xii. 12, xiii. 6, xxi. 3. There is perhaps an association of ideas, suggested by similarity of sound, between *σκηνή* and the Shechinah or *δόξα* mentioned in the next clause. "The idea that the Shechinah, the *σκηνή*, the glory which betokened the Divine Presence in the Holy of Holies, and which was wanting in the second temple, would be restored once more in Messiah's days, was a cherished hope of the Jewish doctors during and after the Apostolic ages. ...S. John more than once avails himself of imagery derived from this expectation.... The two writings (this Gospel and the Apocalypse) which attribute the name of the Word of God to the Incarnate Son, are the same also which especially connect Messiah's Advent with the restitution of the Shechinah, the light or glory which is the visible token of God's presence among men." Lightfoot, *On Revision*, pp. 56, 57. See on xi. 44, xv. 20, xix. 37, xx. 16.

ἐθεασάμεθα. **Contemplated or beheld**: cf. 1 John i. 1. It is a stronger word than *ὁρᾶν*, implying *enjoyment* in beholding.

τὴν δόξαν αὐτοῦ. Cf. ii. 11; xi. 40; xii. 41; xvii. 5, 24; 2 Cor. iii. 7—18; Rev. xxi. 10. Although the Word in becoming incarnate laid aside His Divine prerogatives, and not merely assumed but '*became* flesh,' yet the moral and spiritual grandeur of His unique relationship to the Father remained and was manifest to His disciples. There is probably a special reference to the Transfiguration (Luke ix. 32; 2 Pet. i. 17); and possibly to the vision at the beginning of the Apocalypse.

ὡς. This particle does not necessarily signify *mere* likeness. Here and Matt. vii. 29 it indicates *exact* likeness: the glory is *altogether such as* that of the only-begotten Son of God; He taught *exactly as* one having full authority.

μονογενοῦς. *Only-begotten*, '*unigenitus*.' The word is used of the widow's son (Luke vii. 12), Jairus' daughter (viii. 42), the demoniac boy (ix. 38), Isaac (Heb. xi. 17). As applied to our Lord it occurs only in S. John's writings; here, *v.* 18, iii. 16, 18; 1 John iv. 9. It marks off His unique Sonship from that of the *τέκνα θεοῦ* (*v.* 12). It refers to His eternal generation from the Father, whereas *πρωτότοκος* refers to His incarnation as the Messiah and His relation to creatures. See Lightfoot on Col. i. 15.

παρὰ πατρός. (See on *παρὰ θεοῦ*, *v.* 6.) **From a father**: S. John *never* uses *πατήρ* for the Father without the article: see on iv. 21. The meaning is, 'as of an only son sent on a mission from a father.'

πλήρης. There is no need to make the preceding clause a parenthesis: *πλήρης*, in spite of the case, may go with *αὐτοῦ*. In Luke xx. 27, xxiv. 47, we have equally irregular constructions.—*Πλήρης* looks forward to *πλήρωμα* in *v.* 16. Winer, p. 705.

χάριτος. *Χάρις* from *χαίρω* means originally 'that which causes pleasure.' Hence (1) *comeliness, winsomeness;* from Homer downwards. In Luke iv. 22 *λόγοι τῆς χ.* are 'winning words.' (2) *Kindliness, good will;* both in classical Greek and N.T. Luke ii. 52; Acts ii. 47. (3) The *favour* of God towards sinners. This distinctly theological sense has for its central point the *freeness* of God's gifts: they are not earned, He gives them *spontaneously* through Christ. This notion of spontaneousness is not prominent in classical Greek: it is the main idea in N.T. *Χάρις* is neither earned by works nor prevented by sin; it is thus opposed to *ἔργα, νόμος, ὀφείλημα, ἁμαρτία*, and branches out into various meanings too wide for discussion here. 'Grace' covers all meanings. The third meaning, at its deepest and fullest, is the one in this verse.

ἀληθείας. It is as *τὸ Φῶς* that the Logos is 'full of truth,' as *ἡ Ζωή* that He is 'full of grace,' for it is 'by grace' that we come to eternal life. Eph. ii. 5. Moreover the *ἀληθεία* assures us that the *χάρις* is real and steadfast: comp. the combination of *ἔλεος* and *ἀληθεία* in the LXX. of Ps. lxxxix. 1, 2.

15. **μαρτυρεῖ.** Present tense; **beareth** *witness.* At the end of a long life this testimony of the Baptist still abides fresh in the heart of the aged Apostle. He records three times in twenty verses (15, 27, 30) the cry that was such an epoch in his own life. The testimony abides as a memory for him, as a truth for all.

κέκραγεν. Perfect with present meaning; **cries.** See on v. 42. The word indicates strong emotion, as of a prophet. Cf. vii. 28, 37, xii. 44; Is. xl. 3.

ὃν εἶπον. As if his first utterance under the influence of the Spirit had been hardly intelligible to himself. For *ὅν*=‘*of* whom’ cf. vi. 71, viii. 27.

ὁ ὀπίσω κ.τ.λ. The first and last of these three clauses *must* refer to *time; ὀπίσω*=‘later in time,’ *πρῶτος*=‘first in time.’ The middle clause is ambiguous: *ἔμπροσθεν*=‘before’ either (1) in *time*, or (2) in *dignity*. *Γέγονεν* seems to be decisive against (1). Christ as God was before John in time, as the third clause states; but John could not say, ‘He *has come to be* before me,’ or ‘has *become* before me,’ in *time*. Moreover, to make the second clause refer to time involves tautology with the third. It is better to follow the A. V. ‘*is preferred* before me,’ i.e. ‘has become before me’ in *dignity:* and the meaning will be, ‘He who is coming after me (in His ministry as in His birth) has become superior to me, for He was in existence from all eternity before me.’ Christ's pre-existence in eternity a great deal more than cancelled John's pre-existence in the world: and as soon as He appeared as a teacher He at once eclipsed His forerunner.

πρῶτός μου ἦν. Cf. *v.* 30 and xv. 18, where we again have a genitive after a superlative as if it were a comparative. It is not strange that ‘first of two,’ or ‘former,’ should be sometimes confused with ‘first of many,’ or ‘first,’ and the construction proper to the one be given to the other. Explained thus the words would mean ‘first in reference to me,’ or ‘my first.’ But perhaps there is more than this; viz., ‘He was before me, as no other can be,’ i.e. ‘He was before me and first of all,’ *πρωτότοκος πάσης κτίσεως.*

16. The Baptist's witness to the incarnate Logos confirmed by the experience of all believers. The Evangelist is the speaker.

πληρώματος. “A recognised technical term in theology, denoting the totality of the Divine powers and attributes.” See Lightfoot on *Colossians*, i. 19 and ii. 9, where this meaning is very marked. This fulness of the Divine attributes belonged to Christ (*v.* 14), and by Him was imparted to the Church, which is His Body (Eph. i. 23); and through the Church each individual believer in his degree receives a portion.

ἡμεῖς πάντες. Shews that the Evangelist and not the Baptist is speaking. This appeal to his own experience and that of his fellows is natural as coming from the Apostle; it would not be natural in a writer of a later age. Another indication that S. John is the writer.

καί. Epexegetic, = 'namely' or 'even,' explaining *what* we all received. Comp. 1 Cor. iii. 5, xv. 38; Eph. vi. 18. Winer, p. 545.

χάριν ἀντὶ χάριτος. Literally, *Grace in the place of grace*, one grace succeeding another and as it were taking its place. (On *χάρις* see *v.* 14.) There is no reference to the New Testament displacing the Old: that would have been *χάριν ἀντὶ τοῦ νόμου;* see next verse. Possibly the *ἀντί* may imply that one grace leads on to another, so that the second is, as it were, a reward for the first. Winer, p. 456.

17. The mention of *χάρις* reminds the Evangelist that this was the characteristic of the new dispensation and marked its superiority to the old: the Law condemned transgressors, *χάρις* forgives them.

διὰ Μωυσέως. It is regrettable that the translation of *διὰ* in this prologue is not uniform in the A.V. In verses 3, 10, 17 we have 'by,' in *v.* 7 'through.' 'By means of' is the meaning in all five cases. Moses did not give the Law any more than he gave the manna (vi. 32); he was only the mediate agent, the *μεσίτης* by whose hand it was given (Gal. iii. 19). The form *Μωυσέως* is rightly given in the best MSS. The derivation is said to be from two Egyptian words *mo* = *aqua*, and *ugai* = *servari*. Hence the Septuagint, which was made in Egypt, and the best MSS., which mainly represent the text current in Egypt, keep nearest to the Egyptian form.

ἐδόθη. Not *ἐγένετο*. The Law given through Moses was not his own; the grace and truth that came through Christ were His own.

ἡ χάρις. The asyndeton is remarkable: the Coptic and Peshito supply an equivalent for *δέ*, but this is a common insertion in versions, and no proof that a *δέ* has dropped out of the Greek texts.

ἡ ἀλήθεια. Like *χάρις*, *ἀλήθεια* is opposed to *νόμος*, not as truth to falsehood, but as a perfect to an imperfect revelation.

Ἰησοῦ Χριστοῦ. "To us 'Christ' has become a proper name, and as such rejects the definite article. But in the Gospel narratives, if we except the headings, or prefaces, and the after comments of the Evangelists themselves (e.g. Matt. i. 1; Mark i. 1; John i. 17) no instance of this usage can be found. In the body of the narratives we read only of *ὁ Χριστός*, *the* Christ, *the* Messiah, whom the Jews had long expected......The very exceptions (Mark ix. 41; Luke ii. 11; John ix. 22, xvii. 3) strengthen the rule." Lightfoot, *On Revision*, p. 100. Note that S. John no longer speaks of the Logos: the Logos has become incarnate (*v.* 14) and is spoken of henceforth by the names which He has borne in history.

18. The Evangelist solemnly sums up the purpose of the Incarnation of the Logos,—to be a visible revelation of the invisible God. It was in this way that 'the truth came through Jesus Christ,' for the truth cannot be fully known while God is not fully revealed. Πάσῃ θνητῇ φύσει ἀθεώρητος, ἀπ' αὐτῶν τῶν ἔργων θεωρεῖται ὁ Θεός (Aristotle).

οὐδείς. Not even Moses. Until we see πρόσωπον πρὸς πρόσωπον (1 Cor. xiii. 12) our knowledge is only partial. Symbolical visions, such as Ex. xxiv. 10, xxxiii. 23; 1 Kings xix. 13; Isa. vi. 1, do not transcend the limits of partial knowledge.

ἑώρακεν. Of actual sight. S. John uses no tense of ὁράω but the perfect either in the Gospel or Epistle: in vi. 2 the true reading is ἐθεώρουν.

μονογενὴς θεός. The question of reading here is of much interest. Most MSS. and versions read ὁ μονογενὴς υἱός or μον. υἱός. But the three oldest and best MSS. and two others of great value read μονογενὴς θεός. The test of the value of a MS., or group of MSS., on any disputed point, is the extent to which it admits false readings on other points not disputed. Judged by this test, the group of MSS. reading μονογενὴς θεός is very strong, while the far larger group of MSS. reading υἱός for θεός is comparatively weak, for the same group might be quoted in favour of a multitude of readings which no one would think of defending. Again, the revised Syriac, which is among the minority of versions supporting θεός, is here of special weight, because it agrees with MSS. from which it usually differs. The inference is that the very unusual expression μονογενὴς θεός is the original one, which has been changed into the usual ὁ μονογενὴς υἱός (iii. 16, 18; 1 John iv. 9); a change easily made, as $\overline{\Theta C}$ (=ΘΕΟΣ) is very like $\overline{\Upsilon C}$ (=ΥΙΟΣ). Both readings can be traced back to the second century, which again is evidence that the Gospel was written in the first century. Such differences take time to spread themselves so widely. See on *v.* 13, iii. 6, and ix. 35.

ὁ ὢν εἰς τὸν κόλπον. The preposition of motion (comp. *vv.* 32, 33, 52) *may* point to Christ's *return* to glory, after the Ascension. Comp. Mark ii. 1, xiii. 16; Luke ix. 61. On the other hand ὤν seems to point to a timeless state; 'Whose relation to the Father is eternally that of one admitted to the deepest intimacy and closest fellowship.' But ὤν may be imperf. ('who *was*' rather than 'who *is*'), as in v. 13, xi. 31, 49, xxi. 11. Winer, pp. 429, 517.

ἐκεῖνος. S. John's peculiar retrospective use, to recall and emphasize the main subject: see on *v.* 8, and comp. *v.* 33, v. 11, 37, 39, 43, vi. 57, ix. 37, xii. 48, xiv. 12, 21, 26, xv. 26.

ἐξηγήσατο. Declared, not 'hath declared.' *Only-begotten God as He is, He that is in the bosom of the Father*, He *interpreted* (*God*), supplying an accusative from the beginning of the verse. Ἐξηγεῖσθαι is used both in the LXX. and in classical writers for interpreting the Divine Will.

In this Prologue we notice what may be called a *spiral movement*. An idea comes to the front, like the strand of a rope, retires again, and then reappears later on for development and further definition.

Meanwhile another idea, like another strand, comes before us and retires to reappear in like manner. Thus the Logos is presented to us in *v.* 1, is withdrawn, and again presented to us in *v.* 14. The Creation passes next before us in *v.* 3, to reappear in *v.* 10. Then 'the Light' appears in *v.* 4, and withdraws, to return *vv.* 8, 9. Next the rejection of the Logos is introduced in *v.* 5, and reproduced in in *vv.* 10, 11. Lastly, the testimony of John is mentioned in *vv.* 6, 7, repeated in *v.* 15, taken up again in *v.* 19 and developed through the next two sections of the chapter.

We now enter upon the first main division of the Gospel, which extends to the end of chap. xii., the subject being CHRIST'S MINISTRY, or, HIS REVELATION OF HIMSELF TO THE WORLD, and that in three parts; THE TESTIMONY (i. 19—ii. 11), THE WORK (ii. 13—xi. 57), and THE JUDGMENT (xii.).

19—37. *The Testimony of the Baptist,* (α) to the deputation from Jerusalem, (β) to the people, (γ) to Andrew and John: **31—51.** *The Testimony of the Disciples:* ii. 1—11 *The Testimony of the First Sign.*

19—37. THE TESTIMONY OF THE BAPTIST

19—28. THE TESTIMONY TO THE DEPUTATION FROM JERUSALEM

19—28. This section describes a crisis in the ministry of the Baptist. He had already attracted the attention of the Sanhedrin. It was a time of excitement and expectation respecting the Messiah. John evidently spoke with an authority beyond that of other teachers, and his success was greater than theirs. The miracle which had attended his birth, connected as it was with the public ministry of Zacharias in the Temple, was probably known. He had proclaimed the approach of a new dispensation (Matt. iii. 2), and this was believed to be connected with the Messiah. But what was to be John's relation to the Messiah? or was he the Messiah himself? This uncertainty determined the authorities at Jerusalem to send and question John as to his mission. Apparently no formal deputation from the Sanhedrin was sent. The Sadducee members would not feel so keen an interest in the matter. Their party acquiesced in the Roman dominion and scarcely shared the intense religious and national hopes of their countrymen. But to the Pharisees, who represented the patriotic party in the Sanhedrin, the question was vital; and they seem to have acted for themselves in sending an informal though influential deputation of ministers of religion (*v.* 19) from their own party (*v.* 24). The Evangelist was probably at this time among the Baptist's disciples and heard his master proclaim himself not the Messiah but His Herald. It was a crisis for him as well as for his master, and he records it as such.

19. καί. The narrative is connected with the prologue through the testimony of John common to both. Comp. 1 John i. 5.

οἱ Ἰουδαῖοι. The history of this word is interesting. (1) Originally it meant members of the *tribe* of Judah. After the revolt of the ten tribes, (2) members of the *kingdom* of Judah. After the captivity, because only the kingdom of Judah was restored to national existence, (3) members of the Jewish *nation* (ii. 6, 13, iii. 1, vi. 4, vii. 2). After many Jews and Gentiles had become Christian, (4) members of the Church who were of Jewish descent (Gal. ii. 13). Lastly (5) *members of the nation which had rejected Christ;* the special usage of S. John. With him *οἱ Ἰουδαῖοι* commonly means *the opponents of Christ*, a meaning not found in the Synoptists. With them it is the sects and parties (Pharisees, Scribes, &c.) that are the typical representatives of hostility to Christ. But John writing later, with a fuller consciousness of the national apostasy, and a fuller experience of Jewish malignity in opposing the Gospel, lets the shadow of this knowledge fall back upon his narrative, and 'the Jews' to him are not his fellow-countrymen, but the persecutors and murderers of the Messiah. He uses the term about 70 times, almost always with this shade of meaning.

ἐξ Ἱεροσολύμων. After *ἀπέστειλαν*. S. John never uses the form *Ἱερουσαλήμ* excepting in the *Apocalypse*, where he never uses the form *Ἱεροσόλυμα*. S. Matthew, with the single exception of xxiii. 27, and S. Mark, with the possible exception of xi. 1, never use *Ἱερουσαλήμ*. Both forms are common in S. Luke and the Acts, *Ἱερουσαλήμ* being predominant. As distinguished from *Ἱεροσόλυμα* it is used wherever the name has a *religious* significance, e.g. *ἡ ἄνω Ἱερουσαλήμ* (Gal. iv. 25), cf. Matt. xxiii. 27; Heb. xii. 22; Rev. iii. 12; xxi. 2, 10. *Ἱερουσαλήμ* is found throughout the LXX. It was natural that the sacred name should be preserved in its Hebrew form; but equally natural that the Greek form should be admitted when it was a mere geographical designation.

ἱερεῖς. The Baptist himself was of priestly family (Luke i. 5).

Λευείτας. The Levites were commissioned to *teach* (2 Chron. xxxv. 3; Neh. viii. 7—9) as well as wait in the Temple; and it is as teachers, similar to the Scribes, that they are sent to the Baptist. Probably many of the Scribes were Levites. The mention of Levites as part of this deputation is the mark of an eyewitness. Excepting in the parable of the Good Samaritan (Luke x. 32), Levites are not mentioned by the Synoptists, nor elsewhere in N. T. excepting Acts iv. 36. Had the Evangelist been constructing a story out of borrowed materials, we should probably have had 'scribes' or 'elders' instead of Levites. These indications of eyewitness are among the strong proofs of the authenticity of this Gospel.

20. ὡμολόγησεν καὶ οὐκ ἠρνήσατο. Antithetic parallelism (*v.* 3).

ἐγὼ οὐκ εἰμί. So the best MSS., making *ἐγώ* emphatic; the Received Text having *οὐκ εἰμὶ ἐγώ*. The Baptist hints that though *he* is not the Messiah, the Messiah is near at hand.

ὁ Χριστός. The Evangelist has dropped the philosophic term *Λόγος* and adopted the Jewish title of the Messiah. He was familiar with both aspects of Jesus and makes the transition naturally and easily. See above on *v.* 17.

21. τί οὖν; '*What* art thou *then?*' or, '*What then* are we to think?'

'Ηλίας εἶ σύ; The Scribes taught that Elijah would return before the coming of the Messiah (Matt. xvii. 10), and this belief is repeatedly alluded to in the Talmud. Cf. Mal. iv. 5.

οὐκ εἰμί. A forger would scarcely have written this in the face of Matt. xi. 14, where Christ says that John *is* Elijah (in a figurative sense). John here denies that he is Elijah in a literal sense; he is not Elijah returned to the earth.

ὁ προφήτης. '**The** (well-known) *Prophet*' of Deut. xviii. 15, who some thought would be a second Moses, others a second Elijah, others the Messiah. We see from vii. 40, 41, that some distinguished 'the Prophet' from the Messiah; and from Matt. xvi. 14, it appears that there was an impression that Jeremiah or other prophets might return. Here as in vii. 40, the translation should be '*the* Prophet' not '*that* prophet.' We have a similar error *v.* 25; vi. 14, 48, 69.

This verse alone is almost enough to shew that the writer is a Jew. Who but a Jew would know of these expectations? If a Gentile knew them, would he not explain them?

22. εἶπαν οὖν. See on iii. 25. Their manner has the peremptoriness of officials.

τίς εἶ; They continue asking as to his person; he replies as to his office,—that of Forerunner. In the presence of the Messiah his personality is lost.

23. ἐγὼ φωνὴ κ.τ.λ. *I am a voice, &c.* The Synoptists use these words of John as fulfilling prophecy. From this it seems that they were first so used by himself. The quotation is from the LXX. with the change of *ἑτοιμάσατε* into *εὐθύνατε*. John was a Voice making known the Word, meaningless without the Word. There is a scarcely doubtful reference to this passage in Justin Martyr (c. A.D. 150); *οὐκ εἰμὶ ὁ Χριστὸς, ἀλλὰ φωνὴ βοῶντος. Trypho*, lxxxviii. Comp. iii. 3.

24. ἀπεσταλμένοι ἦσαν. The *οἱ* before the participle is of doubtful authority. Omitting it, we translate *And they had been sent from the Pharisees*, or better (as we have **ἐκ** and not *παρά*), *and* **there had been sent (some) of the Pharisees.** For this use of *ἐκ τῶν* comp. vii. 40, xvi. 17; 2 John 4; Rev. ii. 10. We are not to understand a fresh deputation, as the *οὖν* in the next verse shews. It was precisely the Pharisees who would be jealous about innovations in religious rites. S. John mentions neither Sadducees nor Herodians. Only the sect most opposed to Christ is remembered by the Evangelist who had gone furthest from Judaism.

25. τί οὖν βαπτίζεις. What right have you to treat Jews as if they were proselytes and make them submit to a rite which implies that they are impure? Comp. Zech. xiii. 1. *Βαπτίζω* is the intensive form of *βάπτω*: *βάπτω*, 'I dip,' *βαπτίζω*, 'I immerse:' so *ὀφλήμασι βεβαπτισμένος*, 'over head and ears in debt,' Plut. *Galb.* xxi.

οὐκ εἶ ὁ Χριστός. **Art** *not* **the** *Christ.*

οὐδὲ Ἠλίας οὐδὲ ὁ πρ. *Nor* **yet Elijah,** *nor* **yet the** *Prophet.*

26. The Baptist's words seem scarcely a reply to the question. Perhaps the connexion is—'You ask for my credentials; and all the while He who is far more than credentials to me is among you.'

ἐν ὕδατι. **In** *water:* note the preposition here and *vv.* 26, 33.

27. ὁ ὀπίσω μου ἐρχόμενος. This is the subject of the sentence; **He that cometh after me...is standing in the midst of you, and ye know Him not.** *Ὑμεῖς* is emphatic; 'Whom ye who question me know not, but whom I the questioned know.'

ἄξιος ἵνα. Literally, *worthy in order that I may unloose.* An instance of S. John's preferring *ἵνα* where another construction would have seemed more natural: see on *v.* 8, and comp. ii. 25, v. 40, vi. 7, xi. 50, xv. 8, &c.

αὐτοῦ. This is redundant after *οὗ*, perhaps in imitation of Hebrew construction.

28. Βηθανίᾳ. This, which is the true reading, was altered to *Βηθαβαρᾷ* owing to the powerful influence of Origen, who could find no Bethany beyond Jordan in his day. In 200 years the very name of an obscure place might easily perish. Origen says that almost all the old MSS. had *Βηθανίᾳ*. This Bethany or Bethabara must have been near Galilee: comp. *v.* 29, with *v.* 43, and see on the 'four days,' xi. 17. It is possible to reconcile the two readings. Bethabara has been identified with 'Abârah, one of the main Jordan fords about 14 miles S. of the sea of Galilee: and 'Bethania beyond Jordan' has been identified with Bashan; Bethania or Batanea being the Aramaic form of the Hebrew Bashan, meaning 'soft level ground.' Bethabara is the village or ford; Bethania the district E. of the ford. Conder, *Handbook of the Bible,* pp. 315, 320. The Jordan had grand historical associations: to make men pass through its waters might seem to some a preparation for conquests like those of Joshua.

29—34. THE TESTIMONY OF THE BAPTIST TO THE PEOPLE

29. τῇ ἐπαύριον. These words prevent us from inserting the Temptation between *vv.* 28 and 29. The fact of the Baptist knowing who Jesus is, shews that the Baptism, and therefore the Temptation, must have preceded the deputation from Jerusalem. S. John omits both, as being events well known to his readers. The Baptist's announcements are not a continuous discourse. They come forth like sudden intuitions, of which he did not himself know the full meaning.

ἴδε. S. John uses this form about 20 times (*vv.* 36, 47, 48, iii. 26, v. 14, &c.), and *ἰδού* only four times (iv. 35, [xii. 15,] xvi. 32, xix. 5). The Synoptists use *ἴδε* about 10 times (not in Luke) and *ἰδού* more than 120 times. Both words are interjections, 'Lo! Behold!,' not imperatives, 'See, Look at.' Hence the nominative case. Comp. xix. 14.

ὁ ἀμνὸς τοῦ θεοῦ. The article shews that some Lamb familiar to the Baptist's hearers must be meant, and probably the Lamb of Is. liii. (comp. Acts viii. 32), with perhaps an indirect allusion to the Paschal Lamb (xix. 36). The addition *τοῦ Θεοῦ* may remind us of Gen. xxii. 8. The figure of the Lamb for Christ appears in N. T. elsewhere only 1 Pet. i. 19, and throughout the Apocalypse; but in the Apocalypse the word is always *ἀρνίον*, never *ἀμνός* (v. 6, 8, 12, &c.).

ὁ αἴρων. This seems to make the reference both to Is. liii. esp. *vv.* 4—8, 10, and also to the Paschal Lamb, more clear. The Paschal Lamb was expiatory (Ex. xii. 13). *Taketh away*, rather than *beareth* (margin), is right; comp. 1 John iii. 5. 'Bear' would rather be *φέρω*, as in the LXX. in Is. liii. 4. Christ took away the burden of sin by bearing it; but this is not expressed here, though it may be implied. **Τὴν ἁμαρτίαν.** Regarded as one great burden or plague.

τοῦ κόσμου. Isaiah sees no further than the redemption of the Jews: 'for the transgression of *my people*—*τοῦ λαοῦ μου*—was He stricken' (liii. 8). The Baptist knows that the Messiah comes to make atonement for the whole human race, even His enemies.

31. κἀγὼ οὐκ ᾔδειν αὐτόν. *I* **also** *knew Him not;* I, like you (v. 26), did not at first know Him to be the Messiah. This does not contradict Matt. iii. 14. (1) 'I knew Him not' need not mean 'I had no knowledge of Him whatever.' (2) John's declaration of his need to be baptized by Jesus does not prove that he had already recognized Jesus as the Messiah, but only as superior to himself.

ἀλλ' ἵνα. See on *v.* 8. This is the second half of the Divine purpose respecting the Baptist. He was (1) to prepare for the Messiah by preaching repentance; (2) to point out the Messiah.

φανερωθῇ. One of S. John's favourite words; ii. 11, iii. 21, vii. 4, ix. 3, xvii. 6, xxi. 1, 14; 1 John i. 2, ii. 19, 28, iii. 2, 5, 8, 9; Rev. iii. 18, xv. 4. See on ii. 11.

διὰ τοῦτο. For this cause (xii. 18, 27) **came I:** comp. v. 16, 18, vii. 22, viii. 47, xix. 11. In translation we must distinguish *διὰ τοῦτο* from S. John's favourite particle *οὖν*.

ἐν [τῷ] ὕδατι. Placed before *βαπτίζων* for emphasis, because here he contrasts himself as baptizing with water with Him who baptizes with the Holy Spirit.

32. ἐμαρτ. The Evangelist insists again and again on this aspect of the Baptist: he bears **witness** to the Messiah; 7, 8, 15, 19, 34.

τεθέαμαι. I have beheld (*vv.* 14, 38; 1 John iv. 12, 14). The testimony of the vision still remains; hence the perfect.

ὡς περιστερὰν. Perhaps visible only to Jesus and the Baptist. A real appearance is the natural meaning here, and is insisted on by S. Luke (iii. 22); just as a real voice is the natural meaning in xii. 29. And if we admit the 'bodily shape,' there is no sound reason for rejecting the dove. The marvel is that the Holy Spirit should be visible in any way, not that He should assume the form of a dove or of 'tongues of fire' (Acts ii. 3) in particular. This symbolical vision of the Spirit seems to be analogous to the visions of Jehovah granted to Moses and other Prophets.

The descent of the Spirit made no change in the nature of Christ: but possibly it awoke a *full* consciousness of His relation to God and to man: He had been increasing in favour with both (Luke ii. 52). It served two purposes; (1) to make the Messiah known to the Baptist and through him to the world; (2) to mark the official beginning of His ministry, like the anointing of a king. As at the Transfiguration, Christ is miraculously glorified before setting out to suffer, a voice from heaven bears witness to Him, and 'the goodly fellowship of the Prophets' shares in the glory. For **ἔμεινεν** see next verse.

ἐπ' αὐτόν. Pregnant construction; a preposition of motion with a verb of rest. Thus both the motion and the rest are indicated. Comp. *v.* 18, iii. 36, xix. 13, xx. 19, xxi. 4; Gen. i. 2.

33. κἀγὼ οὐκ ᾔ. αὐ. **I also** *knew Him not.* The Baptist again protests that but for a special revelation he was as ignorant as others that Jesus was the Messiah. Therefore he is here giving not his own opinion about Jesus, but the evidence of a sign from heaven.

ὁ πέμψας. In *v.* 6 the verb used was ἀποστέλλω. Πέμπειν is the most general word for 'send,' implying no special relation between sender and sent: ἀποστέλλειν adds the notion of a *delegated authority* constituting the person sent the envoy or representative of the sender (*vv.* 19, 24). Both verbs are used of the mission of Christ and of the mission of the disciples, as well as that of John. 'Αποστέλλειν is used of the mission of Christ, iii. 17, 34, v. 38, vi. 29, 57, vii. 29, viii. 42, x. 36, xi. 42, xvii. 3, 8, 18, 21, 23, 25; of the mission of the disciples, iv. 38, xvii. 18. Πέμπειν is used of the mission of Christ (always in the aorist participle) iv. 34, v. 23, 24, 30, 37, vi. 38, 39, 40, 44, vii. 16, 18, 28, 33, &c. &c.; of that of the disciples, xiii. 20, xx. 21. Πέμπειν is also used of the mission of the Spirit, xiv. 26, xvi. 7.

ἐκεῖνος. 'That one Himself and no other;' see on *vv.* 8, 18. **'Εφ' ὃν ἄν.** The widest possibility; 'whosoever he may be on whom.'

μένον. Another of S. John's favourite words, a fact which the A.V. obscures by translating it in *seven* different ways. 'Abide' is the most common and the best translation (*v.* 32, iii. 36, iv. 40): besides this we have 'remain' (here, ix. 41, xv. 11, 16), 'dwell' (i. 39, vi. 56, xiv. 10, 17) 'continue' (ii. 12, viii. 31), 'tarry' (iv. 40, xxi. 22, 23), 'endure' (vi. 27), 'be present' (xiv. 25). In *v.* 39, iv. 40, 1 John iii. 24, it is translated in two different ways; in 1 John ii. 24 in three different ways.—The Baptist and the Prophets were moved by the Spirit at times; 'the Spirit of the Lord *came* upon' them from time to time. With Jesus he abode continually.

ὁ βαπτ. ἐν πν. ἁγ. This phrase introduced without explanation assumes that the readers are well aware of this office of the Messiah, i.e. are well-instructed Christians. *Βαπτίζων* is appropriate, (1) to mark the analogy and contrast between the office of the Baptist and that of the Messiah; the one by baptism with water awakens the longing for holiness; the other by baptism with the Spirit satisfies this longing: (2) because the gift of the Spirit is an *out-pouring*.

ἐν πνεύματι ἁγίῳ. The epithet *ἅγιον* is given to the Spirit thrice in this Gospel; here, xiv. 26, and xx. 22 (in vii. 39 the *ἅγιον* is very doubtful). It is not frequent in any Gospel but the third; 5 times in S. Matthew, 4 in S. Mark, 12 in S. Luke. S. Luke rarely omits the epithet, which he uses about 40 times in the Acts. Here and xx. 22 neither substantive nor epithet has the article, in xiv. 26 both have it.

34. ἑώρακα. I have seen, in joyous contrast to 'I knew Him not,' *vv.* 31, 33. See on *v.* 18. The perfects indicate that the results of the seeing and of the testimony remain: comp. *v.* 52, iii. 21, 26, 29.

μεμαρτύρηκα. have borne witness. Our translators have obscured S. John's frequent use of *μαρτυρεῖν*, as of *μένειν*, by capriciously varying the rendering. This is all the more regrettable, because these words serve to connect together the Gospel, the First Epistle, and the Apocalypse. *Μαρτυρεῖν* is translated 'bear witness,' i. 7, 18, 15, iii. 26, 28, v. 31, 32, 33, 36, 37, viii. 18, x. 25, xv. 27, xviii. 23; 1 John i. 2, v. 6; 'bear record,' i. 32, 34, viii. 13, 14, xii. 17, xix. 35; 1 John v. 7; Rev. i. 2; 'give record,' 1 John v. 10; 'testify,' ii. 25, iii. 11, 32, iv. 39, 44, v. 39, vii. 7, xiii. 21, xv. 26, xxi. 24; 1 John iv. 14, v. 9; Rev. xxii. 16, 18, 20: in xv. 26, 27 the translation is changed in the same sentence. *Μαρτυρία* is rendered 'witness,' i. 7, iii. 11, v. 31, 32, 33, 36; 1 John v. 9, 10; Rev. xx. 4; 'record,' i. 19, viii. 13, 14, xix. 35, xxi. 24; 1 John v. 10, 11; 'testimony,' iii. 32, 33, v. 34, viii. 17; Rev. i. 2, 9, vi. 9, xi. 7, xii. 11, 17, xix. 10: in 1 John v. 10 we have two different renderings in the same verse. Neither *μαρτύριον* nor *μάρτυς*, found in all three Synoptists, occurs in this Gospel.

ὁ υἱὸς τοῦ θεοῦ. The incarnate *Λόγος*, the Messiah (*v.* 18). These words of the Baptist confirm the account of the voice from heaven (Matt. iii. 17). The whole passage (*vv.* 32—34) shews that S. John does not, as Philo does, identify the Logos with the Spirit.

35—37. The Testimony of the Baptist to Andrew and John

35. τῇ ἐπ. π. *The next day* **again**; referring to *v.* 29. Thus far we have three days, full of moment to the Evangelist and the Church. On the first the Messiah is proclaimed as already present; on the second He is pointed out; on the third He is followed. In each case the Baptist takes the lead; it is by his own act and will that he decreases while Jesus increases.

The difference between this narrative and that of the Synoptists (Matt. iv. 18; Mark i. 16; Luke v. 2) is satisfactorily explained by supposing this to refer to an earlier and less formal call of these first four disciples, John and Andrew, Peter and James. Their call to be Apostles was a very gradual one. Two of them, and perhaps all four, began by being disciples of the Baptist, who directs them to the Lamb of God (*v.* 36), Who invites them to His abode (*v.* 39): they then witness His miracles (ii. 2, &c.); are next called to be 'fishers of men' (Matt. iv. 19); and are finally enrolled with the rest of the Twelve as Apostles (Mark iii. 13). Their readiness to follow Jesus, as recorded by the Synoptists, implies previous acquaintance with Him, as recorded by S. John. See note on Mark i. 20.

ἐκ τῶν μαθ. αὐτοῦ δύο. One of these was Andrew (*v.* 40); the other was no doubt S. John. The account is that of an eyewitness; and his habitual reserve with regard to himself accounts for his silence, if the other disciple *was* himself. If it was someone else, it is difficult to see why S. John pointedly omits his name.

There was strong antecedent probability that the first followers of Christ would be disciples of the Baptist. The fact of their being so is one reason for the high honour in which the Baptist has been held from the earliest times by the Church.

36. **ἐμβλέψας.** Indicates a fixed, penetrating gaze. Comp. *v.* 42; Mark x. 21, 27; Luke xx. 17, xxii. 61.

ἴδε κ.τ.λ. See on *v.* 28. These disciples were probably present the previous day. Hence there is no need to say more. This is the last recorded meeting between the Baptist and the Christ.

37. **ἤκουσαν.** Although they had not been specially addressed.

ἠκολούθησαν. The first beginning of the Christian Church. But we are not to understand that they had already determined to become His disciples.

38—52. The Testimony of Disciples

This section falls into two divisions, each occupying a day; (1) the call of Andrew, John, Peter, and perhaps James; (2) that of Philip and Nathanael. Of these Peter and James were probably disciples of John. In this also he was the Elijah who was to come first.

38—42. Andrew, John and Peter

38. **θεασάμενος.** Comp. *vv.* 14 and 32. The context shews that He saw into their hearts as well.

39. **Τί ζητεῖτε;** i.e. in Me. He does not ask '*Whom* seek ye?' It was evident that they sought Him.

'Ραββί. A comparatively modern word when S. John wrote, and therefore all the more requiring explanation to Gentile readers. The 'i' termination in Rabbi and Rabboni (xx. 16) = 'my,' but had probably lost its special meaning; comp. '*Mon*sieur.' S. John does not translate '*my* Master.' S. John often interprets between Hebrew and Greek; thrice in this section. (Comp. *vv.* 42, 43.)

ποῦ μένεις; *Where* abidest *thou?* (See on *v.* 33.) They have more to ask than can be answered on the spot. Perhaps they think Him a travelling Rabbi staying close by; and they intend to visit Him at some future time. He bids them come at once: *now* is the day of salvation. In the A.V. *v.* 38 contains *vv.* 38 and 39 of the Greek.

40. ὄψεσθε. The reading *ἴδετε* perhaps comes from *v.* 47.

ἐκείνην. That memorable day.

ὥρα ἦν ὡς δεκάτη. S. John remembers the very hour of this crisis in his life: all the details of the narrative are very lifelike.

It is sometimes contended that S. John reckons the hours of the day according to the modern method, from midnight to midnight, and not according to the *Jewish* method, from sunset to sunset, as everywhere else in N.T. and in Josephus. It is antecedently improbable that S. John should in this point vary from the rest of N.T. writers; and we ought to require strong evidence before accepting this theory, which has been adopted by some in order to escape from the difficulty of xix. 14, where see notes. Setting aside xix. 14 as the cause of the question, we have four passages in which S. John mentions the hour of the day, this, iv. 6, 52 and xi. 9. None of them are decisive: but in no single case is the balance of probability strongly in favour of the modern method. See notes in each place. Here either 10 A.M. or 4 P.M. would suit the context: and while the antecedent probability that S. John reckons time like the rest of the Evangelists will incline us to 4 P.M., the fact that a good deal still remains to be done on this day makes 10 A.M. rather more suitable; and in that case 'abode with him that day' is more natural. Origen knows nothing of S. John's using the modern method of reckoning.

41. ὁ ἀδελφὸς Σ. Π. Before the end of the first century, therefore, it was natural to describe Andrew by his relationship to his far better known brother. In Church History Peter is everything and Andrew nothing: but would there have been an Apostle Peter but for Andrew? In the lists of the Apostles Andrew is always in the first group of four, but outside the chosen three, in spite of this early call.

42. οὗτος. Comp. *vv.* 2, 7, iii. 2, 26.

πρῶτον. The meaning of 'first' becomes almost certain when we remember S. John's characteristic reserve about himself. Both disciples hurry to tell their own brothers the good tidings, that the Messiah has been found: Andrew finds *his own* brother *first*, and afterwards John finds *his*: but we are left to infer the latter point.

Andrew thrice brings others to Christ; Peter, the lad with the loaves (vi. 8), and certain Greeks (xii. 22); and, excepting Mark xiii. 3, we know scarcely anything else about him. Thus it would seem as if in these three incidents S. John had given us the key to his character. And here we have another characteristic of this Gospel—the lifelike way in which the less prominent figures are sketched. Besides Andrew we have Philip, i. 44, vi. 5, xii. 21, xiv. 8; Thomas, xi. 16, xiv. 5; xx. 24—29; Nathanael, i. 45—52; Nicodemus, iii. 1—12, vii. 50—52, xix. 39; Martha and Mary, xi., xii. 1—3.

Εὑρήκαμεν. Does not prove that S. John is still with him, only that they were together when their common desire was fulfilled.

τὸν Μεσσίαν. The Hebrew form of this name is used by S. John only, here and iv. 25. Elsewhere the LXX. translation, *ὁ χριστός*, is used; but here *χριστός* has no article, because S. John is merely interpreting the word, not the title. Comp. iii. 28, iv. 25, 29, vii. 26, 31, 41, x. 24, xi. 27, xii. 34, xx. 31.

43. ἐμβλέψας. Comp. *v.* 36 and Luke xxii. 61: what follows shews that Christ's look penetrated to his heart and read his character.

Ἰωάννου. This, and not Ἰωνᾶ, seems to be the true reading here and xxi. 15, 16, 17: but Ἰωνᾶ might represent two Hebrew names, Jonah and Johanan=John. Tradition gives his mother's name as Johanna. Andrew probably had mentioned his name and parentage.

Κηφᾶς. This Aramaic form occurs elsewhere in N.T. only 1 Cor. i. 12, iii. 22, ix. 5, xv. 5; Gal. i. 18, ii. 9, 11, 14. The second Adam, like (Gen. ii. 19) the first, gives names to those brought to Him. The new name, as in the case of Abraham, Sarah, and Israel, indicates his new position rather than his *character*; for he was 'unstable as water' (xviii. 25; Gal. ii. 11, 12): Simon is designated for a new office. Matt. xvi. 18 presupposes the incident recorded here: here Simon *shall be called*, there he *is*, Peter.

Πέτρος. Translate, **Peter**, with 'a stone,' or 'a mass of rock,' in the margin.—It is quite clear from this narrative that S. Peter was not called first among the Apostles.

44—52. PHILIP AND NATHANAEL

44. τῇ ἐπαύριον. We thus far have four days accurately marked; (1) *v.* 19; (2) *v.* 29; (3) *v.* 35; (4) *v.* 44. A writer of fiction would not have cared for minute details which might entangle him in discrepancies: they are thoroughly natural in an eyewitness profoundly interested in the events, and therefore remembering them distinctly.

ἠθέλησεν. **Willed** or **was minded** *to go forth:* the 'would' of A.V. is too weak (comp. vi. 67, viii. 44). Jesus determined to go from Judaea to Galilee: on His way He finds Philip (see on ix. 35).

ἀκολούθει μοι. In the Gospels these words seem always to be the call to become a disciple: Matt. viii. 22, ix. 9, xix. 21; Mark ii. 14, x. 21; Luke v. 27, ix. 59; John xxi. 19. With two exceptions they are always addressed to those who afterwards became Apostles.

45. ἀπὸ Βηθ. For the change of preposition see on xi. 1. The local knowledge displayed in this verse is very real. S. John would possess it; a writer in the second century would not, and would not care to invent. This is 'Bethsaida of Galilee' (xii. 21) on the western shore, not Bethsaida Julias (see on Matt. iv. 13). In the Synoptists Philip is a mere name: our knowledge of him comes from S. John (see on *v.* 42, vi. 7, xii. 21, xiv. 8).

46. εὑρίσκει Φ. Thus the spiritual *λαμπαδηφορία* proceeds: the receivers of the sacred light hand it on to others, *Et quasi cursores vitai lampada tradunt* (Lucr. ii. 77).

Ναθαναήλ = 'Gift of God.' The name occurs Num. i. 8; 1 Chron. ii. 14; 1 Esdras i. 9, ix. 22. Nathanael is commonly identified with Bartholomew; (1) Bartholomew is only a patronymic and the bearer would be likely to have another name (comp. Barjona of Simon, Barnabas of Joses); (2) S. John never mentions Bartholomew, the Synoptists never mention Nathanael; (3) the Synoptists in their lists place Bartholomew next to Philip, as James next his probable caller John, and Peter (in Matt. and Luke) next his caller Andrew; (4) all the other disciples mentioned in this chapter become Apostles, and none are so highly commended as Nathanael; (5) all Nathanael's companions named in xxi. 2 were Apostles (see note there). But all these reasons do not make the identification more than probable. The framers of our Liturgy do not countenance the identification: this passage appears neither as the Gospel nor as a Lesson for S. Bartholomew's Day.

ὃν ἔγραψεν M. κ.τ.λ. Luthardt contrasts this elaborate profession with the simple declaration of Andrew (*v.* 42). The divisions of the O.T. here given are quite in harmony with Jewish phraseology. Moses wrote of Him not merely in Deut. xviii. 15, but in all the various Messianic types and promises.

τοῦ Ἰωσὴφ τ. ἀπὸ N. The words are Philip's, and express the common contemporary belief about Jesus. As His home was there, *τὸν ἀπὸ Ναζαρέτ* was both natural and true: and *τοῦ Ἰωσὴφ* was natural enough, if untrue. That the Evangelist is ignorant of the birth at Bethlehem, or of its miraculous character, in no way follows from this passage. Rather he is an honest historian, who records exactly what was said, without alterations or additions of his own. "Here we observe for the first time a peculiarity in the narrative of S. John. It seems that the author takes pleasure in recalling certain objections to the Messianic dignity of Jesus, leaving them without reply, because every one acquainted with the Gospel history made short work of them at once; comp. vii. 27, 35, 42, &c." (Godet.)

47. ἐκ Ναζ. κ.τ.λ. All Galileans were despised for their want of culture, their rude dialect, and contact with Gentiles. They were to the Jews what Bœotians were to the Athenians. But here it is a Galilean who reproaches Nazareth in particular. Apart from the Gospels we know nothing to the discredit of Nazareth; neither in O.T. nor in Josephus is it mentioned; but what we are told of the people by the Evangelists is mostly bad. Christ left them and preferred to dwell at Capernaum (Matt. iv. 13); He could do very little among them, 'because of their unbelief' (xiii. 58), which was such as to make Him marvel (Mark vi. 6); and once they tried to kill Him (Luke iv. 29). S. Augustine would omit the question. Nathanael "who knew the Scriptures excellently well, when he heard the name Nazareth, was filled with hope, and said, From Nazareth something good can come." But this is not probable. Possibly he meant 'Can any good thing come out of despised Galilee?' or, 'Can anything so good come out of so insignificant a village?'

ἔρχου κ. ἴδε. The best cure for ill-founded prejudice; at once the simplest and the surest method. Philip shews the strength of his own conviction by suggesting this test, which seems to be in harmony with the practical bent of his own mind. See on xii. 21 and xiv. 8. Here, of course, *ἴδε* is the imperative; not an interjection, as in *vv.* 29, 35, 48.

48. εἶδεν...ἐρχόμενον. This shews that Jesus did not overhear Nathanael's question. S. John represents his knowledge of Nathanael as miraculous: as in *v.* 42 He appears as the searcher of hearts.

ἀληθῶς. In character as well as by birth. The guile may refer to the 'subtilty' of Jacob (Gen. xxvii. 35) before he became Israel: 'Lo a son of Israel, who is in no way a son of Jacob.' The 'supplanter' is gone; the 'prince' remains. His guilelessness is shewn in his making no mock repudiation of Christ's praise: he is free from 'the pride that apes humility.' It is shewn also in the manner of his conversion. Like a true Israelite he longs for the coming of the Messiah, but he will not too lightly believe in the joy that has come, nor does he conceal his doubts. But as soon as he has 'come and seen,' he knows, and knows that he is known: thus 'I know Mine and Mine know Me' (x. 14) is fulfilled beforehand.

S. John uses *ἀληθῶς* about 8 times, and in the rest of N.T. it occurs about 8 times (see on *v.* 8).

49. ὑπὸ τὴν συκῆν. Note the case, implying *motion to* under, and comp. *vv.* 18, 32, 33. The phrase probably means 'at home,' in the retirement of his own garden (1 Kings iv. 25; Mic. iv. 4; Zech. iii. 10). He had perhaps been praying or meditating, and seems to feel that Christ knew what his thoughts there had been. It was under a fig tree that S. Augustine heard the famous '*tolle, lege.*'

50. ὁ υἱὸς τ. θ. Experience of His miraculous knowledge convinces Nathanael, as it convinces the Samaritan woman (iv. 29) and S. Thomas (xx. 28), that Jesus must stand in the closest relation to God: hence he uses this title of the Messiah (xi. 27; Matt. xxvi. 63; Mark iii. 11, v. 7; Luke iv. 41) rather than the more common 'Son of David.'

βασ. εἶ τ. Ἰσρ. No article. The title is not synonymous with 'the Son of God,' though both apply to the same person, and it points to hopes of an earthly king, which since the destruction of Jerusalem even Jews must have ceased to cherish. How could a Christian of the second century have thrown himself back to this?

51. πιστεύεις. As in xvi. 31, xx. 29, the sentence is half a question, half an exclamation. He, who marvelled at the unbelief of the people of Nazareth, expresses joyous surprise at the ready belief of the guileless Israelite of Cana.

52. Ἀμὴν, ἀμὴν. The double *ἀμήν* occurs 25 times in this Gospel, and nowhere else, always in the mouth of Christ. It introduces a truth of special solemnity and importance. The single *ἀμήν* occurs about 30 times in Matt., 14 in Mark, and 7 in Luke. Hence the title of Jesus, 'the Amen' (Rev. iii. 14). The word is originally a verbal adjective, 'firm, worthy of credit,' sometimes used as a substantive; e.g. 'God of truth' (Is. lxv. 16) is literally 'God of (the) Amen.' In the LXX. *ἀμήν* never means 'verily;' in the Gospels it always does. The *ἀμήν* at the end of sentences (xxi. 25; Matt. vi. 13, xxviii. 20; Mark xvi. 20; Luke xxiv. 53) is in every case of doubtful authority.

ὑμῖν. Nathanael alone had been first addressed; now all present.

τ. οὐρ. ἀνεῳγότα. *The heaven* **opened**; made open and remaining so. What Jacob saw in a vision they shall see realised. The Incarnation brings heaven down to earth; the Ascension takes earth up to heaven. These references to Jacob (*v.* 48) were possibly suggested by the locality: Bethel, Mahanaim, and the ford Jabbok, all lay near the road that Jesus would traverse between Judaea and Galilee.

τ. ἀγγέλους τ. θ. The reference is not to the angels which appeared after the Temptation, at the Agony, and at the Ascension; rather to the perpetual intercourse between God and the Messiah during His ministry, and afterwards between God and Christ's Body, the Church; those 'ministering spirits' who link earth to heaven.

ἀναβαίνοντας. Placed first: prayers and needs ascend; then graces and blessings descend. But see Winer, p. 692.

τ. υἱὸν τ. ἀνθρώπου. This phrase in all four Gospels is invariably used by Christ Himself of Himself as the Messiah; upwards of 80 times in all. None of the Evangelists direct our attention to this strict limitation in the use of the expression: their agreement on this striking point is evidently undesigned, and therefore a strong mark of their veracity. See notes on Matt. viii. 20; Mark ii. 10. In O.T. the phrase 'Son of Man' has three distinct uses; (1) in the Psalms, for the ideal man; viii. 4—8, lxxx. 17, cxliv. 3, cxlvi. 3: (2) in Ezekiel, as the name by which the Prophet is addressed by God; ii. 1, 3, 6, 8, iii. 1, 3, 4, &c., &c., more than 80 times in all; probably to remind Ezekiel that in spite of the favour shewn to him, and the wrath denounced against the children of Israel, he, no less than they, had a mortal frailty: (3) in the 'night visions' of Dan. vii. 13, 14, where 'One like a son of man came with the clouds of heaven, and came to the Ancient of Days...and there was given Him dominion, and glory, and a kingdom, that all people, nations, and languages should serve Him, &c.' That 'Son of man henceforth became one of the titles of the looked-for Messiah' may be doubted. Rather, the title was a *new* one assumed by Christ, and as yet only dimly understood (comp. Matt. xvi. 13). Just as 'the Son of David' marked Him as the one in whom the family of David culminated, so 'the Son of Man' as the one in whom the whole human race culminates.

This first chapter alone is enough to shew that the Gospel is the work of a Jew of Palestine, well acquainted with the Messianic hopes, and traditions, and with the phraseology current in Palestine at the time of Christ's ministry; able also to give a lifelike picture of the Baptist and of Christ's first disciples.

CHAPTER II

12. **Καφαρναούμ** (preferred by the best editors to *Καπερναούμ*).

17. **καταφάγεταί** (אABP) has been altered to *κατέφαγε* in order to bring the quotation into harmony with the LXX.

20. **τεσσεράκοντα.** This Ionic form of *τεσσαράκοντα* has good MS. authority here, Rev. xi. 2, xiii. 5, xiv. 1, xxi. 17. Winer, p. 46.

23. **ἐν τοῖς Ἱεροσολύμοις** for *ἐν Ἱερ.* S. John alone gives *Ἱεροσόλυμα* the article, here, v. 2, x. 22, xi. 18; contrast i. 19, iv. 20, 21, ii. 13, v. 1, xi. 55, xii. 12.

Chap. II. 1—11. The Testimony of the First Sign

Jesus is passing from the retirement in which He has lived so long into the publicity of His ministry. The scene which follows lies halfway between—in the family circle, where privacy and publicity meet. It is the same when He returns from temporary retirement in Peraea to the completion of His ministry before His Passion. The last miracle, like the first, is wrought in the circle of family life (xi. 3).

1. **τῇ τρίτῃ.** From the calling of Philip (i. 43), the last date mentioned, making a week in all; the first week, possibly in contrast to the last (xii. 1).

Κανᾷ τ. Γαλ. To distinguish it from Cana of Asher (Josh. xix. 28); an instance of the Evangelist's knowledge of Palestine. This Cana is not mentioned in O. T. It was the home of Nathanael (xxi. 2), which disproves the theory that Jesus and His mother had at one time lived at Cana, for in so small a place Jesus and Nathanael could not have been unknown to one another. Cana is now generally identified with Kánet el-Jelîl, about six miles N. of Nazareth, rather than with Kefr-Kenna.

ἦν. Imperf. in contrast to the aorist in *v.* 2. She was staying there; her Son was invited for the feast: she speaks to the servants as if she were quite at home in the house (*v.* 5). Joseph has disappeared: the inference (not quite certain) is that in the interval between Luke ii. 51 and this marriage—about 17 years—he had died. Mary does not appear again in this Gospel till the Crucifixion.

2. ἐκλήθη. Singular, as if the including of the disciples were an afterthought. There were now five or six; Andrew, John, Peter, Philip, Nathanael, and probably James.

δὲ καὶ ὁ Ἰ. *And Jesus* **also** (iii. 23, xviii. 2, 5, xix. 39).

3. ὑστ. οἴν. When wine failed. The arrival of these six or seven guests might cause the want, and certainly would make it more apparent. To Eastern hospitality such a failure on such an occasion would seem a disgraceful calamity. Whether the feast had already lasted several days (Gen. xxix. 27; Judg. xiv. 17; Tob. ix. 12, x. 1), we do not know.

οἶν. οὐκ ἔχ. Much comment has obscured a simple text. The family in which she was a guest were in a serious difficulty. Perhaps she felt partly responsible for the arrangements; certainly she would wish to help. What more natural than that she should turn to her Son, like the sisters at Bethany afterwards (xi. 3), and tell Him of the trouble? That she wished Him to break up the party, or begin a discourse to distract attention, is quite alien from the context. Whether she expected a miracle, is uncertain: but her appeal for help may well have been accompanied by the thought, that here was an opportunity for her mysterious Son, who had already been proclaimed by the Baptist, to manifest Himself as the Messiah. Elisha had used his powers to relieve ordinary needs; why not her Son?

4. τί ἐμοὶ κ. σοί, γύναι; S. John alone of all the Evangelists never gives the Virgin's name. Here, as so often, he assumes that his readers know the main points in the Gospel narrative: or it may be part of the reserve which he exhibits with regard to all that nearly concerns himself. Christ's Mother had become his mother (xix. 26, 27). He nowhere mentions his brother James.

Treatises have been written to shew that these words do not contain a rebuke; for if Christ here rebukes His Mother, it cannot be maintained that she is immaculate. 'Woman' of course implies no rebuke; the Greek might more fairly be rendered 'Lady' (comp. xix. 26). At the same time it marks a difference between the Divine Son and the earthly parent: He does not say, 'Mother.' The sword is beginning to pierce her heart, as the earthly ties between parent and child begin to be severed. The severance is taken a stage further, Matt. xii. 46—50, and completed on the Cross (xix. 26). But 'what have I to do with thee?' *does* imply rebuke, as is evident from the other passages where the phrase occurs, Judg. xi. 12; 1 Kings xvii. 18; 2 Kings iii. 13; Matt. viii. 29; Mark i. 24; Luke viii. 28. Only in one passage does the meaning seem to vary: in 2 Chron. xxxv. 21 the question seems to mean 'why need we quarrel?' rather than 'what have we in common?' But such a meaning, if possible there, would be quite inappropriate here. The further question has been asked,—what was she rebuked *for?* S. Chrysostom thinks for vanity; she wished to glorify herself through her Son. More probably for interference: He will help, and He will manifest Himself, but in His own way, and in His own time. Comp. Luke ii. 51.

ἡ ὥρα μου. The meaning of 'My hour' and 'His hour' in this Gospel depends in each case on the context. There cannot here be any reference to His death; rather it means His hour for 'manifesting forth His glory' (*v.* 11) as the Messiah by working miracles. The exact moment was still in the future. Comp. vii. 8, where He for the moment refuses what He soon after does; and xii. 23, xvii. 1, which confirm the meaning here given to 'hour.'

5. Between the lines of His refusal her faith reads a better answer to her appeal, and she is content to leave all to Him.

6. λιθ. ὑδρ. ἕξ. As an eyewitness S. John remembers their material, number, and size. The surroundings of the first miracle would not easily be forgotten. Vessels of stone were less liable to impurity: it is idle to seek for special meaning in the number six.

καθαρισμόν. Matt. xv. 2; Mark vii. 3 (see note); Luke xi. 39.

μετρητάς. A *μετρητής* = about nine gallons, so that 'firkin' is an almost exact equivalent. The six, holding from 18 to 27 gallons each, would together hold 106 to 162 gallons. 'Ανά is distributive; it cannot mean 'towards', 'about': Rev. iv. 8. Winer, p. 497.

7. γεμίσατε. What is the meaning of this command, if (as some contend) only the water drawn out was turned into wine? And why such care to state the large size of the vessels? These had been partly emptied by the ceremonial ablutions of the company. Note that in His miracles Christ *never creates;* He increases the quantity, or changes the quality of what already exists.

ἕως ἄνω. His Mother's words (*v.* 5) have done their work. Our attention seems again to be called to the great quantity of water changed into wine. "It is His first miraculous sign; and it must bear strong testimony to His riches, His munificence, and the joy which it gives Him to bestow relief or even gladness: it must become the type of the fulness of grace and joy which the only-begotten Son brings to the earth" (Godet).

8. ἀρχιτρ. Manager *of the feast* (*triclinium*) rather than *ruler:* but it is doubtful whether the head-waiter, who managed the feast and tasted the meat and drink, is meant, or the *rex convivii, arbiter bibendi,* the guest elected by the other guests to preside. The bad taste of his remark inclines one to the former alternative: Ecclus. xxxii. 1, 2 is in favour of the second. In any case the translation should be uniform in these two verses, not sometimes 'governor,' sometimes 'ruler.' The word occurs nowhere else in N. T. Ὑδρία and *ἀντλέω* are also peculiar to this Gospel, and occur again iv. 7, 15, 28.

9. τὸ ὑδ. οἶν. γεγ. *The water now become wine.* This seems to imply that *all* had become wine: there is nothing to distinguish what was now wine from what still remained water. It is idle to ask at what precise moment or in what precise way the water became wine: an instantaneous change seems to be implied. *Γεύεσθαι* c. acc. occurs Heb. vi. 5 and in LXX.: very rare in classical Greek.

10. μεθυσθῶσιν. *Have become drunk,* **are drunk.** The A. V. does not give the full coarseness of the man's joke, although in Matt. xxiv. 49; Acts ii. 15; 1 Cor. xi. 21; 1 Thess. v. 7; Rev. xvii. 2, 6, the same word is rightly translated. The Vulgate has *inebriati fuerint;* Tyndall and Cranmer have 'be dronke'; the error comes from the Geneva Bible. Of course the man does not mean that the guests are intoxicated; it is a jocular statement of his own experience at feasts.

ἕως ἄρτι. This was true in a sense of which he never dreamed. The True Bridegroom was there, and had indeed kept the best dispensation until the last. Ἄρτι occurs about 12 times in this Gospel, 7 in Matt., not at all in Mark or Luke. It expresses the present in relation to the past and the future, 'at this stage,' 'at this crisis,' whereas νῦν regards the present moment only, 'now' absolutely. Comp. v. 17, ix. 19, 25, xiii. 7, 19, 33, 37; xvi. 12, 31, &c.

11. ταύτην ἐπ. ἀρχ. τ. σ. This as a beginning of His signs did Jesus: it is the first miracle of all, not merely the first in Cana. This is quite conclusive against the miracles of Christ's childhood recorded in the Apocryphal Gospels and is evidence of the truthfulness of the writer. If he were inventing, would he not also place miracles throughout the whole of Christ's life? See on *v.* 23, iv. 48; σημεῖον should throughout the Gospel be rendered 'sign' not 'miracle.' Δυνάμεις, so frequent in the Synoptists for 'miracles,' is never used by S. John; τέρατα only once (iv. 48), and then in conjunction with σημεῖα, a word which he uses 17 times. Christ's miracles were 'signs' of His Divine mission: comp. Ex. iv. 8. They were evidence of a perfect humanity working in unison with a perfect Divinity. They were also symbolical of spiritual truths: see on ix. 39.

ἐν Κανᾷ τ. Γαλ. Thus S. John agrees with the Synoptists in representing the Messianic career as beginning in Galilee.

ἐφανέρωσεν. Another of S. John's favourite words (see on i. 31): the rendering should be kept uniform, especially here, vii. 4, xvii. 6, xxi. 1, where the active is used. In the other Gospels the word occurs only Mark iv. 22 [xvi. 12, 14], always in the passive.

τὴν δόξαν αὐτοῦ. This is the final cause of Christ's 'signs,' His own and His Father's glory (xi. 4), and these two are one. Herein lies the difference between His miracles and those wrought by Prophets and others: they never manifested their own glory, but that of Jehovah (Ex. xvi. 7).

ἐπιστ. εἰς αὐ. οἱ μαθ. αὐ. What a strange remark for a writer in the second century to make! His disciples believed on Him? Of course they did. Assume that a disciple himself is the writer, and all is explained: he well remembers how his own imperfect faith was confirmed by the miracle. A forger would rather have given us the effect on the guests. Three times in this chapter does S. John give us the disciples' point of view, here, *v.* 17 and *v.* 22; very natural in a disciple, not natural in a later writer. See on xi. 15, xxi. 12.

This verse gives us four facts respecting the sign; 1. it was the first; 2. it took place in Galilee; 3. its end was Christ's glory; 4. its immediate result was the confirmation of the disciples' faith.

Two objections have been made to this miracle (1) on rationalistic, (2) on 'Temperance' grounds. (1) It is said that it is a wasteful miracle, a parade of power, unworthy of a Divine Agent: a tenth of the quantity of wine would have been ample. But the surplus was not wasted any more than the twelve baskets of fragments (vi. 13); it would be a royal present to the bridal pair. (2) It is urged that Christ would not have supplied the means for gross excess; and to avoid this supposed difficulty it is suggested that the wine made was not intoxicating, i.e. was not wine at all. But in all His dealings with men God allows the possibility of a temptation to excess. All His gifts may be thus abused. The 5000 might have been gluttonous over the loaves and fishes.

Christ's honouring a marriage-feast with His first miracle gives His sanction (1) to marriage, (2) to times of festivity. And here we see the contrast between O. and N. T. The miracles of O. T. are mostly miracles of judgment. Those of N. T. are nearly all miracles of blessing. Moses turns water into blood: Jesus turns water into wine.

Four hundred years had elapsed since the Jews had seen a miracle. The era of Daniel was the last age of Jewish miracles. Since the three children walked in the burning fiery furnace, and Daniel had remained unhurt in the lions' den, and had read the handwriting on the wall, no miracle is recorded in the history of the Jews until Jesus made this beginning of His 'signs' at Cana of Galilee. No wonder that the almost simultaneous appearance of a Prophet like John and a Worker of miracles like Jesus attracted the attention of all classes.

On the symbolical meaning of this first sign see Introduction, chap. v. § 3.

12. This verse alone is almost enough to disprove the theory that the Gospel is a fiction written with a dogmatic object: "why should the author carry his readers thus to Capernaum—for nothing?" If S. John wrote it, all is natural. He records this visit because it took place, and because he well remembers those 'not many days.'

κατέβη. *Down* from the plateau on which Cana and Nazareth stand to the shore of the lake. Capernaum, or Caphar-nahum, the modern Tell-Hûm, was the chief Jewish town, as Tiberias was the chief Roman town, of one of the most busy and populous districts of Palestine: it was therefore a good centre. For **μ. τοῦτο** see on iii. 22.

ἡ μήτ. αὐ. κ. οἱ ἀδ. αὐ.] Natural ties still hold Him; in the next verse they disappear. On the vexed question of the 'brethren of the Lord' see the *Introduction* to the *Epistle of S. James*. It is impossible to determine with certainty whether they are (1) the children of Joseph and Mary, born after the birth of Jesus; (2) the children of Joseph by a former marriage, whether levirate or not; or (3) adopted children. There is nothing in Scripture to warn us against (1), the most natural view antecedently; but it has against it the general consensus of the Fathers, and the prevailing tradition of the perpetual virginity of S. Mary. Jerome's theory, that they were our Lord's cousins, sons of Alphaeus, is the one commonly adopted, but vii. 5 (see note) is fatal to it, and it labours under other difficulties as well.

The fact of His brethren being with Him makes it probable that He returned to Nazareth from Cana before coming down to Capernaum.

οὐ πολλὰς ἡμ. Because the Passover was at hand, and He must be about His Father's business. S. John here corrects the impression, easily derived from S. Matt. (iv. 13, ix. 1), that when Christ moved from Nazareth to Capernaum, the latter at once became His usual abode, 'His own city.'

II. 13—XI. 57. The Work

We enter now on the second and principal portion of the first main division of the Gospel, thus subdivided:—The Work 1. among *Jews* (ii. 13—iii. 36); 2. among *Samaritans* (iv. 1—42); 3. among *Galileans* (iv. 42—54); 4. among *mixed multitudes, chiefly Jews* (v.—ix.). In this last subdivision the Work becomes a conflict between Jesus and 'the Jews.'

II. 13—III. 36. The Work among Jews

13. τὸ πάσχα τ. Ἰ. *The passover* **of the Jews.** Perhaps an indication that this Gospel was written after a Passover *of the Christians* had come into recognition. Passovers were active times in Christ's ministry; and this is the first of them. It was possibly the nearness of the Passover which caused this traffic in the Temple Court. It existed for the convenience of strangers. Certainly the nearness of the Feast would add significance to Christ's action. While the Jews were purifying themselves for the Passover He purified the Temple. S. John groups his narrative round the Jewish festivals: we have (1) Passover; (2) Purim (?), v. 1; (3) Passover, vi. 4; (4) Tabernacles, vii. 2; (5) Dedication, x. 22; (6) Passover, xi. 55.

ἀνέβη. *Up* to the capital. The public ministry of the Messiah opens, as we should expect, in Jerusalem and in the Temple. The place is as appropriate as the time.

14—22. The First Cleansing of the Temple

14. ἐν τῷ ἱερῷ. In the sacred enclosure, viz. the Court of the Gentiles, sometimes called 'the mountain of the house;' whereas *ἐν τῷ ναῷ* (see on *v.* 19) would mean in the sanctuary, in the Temple proper: the traffic would be great on the eve of the Passover. The account is very graphic, as of an eyewitness; note especially *καθημένους*; the money-changers would sit, the others would stand. The animals mentioned are those most often wanted for sacrifice.

τ. κερματιστὰς. From *κέρμα* (*κείρω*) = 'anything cut up, small change:' *the dealers in small change.* The article implies that they were habitually there. Comp. Zech. xiv. 21, where for 'Canaanite' we should perhaps read 'trafficker' or 'merchant.'

15. **ποιήσας φρ.** Peculiar to this account: there is no such incident in the cleansing recorded by the Synoptists. The scourge was probably not used; to raise it would be enough. **Σχοινίων** are literally *twisted rushes*.

τά τε πρόβ. κ.τ.β. **Both** *the sheep and the oxen*, explanatory of *πάντας*, which does not refer to the sellers and exchangers, who probably fled at once: comp. Matt. xxii. 10. The order is natural; first the driving out the cattle, then the pouring out the money and overturning the tables.

κολλυβιστῶν. From *κόλλυβος*=' rate of exchange' (Cic. *Verr.* II. iii. 78; *Att.* XII. vi. 1); this was very high, 10 or 12 per cent. Payments to the Temple were always made in Jewish coin, to avoid profanation by money stamped with idolatrous symbols.

16. **εἶπεν.** The doves could not be driven out, and to let them fly might have caused unseemly and prolonged commotion: He calls to the owners to take the cages away. Throughout He guides His indignation, not it Him. 'The wrath of the Lamb' is mercy here and justice hereafter, never indiscriminating passion.

μὴ ποιεῖτε. Addressed to all, not merely to the dove-sellers.

τ. οἶκ. τοῦ πατρός μου. 'Admiranda auctoritas' (Bengel). A distinct claim to Messiahship: it reminds us of *ἐν τοῖς τοῦ πατρός μου* (Luke ii. 49) spoken in the same place some 17 years before. Possibly some who heard the Child's claim heard the Man's claim also.

οἶκον ἐμπορίου. *A house of* **traffic.** Two years later things seem to have become worse instead of better; the Temple has then become 'a den of robbers, a bandits' cave.' See on Matt. xxi. 13 and Mark xi. 17. He meets with no resistance. As in Gethsemane (xviii. 6) the majesty of His appearance prevails. But His success produces opposite results: those who sympathize are confirmed in faith, those who do not take offence. Later on the Evangelist almost invariably points out this double effect of Christ's teaching.

17. **ἐμνήσθ.** Then and there; contrast *v.* 22. Who could know this but a disciple who was present? Who would think of inventing it? See on *v.* 11.

γεγραμμ. ἐστίν. In quotations S. John almost always uses the perf. part. with the auxiliary (vi. 31, 45, x. 34, xii. 14, [xix. 19]), whereas the Synoptists commonly use the perf. pass.

καταφάγεται. **Will devour,** or **consume me,** i.e. wear me out (Ps. lxix. 9). Excepting the 22nd, no psalm is so often alluded to in N.T. as the 69th; comp. xv. 25, xix. 28; Acts i. 20; Rom. xv. 3, xi. 9, 10. There is no thought of Christ's zeal proving fatal to Him; of that the disciples as yet knew nothing. Nor are we to understand that it was as a 'Zealot,' one who like Phinehas (Num. xxv.) took the execution of God's law into his own hands, that Christ acted on this occasion. If this were so, why did He not do this long before? Rather, He acts as the Messiah, as the Son in His Father's house:

therefore He waits till His hour has come, till His Messianic career has commenced. Just at the time when every Jew was purifying himself for the Feast, the Lord has suddenly come to His Temple to purify the sons of Levi (Mal. iii. 1—3).

It is difficult to believe that this cleansing of the Temple is identical with the one placed by the Synoptists at the *last* Passover in Christ's ministry; difficult also to see what is gained by the identification. If they are the same event, either S. John or the Synoptists have made a gross blunder in chronology. Could S. John, who was with our Lord at both Passovers, make such a mistake? Could S. Matthew, who was with Him at the last Passover, transfer to it an event which took place at the first Passover, a year before his conversion? When we consider the immense differences which distinguish the last Passover from the first in Christ's ministry, it seems incredible that anyone who had contemporary evidence could through any lapse of memory transfer a very remarkable incident indeed from one to the other. On the other hand the difficulty of believing that the Temple was twice cleansed is very slight. Was Christ's preaching so universally successful that one cleansing would be certain to suffice? He was not present at the next Passover (vi. 4), and the evil would have a chance of returning. And if two years later He found that the evil had returned, would He not be certain to drive it out once more? Differences in the details of the narratives corroborate this view.

18. οἱ Ἰουδαῖοι. See on i. 19. On ἀπεκρίθησαν see on x. 32.

Τί σημεῖον. We have a similar question Matt. xxi. 23, but the widely different answer shews that the occasion is different. Such demands, thoroughly characteristic of the Pharisaic spirit (1 Cor. i. 22), would be often made. The Jews failed to see that Christ's words and works were their own credentials. For ὅτι see Winer, p. 557.

19. λύσατε τ. ναὸν τ. The reply is "sudden as a flash of lightning;" (comp. [viii. 7]) and it leaves a lasting impression on all (Matt. xxvi. 61, xxvii. 40): but what it revealed was not comprehended until a fuller and more lasting light revealed it again. It is S. Matthew (xxvi. 61) and S. Mark (xiv. 58) who tell us that this saying was twisted into a charge against Christ, but they do not record the saying. S. John, who records the saying, does not mention the charge. Such coincidence can scarcely be designed, and therefore is evidence of the truth of both statements. See on xviii. 11, xii. 8. Note that in these three verses ναός is used, not ἱερόν; the latter is never used figuratively: *Destroy this* **sanctuary** (see on *v.* 14).

ἐγερῶ. His accusers turn this into 'build' (οἰκοδομῆσαι), which is not appropriate to raising a dead body. There is no contradiction between Christ's declaration and the ordinary N.T. theology, that the Son was raised by the Father. The expression is figurative throughout; and 'I and My Father are one.' Comp. x. 18. This throwing out seeds of thought for the future, which could not bear fruit at the time, is one of the characteristics of Christ's teaching.

20. τεσσ. κ. ἓξ ἔτεσιν. For the dative comp. xiv. 9. This was the third Temple. Solomon's Temple was destroyed by Nebuchadnezzar. Zerubbabel's was rebuilt by Herod the Great. "The building of the Temple, we are told by Josephus (*Ant.* xv. xi. 1), was begun in the 18th year of Herod the Great, 734—735 A.U.C. Reckoning 46 years from this point, we are brought to 781 or 782 A.U.C. = 28 or 29 A.D. Comparing this with the data given in Luke iii. 1, the question arises, whether we are to reckon the 15th year of Tiberius from his joint reign with Augustus, which began A.D. 12; or from his sole reign after the death of Augustus, A.D. 14. This would give us A.D. 27 or 29 for the first public appearance of the Baptist, and at the earliest A.D. 28 or 30 for the Passover mentioned in this chapter." So that there seems to be exact agreement between this date and that of S. Luke, if we count S. Luke's 15 years from the *joint* reign of Tiberius. It is incredible that this can have been planned; it involves intricate calculation, and even with the aid of Josephus absolute certainty cannot be obtained. "By what conceivable process could a Greek in the second century have come to hit upon this roundabout expedient for giving a fictitious date to his invention?" (Sanday).

For other instances of misunderstanding of Christ's words comp. iii. 4, 9, iv. 11, 15, 33, vi. 34, 52, vii. 35, viii. 22, 33, 52, xi. 12, xiv. 5.

21. ἔλεγεν. Was speaking. Even if inspiration be set aside, S. John's explanation must be admitted as the true one. What better interpreter of the mind of Jesus can be found than 'the disciple whom Jesus loved'? And he gives the interpretation not as his only, but as that of the disciples generally. Moreover, it explains the 'three days,' which interpretations about destroying the old Temple-religion and raising up a new spiritual theocracy do not. Ναός is also used of Christians, the *spiritual* Body of Christ, 1 Cor. iii. 16, 17, vi. 19; 2 Cor. vi. 16. For the genitive of apposition see Winer, p. 666.

22. Trusting Belief

ἠγέρθη. *Was* **raised.** Comp. xxi. 14; Acts iii. 15, iv. 10, v. 30. They recollected it when the event which explained it took place; meanwhile what had not been understood had been forgotten. Would any but a disciple give these details about the disciples' thoughts? See on *v.* 11.

τῇ γραφῇ. Not *εἰς τὴν γραφήν*: they believed what the Scripture (Ps. xvi. 10) said. See on i. 12. Ἡ *γραφή* commonly means a particular passage (vii. 38, 42, x. 35, xiii. 18, xix. 24, 28, 36, 37; Mark xii. 10; Luke iv. 21; Acts viii. 32, 35), whereas *αἱ γραφαί* means Scripture generally (v. 39; Matt. xxi. 42, xxii. 29, xxvi. 54, 56; Mark xii. 24, &c.) Of course only the O.T. can be meant.

εἶπεν. Spake, on this occasion.

23—25. Belief without Trust

23. Note the different force of *ἐν* and the exactness of detail: **in** *Jerusalem*, **at** *the Passover*, **during** *the Feast.*

εἰς τὸ ὄνομα. See on i. 12. **θεωροῦντες.** See on vi. 2.

τὰ σημεῖα. None of these 'signs' are recorded; comp. iv. 45, vii. 31, xi. 47, xii. 35, xx. 30, xxi. 25; Mark i. 34, vi. 55, 56. The number of miracles wrought by Jesus during His public life was so great (ἐποίει = was habitually doing), that a writer inventing a Gospel would almost inevitably place them throughout His whole life. That the Evangelists rigidly confine them to the last few years, greatly adds to our confidence in their accuracy. But the faith which was born of wonder would be likely to cease when the wonder ceased, as here: comp. Simon Magus (Acts viii. 13).

24. **ἐπίστευεν.** Antithesis to ἐπιστ. εἰς τ. ὄν αὐτ.—'Many *trusted* in His name, but Jesus did not *trust* Himself to them.'

διὰ τὸ αὐτ. γιν. **For that He of Himself** *knew*. Observe the difference between διὰ τὸ (*for that*), ὅτι (*because*), and γάρ (*for*).

25. **ἵνα τις μαρτ.** See on i. 7, 8: *that any should* **bear witness concerning** *man*; comp. xvi. 30. The article with ἀνθρώπου is generic.

αὐτὸς γὰρ ἐγ. *For He* **of Himself** *knew*: note the repetition of αὐτός in *vv.* 23, 24. We have instances of this supernatural knowledge in the cases of Peter (i. 42), Nathanael (i. 47, 48), Nicodemus (iii. 3), the Samaritan woman (iv. 29), the disciples (vi. 61, 64), Judas (vi. 70, xiii. 11), Peter (xiii. 38, xxi. 17), Thomas (xx. 27). It is remarkable that the word here used for this supernatural knowledge is γινώσκειν, 'to come to know, perceive,' rather than εἰδέναι, 'to know' absolutely (comp. v. 42, x. 14, 15, 27, xvii. 25). This tends to shew that Christ's supernatural knowledge was in some degree analogous to ours. Both verbs are used, 1. in reference to facts, knowledge of which Christ might have obtained in the ordinary manner (γινώσκειν, iv. 1, v. 6, vi. 15; εἰδέναι, vi. 61); 2. in reference to facts, knowledge of which must have been supernatural (γινώσκειν ii. 24, 25, x. 14, 27; εἰδέναι, vi. 64, xiii. 1, 11, xviii. 4); 3. in reference to divine things transcending human experience (γινώσκειν, xvii. 25; εἰδέναι, iii. 11, v. 32, vii. 29, viii. 14, 55, xi. 42, xii. 50, xiii. 3, xix. 28). These references shew that the distinction, though not quite absolute, is very marked between knowledge which in some sense can be regarded as *acquired* (γινώσκειν) and that which is simply regarded as *possessed*.

CHAPTER III

2. **πρὸς αὐτόν** for πρ. τὸν Ἰησοῦν (a correction for clearness at the beginning of a lection: comp. iv. 16, 46, vi. 14, viii. 21, xi. 45).

15. **ἐν αὐτῷ** for εἰς αὐτόν (a correction to S. John's usual construction): μὴ ἀπόληται ἀλλ' before ἔχῃ is an insertion (A) from *v.* 16; ℵBL omit.

25. **μετὰ Ἰουδαίου** for μ. Ἰουδαίων.

34. Omit ὁ θεός (gloss) after **δίδωσιν**, with ℵBC¹L against AC²D.

CHAP. III. 1—21. THE DISCOURSE WITH NICODEMUS

This is the first of the discourses of our Lord which form the main portion, and are among the great characteristics, of this Gospel. They have been used as a powerful argument against its authenticity; (1) because they are unlike the discourses in the Synoptic Gospels, (2) because they are suspiciously like the First Epistle of S. John, which all admit was written by the author of the Fourth Gospel, (3) because this likeness to the First Epistle pervades not only the discourses of our Lord, but those of the Baptist also, as well as the writer's own reflections throughout the Gospel. The inference is that they are, as much as the speeches in Thucydides, if not as much as those in Livy, the ideal compositions of the writer himself.

On the question as a whole we may say at once with Matthew Arnold (*Literature and Dogma*, p. 170), "the doctrine and discourses of Jesus *cannot* in the main be the writer's, because in the main they are clearly out of his reach." 'Never *man* so spake' (vii. 46). Not even S. John could invent such words.

But the objections urged above are serious and ought to be answered. (1) The discourses in S. John are unlike those in the Synoptists, but we must beware of exaggerating the unlikeness. They are longer, more reflective, less popular. But they are for the most part addressed to the educated and learned, to Elders, Pharisees, and Rabbis: even the discourse on the Bread of Life, which is spoken before a mixed multitude at Capernaum, is largely addressed to the educated portion of it (vi. 41, 52), the hierarchical party opposed to Him. The discourses in the first three Gospels are mostly spoken among the rude and simple-minded peasants of Galilee. Contrast the University Sermons with the Parish Sermons of an eminent modern preacher, and we should notice similar differences. This fact will account for a good deal. But (2) the discourses both in S. John and in the Synoptists are translations from an Aramaic dialect. Two translations may differ very widely, and yet both be faithful; they may each bear the impress of the translator's own style, and yet accurately represent the original. This will to a large extent answer objections (2) and (3). And we must remember that it is possible, and perhaps probable, that the peculiar tone of S. John, so unmistakeable, yet so difficult to analyse satisfactorily, may be a reproduction, more or less conscious, of that of his Divine Master.

But on the other hand we must remember that an eventful life of half a century separates the time when S. John heard these discourses from the time when he committed them to writing. Christ had promised (xiv. 26) that the Holy Spirit should 'bring all things to the remembrance' of the Apostles; but we have no right to assume that in so doing He would override the ordinary laws of psychology. Material stored up so long in the breast of the Apostle could not fail to be moulded by the working of his own mind. And therefore we may admit that in his report of the sayings of Christ and of the Baptist there is an element, impossible to separate now, which comes from himself. His report is sometimes a literal translation of the very words used, sometimes the substance of what was said put into his own words: but he gives us no means of distinguishing where the one shades off into the other.

Cardinal Newman has kindly allowed the following to be quoted from a private letter written by him, July 15th, 1878. "Every one writes in his own style. S. John gives our Lord's meaning in his own way. At that time the third person was not so commonly used in history as now. When a reporter gives one of Gladstone's speeches in the newspaper, if he uses the first person, I understand not only the matter, but the style, the words, to be Gladstone's: when the third, I consider the style, &c. to be the reporter's own. But in ancient times this distinction was not made. Thucydides uses the dramatic method, yet Spartan and Athenian speak in Thucydidean Greek. And so every clause of our Lord's speeches in S. John may be in S. John's Greek, yet every clause may contain the matter which our Lord spoke in Aramaic. Again, S. John might and did select or condense (as being inspired for that purpose) the matter of our Lord's discourses, as that with Nicodemus, and thereby the wording might be S. John's, though the matter might still be our Lord's."

1. ἦν δὲ ἄνθ. Now *there was a man*. The *δέ* marks the connexion with what precedes: Nicodemus was one of the 'many' who believed on beholding His signs (ii. 23). *Ἄνθρωπος* probably refers to ii. 25, as in i. 6 to i. 4; Nicodemus was a sample of that humanity whose inmost being Jesus could read. Else we should expect *τις*.

Νικόδημος. He is mentioned only by S. John. It is impossible to say whether he is the Nicodemus (Nakedimon), or Bunai, of the Talmud, who survived the destruction of Jerusalem. Love of truth and fear of man, candour and hesitation, seem to be combined in him. Comp. vii. 50. In xix. 39 his timidity is again noted and illustrated.

ἄρχων. A member of the Sanhedrin (vii. 50: comp. xii. 42; Luke xxiii. 13, xxiv. 20), which was opposed to Jesus; hence, to avoid compromising himself (xii. 42), he comes by night. We do not know whether S. John was present; probably he was. Nicodemus would not be afraid of disciples.

2. οὗτος. S. John's use, to recall a previous subject; comp. i. 2, 7, 42, iv. 47, vi. 71, xxi. 24.

νυκτός. This proved his timidity and illustrated his spiritual condition; he was coming out of the night to the Light of men, as Judas went out from Him into the night (see on xiii. 30, x. 22, xviii. 1, xxi. 19 and Introduction, chap. v. § 3). Jesus welcomes him; He does not quench the smoking flax.

οἴδαμεν. Others also are inclined to believe, and he claims a share in their enlightenment; but there is a touch of Pharisaic complacency in the word: 'some of us are quite disposed to think well of you.' The report of the deputation sent to the Baptist (i. 19—28) and Christ's signs have to this extent influenced even members of the Sanhedrin. On Ῥαββί see i. 39, iv. 31.

ἀπὸ θεοῦ. First for emphasis; it was from God that His commission to be a Rabbi came, not from having gone through the ordinary training (vii. 15, 16). Does 'art come from God' indicate the Messiah, ὁ ἐρχόμενος? If so, Nicodemus again shews his weakness; he begins with admitting Messiahship and ends with the vague word διδάσκαλος: the Messiah was never thought of as a mere teacher. But ἀπὸ θεοῦ may indicate only a Prophet (i. 6), or even less.

ἐὰν μὴ κ.τ.λ. Again a weak conclusion; one expects 'unless he be a Prophet,' or, 'the Messiah.'

3. **ἀπεκρίθη.** He answers his thoughts (v. 17; Luke vii. 40). Nicodemus wonders whether Jesus is about to set up a kingdom. See on ii. 25 and i. 52.

ἐὰν μή τις. *Except one be born:* quite indefinite. Nicodemus changes τις to ἄνθρωπος.

ἄνωθεν. The strict meaning is either 1. 'from above' literally (Matt. xxvii. 51; Mark xv. 38), or 2. 'from above' figuratively (James i. 17, iii. 15, 17), or 3. 'from the beginning' (Luke i. 3; Acts xxvi. 5). S. John uses ἄνωθεν thrice elsewhere; xix. 23, 'from above' literally; iii. 23 and xix. 11, 'from above' figuratively. This favours the rendering 'from above' here, which is generally adopted by the Greek Fathers from Origen onwards. Moreover 'to be born from above' recalls being 'born of God' in i. 13 (comp. 1 John iii. 9, iv. 7, v. 1, 4, 18). But 'from the beginning' easily shades off into 'afresh' or 'over again' (Gal. iv. 9 we have πάλιν ἄνωθεν combined). Hence from very early times this has been one of the interpretations of ἄνωθεν here, preserved in the Peschito, Ethiopic, and Latin Versions. It confirms the rendering 'over again' or 'anew' to find Justin Martyr (*Apol.* I. lxi) quoting ἂν μὴ ἀναγεννηθῆτε, οὐ μὴ εἰσέλθητε εἰς τ. βασ. τ. οὐρανῶν as words of Christ (see on i. 23 and ix. 1): ἀναγεννᾶσθαι *must* mean 'to be reborn.' Comp. Christ's reply to S. Peter in the beautiful legend of the '*Domine, quo vadis?*', ἄνωθεν μέλλω σταυρωθῆναι: where ἄνωθεν σταυροῦν doubtless represents the ἀνασταυροῦν (crucify *afresh*) of Heb. vi. 6.

οὐ δύναται. It is a moral impossibility; not 'shall not' but 'cannot.' See on vii. 7.

ἰδεῖν. i.e. so as to partake of it: so ἰδεῖν θάνατον, Luke ii. 26; θάνατον θεωρεῖν John viii. 51; comp. Ps. xvi. 10, xc. 15.

τ. βασ. τ. θεοῦ. This phrase, so common in the Synoptists, occurs only here and *v.* 5 in S. John. We may conclude that it was the very phrase used. It looks back to the theocracy, and indicates the Messianic kingdom on earth, the new state of salvation.

Had Jesus been a mere enthusiast, would He have given so chilling a reply (comp. *v.* 10) to a member of the Sanhedrin? Would He not have been eager to make the most of such an opening?

4. **γέρων ὤν.** He puts the most impossible case, possibly with reference to himself, '*when he is an old man*, like myself.' New birth as a metaphor for spiritual regeneration cannot have been unknown

to Nicodemus. He purposely misinterprets, in order to force a *reductio ad absurdum:* or, more probably, not knowing what to say, he asks what he knows to be a foolish question.

5. **ἐξ ὕδατος κ. πνεύματος.** The ἐξ answers to the εἰς which follows and reminds us of the ἐν in i. 33. The convert is immersed *in* the material and spiritual elements, rises new-born *out of* them, and enters *into* the kingdom. Christ leaves the foolish question of Nicodemus to answer itself: He goes on to explain what is the real point, and what Nicodemus has not asked, the meaning of ἄνωθεν: 'of water and (the) Spirit.' The outward sign and inward grace of Christian baptism are here clearly given, and an unbiassed mind can scarcely avoid seeing this plain fact. This becomes still more clear when we compare i. 26 and 33, where the Baptist declares 'I baptize with water;' the Messiah 'baptizeth with the Holy Ghost.' The Fathers, both Greek and Latin, thus interpret the passage with singular unanimity. Thus once more S. John assumes without stating the primary elements of Christianity. Baptism is assumed here as well known to his readers, as the Eucharist is assumed in chap. vi. To a well-instructed Christian there was no need to explain what was meant by being born of water and the Spirit. The words therefore had a threefold meaning, past, present, and future. In the past they looked back to the time when the Spirit moved upon the water, causing the new birth from above of Order and Beauty out of Chaos. In the present they pointed to the divinely ordained (i. 33) baptism of John: and through it in the future to that higher rite, to which John himself bore testimony. Thus Nicodemus would see that he and the Pharisees were wrong in rejecting John's baptism (Luke vii. 30). Of the two elements, water signifies the *purifying* power, spirit the *life-giving* power: the one removes hindrances, making the baptized ready to receive the other (Acts ii. 38; Tit. iii. 5). Note that ἐκ is not repeated before πνεύματος, so that the two factors are treated as inseparable: moreover, neither has the article; it is the *kind* of factors rather than a definite instance that is indicated.

The *Sinaiticus* and some other authorities here read τῶν οὐρανῶν for τοῦ Θεοῦ. This reading renders Justin's reference to the passage still more certain (see on *v.* 3).

6. The meaning of γεννηθῆναι ἄνωθεν is still further explained by an analogy. What man inherits from his parents is a body with animal life and passions; what he receives from above is a spiritual nature with heavenly capabilities and aspirations: what is born of sinful human nature is human and sinful; what is born of the Holy Spirit is spiritual and divine.

There is an interesting interpolation here. The old Latin and old Syriac Versions insert *quia Deus spiritus est et de Deo natus est.* No Greek MS. contains the words, which are obviously a gloss. But S. Ambrose (*De Spir.* III. 59) charges the Arians with effacing *quia Deus spiritus est* from their MSS. See on i. 13.

7. **εἶπ. σοι, Δεῖ ὑμᾶς.** Note the change of number and comp. i. 52. The declaration is pressed home: τις in *vv.* 3 and 5 is no vague gene-

rality; excepting Him who says 'ye,' it is of universal application. 'Ye, the chosen people, ye, the Pharisees, ye, the rulers, who know so much (*v.* 2), must all be born of water and spirit.'

8. τὸ πνεῦμα κ.τ.λ. This verse is sometimes rendered thus: *the Spirit breatheth where He willeth, and thou hearest His voice, but canst not tell whence He cometh and whither He goeth: so is every one* (*born*) *who is born of the Spirit.* It is urged in favour of this rendering (1) that it gives to *πνεῦμα* the meaning which it almost invariably has in more than 350 places in N.T., of which more than 20 are in this Gospel: *πνεῦμα* may mean 'breath of the wind,' yet its almost invariable use in N.T. is 'spirit' or 'the spirit,' *ἄνεμος* being used (e.g. vi. 18) for 'wind': (2) that it gives a better meaning to *θέλει*, a word more appropriate to a person than to anything inanimate: that it gives to *φωνή* the meaning which it has in 14 other passages in this Gospel, viz. 'articulate *voice*,' and not 'inarticulate *sound*.' But on the other hand (1) it gives to *πνεῖ* the meaning 'breathes,' which it nowhere has in Scripture: in vi. 18 and elsewhere it is invariably used of the blowing of the wind: (2) it involves the expression 'the voice of the Spirit,' also unknown to Scripture: (3) it requires the insertion of 'born' in the last clause, in order to make sense. The close of the verse, *οὕτως ἐστὶ κ.τ.λ.*, shews that there is a comparison, and this is almost conclusive for 'wind' as the meaning of *πνεῦμα*. Comp. Eccles. xi. 5. The Aramaic word probably used by our Lord has *both* meanings, 'wind' and 'spirit,' to translate which S. John could not use *ἄνεμος*, which has only the meaning of 'wind;' so that the first rather imposing argument for the rendering 'spirit' crumbles away. "At the pauses in the conversation, we may conjecture, they heard the wind without, as it moaned along the narrow streets of Jerusalem; and our Lord, as was His wont, took His creature into His service—the service of spiritual truth. The wind was a figure of the Spirit. Our Lord would have used the same word for both" (Liddon). Socrates uses the same simile; *ἄνεμοι αὐτοὶ οὐχ ὁρῶνται, ἃ δὲ ποιοῦσι φανερὰ ἡμῖν ἐστι, καὶ προσιόντων αὐτῶν αἰσθανόμεθα* (Xen. *Mem.* IV. iii. 14). In the Ignatian Epistles (*Philad.* VII.) we read *τὸ πνεῦμα οὐ πλανᾶται, ἀπὸ Θεοῦ ὄν· οἶδεν γὰρ πόθεν ἔρχεται καὶ ποῦ ὑπάγει, καὶ τὰ κρυπτὰ ἐλέγχει*, which is evidence of this Gospel being known A.D. 150, and probably A.D. 115. See on iv. 10, vi. 33, x. 9.

ὁ γεγεννημένος. *That* **hath been** *born;* perf. pass. It is all over, this spiritual birth, 'he knoweth not how.' He feels that the heavenly influence has done its work; but he finds it incomprehensible in its origin, which is divine, and in its end, which is eternal life. The *Sinaiticus*, supported by the old Latin and old Syriac, inserts *τοῦ ὕδατος καὶ* after *ἐκ*; another proof of the antiquity of corruptions. See on i. 13, and comp. *vv.* 6, 13, 15.

9. γενέσθαι. Come to pass (see on i. 6). He is bewildered; but there is no attempt at a rejoinder, as in *v.* 4. Comp. Job xl. 4, 5.

10. σὺ εἶ ὁ διδάσκ. *Art thou* **the teacher**, a representative of the highest knowledge and supreme authority in the Church? Jesus is astonished at the ignorance of Rabbis, just as He marvelled at the unbelief of His countrymen (Mark vi. 6). **'Ισραήλ**, frequent in Matt., Luke, and Acts, occurs only 4 times in S. John (i. 31, 50, xiii. 13, and here): 'the chosen people' is the idea conveyed. **Οὐ γινώσκεις. Perceivest** *not:* this was knowledge which he might have acquired, had he made the effort. Winer, p. 143.

11. **οἴδαμεν.** The plurals between singulars are to be noted. They may be rhetorical, giving the saying the tone of a proverb; but the next verse seems to shew that they are literal. Jesus and His disciples tell of earthly things, Jesus alone of heavenly. Note the order and the pairing of the verbs; *That which we know, we speak; and of that which we have seen, we bear witness.* See on i. 18. For **καὶ...οὐ λαμβ.** The tragic tone once more; see on i. 5.

12. **τὰ ἐπίγεια.** *Terrena*, things which take place on earth, even though originating in heaven, e.g. the 'new birth,' which though 'of God,' must take place in this world. See on 1 Cor. xv. 40, and James iii. 15. Prophets and other teachers can make known *ἐπίγεια*. **τὰ ἐπουράνια.** The mysteries which are not of this world, the nature of the Son, God's counsels respecting man's salvation.

13. **οὐδεὶς ἀναβ.** No one has been in heaven, so as to see and know these *ἐπουράνια*, excepting the Son of Man (see on i. 52). There is probably no direct reference to the Ascension. **'Εκ τ. οὐρ. Out of** *heaven*, at the Incarnation, when from being *ἐπουράνιος* He became the Son of Man.

ὁ ὢν ἐν τ. οὐρ. These words are wanting in the best MSS. and other authorities. It is much easier to account for their insertion than for their omission. It is, therefore, safest to regard them as a very early expansion of the Greek in ancient Versions. See on i. 13. They mean, 'Whose proper home is heaven,' or, taking *ὢν* as imperf. (vi. 62, ix. 25, xvii. 5), '*Which* **was** *in heaven*' before the Incarnation. Winer, p. 429.

14. **τὸν ὄφιν.** We here have some evidence of the date of the Gospel. The Ophitic is the earliest Gnostic system of which we have full information. The serpent is the centre of the system, at once its good and evil principle. Had this form of Gnosticism been prevalent before this Gospel was written, this verse would scarcely have stood thus. An orthodox writer would have guarded his readers from error: an Ophitic writer would have made more of the serpent.

οὕτως. Christ here testifies to the prophetic and typical character of the O. T. Both Jewish and Christian writers vary much in their explanations of the Brazen Serpent. It is safest in interpreting types and parables to hold fast to the main features and not insist on the details. Here the main points are the *lifting up* of a source of *life* to become effectual through the *faith* of the sufferer. All these points are *expressed* in *vv.* 14, 15. Nicodemus lived to see the fulfilment of the prophecy (xix. 39).

ὑψωθῆναι. On the Cross, as in viii. 28. The exaltation of Christ to glory by means of the Cross (*crux scala coeli*) is probably not included: for this δοξασθῆναι would be the more natural term. In xii. 32 the Ascension is possibly included by ἐκ τῆς γῆς and in Acts ii. 33, v. 31 by τῇ δεξιᾷ τ. Θεοῦ: here and in viii. 28 there is no such addition. Moreover, to include the Ascension spoils the comparison with the Brazen Serpent.

δεῖ. It is so ordered in the counsels of God (Heb. ii. 9, 10). Comp. *v.* 30, ix. 4, x. 16, xii. 34, xx. 9; Matt. xvi. 21, xxvi. 54; Mark viii. 31; Luke ix. 22, xvii. 25, xxii. 37, xxiv. 7, 26, 44.

15. ἵνα. See on i. 8. The eternal life of *all* believers, whether Jew or Gentile, is the *purpose* of the Divine δεῖ. The lifting up on the Cross was the turning-point in the faith of Nicodemus (xix. 39).

ἐν αὐτῷ. This goes with ἔχῃ rather than πιστεύων; *that* **every one** (xi. 25, xii. 46) **that believeth may in Him have** *eternal life*. Authorities are much divided between ἐν and ἐπ' αὐτῷ, εἰς and ἐπ' αὐτόν. The confusion partly arose from the insertion of μὴ ἀπόληται ἀλλ' from *v.* 16 before ἔχῃ, causing the preposition and pronoun to be taken with πιστεύων.

ζωὴν αἰώνιον. This is one of S. John's favourite phrases. It occurs 17 times in the Gospel (8 in the Synoptics) and 6 in the First Epistle. In neither Gospel nor Epistle does he apply αἰώνιος to anything but ζωή. The phrase ἔχειν ζωὴν αἰώνιον is also one of S. John's phrases, *v.* 36, v. 24, vi. 40, 47, 54; 1 John iii. 15, v. 12.

16—21. It is much disputed whether what follows is a continuation of Christ's discourse, or S. John's comment upon it. That expressions characteristic of S. John's diction appear (μονογενής, πιστεύειν εἰς τὸ ὄνομα, ποιεῖν τὴν ἀλήθειαν, τὸ φῶς), cannot settle the question; the substance may still be Christ's though the wording is S. John's. And have we sufficient knowledge of our Lord's phraseology to distinguish S. John's wording from His? In any case we have what was probably a conversation of long duration condensed into one of five minutes. Nor does the cessation of the conversational form prove anything. The more Nicodemus became impressed the less he would be likely to interrupt, like the disciples in the last discourses. It seems unlikely that S. John would give us no indication of the change from the Lord's words to his own, if the discourse with Nicodemus really ended at *v.* 15. See on *vv.* 31—36.

The subject of these six verses is as follows; God's purpose in sending His Son (16, 17); the opposite results (18, 19); the moral cause of these opposite results (20, 21).

16. γάρ. Explaining how God wills life to every believer. **Τὸν κόσμον** = the whole human race (see on i. 10). This would be a revelation to the exclusive Pharisee, brought up to believe that God loved only the Chosen People. **'Αγαπᾶν** is very frequent in the Gospel and First Epistle, and may be considered characteristic of S. John: see on v. 20. **Μονογενῆ**; see on i. 14. This shews the greatness of

God's love: it would remind Nicodemus of the offering of Isaac. Comp. 1 John iv. 9; Heb. xi. 17; Rom. viii. 32. **Ἔδωκεν** is stronger than 'sent:' it was a free gift to the world. Winer, p. 377.

πᾶς ὁ πιστεύων. The only limitation: eternal life is open to all. **Ἀπόληται.** Subj. after a past tense; see on i. 7. The translation of *ζωὴ αἰώνιος* should be uniform; A.V. wavers between 'eternal life' (*v.* 15, v. 39, vi. 54, 68, &c.), 'life eternal' (iv. 36, xii. 25), 'everlasting life' (here, *v.* 36, iv. 14, v. 24, &c.), and 'life everlasting' (xii. 50): 'eternal life' is best.

17. τὸν κόσμον. Thrice for emphasis; characteristic of S. John's style (comp. *v.* 31, i. 10, xii. 36, xv. 19, xvii. 14).

οὐ...ἵνα κρίνῃ. *Not in order to* **judge** (comp. Luke ix. 56). This does not contradict ix. 39. Since there are sinners in the world, Christ's coming involves a separation (*κρίσις*) of them from the good, a judgment, a sentence: but this is not the *purpose* of His coming; the purpose is salvation (xii. 47). The Jews expected both judgment and salvation from the Messiah, judgment for the Gentiles, salvation for themselves. Jesus affirms that the result of the *κρίσις* depends on the faith, not on the race of each. *Κρίνειν* and *κρίσις* are among S. John's characteristic words.

18. οὐ κρίνεται...κέκριται. Change of tense: *is not* **judged...hath been judged.** The Messiah has no need to sentence unbelievers; their unbelief in the self-revelation (*ὄνομα*) of the Messiah is of itself a sentence. They are *self*-condemned; comp. *v.* 36. Note the change from fact to supposition marked by *οὐ* followed by *μή*: Winer, pp. 594, 602.

19. αὕτη δέ ἐσ. ἡ κρ. But the judgment is this; this is what it consists in. We have precisely the same construction 1 John i. 5, v. 11, 14; and almost the same (*ἵνα* for *ὅτι*) xv. 12, xvii. 3.

τὸ φῶς. This is not only S. John's term (i. 4—9) but Christ's (viii. 12, ix. 5, xii. 46). On **ἐλήλ. εἰς τ. κ.** see on xi. 27.

καὶ ἠγαπ. The tragic tone again (see on i. 5). *Men loved* **the** *darkness rather than* **the** *Light.* Litotes or meiosis (vi. 37, viii. 40); they *hated* the Light. *Gravis malae conscientiae lux*, Seneca, *Ep.* 122. No allusion to Nicodemus coming by night: he chose darkness to conceal not an evil work but a good one.

20. φαῦλα. Whereas *πονηρός* (*v.* 19) expresses the *malignity* of evil, its power to cause suffering (*πόνος*), *φαῦλος* (perhaps akin to *paulus*) expresses the *worthlessness* of it. The one is positive, the other negative. Satan is *ὁ πονηρός*, the great *author of mischief* (xvii. 15; 1 John ii. 13, 14, iii. 12, v. 18, 19): *πνεύματα πονηρά* (Luke vii. 21), *ὀφθαλμὸς πον.* (Mark vii. 22), *γενεὰ πον.* (Matt. xii. 39), are *mischief-working* spirits, eye and generation. *Φαῦλος* is the exact opposite of *σπουδαῖος*: the one is 'frivolous, good-for-nothing, *naughty*;' the other is 'serious, earnest, good.'

πράσσων. Is there any difference between *πράσσειν* and *ποιεῖν* in these two verses? *V.* 29 inclines one to think so, and the distinction drawn is that *πράσσειν* (*agere*) expresses mere activity, while *ποιεῖν* (*facere*) implies a permanent result. But in Rom. vii. 15—20, xiii. 4 the two words are interchanged indifferently, each being used both of doing good and of doing evil. *He that* **practiseth worthless things** (the aimless trifler) *hateth the light*, which would shew the true value of the inanities which fill his existence. 1 Kings xxii. 8.

οὐκ. ἔρχ. The hatred is instinctive, the not coming is deliberate.

ἵνα μὴ ἐλεγχθῇ. **In order that his works may not be convicted** of worthlessness, proved to be what they really are. The A.V. translates *ἐλέγχειν* here and xvi. 8 'reprove,' viii. 9 'convict,' viii. 46, 'convince;' and here the margin has 'discovered.' See on xvi. 8; Matt. xviii. 15.

21. ποιῶν τ. ἀλήθ. To *do* **the** *truth* (1 John i. 6) is the opposite of 'doing' or 'making a lie,' *ποιεῖν ψεῦδος* (Rev. xxi. 27, xxii. 15). It is moral rather than intellectual truth that is meant, moral good recognised by the conscience (xviii. 37). To 'do the truth' is to do that which has true moral worth, the opposite of 'practising worthless things.' In 1 Cor. xiii. 6 we have a similar antithesis: 'rejoicing with *the truth*' is opposed to 'rejoicing in *iniquity*.' See on i. 9.

αὐτοῦ τὰ ἔργα. *Αὐτοῦ* is emphatic; '*his* works' as opposed to those of *ὁ φαῦλα πράσσων*. **Φανερωθῇ** (see on i. 31) balances *ἐλεγχθῇ*: the one fears to be convicted; the other seeks the light, not for self-glorification, but as being drawn to that to which he feels that his works are akin. **Ὅτι** is better rendered 'that' than 'because.'

ἐν θεῷ. Note the order and the tense; *that it is* **in God** *that they* **have been** *wrought* and still abide: the permanent result of a past act. 'In God' means in the presence and in the power of God.

These three verses (19—21) shew that *before* the Incarnation there were two classes of men in the world; a majority of evil-doers, whose antecedents led them to shun the Messiah; and a small minority of righteous, whose antecedents led them to welcome the Messiah. They had been given to Him by the Father (vi. 37, xvii. 6); they recognised His teaching as of God, because they desired to do God's will (vii. 17). Such would be Simeon, Anna (Luke ii. 25, 36), Nathanael, the disciples, &c.

We have no means of knowing how Nicodemus was affected by this interview, beyond the incidental notices of him vii. 50, 51, xix. 39, which being so incidental shew that he is no fiction. The discourse exactly harmonizes with his case, teaching that the righteousness of the scribes and Pharisees is powerless to gain admission into the kingdom of heaven. One by one his Pharisaic ideas of the kingdom, the Messiah, salvation and judgment, are challenged: from mere wonder at miracles and interest in the Worker of them he is made to look within and consider his own moral sympathies and spiritual convictions. Again we ask could a writer of the second century throw himself back to this?

22—36. The Baptism and Final Testimony of John

22, 23. A mark of authenticity similar to ii. 12. It is impossible to suppose that these verses were written in the interests of dogma. S. John records these events, not for any theological purpose, but because he was present, and remembers them.

22. μετὰ ταῦτα. Quite vague; a less close connexion than is indicated by *μετὰ τοῦτο*. Contrast v. 1, 14, vi. 1, xix. 38, xxi. 1 with ii. 12, xi. 7, 11, xix. 28. **Εἰς τ. Ἰουδαίαν γῆν.** Occurs here only; comp. *ἡ Ἰ. χώρα* Mark i. 5; Acts xxvi. 20. Both phrases indicate the country as distinct from the capital. The sphere of Christ's ministry widens; first the Temple (ii. 14), then Jerusalem (ii. 23), now Judaea, finally Galilee (iv. 45, vi. 1).

διέτριβεν...ἐβάπτιζεν. Imperfects, implying that this went on for some time. He **was baptizing** through His disciples (iv. 2): not yet in the Name of the Trinity (vii. 39), as ordered to the Apostles (Matt. xxviii. 19), but as a continuation of John's Baptism, accompanied by the operation of the Spirit (*v.* 5). We have abundant evidence that John baptized before Christ's ministry began, and that the Apostles baptized after His ministry closed; yet "this is the one passage in which it is positively stated that our Lord authorised baptism during His lifetime" (Sanday). But how probable that the one baptism should be the offspring of the other!

23. ἦν...βαπτίζων. Not as rival to the Messiah but still in preparation for Him, as Samuel continued to be Judge after the King was appointed. John knew that the Messiah had come; but He had not taken the public position which John expected Him to take, and hence John was not led to suppose that his own office in preaching repentance was at an end. John still went on; Jesus, owing to His rejection in Jerusalem, seems to go back, "becoming in a way His own fore-runner" (Godet). Thus they appear for a moment baptizing side by side. But the Baptist has reached his zenith; whereas the Messiah's career has scarcely begun.

Αἰνών. 'Springs.' The identifications of Aenon and Salim remain uncertain. The Wâdy Fâr'ah, an open vale full of springs, running from Ebal to Jordan, is a tempting conjecture. There is a Salim three miles south, and the name Aenon survives in 'Ainûn, four miles north of the waters.

ὕδατα πολλά. For immersion: the expression points to springs or streams rather than a single river like the Jordan.

24. The Evangelist has not said a word that could imply that the Baptist was in prison. This remark refers to the Synoptists, and guards us against the inference easily drawn from them (Matt. iv. 12; Mark i. 14) that John's imprisonment followed close on the Temptation and preceded the beginning of Christ's ministry. The whole of John i—iii. precedes Matt. iv. 12. In this magisterial interpretation of earlier Gospels we trace the hand of an Apostle writing with sure knowledge and conscious authority.

25. **ἐγένετο οὖν.** *There arose* **therefore**; in consequence of Jesus and John baptizing so near together. The Evangelist's favourite particle to mark a sequence in fact: see Introduction, Chap. v. 6 (c).

ζήτησις ἐκ κ.τ.λ. **Questioning on the part of** *the disciples of John* **with a Jew.** The common reading Ἰουδαίων is respectably supported, but seems quite out of place; with Ἰουδαίου, which has far the strongest support, one expects *τινος*. The questioning may have been as to the efficacy of John's baptism compared with Christ's, or with the ordinary ceremonial purifications. Ἐκ implies that John's disciples started the discussion, and it ends in their going at once to their master for his opinion about Jesus and His success.

26. **ᾧ σὺ μεμ.** *To whom* **thou hast borne witness.** This was what seemed so monstrous; that One who appeared to owe His position to John's testimony should be competing with him and surpassing him: *σύ* and *οὗτος* are in emphatic opposition.

ἴδε οὗτος. **Lo** (see on i. 29) **this fellow,** expressing astonishment and chagrin, and perhaps contempt: they regard baptizing as John's prerogative. In Matt. ix. 14 we find them cavilling again.

πάντες. An exaggeration very natural in their excitement: the picture is thoroughly true to life. Comp. the excited statement of the Samaritan woman, iv. 29; of the Pharisees, xii. 19; contrast *v.* 32, and see on vi. 15.

27. **οὐ δύναται.** Comp. xix. 11. The meaning is disputed; either (1) 'Jesus could not succeed thus without help from Heaven, and this should satisfy you that He is sent by God;' or (2) 'I cannot accept the supremacy which you would thrust on me, because I have not received it from Heaven.' The former is better, as being a more direct answer to 'all men come to Him.' Possibly both meanings are intended.

28. **αὐτοὶ ὑμεῖς.** '*Ye yourselves,* though you are so indignant on my behalf.' They had appealed to his testimony (*v.* 26); he turns it against them. He is not responsible for their error.

ἔμπ. ἐκ. John speaks more plainly in i. 26, 30: now that Jesus has manifested Himself he feels free to declare Him to be the Christ.

29. John explains by a figure his subordination to the Messiah.

τὴν νύμφην. Here only in this Gospel does this well-known symbol occur. It is frequent both in O.T. and N.T. Is. liv. 5; Hos. ii. 19, 20; Eph. v. 32; Rev. xix. 7, xxi. 2, 9. Comp. Matt. ix. 15, xxv. 1. In O.T. it symbolizes the relationship between Jehovah and His chosen people, in N.T. that between Christ and His Church. By 'the friend of the bridegroom' is meant the special friend, appointed to arrange the preliminaries of the wedding, to manage and preside at the marriage-feast. Somewhat analogous to our 'best man,' but his duties were very much more considerable. A much closer analogy may be found among the lower orders in the Tyrol at the present day. Here the Messiah is the Bridegroom and the Church His Bride;

John is His friend who has prepared the heart of the Bride and arranged the espousal. He rejoices to see the consummation of his labours.

ἑστηκὼς καὶ ἀκούων. In the attitude of a devoted attendant.

χαρᾷ χαίρει. A Hebraism: comp. Luke xxii. 15; Acts iv. 17, v. 28, xxiii. 14; James v. 17; Matt. xiii. 14, xv. 4 (from LXX., where the idiom is common). Winer, p. 584. It is in the marriage festivities that the Bridegroom's voice is heard.

πεπλήρωται. *Has been fulfilled* and still remains complete: comp. *vv.* 18, 21, 26, i. 34, 52, &c. To speak of *joy being fulfilled* is an expression peculiar to S. John (xv. 11, xvi. 24, xvii. 13; 1 John i. 4; 2 John 12): the active occurs Phil. ii. 2.

30. δεῖ. See on *v.* 14. This joy of the Bridegroom's friend, in full view of the certain wane of his own influence and dignity, is in marked contrast to the jealousy of his disciples. With this triumphant self-effacement he ceases to speak of himself, and the second half of his discourse begins: 1. the Christ and the Baptist (27—30); 2. the Christ and the world (31—36).

31—36. A question is raised with regard to this section similar to that raised about *vv.* 16—21. Some regard what follows not as a continuation of the Baptist's speech, but as the Evangelist's comment upon it. But, as in the former case, seeing that the Evangelist gives us no intimation that he is taking the place of the speaker, and that there is nothing in what follows to compel us to suppose that there is such a transition, it is best to regard the Baptist as still speaking. It is, however, quite possible that this latter part of the discourse is more strongly coloured with the Evangelist's own style and phraseology, while the substance still remains the Baptist's. Indeed a change of style may be noticed. The sentences becomes less abrupt and more connected; the stream of thought is continuous.

"The Baptist, with the growing inspiration of the prophet, unveils before his narrowing circle of disciples the full majesty of Jesus; and then, as with a swan-like song, completes his testimony before vanishing from history" (Meyer).

There is no contradiction between this passage and Matt. xi. 2—6, whatever construction we put on the latter (see notes there). John was 'of the earth,' and therefore there is nothing improbable in his here impressing on his disciples the peril of not-believing on the Messiah, and yet in prison feeling impatience, or despondency, or even doubt about the position and career of Jesus.

31. ὁ ἄνωθεν ἐρχ. Christ: *v.* 13, viii. 23: *ἄνωθεν* here *must* mean 'from above'; see on *v.* 3. He is above all, John included, little as John's disciples may like the fact. Comp. Matt. xi. 11.

ὁ ὢν ἐκ τ. γῆς. *Εἶναι ἐκ*, expressing a moral relation, is characteristic of S. John, vii. 17, viii. 23, 44, 47, xv. 19, xvii. 14, 16, xviii. 36, 37; 1 John ii. 16, 19, 21, iii. 8, 10, 12, 19, iv. 1—7, v. 16, 3 John 11; elsewhere in N.T. not common. Comp. *γεγεννῆσθαι ἐκ*, *vv.* 5, 6, 8,

i. 13, viii. 41; 1 John ii. 29, iii. 9, iv. 7, v. 1, 4, 18. Note the emphatic repetition of ἐκ τ. γῆς, as of κόσμος in *v.* 17. Comp. xii. 36, xv. 19. *He that is of the earth, of the earth he is, and of the earth he speaketh.* This was John's case: he spoke of 'earthly things' (*v.* 12). Divine Truth *as manifested in the world*, and as revealed to him. He could not, like Christ, speak from immediate knowledge of 'heavenly things.' Ἐκ τ. γῆς λαλεῖν is very different from ἐκ τ. κόσμου λαλεῖν (1 John iv. 5); the one is to speak of God's work on earth; the other of what is not God's work but opposes it.

ὁ ἐκ τ. οὐρ. ἐρχ. Repeating and defining ὁ ἄνωθεν ἐρχ., thoroughly in S. John's style. In what follows we have another (see *vv.* 13, 15) interesting question of reading. T. R. has ἐπάνω πάντων ἐστί, καί. The καί must be omitted on overwhelming evidence (ℵBDL against A): asyndeton is the rule throughout this passage. The evidence as to ἐπάνω π. ἐστί is very divided, the balance being against the words. Omitting them, we translate: *He that cometh from heaven beareth witness to that which He hath seen and heard.*

32. ὃ ἑώρακεν κ. ἤκ. In His pre-existence with God; *v.* 11, i. 18. He has immediate knowledge of τὰ ἐπουράνια. Τοῦτο, precisely this is the substance of His witness: comp. xiv. 13. This use of a retrospective pronoun for emphasis is frequent in S. John; v. 38, vi. 46, vii. 18, viii. 26, x. 25, xv. 5.

καὶ...οὐδεὶς λαμβ. The tragic tone again; see on i. 5, and comp. *v.* 11. 'No man' is an exaggeration resulting from deep feeling: comparatively speaking none, so few were those who accepted the Messiah. Comp. the similar exaggeration on the other side, *v.* 26, '*all* men come to Him.' These extreme contradictory statements, placed in such close proximity, confirm our trust in the Evangelist as faithfully reporting what was actually said. He does not soften it down to make it look plausible.

33. The Baptist at once shews that οὐδείς is hyperbolical: some did receive the witness; 'but what are they among so many?'

ἐσφράγισεν. Of sealing a document to express one's trust in it and adherence to it (vi. 27; 1 Cor. ix. 2): but in this figurative sense the middle is more usual (Rom. xv. 28; 2 Cor. i. 22; Eph. i. 13, iv. 30); the active in the literal sense (Matt. xxvii. 66). Αὐτοῦ is emphatic, balancing ὁ Θεός: 'he that receiveth *Christ's* witness, set his seal that *God* is true.' To believe the Messiah is to believe God, for the Messiah is God's ambassador and interpreter (i. 18). Ἀληθής not ἀληθινός; see on i. 9.

34. τὰ ῥήματα. S. John uses this word only in the plural (v. 47, vi. 63, 68, viii. 47, xii. 47, xv. 7); it means the separate utterances, as distinct from ὁ λόγος (vi. 60, viii. 43, 51, xii. 48, xv. 3), which is the communication as a whole.

οὐ γὰρ ἐκ μ. Ὁ Θεός is a gloss of interpretation. Omitting it, we translate, **He** *giveth not the Spirit by measure;* or, **the Spirit** *giveth not by measure.* The former is better, and 'He' is probably God.

'Unto Him' should not be supplied, though there is a direct reference to Jesus. 'Not by measure' (first for emphasis) 'giveth He the Spirit,' least of all to Jesus, 'for it pleased (the Father) that in Him the whole plenitude (of Divinity) should have its permanent abode' (Col. i. 19). Some make Christ the nominative, as giving the Spirit fully to His disciples; but this does not agree with *v.* 35.

35. ἀγαπᾷ. See on *v.* 16 and comp. v. 10. The words seem to be an echo of the voice from heaven which John had so lately heard; *οὗτός ἐστιν ὁ υἱός μου ὁ ἀγαπητός*. The love explains the giving all into His hand, so that He becomes *πάντων κύριος* (Acts x. 36), and *κεφαλὴ ὑπὲρ πάντα* (Eph. i. 22).

δέδωκεν. In S. John statements respecting the Father's gifts to the Son are specially frequent. He has given Him all things (xiii. 3); to have life in Himself (*v.* 26); all judgment (*v.* 22, 27); His name and glory (xvii. 11, 24); authority over all flesh (xvii. 2); faithful disciples (vi. 39); commandment what to say (xii. 49) and do (xiv. 31, xvii. 4). Here the hand signifies power to dispose of and control. Note the pregnant construction; '*has given* into, so that they remain *in His hand;*' in i. 18, 32, 33, we have the converse, a verb of rest with a preposition of motion.

36. ἔχει ζ. αἰώνιον. See on *v.* 16. Present; 'hath,' not 'shall have.' Believers already *have* eternal life. We often think of it as something to be won; but it has already been given. The struggle is not to gain, but to retain: v. 24, vi. 47, 54, xvii. 3. Winer, p. 332.

ὁ ἀπειθῶν. *He that* **disobeyeth**, rather than 'he that believeth not.' Unbelief may be the result of ignorance; disobedience must be voluntary. A similar correction of A. V. seems to be needed Acts xiv. 2, xix. 9; Rom. xi. 30 (margin). Comp. Heb. iv. 6, 11; 1 Pet. iv. 1.

οὐκ ὄψεται. Has not seen and has no prospect of seeing.

ἡ ὀργὴ τ. θεοῦ. This phrase occurs nowhere else in the Gospels, and its unique character is against this passage (31—36) being the comment of the Evangelist and not the Baptist's speech. The wrath of God is the necessary complement of the love of God. If there is love for those who believe, there must be wrath for those who refuse. Comp. Matt. iii. 7; Luke iii. 7; Rom. i. 18, ix. 22, xii. 19; 1 John iii. 14.

μένει, not *μενεῖ*; *abideth*, not 'will abide.' He is under a ban until he believes, and he refuses; therefore his ban remains (comp. 1 John v. 12). He, like the believer, not only *will* have, but *has* his portion. It rests with him also, whether the portion continues his. He has to struggle, not to avert a sentence, but to be freed from it. Thus the last-spoken words of O. T. prophecy resemble its last-written words. We have here the last utterance of the Baptist. Its sternness recalls and enforces the last solemn warning of Malachi;—'lest I come and smite the earth with a curse.'

CHAPTER IV

14. **διψήσει** for διψήσῃ (correction to the usual construction: comp. vi. 42, x. 5, Luke x. 19).

16. Omit ὁ Ἰησοῦς after **αὐτῇ**: comp. iii. 2.

21. **πίστευέ μοι, γύναι** (ℵBL) for γύναι, πίστευσόν μοι (A).

27. **ἐθαύμαζον**, with all the best MSS., for ἐθαύμασαν, which has been substituted to harmonize with ἦλθαν.

42. Omit ὁ Χριστός after **κόσμου**, with ℵBC[1] and most versions and Fathers against AC[3]D.

43. Omit καὶ ἀπῆλθεν after **ἐκεῖθεν**, with ℵBCD.

46. Omit ὁ Ἰησοῦς after **οὖν**: comp. iii. 2. **Καφαρναούμ** for Καπερναούμ: comp. ii. 12.

51. **ὑπήντησαν** (always used by S. John; xi. 20, 30, xii. 18) for ἀπήντησαν (never used by him), with ℵBCDKL against A.

52. **τὴν ὥραν παρ' αὐτῶν** for παρ' αὐ. τ. ὥρ., a correction to bring παρ' αὐτῶν nearer to ἐπύθετο.

1—42. The Work among Samaritans

The whole section is peculiar to S. John, and is evidently the narrative of an eyewitness: of the Synoptists S. Luke alone, the writer of 'the Universal Gospel,' mentions any intercourse of Christ with Samaritans (ix. 52, xvii. 16; comp. x. 33). *Vv.* 1—4 are introductory, explaining the change of scene, like ii. 13 in the previous section.

1. **οὖν.** This refers back to iii. 22—26. Of the many who came to Jesus some told the Pharisees (see on i. 24) of His success, as others told the Baptist, and this was reported to Him again: ὁ κύριος here, which is rarely used except by S. Luke of Christ before the Resurrection (vi. 23, xi. 2; Luke x. 1, xi. 39, xii. 42, xvii. 5, 6, &c.) is no evidence that the knowledge was supernatural. See on ii. 25.

ποιεῖ κ. βαπτ. **Is making and baptizing**; the very words of the report. This is important for the meaning of *v.* 2, which is a correction not of S. John's statement, but of the report to the Pharisees: in A.V. the Evangelist seems to be correcting himself.

ἢ Ἰωάν. They had less objection to John's success. He disclaimed being the Messiah, he 'did no miracle,' and he took his stand on the Law. They understood his position better than that of Jesus, and feared it less. Jesus had been proclaimed as the Messiah, He wrought miracles, and He shewed scant respect to traditions.

2. **αὐτὸς οὐκ.** Because baptizing is the work of a minister, not of the Lord: Jesus baptizes with the Holy Spirit (i. 33).

3. **ἀφῆκεν.** 'He left it *alone*, let it *go*' (*v.* 28) as something that He would have retained, but now left to itself. First the Temple, then Jerusalem, and now Judaea has to be abandoned, because He can win no welcome. On the contrary, the report of His very partial success seems at once to have provoked opposition, which He avoids by retiring. Perhaps also He wished to avoid the appearance of being a rival of John. There is no trace of His continuing to baptize in Galilee.

πάλιν. Omitted by some important witnesses. It points to i. 43—ii. 12. He had come from Capernaum to Jerusalem for the Passover (ii. 13); He now returns to Galilee, where His opponents would have less influence. That this return is the beginning of the Galilean ministry recorded by the Synoptists (Matt. iv. 12) is possibly but by no means certainly correct. See on vi. 1 and Mark i. 14, 15.

4. **ἔδει.** There was no other way, unless He crossed the Jordan, and went round by Perea, as Jews sometimes did to avoid annoyance from the Samaritans (see on Matt. x. 5). As Jesus was on His way *from* Jerusalem, He had less reason to fear molestation. Contrast Luke ix. 53.

5—42. Doubt has been thrown on this narrative in four different ways. (1) On *a priori* grounds. How could the Samaritans, who rejected the prophetical books, and were such bitter enemies of the Jews, be expecting a Messiah? The narrative is based on a fundamental mistake. But it is notorious that the Samaritans did look for a Messiah, and are looking for one to the present day. Though they rejected the Prophets, they accepted the Pentateuch, with all its Messianic prophecies. (2) On account of *Matt. x.* 5. Would Christ do what He forbad His disciples to do? But what He forbad them was to undertake a mission to the Samaritans until the lost sheep of Israel had been sought after; whereas, 1. He had already been seeking after Israel; 2. this was no mission to the Samaritans. He went thither, we are expressly told, because He could not help going, ἔδει. Was it to be expected that being there He should abstain from doing good? (3) On account of *Acts viii.* 5. How could Philip go and convert the Samaritans, if Christ had already done so? But is it to be supposed that *in two days* Christ perfected Christianity in Samaria (even supposing, what is not certain, that Christ and Philip went to the same town), so as to leave nothing for a preacher to do afterwards? Many acknowledged Jesus as the Messiah who afterwards, on finding Him to be very different from the Messiah they expected, fell away. This would be likely enough at Samaria. The seed had fallen on rocky ground. (4) On the supposition that the narrative is an *allegory*, of which the whole point lies in the words 'thou hast had five husbands, and he whom thou now hast is not thy husband.' The five husbands are the five religions from Babylon, Cuthah, Ava, Hamath, and Sepharvaim, brought to Samaria by the colonists from Assyria (2 Kings xvii. 24); and the sixth is the adulterated worship of Jehovah. If our interpreting Scripture depends upon our guessing such riddles as this, we may well give up the task in despair. But the allegory is a pure fiction. 1. When S. John gives us an allegory, he leaves no doubt that it is an allegory. There is not the faintest hint here. 2. It would be extraordinary that in a narrative of 38 verses the whole allegory should be contained in less than one verse, the rest being mere setting. This is like a frame a yard wide round a miniature. 3. Though there were five nations, there were seven or eight worships (2 Kings xvii. 30, 31), and the worships were simultaneous, not successive like the husbands. 4. There is a singular impropriety in making the heathen religions 'husbands,' while the worship of Jehovah is represented by a paramour.

The narrative is true to what we know of Jews and Samaritans at this time. The topography is well preserved. 'The gradual development of the woman's belief is psychologically true.' These and other points to be noticed as they occur may convince us that this narrative cannot be a fiction. Far the easiest supposition is that it is a faithful record of actual facts.

5. ἔρχ. οὖν. *He cometh* **therefore**; because that was the route.

πόλιν. Town; the word does not imply anything very large. Capernaum, which Josephus calls a *κώμη*, the Evangelists call a *πόλις*. Samaria here is the insignificant province into which the old kingdom of Jeroboam had dwindled.

λεγομένην Συχάρ. *Λεγομ.* may be another indication that this Gospel was written outside Palestine, or it may mean that Sychar was a nickname ('liar' or 'drunkard'). In the one case Sychar is different from Sychem or Shechem, and is the mediaeval Ischar and modern 'Askar; in the other it is another name for Sychem, the Neapolis of S. John's day, a name which survives in Naplûs, the home of the Samaritans at the present day. The former is very preferable. Would not S. John have written *Νεαπόλις* if he had meant Sychem? He writes Tiberias (vi. 1, 23, xxi. 1): but Tiberias was probably a new town with a new name, whereas Neapolis was a new name for an old town; so the analogy is not perfect. Eusebius and Jerome distinguish Sychar from Sychem: and Naplûs has many wells close at hand.

τ. χωρίου. *The* **portion** *of ground;* Shechem means 'portion.' Abraham bought it, Jacob gave it to Joseph, and Joseph was buried there (Gen. xxxiii. 19, xlviii. 22; Josh. xxiv. 32).

6. πηγή. Spring; *v.* 14; Rev. vii. 17, viii. 10, xiv. 7, xvi. 4, xxi. 6; elsewhere in N. T. rare. Similarly *φρέαρ*, *well*, occurs *vv.* 11, 12; Rev. ix. 1, 2; elsewhere only Luke xiv. 5. See on vii. 30. It still exists, but without spring-water, in the entrance to the valley between Ebal and Gerizim; one of the few undisputed sites. Samaria was now to receive the fulfilment of the promises in Gen. xlix. 22; Deut. xxxiii. 28, and become the heir of the patriarchs. Jacob's well was a pledge of this.

ἐκαθ. οὕτως ἐπὶ τ. π. **Was sitting** *thus* (just as He was) **by** (v. 2) *the spring*. These details shew full information. He is willing at once to surrender His rest by day to the Samaritan woman, as His rest by night to Nicodemus (iii. 2) and His retirement on the mountain to the multitude (vi. 5). On **ἐκ** expressing result see Winer, pp. 459, 772.

ὡς ἕκτη. This case again is not decisive as to S. John's mode of reckoning the hours. On the one hand, noon was an unusual hour for travelling and for drawing water, while evening was the usual time for the meal (*vv*. 8, 31). On the other, a woman whose life was under a cloud (*v*. 18) might select an unusual hour; and at 6 P.M. numbers would probably have been coming to draw, and the conversation would have been disturbed. Again, after 6 P.M. there would be rather short time for all that follows. These two instances (i. 39 and this) lend no strong support to the antecedently improbable theory that S. John's method of counting the hours is different from the Synoptists'.

7. ἐκ τ. Σαμ. Of the *province*, not of the *city* of Samaria. A woman of the city would not have come all that distance for water. The city was at that time called Sebaste, a name given to it by Herod the Great in honour of Augustus (Σεβαστός), who had granted the place to Herod on the death of Antony and Cleopatra (see on vi. 1). Herod's name Sebaste survives in the modern Sebustieh. In legends this woman is called Photina. For **ἀντλῆσαι**, comp. ii. 8.

δός μοι πεῖν. Quite literal, as the next verse shews: He asked her for refreshment *because* His disciples were not there to give it. 'Give Me the spiritual refreshment of thy conversion' is a meaning read into the words, not found in them. This request and *κεκοπιακὼς ἐκ τ. ὁδ.* (*v*. 6) shew how untenable is the view that the Fourth Evangelist held Docetic views: the reality of Christ's human form is very plain here (see on xix. 35). The reality of His human sympathy appears also; for often the best way to win a person is to ask a favour.

9. ἡ Σαμαρ. The adjective, as distinct from *ἐκ τῆς Σ.* in *v*. 7, lays stress on the national and religious characteristics. The repetition of the article, *ἡ γυνὴ ἡ Σ.*, giving emphasis to the adjective, is very frequent in S. John; v. 30, vi. 38, 42, 44, 50, 51, 58, &c. &c.

πῶς σὺ—παρ' ἐμοῦ. The pronouns are in emphatic opposition: she is half amused and half triumphant. She would know Him to be a Jew by His dress and speech In His request He would use the testing letter (Judg. xii. 6), 'Teni li*sch*ekoth,' which a Samaritan would pronounce 'li*s*ekoth.'

οὐ γὰρ συγχ. *For Jews have no dealings with Samaritans;* no articles. The remark is not the woman's, but S. John's, to explain her question. Comp. Luke ix. 53. As He was on His way from Judaea she would suppose Him to be a Judaean. Galileans seem to have been less strict, and hence His disciples had gone to buy food of Samaritans. But even Pharisees allowed Samaritan fruit, vegetables, and eggs. Some important authorities omit the remark.

10. εἰ ᾔδεις. *If thou* **hadst known**; on account of the aorists which follow: *οἶδα* has no aorist; comp. xi. 21, 32, xiv. 28, for the same construction; and contrast v. 46 and viii. 19, where A.V. makes the converse mistake of translating imperfects as aorists.

τ. δωρεὰν τ. θεοῦ. What He is ready to give to all, what is now held out to thee, salvation, or the living water. Comp. Rom. v. 15; 2 Cor. ix. 15.

σὺ ἂν ᾔτ. *Σύ* is emphatic; 'instead of His asking of thee.' 'Spiritually our positions are reversed. It is thou who art weary, and footsore, and parched, close to the well, yet unable to drink; it is I who can give thee the water from the well, and quench thy thirst for ever.' There is a scarcely doubtful reference to this passage in the Ignatian Epistles, *Romans*, VII. See p. xxi. and on vi. 33, to which there is a clear reference in this same chapter, and on iii. 8. The passage with these references to the Fourth Gospel is found in the Syriac as well as in the shorter Greek versions of Ignatius; so that we have almost certain evidence of this Gospel being known A.D. 115.

11. Κύριε. *Sir*, not 'Lord.' Having no neutral word in English, we must, as A.V., translate *Κύριε* sometimes 'Sir,' sometimes 'Lord.' But 'Sir' is a marked change from the feminine pertness of *v.* 9: His words and manner already begin to impress her.

βαθύ. Earlier travellers say over 100 feet; now it is about 75 feet deep. For **φρέαρ** see on *v.* 6: **ἄντλημα** here only in N. T.

τὸ ὕδ. τὸ ζ. *The water, the living* water (see on *v.* 9), of which Thou speakest. She thinks He means spring-water as distinct from cistern-water. Comp. Jer. ii. 13, where the two are strongly contrasted. In Gen. xxvi. 19, as the margin shews, 'springing water' is literally 'living water,' *viva aqua*. What did Christ mean by the 'living water'? Christ here and vii. 38 uses the figure of water, as elsewhere of bread (vi.) and light (viii. 12), the three most necessary things for life. But he does not *identify* Himself with the living water, as He does with the Bread, and the Light: therefore it seems better to understand the living water as the 'grace and truth' of which He is full (i. 14). Comp. Ecclus. xv. 3; Baruch iii. 12; Rev. vii. 17, xxi. 6, xxii. 1.

12. μὴ σὺ μείζ. *Σύ* is very emphatic; *Surely* Thou *art not greater:* comp. viii. 53, xviii. 33. Her loquacity as contrasted with the sententiousness of Nicodemus is very natural, while she shews a similar perverseness in misunderstanding spiritual metaphors.

τοῦ πατρὸς ἡμῶν. The Samaritans claimed to be descended from Joseph; with how much justice is a question very much debated. Some maintain that they were of purely heathen origin, although they were driven by calamity to unite the worship of Jehovah with their own idolatries: and this view seems to be in strict accordance with 2 Kings xvii. 23—41. Renegade Jews took refuge among them from time to time; but such immigrants would not affect the texture of the nation more than French refugees among ourselves. Others hold that the Samaritans were from the first a mongrel nation, a mixture of heathen colonists with Jewish inhabitants, left behind by Shalmaneser. There is nothing to shew that he did leave any (2 Kings xviii. 11); Josephus says (*Ant.* IX. xiv. 1) that 'he transplanted *all* the people.' When the Samaritans asked Alexander the Great to excuse them from tribute in the Sabbatical year, because as true sons of Joseph they did not till their land in the seventh year, he pronounced their claim an imposture, and destroyed Samaria. Our Lord calls a Samaritan 'one of a different race,' ἀλλογενής (Luke xvii. 18).

ἔδωκεν ἡμῖν. This has no foundation in Scripture, but no doubt was a Samaritan tradition. She means, 'the well was good enough for him, his sons, and his cattle, and is good enough for us; hast Thou a better?' The energetic diffuseness of her statement is very natural. **Θρέμματα** might mean 'slaves.'

13, 14. He leaves her question unanswered, like that of Nicodemus, and passes on to develope the metaphor rather than explain it, contrasting the literal with the figurative sense. Comp. iii. 6, vi. 35, 48—58, x. 7—9. Note the change from πᾶς ὁ πίνων, **every one that** *drinketh* (habitually) to ὃς ἂν πίῃ, *whosoever* **hath drunk** (once for all).

14. οὐ μὴ διψ. εἰς τ. αἰ. Strongest negation (*v.* 48), **will certainly not thirst for ever** (see on viii. 51), for it is the nature of the living water to reproduce itself perpetually, so that the thirst is quenched as soon as it recurs. And this inexhaustible fount not only satisfies the possessor but refreshes others also (vii. 38).

εἰς ζωὴν αἰών. This is the immediate result; the soul in which the living water flows *has* eternal life: see on *v.* 36 and iii. 16, 34. Comp. vi. 27, where the living bread is said to abide εἰς ζωὴν αἰώνιον.

15. She still does not understand, but does not wilfully misunderstand. This wonderful water will at any rate be worth having, and she asks quite sincerely (not ironically) for it. Had she been a Jew, she could scarcely have thus misunderstood; this metaphor of 'water' and 'living water' is so frequent in the Prophets. Comp. Isa. xii. 3, xliv. 3; Jer. ii. 13; Zech. xiii. 1, xiv. 8. But the Samaritans rejected all but the Pentateuch. With **δι**έρχωμαι comp. Luke ii. 15; Acts ix. 38.

16. φών. τ. ἄνδρα σοῦ. Not that the man was wanted, either as a concession to Jewish propriety, which forbad a Rabbi to talk with a woman alone, or for any other reason. By a seemingly casual request Christ lays hold of her inner life, convinces her of sin, and leads her to repentance, without which her request, 'Give me this water,' could not be granted. The husband who was no husband was the plague-spot where her healing must begin.

17. οὐκ ἔχω ἄνδ. Her volubility is checked: in the fewest possible words she tries to stop a dangerous subject at once.

καλῶς. There is perhaps a touch of irony, as in Matt. xv. 7; 2 Cor. xi. 4. Comp. viii. 48; Luke xx. 39.

18. πέντε ἄνδ. Quite literally; they were either dead or divorced, and she was now living with a man without being married to him. The emphatic position of *σου* may possibly mean that he is the husband of some one else.

τοῦτο ἀλ. εἴρ. **This thou hast said** *truly*, literally **'a true thing.'** Christ exposes the falsehood lurking under the literal truth.

19. προφήτης. One divinely inspired with supernatural knowledge, 1 Sam. ix. 9. The declaration contains an undoubted, though indirect, confession of sin. Note the gradual change in her attitude of mind towards Him. First, off-hand pertness (*v.* 9); then, respect to His gravity of manner and serious words (*v.* 11); next, a misunderstanding belief in what He says (*v.* 15); and now, reverence for Him as a 'man of God.' Comp. the parallel development of faith in the man born blind (see on ix. 11) and in Martha (see on xi. 21).

20. Convinced that He can read her life she shrinks from inspection and hastily turns the conversation from herself. In seeking a new subject she naturally catches at one of absorbing interest to every Samaritan. Or possibly she has had her religious yearnings before this, and eagerly grasps a chance of satisfying them. Mount Gerizim shorn of its temple recalls the great national religious question ever in dispute between them and the Jews. Here was One who could give an authoritative answer about it; she will ask Him. To urge that such a woman would care nothing about the matter is unsound reasoning. Are irreligious people never keen about religious questions now-a-days?

ἐν τ. ὄρει τ. Gerizim; her not naming it is very lifelike. The Samaritans contended that here Abraham offered up Isaac, and afterwards met Melchisedek. The former is more credible than the latter. A certain Manasseh, a man of priestly family, married the daughter of Sanballat the Horonite (Neh. xiii. 28), and was thereupon expelled from Jerusalem. He fled to Samaria and helped Sanballat to set up a rival worship on Gerizim. It is uncertain whether the temple on Gerizim was built then (about B.C. 410) or a century later; but it was destroyed by John Hyrcanus B.C. 130, after it had stood 200 years or more. Yet the Samaritans in no way receded from their claims, but continue their worship on Gerizim to the present day.

ὑμεῖς λέγ. Unconsciously she admits that One, whom she has confessed to be a Prophet, is against her in the controversy. Comp. Deut. xii. 13. **Δεῖ, must** *worship* (*v.* 24) according to God's will.

21—24. "We shall surely be justified in attributing the wonderful words of verses 21, 23, 24, to One greater even than S. John. They seem to breathe the spirit of other worlds than ours—'of worlds whose course is equable and pure;' where media and vehicles of grace are unneeded, and the soul knows even as it is known. There is nothing so like them in their sublime infinitude of comprehension, and intense penetration to the deepest roots of things, as some of the sayings in the Sermon on the Mount (Matt. v. 45, vi. 6). It is words like these that strike home to the hearts of men, as in the most literal sense Divine"—(Sandday).

21. πίστευέ μοι. See on i. 12, vi. 30. This formula occurs here only; the usual one is *ἀμὴν, ἀμὴν, λέγω σοι* (iii. 3, 5, 11, xiii. 38, xxi. 18; comp. i. 52, iv. 35, v. 24, 25, &c.). The present, as distinct from the aorist, means 'believe, and continue to believe' (x. 38, xii. 36, xiv. 1, 11). T. R. here reads *πίστευσον*.

ἔρχεται ὥρα. There cometh an hour (v. 25, 28, xvi. 2, 4, 25, 32). He decides neither for nor against either place. The claims of both will ere long be lost in something higher. The ruin on Gerizim and the Temple at Jerusalem will soon be on an equality, but without any privileges being transferred from the one to the other. Those who worship 'the Father' must rise above distinctions of place; for a time is coming when limitations of worship will disappear. 'The Father' (*ὁ πατήρ*, never *πατήρ*) used absolutely of God is very common in S. John, very rare elsewhere in N. T. (Matt. xi. 27; Acts i. 4, 7; Rom. vi. 4; Eph. ii. 18).

22. ὃ οὐκ οἴδ. That which ye know not. The higher truth having been planted for the future, Christ proceeds to answer her question as to the present controversy. The Samaritan religion, even after being purified from the original mixture with idolatry (2 Kings xvii. 33, 41), remained a mutilated religion; the obscurity of the Pentateuch (and of that a garbled text) unenlightened by the clearer revelations in the Prophets and other books of O. T. Such a religion when contrasted with the Jewish, which had developed in constant contact with Divine revelation, might well be called ignorance.

ἡμεῖς κ.τ.λ. We worship that which we know. The abstract form conveyed by the neuter should be preserved in both clauses (Acts xvii. 23). The first person plural here is not similar to that in iii. 11 (see note there), though some would take it so. Christ here speaks as a Jew, and in such a passage there is nothing surprising in His so doing. As a rule Christ gives no countenance to the view that He belongs to the Jewish nation in any special way, though the Jewish nation specially belongs to Him (i. 11): He is the Saviour of the world, not of the Jews only. But here, where it is a question whether Jew or Samaritan has the larger share of religious truth, He ranks Himself both by birth and by religion among the Jews. 'We,' therefore, means 'we Jews.'

ὅτι. The importance of the conjunction must not be missed: the Jews know their God **because** *the salvation of the world issues from them.* Their religion was not, like the Samaritan, mere deism, but a *παιδαγωγὸς* leading on to the Messiah (Gal. iii. 24).

ἡ σωτηρία ἐκ τ. Ἰ. ἐ. The *salvation*, the expected salvation, *is of the Jews;* i.e. *proceeds from* them (not *belongs to* them), in virtue of the promises to Abraham (Gen. xii. 3, xviii. 18, xxii. 18) and Isaac (xxvi. 4): comp. Is. ii. 3; Obad. 17. This verse is absolutely fatal to the theory that this Gospel is the work of a Gnostic Greek in the second century (see on xix. 35). That salvation proceeded from the Jews contradicts the fundamental principle of Gnosticism, that salvation was to be sought in the higher knowledge of which Gnostics had the key. Hence those who uphold such a theory of authorship assume, in defiance of all evidence, that this verse is a later interpolation. The verse is found in all MSS. and versions. See Introduction, Chap. II. ii. For **τῶν Ἰουδαίων** see on xiii. 33.

23. καὶ νῦν ἐστίν. These words could not be added in *v.* 21. The local worship on Zion and Gerizim must continue for a while. But already a few are rising above these externals to the spirit of true worship, in which the differences between Jew and Samaritan disappear. In the heavenly Jerusalem there is 'no temple therein; for the Lord God Almighty is the temple of it, and the Lamb' (Rev. xxi. 22). Perhaps Jesus sees His disciples returning, and the sight of them prompts the joyous *καὶ νῦν ἐστι.*

οἱ ἀληθινοὶ πρ. *True* as opposed to unreal and spurious (see on i. 9), not to insincere and lying worshippers. Jewish types and shadows no less than Samaritan and Gentile imitations and delusions must pass away. Worship to be perfect and real must be offered in spirit and truth.

ἐν πνεύματι. This is opposed to what is material, carnal, and of the earth, earthy; 'this mountain,' the Temple, limitations of time, and space and nation. Not that such limitations are wrong; but they are not of the essence of religion and become wrong when they are mistaken for it. In the 'holy ground' of his own heart every one, whatever his race, may at all times worship the Father.

καὶ ἀληθείᾳ. Just as *ἐν πνεύματι* confirms the declaration against local claims in *v.* 21, so *ἐν ἀληθείᾳ* confirms the condemnation of an ignorant worship, that sins against light, in *v.* 22. True worship must be in harmony with the Nature and Will of God. In the sphere of intellect, this means recognition of His Presence and Omniscience; in the sphere of action, conformity with His absolute Holiness. 'Worship in spirit and truth,' therefore, implies prostration of the inmost soul before the Divine Perfection, submission of every thought and feeling to the Divine Will. The two words express two aspects of one truth; hence *ἐν* is not repeated: Winer, p. 522.

καὶ γὰρ ὁ πατὴρ τ. For such the Father also seeketh for His worshippers. 'Such' is emphatic; 'this is the character which He also desires in His worshippers.' The 'also' must not be lost. That worship should be 'in spirit and truth' is required by the fitness of things: moreover God Himself desires to have it so, and works for this end. *Intus exhibe te templum Deo. In templo vis orare, in te ora* (S. Augustine). Note how three times in succession Christ speaks of God as *the Father* (*vv.* 21, 23): perhaps it was a new aspect of Him to the woman.

24. God is spirit (not '*a* spirit'), and must be approached in that part of us which is spirit, in the true temple of God, 'which temple ye are.' The premise was old (1 Kings viii. 27); it is the deduction from it which though necessary (δεῖ) is new. Even to the chosen three Christ imparts no truths more profound than these. He admits this poor schismatic to the very fountain-head of religion.

25. **Μεσσίας.** See on i. 41. There is nothing improbable in her knowing the Jewish name and using it to a Jew. The word being rare in N. T. we are perhaps to understand that it was the very word used; but it may be S. John's equivalent for what she said. Comp. *v.* 29. Throughout this discourse it is impossible to say how much of it is a translation of the very words used, how much merely the substance of what was said. S. John would obtain his information from Christ, and possibly from the woman also during their two days' stay. The idea that S. John was left behind by the disciples, and *heard* the conversation, is against the tenour of the narrative and is contradicted by *vv.* 8 and 27.

ὁ λ. Χριστός. Probably the Evangelist's parenthetic explanation (but contrast i. 42), not the woman's. The Samaritan name for the expected Saviour was 'the Returning One,' or (according to a less probable derivation) 'the Converter.' 'The Returner' points to the belief that Moses was to appear again. Comp. xi. 16, xx. 24.

ἐκεῖνος. Emphatic; in contrast with other Prophets and teachers; the pronoun implies the exclusion of her present Teacher also.

ἀναγγελεῖ. *He will* **announce** *to us all things:* the revelation will be complete.

26. **Ἐγώ εἰμι.** It is the ordinary Greek affirmative (Luke xxii. 70). There is no reference to the Divine name 'I AM,' Ex. iii. 14; Deut. xxxii. 39. This open declaration of His Messiahship is startling when we remember Matt. xvi. 20, xvii. 9; Mark viii. 30. But one reason for reserve on this subject, lest the people should 'take Him by force to make Him a king' (vi. 15), is entirely wanting here. There was no fear of the Samaritans making political capital out of Him. Moreover it was one thing for Christ to avow Himself when He saw that hearts were ready for it; quite another for disciples to make Him known promiscuously. Contrast Matt. xxvi. 63.

27. **ἐθαύμαζον.** Change of tense; their coming was a single act, *they continued wondering* (*vv.* 30, 40) *that He* **was talking with a woman,** contrary to the precepts of the Rabbis. 'Let no man talk with a woman in the street, no not with his own wife. Rather burn the words of the Law than teach them to women.' This was probably the first time that they had seen Him ignore this prejudice, and the woman's being a Samaritan would increase their astonishment.

οὐδείς. Out of reverence: comp. xxi. 12.

μέντοι. Only thrice (2 Tim. ii. 19; James ii. 8; Jude 8) outside this Gospel (vii. 13, xii. 42, xx. 5, xxi. 4). The two questions are probably both addressed (hypothetically) to Christ. The word λαλεῖν, thrice in two verses, seems to point to the freedom with which He had conversed with her.

28. οὖν. **Therefore**, because of the interruption: see on iii. 25. Ὑδρία occurs ii. 6, 7 and nowhere else. Her leaving it to take care of itself (*v.* 3) shews that her original errand is of no moment compared with what now lies before her; it is also a pledge for her speedy return. This graphic touch is from one who was there, and saw, and remembered.

τοῖς ἀνθρώποις. **The** *people*, those whom she met anywhere. She feels that the wonderful news is for all, not for her 'husband' only (*v.* 16). Like Andrew, John, and Philip, her first impulse is to tell others of what she has found, and in almost the same words; 'Come, see' (i. 41—46). The learned Nicodemus had given no sign of being convinced. This ignorant schismatic goes forth in the enthusiasm of conviction to proclaim her belief.

29. πάντα ἅ. ἐπ. How natural is this exaggeration! In her excitement she states not what He had really told her, but what she is convinced He could have told her. Comp. *πάντες* in iii. 26, and *οὐδεὶς* in iii. 32. This strong language is in all three cases thoroughly in keeping with the circumstances. See on i. 50, xx. 28.

μήτι οὗτος. Can this be the Christ? not 'Is not this,' as A.V., which has a similar error xviii. 17, 25. Comp. *v.* 33, vii. 31, 48, viii. 22, xviii. 35, xxi. 5; where in all cases a negative answer is anticipated; *num* not *nonne*. Here, although she believes that He is the Christ, she states it as almost too good to be true. Moreover she does not wish to seem too positive and dogmatic to those who do not yet know the evidence.

30. ἐξῆλθον...ἤρχοντο. *Went out*...**were coming** (comp. *v.* 27): the single act (aorist) is contrasted with what took some time (imperf.). See on xi. 29. We are to see them coming across the fields as we listen to the conversation that follows (31—38).

31. ἐν τῷ μετ. Between her departure and their arrival.

ἠρώτων. Were beseeching Him (*vv.* 40, 47): they had left him exhausted with the journey (*v.* 6), and they urge, not their own wonder (*v.* 27), but His needs.

'Ραββί. See on i. 39. Here and in ix. 2 and xi. 8 our translators have rather regrettably turned 'Rabbi' into 'Master' (comp. Matt. xxvi. 25, 49; Mark ix. 5, xi. 21, xiv. 45); while 'Rabbi' is retained i. 38, 49, iii. 2, 26, vi. 25 (comp. Matt. xxiii. 7, 8). Apparently their principle was that wherever a disciple addresses Christ, 'Rabbi' is to be translated 'Master;' in other cases 'Rabbi' is to be retained; thus obscuring the view which the disciples took of their own relation to Jesus. He was their Rabbi.

32. ἐγὼ...ὑμεῖς. In emphatic opposition: they have their food; He has His. Joy at the fruit of His teaching prompts Him to refuse food; not of course that His human frame could do without it, but that in His delight He for the time feels no need of it. **Βρῶσις** is rather 'eating' than food, which is *βρῶμα*, as in *v.* 34; comp. vi. 27, 55. S. Paul accurately distinguishes the two; Col. ii. 16; Rom. xiv.

17; 1 Cor. viii. 4; 2 Cor. ix. 10; so also Heb. xii. 16: *πόσις* and *πόμα* the same; Rom. xiv. 17; 1 Cor. x. 3; also Heb. ix. 10.

οὐκ οἴδατε. *Know not;* not (as A.V.) 'know not *of*,' which spoils the sense. The point is, not that He has had food without their knowledge, but a kind of food of which they have no conception.

33. πρὸς ἀλλ. Comp. *v.* 27, xvi. 17. They refrain from pressing Him with their difficulty.

ἤνεγκεν. Emphatic: 'Surely no one hath *brought* Him anything to eat.' This would be specially unlikely among Samaritans. Another instance of dulness as to spiritual meaning. In ii. 20 it was the Jews; in iii. 4 Nicodemus; in *v.* 11 the Samaritan woman; and now the disciples. 'What wonder that the woman did not understand the water? The disciples do not understand the food!' (Augustine). Comp. xi. 12, xiv. 5. These candid reports of what tells against the disciples add to the trust which we place in the narratives of the Evangelists.

34. ἐμὸν βρ. ἐστιν ἵνα. 'Εμόν is emphatic: *My food is* **that I may** *do the will of Him that sent Me and* (*thus*) **perfect** *His work.* Christ's aim and purpose is His food. See on i. 8; *ἵνα* is no mere periphrasis for the infinitive (vi. 29, 40, xvii. 3; 1 John iii. 11, v. 3; comp. i. 27, ii. 25, v. 40). This verse recalls the reply to the tempter 'man doth not live by bread alone,' and to His parents 'Wist ye not that I must be about My Father's business?' Luke iv. 4, ii. 49. It is the first of many such sayings in this Gospel, expressing Christ's complete conformity to His Father's will in doing His work (v. 30, vi. 38, xi. 4, xii. 49, 50, xiv. 31, xv. 10, xvii. 4). **Τελειοῦν** (not merely *τελεῖν*) means 'to bring to a full end, make perfect;' frequent in S. John (v. 36, xvii. 4, 23, xix. 28; 1 John ii. 5, iv. 12, 17) and in Hebrews.

35. ἔτι τετράμ. κ.τ.λ. This cannot be a proverb. No such proverb is known; and a proverb on the subject would have to be differently shaped; e.g. 'From seedtime to harvest is four months;' *ἔτι* points to a single case. So that we may regard this saying as a mark of time. Harvest began in the middle of Nisan or April. Four months from that would place this event in the middle of December: or, if (as some suppose) this was a year in which an extra month was inserted, in the middle of January. The words form an iambic verse.

ὅτι λευκαί εἰσιν. In the green blades just shewing through the soil the faith of the sower sees the white ears that will soon be there. So also in the flocking of these ignorant Samaritans to Him for instruction Christ sees the abundant harvest of souls that is to follow. *Ὅτι* should be taken after *θεάσασθε*, *behold* **that**, not as A.V. 'for,' or 'because.' The punctuation is very uncertain, as to whether *ἤδη* belongs to this verse or the next. The balance of authority gives *ἤδη* to *v.* 36; but in punctuation MSS. are not of great authority, and *ἤδη* at the end of *v.* 35 seems intended to balance *ἔτι* at the beginning of it. Comp. 1 John iv. 3.

36. εἰς ζωὴν αἰ. See on iii. 15, 16. Eternal life is regarded as the granary *into* which the fruit is gathered; comp. *v.* 14, and for similar imagery Matt. ix. 37, 38.

ἵνα. This is God's purpose. Ps. cxxvi. 5, 6 promises that the toil of sowing shall be rewarded with the joy of reaping; but in the Gospel the gracious work is so rapid that the sower shares in the joys of harvest. The contrast between His failure in Judaea and His success in Samaria fills Jesus with joy. Christ, not the Prophets, is the Sower. The Gospel is not the fruit of which the O.T. is the seed; rather the Gospel is the seed for which the O.T. prepared the ground. And His ministers are the reapers; in this case the Apostles.

37. ἐν γὰρ...ἀληθινός. *For herein is the saying* (*proved*) *a true one*, shewn by fulfilment to be a genuine proverb and not an empty phrase. See on *v.* 23, vii. 28, xix. 35. Ἐν τούτῳ refers to what precedes (comp. xv. 8, xvi. 30), in your reaping what others sowed (*vv.* 35, 36).

38. κεκοπιάκατε. *Ye have laboured.* The pronouns, as in *v.* 32, are emphatic and opposed. This will be the rule throughout; *sic vos non vobis.*

ἄλλοι. Christ, the Sower; but put in the plural to balance ὑμεῖς. In *v.* 37 both are in the *singular* for the sake of harmony; ὁ σπείρων, Christ; ὁ θερίζων, His ministers.

39. πολλοὶ ἐπ. εἰς αὐ. Strong proof of the truth of *v.* 35. These Samaritans outstrip the Jews, and even the Apostles, in their readiness to believe. The Jews rejected the testimony of their own Scriptures, of the Baptist, of Christ's miracles and teaching. The Samaritans accept the testimony of the woman, who had suddenly become an Apostle to her countrymen. The miraculous knowledge displayed by Jesus for a second time (i. 49) produces immediate and complete conviction, and in this case the conviction spreads to others.

40. ἠρώτων. **Kept beseeching** (*vv.* 30, 31, 47). How different from His own people at Nazareth (Matt. xiii. 58; Luke iv. 29) and from the Jews at Jerusalem after many miracles and much teaching (v. 18, &c.). And yet he had uncompromisingly pronounced against Samaritan claims (*v.* 22). Comp. the thankful Samaritan leper (Luke xvii. 16, 17).

μεῖναι. See on i. 33. They wished him to take up his abode permanently with them, or at least for a time.

42. οὐκέτι κ.τ.λ. Note the order: **No longer is it because of thy speech that we believe** (see on i. 7). Λαλιά and λόγος should be distinguished in translation. In classical Greek λαλιά has a slightly uncomplimentary turn, 'gossip, chatter.' But this shade of meaning is lost in later Greek, though there is *perhaps* a tinge of it here, 'not because of *thy talk;*' but this being doubtful, 'speech' will be safer. S. John uses λόγος both for her word (*v.* 39) and Christ's (*v.* 41). See on viii. 43, where Christ uses λαλιά of His own teaching.

αὐτοὶ γ. ἀκ. *For we have heard* **for** *ourselves.*

ἀληθῶς ὁ σ. τ. κ. See on i. 48 and 10. It is not improbable that such ready hearers should arrive at this great truth so rapidly. They had the Pentateuch (comp. Gen. xii. 3, xviii. 18, xxii. 18, xxvi. 4), and not being in the trammels of Jewish exclusiveness would believe that the Messiah was not for the Jew alone. The Samaritan gave up less than the Jew when he accepted Christ. It is therefore unnecessary to suppose that S. John is unconsciously giving his own expression (1 John iv. 14) for theirs.

43—54. The Work among Galileans

43. τὰς δ. ἡμ. The *two days* mentioned in *v.* 40. These three verses (43—45) form a sort of introduction to this section, as ii. 13 and iv. 1—4 to the two previous sections.

44. αὐτὸς γὰρ κ.τ.λ. This is a well-known difficulty. As in xx. 17, we have a reason assigned which seems to be the very opposite of what we should expect. This witness of Jesus would account for His *not* going into Galilee: how does it account for His going thither? It seems best to fall back on the old explanation of Origen, that by 'His own country' is meant Judaea, 'the home of the Prophets,' and, we may add, the land of His birth, for centuries connected with Him by prophecy. Moreover, Judaea fits in with the circumstances. He had not only met with little honour in Judaea; He had been forced to retreat from it. No Apostle had been found there. The appeal to Judaea had in the main been a failure. True that the Synoptists record a similar saying (Matt. xiii. 57; Mark vi. 4; Luke iv. 24) *not* in relation to *Judaea*, but to *Nazareth*, 'where He had been brought up.' But as they record the Galilaean, and S. John the Judaean ministry, it is only natural that a saying capable of various shades of meaning, and perhaps uttered on more than one occasion, should be applied in different ways by them and by S. John. Origen's explanation accounts quite satisfactorily not only for the *γάρ* here, but also for the *οὖν* in *v.* 45, which means *When* **therefore** *He came into Galilee*, the welcome which He received proved the truth of the saying; 'Galilee of the Gentiles' received Him whom *οἱ ἴδιοι* (i. 11), the Jews of Jerusalem and Judaea, had rejected.

45. ἐν τῇ ἑορτῇ. The Passover; but there is no need to name it, because it has already been mentioned in connexion with these miracles, ii. 23. Perhaps these Galilaeans who then witnessed the miracles were the chief of the *πολλοί* who then believed.

46. ἦλθεν οὖν. *He came* **therefore**, because of the previous invitation and welcome: see Introduction, chap. v. 6, c.

βασιλικός. **Royal official** of Herod Antipas, who though only tetrarch was given his father's title of *βασιλεύς*. The word has nothing to do with birth ('nobleman' A.V.), nor can we tell whether a civil or military officer is intended. That he was Chusa (Luke viii. 3) or Manaen (Acts xiii. 1) is pure conjecture. Here and in *v.* 49 the form *βασιλίσκος* is strongly supported.

47. ἀπῆλθεν...ἠρώτα. Comp. *vv.* 27, 30, 40, 50, and see on xi. 29. The leaving his son was a single act (aor.), the beseeching (*vv.* 31, 40) was continuous (imp.). For *ἵνα* see on i. 8. Some scholars think that in constructions like this *ἵνα* does not mean 'in order that,' but 'that,' and simply *defines the scope* of the request or command; comp. xi. 57, xvii. 15, 21, xix. 31, 38, xv. 17, 12, xi. 57. Winer, pp. 425, 573.

καταβῇ. *Down* to the lake (ii. 12); about 20 miles. See on i. 7.

ἤμελλε. *Μέλλειν* here simply means 'to be likely' without any further notion either of *intention* (vi. 6, 15, vii. 35, xiv. 22), or of being *fore-ordained* (xi. 51, xii. 33, xviii. 32).

48. σημεῖα κ. τέρατα. Christ's miracles are never mere *τέρατα*, wonders to excite astonishment; they are 'signs' of heavenly truths as well, and this is their primary characteristic. Where the two words are combined *σημεῖα* always precedes, excepting Acts ii. 22, 43, vi. 8, vii. 36. S. John nowhere else uses *τέρατα*: his words for miracles are *σημεῖα* and *ἔργα*.

οὐ μὴ πιστεύσητε. Strongest negation (*v.* 14). *Ye will* **in no wise** *believe:* or interrogatively; *Will ye in no wise believe?* Comp. *οὐ μὴ πίω*; xviii. 11. The words are addressed to him (*πρὸς αὐτόν*), but as the representative of the many who demanded a sign before believing (see on 1 Cor. i. 22). Faith of this low type is not rejected (x. 38, xiv. 11, xx. 29); it may grow into something better, as here, by being tested and braced (*v.* 50). But it may also go back into sheer unbelief, as with most of those who were won over by His miracles. The verse tells of the depressing change which Christ experienced in returning from Samaria to the land of Israel.

49. Κύριε. See on *v.* 11. His words shew both his faith and its weakness. He believes that Christ's presence can heal; he does not believe that He can heal without being present. The words for the child are characteristic: the father uses *παιδίον*, the term of endearment; Jesus and the Evangelist use *υἱός*, the term of dignity; the servants the more familiar *παῖς*.

50. ἐπίστ. τῷ λόγῳ. Not yet *ἐπίστ. εἰς αὐτόν*: but this is an advance on *κατάβηθι πρὶν ἀποθανεῖν*.

52. κομψότερον ἔσχεν. Literally, **got somewhat better**; a colloquial expression: *κομψῶς ἔχεις*, 'you are getting on nicely,' occurs as a doctor's expression, Arrian, *Diss. Epict.* III. x. 13. The father expects the cure to be gradual: the fever will depart at Christ's word, but in the ordinary way. He has not yet fully realised Christ's power. The servants' reply shews that the cure was instantaneous.

ἐχθὲς ὥραν ἑβδ. Accusative; *during* or *in the seventh hour*. Once more we have to discuss S. John's method of counting the hours. (See on i. 39, iv. 6.) Obviously the father set out as soon after Jesus said 'thy son liveth' as possible; he had 20 or 25 miles to go to reach home, and would not be likely to loiter. 7 A.M. is incredible; he would have been home long before nightfall, and the servants met him some distance from home. 7 P.M. is improbable; the servants would meet him before midnight. Thus the modern method of reckoning from midnight to midnight does not suit. Adopting the Jewish method from sunset to sunset, the seventh hour is 1 P.M. He would scarcely start at once in the mid-day heat; nor would the servants. Supposing they met him after sunset, they might speak of 1 P.M. as 'yesterday.' (But see on xx. 19, where S. John speaks of the late hours of the evening as belonging to the day *before* sunset.) Still, 7 P.M. is not impossible, and this third instance must be regarded as not decisive. But the balance here seems to incline to what is antecedently more probable, that S. John reckons the hours, like the rest of the Evangelists, according to the Jewish method.

53. ἔγνω. *Recognised*, perceived.

ἐπίστευσεν. *Εἰς αὐτόν*, i.e. as the Messiah: comp. *v.* 42, i. 7, 51, vi. 36, xi. 15, where, as here, *πιστεύω* is used absolutely. The growth of this official's faith is sketched for us in the same natural and incidental way as in the cases of the Samaritan woman (*v.* 19), the man born blind (ix. 11), and Martha (xi. 21).

ἡ οἰκία αὐ. ὅλη. The first converted family. Comp. Cornelius, Lydia, and the Philippian gaoler (Acts x. 24, xvi. 15, 34).

54. τοῦτο π. δ. σ. *This again as a second sign did Jesus, after He had come out of Judaea into Galilee.* Once more S. John carefully distinguishes two visits to Galilee, which any one with only the Synoptic account might easily confuse. Both signs confirmed imperfect faith, the first that of the disciples, the second that of this official and his household.

The question whether this foregoing narrative is a discordant account of the healing of the centurion's servant (Matt. viii. 5; Luke vii. 2) has been discussed from very early times, for Origen and Chrysostom contend against it. Irenaeus seems to be in favour of the identification, but we cannot be sure that he is. He says, 'He healed the son of the centurion though absent with a word, saying, Go, thy son liveth.' Irenaeus may have supposed that this official was a centurion, or 'centurion' may be a slip. Eight very marked points of difference between the two narratives have been noted. Together they amount to something like proof that the two narratives cannot refer to one and the same fact, unless we are to attribute an astonishing amount of carelessness or misinformation either to the Synoptists or to S. John.

(1) Here a 'king's man' pleads for his son; there a centurion for his servant.

(2) Here he pleads in person; there the elders plead for him.

(3) The father is probably a Jew; the centurion is certainly a Gentile.

(4) Here the healing words are spoken at Cana; there at Capernaum.

(5) Here the malady is fever; there paralysis.

(6) The father wishes Jesus to come; the centurion begs Him not to come.

(7) Here Christ does not go; there apparently He does.

(8) The father has weak faith and is blamed (*v.* 48); the centurion has strong faith and is commended.

And what difficulty is there in supposing two somewhat similar miracles? Christ's miracles were 'signs;' they were vehicles for conveying the spiritual truths which Christ came to teach. If, as is almost certain, He often repeated the same instructive sayings, may He not sometimes have repeated the same instructive acts? Here, therefore, as in the case of the cleansing of the Temple (ii. 13—17), it seems wisest to believe that S. John and the Synoptists record different events.

Chaps. V. to XI. The Work among mixed Multitudes, chiefly Jews

The Work now becomes a conflict between Christ and 'the Jews;' for as Christ reveals Himself more fully, the opposition between Him and the ruling party becomes more intense; and the fuller revelation which excites the hatred of His opponents serves also to sift the disciples; some turn back, others are strengthened in their faith by what they see and hear. The Evangelist from time to time points out the opposite results of Christ's work: vi. 60—71, vii. 40—52, ix. 13—41, x. 19, 21, 39—42, xi. 45—57. Three miracles form crises in the conflict; the healing of the impotent man (v.), of the man born blind (ix.), and the raising of Lazarus (xi).

Thus far we have had the announcement of the Gospel to the world, and the reception it is destined to meet with, set forth in four typical instances; *Nathanael*, the guileless Israelite, truly religious according to the light allowed him; *Nicodemus*, the learned ecclesiastic, skilled in the Scriptures, but ignorant of the first elements of religion; the *Samaritan woman*, immoral in life and schismatical in religion, but simple in heart and readily convinced; and the *royal official*, weak in faith, but progressing gradually to a full conviction. But as yet there is little evidence of hostility to Christ, although the Evangelist prepares us for it (i. 11, ii. 18—20, iii. 18, 19, 26, iv. 44). Henceforth, however, hostility to Him is manifested in every chapter of this division. Two elements are placed in the sharpest contrast throughout; the Messiah's clearer manifestation of His Person and Work, and the growing animosity of 'the Jews' in consequence of it. The opposition is stronger in Judaea than elsewhere; strongest of all at Jerusalem. In Galilee they abandon Him, in Jerusalem they compass His death. Two miracles form the introduction to two great discourses: two miracles illustrate two discourses. The healing at Bethesda and the feeding of the 5000 lead to discourses in which Christ is set forth as *the Source and the Support of Life* (v., vi.). Then He is set forth as *the Source of Truth and Light;* and this is illustrated by His giving physical and spiritual sight to the blind (vii.—ix.). Finally He is set forth as *Love* under the figure of the Good Shepherd giving His life for the sheep; and this is illustrated by the raising of Lazarus, a work of love which costs Him His life (x., xi.). Thus, of four typical miracles, two form the introduction and two form the sequel to great discourses. The prevailing idea throughout is truth and love provoking contradiction and enmity.

CHAPTER V

3. Omit *ἐκδεχομένων τὴν τοῦ ὕδατος κίνησιν* after **ξηρῶν,** with ℵA[1]BC[1]L against D and the great mass of later authorities; a gloss suggested by *v.* 7, and added before *v.* 4.

4. Omit the whole verse, with ℵBC[1]D against AL and the majority of later authorities; a gloss probably embodying an ancient tradition. Insertion in this case is easily explained, omission not.

5. Insert **αὐτοῦ** (overlooked between *-ᾳ* and *του-*) after *ἀσθενείᾳ*.

8—11. **κράβαττον** is the form now generally received in N. T. for *κράββατον*.

16. Omit *καὶ ἐζήτουν αὐτὸν ἀποκτεῖναι* (inserted from *v.* 18) with ℵBCDL against A.

25, 28. **ἀκούσουσιν.** We cannot determine with certainty between this form (xvi. 13?) and *ἀκούσονται*: *ἀκούσομαι* is the more common future in N. T. On **ζήσουσιν** (*v.* 25) see on vi. 57.

36. **μείζων** (ABEGMΛ) is to be preferred to *μείζω* (ℵ), **δέδωκεν** (ℵBL) to *ἔδωκε* (AD), which has been influenced by *vv.* 26, 27.

37. **ἐκεῖνος** (ℵBL) for *αὐτός*, which was first inserted along with *ἐκεῖνος* (D), and then drove it out (A).

43. **λήμψεσθε** for *λήψεσθε*: xvi. 14, 15, 24. Winer, p. 53.

Chap. V. Christ the Source of Life

In chaps. v. and vi. the word 'life' occurs 18 times; in the rest of the Gospel 18 times. 'Thy son liveth' (iv. 51) leads up to this subject.

This chapter falls into two main divisions; (1) *The Sign at the Pool of Bethesda and its Sequel* (1—16); (2) *The Discourse on the Son as the Source of Life* (17—47).

1—9. The Sign at the Pool of Bethesda

1. **μετὰ ταῦτα.** See on iii. 22.

ἑορτὴ τ. 'Ι ABD, Origen, and many later authorities omit the article, which though very ancient, was probably inserted owing to a belief that Tabernacles or the Passover was the feast intended.

Insertion would be more likely than omission. If ἑορτή is the true reading, this alone is almost conclusive against its being the Passover; S. John would not call the Passover '*a* feast of the Jews.' Moreover in all other cases where he mentions Passovers he lets us know that they are Passovers and not simply feasts, ii. 13, vi. 4, xi. 55, &c. He gives us three Passovers; to make this a fourth would be to put an extra year into our Lord's ministry for which scarcely any events can be found, and of which there is no trace elsewhere. In vii. 19—24 Jesus justifies the healing at this feast. Would He go back to an event like this after a year and a half? Almost every other feast, and even the Day of Atonement, has been suggested; but the only one which fits in satisfactorily is Purim. We saw from iv. 35 that the two days in Samaria were either in December or January. The next certain date is vi. 4, the eve of the Passover, i.e. April. Purim, which was celebrated in March (14th and 15th Adar), falls just in the right place in the interval. This feast commemorated the deliverance of the Jews from Haman, and took its name from the *lots* which he caused to be cast (Esther iii. 7, ix. 24, 26, 28). It was a boisterous feast, and some have thought it unlikely that Christ would have anything to do with it. But we are not told that He went to Jerusalem *in order to keep the feast;* Purim might be kept anywhere. More probably He went because the multitudes at the feast would afford great opportunities for teaching. Moreover, it does not follow that because some made this feast a scene of unseemly jollity, therefore Christ would discountenance the feast itself. Assuming Purim to be right, why does S. John not name it? Not because it was without express Divine sanction; the Dedication (x. 22) was a feast of man's institution. More probably because Purim had no reference to either Christ or His work. 'The promised salvation is of the Jews,' and S. John is ever watchful to point out the connexion between Jesus and the O. T. The Passover and Feast of Tabernacles pointed clearly to Him; the Feast of Dedication pointed to His work, the reconsecration of the Jewish people to Jehovah. To refer the political festival of Purim to Him whose kingdom was not of this world (xviii. 36), might cause the gravest misunderstanding. The feast here has no symbolical meaning, but is a barren historical fact; and the Evangelist leaves it in obscurity.

ἀνέβη. Went *up*, because to the capital.

2. **ἔστιν.** The present tense is no evidence that this Gospel was written before the destruction of Jerusalem. S. John might easily write of the place as he remembered it. Even if the building were destroyed the pool would remain; and such a building, being of the nature of a hospital, would possibly be spared. See on xi. 18.

ἐπὶ τῇ προβατικῇ κ.τ.λ. Reading and interpretation are somewhat uncertain: κολυμβήθρα is preferable to κολυμβήθρᾳ, ἡ ἐπιλεγομένη to τὸ λεγόμενον, and Βηθζαθά to Βηθεσδά or Βηθσαϊδά. It is better to supply πύλῃ rather than ἀγορᾷ with προβατικῇ, although the ellipse of πύλη occurs nowhere else; for we know from Neh. iii. 1, 32, xii. 39, that there was a sheep-gate. It was near the Temple, for by it sacrifices probably entered the Temple. There is evidence, however, that there were *two* pools at this place, and so we may translate, *Now there is at Jerusalem, by the sheep-pool, the pool* (or, reading τὸ λεγ., *the place*) *called, &c.* We cannot be sure from ἐπιλεγομένη ('surnamed') that the pool had some other name as well. 'The pool' might be the name, Bethzatha the *sur*name. Beth-*esda*='House of Mercy,' or (-*Aschada*) 'of outpouring,' or (*estâu*) 'of the Portico.' Beth-*zatha* may mean 'House of the Olive.' The traditional identification with *Birket Israel* is not commonly advocated now. The 'Fountain of the Virgin' is an attractive identification, as the water is intermittent to this day. This fountain is connected with the pool of Siloam, and some think that Siloam is Bethesda. That S. John speaks of Bethesda here and Siloam in ix. 7, is not conclusive against this: for Bethesda might be the name of the building and Siloam of the pool, which would agree with ἐπιλεγομένη, as above.

Ἑβραϊστί. In Aramaic, the language spoken at the time, not the old Hebrew of the Scriptures. See on xx. 16. The word occurs only in this Gospel (xix. 13, 17, 20, xx. 16) and in Revelation (ix. 11, xvi. 16). See on i. 14, iv. 6, vii. 30, xi. 44, xv. 20, xix. 37, xx. 16.

στοάς. *Colonnades* or cloisters. These would shelter the sick. The place seems to have been a kind of charitable institution, and Jesus, we may suppose, had come to heal this patient.

3. **τυφλ., χ., ξ.** The special kinds of ἀσθενοῦντες. The words which follow in T.R., and the whole of *v.* 4 are an interpolation, though a very ancient one, for it was known to Tertullian (*De Bapt.* v.). "The whole passage is omitted by the oldest representatives of each great group of authorities" (Westcott). The conclusion of *v.* 3 was added first as a gloss on *v.* 7; and *v.* 4 may represent the popular belief with regard to the intermittent bubbling of the healing water, first added as a gloss, and then inserted into the text. The water was probably mineral, and the people may have been right in supposing that it was most efficacious when it was most violent. The MSS. which contain the insertion vary very much.

5. **ἔτη.** Accusative after ἔχων, like χρόνον in *v.* 6; *having* (*passed*) *thirty-eight years in his infirmity*. Not that he was 38 years old, but had had this malady 38 years. To suppose that S. John regards him as typical of the nation, wandering 38 years in the wilderness and found paralysed by the Messiah, is perhaps fanciful.

6. **γνούς.** Perhaps supernaturally, as He knew the past life of the Samaritan woman (see on ii. 25): but He might learn it from the bystanders; the fact would be well known.

θέλεις. Dost thou wish? Note that the man does not ask first. Here and in the case of the man born blind (ix.), as also of Malchus' ear (Luke xxii. 51), Christ heals without being asked to do so. Excepting the healing of the royal official's son all Christ's miracles in the Fourth Gospel are spontaneous. On no other occasion does Christ ask a question without being addressed first: why does He now ask a question of which the answer was so obvious? Probably in order to rouse the sick man out of his lethargy and despondency. It was the first step towards the man's having sufficient faith: he must be inspired with some expectation of being cured. Comp. S. Peter's Βλέψον εἰς ἡμᾶς (Acts iii. 4). The question has nothing to do with religious scruples; 'Art thou willing to be made whole, although it is the Sabbath?'

7. ἄνθρ. οὐκ ἔχω. Not only sick, but friendless. See on iv. 11.

ὅταν ταραχθῇ. **Whenever** &c. The disturbance took place at irregular intervals: hence the need to wait and watch for it.

βάλῃ. Literally, **throw** *me in;* perhaps implying that the gush of water did not last long, and there was no time to be lost in quiet carrying. But in this late Greek *βάλλειν* has become weakened in meaning: xii. 6, xiii. 2, xviii. 11, xx. 25; Matt. ix. 2, 17, x. 34.

ἔρχομαι ἐγώ. Unaided and therefore slowly.

ἄλλος. Not *ἄλλοι*; one other is hindrance enough, so small is the place in which the bubbling appeared.

8. ἔγειρε, ἆρον. As with the paralytic (Mark ii. 9), Christ does not ask as to the man's faith: He knew that he had it; and the man's attempting to rise and carry his bed after 38 years of impotence was an open confession of faith.

κράβαττον. *Grabatus* (Cic. *Div.* II. LXIII.); a *pallet:* probably only a mat or rug, still common in the East. The word is said to be Macedonian (Mark ii. 4, vi. 55; Acts v. 15, ix. 33).

9. ἦρεν...περιεπάτει. The taking up took place once for all (aor.), the walking continued (imp.): comp. iv. 27, 30, 40, 47, 50, vi. 66, xi. 27. It is scarcely necessary to discuss whether this miracle can be identical with the healing of the paralytic let down through the roof (Matt. ix.; Mark ii.; Luke v.). Time, place, details and context are all different, especially the important point that this miracle was wrought on the Sabbath.

9—16. The Sequel of the Sign

ἦν δὲ σάββατον. **Now on that day was a Sabbath.** This is the text for what follows. Jesus had proclaimed Himself Lord of the Temple (see on ii. 17); He now proclaims Himself Lord of the Sabbath. This is a new departure: ritual must give way to love. The fourth commandment was the favourite sphere of Jewish religiousness. By ostentatious rigour in enforcing it the Pharisees exhibited their zeal for the Law. Here, therefore, Jesus confronted them. He came to vindicate the Law and make it once more lovable. So long as it remained an iron taskmaster it would keep men from Christ, instead of being a *παιδαγωγός* to bring them to Him (Gal. iii. 24).

10. οἱ Ἰουδαῖοι. The hostile party, as usual, and perhaps members of the Sanhedrin (i. 19). They ignore the cure, and notice only what can be attacked. They had the letter of the law strongly on their side: comp. Exod. xxiii. 12, xxxi. 14, xxxv. 2, 3; Num. xv. 32;

Neh. xiii. 15; and especially Jer. xvii. 21. Acts of healing (except in urgent cases) and carrying furniture were among the thirty kinds of work forbidden by the fourth commandment, according to Rabbinical interpretation.

τῷ τεθεραπευομένῳ. *To the man that had been cured.* Contrast ὁ ἰαθεὶς in *v.* 13.

11. **ὁ ποιήσας.** The man's defiance of them in the first flush of his recovered health is very natural. He means, 'if He could cure me of a sickness of 38 years, He had authority to tell me to take up my bed.' They will not mention the cure; he flings it in their face. There is a higher law than that of the Sabbath, and higher authority than theirs. Comp. the conduct of the blind man, chap. ix. The attitude of both parties throughout is thoroughly natural.

ἐκεῖνος. **Even He**, with emphasis: S. John's characteristic use of ἐκεῖνος; see on i. 18, and comp. Mark vii. 15, 20; Rom. xiv. 14.

12. **ὁ ἄνθρ.** **Who is the man?** 'man,' implying a contemptuous contrast with the law of God. Again they ignore the miracle and attack the command. They do not ask, 'Who cured thee, and therefore must have Divine authority?' but, 'Who told thee to break the Sabbath, and therefore could not have it?' Christ's command was perhaps aimed at erroneous views about the Sabbath.

13. **ἐξένευσεν.** **Withdrew** or **turned aside**: literally (νεύω) 'stooped out of the way of,' 'bent aside to avoid.' Here only in N. T. It might mean (νέω) '*swam* out of,' which would be a graphic expression for making one's way through a surging crowd and natural in a fisherman of the sea of Galilee: but LXX. in Judg. iv. 18 is certainly νεύω not νέω (comp. 2 K. ii. 24, xxiii. 16).

ὄχλου ὄντος. This is ambiguous: it may mean *why* He withdrew, viz. to avoid the crowd, or *how* He withdrew, viz. by disappearing in the crowd. Both make good sense.

14. **μετὰ ταῦτα.** See on iii. 22, ix. 35. Probably the same day; we may suppose that one of his first acts after his cure would be to offer his thanks in the Temple. On *vv.* 13 and 14 S. Augustine writes, "It is difficult in a crowd to see Christ; a certain solitude is necessary for our mind; it is by a certain solitude of contemplation that God is seen......He did not see Jesus in the crowd, he saw Him in the Temple. The Lord Jesus indeed saw him both in the crowd and in the Temple. The impotent man, however, does not know Jesus in the crowd; but he knows Him in the Temple." For **ἴδε** see on i. 29.

μηκέτι ἁμάρτανε. Present imperative; **continue no longer in sin.** Comp. [viii. 11,] xx. 17; 1 John iii. 6 The man's conscience would tell him what sin. Comp. [viii. 7]. What follows shews plainly not merely that physical suffering in the aggregate is the result of sin in the aggregate, but that this man's 38 years of sickness were the result of his own sin. This was known to Christ's heart-searching eye (ii. 24, 25), but it is a conclusion which we may not draw without the clearest evidence in any given case. Suffering serves other ends than punishment: 'whom the Lord loveth He chasteneth;' and comp. **ix. 3.**

χεῖρον. Not necessarily hell: even in this life there might be a worse thing than the sickness which had consumed more than half man's threescore and ten. So terrible are God's judgments; so awful is our responsibility. Comp. Matt. xii. 45; 2 Pet. ii. 20.

15. τοῖς Ἰουδαίοις. See on i. 19. Authorities differ as to whether *εἶπεν* or *ἀνήγγειλεν* is the verb. If the latter is correct, S. John perhaps intimates that the man's announcement was virtually a prophetic declaration (comp. iv. 25, xvi. 13, 14, 15, 25; 1 John i. 5; the only places where he uses the word). But in no case need we suppose that the man *purposes* to convert 'the Jews.' On the other hand he does not act in malice against Jesus; in that case he would have said 'He that bade me carry my bed.' But he retains his old defiance (*v.* 11). He had good authority for breaking the Sabbath—One who could work miracles; and this was the famous Teacher from Galilee.

16. διὰ τοῦτο. For this cause. We should mark the difference between *διὰ τοῦτο* (*v.* 18, vi. 65, vii. 21, 22, viii. 47, ix. 23, x. 17, xii. 39, xiii. 11, xv. 19, xvi. 15) and *οὖν*, *therefore.*

ἐδίωκον. Once more we have contrasted effects of Christ's work (see on ii. 16). The man healed returns thanks in the Temple, and maintains the authority of Jesus over the Sabbath: 'the Jews' persecute Him. This is the first declaration of hostility, and it comes very early in the ministry. Note the imperfects *ἐδίωκον*, 'continued to persecute'; the hostility is permanent: *ἐποίει*, 'was wont to do'; He went counter to the Law on principle. *Ὅτι ἐποίει* may be either the Jews' or S. John's statement. Perhaps some of the unrecorded miracles (ii. 23, iv. 45) were wrought on the Sabbath. His having convicted them of publicly profaning the Temple (ii. 14) would make them the more eager to retaliate for a public profanation of the Sabbath. Comp. a similar result in Galilee (Luke vi. 1—11).

17—47. THE DISCOURSE ON THE SON AS THE SOURCE OF LIFE

17. ἀπεκρίνατο. The middle occurs in S. John only here, *v.* 19, and xii. 23 (?). This was how He met their constant persecution. The discourse which follows (see introductory note to chap. iii.) may be thus analysed. (Sanday, p. 106.) It has two main divisions—I. *The prerogatives of the Son of God* (17—30). II. *The unbelief of the Jews* (31—47). These two are subdivided as follows: I. 1. Defence of healing on the Sabbath based on the relation of the Son to the Father (17, 18). 2. Intimacy of the Son with the Father further enforced (19, 20). 3. This intimacy proved by the twofold power committed to the Son (*a*) of communicating spiritual life (21—27), (*b*) of raising the dead (28, 29). 4. The Son's qualification for these high powers is the perfect harmony of His Will with that of the Father (30). II. 1. The Son's claims rest not on His testimony alone, nor on that of John, but on that of the Father (31—35). 2.

The Father's testimony is evident (*a*) in the works assigned to the Son (36), (*b*) in the revelation which the Jews reject (37—40). 3. Not that the Son needs honour from men, who are too worldly to receive Him (41—44). 4. Their appeal to Moses is vain; his writings condemn them.

17—30. THE PREROGATIVES AND POWERS OF THE SON OF GOD

17, 18. *Defence of healing on the Sabbath based on the relation of the Son to the Father.*

17. ἕως ἄρτι. See on ii. 10. *My Father* **is working even until now; I am working also.** From the Creation up to this moment God has been ceaselessly working for man's salvation. From such activity there is no rest, no Sabbath: for mere cessation from activity is not of the essence of the Sabbath; and to cease to do good is not to keep the Sabbath but to sin. Sabbaths have never hindered the Father's work; they must not hinder the Son's. Elsewhere (Mark ii. 27) Christ says that the Sabbath is a blessing not a burden; it was made for man, not man for it. Here He takes far higher ground for Himself. He is equal to the Father, and does what the Father does. Mark ii. 28 helps to connect the two positions. If the Sabbath is subject to man, much more to the Son of Man, who is equal to the Father. Is not the Law-Giver greater than His laws? Note the co-ordination of the Son's work with the Father's.

18. διὰ τοῦτο. See on *v.* 16. Μᾶλλον shews that ἐδίωκον in *v.* 16 includes attempts to compass His death. Comp. Mark iii. 6. This is the blood-red thread which runs through the whole of this section of the Gospel; vii. 1, 19, 25, viii. 37, 40, 59, x. 31, xi. 53, xii. 10.

ἔλυεν. *Was loosing* or *relaxing,* making less binding; *solvebat.* Not a single occasion, but a general principle, was in question. Comp. vii. 23, and see on x. 35: Matt. v. 19, xviii. 18.

ἴσον ἑ. π. τ. θ. They fully understand the force of the parallel statements, 'My Father is working; I am working also,' and the exclusive expression '*My* Father,' not '*our* Father' (viii. 41). 'Behold,' says S. Augustine, 'the Jews understand what the Arians fail to understand.' If Arian or Unitarian views were right, would not Christ at once have explained that what they imputed to Him as blasphemy was not in His mind at all? But instead of explaining that He by no means claims equality with the Father, He goes on to reaffirm this equality from other points of view: see especially *v.* 23.

19, 20. *Intimacy of the Son with the Father further enforced.*

19. οὐ δ. ὁ υἱὸς π. ἀφ' ἑ. οὐδέν. It is morally impossible for Him to act with individual self-assertion independent of God, because He is the Son: Their Will and working are one. It was to this independent action that Satan had tempted Him (comp. 'Better to reign in hell than serve in heaven'). The Jews accuse Him of blasphemy; and blasphemy implies opposition to God: but He and the Father are most intimately united. See on i. 52.

ἀφ' ἑαυτοῦ. The expression is peculiar to S. John: comp. *v.* 30, vii. 17, 28, viii. 28, 42, xi. 51, xiv. 10, xv. 4, xvi. 13. There is only one *πηγὴ τῆς Θεότητος*: the Son must in some sense be dependent; the very idea implies it. Comp. 'I have not done them of mine own mind' (*ἀπ' ἐμαυτοῦ*), Numb. xvi. 28.

ἐὰν μή τι βλ. Unless He seeth the Father doing it.

ἃ γὰρ ἄν. The negative statement is explained by a positive one. The Son cannot act of Himself, *for* He is ever engaged in doing the Father's work, whatsoever it may be.

20. **ὁ γὰρ π.** Moral necessity for the Son's doing what the Father does. The Father's love for the Son compels Him to make known all His works to Him; the Son's relation to the Father compels Him to do what the Father does. The Son continues on earth what He had seen in heaven before the Incarnation.

φιλεῖ. Some good authorities read *ἀγαπᾷ* (perhaps from iii. 35), but *φιλεῖ* is right. *Φιλεῖν* (*amare*) denotes affection resulting from personal relationship; *ἀγαπᾶν* (*diligere*) denotes affection resulting from deliberate choice: see on xi. 5, xxi. 15.

μείζονα τ. Greater works than these will He shew Him. 'The Father will give the Son an example of greater works than these healings, the Son will do the like, and ye unbelievers will be shamed into admiration.' He does not say that they will *believe*. 'Works' is a favourite term with S. John to express the *details* of Christ's *work* of redemption, much as *ῥήματα* in relation to *λόγος* (see on iii. 34). Comp. *v.* 36, ix. 4, x. 25, 32, 37, xiv. 11, 12, xv. 24. Of these passages, xiv. 12 is analogous to this, shewing that what the Father does for the Son, the Son does for those who believe on Him.

21—29. *The intimacy of the Son with the Father proved by the twofold power committed to the Son* (a) *of communicating spiritual life*, (b) *of causing the bodily resurrection of the dead.*

21—27. The Father imparts to the Son the power of raising the spiritually dead. It is very important to notice that 'raising the dead' in this section is *figurative;* raising from moral and spiritual death: whereas the resurrection (*vv.* 28, 29) is *literal;* the rising of dead bodies from the graves. It is impossible to take both sections in one and the same sense, either figurative or literal. The wording of *v.* 28 and still more of *v.* 29 is quite conclusive against spiritual resurrection being meant there: what in that case could 'the resurrection of damnation' mean? Verses 24 and 25 are equally conclusive against a bodily resurrection being meant here: what in that case can 'an hour is coming, *and now is*' mean?

21. **ἐγείρει τ. ν.** This is one of the 'greater works' which the Father sheweth the Son, and which the Son imitates, the raising up those who are spiritually dead. Not all of them: the Son imparts life only to 'whom He will:' and He wills not to impart it to those

who will not believe. The 'whom He will' would be almost unintelligible if actual resurrection from the grave were intended.

22. **οὐδὲ γὰρ ὁ π.** *For* **not even doth the Father** (to Whom judgment belongs) **judge any** *man*. The Son therefore has both powers, to make alive whom He will, and to judge: but the second is only the corollary of the first. Those whom He does not will to make alive are by that very fact judged, separated off from the living, and left in the death which they have chosen. He does not make them dead, does not slay them. They are spiritually dead already, and will not be made alive. As in iii. 17, 18, the context shews that the judgment is one of condemnation. Note the emphatic position of **πᾶσαν.**

23. **οὐ τιμᾷ.** By not knowing the Father's representative.

24. **ὁ τ. λ. μ. ἀκούων.** This shews that *οὓς θέλει* (*v*. 21) implies no arbitrary selection. Each decides for himself whether he will hear and believe and thus have life.

πιστ. τῷ πέμψαντι. **Believeth Him** *that sent* (see on i. 33). Here and viii. 31; Acts xvi. 34, xviii. 8; Tit. ii. 8, the A. V. renders *πιστ. τινί*, 'to believe a man's *word*,' as if it were *πιστ. εἰς τινα*, 'to believe *on* a man.' Here the meaning is, 'believeth God's word respecting His Son:' see on i. 12, vi. 20.

ἔχει ζ. αἰών. Hath it *already:* see on iii. 36 and 16.

εἰς κρ. οὐκ ἔρχ. **Cometh not into judgment.**

μεταβ. κ.τ.λ. *Is passed* **over out of** *death* **into** *life:* comp. xiii. 1; 1 John iii. 14. This cannot refer to the resurrection of the *body:* it is equivalent to escaping judgment and obtaining eternal life; shewing that the death is spiritual and the resurrection spiritual also.

25. Repetition of *v*. 24 in a more definite form, with a cheering addition: *v*. 24 says that whoever hears and believes God has eternal life; *v*. 25 states that already some are in this happy case.

ἔρχ. ὥρα. **There cometh an hour**: comp. iv. 21, 23.

καὶ νῦν ἐστιν. These words also exclude the meaning of a *bodily* resurrection; the hour for which had not yet arrived. The few cases in which Christ raised the dead cannot be meant; (1) the statement evidently has a much wider range; (2) the widow's son, Jairus' daughter, and Lazarus were not yet dead, so that even of them 'and *now is*' would not be true; (3) they died again after their return from death, and 'they that hear shall live' clearly refers to *eternal* life, as a comparison with *v*. 24 shews. If a *spiritual* resurrection be understood, 'and now is' is perfectly intelligible: Christ's ministry was already winning souls from spiritual death.

26. *So* **gave He also** *to the Son*. Comp. 'the living Father sent Me, and I live by the Father' (vi. 57). The Father is the absolutely living One, the Fount of all Life. The Messiah, however, imparts life to all who believe; which He could not do unless He had in Himself a fountain of life; and this the Father *gave* Him when He

sent Him into the world. The Eternal Generation of the Son from the Father is not here in question; it is the Father's communication of Divine attributes to the Incarnate Word that is meant.

27. **ἐξουσίαν ἔδωκεν.** **Gave** *Him authority* (i. 12, x. 18), when He sent Him into the world. Aorists mark what was done once for all.

ὅτι υἱὸς ἀνθρ. ἐστίν. *Because He is* **a son of man**, i.e. not because He is the Messiah, but because He is a human being. Neither 'son' nor 'man' has the article. Where 'the Son of Man,' i.e. the Messiah, is meant, both words have the article: comp. i. 52, iii. 13, 14, vi. 27, 53, 62, viii. 28, &c. Because the Son emptied Himself of His glory and became a man, therefore the Father endowed Him with these two powers; to have life in Himself, and to execute judgment.

Before passing on to the last section of this half of the discourse we may remark that "the relation of the Son to the Father is seldom alluded to in the Synoptic Gospels. But a single verse in which it is, seems to contain the essence of the Johannean theology, Matt. xi. 27: 'All things are delivered unto Me of My Father; and no man knoweth the Son but the Father; neither knoweth any man the Father, save the Son, and he to whomsoever the Son will reveal Him.' This passage is one of the best authenticated in the Synoptic Gospels. It is found in exact parallelism both in S. Matthew and S. Luke...... And yet once grant the authenticity of this passage, and there is nothing in the Johannean Christology that it does not cover." Sanday. The theory, therefore, that this discourse is the composition of the Evangelist, who puts forward his own theology as the teaching of Christ, has no basis. If the passage in S. Matthew and S. Luke represents the teaching of Christ, what reason have we for doubting that this discourse does so? To invent the substance of it was beyond the reach even of S. John; how far the precise wording is his we cannot tell. This section (21—27) bears strong impress of his style.

28, 29. The intimacy between the Father and the Son further proved by the power committed to the Son of causing the bodily resurrection of the dead.

28. **μὴ θαυμ.** Comp. iii. 7. Marvel not that the Son can grant spiritual life to them that believe, and separate from them those who will not believe. There cometh an hour when He shall cause a general resurrection of men's bodies, and a final separation of good from bad, a final judgment. He does not add 'and now is,' which is in favour of the resurrection being *literal*.

πάντ. οἱ ἐν τ. μν. Not 'whom He will;' there are none whom He does not will to come forth from their sepulchres (see on xi. 7). All, whether believers or not, must rise. This shews that spiritual resurrection cannot be meant.

29. **τὰ φ. πράξ.** **Practised worthless things.** See on iii. 20.

εἰς ἀνάστ. κρ. *Unto the resurrection of* **judgment.** These words are the strongest proof that spiritual resurrection cannot be meant.

Spiritual resurrection must always be a resurrection of life, a passing from spiritual death to spiritual life. A passing from spiritual death to *judgment* is not spiritual resurrection. This passage, and Acts xxiv. 15, are the only *direct* assertions in N. T. of a bodily resurrection of the wicked. It is implied, Matt. x. 28; Rev. xx. 12, 13. Comp. Dan. xii. 2. A satisfactory translation for *κρίνειν* and *κρίσις* is not easy to find: they combine the notions of 'separating' and 'judging,' and from the context often acquire the further notion of 'condemning.' See on iii. 17, 18, and for the genitive Winer, p. 235.

30. *The Son's qualification for these high powers is the perfect harmony between His Will and that of the Father.*

οὐ δύν. ἐγώ. Change to the first person, as in vi. 35. He identifies Himself with the Son. It is because He is the Son that He cannot act independently: it is impossible for Him to will to do anything but what the Father wills. See on *v.* 19.

καθὼς ἀκούω. From the Father: Christ's judgment is the declaration of that which the Father communicates to Him. Hence Christ's judgment must be just, for it is in accordance with the Divine Will; and this is the strongest possible guarantee of its justice. Matt. xxvi. 39. The Jews were seeking to do their own will, and their judgment was not just.

31—47. THE UNBELIEF OF THE JEWS

31—35. *These claims rest not on My testimony alone, nor on that of John, but on that of the Father.*

31. οὐκ ἔστιν ἀληθής. Nothing is to be understood; the words are to be taken literally: 'If I bear any witness other than that which My Father bears, that witness of Mine is not true.' In viii. 14, we have an apparent contradiction to this, but it is only the other side of the same truth: 'My witness is true because it is really My Father's.'

32. ἄλλος ἐστίν. Not the Baptist (*v.* 34), but the Father (vii. 28, viii. 26). On **μαρτυρῶ** see on i. 7.

33. ἀπεστάλκ....μεμαρτ. *Ye* **have sent** *unto J., and he* **hath borne** *witness.* The perfects express the abiding results of past actions. 'What ye have heard from him is true; but I do not accept it; the testimony which I accept comes not from man. I mention it for your sakes, not My own. If ye believe John ye will believe Me and be saved.' 'Ye' and 'I' in these two verses (33, 34) are in emphatic opposition. Note the article before *μαρτυρίαν*.

35. ἐκεῖνος κ.τ.λ. The A. V. is here grievously wrong, ignoring the Greek article twice over, and also the meaning of the words; and thus obscuring the marked difference between the Baptist and the Messiah: better, *he was* **the lamp which is kindled and (so) shineth.** Christ is the Light; John is only the lamp kindled at the Light, and shining only after being so kindled, having no light but what is derived. *Λύχνος* is again rendered 'light' Matt. vi. 22, but 'candle'

Matt. v. 15; Mark iv. 21; Luke viii. 16, xi. 33, 36, xv. 8; Rev. xviii. 23, xxii. 5. 'Lamp' would be best in all places. No O.T. prophecy speaks of the Baptist under this figure. David is so called 2 Sam. xxi. 17 (see margin), and Elijah (Ecclus. xlviii. 1); and S. Augustine applies *ἡτοίμασα τῷ Χριστῷ μου λύχνον, paravi lucernam Christo Meo* (Ps. cxxxii. 18), to the Baptist. The imperfects in this verse seem to imply that John's career is closed; he is in prison, if not dead.

ἠθελ. ἀγαλλ. Like children, they were glad to disport themselves in the blaze, instead of seriously considering its meaning. And even that only for a season: their pilgrimages to the banks of the Jordan had soon ended; when John began to preach repentance they left him, sated with the novelty and offended at his doctrine.—For another charge of frivolity and fickleness against them in reference to John comp. Matt. xi. 16—19.

36—40. *The Father's testimony is evident,* (a) *in the works assigned to Me,* (b) *in the revelation which ye do not receive.*

36. ἐγὼ δὲ ἔχω. *I have* **the witness which is greater than John**; or, **the witness which I have is greater than John**, viz. the works (see on *v.* 20) which as the Messiah I have been commissioned to do. Among these works would be raising the spiritually dead to life, judging unbelievers, as well as miracles: certainly not miracles only; vii. 3, x. 38. See on iii. 35.

ἵνα τελ. Literally, **in order that I may accomplish**; comp. xvii. 4. This was God's purpose. See on iv. 34, 47, ix. 3. S. John is very fond of constructions with *ἵνα*, especially of the Divine purpose.

37—40. The connexion of thought in the next few verses is very difficult to catch, and cannot be affirmed with certainty. This is often the case in S. John's writings. A number of simple sentences follow one another with an even flow; but it is by no means easy to see how each leads on to the next. Here there is a transition from the *indirect* testimony to the Messiahship of Jesus given by the *works* which He is commissioned to do (*v.* 36) to the *direct* testimony to the same given by the *words* of Scripture (37—40). The Jews were rejecting both.

37. ὁ πέμψας. See on i. 33: *ἐκεῖνος*, see on i. 18, iii. 32. Note the change from aorist to perfect; *The Father which* **sent** *Me* (once for all at the Incarnation) *He* **hath borne** *witness* (for a long time past, and is still doing so) *of Me.* For the conjunctions see Winer, p. 613.

οὔτε φωνὴν κ.τ.λ. These words are a *reproach;* therefore there can be no allusion (as suggested in the margin) to the Baptism or the Transfiguration. The Transfiguration had not yet taken place, and very few if any of Christ's hearers could have heard the voice from heaven at the Baptism. Moreover, if that particular utterance were meant, *φωνήν* would have had the article. Nor can there be any reference to the theophanies, or symbolical visions of God, in O.T. It could be no matter of *reproach* to these Jews that they had never beheld a theophany. A paraphrase will shew the meaning; 'neither with the ear of the heart have ye ever heard Him, nor with the eye of the heart have ye ever seen Him, in the revelation of Himself given in the Scriptures; and so ye have not the testimony of His word present as an abiding power within you.' There should be no full stop at 'shape,' only a comma or semi-colon. Had they studied Scripture rightly they would have had a less narrow view of the Sabbath (*v.* 16), and would have recognised the Messiah.

38. 'And hence it is that ye have no inner appropriation of the word'—seeing that ye have never received it either by hearing or vision. Ὁ λόγος is not a fresh testimony different from *φωνή* and *εἶδος*: all refer to the same—the witness of Scripture to the Messiah.

ὅτι ὃν ἀπ. **Because** *whom He sent:* see on i. 33. Proof of the previous negation. One who had the word abiding in his heart could not reject Him to whom that word bears witness. 1 John ii. 14, 24.

τούτῳ ὑμεῖς. In emphatic opposition. See on i. 12, vi. 30, iii. 32.

39. **ἐραυνᾶτε τ. γρ.** It will never be settled beyond dispute whether the verb here is *imperative* or *indicative.* As far as the Greek shews, it may be either, 'search,' or 'ye search,' and both make sense. Comp. xii. 19, xvi. 31. The question is, which makes the best sense, and this the context must decide. The context seems to be strongly in favour of the indicative, **ye search** *the Scriptures.* All the verbs on either side are in the indicative; and more especially the one with which it is so closely connected, *οὐ θέλετε.* *Ye search the Scriptures, and* (instead of their leading you to Me) *ye are not willing to come to Me.* The tragic tone once more: see on i. 5. The reproach lies not in their searching, but in their searching to so little purpose. Jewish study of the Scriptures was too often learned trifling and worse; obscuring the text by frivolous interpretations, 'making it of none effect' by unholy traditions. **Ὑμεῖς** is emphatic: *because ye are the people who think.* Not that they were wrong in thinking that eternal life was contained in the Scriptures: their error was in thinking that by their dissection of them, letter by letter, they had found it. They had scrutinised with the utmost minuteness the written word (*γραφαί*), and missed the living word (λόγος) which spoke of the Messiah; *ἐκεῖναι* (i. 8, 18), precisely they, the very books ye study so diligently.

40. **οὐ θέλετε.** **Ye are not willing** *to come to Me.* This is at the root of their failure to read Scripture aright; their hearts are estranged. They have no *will* to find the truth, and without that no intellectual searching will avail. Here again man's will is shewn to be free; the truth is not forced upon him; he can reject if he likes: iii. 19, vii. 17, viii. 44.

41—44. *Not that I seek glory from men; had I done so, you would have received Me. Your worldliness prevents you from receiving One whose motives are not worldly.*

41. **οὐ λαμβ.** It is nothing to Me; I have no need of it, and refuse it (*v.* 34). **Glory** would perhaps be better than 'honour' both here and in *v.* 44, and than 'praise' in ix. 24 and xii. 43; see notes there. Christ is anticipating an objection, and at the same time shewing what is the real cause of their unbelief. 'Glory from men is not what I seek; think not the want of that is the cause of My complaint. The desire of glory from men is what blinds your eyes to the truth.'

42. ἔγνωκα. *I have come to know* and therefore **I know**: comp. *κέκραγα* (i. 15), *ἤλπικα* (*v.* 45), *οἶδα* (*v.* 32). Once more Christ appears as the searcher of hearts; comp. i. 47, 50, ii. 24, 25 (see note), iv. 17, 18, 48, v. 14.

ἐν ἑαυτοῖς. *In* **yourselves**, *in your hearts.* 'Thou shalt love the Lord thy God with all thy heart' (Deut. vii. 5) was written on their broad phylacteries (see note on Matt. xxiii. 5), but it had no place in their hearts and no influence on their lives. It is the want of *love*, the want of *will* (*v.* 40), that makes them reject and persecute the Messiah. The phrase *ἡ ἀγάπη τ. θεοῦ* occurs 1 John ii. 5, iii. 17, iv. 9, v. 3; elsewhere in the Gospels only Luke xi. 42.

43. καὶ οὐ λαμβ. The *καί* of tragic contrast, as in *v.* 40. 'I come with the highest credentials (x. 25), as My Father's representative (viii. 42), and ye reject Me (see on i. 5).

ἐν τ. ὀν τ. ἰδίῳ. Double article; *in the name that is his own*, as a false Messiah (Matt. xxiv. 5, 24). Both the verb, *ἔλθῃ*, and *ἄλλος* (not *ἕτερος*), which implies some kind of likeness, point to a pretended Messiah. Sixty-four such have been counted. On *ἐκεῖνον* see on i. 18.

44. ὑμεῖς. Emphatic; 'such men as you.' It is morally impossible for *you*, who care only for the glory that man bestows, to believe on One who rejects such glory. This is the climax of Christ's accusation. They have reduced themselves to such a condition that they *cannot* believe. They must change their whole view and manner of life before they can do so: comp. *v.* 47. On **πιστεῦσαι** see on i. 7.

π. τ. μόνου θ. *From* **the only God**, from Him who alone is God: whereas by receiving glory they were making gods of themselves. So that it is they who really make themselves equal with God (*v.* 18). 'The only God,' as in xvii. 3; 1 Tim. vi. 16: 'God only' would be *τοῦ θ. μόνου* (Matt. xii. 4, xvii. 8) or *μόνου τ. θ.* (Luke v. 21, vi. 4). The second *δόξαν* has the article, the first has not: they receive glory, such as it is, from one another, and are indifferent to *the* glory, which alone deserves the name. They pride themselves on the external glory of Israel and reject the true glory which God would give them in the Messiah. The whole should run thus, *How can ye believe,* seeing **that ye receive glory** *one of another: and the glory which cometh from* **the only God** *ye seek* **not.** Winer, p. 723.

45—47. *Do not appeal to Moses: his writings condemn you.*

Thus the whole basis of their confidence is cut away. Moses on whom they trust as a defender is their accuser.

45. μὴ δοκεῖτε. '*Think not*, because I reproach you now, *that it is I who will accuse you.*' If this refers to the day of judgment (and the future tense seems to point to that), there are two reasons why Christ will not act as accuser (1) because it would be needless; there is another accuser ready; (2) because He will be acting as Judge.

ἔστιν ὁ κατ. Your accuser exists already; he is there with his charge. Note the change from future to present: Christ *will* not be, because Moses *is*, their accuser.

Μωυσῆς. See on i. 17. Moses represents the Law. It was zeal for the Mosaic Law which stirred the Jews on this occasion.

ἠλπίκατε. *On whom ye* **have set your hope**; present result of past action. Ἤλπικα is *spero* not *speravi:* see on *v.* 42 and comp. 1 Tim. v. 5. The Jews eagerly claimed him as their own (ix. 28, 29).

46. εἰ...ἐπιστεύετε. If ye believed (as in *v.* 47) *M., ye* **would believe** *Me:* not 'had ye believed,' 'would have believed,' which would have required aorists. Comp. viii. 19 (where A.V. has a similar error), 42, ix. 41, xv. 19, xviii. 36; and contrast iv. 10, xi. 21, 32, xiv. 28, where we have the aorist. The **γάρ** introduces the proof that Moses is their accuser; his statements and Christ's agree: see on vi. 30.

περὶ γ. ἐμοῦ. Emphatic: *For* **it was of Me** *he wrote.* Christ here stamps the Pentateuch with His authority; accepting, as referring to Himself, its Messianic types and prophecies. Luke xxiv. 27, 44.

47. ἐκείνου...ἐμοῖς. These are the emphatic words, not *γράμμασιν* and *ῥήμασιν*. The comparison is between Moses and Christ; the contrast between writings and words is no part of the argument. It was a mere matter of fact that Moses had written and Christ had not. Comp. 'If they hear not Moses and the prophets, &c.' (Luke xvi. 31). For **εἰ οὐ** see on x. 37. On **ῥήμασιν** see on iii. 34.

We pass now from a crisis in the work at Jerusalem to a crisis in the work in Galilee, each typical of the section to which it belongs and exhibiting the development of national unbelief.

CHAPTER VI

2. ἐθεώρουν for *ἑώρων*, a tense of *ὁράω* never used by S. John.

9. Omit *ἓν* after **παιδάριον**, with ℵBDL, *Lat. vet.*, *Syr. vet.*, and Origen, i.e. the oldest MSS., oldest versions, and oldest Father who quotes the passage.

11. ἔλαβεν οὖν (S. John's favourite particle) for *ἔλαβε δέ*. Omit (ℵ[1]ABL) *τοῖς μαθηταῖς, οἱ δὲ μαθηταὶ* after *διέδωκεν*. The insertion (D) comes from the Synoptic narrative.

14. Omit *ὁ Ἰησοῦς* after **σημεῖον** with ℵBD against A: comp. iii. 2, iv. 46, viii. 21.

22. εἶδον for *ἰδών* (misconception of the construction). After **εἰ μὴ ἓν** omit *ἐκεῖνο εἰς ὃ ἐνέβησαν οἱ μαθηταὶ αὐτοῦ* (explanatory gloss).

35. **διψήσει** for *διψήσῃ* (correction to usual construction: comp. iv. 14, x. 5).

38. **ἀπό** for *ἐκ* (from *vv.* 33, 41, 51).

40. **γάρ** for *δέ*. **πατρός μου** for *πέμψαντός με* (from *v.* 39) with ℵBCDLTU against A.

51. Omit *ἣν ἐγὼ δώσω* after **ἐστίν**, with ℵBCDLT against the mass of later MSS. A is defective here.

55. **ἀληθής** for *ἀληθῶς* twice: Origen substitutes *ἀληθίνη*.

57. **ζήσει** for *ζήσεται*. The future of *ζάω* occurs 20 times in N.T. In 6 quotations from LXX. *ζήσομαι* is used: 4 times in S. John (v. 25, vi. 57, 58, xiv. 19) *ζήσω* is used; so also probably in vi. 51. *ζήσεται* occurs xi. 25.

63. **λελάληκα** for λαλῶ, with all the oldest MSS., versions, and Fathers.

69. **ὁ ἅγιος τοῦ θεοῦ** for *ὁ Χριστὸς ὁ υἱὸς τοῦ θεοῦ τοῦ ζῶντος* (from Matt. xvi. 16), with ℵBC[1]DL against the mass of later MSS. A and T are defective.

71. **Ἰσκαριώτου** for *Ἰσκαριώτην*, with the earlier MSS. and best copies of the Vulgate.

We see more and more as we go on, that this Gospel makes no attempt to be a complete or connected whole. There are large gaps in the chronology. The Evangelist gives us not a biography, but a series of typical scenes, very carefully selected, and painted with great accuracy and minuteness, but not closely connected. As to what guided him in his selection, we know no more than the general purpose stated xx. 31, and it is sufficient for us. Those words and works of Jesus, which seemed most calculated to convince men that He 'is the Christ, the Son of God,' were recorded by the beloved Apostle. And the fact that they had already been recorded by one or more of the first Evangelists did not deter him from insisting on them again; although he naturally more often chose what they had omitted. In this chapter we have a notable instance of readiness to go over old ground in order to work out his own purpose. The miracle of feeding the Five Thousand is recorded by all four Evangelists, the only miracle that is so. Moreover, it is outside the Judaean ministry; so that for this reason also we might have expected S. John to omit it. But he needs it as a text for the great discourse on the Bread of Life; and this though spoken in Galilee was in a great measure addressed to Jews from Jerusalem; so that both text and discourse fall naturally within the range of S. John's plan. Moreover by producing an outburst of popular enthusiasm (*v.* 15) it shewed how utterly the current ideas about the Messiah were at variance with Christ's work.

As in chap. v. Christ is set forth as the *Source of Life*, so in this chapter He is set forth as the *Support of Life*. In the one the main idea is the Son's relation to the Father, in the other it is the Son's relation to the believer.

Chap. VI. Christ the Support of Life

This chapter, like the last, contains a discourse arising out of a miracle. It contains moreover an element wanting in the previous chapter,—the results of the discourse. Thus we obtain three divisions; 1. *The Sign on the Land, the Sign on the Lake, and the Sequel of the Signs* (1—25). 2. *The Discourse on the Son as the Support of Life* (26—59). (3) *The opposite Results of the Discourse* (60—71).

1—15. The Sign on the Land; Feeding the Five Thousand

1. μετὰ ταῦτα. See on v. 1. How long after we cannot tell; but if the feast in v. 1 is rightly conjectured to be Purim, this would be about a month later in the same year, which is probably A.D. 29. But S. John is not careful to mark the precise interval between the various scenes which he gives us. Comp. the indefinite transitions from the First Passover to Nicodemus, ii. 23, iii. 1; from Nicodemus to the Baptist's discourse, iii. 22, 25; from that to the scene at Sychar, iv. 1—4; &c., &c. The chronology is doubtless correct, but it is not clear: chronology is not what S. John cares to give us. The historical connexion with what precedes is not the same in the four accounts. Here it is in connexion with the miracles at Bethesda and probably after the death of the Baptist: in S. Matthew it is in connexion with the death of the Baptist: in S. Mark and S. Luke it is after the death of the Baptist, but in connexion with the return of the Twelve. The notes on Matt. xiv. 13—21, Mark vi. 40—44, and Luke ix. 10—17 should be compared throughout.

ἀπῆλθεν. Departed, we do not know from what place. The scene suddenly shifts from Judaea (v. 18) to Galilee; but we are told nothing about the transit or the reason for it.

From the Synoptists we gather that the murder of the Baptist (Matt. xiv. 13), and the curiosity of Herod (Luke ix. 9), rendered it expedient to leave Herod's dominions; moreover the return of the Twelve (Luke ix. 10) made retirement easy and perhaps desirable (Mark vi. 30, 31). Thus the four narratives combine.

τῆς Τιβεριάδος. Here, *v.* 23 and xxi. 1 only. The name is added to describe the sea more exactly, especially for the sake of foreign readers. Another slight indication that this Gospel was written outside Palestine: inside Palestine such minute description would be less natural. The Greek geographer Pausanias writes *λίμνη Τιβερίς*; Josephus uses one or other of the names here combined by S. John; S. Matt. and S. Mark have *θάλ. τῆς Γαλιλαίας*; S. Luke *λίμνη Γεννησαρέτ*. Perhaps we are to understand that the *southern* half of the lake is specially intended; for here on the western shore Tiberias was situated. The name Tiberias is not found in the first three Gospels.

The magnificent town was built during our Lord's lifetime by Herod Antipas, who called it Tiberias out of compliment to the reigning Emperor; one of many instances of the Herods paying court to Rome. Comp. Bethsaida Julias, where this miracle took place, called Julias by Herod Philip after the infamous daughter of Augustus, and Sebaste, so called in honour of Augustus (see on iv. 7). The new town would naturally be much better known and more likely to be mentioned when S. John wrote than when the earlier Evangelists wrote.

2. **ἠκολούθει.** Imperfects of continued action throughout the verse in contrast to *ἀπῆλθεν* and *ἀνῆλθεν* in *vv.* 1 and 3. **Ἐθεώρουν** implies reflecting attention; *v.* 19, ii. 23, vii. 3, xii. 45, xiv. 19, xvi. 16. The multitude went round by land, while Jesus crossed the lake: it would be all the greater because the Baptist was no longer a counter-attraction, and the Twelve had returned from a mission which must have excited attention. Jesus kept on working miracles (*ἐποίει*), and these continually attracted fresh crowds.

3. **τὸ ὄρος.** The *mountain*, or *the mountainous part*, of the district: the article indicates familiarity with the neighbourhood (*v.* 15). We cannot determine the precise eminence. The object is retirement.

4. **ἡ ἑορτὴ τ. Ἰ.** The *feast of the Jews.* Possibly a mere date to mark the time. As already noticed (see on ii. 13), S. John groups his narrative round the Jewish festivals. But the statement may also be made as a further explanation of the multitude. Just before the Passover large bands of pilgrims on their way to Jerusalem would be passing along the east shore of the lake. But we find that the multitude in this case are quite ready (*v.* 24) to cross over to Capernaum, as if they had no intention of going to Jerusalem; so that this interpretation of the verse is uncertain. Equally doubtful is the theory that this verse gives a key of interpretation to the discourse which follows, the eating of Christ's Flesh and Blood being the antitype of the Passover. From vii. 1 it would seem that Jesus did not go up to Jerusalem for this Passover.

5. **ἔρχεται.** **Is coming**; present of graphic description. The quiet which He sought is being invaded; yet He welcomes the opportunity and at once surrenders His rest to His Father's work, as in the case of Nicodemus and the Samaritan woman. But why does He address Philip? Because he was nearest to Him; or because his forward spirit (xiv. 8) needed to be convinced of its own helplessness; or because, as living on the lake (i. 44), he would know the neighbourhood. Any or all of these suggestions may be correct. Throughout we see how Jesus uses events for the education of His disciples. As Judas kept the purse it is not likely that Philip commonly provided food for the party. A more important question remains: "we notice that the impulse to the performance of the miracle comes in the Synoptists from the disciples; in S. John, solely from our Lord Himself." This is difference, but not contradiction: S. John's narrative does not preclude the possibility of the disciples having spontaneously applied to Christ for help either before or after this conversation with

Philip. "For the rest the superiority in distinctness and precision is all on the side of S. John. He knows to whom the question was put; he knows exactly what Philip answered; and again the remark of Andrew, Simon Peter's brother......Some memories are essentially pictorial; and the Apostle's appears to have been one of these. It is wonderful with what precision every stroke is thrown in. Most minds would have become confused in reproducing events which had occurred so long ago; but there is no confusion here" (Sanday).

ἀγοράσωμεν. Must *we buy:* deliberative subjunctive.

6. **πειράζων.** This *need* not mean more than to try whether he could suggest anything; but more probably, to test his faith, to prove to him how imperfect it still was in spite of His having been so long with him (xiv. 9). Jesus had no need to inform Himself as to Philip's faith: He 'knew what was in man.' *In Philippo non desideravit panem, sed fidem* (S. Augustine).

αὐτός. Without suggestions from others; xv. 27. The Evangelist knows the Lord's motives (ii. 24, 25, iv. 1—3, v. 6, vii. 1, xiii. 1, 3, 11, xvi. 19, xviii. 4, xix. 28). Unless this is most audacious invention it almost amounts to proof that the Evangelist is the Apostle S. John.

τί ἔμελλεν ποιεῖν. The miracle and the lesson deduced from it.

7. **διακοσίων δην.** *Two hundred shillingsworth* would fairly represent the original. The *denarius* was the ordinary wage for a day's work (Matt. xx. 2; comp. Luke x. 35); in weight of silver it was less than a shilling; in purchasing power it was more. Two hundred *denarii* from the one point of view would be about £7, from the other, nearly double that. S. Philip does not solve the difficulty; he merely states it in a practical way; a much larger amount than they can command would still be insufficient. See on Mark viii. 4.

8. **εἷς ἐκ τ. μαθ.** Of course this does not imply that Philip was *not* a disciple; the meaning rather is, that a disciple had been appealed to without results, and now a disciple makes a communication out of which good results flow. The *name* of this second disciple comes in as a sort of afterthought. There seems to have been some connexion between S. Andrew and S. Philip (i. 44, xii. 22). In the lists of the Apostles in Mark iii. and Acts i. S. Philip's name immediately follows S. Andrew's. On S. Andrew see notes on i. 40, 41. The particulars about Philip and Andrew here are not found in the Synoptists' account.

9. **παιδάριον.** *A little lad,* or (less probably) servant. The ἕν of some MSS., if genuine, would emphasize the poverty of their resources; the provisions of a single boy. S. Andrew has been making enquiries; which shews that the disciples had considered the matter before Jesus addressed S. Philip, as the Synoptists tell us.

κριθίνους. The ordinary coarse food of the lower orders; Judg. vii. 13. S. John alone mentions their being of barley, and that they belonged to the lad, who was probably selling them. With homely food from so scanty a store Christ will feed them all. These minute details are the touches of an eyewitness.

ὀψάρια. The force of the diminutive is lost; **fishes**, not '*small* fishes.' The word occurs in this Gospel only (*v.* 11, xxi. 9, 10, 13), and literally means a *little relish*, i.e. anything eaten with bread or other food: and as salt fish was most commonly used for this purpose, the word came gradually to mean 'fish' in particular. S. Philip had enlarged on the greatness of the difficulty; S. Andrew insists rather on the smallness of the resources for meeting it.

10. χόρτος πολύς. As we might expect early in April (*v.* 4). S. Mark (vi. 39, 40) mentions how they reclined in parterres (*πρασιαὶ πρασιαί*), by hundreds and by fifties, *on the green grass.* This arrangement would make it easy to count them.

οἱ ἄνδρες. *The men*, as distinct from the women and children, who would not be very numerous: *τοὺς ἀνθρώπους*, *the people*, includes all three. S. Matthew (xiv. 21) says that the 5000 included the men only. **Τὸν ἀριθμόν**, accusative of closer definition; Winer, p. 288.

11. εὐχαριστ. The usual grace before meat said by the head of the house or the host. 'He that enjoys aught without thanksgiving, is as though he robbed God.' Talmud. But it seems clear that this giving of thanks or blessing of the food (Luke ix. 16) was the *means* of the miracle, because (1) all four narratives notice it; (2) it is pointedly mentioned again *v.* 23; (3) it is also mentioned in both accounts of the feeding of the 4000 (Matt. xv. 36; Mark viii. 6). It should be remembered that this act is again prominent at the institution of the Eucharist (Matt. xxvi. 26; Mark xiv. 22; Luke xxii. 17, 19; 2 Cor. xi. 24). It is futile to ask whether the multiplication took place in Christ's hands only: the *manner* of the miracle eludes us, as in the turning of the water into wine. That was a change of quality, this of quantity. This is a literal fulfilment of Matt. vi. 33.

12. συναγάγετε. S. John alone tells of this command, though the others tell us that the fragments were gathered up. It has been noticed as a strong mark of truth, most unlikely to have been invented by the writer of a fiction. We do not find the owner of Fortunatus' purse careful against extravagance. How improbable, from a human point of view, that one who could multiply food at will should give directions about saving fragments!

13. κοφίνους. All four Evangelists here use *κόφινος* for basket, as does S. Matthew (xvi. 9) in referring to this miracle. It is the wallet which every Jew carried when on a journey, to keep himself independent of Gentile food (Juv. III. 14). In the feeding of the 4000 (Matt. xv. 37; Mark viii. 8), and in referring to it (Matt. xvi. 10), *σπυρίς* is the word for basket. See on Mark viii. 8; Acts ix. 25.

ἄρτ. τ. κριθ. S. John insists on the identity of the fragments with the original loaves. He mentions the bread only, because only the bread has a symbolical meaning in the subsequent discourse. S. Mark says that fragments of fish were gathered also. Each of the Twelve filled his wallet full, so that the remnants far exceeded the original store. For the plural verb with a neut. nom. comp. xix. 31.

The expedients to evade the obvious meaning of the narrative are worth mentioning, as shewing how some readers are willing to 'violate all the canons of historical evidence,' rather than admit the possibility of a miracle: (1) that food had been brought over and concealed in the boat; (2) that some among the multitude were abundantly supplied with food and were induced by Christ's example to share their supply with others; (3) that the whole is an allegorical illustration of Matt. vi. 33. How could either (1) or (2) excite even a suspicion that He was the Messiah, much less kindle such an enthusiasm as is recorded in *v.* 15? And if the whole is an allegory what meaning can be given to this popular enthusiasm?

14. οἱ οὖν ἄνθρ. The people therefore, the whole multitude. The plural, *ἃ ἐπ. σημεῖα*, which some authorities read, includes the effect of previous miracles. The imperf., *ἔλεγον*, indicates that this was repeatedly said. 'Ο Ἰησοῦς has been inserted here, as elsewhere, in some MSS., because this was once the beginning of a lesson read in church. The same thing has been done in our own Prayer Book in the Gospels for Quinquagesima and the 3rd Sunday in Lent: in the Gospel for S. John's day the names of both Jesus and Peter have been inserted; and in those for the 5th S. in Lent and 2nd S. after Easter the words 'Jesus said' have been inserted. In all cases a desire for clearness has caused the insertion. Comp. viii. 21.

ὁ πρ. ὁ ἐρχ. The *Prophet that* **cometh**; the Prophet of Deut. xviii. 15 (see on i. 21 and xi. 27). The miracle perhaps reminded them of the manna, and Moses, and his promise of a greater than himself. S. John alone tells us of the effect of the miracle on the spectators (comp. ii. 11, 23). It exactly corresponds with what we know of the prevailing Messianic expectations, and explains the strange fluctuations of opinion about Jesus. His 'signs' pointed to His being the Messiah, or at least a great Prophet: but He steadfastly refused to act the part expected from the Messiah.

15. μέλλουσιν. Are about to (*v.* 6) *take Him by force and* **make Him king**; carry Him, whether He will or no, to Jerusalem and proclaim Him king at the Passover. They will have a *σωτηρία* according to their own ideas, not according to God's decree: earthly deliverance and glory, not spiritual regeneration. This also is peculiar to S. John; but S. Luke (ix. 11) tells us that He had been speaking of 'the kingdom of God;' and this would turn their thoughts to the Messianic King. The whole incident explains the remarkable expression 'He immediately *compelled* (*ἠνάγκασε*) His disciples to embark' (Matt. xiv. 22; Mark vi. 45). There was danger of the Twelve being infected with this wrongheaded enthusiasm. Some such command is implied here; for they would not have left Him behind without orders.

In his Divine Epic S. John points out the steady increase of the enmity against Jesus; and nothing increased it so much as popular enthusiasm for Him: iii. 26, iv. 1—3, vii. 40, 41, 46, viii. 30, ix. 30—38, x. 21, 42, xi. 45, 46, xii. 9—11.

πάλιν. He had come down to feed them: 'again' refers to *v.* 3. After dismissing first the disciples and then the bulk of the multitude, He ascended again, but this time *alone*, to *pray* (Matt. xiv. 23; Mark vi. 46).

16—21. The Sign on the Lake; Walking on the Water

16. ὀψία. The second (6 P.M. to dark) of the two evenings which S. Matthew (xiv. 15, 23) gives in accordance with Jewish usage. The narrative here makes a fresh start: *κατέβησαν* does not imply that the disciples went up again with Jesus; this is excluded by *αὐτὸς μόνος*.

17. ἤρχοντο. The imperfect expresses their continued efforts to reach Capernaum. S. Mark says 'unto Bethsaida,' which was close to Capernaum. See on Matt. iv. 13; Luke v. 1.

οὔπω. *Not* **yet**, implying that they expected Him. Perhaps they had arranged to meet Him at some place along the shore. He is training them gradually to be without His visible presence; in the earlier storm He was with them (Matt. viii. 23—26). The description is singularly graphic. Darkness had come on; their Master was not there; a storm had burst on them, and the lake was becoming very rough: 25 or 30 furlongs would bring them about 'the midst of the sea' (Mark vi. 47), which is 6 or 7 miles across. Many travellers have testified to the violent squalls to which the lake is subject.

19. ἐπὶ τῆς θαλάσσης. Although this might mean 'on the seashore' (xxi. 1), yet the context plainly shews that here it means 'on the surface of the sea.' Winer, p. 468. Would they have been frightened by seeing Jesus walking on the shore? S. Mark says it was about the fourth watch, i.e. between 3.0 and 6.0 A.M. S. Matthew alone gives S. Peter's walking on the sea. S. Luke omits the whole incident.

20. ἐγώ εἰμι. All three narratives preserve these words; we infer that they made a deep impression. Comp. viii. 24, 28, 58, xiii. 13, 19, xviii. 5, 6, 8.

21. ἤθελον. *They* **were willing therefore to receive** *Him*. The 'willingly received' of A.V. is perhaps due to Beza, who substitutes *volente animo receperunt* for the Vulgate's *voluerunt recipere*. *Ἤθελον λαβεῖν αὐτόν* here seems to contrast with *ἤθελεν παρελθεῖν αὐτούς* in Mark vi. 48. His will to pass them by was changed by their will to receive Him. But (comp. i. 43, v. 35) S. John does not mean that He did not enter the boat: he is not correcting S. Matthew and S. Mark: this would require *ἀλλ' εὐθέως κ.τ.λ.*, 'but (before He could enter) the boat was at the land.' *Ἦλθον* conjectured by Michaelis for *ἤθελον*, and found in the Sinaiticus, is an attempt to avoid a difficulty. **Εὐθέως** *probably* points to something miraculous: He who had just imparted to S. Peter His own royal power over gravity and space, now does the like to the boat which bore them all.

ὑπῆγον. Were going, or intending to go; comp. ἤρχοντο (*v.* 17). The imperfects mark the contrast between the difficulty of the first part of the voyage, when they were alone, with the ease of the last part, when He was with them. 'Then are they glad, because they are at rest: and so He bringeth them unto the haven where they would be.' Ὑπάγειν implies departure, and looks back to the place left (*v.* 67, vii. 33, xii. 11, xviii. 8).

The Walking on the Sea is no evidence that the writer was a Docetist, i.e. believed that Christ's Body was a mere phantom: on the contrary, the event is narrated as extraordinary, quite different from their usual experience of His bodily presence. A Docetist would have presented it otherwise, and would hardly have omitted the disciples' cry, φάντασμά ἐστι (Matt. xiv. 26; comp. Mark vi. 49). Docetism is absolutely excluded from this Gospel by i. 14 and by the general tone throughout; see on xix. 34, 35, xx. 20, 27. The whole incident should be compared with Luke xxiv. 36—41; in both Christ's supernatural return aggravates their distress, *until* they know who He is. And the meaning of both is the same. In times of trouble Jesus is near His own, and His presence is their deliverance and protection.

22—25. The Sequel of the two Signs

The people had wished to make Jesus a Jewish king. He has just manifested Himself to His disciples as King of the whole realm of nature. The wrongheaded multitude, to which we return, are now taught in parables.

22—24. A complicated sentence very unusual in S. John (comp. xiii. 1—4); but its very intricacy is evidence of its accuracy. A writer of fiction would have given fewer details and stated them with greater freedom. S. John explains what is well known to him.

22. **πέραν τ. θ.** On the eastern side, where the miracle took place.

23. This awkward parenthesis explains how there came to be boats to transport the people to the western shore.

εὐχαριστ. Unless the thanksgiving (*v.* 11) was the turning-point of the miracle, it is hard to see why it is mentioned again here.

24. **εἶδεν.** A fresh seeing; not a resumption of εἶδον in *v.* 22.

εἰς τὰ πλ. The boats from Tiberias, driven in probably by the contrary wind (Matt. xiv. 24; Mark vi. 48) which had delayed the Apostles. There is no need to suppose that *all* the 5000 crossed over.

25. **πέραν τ. θ.** This is now the western shore, Capernaum (*v.* 59).

πότε ὧδε γ.; Comp. i. 15. They suspect something miraculous, but He does not gratify their curiosity. If the feeding of the 5000 taught them nothing, what good would it do them to hear of the crossing of the lake?

26—59. The Discourse on the Son as the Support of Life

God's revealed word and created world are unhappily alike in this; that the most beautiful places in each are often the scene and subject of strife. This marvellous discourse is a well-known field of controversy, as to whether it does or does not refer to the Eucharist. That it has no reference whatever to the Eucharist seems incredible, when we remember (1) the startling words here used about eating the Flesh of the Son of Man and drinking His Blood; (2) that just a year from this time Christ instituted the Eucharist; (3) that the primitive Church is something like unanimous in interpreting this discourse as referring to the Eucharist. A few words are necessary on each of these points. (1) Probably nowhere in any literature, not even among the luxuriant imagery of the East, can we find an instance of a teacher speaking of the reception of his doctrine under so astounding a metaphor as eating his flesh and drinking his blood. Something more than this must at any rate be meant here. The metaphor 'eating a man's flesh' elsewhere means to injure or destroy him. Ps. xxvii. 2 (xiv. 4); James v. 3. (2) The founding of new religions, especially of those which have had any great hold on the minds of men, has ever been the result of much thought and deliberation. Let us leave out of the account the Divinity of Jesus Christ, and place Him for the moment on a level with other great teachers. Are we to suppose that just a year before the Eucharist was instituted, the Founder of this, the most distinctive element of Christian worship, had no thought of it in His mind? Surely for long beforehand that institution was in His thoughts; and if so, 'Except ye eat the Flesh of the Son of Man and drink His Blood, ye have no life in you' cannot but have some reference to 'Take eat, this is My Body,' 'Drink ye all of it, for this is My Blood.' The coincidence is too exact to be fortuitous, even if it were probable that a year before it was instituted the Eucharist was still unknown to the Founder of it. That the audience at Capernaum could not thus understand Christ's words is nothing to the point: He was speaking less to them than to Christians throughout all ages. How often did He utter words which even Apostles could not understand at the time. (3) The interpretations of the primitive Church are not infallible, even when they are almost unanimous: but they carry great weight. And in a case of this kind, where spiritual insight and Apostolic tradition are needed, rather than scholarship and critical power, patristic authority may be allowed very great weight.

But while it is incredible that there is *no* reference to the Eucharist in this discourse, it is equally incredible that the reference is solely or primarily to the Eucharist. The wording of the larger portion of the discourse is against any such exclusive interpretation; not until *v.* 51 does the reference to the Eucharist become clear and direct. Rather the discourse refers to *all* the various channels of grace by means of which Christ imparts Himself to the believing soul: and who will dare to limit these in number or efficacy?

To quote the words of Dr Westcott, the discourse "cannot refer primarily to the Holy Communion; nor again can it be simply prophetic of that Sacrament. The teaching has a full and consistent meaning in connexion with the actual circumstances, and it treats essentially of spiritual realities with which no external act, as such, can be coextensive. The well-known words of Augustine, *crede et man-*

ducasti, 'believe and thou *hast* eaten,' give the sum of the thoughts in a luminous and pregnant sentence.

"But, on the other hand, there can be no doubt that the truth which is presented in its absolute form in these discourses is presented in a specific act and in a concrete form in the Holy Communion; and yet further that the Holy Communion is the divinely appointed means whereby men may realise the truth. Nor can there be any difficulty to any one who acknowledges a divine fitness in the ordinances of the Church, an eternal correspondence in the parts of the one counsel of God, in believing that the Lord, while speaking intelligibly to those who heard Him at the time, gave by anticipation a commentary, so to speak, on the Sacrament which He afterwards instituted." *Speaker's Commentary*, N. T. Vol. II. p. 113.

The discourse has been thus divided; I. 26—34, Distinction between the material bread and the Spiritual Bread; II. 35—50 (with two digressions, 37—40; 43—46), Identification of the Spiritual Bread with Christ; III. 51—58, Further definition of the identification as consisting in the giving of His Body and outpouring of His Blood. On the language and style see introductory note to chap. iii.

26—34. *Distinction between the material bread and the Spiritual Bread*

26. ἀμὴν ἀμήν. See on i. 52. As so often, He answers, not the question, but the thought which prompted it (ii. 4, iii. 3, 10, iv. 16): *not because ye* **saw signs.** They *had* seen the *miracle*, but it had *not* been a *sign* to them: instead of seeing a sign in the bread, they had seen only bread in the sign; it had excited mere curiosity and greed. **Σημεῖα** may be the generic plural and refer only to the Feeding; or it may include the previous miracles (*v.* 2). As in the case of *λαλιά* (iv. 42), we are in doubt whether there is any shade of disparagement in *ἐχορτάσθητε*, *were fed as with fodder.* Luke xv. 16, xvi. 21; Rev. xix. 21 incline us to think so; Matt. v. 6, xiv. 20 and parallels, Mark vii. 27 incline us to think not. *Quam multi non quaerunt Jesum, nisi ut illis faciat bene secundum tempus...Vix quaeritur Jesus propter Jesum* (S. Augustine).

27. ἐργάζεσθε. Work, not 'labour,' to keep up the connexion with *vv.* 28—30. They keep harping on the word 'work.' The meaning 'work *for*' is rare: *ἐργ. χρήματα*, Herod. I. 24. Comp. 'Whosoever drinketh of this water shall thirst again' (iv. 13). The discourse with the woman should be compared throughout: 'the food which abideth' (see on i. 33) corresponds with 'the living water' (see on iv. 14); 'the food that perisheth' with the water of the well. 'Perisheth' not only in its sustaining power but in itself; it is digested and dispersed (Matt. xv. 17; 1 Cor. vi. 13). Comp. 'Take no thought what ye shall eat' (Matt. vi. 25). Work, however, is needed to win the food that abides. Comp. the lines of Joan. Audenus;

Mandere qui panem jubet in sudore diurnum
Non dabit aeternas absque labore dapes.

ὁ υἱὸς τ. ἀνθρ. See on i. 52. It is as the perfect Man that Christ in His communion with men sustains the life which He has bestowed

(v. 25). Hence He says, '*the* Father' (of men as well as of Himself, xx. 17), not 'My Father.'

τοῦτον γάρ. Keep the emphatic order; *for Him* **the Father sealed, even God.** To God belongs the authority to seal: He sealed, i.e. authenticated (iii. 33) Christ as the true giver of the food that abideth (1) by direct testimony in the Scriptures, (2) by the same in the voice from Heaven at His Baptism, (3) by indirect testimony in His miracles and Messianic work.

28. **τί ποιῶμεν...;** *What* **must** *we do* (*v.* 5) *that we* **may** *work?* Perhaps they understood Him to mean that they must *earn* what they desire; certainly they see that Christ's words have a moral meaning; they must do the works required by God. But how?

29. **τὸ ἔργον.** They probably thought of works of the law, tithes, sacrifices, &c. He tells them of one work, one moral act, from which all the rest derive their value, continuous belief (*πιστεύητε*, not *πιστεύσητε*) in Him whom God has sent. Comp. Acts xvi. 31. On **ἵνα** and **ἀπέστειλεν** see on i. 8, 33, iv. 47, xvii. 3.

30. **τί...σὺ σημ.;** *Σύ* is emphatic: 'Thou urgest us to work; what doest Thou on Thy part?' They quite see that in *ὃν ἀπέστ. ἐκ.* He is claiming to be the Messiah, and they require proof. The feeding of the 5000 was less marvellous than the manna, and the Messiah must shew greater signs than Moses. They demand 'a sign *from heaven*,' as so often in the Synoptists. Note that whereas He used the strong *πιστεύειν εἰς ὅν* they use the weak *πιστεύειν σοι* (see on i. 12): *πιστεύειν τινί* occurs iv. 21, v. 24, 38, 46, xiv. 11; comp. ii. 22, iv. 50; it means no more than to believe a man's statements, as distinct from trusting in his person and character.

τί ἐργάζῃ; They use the very word that He used in *v.* 29.

31. **ἐστιν γεγραμ.** See on ii. 17. What follows is a rough quotation of 'had rained down manna upon them to eat' (Ps. lxxviii. 24), or possibly of Neh. ix. 15. In either case they artfully suppress the nominative, 'God,' and leave 'Moses' to be understood. The *ἐκ* points to Neh. ix. 15; not merely from above, but **out of** *heaven* **itself.**

32. **Μωυσῆς.** See on i. 17. Christ answers their thought rather than their questions, *τί ποιεῖς; τί ἐργάζῃ;* He shews them that He understands their insinuation, that He is inferior to Moses, and He denies both their points; (1) that Moses gave the manna; (2) that the manna was in the truest sense bread out of heaven.

τὸν ἄρτον...τὸν ἀληθινόν. Emphatic repetition of the article; *the bread out of heaven, the true* bread; 'true' in the sense of 'real' and 'perfect,' a complete realisation of what it professes to be; see on i. 9. The manna was only a type, and therefore imperfect. Note the change from *ἔδωκεν* to *δίδωσιν*: God *is continually giving* the true bread; it is not given at one time and then no more, like the manna.

33. **ὁ καταβαίνων.** **That which** *cometh down.* Jesus has not yet identified Himself with the Bread, which is still impersonal, and hence

the present participle: contrast *v.* 41. There is a clear reference to this passage in the Ignatian Epistles, *Romans* vii.; the whole chapter is impregnated with the Fourth Gospel. See on iv. 10, iii. 8, x. 9.

τῷ κόσμῳ. See on i. 10. Not to the Jews only, but to all. We have evidence (the *γάρ* introduces an argument) that it is the Father who gives the really heavenly Bread, *for* it is His Bread that quickens the whole human race.

34. κύριε. 'Lord' is too strong, making the request too much like the prayer of a humble believer: as in iv. 11, 15, 19, 'Sir' would be better (see on iv. 11). Not that the request is ironical, the mocking prayer of the sceptic. Rather it is the selfish petition of those whose beliefs and aspirations are low. Like the Samaritan woman (iv. 15) they think that this wonderful food is at any rate worth having. He fed them yesterday, and they are hungry again. He speaks of bread that abideth, and it will be well to obtain it. But their only idea of 'abiding' is a supply constantly (*πάντοτε*) repeated, like the manna; and for this they ask in good faith. They do not disbelieve in His power, but in His mission.

35—50. *Identification of the Spiritual Bread with Christ*

35. ἐγώ εἰμι. Comp. *vv.* 41, 48, 51: the pronoun is very emphatic as in iv. 56. As in v. 30, He passes from the third person to the first. These identifications are characteristic of this Gospel: Christ declares Himself to be the Light of the world (viii. 12), the Door of the Fold (x. 7, 9), the Good Shepherd (x. 11, 14), the Resurrection and the Life (xi. 25), the Way, the Truth, and the Life (xiv. 6), the True Vine (xv. 1, 5). Ὁ *ἄρτος τ. ζωῆς* means *ὁ ἄρτ. ζωὴν διδούς*: comp. *τὸ ὕδωρ τ. ζ.*, Rev. xxi. 6 (xxii. 1), and *τὸ ξύλον τ. ζ.*, Gen. ii. 9, iii. 22, 24. 'He that cometh to Me'='he that believeth on Me,' and 'shall in no wise hunger'='shall in no wise ever thirst' (*πώποτε*, not, as in iv. 14, *εἰς τὸν αἰῶνα*); i.e. the believer shall experience the immediate and continual satisfaction of his highest spiritual needs. Christ's superiority to the manna is this, that it satisfied only bodily needs for a time, He satisfies spiritual needs for ever. Note the Hebraic parallelism.

36. εἶπον ὑμῖν. When? no such saying is recorded. Ewald thus finds some slight evidence for his theory that a whole sheet of this Gospel has been lost between chapters v. and vi. But the reference may easily be to one of the countless unrecorded sayings of Christ, or possibly to the general sense of v. 37—44. In the latter case 'you' must mean the Jewish nation, for those verses were addressed to Jews at Jerusalem. Or the reference may be to the *spirit* of *v.* 26, which accuses them of having seen His miracles without believing that they were signs.

καὶ ἑωράκ. See on i. 18, *Ye have* **even** *seen Me* (not merely heard of Me) *and* (yet) *do not believe*. The tragic tone again (see on i. 5), followed by a pause. The next sentence has no conjunction.

37—40. Digression on the blessedness of those who come to Christ as believers.

37. πᾶν ὃ...τὸν ἐρχ. Note the significant change of gender. What is given (see on iii. 35) is treated as impersonal and neuter, mankind *en masse* (comp. iii. 6); what comes, with free will, is masculine. Men are given to Christ without being consulted; but each, if he likes, can refuse to come, as the Jews did: there is no coercion. Comp. xvii. 2; i. 11. Note also the different verbs for 'come'; *ἥκω* expresses the arrival (Rev. xv. 4), *ἔρχομαι* the coming. Comp. 'Come unto Me, all ye that labour' (Matt. xi. 28).

οὐ μὴ ἐκβ. Litotes (iii. 19, viii. 40): so far from casting out, will keep and protect, x. 28. *Quale intus illud est, unde non exitur foras? Magnum penetrale et dulce secretum* (S. Augustine).

38. ὅτι καταβ. Because I am come down. Four times in this discourse Christ declares His descent from heaven; *vv.* 38, 50, 51, 58. The drift of *vv.* 38—40 is; 'How could I cast them out, seeing that I am come to do My Father's will, and He wills that they should be received?' See on viii. 31.

39. τὸ θέλημα...ἵνα. See on i. 8, iv. 47, xvii. 3, and comp. *v.* 29.

πᾶν. *Casus pendens:* comp. vii. 38, xv. 2, xvii. 2; Luke xxi. 6. 'Credentes dantur, credentibus datur.' **μὴ ἀπολέσω.** His care for the fragments (*v.* 12) would not be greater than His care for men's souls. With **ἐξ αὐτοῦ** comp. *ἐκ τῶν τ.* in 2 John 4, *ἐξ ὑμῶν* Rev. ii. 10.

ἀναστήσω. The same gracious utterance is repeated as a kind of refrain, *vv.* 40, 44, 54: but here *ἀναστήσω* probably depends on *ἵνα*, although it *may* be an independent future as in *vv.* 44, 54. This is the *ἀνάστασις ζωῆς* (v. 29), *ἡ ἀν. ἡ πρώτη* (Rev. xx. 5, 6), *ἡ ἀν. τῶν δικαίων* (Luke xiv. 14); the ultimate end of Christ's work.

τῇ ἐσχ. ἡμέρᾳ. The phrase is peculiar to S. John; *vv.* 40, 44, 54, xi. 24, xii. 48; comp. vii. 37. Elsewhere *ἡ ἡμέρα τῆς κρίσεως* (1 John iv. 17); *ἡ ἡμ. ἡ μεγάλη* (Rev. vi. 17; comp. xvi. 14); *ἐκείνη ἡ ἡμ.* (Matt. vii. 22); *ἡ ἡμ. τ. κυρίου* (1 Cor. v. 5); *ἡ τ. θεοῦ ἡμ.* (2 Pet. iii. 12); *ἡμ. Χριστοῦ* (Phil. i. 10); *ἡμ. αἰῶνος* (2 Pet. iii. 18); or simply *ἡ ἡμέρα* (Heb. x. 25). The phrases from 2 Peter occur nowhere else.

40. τοῦτο γὰρ...πατρός μου. This is the true reading; but the opening words of *vv.* 39 and 40, being very similar, have become confused in inferior MSS. The best have *πατρός* in *v.* 40, where the Son is mentioned, not in *v.* 39, where He is not. Moreover *v.* 40 is explanatory of *v.* 39, and opens with *γάρ*; it shews who are meant by *πᾶν ὃ δέδ. μοι*, viz. *every one that contemplateth the Son and believeth on Him.* Not *ὁρῶν* but *θεωρῶν*: the Jews had seen Jesus; they had not contemplated Him so as to believe. *Θεωρεῖν* is frequent in S. John and the Acts, elsewhere not; vii. 3, xii. 45, xiv. 19, xvi. 10, 16, 19, xvii. 24, xx. 6, 12, 14.

ἀναστήσω. Here, still more easily than in *v.* 39, *ἀναστήσω* may be future. **'Εγὼ** is very emphatic; 'by My power as Messiah.'

Some think that a break in the discourse must be made here; *vv.* 25—40 being spoken on the shore of the lake, *vv.* 41—58 in the synagogue at Capernaum to a somewhat different audience.

41. ἐγόγγυζον. Talked in an undertone respecting Him: the word in itself does not necessarily mean that they found fault, but the context shews that they did (comp. *v.* 61, vii. 12; Matt. xx. 11; Luke v. 30). Moreover, O. T. associations have given this shade of meaning to the word, which is frequent in LXX. for the murmurings in the wilderness, especially in the compound *διαγογγύζω*: comp. 1 Cor. x. 10. Some members of the hostile party (*οἱ Ἰουδαῖοι*), and possibly some of the Sanhedrin, were now present; but we are not to understand that the whole multitude were hostile, though carnally-minded and demanding a further sign: i. 19, ii. 18, v. 10, vii. 11, &c.

ἐγώ εἰμι...οὐρανοῦ. They put together *vv.* 33, 35, 38.

42. οὗτος. Contemptuous; *this* **fellow.** 'We know all about His parentage; there is nothing supernatural about His origin.' Nothing can be inferred from this as to Joseph's being still alive (see on ii. 1). **Ἡμεῖς** is emphatic; 'we know it for ourselves.' This is in favour of the speakers being of Galilee rather than from Jerusalem.

43—46. Digression on the difficulty of coming to Christ as a believer

43. Christ does not answer their objections or explain. Even among the first Christians the fact of His miraculous conception seems to have been made known only gradually, so foul were the calumnies which the Jews had spread respecting His Mother. This certainly was not the place to proclaim it. He directs them to something of more vital importance than the way by which He came into the world, viz. the way by which they may come to Him.

44. οὐδεὶς δύναται. It is a moral impossibility: comp. iii. 3, 5, v. 44, viii. 43, xii. 39, xiv. 17, xv. 4, 5. The *οὐδείς* corresponds to the *πᾶν* in *v.* 37, as *ἑλκύσῃ* to *δίδωσιν*: *all* that are given shall reach Christ; *none* but those who are drawn are able to come to Him. The aor. *ἐλθεῖν* expresses the result, rather than the process, as in *τὸν ἐρχόμενον* (*v.* 37), and *ἔρχεται* (*v.* 45).

ἑλκύσῃ. Comp. xii. 32, *πάντας ἑλκύσω πρὸς ἐμαυτόν.* Unlike *σύρειν*, 'to drag' (Acts viii. 3, xiv. 19, xvii. 6), *ἑλκύειν* does not necessarily imply force, but mere *attraction* of some kind, some inducement to come. Comp. Jer. xxxi. 3, 'with lovingkindness have I *drawn* thee' (*εἵλκυσά σε*), and Virgil's *trahit sua quemque voluptas.* Ἑλκύσῃ expresses the internal process, *δίδωσιν* (*v.* 37) the result.

κἀγώ. The Father begins the work of salvation, the Son completes it. The Father draws and gives; the Son receives, preserves, and raises up to eternal life.

45. ἔστιν γεγρ. See on ii. 17. Here, as in xiii. 18 and xix. 37, the quotation agrees with the Hebrew against the LXX. This is evidence that the writer knew Hebrew, and was probably a Jew of Palestine.

ἐν τοῖς προφήταις. In the division of the Scriptures, so called as distinct from the Law (i. 45), and the Psalms or Hagiographa (Luke xxiv. 44): comp. Acts xiii. 40, and (*ἐν βίβλῳ τῶν πρ.*) vii. 42. The direct reference is to Isa. liv. 13, which may have been part of the synagogue-lesson for the day (Luke iv. 17); but comp. Jer. xxxi. 33, 34; Joel iii. 16, 17. The quotation explains how the Father *draws* men, viz. by enlightening them. Note that Jesus does not *derive* His teaching *from* the O. T. but *confirms* it by an *appeal* to the O. T. Comp. viii. 17, 56, x. 34.

διδακτοὶ θεοῦ. In classical Greek *διδακτός* is applied to doctrine rather than pupils, the things that can be taught rather than the persons taught. The Hebrew *limmûd* in Is. liv. 13 is perhaps a substantive, and hence the genitive here without *ὑπό*; 'God's instructed ones,' *i.e.* prophets in the wider sense. Comp. *διδακτοῖς πνεύματος* (1 Cor. ii. 13) for the genitive, and *θεοδίδακτοι* (1 Thes. iv. 9) for the meaning.

πᾶς ὁ ἀκ....κ. μαθ. *Every one that hath heard and hath learned* **from** (viii. 26, 40, xv. 15) *the Father*, and no others; only those who have been 'taught of God' can come to the Son. The *οὖν* after *πᾶς* in T. R. is not genuine; very common in S. John's narrative, it is very rare in discourses. Omit with ℵBCDLST against A.

46. ἑώρακεν. See on i. 18. Hearing is not the same as seeing, and in order to hear and learn from the Father it is not necessary to see Him. The result of hearing is to lead men to the only One who has seen (i. 18), and in whom the Father may be seen (xiv. 9).

ὁ ὢν παρὰ τ. θ. The expression, as in vii. 29, implies a permanent relation, and points to the generation rather than the mission of the Son. On **οὗτος** see on iii. 32.

47—50. Christ returns from answering the Jews to the main subject

47. ἀμὴν ἀμ. With the authority of Him who alone has seen the Father, Jesus solemnly assures them that the believer is already in possession (*ἔχει*) of eternal life: see on iii. 36, v. 24.

48. ἐγώ εἰμι. See on *v.* 35 and i. 21.

49. ἔφαγον...ἀπέθ. **Ate the** *manna...and* **they died**, see on viii. 52. The point is, not that they are dead now, but that they died then; the manna did not save them. He answers them out of their own mouths. On the other hand, the Bread of Life is a permanent source of spiritual life here and a pledge of resurrection hereafter.

50. οὗτος. May be subject or predicate; the latter seems to be better, as in xv. 12, xvii. 3; 1 John v. 3, where *αὕτη* anticipates *ἵνα*. *Of this purpose is the Bread which cometh down* (see on *v.* 58) *from heaven that a man may eat thereof and* (*so*) *not die* (comp. iii. 19). The *ἵνα* indicates the Divine intention (see on i. 9, iv. 47); the indefinite *τις* shews the unbounded character of the offer.

μὴ ἀποθάνῃ. The *ἀπέθανον* in *v.* 49 seems to shew that physical death is intended, otherwise the antithesis fails. The death of the believer is only sleep: he has partaken of the Bread of Life and will be raised up at the last day; *vv.* 40, 44, 54; comp. viii. 51, xi. 25, 26.

51—58. *Further definition of the identification of the Spiritual Bread with Christ as consisting in the giving of His Body and the outpouring of His Blood.*

In *vv.* 35—50 Christ in His *Person* is the Bread of Life: here He is the spiritual food of believers in the Redemptive *work* of His Death.

51. ὁ ζῶν. Τῆς ζωῆς referred to its *effects*, like the Tree of Life, which was a mere instrument; ὁ ζῶν refers to its *nature;* not merely the Bread of life (*v.* 48), the life-giving Bread, but the living Bread, having life in itself, which life is imparted to those who partake of the Bread.

ὁ ἐκ τ. οὐρ. καταβάς. At the Incarnation. Now that the Bread is identified with Christ, we have the past tense of what took place once for all. Previously (verses 33, 50) the present tense is used of what is continually going on. In one sense Christ is perpetually coming down from heaven, in the other He came but once. He is ever imparting Himself to man; He only once became man.

ζήσ. εἰς τ. αἰῶνα. Just as ὁ ζῶν is stronger than τῆς ζωῆς, so ζήσ. εἰς τ. αἰῶνα is stronger than μὴ ἀποθάνῃ. With ὁ ἄρτος ὁ ἐκ τ. οὐρ. κ., ὃν ἐγὼ δώσω comp. γευσαμένους τ. δωρεᾶς τ. ἐπουρανίου, Heb. vi. 4.

ἡ σάρξ μου ἐστίν. The *Sinaiticus* transfers these words to the end of the verse to avoid the harsh construction. Later MSS. insert ἣν ἐγὼ δώσω between ἐστίν and ὑπέρ, with the same object. Both are corruptions of the true text, which is quite in S. John's style, ὑπὲρ τ. τ. κ. ζωῆς being an expansion of what is expressed in the main sentence. Note the καὶ...δὲ...*But, moreover*, or *Yea and indeed* (He will tell them this startling truth right out to the end) *the Bread which I will give you is my Flesh,—for the life of the world.* Comp. viii. 16, 17, xv. 27; and esp. 1 John i. 3. Note also the emphatic ἐγώ; 'I, in contrast to Moses.' That in these words Christ looked onwards to the Eucharist, and that in thus speaking to believers throughout all time He included a reference to the Eucharist, has already been stated to be highly probable. (See above, Introduction to 26—58.) But that the reference is not exclusively nor even directly to the Eucharist is shewn from the use of σάρξ and not σῶμα. In all places where the Eucharist is mentioned in N.T. we have σῶμα, not σάρξ; Matt. xxvi. 26; Mark xiv. 22; Luke xxii. 19; 1 Cor. xi. 24 ff. Moreover the words must have had some meaning for those who heard them at Capernaum. Evidently they have a wider range than any one Sacrament. Christ promises to give His Flesh (by His bloody death soon to come) for the benefit of the whole world. But this benefit can only be appropriated by the faith of each individual; and so that which when offered by Christ is His Flesh appears under the figure of bread when partaken of by the believer. The primary reference therefore is to Christ's propitiatory death; the secondary reference is to *all* those means by which the death of Christ is appropriated, especially the Eucharist.

ἡ σάρξ. Human nature regarded from its lower side (see on i. 14): here it is Christ's perfect humanity given to sustain the spiritual life of mankind. He proceeds to state (53—58) *how* it is given.

τοῦ κόσμου. The true Paschal Lamb is for the whole human race: contrast, 'There shall no stranger eat thereof' (Exod. xii. 43—45).

52. πρὸς ἀλλήλους. One with another (iv. 33, xvi. 17): their excitement increases; they have got beyond murmuring about Him (*v.* 4), but they are not all equally hostile (vii. 12, 43; x. 19). "They strove, and that with one another, for they understood not, neither wished to take the Bread of concord" (S. Augustine).

Πῶς. This is the old vain question (iii. 4, 9) which continues to distract the Church and the world. All that men need know is the fact; but they insist in asking as to the manner. '*Cur*' *et* '*Quomodo*' *exitiales voculae*—'Why' and 'How' are deadly little words (Luther). *Οὗτος* is contemptuous (*v.* 42): *φαγεῖν* is their own addition; they wish to bring out in full the strangeness of His declaration.

53. πίητε αὐτ. τ. αἷμα. Christ not only accepts what they have added to His words, but still further startles them by telling them that they must drink His Blood; an amazing statement to a Jew, who was forbidden to taste even the blood of animals (Gen. ix. 4; Lev. xvii. 10—16). These words are the answer to their *πῶς*; by an expansion of the previous statement (comp. the answer to the *πῶς*; of Nicodemus, iv. 5). The words point still more distinctly to His propitiatory death; for 'the blood is the life' which He offered up for the sins of the world. The eating and drinking are not faith, but the appropriation of His death; faith leads us to eat and drink and is the means of appropriation. Taken separately, the Flesh represents sacrifice and sustenance, the Blood represents atonement and life, life by means of His death.

ἐν ἑαυτοῖς. In yourselves; for the source of life is absent.

54. The gracious positive of the previous minatory negative. From warning as to the ruinous consequences of not partaking He goes on to declare the blessed consequences of partaking, viz. eternal life, and that at once, with resurrection among the just hereafter.

ὁ τρώγων. Present; it is a continuous action, not one that may be done once for all (*v.* 45). *Φαγεῖν* has no present, so that the same word could not be used; but the change to *τρώγειν* rather than to *ἐσθίειν* is not meaningless: *τρώγειν* is 'to eat with enjoyment' (Matt. xxiv. 38); see on xiii. 18. Excepting these two texts the word occurs here only (*vv.* 54—58) in N.T.

55. ἀληθής. This reading has the highest authority; *ἀληθῶς* and *ἀληθινή* are corrections to make the passage easier. In iv. 37 we had *ἀληθινός* where we might have expected *ἀληθής*. The eating and drinking is no misleading metaphor, but a fact. See on i. 9.

56. ἐν ἐμοὶ μένει, κἀγὼ ἐν αὐτῷ. This is one of S. John's very characteristic phrases to express the most intimate mutual fellowship and union; xiv. 10, 20, xv. 4, 5, xvii. 21; 1 John iii. 24, iv. 15, 16. Christ is at once the centre and the circumference of the life of the Christian; the source from which it springs and the ocean into which it flows. See on i. 33.

57. Not a mere repetition, but an enlargement. In S. John there are no mere repetitions; the thought is always recut or reset, and frequently with additions. The result of this close union is perfect life, proceeding as from the Father to the Son, so from the Son to all believers. For **καθὼς...καὶ...**comp. xiii. 15, 1 John ii. 6, iv. 17.

ὁ ζῶν πατήρ. The absolutely Living One, the Fount of all life. The expression occurs here only. Comp. Matt. xvi. 16; 2 Cor. vi. 16; Heb. vii. 25.

διὰ τὸν π....δι' ἐμέ. **Because of** *the Father*, because the Father is the Living One (v. 26); **because of** *Me*, because he thus derives life from Me. '*By* the Father ..*by* Me' would require the genitive.

ὁ τρ. με. Instead of the Flesh and Blood we have Christ Himself: the two modes of partaking are merged in one, the more appropriate of the two being retained.

κἀκεῖνος. He also. The retrospective pronoun repeats and emphasizes the subject: xiv. 12 (where again it immediately follows the subject), i. 18, 33, v. 11, 39, ix. 37, x. 1, xii. 48, xiv. 21, 26, xv. 26.

58. A general summing-up of the whole, returning from the Flesh and Blood to the main theme,—the Bread from heaven and its superiority to the highest earthly food. **Οὗτος** again may be subject or predicate; there is no *ἵνα* (*v.* 50) or *ὅτι* to lead up to, but the *οὐ καθὼς κ.τ.λ.* seems to shew that *οὗτος* is the predicate. Ὁ *καταβάς* corresponds to *ἀπέστειλε* in *v.* 57; both aorists refer to the historic fact of the Incarnation. In this sense Christ came once for all: in another sense He is always coming, *ὁ καταβαίνων* (*v.* 50).

οὐ καθὼς κ.τ.λ. Irregularly expressed contrast to *οὗτος*: *Of this nature* (giving eternal life) *is the Bread which came down from heaven; not as* **the fathers did eat and died** (*v.* 49). Comp. 1 John iii. 11, 12.

59. ἐν συναγωγῇ. *In synagogue* (no article), as we say 'in church;' comp. xviii. 20. The verse is a historical note, stating definitely what was stated vaguely in *v.* 22 as 'on the other side of the sea.' S. John cannot forget the circumstances of this solemn discourse, and he records them one by one; 'these things He said—in full synagogue—while teaching—in Capernaum;' a very early gloss (D) adds 'on a sabbath.' The verse shews that the Evangelist is aware of the Synoptic ministry in Galilee. 'These things' naturally refers to the whole discourse from *v.* 26; we have no sufficient evidence of a break between *v.* 40 and *v.* 41. On the other hand there is strong evidence that from *v.* 26 to *v.* 58 forms one connected discourse spoken at one time in the synagogue at Capernaum. The site of Capernaum is not undisputed (see on Matt. iv. 13); but assuming Tell Hûm to be correct, the ruins of the synagogue there are probably those of the very building in which these words were uttered. On one of the stones a pot of manna is sculptured.

60—71. Opposite Results of the Discourse

60. τῶν μαθητῶν. The more numerous and somewhat shifting company out of which He had chosen the Twelve.

σκληρός. Not hard to understand, but hard to accept: σκληρός (σκέλλω) means originally 'dry' and so 'rough;' and then in a moral sense, 'rough, harsh, offensive.' Nabal the churl is σκληρός, 1 Sam. xxv. 3, and the slothful servant calls his master σκληρός, Matt. xxv. 24. Λόγος is more than 'saying' (iii. 34), and might cover the whole discourse. It was the notion of eating His Flesh and drinking His Blood that specially scandalized them: 'This is a revolting speech; who can listen to it?' Αὐτοῦ no doubt refers to λόγος; but it *might* mean 'listen to *Him*.' A century later we find the same thing: not only opponents but disciples take offence at such language; "They abstain from (public) thanksgiving and prayer, because they allow not that the Eucharist is the Flesh of our Saviour Jesus Christ, which Flesh suffered for our sins." Ignat. *Smyrn.* VI.

61. ἐν ἑαυτῷ. They talked in a low tone, but He knew without hearing; see on *v.* 41 and ii. 24. As in i. 42, 47, iv. 18, v. 14, 42, vi. 26, &c., Jesus reads men's hearts. For **σκανδαλίζει** see on xvi. 1.

62. ἐὰν οὖν θ. Literally, **If therefore ye should behold the Son of man ascending** *where He was before?* The sentence breaks off (*aposiopesis*) leaving something to be understood: but what is to be understood? The answer to this depends on the meaning assigned to 'behold the Son of man ascending.' The most literal and obvious interpretation is of an actual beholding of the Ascension: and in that case we supply; 'Would ye still take offence then?' The Ascension would prove that their carnal interpretation of the eating and drinking *must* be wrong. Against this interpretation it is urged (1) that S. John does not record the Ascension. But it is assumed, if not here and iii. 13, yet certainly xx. 17 as a fact; and in all three cases it is in the words of our Lord that the reference occurs. S. John throughout assumes that the main events of Christ's life and the fundamental elements of Christianity are well known to his readers. (2) That none but the Twelve witnessed the Ascension, while this is addressed to a multitude of doubting disciples. But some of the Twelve were present: and Christ speaks hypothetically; '*if* ye *should* behold,' not '*when* ye *shall* behold.' (3) That in this case we should expect ἀλλά instead of οὖν. Possibly, but not necessarily. The alternative interpretation is to make the 'ascending' refer to the whole drama which led to Christ's return to glory, especially the Passion (comp. vii. 33, xiii. 3, xiv. 12, 28, xvi. 5, 28,

xvii. 11, 13): and in that case we supply; 'Will not the sight of a suffering Messiah offend you still more?' Winer, p. 750.

63. τὸ ζωοποιοῦν] *That maketh to live* or *giveth life.* 'Quickeneth' obscures the connexion with *ζωή ἐστιν.*

ἡ σάρξ. Not *ἡ σάρξ μου,* which would contradict *v.* 51. The statement is quite general, affirming the superiority of what is unseen and eternal to what is seen and temporal (2 Cor. iv. 18, iii. 6; 1 Cor. xv. 45), but with a reference to Himself. 'My flesh' in *v.* 51 means 'My human nature sacrificed in death,' to be *spiritually* appropriated by every Christian, and best appropriated in the Eucharist. 'The flesh' here means the flesh without the spirit; that which can only be appropriated *physically,* like the manna. In this sense even Christ's flesh 'profiteth nothing.' "The flesh was a vessel," says S. Augustine; "consider what it held, not what it was." Comp. iii. 6. Perhaps there is a reference to their carnal ideas about the Messiah.

τὰ ῥήματα. See on iii. 34. The authoritative **ἐγώ,** so frequent throughout this discourse (*vv.* 35, 40, 41, 44, 48, 51, 54), appears again: I, in contrast to mere human teachers. **Λελάληκα,** *have spoken,* in the discourse just concluded.

64. ἐξ ὑμῶν τινες. Of you some; for the order comp. *ἐξ ὑμ. εἷς, v.* 70. Some followed Him without believing on Him.

ἐξ ἀρχῆς. The meaning of *ἀρχή* always depends on the context (see on i. 1, xv. 27). Here the most natural limit is 'from the beginning of their discipleship.' Comp. ii. 24, 25. **Οἱ** *οὐ πιστ.* expresses a fact, **οἱ μὴ** *π.* a thought; 'those, whoever they might be, who believed not:' v. 33, xiv. 24, xv. 24.

τίς ἐστιν ὁ π. αὐ. *Who* **it was that would** *betray Him.* To ask, 'Why then did Jesus choose Judas as an Apostle?' is to ask in a special instance for an answer to the insoluble enigma 'Why does Omniscience allow wicked persons to be born? Why does Omnipotence allow evil to exist?' The tares once sown among the wheat, both 'grow together till the harvest,' and share sunshine and rain alike. *Παραδίδοναι* means to 'hand over, deliver up;' xviii. 30, 35, xix. 16.

65. Διὰ τοῦτο. For this cause; v. 16, 18, vii. 22, viii. 47, ix. 23, x. 17, xii. 18, 27, 39, &c.

οὐδεὶς δύναται. See on *vv.* 44, 37. The necessity for the internal preparation, the drawing by the Father, was strongly shewn in the case of Judas, who would be still more alienated by Christ's refusal to be made a king (*v.* 15) and by the *σκληρὸς λόγος* (*v.* 60). The *ἐκ* indicates the Father as the *source* of conversion; *except it* **have been** *given him* **from the** *Father:* comp. iii. 27.

66. ἐκ τούτου. Combines the notions of 'from that time' and 'in consequence of that;' **Upon this**: we are to understand a *continual* drifting away. The phrase occurs in N.T. here and xix. 12 only.

ἀπῆλθον εἰς τὰ ὀπίσω. Not only *deserted* Him, but went *back* to their old life. This is the *κρίσις*, the separation of bad from good, which Christ's coming necessarily involved; iii. 18, 19.

οὐκέτι. No longer. 'No more' may mean 'never again,' which *οὐκέτι* does not mean; some may have returned again. *Περιεπάτουν* graphically expresses Christ's wandering life; comp. vii. 1, xi. 54, Luke viii. 1, ix. 58.

67. τοῖς δώδεκα. The first mention of them; S. John speaks of them familiarly as a well-known body, assuming that his readers are well acquainted with the expression (see on *v.* 62). This is a mark of truth: all the more so because the expression does not occur in the earlier chapters; for it is probable that down to the end of chap. iv. at any rate 'the Twelve' did not yet exist. Pilate, Martha and Mary, and Mary Magdalene are introduced in the same abrupt way as persons well-known (xviii. 29, xix. 25). **Οὖν**, in consequence of the frequent desertions.

μὴ κ. ὑμ. θέλετε. Surely ye also do not wish to go: we must avoid rendering *θέλειν* by the 'will' of the simple future: comp. vii. 17, viii. 44. Christ knows not only the unbelief of the many, but the belief and loyalty of the few.

68. Σίμων Πέτρος. See on i. 42. S. Peter, as leader, *primus inter pares*, answers here as elsewhere in the name of the Twelve (see on Mark iii. 17), and with characteristic impetuosity. His answer contains three reasons in logical order why they cannot desert their Master: (1) there is no one else to whom they can go; the Baptist is dead. Even if there were (2) Jesus has all that they need; He has 'sayings of eternal life.' And if there be other teachers who have them also, yet (3) there is but one Messiah, and Jesus is He. Contrast his earlier utterance, 'Depart from me' (Luke v. 8).

ῥήματα ζ. αἰων. See on iii. 34. No article; the expression is quite general, and seems to be an echo of *v.* 63, the truth of which S. Peter's experience could already affirm. It may mean either utterances *about* eternal life, or *leading to* eternal life. The analogy of the *Bread of life*, *Light of life*, *Tree of life*, and *Water of life* (*v.* 35, viii. 12; Rev. ii. 7, xxi. 6) is strongly in favour of the latter.

69. ἡμεῖς. Emphatic; **we** (in contrast to the deserters) **have believed and have come to know** (vii. 17, 26, viii. 32, 51): this has been the case for some time. Note the order; by believing they have come to know; sometimes (1 John iv. 16) knowledge precedes faith.

ὁ ἅγιος τ. Θ. S. Peter's confessions are worth comparing. 1. 'Thou art the Son of God' (Matt. xiv. 33); in this the other Apostles joined. 2. 'Thou art the Holy One of God' (John vi. 69). 3. 'Thou art the Christ, the Son of the living God' (Matt. xvi. 16). They increase in fulness, as we might expect. For the last he is pronounced 'blessed' by Christ. See on i. 21.

70. αὐτοῖς. He replies to all, not to their spokesman only.

οὐκ ἐγὼ ὑμᾶς τ. δ. ἐξ. Note the order throughout. **Did not I choose** (xiii. 18, xv. 16) **you the Twelve?** Here probably the question ends: *and of you one is a devil* is best punctuated without an interrogation; it is a single statement in tragic contrast to the preceding question (comp. vii. 19). It would be closer to the Greek to omit the article before 'devil' and make it a kind of adjective; *and of you one is devil*, i.e. devilish in nature: but this is hardly English. The words contain a half-rebuke to S. Peter for his impetuous avowal of loyalty in the name of them *all.* The passage stands alone in the N.T. (comp. Matt. xvi. 23), but its very singularity is evidence of its truth. S. John is not likely to have forgotten what was said, or in translating to have made any serious change.

71. ἔλεγεν δέ. Now *He spake*, was meaning. For the accusative instead of *περί* c. gen. comp. viii. 54, ix. 19, i. 15.

Ἰσκαριώτου. Here and in xiii. 26 the true reading adds Iscariot not to the name of Judas (xii. 4, xiii. 2, xiv. 22), but to that of his father. If Iscariot means 'man of Kerioth,' a place in Judah (Josh. xv. 25), or possibly Moab (Jer. xlviii. 24), it would be natural for both father and son to have the name. In this case Judas was the only Apostle who was not a Galilean, and this would place a barrier between him and the Eleven.

ἔμελλεν. Was about to; xii. 4; Luke xxii. 23; comp. *v.* 64. There is no need to include either predestinarian views on the one hand or the intention of Judas on the other. What *has* taken place, when viewed from a point before the event, may be regarded as *sure* to take place. **εἷς ἐκ τ. δ.** is in tragic contrast with what precedes; *for he was to betray Him—one of the Twelve.* "Clean and unclean birds, the dove and the raven, are still in the Ark" (S. Augustine).

With regard to the difficulty of understanding Christ's words in this sixth chapter, Meyer's concluding remark is to be borne in mind. "The difficulty is partly exaggerated; and partly the fact is overlooked that in all references to His death and the purpose of it Jesus could rely upon the light which the *future* would throw on these utterances: and sowing, as He generally did, for the future in the bosom of the present, He was compelled to utter much that was mysterious, but which would supply material and support for the further development and purification of faith and knowledge. The wisdom thus displayed in His teaching has been justified by *History.*"

CHAPTER VII

8. Omit *ταύτην* after first **ἑορτήν**. Between *οὔπω* (BLT) and *οὐκ* (ℵDKM) before **ἀναβαίνω** it is impossible to decide with certainty.

10. εἰς τὴν ἑορτήν, τότε καὶ αὐτὸς ἀνέβη for *τότε κ. αὐ. ἀν. εἰς τ. ἑορ.* on overwhelming evidence.

26. Omit ἀληθῶς after **ἐστιν.**

32. **οἱ ἀρχιερεῖς καὶ οἱ Φαρισαῖοι** (S. John's invariable order; *v.* 45, xi. 47, 57, xviii. 3) for *οἱ Φ. κ. οἱ ἀρχ.*, on overwhelming evidence.

39. After **πνεῦμα** omit *ἅγιον* (assimilation to xx. 22), with ℵT. D adds *ἐπ' αὐτοῖς* and B adds *δεδομένον* after *ἅγιον*. **Οὔπω** for *οὐδέπω*.

46. **ἐλάλησεν οὕτως** for *οὕτως ἐλ.* Omit *ὡς οὗτος ὁ ἄνθρωπος* after **ἄνθρωπος**, with BLT: other MSS. exhibit great variation.

50. **πρὸς αὐτὸν πρότερον** for *νυκτὸς πρὸς αὐτόν*. Here also there is much variation in the readings.

52. **ἐγείρεται** for *ἐγήγερται*.

"Chapter vii., like chapter vi., is very important for the estimate of the fourth Gospel. In it the scene of the Messianic crisis shifts from Galilee to Jerusalem; and, as we should naturally expect, the crisis itself becomes hotter. The divisions, the doubts, the hopes, the jealousies, and the casuistry of the Jews are vividly portrayed. We see the mass of the populace, especially those who had come up from Galilee, swaying to and fro, hardly knowing which way to turn, inclined to believe, but held back by the more sophisticated citizens of the metropolis. These meanwhile apply the fragments of Rabbinical learning at their command in order to test the claims of the new prophet. In the background looms the dark shadow of the hierarchy itself, entrenched behind its prejudices and refusing to hear the cause that it has already prejudged. A single timid voice is raised against this injustice, but is at once fiercely silenced" (Sanday).

As in chapters v. and vi. Christ is set forth as the *Source and Support of Life*, so in chapters vii. viii. and ix. He is set forth as the *Source of Truth and Light*. The Fulfiller of the Sabbath and of the Passover fulfils the Feast of Tabernacles also.

Chap. VII. Christ the Source of Truth and Light

Chap. vii. has three main divisions: 1. *The controversy with His brethren* (1—9); 2. *His teaching at the Feast of Tabernacles* (10—39); 3. *The opposite results;* division in the multitude and in the Sanhedrin (40—52).

1—9. The Controversy with His Brethren

1. **μετὰ ταῦτα.** See on iii. 22. The interval is again vague (Introduction to Chap. vi.): it covers five or six months, the interval between the Passover (vi. 4) and the Feast of Tabernacles.

περιεπάτει. See on vi. 66. The imperfects imply continued action. To this ministry in Galilee, which S. John thus passes over, much of Matt. xiv. 34—xviii. 35 belongs.

οὐ γὰρ κ.τ.λ. See v. 18. From this we understand that He did not go up to Jerusalem foı the Passover of vi. 4. 'Jewry' is found here in all English Versions except Wiclif's; it was common in the earlier translations. But in A.V. it has been retained (probably by an oversight) only here, Luke xxiii. 5, and Dan. v. 13: elsewhere **Judæa** has been substituted. In Dan. v. 13 the same word is translated both 'Jewry' and 'Judah'! Comp. the Prayer-Book version of Ps. lxxvi. 1.

2. ἡ ἑορ. τ. Ἰουδ. ἡ σκ. Tabernacles, or 'the Feast of the 7th month,' or 'of ingathering,' was the most joyous of the Jewish festivals. It had two aspects: (1) a commemoration of their dwelling in tents in the wilderness, (2) a harvest-home. It was therefore a thanksgiving (1) for a permanent abode, and especially for a permanent place of worship, (2) for the crops of the year. *Celebrebant hoc Judaei, velut reminiscentes beneficia Domini, qui occisuri erant Dominum* (S. Augustine). It began on the 15th of the 7th month, Ethanim or Tisri (about our September), and lasted seven days, during which all who were not exempted through illness or weakness were obliged to live in booths, which involved much both of the discomfort and also of the merriment of a picnic. The distinctions between rich and poor were to a large extent obliterated in the general encampment, and the Feast thus became a great levelling institution. On the eighth day the booths were broken up and the people returned home: but it had special sacrifices of its own and was often counted as part of the Feast itself. The Feast is mentioned here, partly as a date, partly to shew what after all induced Christ to go up to Jerusalem, partly perhaps for its symbolical meaning. 'The Word was made flesh and *tabernacled* among us' (i. 14). Tabernacles was a type of the Incarnation, as the Passover of the Passion.

3. οὖν. Because He had not attended the previous Passover.

οἱ ἀδελφοὶ αὐτοῦ. See on ii. 12. The bluntness of this suggestion, given almost as a command, shews that they presumed upon their near relationship. It would be more natural in the mouths of men *older* than Christ, and therefore is in favour of their being sons of Joseph by a former marriage rather than sons of Joseph and Mary (comp. Mark iii. 21, 31). They shared the ordinary beliefs of the Jews about the Messiah, and therefore did not believe in their Brother. But His miracles perplexed them, and they wished the point brought to a decisive issue. There is no treachery in their suggestion; its object is not to put Him in the power of His enemies. Comp. ii. 3, 4, where His Mother's suggestion and His treatment of it are somewhat similar to what we have here.

οἱ μαθηταί σου. Any of them, whether pilgrims to Jerusalem for the Feast or living there. His brethren seem to imply that they themselves are not disciples. *Θεωρήσουσιν*, not merely 'see,' but 'contemplate;' see on vi. 40.

4. οὐδεὶς γ. *For no man doeth anything in secret and himself seeketh to be in openness:* or, according to BD[1], *and seeketh it* (*αὐτό*) *to* *be in openness.* They imply that He works miracles to prove His Messiahship and hides them from those who would be convinced by them. To conceal His miracles is to deny His Messiahship; the Messiah must assert His position. Winer, p. 786.

ἐν παῤῥησίᾳ. Here and xvi. 29 only with a preposition; see on *v.* 13.

εἰ ταῦτα ποιεῖς. *If Thou* **doest** *these things*, not 'If Thou *do* these things;' no doubt as to the fact of His miracles is expressed. 'If Thou doest miracles at all, do them before the whole nation, instead of in obscure parts of Galilee.'

φανέρωσον σ. **Manifest** *Thyself;* see on i. 31 and xxi. 1.

οὐδὲ γ. Evidence of the Evangelist's candour; he admits that those who were thus closely connected with Jesus did not put their trust in Him: *For* **not even** *did His brethren* (as one would certainly expect) *believe on Him.* It is marvellous that in the face of this verse any one should have maintained that three of His brethren (James, Simon, and Judas) were Apostles. This verse is also fatal to the common theory, that these 'brethren' are really our Lord's cousins, the sons of Alphæus. Certainly *one* of the sons of Alphæus (James) was an Apostle; probably a *second* was (Matthew, if Levi and Matthew are the same person, as is almost universally admitted); possibly a third was (Judas, if 'Judas of James' means 'Judas, *brother* of James,' as is commonly supposed). By this time the company of the Twelve was complete (vi. 67, 70, 71); so that we cannot suppose that some of the Twelve have still to be converted. If then one, two, or three sons of Alphæus were Apostles, how could it be true that the sons of Alphæus 'did not believe on Him?' 'His brethren' cannot be the sons of Alphæus. They seem to have been converted by the Resurrection. Immediately after the Ascension we find them with the Apostles and the holy women (Acts i. 14; comp. 1 Cor. ix. 5; Gal. i. 19).

6. **ὁ καιρὸς ὁ ἐμ.** See on viii. 31. *My time* for manifesting Myself to the world *is not yet* **present**; with special reference to the Passion. It is inadequate to interpret it of the time for going up to the Feast. Moreover, what sense would there be in 'Your time *for going up to the Feast* is always ready?' Whereas 'You can always manifest yourselves' makes excellent sense. See last note on ii. 4. *Καιρός*, frequent in the Synoptists, occurs here only in S. John, v. 4 being a gloss: S. John's word is *ὥρα*. *Καιρός* is Christ's *opportunity* on the human side, *ὥρα* is His *hour* on the Divine side, i.e. as ordained by God.

7. **ὁ κόσμος.** Unbelievers; the common use in S. John: in *v.* 4 it meant all mankind (see on i. 10). He takes up their word and gives it a meaning far deeper than theirs. The world cannot hate them because they are part of itself (xv. 19). Hence it is that they can always manifest themselves; they can always count upon a favourable reception. As in iii. 3, 5, v. 19, vi. 44, 65, *οὐ δύναται* expresses a moral impossibility; comp. *vv.* 34, 36, viii. 21, 43, xii. 39, xiii. 33, 36, xiv. 17, xvi. 12. For **μαρτυρῶ** see on i. 7.

8. **ὑμεῖς.** Emphatic; ***you*, with all your fondness for publicity.**

ἐγὼ οὐκ ἀν. Οὔπω, certainly very ancient, is *possibly* a correction. It may have been substituted for οὐκ to avoid the charge of the heathen critic Porphyry, that Jesus here shews fickleness or deceit, and therefore cannot be Divine. But the sense is the same, whether we read οὐκ or οὔπω; 'I am not going now, publicly, in the general caravan of pilgrims; not going with you, who do not believe on Me.' He does not say 'I shall not go.' The next two verses shew exactly what the negative means.

9. Once more we see (*v.* 1, i. 43, ii. 1, 12, iv. 2, 43, vi. 1, 59) that S. John is quite aware that Galilee is the main scene of Christ's ministry, as the Synoptists represent. The gaps in his narrative leave ample room for the Galilean ministry.

10—39. The Discourses at the Feast of Tabernacles

Of this section *vv.* 10—13 are introductory.

10. εἰς τὴν ἑορτήν. These words, transposed in T.R., belong to ἀνέβησαν, not ἀνέβη. We are not told that Christ went up to the Feast, i.e. to keep it; so that His words 'I go not up to this Feast' may be true even in the sense 'I shall not go up for it at all.' All that is certain is that He appeared when the Feast was half over (*v.* 14).

οὐ φανερῶς. *Not* **manifestly**; He did not follow the worldly advice of His brethren: comp. φανέρωσον in *v.* 4. Had He gone in the general caravan there might have been another outburst of enthusiasm (vi. 14, 15), such as actually took effect at the next Passover (xii. 12—18). Perhaps He went by a different route (e.g. through Samaria, as in iv. 4, instead of down the eastern bank of Jordan), or several days later. One suspects that traces of Docetism are difficult to find in this Gospel when it is maintained that this verse contains such. See on i. 14, vi. 21, xix. 35.

11. οἱ οὖν 'I. The hostile party *therefore;* because they did not find Him in the caravan of pilgrims from Galilee. Note the imperfects, implying continued action.

ἐκεῖνος. That man of whom we have heard so much; ix. 12, 28.

12. γογγυσμός. Muttering; see on vi. 41. Some are for and some are against Him.

ἐν τοῖς ὄχλοις. Perhaps, *in the bands of pilgrims.* Here only does S. John use ὄχλοι; ὄχλος is frequent, and is read here in ℵD.

πλανᾷ. Leadeth astray.

13. οὐδεὶς μέντοι. Quite literally; no man dared speak openly either for or against Him, they were so afraid of the hierarchy. Experience had taught them that it was dangerous to take any line which the rulers had not formally sanctioned; and though the rulers were known to be against Christ, yet they had not committed themselves beyond recall, and might turn against either side. "A true indication of an utterly jesuitical domination of the people" (Meyer). See on iv. 27.

13. παῤῥησίᾳ. The word occurs nine times in the Gospel and four in the First Epistle, not in Matt. or Luke, and only once in Mark. It means either 'without reserve' (*v.* 4, x. 24, xi. 14, xvi. 25, 29, xviii. 20), or 'without fear' (*vv.* 13, 26, xi. 54). Originally it was confined to unreserved or fearless *speech*, but v. 4 and xi. 54 break through this restriction.

διὰ τὸν φ. τ. Ἰ. **Because of the** (prevalent) *fear of the Jews.* Thus 'the sins of the teachers are the teachers of sin.'

14—39. We have (1) a discourse in the midst of the Feast in which three groups take part; 'the Jews' (14—24); some of the people of Jerusalem (25—31); the envoys of the Sanhedrin (32—36): (2) a discourse on the last day of the Feast (37—39). The report is no doubt greatly condensed, but the divisions and vacillations in the multitude are vividly preserved.

14. ἤδη δὲ τ. ἑ. μ. *But when it was already the midst of the feast;* i.e. about the fourth day. Whether He had been in Jerusalem for the first half is uncertain: see on *v.* 10. Once more the Lord, whom they sought, suddenly visits His Temple, and perhaps for the first time teaches in public there: at the cleansing (ii. 13—17) He delivered no discourse. Note the change from aorist to imperfect.

15. οὗτος. Contemptuous, as in vi. 32. Their question is so eminently characteristic, that it is very unlikely that a Greek writer of the second century would have been able to invent it for them; he would probably have made them too cautious to commit themselves to any expression of astonishment about Him. The substance of His doctrine excites no emotion in them, but they are astounded that He should possess learning without having got it according to ordinary routine. He had never attended the schools of the Rabbis, and yet His interpretations of Scripture shewed a large amount of biblical and other knowledge. That *does* excite them. Their questions and comments throughout this section are too exactly in keeping with what we know of the Jews in our Lord's time to be the invention of a Greek a century or more later. By *γράμματα* is meant literature in general, not merely the Scriptures, which would be *τὰ ἱερὰ γρ.* (2 Tim. iii. 15), or *αἱ γραφαί* (v. 39; Acts xviii. 24, 28, &c.). Comp. *τὰ πολλά σε γράμματα εἰς μανίαν περιτρέπει,* Acts xxvi. 24.

16. οὐκ ἔστιν ἐμή. Jewish teachers commonly quoted their authorities. These Jews thought that Jesus was self-taught, and marvelled at His literary proficiency. Jesus here gives the authority for His teaching and accounts for its power. 'My teaching does not originate with Me; that is why I have no need to learn in the schools. He who sent Me communicates it to Me.'

17. ἐάν τις θέλῃ. *If any man* **willeth to do** *His will;* see on i. 44, vi. 67, viii. 44. The mere mechanical performance of God's will is not enough; there must be an inclination towards Him, a wish to make our conduct agree with His will; and without this agreement Divine doctrine cannot be recognised as such. There must be a moral harmony between the teaching and the taught, and this harmony is in the first instance God's gift (vi. 44, 45), which each can accept or refuse at will. Comp. xiv. 21. Doing the will of God means personal holiness, not mere belief: it is the ποιεῖν τὴν ἀλήθειαν of iii. 21.

γνώσεται. *He will come to know,* recognise; comp. *v.* 26, viii. 32. No time is stated; but sooner or later the knowledge will come. 'Will' rather than 'shall'; the words are partly a promise, partly a statement of fact. The test would be a strange one to men who were always seeking for 'signs,' i.e. miraculous proofs.

πότερον ἐκ τ. Θ. *Whether it proceeds from God* (as its Fount), *or I speak from Myself.* Note the change from ἐκ to ἀπό and comp. v. 19, 30, xv. 4.

18. Proof almost in the form of a syllogism that He does not speak of Himself. It applies to Christ alone. Human teachers who seek God's glory are not thereby secured from erroneous teaching. These verses (16—18) remind us, and might remind some of His hearers, of an earlier discourse delivered in Jerusalem some seven months before: comp. v. 19, 30, 37, 44.

οὗτος ἀληθής ἐστιν. Emphatic retrospective pronoun; see on iii. 32. Any one who speaks from himself seeks his own glory: but an *ambassador* who speaks from himself is not only vain-glorious but *false;* he claims his master's message as his own. The ambassador who seeks his master's glory is *true.*

ἀδικία. Unrighteousness is not in him. S. John does not say 'falsehood' as we might expect, but uses a wider word which points out the moral root of the falsehood. Comp. viii. 46. Throughout S. John's writings the connexion between truth and righteousness, falsehood and unrighteousness, is often brought before us. Hence his peculiar phrases 'to *do* the truth' (1 John i. 6), 'to *do* a lie' (Rev. xxi. 27, xxii. 15).

There is no need to suppose that anything is omitted between 18 and 19, though the transition is abrupt. Christ has answered them and now takes the offensive. He exposes the real meaning of their cavillings; they seek His life.

19. οὐ Μ. ἔδ. ὑ τ. νόμον; Here the interrogation probably ends (comp. vi. 70); the next clause is a statement of fact. The words are possibly an allusion to the custom of reading the Law in public every day of the Feast of Tabernacles, when the Feast fell in a Sabbatical year (Deut. xxxi. 10—13). The argument is similar to v. 45; Moses (see on i. 17) in whom they trust condemns them. Moreover it is an *argumentum ad hominem:* 'Ye are all breakers of the law, and yet would put Me to death as a breaker of it.'

20. Δαιμ. ἔχεις. *Thou hast a* **demon** (see on viii. 48). The multitude from the provinces know nothing of the designs of the hierarchy, although dwellers in Jerusalem (*v.* 25) are better informed. These provincials think He must be possessed to have such an idea.

Comp. x. 20, and also Matt. xi. 18, where the same is quoted as said of the Baptist. In both cases extraordinary conduct is supposed to be evidence of insanity, and the insanity is attributed to demoniacal possession, the *κακοδαιμονᾷν* of the Greeks. In viii. 48 the same remark is made, but in a much more hostile spirit, and there Christ answers the charge. Here, where it is the mere ignorant rejoinder of a perplexed multitude, He takes no notice of the interruption.

21. ἓν ἔρ. ἐπ. *I* **did** *one work;* the healing at Bethesda, which (He reminds them) excited the astonishment and indignation of *all*, not of the rulers only, as being wrought on the Sabbath. Ἕν, a single work, in contrast to frequent circumcisions on the Sabbath, or possibly to the many works which excited comparatively little attention: *ἕν* balances *πάντες*, one act sets all in amazement.

Many modern editors add *διὰ τοῦτο* from *v.* 22 to this verse; 'and ye all marvel on account of this.' But this is cumbrous, and unlike S. John, who begins sentences with *διὰ τοῦτο* (v. 16, 18, vi. 65, viii. 47, x. 17, xii. 18, 39) rather than ends them with it.

22. διὰ τ. M. For this cause M. hath given you: the perfect indicates that the gift abides, the present result of a past act.

οὐκ ὅτι. *Not* **that**; the sentence is a parenthesis, and *ὅτι* does not answer to *διὰ τοῦτο*. The meaning is not, '*For this cause* M. hath given you circumcision, *because* it originated (*ἐκ*) not with him but with the fathers:' which spoils the argument. *Διὰ τοῦτο* means, 'in order to teach the same lesson as I do.' It is not easy to determine the object of the parenthesis: whether it states (1) a mere matter of fact; or (2) the reason why circumcision on the eighth day (as being the older law, reaffirmed side by side with the later one) prevailed over the Sabbath; or (3) a reason why it might have been expected that the Sabbath (as being of Moses and in the Decalogue, whereas circumcision was not) would have prevailed over the law about circumcision. Anyhow the national conscience felt that it was better that the Sabbath should be broken, than that circumcision, the sign of the covenant and token of sanctification, should be postponed, and Jesus claims this right instinct as justifying Him. If then the Sabbath could give way to ceremonial ordinance, how much more to a work of mercy? The law of charity is higher than any ceremonial law. **'Eν** *σάββατῳ*, *on* **a** *Sabbath;* any that fell on the eighth day.

23. ἵνα μὴ λ. ὁ ν. M. The law about circumcision on the eighth day (Lev. xii. 3), which was a re-enactment of the patriarchal law (Gen. xvii. 12). Some adopt the inferior rendering in the margin; 'without breaking the law of Moses,' or 'without the law of Moses being broken;' in which case 'the law of Moses' means the law about the Sabbath. But this is not the natural meaning of *ἵνα μή*. Comp. v. 18, and see on x. 35.

χολᾶτε. Here only in N.T. It signifies bitter resentment.

ὅτι...σαββάτῳ. *Because* **I made a whole man sound** *on* **a** *Sabbath*, whereas circumcision purified one part only.

24. κατ' ὄψιν. *According to appearance* Christ's act was a breach of the Sabbath. Ὄψις may mean 'face,' as in xi. 44 (see note there); but there is no reference to Christ's having 'no form nor comeliness,' as if He meant 'Judge not by My mean appearance.'

τὴν δικ. κρ. **The** *righteous judgment:* there is only one.

25. ἐλ. οὖν τ. *Some* **therefore** *of them of Jerusalem said;* i.e. in consequence of Christ's vindication of Himself. Living in the capital, they know better than the provincials (*v.* 20) what the intentions of the hierarchy are. Ἱεροσολυμῖται occurs only here and Mark i. 5.

26. ἴδε παῤῥησίᾳ. See on i. 29 and vii. 13.

μήποτε κ.τ.λ. **Can it be that the rulers indeed have come to know that this man is the Christ?** Surely they have not; and yet why do they allow such language? Comp. *v.* 31, iv. 29, 33, and see on i. 48. The suggestion is only momentary: they at once raise a technical difficulty which suffices with them to cancel the moral impression produced by His words.

27. ὁ δὲ Χρ. ὅταν ἔρχ. *But when* **the** *Christ cometh;* see on i. 20. **οὐδεὶς γινώσκει.** *No one* **cometh to know** (*v.* 26) or **perceiveth.** Note the change from οἴδαμεν to γινώσκει and comp. viii. 55, xiii. 7, xiv. 7, xxi. 17. Πόθεν does not refer to the Messiah's *birthplace*, which was known (*vv.* 41, 42); nor to His *remote descent*, for He was to be the Son of David (*ibid.*); but to His parentage (vi. 42), immediate and actual. This text is the strongest, if not the only evidence that we have of the belief that the immediate parents of the Messiah would be unknown: but the precision and vivacity of this passage carry conviction with them, and shew how familiar the ideas current among the Jews at that time were to S. John. It never occurs to him to explain. The belief might easily grow out of Isai. liii. 8, 'Who shall declare His generation?' Justin Martyr tells us of a kindred belief, that the Messiahship of the Messiah would be unknown, even to Himself, until He was anointed by Elijah (*Trypho*, pp. 226, 336).

28. ἔκραξεν οὖν. **Jesus therefore** (moved by their gross misconceptions) **cried aloud.** The word expresses loud expression of strong emotion; comp. *v.* 37, i. 15, xii. 44. S. John well remembers that moving cry in the midst of Christ's teaching in the Temple. The scene is still before him and he puts it before us, although neither ἐν τῷ ἱερῷ nor διδάσκων is needed for the narrative (*v.* 14).

κἀμὲ οἴδ. κ.τ.λ. Various constructions have been put upon this: (1) that it is a question; (2) ironical; (3) a mixture of the two; (4) a reproach, i.e. that they knew His Divine nature and maliciously concealed it. None of these are satisfactory. The words are best understood quite simply and literally. Christ admits the truth of what they say: they have an outward knowledge of Him and His origin (vi. 42); but He has an inner and higher origin, of which they know nothing. So that even their self-made test, for which they are willing to resist the evidence both of Scripture and of His works, is complied with; for they know not His real immediate origin.

καὶ ἀπ' ἐμαυτοῦ. Καί introduces a contrast, as so often in S. John (*v.* 30); ἀπ. ἐμ. is emphatic; *and* (*yet*) *of Myself I am not come* (viii. 42). 'Ye know My person, and ye know My parentage; and yet of the chief thing of all, My Divine mission, ye know nothing.'

ἀληθινὸς ὁ π.] *He that sent Me is a true Sender*, One who in the most real and perfect sense can give a mission; or possibly, a really existing Sender, and not a fiction. In either case the meaning is 'I have a valid commission.'

29. ἐγώ. Emphatic, in contrast to the preceding emphatic ὑμεῖς.

ὅτι παρ' αὐ. εἰμι. **Because** *I am from Him, and He*, and no other, *sent Me.* Jesus knows God (1) because of His Divine generation, (2) because of His Divine mission. Comp. the very remarkable passage, Matt. xi. 27.

30. ἐζήτουν οὖν. *They sought* **therefore**, in consequence of His claiming Divine origin and mission; for though He has not mentioned God, they understand His meaning. Imperfect of continued action (xi. 27), the nominative being οἱ ἄρχοντες or οἱ Ἰουδαῖοι, not ὁ ὄχλος. **Πιάζειν** occurs Rev. xix. 20, and 7 times in this Gospel; elsewhere only Acts iii. 7, xii. 4; 2 Cor. xi. 32. See on i. 14, iv. 6, xi. 44 and xix. 37.

καὶ οὐδεὶς ἐπ. **And** (*yet*) *no one laid hands.* That καί in S. John often = 'and yet,' as here and *v.* 28, is most true; that καί ever = 'but' is true neither of S. John nor of any other Greek writer. In A.V. καί is rendered 'but' here and in *v.* 26, while in *v.* 31 δέ is rendered 'and.' See on i. 5 and viii. 20.

ἡ ὥρα αὐ. The hour appointed by God for His Passion (xiii. 1), this meaning being clearly marked by the context (see on *v.* 6 and ii. 4). The immediate cause of their not seizing Him was that they were as yet afraid to do so; but S. John passes through proximate causes to the prime cause of all, the Will of God. When the hour was come God no longer allowed their fear, which still existed (Matt. xxvi. 5), to deter them.

31. ἐκ τ. ὀχλ. δὲ π. **But** (on the other hand, i.e. in contrast to the rulers) **of the multitude** *many believed on Him* (as the Messiah) *and* **kept saying** (in answer to objectors), *When* **the** *Christ* (see on *v.* 27 and i. 20) *cometh, will He do more* **signs** *than those which this man* **did**? They express, not their own doubts, but those of objectors in saying, '*when* the Christ cometh:' *they* believe that He has come. Some of them perhaps had witnessed the numerous Galilean miracles; they have at any rate heard of them, and it is on them, not on His teaching and work, that their faith is based; hence its weakness. Winer, p. 641.

32. γογγύζοντος. Here, as in *v.* 12, mere **muttering**, as distinct from murmuring, seems to be meant: see on vi. 41. But they are restless at all this uncertainty. The Pharisees (comp. iv. 1) hear what they say and report it to the Sanhedrin, which orders His arrest.

ἀρχιερεῖς. First mention of them by S. John. The word signifies, not the heads of the 24 courses of priests, but Caiaphas, Annas, and the other ex-high-priests, with, perhaps, their relations in the Sanhedrin (Acts iv. 6). See on xi. 48, xviii. 13. Note that in this the reckless hierarchy, who were mainly Sadducees, combine with the Pharisees; comp. *v.* 45, xi. 47, 57, xviii. 3. On *πιάσωσιν* see on *v.* 30.

33. εἶπεν οὖν ὁ Ἰ. Therefore *said Jesus*, i.e. in consequence of their sending to arrest Him: probably He recognised the officers waiting for an opportunity to take Him. Christ's words are addressed to the officers and those who sent them, and it is very difficult to decide on their precise meaning. Perhaps the simplest interpretation is the best. 'I must remain on earth a little while longer, and during this time ye cannot kill Me: then ye will succeed, and I shall go to My Father. Thither ye will wish to come, but ye cannot; for ye know Him not (*v.* 28), and such as ye cannot enter there.' This is the first formal attempt upon His life. It reminds Him that His death is not far off, and that it will place a tremendous barrier between Him and those who compass it. It is the beginning of the end; an end that will bring a short-lived loss and eternal triumph to Him, a short-lived triumph and eternal loss to them.

χρόν. μικρόν. About six months; from the F. of Tabernacles to the Passover.

ὑπάγω. The voluntariness of His dying is implied in the word: see on x. 17, 18, xix. 30, 34, and on xvi. 7.

πρὸς τ. πέμψ. με. See on i. 33. One suspects that here S. John is translating Christ's words into plainer language than He actually used. Had He said thus clearly 'unto Him that sent Me,' a phrase which they elsewhere understand at once of God (see on *v.* 30), they could scarcely have asked the questions which follow in *v.* 35. Unless we are to suppose that they here *pretend* not to understand; which is unlikely, as they speak not to Him but 'among themselves.'

34. ζητήσετέ με. In spite of *vv.* 1, 19, 20, 25, 30, v. 18, viii. 37, 40, x. 39, xi. 8, it seems clear from xiii. 33 that these words are not to be understood of seeking His *life:* no infinitive is added here; in all the other cases we have *ἀποκτεῖναι*, *πιάσαι*, or *λιθάσαι*. Nor can *repentance* be meant; repentance could not be in vain. Rather *distress* is meant; they will seek for *help* at His hands and not find it (comp. viii. 21). But it is best not to limit the application to any particular occasion, such as the destruction of Jerusalem, the great hour of Jewish need.

ὅπου εἰμὶ ἐγώ, ὑμεῖς. The pronouns are again in emphatic opposition as in *vv.* 28, 29; comp. *vv.* 7, 8. *Εἰμί*, not *εἶμι*, which does not occur in N.T. Winer, p. 61. The present tense implies His continual presence with the Father; 'where I *am*,' not 'where I *shall be*.'

οὐ δύνασθε. It is morally impossible: see on *v.* 7.

Ποῦ οὗτος μέλλει. Where is this fellow (iii. 26, vi. 42, 52) **about to** (vi. 71) go, **seeing** *that we shall not find Him.* **Is He about to go unto the Dispersion** *among the Gentiles?* Ἡ *διασπορά τ.* Ἑλλ. means those Jews who were *dispersed among the heathen* outside Palestine; the abstract for the concrete, like *ἡ περιτομή* for the Jews generally. *Διασπορά* occurs James i. 1 and 1 Pet. i. 1 (see notes there), and nowhere else in N.T. There were three chief colonies of these 'dispersed' or 'scattered' Jews, in Babylonia, Egypt, and Syria, whence they spread over the whole world. 'Moses from generations of old hath in every city them that preach him,' Acts xv. 21. These opponents of Christ, therefore, suggest that He means to go to the Jews scattered among the Gentiles in order to reach the Gentiles and teach them—the very mode of proceeding afterwards adopted by the Apostles; so that their saying, like that of Caiaphas (xi. 50), was an involuntary prophecy. But here it is spoken in sarcasm. Christ's utter disregard of Jewish exclusiveness and apparent non-observance of the ceremonial law gave a handle to the sneer; which would be pointless if Ἑλλήνων were rendered 'Hellenists,' i.e. Grecised Jews. Ἕλληνες in N.T. *always* means Gentiles or heathen. See on xii. 20.

36. **ὁ λόγος οὗτος.** *Οὗτος* is again contemptuous, like '**this** precious word.' But they cannot shake the impression which it has made on them. Their own scornful suggestion does not satisfy them, for they know that it is not true.

37. **ἐν......μεγάλῃ.** **Now on** *the last day*, **the** *great day*. This was probably not the seventh day, but the eighth day, which according to Lev. xxiii. 36, 39; Num. xxix. 35; Neh. viii. 18, was reckoned along with the seven days of the feast proper. To speak of the seventh day as 'the great day of the feast' would not be very appropriate; whereas the eighth day on which the people returned home was, like the first day, kept as a Sabbath (Lev. xxiii. 39), and had special sacrifices (Num. xxix. 36—38). Comp. 2 Macc. x. 6. In keeping with the solemnity of the day Christ solemnly takes up His position and cries aloud with deep emotion (see on *v.* 28). The *εἱστήκει* and *ἔκραξεν* are very graphic: comp. i. 35, xviii. 5, 16, 18, xix. 25, xx. 11. He **was standing**, beholding the multitude engaged in the ceremonies of the last day of the Feast, and moved by the sight He **cried aloud.**

ἐάν τις διψᾷ. The words recall Isa. lv. 1 and Rev. xxii. 17, *ὁ διψῶν ἐρχέσθω*. See on *v.* 30. The conjectured reference to the custom of pouring water at the Feast of Tabernacles is probably correct. On all seven days water was brought from the pool of Siloam and poured into a silver basin on the western side of the altar of burnt offering, a ceremony not mentioned in O.T. Apparently this was *not* done on the *eighth* day. Accordingly Christ comes forward and fills the gap, directing them to a better water than that of Siloam. The fact that the water was poured and not drunk, does not seem to be a reason for denying the reference, especially when we remember how frequently Christ took an external fact as a text (comp. iv. 10, v. 17, 19, vi. 26, 27, (viii. 12?) ix. 39, xiii. 8, 10, 12—17; Mark x. 15, 16, 23, 24, &c.). The pouring of the water would be suggestive enough, especially as it represented the water from the rock (1 Cor. x. 4). In such cases there is no need for the analogy to be complete, and in the present case it would add point to the reference that it was not complete. Mere pouring of water could not quench even bodily thirst; Christ could satisfy spiritual thirst. 'Therefore with joy shall ye draw water out of the wells of salvation.' Isa. xii. 3. Thus S. John, having shewn us Christ as typified by the Brazen Serpent (iii. 14) and the Manna (vi. 51), now shews Him as the Rock.

38. ὁ πιστεύων. *Nominativus pendens;* comp. vi. 39; xv. 2.

καθὼς εἶπεν ἡ γρ. *As the scripture* said; as if some passage to this effect had recently been read. See on ii. 22. The phrase undoubtedly refers to the words that follow: but inasmuch as no such text is found in Scripture, some have tried to force the phrase into connexion with what precedes, as if the meaning were 'He that believeth on me in the way that Scripture prescribes.' Although the exact words are not found in Scripture there are various texts of similar import: Isa. xliv. 3, lviii. 11; Zech. xiii. 1, xiv. 8, &c. But none of them contain the very remarkable expression 'out of his belly.' Godet contends for Ex. xvii. 6 and Num. xx. 11, and thinks that 'out of it' (Heb. 'from within him') is the source of *ἐκ τῆς κοιλίας αὐτοῦ*, and 'abundant waters' of *ποταμοὶ ὕδατος*, while 'I will stand' may possibly be alluded to in 'Jesus was standing.' In the LXX. there is no resemblance to the Greek here. Ποταμοὶ stands first with great emphasis; *rivers out of his belly shall flow*, rivers *of living water;* in marked contrast to the *ewer* of water poured each day of the Feast. (For the form *ῥεύσουσιν* see Winer, p. 109.) Note how, as so often in S. John, the conclusion of one thought is the starting-point of another. As in vi. 35, 'coming to Christ' is equivalent to 'believing on Christ;' and believing on Him is far in advance of thirsting for spiritual satisfaction, for a man may thirst and refuse to believe. But the believer cannot end in satisfying his own thirst; he at once becomes a fount whence others may derive refreshment. Whether he wills to be a teacher or no, the true Christian cannot fail to impart the spirit of Christianity to others. Thus we have three stages; (1) thirsting; (2) coming or believing; (3) being filled and supplying others.

39. περὶ τ. πν. S. John's interpretation is to be accepted, whatever may be our theory of inspiration, (1) because no better interpreter of Christ's words ever lived, even among the Apostles; (2) because it is the result of his own inmost experience. The principle of Christian activity has ever been the Spirit. He moves the waters, and they overflowed at Pentecost. Till then 'the Spirit was not yet;' the dispensation of the Spirit had not come.

οὗ ἔμελλον. *Which they that* believed *on Him* were about to (vi. 71) *receive: οἱ πιστεύσαντες*, those who did believe, the first disciples.

οὔπω γὰρ ἦν πν. As in i. 33 and xx. 22 there is no article, and an *influence* of the Spirit rather than the Third Person is meant: the spiritual life was not yet. *Christus Legis, Spiritus Evangelii complementum;* Christ completes the Law, the Spirit completes the Gospel.

ὅτι...ἐδοξάσθη. Comp. xvi. 7, xvii. 1, 5; Ps. lxviii. 18. The Spirit, "though given in His fulness to Christ Himself (iii. 34), and operating through Him in His people (vi. 63), was not, until after Christ's return to glory, to be given to the faithful as the Paraclete and representative of Christ for the carrying on of His work" (Meyer). Christ did not send the Paraclete until He Himself had resumed the fulness of Divinity; and the Spirit did not give Christ to be the life of the Church until Christ was perfected.

40—52. Opposite Results of the Discourses

40. ἐκ τ. ὄχλ. οὖν. **Of the multitude, therefore, some, when they heard these words, kept saying**, or, **began to say.** For *ἐκ τῶν* as a nominative comp. i. 24, xvi. 17, and as an accusative 2 John 4; Rev. ii. 10. The *λόγοι* probably mean the discourses from *v.* 14 onwards.

ὁ προφήτης. The Prophet of Deut. xviii. 15, who is here distinguished from the Messiah. See on i. 21 and vi. 14.

41. μὴ γὰρ...ὁ Χρ. ἐρ. We have here an instance how little attention our translators paid to the Greek article; in the same verse they translate the article in one place and ignore it in another. In the next verse they ignore it again. In all three places it should be '*the* Christ' (see on i. 20). **What, doth the Christ** *come out of Galilee?* Comp. Nathanael's difficulty (i. 46). It is quite inadmissible to infer, because S. John does not correct this mistake of supposing that Jesus came from Galilee, that he is either ignorant of the truth or indifferent to it. He knew that his readers would be well aware of the facts, and he leaves the error without comment to their pity or disdain; comp. i. 45, vi. 42, 43, vii. 20, 52. On the other hand, could a Greek of the second century invent these discussions of the Jewish multitude?

42. ἐκ τ. σπ. Δ. Ps. cxxxii. 11; Jer. xxiii. 5; Isa. xi. 1, 10. See on ii. 22.

ἀπὸ Βηθλεέμ. Mic. v. 2; 1 Sam. xvi. 1; comp. Matt. ii. 6. Like Oedipus they are tragically ignorant that the very test which they so confidently apply tells against them.

43. σχίσμα. Whence our word 'schism.' It means a serious and possibly violent division: ix. 16, x. 19; 1 Cor. i. 10, xii. 25; comp. Acts xiv. 4, xxiii. 7. In N.T. it is never used in the modern sense of a separation *from* the Church, but of parties *in* the Church. In the Synoptists it is used only in its original sense of *physical* severing; 'a worse *rent* is made;' Matt. ix. 16; Mark ii. 21.

44. τινές. Not the officers, but some zealots who would have arrested Him on their own responsibility. See on xi. 27.

45. ἦλθ. οὖν οἱ ὑπ. **Therefore** *came the officers*, i.e. because neither they nor any of the multitude had ventured to arrest Him. Under the control of God's providence (*v.* 30), they had been unable to find any good opportunity for taking Him, and had been overawed by the majesty of His words (*v.* 46). The influence which Christ exercised over His enemies shews again and again that they had no power over Him until He and His Father willed to allow it; comp. xiii. 27, xviii. 6, xix. 11. It would seem as if the Sanhedrin had continued sitting, waiting for the return of its officers; an extraordinary proceeding on so great a day (see on *v.* 37), shewing the intensity of their hostility. Their question is quite in harmony with this. See on *v.* 32. The omission of *τούς* before Φαρ. shews that the chief priests and Pharisees are now regarded as one body.

ἐκεῖνοι. The pronoun marks the Evangelist's aversion: comp. x. 6.

47. οἱ Φαρ. That part of the Sanhedrin which was most jealous of orthodoxy, regarded both by themselves and others as models of correct belief, **therefore** *answered them; Surely ye also have not been* **led astray** (*v.* 12), ye, the officers of the Sanhedrin! *ὑμεῖς* is very emphatic. Comp. *vv.* 26, 31, 41, vi. 67. **Πλανᾶσθαι** implies fundamental departure from the truth, not mere error; 1 John i. 7, ii. 26, iii. 7; Rev. *passim.*

48. What right have you to judge for yourselves, contrary to the declared opinion of the Sanhedrin and of the orthodox party? What right have you to wear our livery and dispute our resolutions? Note the singular; *Hath any* **one**? '*Have* any' weakens it.

49. ὁ ὄχ. οὗτος. Very contemptuous; *this* **multitude** *of yours, iste* (35, 36), whose ignorant fancies you prefer to our deliberate decisions.

ὁ μὴ γιν. The *μή* implies censure; knoweth not when it ought to know. They ought to know that a sabbath-breaker cannot be the Messiah. Ὁ *οὐ γιν.* would express a mere fact; comp. vi. 64.

ἐπάρατοι. A mere outburst of theological fury. A formal excommunication of the whole multitude by the Sanhedrin (comp. ix. 22) would be impossible. How could such a sentence be executed on the right individuals? It was reserved for a Christian hierarchy to invent the interdict. Excommunication *en masse* was unknown to the Jews. Rabbinical writings abound in contempt for the "people of the earth."

50. ὁ ἐλθὼν πρότερον. See on iii. 1, 2. His being 'one of them' answers the challenge in *v.* 48, 'Hath any one of the rulers believed on Him?' But he does not yet declare himself His disciple. Comp. the attitude of Gamaliel, Acts v. 34—42.

51. μὴ ὁ νόμος. Ὁ *νόμος* is emphatic. 'You condemn the multitude for not knowing the law; but are we not forgetting the law in condemning a man unheard?' These learned theologians and lawyers were forgetting such plain and simple texts as Deut. i. 16, 17, xvii. 8, xix. 15, involving the most elementary principles of justice.

τὸν ἄνθρ. **The** *man* (prosecuted), **except it first hear** from himself, or perhaps **hear his defence.**

52. μὴ καὶ σύ. 'Surely *thou* dost not sympathize with Him as being a fellow-countryman?' They share the popular belief that Jesus was by birth a Galilean (see on *v.* 41).

ἐρ. κ. ἴδε. *Search and* see; i.e. search and thou wilt see: like *Divide et impera.* The ὅτι may be either 'that' after 'see,' or 'because:' the former seems better.

ἐκ τ. Γαλ....οὐκ ἐγείρεται. Jonah of Gath-hepher (2 Kings xiv. 25) was certainly of Galilee; Nahum of Elkosh may have been, but the situation of Elkosh is uncertain; Hosea was of the northern kingdom, but whether of Galilee or not is unknown; Abelmeholah, whence Elisha came, was in the north part of the Jordan valley, possibly in Galilee. Anyhow, their statement is only a slight and very natural exaggeration (comp. iv. 29). Moreover they speak of the present and future, rather than of the past; *ἐγείρεται*, not (as T. R.) *ἐγήγερται*. Judging from the past, Galilee was not very likely to produce a prophet, much less the Messiah.

Of the various questions which arise respecting the paragraph that follows (vii. 53—viii. 11) one at least may be answered with something like certainty,—that it is *no part of the Gospel of S. John.* (1) In both tone and style it is very unlike his writings. His favourite words and expressions are wanting; others that he rarely or never uses are found. (2) It breaks the course of the narrative by severing the two closely connected declarations of Christ, Ἐάν τις διψᾷ κ.τ.λ. and Ἐγώ εἰμι τὸ φῶς τ. κόσμου, with the two equally closely connected promises, ὁ πιστεύων εἰς ἐμὲ κ.τ.λ. and ὁ ἀκολουθῶν μοι κ.τ.λ. (vii. 37, 38, viii. 12); and hence a few of the MSS. which contain it place it at the end of the Gospel, and one places it after vii. 36. (3) All the very serious amount of external evidence (see Appendix D.) which tells against the passage being part of the Gospel narrative at all of course tells against its being by S. John, and in this respect is not counterbalanced by other considerations. So that the internal and external evidence when put together is overwhelmingly against the paragraph being part of the Fourth Gospel.

With regard to the question whether the section is *a genuine portion of the Gospel history*, the internal evidence is wholly in favour of its being so, while the balance of external testimony is decidedly on the same side. (1) The style is similar to the Synoptic Gospels, especially to S. Luke; and four inferior MSS. insert the passage at the end of Luke xxi., the place in the history into which it fits best. (2) It bears the impress of truth and is fully in harmony with Christ's conduct on other occasions; yet it is quite original and cannot be a divergent account of any other incident in the Gospels. (3) It is easy to see how prudential reasons *might* in some cases have caused its omission (the fear of giving, as S. Augustine says, *peccandi impunitatem mulieribus*); difficult to see what, excepting its truth, can have caused its insertion. But "the utmost licence of the boldest transcribers never makes even a remote approach to the excision of a complete narrative from the Gospels" (W. and H.). (4) Though it is found in no Greek MS. earlier than the sixth century, nor in the earliest versions, nor is quoted as by S. John until late in the fourth century, yet Jerome says that in his time it was contained '*in many Greek and Latin MSS.*' (*Adv. Pelag.* II. 17). But if it be thought that these must have been as good as the best MSS. which we now possess, we must remember that most of the worst corruptions of the text were already in existence in Jerome's time.

The question as to *who is the author*, cannot be answered. There is not sufficient material for a satisfactory conjecture, and mere guesswork is worthless. The extraordinary number of various readings (80 in 183 words) points to more than one source.

One more question remains. *How is it that nearly all the MSS. that do contain it* (several uncials, including the Cambridge MS., and more than 300 cursives) *agree in inserting it here?* This cannot be answered with certainty. *Similarity of matter* may have caused it to have been placed in the margin in one copy, and thence it may have passed, as other things have done, into the text of the Cambridge and other MSS. In chap. vii. we have an unsuccessful attempt to ruin Jesus: this paragraph contains the history of another attempt, equally unsuccessful. Or, the incident may have been inserted in the margin (very possibly from Papias) in illustration of viii. 15, and hence have got into the text.

53. That this verse, as well as viii. 1, 2, is omitted in most MSS. shews that prudential reasons could not explain the omission of the paragraph in more than a *very* limited number of cases. It is a minority of MSS. which omit only viii. 3—11.

καὶ ἐπορ. ἕκαστος. See on viii. 1. *And* **they went each man** *unto his own house.* **But** *Jesus went, &c.* It is unfortunate that the verse should have been placed at the end of this chapter instead of at the beginning of the next: this arrangement destroys the contrast between Jesus and the others, and creates an impression that the verse records the breaking up of the meeting of the Sanhedrin.

CHAPTER VIII

1—11. The number of various readings in this section is very large, and we have not the data for constructing a satisfactory text.

4. **κατείληπται** for *κατελήφθη*.

5. **λιθάζειν** for *λιθοβολεῖσθαι*.

7. **ἀνέκυψεν καὶ εἶπεν αὐτοῖς** for *ἀνακύψας εἶπε πρὸς αὐτούς*, and **πρῶτος ἐπ' αὐτὴν βαλέτω λίθον** for *πρ. τὸν λ. ἐπ' αὐτῇ β.*

9. Omit *καὶ ὑπὸ τῆς συνειδήσεως ἐλεγχόμενοι* after **ἀκούσαντες**, and *ἕως τῶν ἐσχάτων* after **πρεσβυτέρων** (both obvious glosses). **Οὖσα** for *ἑστῶσα*.

10. Omit *καὶ μηδένα θεασάμενος πλὴν τῆς γυναικός* after **Ἰησοῦς**, and *ἐκεῖνοι οἱ κατήγοροί σου* after **εἰσιν**. **Γύναι** for *ἡ γυνή*.

11. **ἀπὸ τοῦ νῦν** for *καί*.

16. **ἀληθινή** (BDLTX) for *ἀληθής* (from *vv.* 13, 14).

20, 21. Omit (ℵBDLT) *ὁ Ἰησοῦς*: comp. iii. 2, iv. 46, vi. 14.

26. **λαλῶ** (ℵBDLTX) for *λέγω* (E).

29. Omit (ℵBDLTX) *ὁ πατήρ* after **μόνον** (a gloss).

38. **ἃ ἐγώ** for *ἐγὼ ὅ*. Omit *μου* after **πατρί**. **ἃ ἠκούσατε** for *ὃ ἑωράκατε* and **τοῦ πατρός** for *τῷ πατρὶ ὑμῶν* (both for the sake of harmony with the first clause).

39. **ἐστε** (ℵBDLT) for *ἦτε* (C). Omit *ἂν* after **ἐποιεῖτε**.

41. **οὐκ ἐγεννήθημεν** (BD¹) for *οὐ γεγεννήμεθα* (CD²).

51. **τὸν ἐμὸν λόγον** for *τ. λ. τ. ἐμ.* (S. John's common use).

54. **ἡμῶν** (AB²C) for *ὑμῶν* (B¹DFX); *ὑμῶν* seems preferable.

59. Omit *διελθὼν διὰ μέσου αὐτῶν καὶ παρῆγεν οὕτω* after **ἱεροῦ** (an addition from ix. 1 combined with Luke iv. 30) with ℵ¹BD against ℵ³A. Other MSS. have the addition in another form. No English Version earlier than 1611 recognises the addition.

1. τὸ ὄρος τῶν Ἐ. The M. of Olives, which is mentioned 10 times by the Synoptists, is not mentioned by S. John (comp. xviii. 1); and when he introduces a new place he commonly adds an explanation: i. 44, iv. 5, v. 2, vi. 1, xix. 13, 17. *Πορεύεσθαι εἰς*, frequent in the Synoptists, does not occur in S. John.

2. ὄρθρου δὲ κ.τ.λ. Comp. Luke xxi. 38; *καὶ πᾶς ὁ λαὸς ὤρθριζε πρὸς αὐτὸν ἐν τῷ ἱερῷ ἀκούειν αὐτοῦ*. S. John never uses *πᾶς ὁ λαός*, S. Luke frequently does. S. John uses *λαός* only twice; it occurs more than 30 times in S. Luke, more than 20 in the Acts: *καθίζειν* is frequent in the Synoptists and the Acts; only twice in S. John: *καθίσας ἐδίδασκεν* occurs Luke v. 3. He sat to teach with authority; Matt. v. 1, xxiii. 2; Mark ix. 35. *Ὄρθρου, ὀρθρινός, ὀρθρίζειν* occur Luke xxiv. 1, 22, xxi. 38; none of them in S. John, who uses *πρωΐ* or *πρωΐας* and *πρωϊνός* (xviii. 33, xxi. 4; Rev. ii. 28, xxii. 16). See on vii. 20.

3. οἱ γραμμ. κ. οἱ Φαρ. This phrase occurs in all three Synoptists, in S. Luke thrice. S. John nowhere mentions the scribes. He speaks of the hierarchy as *οἱ ἀρχιερεῖς* or *οἱ ἄρχοντες* with or without *οἱ Φαρισαῖοι*, or else simply as *οἱ Ἰουδαῖοι*. This is probably not an official deputation from the Sanhedrin; there is nothing to shew that the woman had been before the Sanhedrin. Their bringing her was a wanton outrage both on her and all generous and modest spectators. She might have been detained while the case was referred to Christ.

4. κατείληπται. Hath been *taken.* The vividness of this, and still more of *ἐπαυτοφώρῳ* (literally, 'in the very act of theft'), is another piece of brutal indelicacy.

5. ἐν δὲ τῷ νόμῳ. Of the two texts given in the margin of our Bible, Lev. xx. 10 and Deut. xxii. 22, probably neither is correct. It is often assumed that 'put to death' in Jewish Law means stoning: such however is not Jewish tradition. The Rabbis taught that it meant strangulation; i.e. the criminal was smothered in mud and then a cord was twisted round his neck. But, for the case of a betrothed woman sinning in the city, stoning is specified as the punishment (Deut. xxii. 23, 24), and this is probably what is indicated here. Such cases would be rare, and therefore all the better suited for a casuistical question.

σὺ οὖν τί λέγεις; What therefore *sayest Thou?* This is the only place in the whole paragraph where S. John's favourite particle *οὖν* occurs; and that not in the narrative, where S. John makes such frequent use of it, but in the dialogue, where he very rarely employs it. Scarcely anywhere in this Gospel are there 12 verses of *narrative* without an *οὖν*; but see ii. 1—17, and contrast iv. 1—26, xx. 1—9.

6. πειράζοντες. This verb is frequent in the Synoptists of trying to place Christ in a difficulty; never so used by S. John, who, however, uses it once of Christ 'proving' Philip (vi. 6).

ἵνα ἔχ. κατ. This clause must be borne in mind in determining what the difficulty was in which they wished to place Him. It seems to exclude the supposition that they hoped to undermine His popularity, in case He should decide for the extreme rigour of the law; the people having become accustomed to a lax morality (Matt. xii. 39; Mark viii. 38). Probably the case is somewhat parallel to the question about tribute, and they hoped to bring Him into collision either with the Law and Sanhedrin or with the Roman Government. If He said she was *not* to be stoned, He contradicted Jewish Law; if He said she *was* to be stoned, He ran counter to Roman Law, for the Romans had deprived the Jews of the right to inflict capital punishment (xviii. 31). The Sanhedrin might of course pronounce sentence of death (Matt. xxvi. 66; Mark xiv. 64; comp. John xix. 7), but it rested with the Roman governor whether he would allow the sentence to be carried out or not (xix. 16): see on xviii. 31 and xix. 6.

κάτω κύψας κ.τ.λ. It is said that this gesture was a recognised sign of unwillingness to attend to what was being said; a call for a change of subject. McClellan quotes Plut. II. 532: 'Without uttering a syllable, by merely raising the eyebrows, or *stooping down*, or *fixing the eyes upon the ground*, you may baffle unreasonable importunities.' Κατέγραφεν means '*kept writing*' (comp. vii. 40, 41), or '*began to write*, made as though He would write' (comp. Luke i. 59). Either rendering would agree with this interpretation, which our translators have insisted on as certain by inserting the gloss (not found in any earlier English Version except the Bishops' Bible), 'as though He heard them not.' The Greek is *μὴ προσποιούμενος*, which Stephens admitted into his editions of 1546 and 1549, but not into that of 1550, which became the *Textus Receptus*. But it is just possible that by writing on the stone pavement of the Temple He wished to remind them of the 'tables of stone, written with the finger of God' (Ex. xxxi. 18; Deut. ix. 10). They were hoping that He would explain away the seventh commandment, in order that they themselves might break the sixth.

7. They will not take the hint; and therefore with marvellous skill He lifts the whole question from the judicial sphere, into which He declined to enter (comp. Luke xii. 14), to the moral one, in which their guilty consciences rendered them powerless. Thus the self-made judges were foiled, while the majesty of the Law remained intact. The abruptness of the reply reminds us of ii. 19.

ἀναμάρτητος. Quite classical, but here only in N.T. It may mean either 'free from the possibility of sin, *impeccable;*' or 'free from actual sin, *sinless:*' if the latter, it may mean either 'free from sin in general, *guiltless;*' or 'free from a particular sin, *not guilty.*' The context shews that the last is the meaning here, 'free from the sin of impurity:' comp. '*sin* no more,' *v.* 11, and 'sinner,' Luke vii. 37, 39. The practical maxim involved in Christ's words is that of Matt. vii. 1—5; Rom. xiv. 4. As to its application to them comp. Matt. xii. 39; Mark viii. 38. He is contending not against punishment being inflicted by human law, but against men taking the law into their own hands.

λίθον. Some authorities have *τὸν λίθον*, the *stone* required for executing the sentence. Others take it of the *first* stone, which in stoning for idolatry was to be thrown by the witnesses (Deut. xiii. 9, xvii. 7); probably as a check on rash testimony. Thus in stoning Stephen the witnesses take off their upper garments in order to throw the better (Acts vii. 58).

8. πάλιν κ. ἑ. He again refuses to have the office of judge thrust upon Him. The Reader of men's hearts knew how His challenge would work: no one would respond to it.

ἔγραφεν. Imperfect, as in *v.* 6. A Venetian MS. ascribed to the 10th century has the remarkable reading 'wrote on the ground the sins of each one of them.' The same strange idea appears in Jerome and elsewhere, shewing how soon men began to conjecture *what* He wrote. Others suppose that He wrote the answer in *v.* 7. As has been shewn on *v.* 6, it is not certain that He wrote anything.

9. The variations in this verse are considerable, but the substance is the same. *Καὶ ὑπὸ τ. συνειδήσεως ἐλεγχόμενοι* is probably a gloss like *μὴ προσποιούμενος* in *v.* 6. Another gloss here is 'understanding His upbraiding.' Both additions are right as *interpretations*. The word of God, 'sharper than any two-edged sword,' had pierced them and proved 'a discerner of the thoughts of their hearts' (Heb. iv. 12).

ἀρξ. ἀπὸ τ. πρεσβυτέρων. The elders in years, not the official Elders. Meyer suggests that the oldest would be shrewd enough to slip away without compromising themselves further: certainly they would have the largest experience of life and its temptations.

μόνος. The multitude may or may not have withdrawn with the woman's accusers; the disciples probably had not moved. But of the actors in the scene only two were left, she who needed compassion and He who could bestow it: *relicti sunt duo, misera et Misericordia* (S. Augustine). The woman was *in the midst*, where the brutality of her accusers had placed her (*v.* 3).

10. A gloss, *καὶ μηδένα θεασάμενος πλὴν τῆς γυναικός*, has been inserted here, as in *vv.* 6 and 9: *πλήν* occurs nowhere in S. John's writings excepting Rev. ii. 25. *'Εκεῖνοι οἱ κατήγοροί σου* is another insertion.

οὐδείς σε κατέκρινεν; Did no man condemn thee? shewing how long He had waited for an answer to His challenge. *Κατακρίνω* occurs nine times in the Synoptists, but not in S. John, who uses *κρίνω*.

11. οὐδείς, κύριε. We must remember that *κύριε* need not mean more than 'Sir' (see on vi. 34): but as we have no such ambiguous word in English, 'Lord,' though possibly too strong, is best.

οὐδὲ ἐγώ. *'Εγώ* is very emphatic, 'not even I, though *ἀναμάρτητος*.' He maintains in tenderness towards her the attitude which He had assumed in sternness towards her accusers: He declines the office of judge. He came not to condemn, but to seek and to save. And yet He did condemn, as S. Augustine remarks, not the woman, but the sin. With regard to the woman, though He does not condemn, yet He does not pardon: He does not say 'thy sins have been forgiven thee' (Matt. ix. 2; Luke vii. 48), or even 'go in peace' (Luke vii. 50, viii. 48). "We must not apply in all cases a sentence, which requires His Divine knowledge to make it a just one" (Alford). He knew, what her accusers did not know, whether she was penitent or not.

ἀπὸ τ. ν. μ. ἁμάρτανε. From henceforth continue no longer in sin (see on v. 14). The contrast between the mere negative declaration and the very positive exhortation is striking. There is *πάρεσις*, but not *ἄφεσις, τῶν ἁμαρτημάτων* (Rom. iii. 25); her sins are *passed by* for the present, while she has time to amend.

VIII. 12—IX. 41. Christ the Source of Truth and Light (*Continued.*)

In viii. 12—46 *ἀλήθεια* occurs 7 times, *ἀληθής* 4 times, *ἀληθινός* and *ἀληθῶς* each once.

12. πάλιν οὖν. The paragraph vii. 53—viii. 11 being omitted, these words must be connected with vii. 52. The officers have made their report to the Sanhedrin, leaving Jesus unmolested. After an interval He continues His discourse: *again*, **therefore**, *Jesus spake unto them*, i.e. because the attempt to interfere with Him had failed. How long the interval was we do not know, but probably a few hours.

ἐγώ εἰμι τ. φῶς τ. κ. See on vi. 35. Once more we have a possible reference to the ceremonies of the Feast of Tabernacles, somewhat less probable than the other (see on vii. 37), but not improbable. Large candelabra were lighted in the Court of the Women on the evening of the first day of the Feast in memory of the pillar of fire at the Exodus, and these flung their light over the whole city. Authorities differ as to whether this illumination was repeated, but all are agreed that it did not take place on the last evening. Here, therefore, there was once more a gap, which Christ Himself may have designed to fill; and while the multitude were missing the festal light of the great lamps, He declares, 'I am the Light of the world.' 'Light,' according to tradition, was one of the names of the Messiah. In the case of the water we know that it was poured on each of the seven days, and that Christ spoke the probable reference to it on the last day of the Feast. But in this case the illumination took place possibly on the first night *only*, and Christ certainly did not utter this possible reference to it until the last day of the Feast, or perhaps not until the Feast was all over. But the fact that the words were spoken in the Court of the Women (see on *v.* 20) makes the reference not improbable; and *πάλιν* may point to this: Jesus having appropriated the type of the Rock, now appropriates that of the Pillar of Fire.

ὁ ἀκολουθῶν. This expression also is in favour of the reference. 'The Lord went before them by day in a pillar of a cloud *to lead them the way;* and by night in a pillar of fire, *to give them light*' (Exod. xiii. 21). So Christ here declares that those who *follow* Him *shall* **in nowise** *walk in* **the** *darkness*. The negative (*οὐ μή*) is very strong. This use of 'darkness' for moral evil is peculiar to S. John: see on i. 5, where (as here) we have light and life (*v.* 4) closely connected, while darkness is opposed to both.

ἕξει. Not only *with* him but *in* him, so that he also becomes a source of light. See on vii. 38 and comp. 'Ye are the light of the world' Matt. v. 14. *Τῆς ζωῆς* means 'giving life' not merely 'leading to life:' see on vi. 35 and i. 4. Note that as in the case of the living bread and the living water so also here the believer is not a mere *passive recipient;* he has to eat and to drink to appropriate the heavenly food, and here he has to follow to appropriate the heavenly light. In the early Church candidates for baptism first turned to the West and renounced Satan and his works and then to the East, 'the place of light,' and professed allegiance to Christ (the Light of the world and the Sun of righteousness) and a belief in the Trinity (Dionys. Areop. *Eccl. Hier.*; S. Cyril *Cat. Myst.* I.) From this very ancient custom the practice of turning to the east at the Creed is derived. Comp. Tert. *Apol.* XVI.; *In Valent.* III.; *Apost. Const.* II. vii. 57; Clem. Alex. *Strom.* VII. vii.; &c.

13—59. A comparison of the discourses in chapters v.—viii. shews how the conflict increases in intensity. In v. and vi. Christ proceeds almost without interruption, and the Jews demur rather than contradict. In vii. the interruptions are stronger. Here He is interrupted and contradicted at every turn.

13. μαρτυρεῖς. *Bearest* **witness** (see on i. 7). The Pharisees try to cancel the effect of His impressive declaration by a formal objection, the validity of which He had been heard to admit (*v.* 31).

14. κἂν ἐγὼ μ. Even if *I should bear* **witness.** Strong emphasis on *ἐγώ*. God can testify respecting Himself, and there are truths to which He alone can testify. Yet He condescends to conform to the standard of human testimony, and adds to His witness the words and works of His incarnate Son; who in like manner can bear witness of Himself, being supported by the witness of the Father (*v.* 16).

ποῦ ὑπάγω. By Death and Ascension. *Ὑμεῖς* is emphatic: they knew neither the whence nor the whither of their own lives, and how could they know His? Throughout the chapter we find *ἐγώ* and *ὑμεῖς* in constant opposition.

15. κατὰ τ. σάρκα. According to His humanity, the form of a servant: comp. vii. 24; vi. 63. Treating Him as a mere man they had condemned His witness concerning Himself as invalid. *Κρίνω* acquires an adverse sense from the context: comp. iii. 17, 18, vii. 51.

οὐ κρ. οὐδένα. Neither *κατὰ τ. σάρκα* nor anything else is to be supplied. No such addition can be made in *v.* 16, and therefore cannot be made here. The words are best taken quite literally. 'My mission is not to condemn, but to save and bless.' Comp. xii. 47; iii. 17.

16. καὶ ἐὰν κρ. δὲ ἐγώ. But even *if I should judge*, like 'even if I should bear witness' (*v.* 14). 'I judge no man; not because I have no authority, but because judging is not what I came to do. Even if I do in exceptional cases judge, My judgment is a genuine and authoritative one (see on i. 9), not the mock sentence of an impostor. It is the sentence not of a mere man, nor even of one with a divine commission yet acting independently; but of One sent by God acting in union with His Sender.' Comp. v. 30. For *καὶ...δέ* comp. *v.* 17, vi. 51, xv. 27; 1 John i. 3; Matt. xvi. 18; Acts xxii. 29; Heb. ix. 21; 2 Pet. i. 5. It is important to note which of the two conjunctions connects the clauses and leads: here and xv. 27 it is *δέ*, but in vi. 51 *καί*. See on *v.* 31.

17. καὶ ἐν τ. ν. δέ. But in the law also, your law (about which you profess to be so jealous), *it is written*. Comp. 'Thou art called a Jew and restest on the Law' (Rom. ii. 17). The *Sinaiticus* here gives S. John's usual *γεγραμμένον ἐστίν* (see on ii. 17), instead of *γέγραπται*, which he uses nowhere else of O.T. quotations; comp. xx. 31.

δύο ἀνθρώπων. Not so much a quotation as a reference to Deut. xix. 15, xvii. 6. Note that the Law speaks of 'two or three *witnesses*:' here we have 'two *men*.' The change is not accidental, but introduces an argument *à fortiori*: if the testimony of two *men* is valid, how much more the testimony of two Divine Witnesses. Comp. 'If we receive the witness of men, the witness of God is greater; for this is the witness of God which He hath testified of His Son' (1 John v. 9).

18. ἐγώ εἰμι. There is I who bear witness of Myself (in My words and works), **and there beareth witness of Me the Father** (in Scripture and the voice from Heaven).

19. ποῦ ἐστίν. They do not ask 'who' but 'where;' they know well enough by this time the meaning of Christ's frequent reference to 'Him that sent Me:' v. 23, 24, 30, 37, 38, vi. 38, 39, 40, 44, vii. 16, 18, 28, 33. They ask, therefore, in mockery, what Philip (xiv. 8) asks with earnest longing, '*Shew us the Father:* we see one of Thy two witnesses; shew us the other. Any liar can appeal to God.'

οὔτε ἐμὲ οἴδ. Ye know neither Me...If ye knew Me, ye would know, as in *v.* 42: here and in v. 46 the A.V. translates imperfects as aorists. It is in the Son that the Father reveals Himself: xiv. 9, xvi. 3. By learning to know the Son the disciples came to know the Father: the Jews could not know the Father because they refused to know the Son.

20. ἐν τῷ γαζοφ. At *the treasury* is an admissible and in one respect safer translation. It is not certain that there was a separate building called the treasury, but comp. 1 Macc. xiv. 49; and if there was, it is not probable that Christ would be able to address the multitude there. But the thirteen brazen chests, into which people put their offerings for the temple and other charitable objects, stood in the Court of the Women (see on Mark xii. 41), and these chests seem to have been called 'the treasury.' The point appears to be that in so public and frequented a place as this did He say all this, and yet no man laid hands on Him (see on vii. 30). Moreover the Hall Gazith, where the Sanhedrin met, was close to the Court of the Women; so that He was teaching close to His enemies' head-quarters.

καὶ οὐδεὶς ἐπ. *And* (yet) *no one* **took** *Him;* see on vii. 30. Comp. vi. 70, ix. 30, xvi. 32.

21. εἶπεν οὖν πάλιν. *He said* **therefore** *again.* The 'therefore' does not compel us to place what follows on the same day with what precedes; 'therefore' merely signifies that, as no one laid hands on Him, He was able to address them again. 'Again' shews that there is some interval, but whether of minutes, hours, or days, we have no means of determining. The connexion is in thought rather than in time. There is no distinct mark of time between vii. 37 (the close of the Feast of Tabernacles) and x. 22 (the Feast of the Dedication), an interval of two months. See introductory note to chap. vi.

ὑπάγω. Comp. *v.* 14 and vii. 33. Possibly in all three places there is a side reference to the Jews who were now leaving Jerusalem in great numbers, the Feast of Tabernacles being over.

ζητήσετε. See on vii. 33, 34. Here Christ is more explicit: so far from finding Him and being delivered by Him, they will perish most miserably; *in your sin shall ye die.* The singular means '*state* of sin.' Note the order, and contrast *v.* 24.

22. μήτι ἀποκτενεῖ ἑαυτόν. They see that He speaks of a voluntary departure, and perhaps they suspect that He alludes to His death. So with sarcasm still more bitter than the sneer in vii. 35 they exclaim 'Surely He does not mean to commit suicide? We certainly shall not be able to follow Him if He takes refuge in that!'

23. ἐκ τῶν κάτω ἐστέ. At first sight it might seem as if this meant 'ye are from hell.' Christ uses strong language later on (*v.* 44), and this interpretation would make good sense with what precedes. 'Ye suggest that I am going to hell by self-destruction: it is ye who come from thence.' But what follows forbids this. The two halves of the verse are manifestly equivalent, and 'ye are from beneath' = 'ye are of this world.' They were *σὰρξ ἐκ τῆς σαρκός* (iii. 6) and judged *κατὰ τ. σάρκα* (*v.* 15): He was *ἐκ τοῦ οὐράνου* (iii. 31). The pronouns throughout are emphatically opposed. The whole verse is a good instance of 'the spirit of parallelism, the informing power of Hebrew poetry,' which runs more or less through the whole Gospel. Comp. xiii. 16, xiv. 27.

24. ἀποθανεῖσθε. This is the emphatic word here, not *ἐν τ. ἁμαρτ.*, as in *v.* 21 The plural expresses the separate sins of each. "No reckoning made, but sent to your account with all your imperfections on your head." But the sentence is not irreversible; it is pronounced conditionally, **unless ye believe.** Comp. i. 12, iii. 15—18, vi. 40.

ὅτι ἐγώ εἰμι. *That* **I am**, implying the self-existence of Divinity. Here and in *vv.* 24, 28, 58, xiii. 19, the context supplies no predicate; elsewhere (iv. 26, ix. 9, xviii. 5, 6, 8) it does. I AM is the great Name, which every Jew understood; Ex. iii. 14; Deut. xxxii. 39; Isa. xliii. 10.

25. σὺ τίς εἶ; It is incredible that the Jews can have failed to understand. Christ had just declared that He was from above, and not of this world. Even if the words 'I am' were ambiguous in themselves, in this context they are plain enough. As in *v.* 19, they pretend not to understand, and contemptuously ask, *Thou, who art Thou?* The pronoun is scornfully emphatic. Comp. Acts xix. 15. Possibly both in *v.* 19 and here they wish to draw from Him something more definite, more capable of being stated in a formal charge against Him. The tone of their question must be considered in determining the meaning of Christ's reply.

τὴν ἀρχὴν ὅ τι καὶ λαλῶ ὑμῖν. The meaning of this obscure passage (comp. *v.* 44) cannot be determined with certainty. There is doubt as to (1) whether it is a question or not; (2) whether we should read *ὅ τι* or *ὅτι*; (3) the meaning of every word except *ὑμῖν.* Under (3) the chief doubt is whether *τὴν ἀρχήν* is to be taken as an adverb ('altogether, absolutely,' or 'first of all,' or possibly 'from the first'), or as a substantive ('the Beginning'). The chief renderings of the whole sentence will be found in Godet, Meyer, or Westcott. Three may be noticed here. (i) *How is it that I even speak to you* **at all?** *Τὴν ἀρχήν* has the meaning of 'at all' in negative sentences, and the question or exclamation makes the sentence virtually negative. The Greek Fathers, whose authority in interpreting Greek dialogue is very great, seem almost to have taken this rendering for granted as the only one that occurred to them. It may remind us of Matt. xvii. 17, 'O faithless and perverse generation! How long shall I be with you? How long shall I suffer you?' Comp. *οὐκ ἀγαπᾷς ὅτι σοι καὶ λαλῶ;* Art thou not content that I condescend to speak to thee? Ach. Tat. vi. 20. (ii) *What I* **from the beginning** *am even speaking to you of*, or *even that which I have spoken to you* **all along**; i.e. My words from the first have been and are a revelation of My Person. This may be made interrogative by understanding 'Do ye ask?' before 'what.' Comp. *Quis igitur ille est? Quem dudum dixi a principio tibi.* Plaut. *Captiv.* III. iv. 91. (iii) **The Beginning** (Rev. xxi. 6), *that which I am even saying to you*, which seems to be the interpretation of the early Latin Fathers; *Initium quod et loquor vobis.* But this would require λέγω; λαλῶ means 'I speak,' never 'I say.' Moreover, the attraction of *τὴν ἀρχήν* from the nominative ('I am the Beginning') to the accusative is awkward. The later Latin rendering of S. Augustine and others, *Principium, quia et loquor vobis*, 'The Beginning, because I even (humble Myself to) speak with you,' ignores the Greek.

26. Here again we have a series of simple sentences, the precise meaning of which and their connexion with one another cannot be determined with certainty. See on vii. 33. The following seems to be the drift of the verse: 'I have very much to speak concerning you, very much to blame. But I keep to My immediate task of speaking to the world those truths which before the world was I heard from God that cannot lie, Who sent Me:' i.e. Christ will not desist from teaching Divine truth in order to blame the Jews. It is as the Truth and the Light that He appears in these discourses. If this seems unsatisfactory, we may adopt: 'I have very much to speak and to blame concerning you. It will offend you still more. But nevertheless it must be spoken; for He who cannot lie commissioned Me thus to speak,' i.e. it is both true in itself and is spoken with authority. Note the emphatic position of πόλλα.

κἀγὼ ἃ ἤκ. *And* **the things which I heard from Him, these I** on My part **speak unto the world**: literally, '*into* the world,' so as to be sounded through it. Christ speaks as 'not of the world' (*v.* 23).

27. οὐκ ἔγνωσαν. *They* **perceived** *not that He* **was speaking.** This statement of the Evangelist has seemed to some so unaccountable after *v.* 18, that they have attempted to make his words mean something else. But the meaning of the words is quite unambiguous, and is not incredible. Even Apostles were sometimes strangely wanting. We have seen that there is an interval, possibly of days, between *v.* 20 and *v.* 21. The audience may have changed very considerably: but if not, experience shews that the ignorance and stupidity of unbelief are sometimes almost unbounded. Still we may admit that the dulness exhibited here is extraordinary; and it is precisely because it is so extraordinary that S. John records it.

28. εἶπεν οὖν ὁ Ἰ. *Jesus* **therefore** *said;* because of their gross dulness.

ὑψώσητε. On the Cross: see on iii. 14 and xii. 32. The Crucifixion was the act of the Jews, as S. Peter tells them (Acts iii. 13—15).

τότε γνώσεσθε. *Then shall ye* **perceive**, as in *v.* 27; the same verb is purposely used in both places (comp. *v.* 43). Had they known the Messiah they would have known His Father also (xiv. 9). But when by crucifying Him they have brought about His glory, then and not till then will their eyes be opened. Then will facts force upon them what no words could teach them. Comp. xii. 32.

ὅτι ἐγώ εἰμι. *That* **I am** (see on *v.* 24), *and* (*that*) **of Myself** *I do nothing* (v. 19), *but* (**that**) *even as the Father* **taught** *Me, I speak these things.* The construction depends on γνώσεσθε probably as far as λαλῶ, and possibly as far as ἐστιν: but it would be quite in S. John's style to begin an independent sentence with each καί. These aorists, ἤκουσα (*vv.* 26, 40; iii. 32, xv. 15) and ἐδίδαξεν, refer back to the point before the Incarnation when the Son was commissioned and furnished for His work. Ταῦτα λαλῶ is not put for οὕτω λαλῶ (xii. 50). There is a reminiscence of this verse in the Ignatian Epistles (*Magn.* VII.); ὁ κύριος ἄνευ τοῦ πατρὸς οὐδὲν ἐποίησεν. See on *v.* 29, x. 9.

29. ἀφῆκεν. It will depend on the interpretation whether the aorist or perfect is to be used in English. If it refers to God sending the Messiah into the world, then, as in the cases of ἤκουσα and ἐδίδαξεν, we must keep the aorist; *He left.* But if it refers to Christ's experience in each particular case, the perfect may be substituted; *He hath left.* In some cases (comp. xiii. 13, 34, xv. 9, 12) it is the idiom in English to use the perfect where the aorist is used in Greek, and then to translate the Greek aorist by the English aorist would be misleading. See on xvi. 32 and comp. οὐκ ἀμάρτυρον αὐτὸν ἀφῆκεν (Acts xiv. 17).

ὅτι ἐγὼ κ.τ.λ. Because the things pleasing to Him I always do: πάντοτε is emphatic, and means 'on every occasion,' which is somewhat in favour of the second interpretation of οὐκ ἀφῆκέν με: 'He hath never left Me alone because in every case I do what pleaseth Him.' The emphasis on ἐγώ is perhaps in mournful contrast to the Jews. In any case it is a distinct claim to Divinity. What blasphemous effrontery would such a declaration be in the mouth of any but the Incarnate Deity! The theory that Jesus was the noblest and holiest of teachers, but nothing more, shatters against such words as these. What saint or prophet ever dared to say, 'The things which are pleasing to God I in every instance do'? Comp. *v.* 46, xiv. 30, xv. 10. And if it be said, that perhaps Jesus never uttered these words, then it may also be said that perhaps He never uttered any of the words attributed to Him. We have the same authority for what is accepted as His as for what is rejected as not His. History becomes impossible if we are to admit evidence that we like, and refuse evidence that we dislike. Comp. 1 John iii. 22, and Ign. *Magn.* VIII.; ὃς κατὰ πάντα εὐηρέστησεν τῷ πέμψαντι αὐτόν. See on iii. 8, iv. 10.

30. ἐπίστευσαν εἰς αὐτόν. Not merely αὐτῷ; see on i. 12. Nothing exasperated His enemies so much as His success; and therefore in leading us on to the final catastrophe, the Evangelist carefully notes the instances in which He won, though often only for a time, adherents and believers. See on vi. 15.

31. Besides the 'many' who had full faith in Him there were some of His opponents disposed to believe His statements. Their faith, poor as it proves, is better than that of the many in ii. 23; belief that results from teaching is higher than that which results from miracles. Jesus recognises both its worth and its weakness, and applies a test, which might have raised it higher, but under which it breaks down.

πεπιστ. αὐτῷ. The change from 'believed *on* Him' to the weaker **had believed Him** is significant, as if S. John would prepare us for their collapse of faith. The expression *οἱ πεπ. αὐτῷ Ἰουδαῖοι* is remarkable; in this Gospel it almost amounts to a contradiction in terms.

ἐὰν ὑμεῖς μ. *If ye* **abide** (i. 33) *in My word, ye* **are truly** (i. 48) **My disciples.** Emphasis on 'ye' and 'My;' 'you on your part'—'the word that is Mine.' 'If ye abide in My word, so that it becomes the permanent condition of your life, then truly are ye My disciples, and not merely in appearance under a passing impulse.' Comp. v. 38, vi. 56, xv. 4—10. The form of expression, **ὁ λόγος ὁ ἐμός**, *the word that is Mine* (*vv.* 43, 51), is very frequent in this Gospel: comp. *ἡ χαρὰ ἡ ἐμή* (iii. 29, xv. 11, xvii. 13), *ἡ κρίσις ἡ ἐμή* (v. 30, viii. 16), *τὸ θέλημα τὸ ἐμόν* (v. 30, vi. 38), *ὁ καιρὸς ὁ ἐμός* (vii. 6, 8), *ἡ εἰρήνη ἡ ἐμή* (xiv. 27), *αἱ ἐντολαὶ αἱ ἐμαί* (xiv. 15), *ὁ διάκονος ὁ ἐμός* (xii. 26), *ἡ ἀγάπη ἡ ἐμή* (xv. 9), *ἡ δόξα ἡ ἐμή* (xvii. 24), *ἡ βασιλεία ἡ ἐμή* (xviii. 36).

32. **γνώσεσθε.** *Ye shall come to know* (vi. 69, vii. 17, 26).

τὴν ἀλήθειαν. Divine doctrine (i. 17, xvii. 17) and Christ Himself (xiv. 6, v. 33), 'whose service is perfect freedom.' See xviii. 37.

ἐλευθερώσει. Free from the moral slavery of sin. The power of sin is based on a delusion, a fascination, the real nature of which the truth exposes, and so breaks the spell. Truth and freedom are inseparable. Truth destroys the bondage to appearances, whether attractive or repulsive; the seductions of sin and the servile fears of an ignorant conscience. Socrates taught that vice is ignorance, and the Stoics that the wise man alone is free. Plato *Rep.* IX. 589 E.

33. **ἀπεκρίθησαν πρὸς αὐ.** *They answered* **unto Him.** The subject is *οἱ πεπιστευκότες αὐτῷ Ἰ.* (*v.* 31): it is quite arbitrary to suppose any one else. The severe words which follow (*v.* 44) are addressed to them, for turning back, after their momentary belief, as well as to those who had never believed at all.

σπέρμα Ἀβρ. Comp. 'kings of peoples shall be of her' (Sarah), and 'thy seed shall possess the gate of his enemies' (Gen. xvii. 16, xxii. 17). On texts like these they build the proud belief that Jews **have never yet been** *in bondage to any man.* But passion once more blinds them to historical facts (see on vii. 52). The bondage in Egypt, the oppressions in the times of the Judges, the captivity in Babylon, and the Roman yoke, are all forgotten. "They have an immovable love of liberty, and maintain that God is their only ruler and master" (Josephus, *Ant.* XVIII. i. 6). Some, who think such forgetfulness incredible, interpret 'we have never been *lawfully* in bondage.' 'The Truth' would not free them from *enforced* slavery. It might free them from *voluntary* slavery, by teaching them that it was unlawful for them to be slaves. 'But we know that already.' This, however, is somewhat subtle, and the more literal interpretation is not incredible. The power which the human mind possesses of keeping inconvenient facts out of sight is very considerable. In either case we have another instance of gross inability to perceive the spiritual meaning of Christ's words. Comp. iii. 4, iv. 15, vi. 34.

34. Ἀμὴν ἀμήν. With great solemnity He points them to a bondage far worse than political servitude. See on i. 52.

πᾶς ὁ ποιῶν τ. ἁμ. Everyone who continueth to do sin is the bond-servant *of sin.* Christ does not say that a single act (ὁ ποιήσας) of sin enslaves; it is a life of sin that makes a man a slave and the child of the devil (1 John iii. 8). Ποιεῖν τὴν ἁμαρτ. is the opposite of ποιεῖν τὴν ἀλήθειαν (iii. 21) and of π. τὴν δικαιοσύνην (1 John ii. 29, iii. 7). 'Servant' is a good rendering of δοῦλος where nothing degrading is implied (Rom. i. 1; Phil. i. 1; Tit. i. 1, &c.), but is too weak, where, as here, the degradation is the main point. Moreover, the connexion with δεδουλεύκαμεν must be preserved; 'have been in bondage' or 'in slavery,' and 'bond-servants' or 'slaves,' must be our renderings.

Some have thought that we have here an echo of Rom. vi. 16, which S. John may have seen. But may not both passages be original? The idea that vice is slavery—*tot dominorum quot vitiorum*—is common in all literature: frequent in the classics. 2 Pet. ii. 19 is probably an echo of this passage or of Rom. vi. 16. Comp. Matt. vi. 24.

35. ὁ δὲ δοῦλος. The transition is somewhat abrupt, the mention of 'bond-servant' suggesting a fresh thought. **Now the bond-servant** (not the bond-servant *of sin*, but any slave) *abideth not in the house for ever:* **the son** (not the Son of God, but any son) *abideth* **for** *ever.* It is perhaps to avoid this abruptness that some important authorities omit τῆς ἁμαρτίας.

36. ἐὰν οὖν ὁ υἱός. As before, any son is meant. 'If the son emancipates you, your freedom is secured; for he is always on the spot to see that the emancipation is carried out.' The statement is general, but with special reference to the Son of God, who frees men by granting them a share in His Sonship. If they will abide in His word (*v.* 31), He will abide in them (vi. 56), and will take care that the bondage from which He has freed them is not thrust upon them again.

ὄντως. Here only in S. John: comp. Luke xxiii. 47, xxiv. 34; 1 Tim. v. 3, 5, 16. It expresses reality as opposed to appearance; ἀληθῶς (*v.* 31, iv. 42, vi. 14, vii. 40) implies that this reality is known.

37. Having answered the conclusion οὐδενὶ δεδουλεύκαμεν πώποτε (*v.* 33), Jesus proceeds to deal with the premise from which it was drawn. He admits their claim in their own narrow sense. They are the natural descendants of Abraham: his children in any higher sense they are not (*v.* 39). Comp. 'neither, because they are the seed of Abraham, are they all children' (Rom. ix. 8).

οὐ χωρεῖ ἐν ὑμῖν. Maketh no advance in you. His word had found place in them for a very short time; but it made no progress in their hearts: it did not abide in them and they did not abide in it (*v*. 31). They had stifled it and cast it out. See on *v*. 31.

38. The text is somewhat uncertain. **The things which** *I* (in My own Person) *have seen* (see on i. 18) *with the Father I speak: ye* **also, therefore, do the things which ye heard from** *your father*. We are uncertain whether *ποιεῖτε* is indicative or imperative: if indicative, *παρὰ τ. π.* means 'from *your* father,' the devil, as in *v*. 41; if imperative, it means 'from *the* Father,' as in the first half of the verse. In the former case *οὖν* (rare in discourses) is severely ironical; 'I speak those truths of which I have direct knowledge from all eternity with the Father: you, therefore, following My relation to My Father, are doing those sins which your father suggested to you.' In the latter case the *οὖν* is simple; 'I in My words follow the Father, of whom I have direct knowledge: you also, therefore, in your acts must follow the Father, of whom you have had indirect knowledge.' This appeal to Christ's having seen God is peculiar to S. John; it is made sometimes by Christ Himself (iii. 11, vi. 46), sometimes by the Evangelist or the Baptist (i. 18, iii. 32). The connexion of *v*. 38 with *v*. 37 is not quite obvious: perhaps it is—'My words make no progress in you, because they are so opposite in origin and nature to your deeds.'

39. Ἀβρ. ἐστε. They see that He means some other father than Abraham; but they hold fast to their descent.

εἰ ..ἐστε. *If ye* **are** *children of Abraham: ἐστέ* has been altered to *ἦτε* in some MSS. to bring the protasis into harmony with the supposed apodosis *ἐποιεῖτε* or *ἐποιεῖτε ἄν*. But the true reading is probably *ποιεῖτε*, either imperative or indicative: 'If ye are children of Abraham, **do** the works of Abraham,' or '**ye do** the works of Abraham;' and these they manifestly did not do, and therefore could not be his children. Authorities are much divided between *ἐστέ* and *ἦτε*, *ποιεῖτε* and *ἐποιεῖτε* or *ἐποιεῖτε ἄν*.

40. 'But, as it is, ye seek to commit murder of the most heinous kind. Ye would kill One who is your fellow-man, and that for telling you the truth, truth which He heard from God.' The insertion of *ἄνθρωπον*, which the Lord nowhere else uses of Himself, involves His claim to their sympathy, and perhaps anticipates *v*. 44, where they are called the children of the great *ἀνθρωποκτόνος*, lusting like him for blood.

τοῦτο Ἀβ. οὐκ ἐποί. Litotes, or understatement: comp. iii. 19, vi. 37. Abraham's life was utterly unlike theirs. What had 'the Friend of God' (Jas. ii. 23) in common with the foes of God's Son?

41. ὑμεῖς π. τ. ἐρ. *Ye* **are doing** *the* **works** *of your father: ὑμεῖς* in emphatic contrast to *Ἀβραάμ*. This shews them that He means spiritual not literal descent; so they accept His figurative language, but indignantly deny any evil parentage. 'Thou art speaking of spiritual parentage. Well, our spiritual Father is God.'

ἡμεῖς ἐκ πορνείας. The meaning of this is very much disputed. The following are the chief explanations: (1) Thou hast denied that we are the children of Abraham, then we must be the children of some one sinning with Sarah: which is false.' But this would be adultery, not fornication. (2) 'We are the children of Sarah, not of Hagar.' But this was lawful concubinage, not fornication. (3) 'We are not a mongrel race, like the Samaritans; we are pure Jews.' This is far-fetched, and does not suit the context. (4) 'We **were** not born of fornication, *as Thou art*.' But His miraculous birth was not yet commonly known, and this foul Jewish lie, perpetuated from the second century onwards (Origen, *c. Celsum* I. xxxii.), was not yet in existence. (5) 'We **were** not born of spiritual fornication; our sonship has not been polluted with idolatry. If thou art speaking of spiritual parentage, we have one Father, even God.' This last seems the best. Idolatry is so constantly spoken of as whoredom and fornication throughout the whole of the O. T., that in a discussion about spiritual fatherhood this image would be perfectly natural in the mouth of a Jew. Exod. xxxiv. 15, 16; Lev. xvii. 7; Judg. ii. 17; 2 Kgs. ix. 22; Ps. lxxiii. 27; Isa. i. 21; Jer. iii. 1, 9, 20; Ezek. xvi. 15; &c. &c. See esp. Hos. ii. 4. There is a proud emphasis on 'we;'—'*we* are not idolaters, like Thy friends the Gentiles' (comp. vii. 35). Ἕνα also is emphatic: **One Father we have**, in contrast to the many gods of the heathen and of the first Samaritans (2 K. xvii. 33): comp. *v.* 48.

42. Moral proof that God is *not* their Father; if He were, they would love His Son. Comp. xv. 23 and 'Every one that loveth Him that begat loveth Him also that is begotten of Him' (1 John v. 1). Here, as in *v.* 19, v. 46, ix. 41, xv. 19, xiii. 36, we have imperfects, not aorists: contrast iv. 10, xi. 21, 32, xiv. 28.

ἐκ. τ. θ. ἐξῆλθον κ. ἥκω. **I came out** *from God and* **am here** from God among you. See on xvi. 28, the only other place where ἐκ τ. Θ. ἐξῆλθον occurs: it includes the Divine Generation of the Son. In the highest and fullest sense He is 'of God:' if they were God's children they would recognise and love Him.

οὐδὲ γάρ. Proof of His Divine origin: **for not even of Myself have I come.** 'So far from having come from any other than God, I have not even come of My own self-determination.'

43. τ. λαλιὰν τ. ἐμ...τ. λόγον τ. ἐμ. See on *v.* 31. Λαλιά is the *outward expression*, the language used: ἡ λαλιά σου δῆλόν σε ποιεῖ (Matt. xxvi. 73), ἡ λαλιά σου ὁμοιάζει (Mark xiv. 70). Elsewhere **λαλιά** occurs only iv. 42 and here. Λόγος is the *meaning* of the expression, the thoughts conveyed in the language. They perpetually misunderstand His language because they cannot appreciate His meaning. They are ἐκ τῶν κάτω (*v.* 23), and He is speaking of τὰ ἄνω (Col. iii. 1); they are ἐκ τ. κόσμου τούτου (*v.* 23), and He is telling of τὰ ἐπουράνια (iii. 12); they are ψυχικοί, and He is teaching πνευματικά (1 Cor. ii. 13; see notes there). They '*cannot* hear:' it is a moral impossibility (see on vi. 44): they have their whole character to change before they can understand spiritual truths. Ἀκούειν, as in *v.* 47, means 'listen to, obey:' comp. Ps. lxxxi. 11.

44. ὑμεῖς ἐκ τ. π. τ. δ. ἐστέ. At last Christ says plainly, what He has implied in *vv.* 38 and 41. 'Ye' is emphatic; 'ye, who boast that ye have Abraham and God as your Father, ye are morally the devil's children.' 1 John iii. 8, 10 is perhaps an echo of Christ's words.

This passage seems to be conclusive as to the real personal existence of the devil. It can scarcely be an economy, a concession to ordinary modes of thought and language. Would Christ have resorted to a popular delusion in a denunciation of such solemn and awful severity? Comp. 'the children of the wicked one' (Matt. xiii. 38); 'ye make him twofold more the child of hell than yourselves' (Matt. xxiii. 15). With this denunciation generally comp. Matt. xi. 20—24, xxiii. 13—36.

A monstrous but grammatically possible translation of these words is adopted by some who attribute a Gnostic origin to this Gospel;—'ye are descended from the father of the devil.' This Gnostic demonology, according to which the father of the devil is the God of the Jews, is utterly unscriptural, and does not suit the context here.

θέλετε ποιεῖν. **Ye will to do**: see on vi. 67, vii. 17; comp. *v.* 40. 'Ye love to gratify the lusts which characterize him, especially the lust for blood; this shews your moral relationship to him.' The *θέλετε* brings out their full consent and sympathy.

ἀνθρωποκτόνος. See on *v.* 40. The devil was a murderer by causing the Fall, and thus bringing death into the world. In the Gospel of Nicodemus, he is called *ἡ τοῦ θανάτου ἀρχή.* Comp. 'God created man to be immortal, and made him to be an image of His own eternity. Nevertheless, *through envy of the devil came death into the world*, and they that do hold of his side shall find it' (Wisd. ii. 23, 24): and 'Cain was of that wicked one and slew his brother:' and 'whosoever hateth his brother is a murderer' (1 John iii. 12, 15).

οὐχ ἕστηκεν. **Standeth** *not in the truth* (iii. 29, vi. 22, &c.). The true reading however is probably *ἔστηκεν*, imperf. of *στήκειν* (i. 26; Rom. xiv. 4), a stronger form; **stood firm.** The truth is a region from which the devil has long since departed, *because truth* (no article) *is not in him.* In S. John the most complete union is expressed by mutual indwelling, 'I in you, and you in Me:' this is the converse of it. The devil is not in the truth because truth is not in him: there is absolute separation. The truth cannot be possessed by one who is internally alien to it.

τὸ ψεῦδος. Falsehood as a whole as opposed to *ἡ ἀλήθεια* as a whole: in English we speak of 'the truth,' but not of 'the falsehood.' But the article may mean 'the lie that is natural to him:' **whenever** *he speaketh* **his** *lie.*

ἐκ τῶν ἰδίων. Out of his own resources, or nature: the outcome is what may be expected from him: comp. 2 Cor. iii. 5.

ὅτι ψ. ἐ. κ. ὁ π. αὐ. **Because** *he is a liar and the father* **thereof,** either of the liar, or of the lie. Thus he lied to Eve, "Ye shall not surely die" (Gen. iii. 4). The article before *πατήρ* does not at all prevent *πατήρ* being included in the predicate. It is, however, possible to take this obscure sentence (comp. *v.* 26) very differently, and to make *ὁ πατήρ* the subject of the last clause; **Whenever a man** *speaketh* **his** *lie, he speaketh of his own, for* **his father also is a liar:** i.e. a man by lying proclaims himself to be a child of the devil acting in harmony with his parentage. But the change of subject from 'the devil' to 'a man' understood is very awkward. And here again a monstrous misinterpretation is grammatically possible;—'for the devil is a liar, and his father also.' It is not strange that Gnostics of the second and third centuries should have tried to wring a sanction for their fantastic systems out of the writings of S. John. It *is* strange that any modern critics should have thought demonology so extravagant compatible with the theology of the Fourth Gospel.

45. ἐγὼ δὲ ὅτι. But *as for Me, because I* **say** *the truth, ye believe Me not:* ἐγώ is in emphatic contrast to the ψεύστης. Just as the devil 'stood not in the truth' because of his natural alienation from it, so they do not accept the truth when Jesus offers it to them. They will listen to the devil (*v.* 38); they will believe a lie: but the Messiah speaking the truth they will not believe. The tragic tone once more, but more definitely expressed: comp. i. 5, 10, 11, ii. 24; iii. 10, 19.

46. τίς ἐξ ὑ. ἐλέγχει. *Which of you* **convicteth** *Me of sin?* See on iii. 20, xvi. 8. For περὶ comp. x. 33; 1 John ii. 2. Many rebuked Christ and laid sin to His charge: none brought sin home to His conscience. There is the majesty of Divinity in the challenge. What mortal man would dare to make it? See on *v.* 29, and comp. xiv. 30, xv. 10; 1 John iii. 5; 1 Pet. i. 19, ii. 22. Note the implied connexion between sin generally and falsehood, as between righteousness and truth, vii. 18. Perhaps we are to understand a pause in which He waits for their answer to His challenge. But they are as unable to charge Him with sin as to acquit themselves (*v.* 7) of it: and he makes the admission implied by their silence the basis for a fresh question. 'If I am free from sin (and none of you can convict Me of it), I am free from falsehood. Therefore, **if I say truth** *why do ye on your part not believe Me?*'

47. There is a pause, and then Christ answers His own question and gives a final disproof of their claim to be God's children (*v.* 41).

ὁ ὢν ἐκ τ. θ. The true child of God, deriving his whole being from Him: comp. *v.* 23, iii. 31, xv. 19, xvii. 14, 16, xviii. 36, 37.

τὰ ῥήματα τ. θ. See on iii. 34. Christ here assumes, what He elsewhere states, that He speaks the words of God (*v.* 26, vii. 16, xvii. 8).

διὰ τοῦτο. For this cause: see on vii. 21, 22. S. John uses the same test; 'We are of God: he that knoweth God heareth us; he that is not of God heareth not us. Hereby know we the spirit of truth and the spirit of error' (1 John iv. 6).

48. οἱ Ἰουδαῖοι. Not those who for the moment believed on Him (*v.* 31), but the hostile party as a whole. This denial of their national prerogative of being sons of God seems to them malicious frenzy. He must be an enemy of the Chosen People and be possessed. Καλῶς = 'rightly;' comp. iv. 17, xiii. 13, xviii. 23: ἡμεῖς is emphatic;

'we at any rate are right.' For the position of *ἡμεῖς* comp. 1 John i. 4.

Σαμαρ. εἶ σύ. *Σύ* last, with contemptuous emphasis. The passage implies that this was a common reproach, but it is stated nowhere else. Yet it was most natural that one whose teaching so often contradicted Jewish traditions and Jewish exclusiveness should be called a Samaritan. It is therefore a striking touch of reality, and another instance of the Evangelist's complete familiarity with the ideas and expressions current in Palestine at this time. Possibly this term of reproach contains a sneer at His visit to Samaria in chap. iv., and at His having chosen the unusual route through Samaria, as He probably did (see on vii. 10), in coming up to the Feast of Tabernacles. The parable of the Good Samaritan was probably not yet spoken. The two reproaches possibly refer to what He had said against them. He had said that they were no true children of Abraham; they say that He is a Samaritan. He had said that they were not of God: they say that He has a demon.

δαιμόνιον. It is unfortunate that we have not two words in our Bible to distinguish *ὁ διάβολος*, '*the* Devil' (*v.* 44, xiii. 2; Matt. iv. 1; Luke viii. 12, &c.), from *δαιμόνιον* (vii. 20, x. 20, Matt. vii. 22, &c.) and *δαίμων* (Matt. viii. 31; Mark v. 12; Luke viii. 29; Rev. xviii. 2), '*a* devil,' or 'unclean spirit.' 'Fiend,' which Wiclif *sometimes* employs (Matt. xii. 24, 28; Mark i. 34, 39, &c.), might have been used, had Tyndale and Cranmer adopted it: **demon** would have been better still. But here Tyndale, Cranmer, and the Geneva Version make the confusion complete by rendering 'and hast *the* devil,' a mistake which they make also in vii. 20 and x. 20. The charge here is more bitter than either vii. 20 or x. 20, where it simply means that His conduct is so extraordinary that He must be demented. We have instances more similar to this in the Synoptists; Matt. ix. 34, xii. 24; Mark iii. 22; Luke xi. 15.

49. ἐγὼ δ. οὐκ ἔχω. He does not notice the charge of being a Samaritan. For Him it contained nothing offensive, for He knew that Samaritans might equal or excel Jews (iv. 39—42; Luke x. 33, xvii. 16) in faith, benevolence, and gratitude. There is an emphasis on 'I,' but the meaning of the emphasis is not '*I* have not a demon, *but ye have;*' which would require *οὐκ ἐγώ* for *ἐγὼ οὐκ*. Rather it means '*I* have not a demon, but honour My Father; while *you* on the contrary dishonour My Father through Me.'

50. ἐγὼ δὲ οὐ ζ. But it is not I who seek. 'It is not because I seek glory for Myself that I speak of your dishonouring Me: the Father seeks that for Me and pronounces judgment on you.' Comp. *v.* 54 and v. 41. There is no contradiction between this and v. 22. In both cases God's law operates of itself: the wicked sentence themselves, rather than are sentenced by Him or by the Son.

51. ἐμὸν λόγον τηρήσῃ. *Keep My* **word**. The connexion with *vv.* 31, 43 and v. 24 must be preserved by retaining the same translation for *λόγος*: 'keeping My word' here corresponds to 'abiding in

My word' in *v.* 31. Τὸν λόγον τηρεῖν is a phrase of frequent occurrence in S. John; *vv.* 52, 55, xiv. 23, xv. 20, xvii. 6; Rev. iii. 8, 10: τοὺς λόγους τηρεῖν, xiv. 24; Rev. xxii. 7, 9: so also the analogous phrase τὰς ἐντολὰς τηρεῖν; xiv. 15, 21, xv. 10; 1 John ii. 3, 4, 5, iii. 22, 24, v. 2, 3; Rev. xii. 17, xiv. 12. Of the three phrases the first is the most comprehensive; τὸν λόγον τ. is to observe the Divine revelation as a whole; τοὺς λ. or τὰς ἐντ. τ. is to observe certain definite injunctions. Τηρεῖν is not merely keeping in mind, but being on the watch to obey and fulfil. Comp. φυλάσσειν (τὸν νόμον, τὰ δόγματα, τὴν παραθήκην), which is being on the watch to guard and protect. By 'keeping His word' they may escape the judgment just mentioned. There is no need to suppose, therefore, that *vv.* 49, 50 are addressed to His opponents, and *v.* 51 to a more friendly group; a change of which there is no hint.

θ. οὐ μὴ θ. εἰς τ. αἰῶνα. *Shall certainly not behold death for ever:* i.e. *shall never behold* or experience *death.* Εἰς τ. αἰῶνα belongs like οὐ μή to θεωρήσῃ, not to θάνατον: it does not mean 'he shall see death,' but 'death shall not be eternal.' This is evident from iv. 14, which cannot mean 'shall thirst,' but 'the thirst shall not be eternal,' and from xiii. 8, which cannot mean 'shalt wash my feet,' but 'the washing shall not be eternal.' In all three cases the meaning is 'shall certainly never.' Comp. x. 28, xi. 26; 1 Cor. viii. 13.

θεωρήσῃ. Θεωρεῖν θάνατον occurs here only in N.T. It is stronger than ἰδεῖν θαν. (Luke ii. 26; Heb. xi. 5) and ἰδεῖν διαφθοράν (Acts ii. 27, 31, xiii. 35), expressing fixed contemplation and full acquaintance. Just as 'keep My word' here corresponds to 'abide in My word' in *v.* 31, so 'exemption from death' here corresponds to 'freedom' there: εἰς τ. αἰῶνα occurs in both passages. The firm believer *has* (not *shall* have) eternal life and real freedom, and shall never lose either. Of this Christ solemnly (ἀμὴν ἀμήν *vv.* 34, 51) assures them.

52. νῦν ἐγνώκαμεν. 'It was somewhat of a conjecture before (*v.* 48), but *now we have* **come to know** *it:*' comp. *v.* 55, v. 42, vi. 69. First they thought it; then they said it; then they knew it.

ἀπέθανεν. **Died.** As in vi. 49, the point is that he perished then, not that he is dead now: keeping God's word did not save him.

γεύσηται. They misunderstand and therefore exaggerate His language, all the more naturally as 'taste of death' was a more familiar metaphor than 'contemplate death.' The believer *does taste* of death, though he does not have a complete experience of it; to him it is but a passing phase. The metaphor 'taste of death' is not taken from a death-cup, but from the general idea of bitterness; Matt. xvi. 28; Heb. ii. 9; comp. xviii. 11; Rev. xiv. 10.

53. μὴ σὺ μείζων. Exactly parallel to iv. 12. 'Surely *Thou*, the mad Galilean, art not greater than our father Abraham, **seeing that he died**? and the prophets **died**.' The anacoluthon, like their exaggeration, is very natural. The sentence should run καὶ τ. προφήτων οἵτινες ἀπέθανον. For **ὅστις** comp. 1 John i. 2; Heb. x. 35. For

σεαυτὸν ποιεῖν comp. v. 18, x. 33, xix. 7, 12; 1 John i. 10: it is a Johannean phrase, meaning to declare oneself to be such by word and deed.

54—56. Christ first answers the insinuation that He is vainglorious, implied in the question 'whom makest Thou Thyself? Then He shews that He really is greater than Abraham.

54. ἐὰν ἐγὼ δοξ. *If I* **shall have glorified** *Myself, My* **glory** *is nothing.* **There** *is* (*v.* 50) *My Father who* **glorifieth** *Me*—in miracles and the Messianic work generally. In translation distinguish between *τιμᾷν* (*v.* 49) and *δοξάζειν*. See on vi. 71.

55. ἐγνώκατε...οἶδα. And *ye have not* **learned to know** *Him* (*v.* 52); *but I know Him.* Οἶδα refers to His immediate essential knowledge of the Father, *ἐγνώκατε* to the progressive knowledge of mankind by means of revelation. Here and elsewhere (vii. 15, 17, 26, 27, xiii. 7, xxi. 17) A.V. obliterates the distinction between the two verbs. Comp. xiv. 7. **ἔσομαι...ψεύστης.** Preserve the order; *I shall be* **like unto you, a liar**: referring back to *v.* 44. Winer, p. 243.

τ. λ. αὐ. τηρῶ. Christ's whole life is a continual practice of obedience (Heb. v. 8; Rom. v. 19; Phil. ii. 8): His relation to the Father is analogous to that of the believer to Christ (xv. 10, xvii. 11, 18).

56. ὁ πατὴρ ὑμῶν. Whom you so confidently claim (*vv.* 39, 53): *he* rejoiced in expecting One whom *ye* scornfully reject.

ἠγαλλιάσατο ἵνα ἴδῃ. Exulted that he might *see My day;* the object of his joy being represented as the goal to which his heart is directed. This is a remarkable instance of S. John's preference for the construction expressing a purpose, where other constructions would seem more natural. Comp. iv. 34, 47, vi. 29, 50, ix. 2, 3, 22, xi. 50, xvi. 7. Abraham exulted in anticipation of the coming of the Messiah through implicit belief in the Divine promises. Winer, p. 426. 'My day' is most naturally interpreted of the Birth of Christ: comp. Luke xvii. 22. The aorists *εἶδεν* and *ἐχάρη* point to a definite event.

καὶ εἶδεν κ. ἐχάρη. A very important passage with regard to the intermediate state, shewing that the soul does not, as some maintain, remain unconscious between death and the Day of Judgment. The Old Testament saints in Paradise were allowed to know that the Messiah had come. *How* this was revealed to them we are not told; but here is a statement of the fact. 'Εχάρη expresses a calmer, less emotional joy than *ἠγαλλιάσατο* and therefore both are appropriate: 'exulted' while still on earth; 'was glad' in Hades: 'exulted' in tumultuous anticipation; 'was glad' in calm beholding. Thus the 'Communion of Saints' is assured, not merely in parables (Luke xvi. 27, 28), but in the plain words of Scripture. Heb. xii. 1.

57. πεντήκοντα ἔτη. The reading *τεσσαράκοντα* which Chrysostom and a few authorities give, is no doubt incorrect. It has arisen from a wish to make the number less wide of the mark; for our Lord was probably not yet thirty-five, although Irenaeus preserves a tradition that He taught at a much later age. He says (II. xxii. 5), *a quadrigesimo autem et quinquagesimo anno declinat jam in aetatem seniorem, quam habens Dominus noster docebat, sicut evangelium et omnes seniores testantur qui in Asia apud Joannem discipulum Domini convenerunt.* By 'evangelium' he probably means this passage. But 'fifty years' is a round number, the Jewish traditional age of full manhood (Num. iv. 3, 39, viii. 24, 25). There is no reason to suppose that Jesus was nearly fifty, or looked nearly fifty. In comparing His age with the 2000 years since Abraham the Jews would not care to be precise so long as they were within the mark.

ἑώρακας. See on i. 18. They again misunderstand and misquote His words. Abraham's seeing Christ's day was not the same as Christ seeing Abraham.

58. **Ἀμὴν ἀμήν.** For the third time in this discourse (*vv.* 34, 51) Jesus uses this asseveration. Having answered the charge of self-glorification (*vv.* 54, 55), and shewn that Abraham was on His side not theirs (*v.* 57), He now solemnly declares His superiority to him.

πρὶν Ἀβρ. γ. ἐγώ εἰμι. Here A.V. has lamentably gone back from earlier translations. Cranmer has, 'Ere Abraham *was born*, I am,' perhaps following Erasmus' *Antequam nasceretur A., Ego sum;* and the Rhemish has, 'Before that Abraham *was made*, I am,' following the Vulgate, *Antequam Abraham fieret, Ego sum.* See notes on ἦν in i. 1, 6. 'I am,' denotes absolute existence, and in this passage clearly involves the pre-existence and Divinity of Christ, as the Jews see. Comp. *vv.* 24, 28; Rev. i. 4, 8; and see on *v.* 24. 'I was' would have been less comprehensive, and *need* not have meant more than that Christ was prior to Abraham. In O.T. we have the same thought, *πρὸ τοῦ ὄρη γενηθῆναι...σὺ εἶ*, Ps. xc. 2; cii. 27.

59. **ἦραν οὖν.** *They took up* **therefore**; i.e. in consequence of His last words. They clearly understand Him to have taken to Himself the Divine Name, and they prepare to stone Him for blasphemy. Building materials for completing and repairing the Temple would supply them with missiles (comp. x. 31—33): Josephus mentions a stoning in the Temple (*Ant.* XVII. ix. 3). They would not have stoned Him for merely claiming to be the Messiah (x. 24).

ἐκρύβη κ. ἐξῆλθεν. Probably we are not to understand a miraculous withdrawal as in Luke iv. 30, where the 'passing through the midst of them' seems to be miraculous. Comp. *ἄφαντος ἐγένετο*, Luke xxiv. 31. Here we need not suppose more than that He drew back into the crowd away from those who had taken up stones. The Providence which ordered that as yet the fears of the hierarchy should prevail over their hostility (vii. 30, viii. 20), ruled that the less hostile in this multitude should screen Him from the fury of the more fanatical. It is quite arbitrary to invert the clauses and render, 'Jesus went out of the Temple and hid Himself.'

As a comment on the whole discourse see 1 Pet. ii. 22, 23, remembering that S. Peter was very possibly present on the occasion.

"The whole of the Jews' reasoning is strictly what we should expect from them. These constant appeals to their descent from Abraham, these repeated imputations of diabolic possession, this narrow intelligence bounded by the letter, this jealousy of anything that seemed in the slightest degree to trench on their own rigid monotheism—all these, down to the touch in *v.* 57, in which the age they fix upon in round numbers is that assigned to completed manhood, give local truth and accuracy to the picture; which in any case, we may say confidently, must have been drawn by a Palestinian Jew, and in all probability by a Jew who had been himself an early disciple of Christ" (Sanday).

CHAPTER IX

4. **ἡμᾶς** for *ἐμέ* (a correction to harmonize with *με*) with ℵ[1]BL against ℵ[3]AC.

6. **ἐπέχρισεν αὐτοῦ** for *ἐπέχρισε*. Omit *τοῦ τυφλοῦ* (explanatory gloss) after **ὀφθαλμούς** with ℵBL against AC.

8. **προσαίτης** (all the best MSS. and versions) for *τυφλός*.

10. **ἠνεῴχθησαν** (ℵBCD) for *ἀνεωχθησαν* (AKUS). For this triple augment comp. Matt. ix. 30, Acts xvi. 26, Rev. xix. 11.

11. After **ἐκεῖνος** omit *καὶ εἶπεν* with ℵBCDL against A. **ὁ ἄνθρωπος ὁ λεγόμενος** (ℵBL) for *ἄνθρ. λεγ.* (AD). **τὸν** (ℵBDLX) for *τὴν κολυμβήθραν τοῦ* (A).

14. **ἐν ᾗ ἡμέρᾳ** for *ὅτε* (simplification) with ℵBLX against AD.

36. Insert **καὶ** before *τίς.* Confusion with *κύριε* may have caused the omission. KAI and $\overline{\text{KE}}$ (=KΥPIE) are easily confounded, and *κε τις εστιν κε* would seem to have a superfluous *κύριε*.

Christ the Source of Truth and Light illustrated by a Sign

Light is given to the eyes of the man born blind and the Truth is revealed to His soul. The Jews who cast Him out for accepting the Truth rejected by themselves are left in their blindness, the faith of those who began to believe on Him (viii. 30) having failed under the test applied by Jesus (viii. 31—59).

1—5. The Prelude to the Sign

1. **καὶ παράγων.** Possibly on His way from the Temple (viii. 59), or (if *ἐγένετο τότε* be the right reading in x. 22) more probably on a later occasion near the F. of the Dedication. Comp. *καὶ παράγων εἶδε Λευὶν* (Mark ii. 14). We know that this man was a beggar (*v.* 8), and that beggars frequented the gates of the Temple (Acts iii. 2), as they frequent the doors of foreign churches now; but we are not told where this man was begging.

ἐκ γενετῆς. The phrase occurs nowhere else in N.T. Justin Martyr uses it twice of those healed by Christ; *Trypho* LXIX.; *Apol.* I. xxii. No source is so probable as this verse, for nowhere else is Christ said to have healed a congenital disease. See on i. 23 and iii. 3. There is an indubitable reference to this passage in the *Clementine Homilies* (XIX. xxii.), the date of which is c. A.D. 150. See on x. 9, 27. For other instances of Christ giving sight to the blind see Matt. ix. 27, xx. 29; Mark viii. 22.

2. Rabbi. See on i. 39, iv. 31.

ἵνα τ. γεννηθῇ. *That he* **should be** *born blind*, in accordance with the Divine decree; comp. iv. 34, vi. 29, 40, and see on viii. 56. They probably knew the fact from the man himself, who would often state it to the passers-by. This question has given rise to much discussion. It implies a belief that some one *must* have sinned, or there would have been no such suffering: who then was it that sinned? Possibly the question means no more than this; the persons most closely connected with the suffering being specially mentioned, without much thought as to possibilities or probabilities. But this is not quite satisfactory. The disciples name two very definite alternatives; we must not assume that one of them was meaningless. That the sins of the fathers are visited on the children is the teaching of the Second Commandment and of every one's experience. But how could a man be born blind for his own sin?

Four answers have been suggested. (1) The predestinarian notion that the man was punished for sins which God knew he would commit in his life. This is utterly unscriptural and scarcely fits the context.

(2) The doctrine of the transmigration of souls, which was held by some Jews: he might have sinned in another body. But it is doubtful whether this philosophic tenet would be familiar to the disciples.

(3) The doctrine of the pre-existence of the soul, which appears Wisdom viii. 20: the man's soul sinned before it was united to the body. This again can hardly have been familiar to illiterate men.

(4) The current Jewish interpretation of Gen. xxv. 22, Ps. li. 5, and similar passages; that it was possible for a babe yet unborn to have emotions (comp. Luke i. 41—44) and that these might be and often were sinful. On the whole, this seems to be the simplest and most natural interpretation, and *v.* 34 seems to confirm it.

3. Christ shews that there is a third alternative, which their question assumes that there is not. Moreover He by implication warns them against assuming, like Job's friends, a connexion between suffering and sin in individuals (see on v. 14). *Neither* **did** *this man* **sin** (not 'hath sinned'), *nor his parents.* The answer, like the question, points to a definite act of sin causing this retribution.

ἀλλ' ἵνα. *But* he was born blind *in order that:* Jesus affirms the Divine purpose. This elliptical use of 'but (in order) that' is common in S. John, and illustrates his fondness for the construction expressing a purpose: see on i. 8. Winer, p. 398.

φανερωθῇ. First for emphasis: see on i. 31.

τὰ ἔργα τ. θ. Including not only the miracle but its effects.

4. ἡμᾶς δεῖ...με. The readings are doubtful as to whether *ἡμᾶς* or *ἐμέ*, *με* or *ἡμᾶς* is right in each place. The more difficult reading is the best supported: **We** *must work the works of Him that sent* **Me.** Some copyists changed *ἡμᾶς* to *ἐμέ* to agree with *με*; others changed *με* to *ἡμᾶς* to agree with *ἡμᾶς*. '*We* must work:' Christ identifies Himself with His disciples in the work of converting the world. 'Him that sent *Me*:' Christ does *not* identify His *mission* with that of the disciples. They were both sent, but not in the same sense: the Son is sent by the Father, the disciples by the Son. So also He says 'My Father' and 'your Father,' 'My God' and 'your God;' but not 'our Father,' or 'our God' (xx. 17). *Τὰ ἔργα* refers to *v.* 3.

ἕως ἡμέρα ἐστίν. **So long as** *it is day*, i.e. so long as we have life. Day and night here mean, as so often in literature of all kinds, life and death. Other explanations, e.g. opportune and inopportune moment, the presence of Christ in the world and His withdrawal from it,—are less simple and less suitable to the context. *If* all that is recorded from vii. 37 takes place on one day, these words would probably be spoken in the evening, when the failing light would add force to the warning, **night** *cometh* (no article), *when no* **one** *can work;* not even Christ Himself as man upon earth: comp. xi. 7—10; Ps. civ. 23.

5. ὅταν ἐν τ. κ. ὦ. **Whensoever** *I am in the world:* distinguish between *ἕως ἐστί* and *ὅταν ὦ*. *Ὅταν* is important; it shews the comprehensiveness of the statement. The Light shines at various times and in various degrees, whether the world chooses to be illuminated or not. Comp. i. 5, viii. 12. Here there is special reference to His giving light both to the man's eyes and to his soul. The Pharisees prove the truth of the saying that 'the darkness comprehended it not.'

φῶς εἰμὶ τ. κ. *I am* **light to** *the world;* not quite the same as *τὸ φ. τ. κ.* (viii. 2), **the Light of** *the world.* Note also the absence of *ἐγώ* in both clauses: it is not Christ's Person, but the effect of His presence that is prominent here.

6—12. THE SIGN

6. ἐπέχρισεν αὐτοῦ τ. π. Either **spread the clay thereof** (made with the spittle), or **spread His clay** (made by Him) **upon his eyes.** Jewish tradition expressly forbade putting spittle to the eyes on the Sabbath: of course it would forbid making clay on the Sabbath: comp. v. 10. Regard for Christ's truthfulness compels us to regard the clay as the *means* of healing; not that He could not heal without it, but that He willed this to be the channel of His power. Elsewhere He uses spittle; to heal a blind man (Mark viii. 23); to heal a deaf and dumb man (Mark vii. 33). Spittle was believed to be a remedy for diseased eyes (comp. Vespasian's reputed miracle, Tac. *Hist.* IV. 8, and other instances); clay also, though less commonly. So that Christ selects an ordinary remedy and gives it success in a case confessedly beyond its supposed powers (*v.* 32). This helps us to conclude *why* He willed to use means, instead of healing without even a word; viz. to help the faith of the sufferer. It is easier to believe, when means can be perceived; it is still easier, when the means seem to be appropriate.

Perhaps the whole act was symbolical. To the man's natural blindness Jesus added an artificial blindness, and pointed out a cure for the latter, which, being accepted by the man's faith, cured the former also. To the natural blindness of the Jews Jesus added an artificial blindness by teaching in parables (Mark iv. 11, 12). The interpretation of the teaching would have cured both forms of blindness. But the Jews rejected it.

7. νίψαι εἰς τ. κ. Either, *Wash* the clay off *into the pool*, or, *Go to the pool and wash.* Νίπτω, Attic νίζω, besides *vv.* 11, 15 and xiii. 5—14 occurs only Matt. vi. 17, xv. 2; Mark vii. 3; 1 Tim. v. 10, and is always used of washing *part* of the body. For bathing the whole either λούειν (xiii. 10; Acts ix. 37; Heb. x. 22; 2 Pet. ii. 22; Rev. i. 5) or βαπτίζειν is used; the latter in N.T. always of ceremonial immersion (i. 25—33, &c.). Πλύνειν (Rev. vii. 14, xxii. 14; Luke v. 2) is to wash inanimate objects, as clothes and nets. Comp. LXX. in Lev. xv. 11, *τὰς χεῖρας οὐ νένιπται ὕδατι, πλυνεῖ τὰ ἱμάτια, καὶ λούσεται τὸ σῶμα.* See on xiii. 10. The washing was probably part of the means of healing (comp. Naaman) and was a strong test of the man's faith.

Σιλωάμ. Satisfactorily identified with *Birket Silwân* in the lower Tyropoean valley, S.E. of the hill of Zion. This is probably the Siloah of Neh. iii. 15 and the Shiloah of Isa. viii. 6. 'The tower in Siloam' (Luke xiii. 4) was very possibly a building connected with the water; perhaps part of an aqueduct.

ὁ ἑρμ. ἀπεσταλμένος. *Which is* **interpreted**, *Sent.* The interpretation is admissible; but the original meaning is rather *Sending, Missio* or *Emissio aquarum*, 'outlet of waters.' Comp. 'the waters of Shiloah that go softly' (Isa. viii. 6). S. John sees in the word '*nomen et omen*' of the man's cure: and he also appears to see that this water from the rock is again (see on vii. 37) an image of Him who was sent (iii. 17, viii. 42, xviii. 3, &c.) by the Father, *τὸν ἀπόστολον* (Heb. iii. 1).

ἀπῆλθεν...ἦλθεν. *He* **went away** to Siloam *and came* home, as what follows seems to shew. Jesus had gone away (*v.* 12); the man did not return to Him. Has any poet attempted to describe this man's emotions on first seeing the world in which he had lived so long?

8. οἱ θεωροῦντες. *They* **who used to behold him aforetime,** *that* (iv. 19, xii. 19) *he was a* **beggar,** or **because** *he was a beggar*, and was therefore often to be seen in public places.

9. ἄλλοι ἐλ. οὐχί. A third group said, *No, but he is like him.* The opening of his eyes would greatly change him: this added to the improbability of a cure made them doubt his identity.

11. ἐκεῖνος. S. John's fondness for this pronoun has been remarked. Here and in *vv.* 25, 36 it marks the man's prominence in the scene. Comp. i. 8, ii. 21, xiii. 25, xviii. 17, 25, xx. 15, 16.

ὁ ἄνθρ. ὁ λεγ. The *man that is called;* implying that Jesus was well known. Was he thinking of the meaning of the name 'Jesus'?

πηλὸν ἐπ. He had not seen how: the rest he tells in order.

ἀνέβλεψα. This may mean either 'I looked up' (Mark vi. 41, vii. 34, xvi. 4, &c.); or 'I recovered sight' (Matt. xi. 5; Mark x. 51, 52, &c.). 'I looked up' does not suit *vv.* 15 and 18, where the word occurs again: and though 'I recovered sight' is not strictly accurate of a man *born* blind, yet it is admissible, as sight is natural to man.

Note the gradual development of faith in the man's soul, and compare it with that of the Samaritan woman (see on iv. 19) and of Martha (see on xi. 21). Here he merely knows Jesus' name and the miracle; in *v.* 17 he thinks Him 'a Prophet;' in *v.* 33 He is 'of God;' in *v.* 39 He is 'the Son of God.' What writer of fiction in the second century could have executed such a study in psychology?

12. **ἐκεῖνος.** That strange Rabbi who perplexes us so much: comp. *v.* 28, vii. 12, xix. 21.

οὐκ οἶδα rather implies that He did not return to Jesus (*v.* 7).

13—41. Opposite Results of the Sign

13. **ἄγουσιν.** These friends and neighbours are perhaps well-meaning people, not intending to make mischief. But they are uncomfortable because work has been done on the Sabbath, and they think it best to refer the matter to the Pharisees, the great authorities in matters of legal observance and orthodoxy (comp. vii. 47, 48). This is not a meeting of the Sanhedrin. S. John's formula for the Sanhedrin is *οἱ ἀρχιερεῖς κ.* (*οἱ*) *Φαρ.* (vii. 32, 45, xi. 47, 57, xviii. 3). Possibly one of the smaller Synagogue Councils is here meant. Apparently this is the day after the miracle.

14. **ἦν δὲ σ. ἐν ᾗ ἡμ.** *Now it was a Sabbath on the day on which: τ. πηλὸν ἐποίησεν* is specially stated as being an aggravation of the offence of healing on the Sabbath: see on v. 9. There were seven miracles of mercy wrought on the Sabbath: 1. Withered hand (Matt. xii. 9); 2. Demoniac at Capernaum (Mark i. 21); 3. Simon's wife's mother (Mark i. 29); 4. Woman bowed down 18 years (Luke xiii. 14); 5. Dropsical man (Luke xiv. 1); 6. Paralytic at Bethesda (John v. 10); 7. Man born blind. In all cases, excepting 2 and 3, the Jews charged the Lord with breaking the Sabbath by healing on it.

15. **πηλὸν ἐπ.** The man is becoming impatient of this cross-questioning and answers more briefly than at first. He omits the aggravating circumstance of making the clay as well as the sending to Siloam.

16. **οὗτος.** Contemptuous: comp. iii. 26, vi. 42, 52, vii. 15, 35, 49, xii. 34. The fact of the miracle is as yet not denied; but it cannot have been done with God's help. Comp. 'He casteth out devils through the prince of the devils' (Matt. ix. 34); like this, an argument of the Pharisees.

πῶς δύναται. The less bigoted, men like Nicodemus (iii. 2) and Joseph of Arimathea, shew that the argument cuts both ways. They also start from the 'sign,' but arrive at an opposite conclusion. Their timidity in contrast with the man's positiveness is very characteristic.

Comp. Nicodemus' question, v. 51. Perhaps Christ's teaching about the Sabbath (v. 17—23) has had some effect.

σχίσμα ἦν. See on vii. 43 and comp. x. 19.

17. There being a division among them they appeal to the man himself, each side wishing to gain him. 'They' includes both sides, the whole body of Pharisees present. Their question is not twofold, but single; not 'What sayest thou of Him? that He hath opened thine eyes?' but *What sayest thou of Him*, **because He opened** *thine eyes?* Comp. ii. 18. 'Thou' is emphatic: '*thou* shouldest know something of Him.' They do not raise the question of fact; the miracle is still undisputed. His answer shews that only one question is asked, and that it is not the question of fact.

προφήτης. i.e. one sent by God to declare His will; a man with a special and Divine mission; not necessarily predicting the future. Comp. iv. 19, iii. 2. His answer is short and decided.

18. οὐκ ἐπ. οὖν οἱ 'Ι. *The Jews* **therefore** *did not believe.* The man having pronounced for the moderates, the bigoted and hostile party begin to question the *fact* of the miracle. Note that here and in *v.* 22 S. John no longer speaks of the Pharisees, some of whom were not unfriendly to Christ, but 'the Jews,' His enemies, the official representatives of the nation that rejected the Messiah (see on i. 19).

αὐτοῦ τ. ἀναβλ. *Of* **the man himself** *that had received his sight.*

19. Three questions in legal form. Is this your son? Was he born blind? How does he now see?

ὃν ὑμεῖς λ. **Of whom** *ye say* **that he** *was born blind* (see on vi. 71). The emphatic *ὑμεῖς* implies 'we do not believe it.'

20. In their timidity they keep close to the questions asked.

21. τίς ἤνοιξεν. This is the dangerous point, and they become more eager and passionate. Hitherto there has been nothing emphatic in their reply; but now there is a marked stress on all the pronouns, the parents contrasting their ignorance with their son's responsibility. 'Who opened his eyes, *we* know not: ask *himself; he* [*himself*] is of full age; *he himself* will speak concerning himself.' See on *v.* 23.

22. συνετέθειντο. It does not appear when; but the tense and *ἤδη* indicate some previous arrangement, and probably an informal agreement among themselves. A formal decree of the Sanhedrin would be easily obtained afterwards. *Συντίθεσθαι* occurs in Luke xxii. 5 of the compact with Judas, and in Acts xxiii. 20 of the Jews' compact to kill S. Paul, and nowhere else.

ἀποσυνάγωγος. *Put away from the synagogue*, or excommunicated. The word is peculiar to S. John, occurring here, xii. 42, and xvi. 2, only. The Jews had three kinds of anathema. (1) Excommunication for thirty days, during which the excommunicated might not come within four cubits of any one. (2) Absolute exclusion from all intercourse and worship for an indefinite period. (3) Absolute exclusion for ever; an irrevocable sentence. This third form was very rarely if ever used. It is doubtful whether the second was in use at this time for Jews;

but it would be the ban under which all Samaritans were placed. This passage and 'separate' in Luke vi. 22 probably refer to the first and mildest kind of anathema. The principle of all anathema was found in the Divine sentence on Meroz (Judg. v. 23): comp. Ezra x. 8.

23. διὰ τοῦτο. For this cause: i. 31, v. 16, 18, vi. 65, viii. 47, &c.

ἡλικ. ἔχ. αἰ. ἐ. This is the right order here: in T. R. the clauses have been transposed in *v.* 21 to match this verse.

24. ἐφών. οὖν. *They called*, **therefore, a second time.** Having questioned the parents apart from the son, they now try to browbeat the son, before he learns that his parents have not discredited his story.

δὸς δ. τ. θ. Give glory to God. 'Glory,' not 'praise' (xii. 43), which would be *αἶνος* or *ἔπαινος* (Matt. xxi. 16; Luke xviii. 43; Rom. ii. 29), nor 'honour' (v. 41, 44, viii. 54), which would be *τιμή* (iv. 44; Rev. iv. 9, 11, v. 12, 13). Even thus the meaning remains obscure: but 'Give God *the* praise' is absolutely misleading. The meaning is not 'Give God the praise for the cure;' they were trying to deny that there had been any cure: but, 'Give glory to God *by speaking the truth.* The words are an adjuration to confess. Comp. Josh. vii. 19; 1 Sam. vi. 5; Ezra x. 11; 1 Esdr. ix. 8; 2 Cor. xi. 31. Wiclif, with the Genevan and Rhemish Versions, is right here. Tyndale and Cranmer have misled our translators. See on Jer. xiii. 16.

ἡμεῖς οἴδαμεν. Ἡ*μεῖς* is emphatic. 'We, the people in authority, who have a right to decide, know that this person (contemptuous, as in *v.* 16) is a Sabbath-breaker. It is useless, therefore, for you to maintain that He is a Prophet.'

25. ἐκεῖνος. See on *v.* 11. He will not argue or commit himself, but keeps to the incontrovertible facts of the case.

τυφλὸς ὤν. As in iii. 13 and xix. 38, we are in doubt whether the participle is present or imperfect; either 'being by nature a blind man,' or 'being formerly blind:' so also in *v.* 8. Winer, p. 429.

ἄρτι. *Now*, in contrast to the past; see on ii. 10.

26. Being baffled, they return to the details, either to try once more to shake the evidence, or for want of something better to say.

27. καὶ οὐκ ἠκούσατε. Possibly interrogative, **Did ye not hear?** This avoids taking *ἀκούειν* in two senses; (1) 'hearken,' (2) 'hear.' The man loses all patience, and will not go through it again.

μὴ καὶ ὑμεῖς. Surely ye also do not wish to become: comp. iv. 29, vi. 67, vii. 35, 52. For *θέλειν* comp. v. 40, vi. 67, vii. 17, viii. 44. For *γένεσθαι* comp. i. 6, viii. 58, x. 19. The meaning of 'also' has been misunderstood. It can scarcely mean 'as well as I:' the man has not advanced so far in faith as to count himself a disciple of Jesus; and if he had, he would not avow the fact to the Jews. 'Also' means 'as well as His well-known disciples.' That Christ had a band of followers was notorious.

28. ἐλοιδόρησαν. The word occurs here only in the Gospels: comp. 1 Pet. ii. 23. Argument fails, so they resort to abuse.

ἐκείνου. That man's ***disciple:*** the pronoun expresses that they have nothing to do with Him: comp. *v.* 12, vii. 12, xix. 21.

The pronouns are emphatic in both *v.* 28 and *v.* 29 : '*Thou* art His disciple; but *we* are Moses' disciples. *We* know that *God* hath spoken to Moses; but as for *this* fellow, &c.' See on *v.* 16 and i. 17.

29. **λελάληκεν. Hath spoken,** i.e. that Moses received a revelation *which still remains.* This is a frequent meaning of the perfect tense—to express the permanent result of a past action. Thus the frequent formula *γέγραπται* is strictly 'it has been written,' or 'it *stands* written:' i.e. it once was written, and the writing still remains. But as there are cases where the Greek aorist is best represented by the English perfect (viii. 10, 29), so there are cases where the Greek perfect is best represented by the English aorist; and this perhaps is one. The meaning is, Moses had a mission plainly declared by God.

οὐκ οἴδ. πόθεν. We know neither His mission, nor who sent Him. In a different sense they declared the very opposite, vii. 27. Comp. Pilate's question (xix. 9), and Christ's declaration (viii. 14). As at Capernaum (vi. 31, 32), He is compared unfavourably with Moses.

30. **τὸ θαυμαστόν. The** ***marvellous thing,*** or ***the marvel.*** '*You*, the very people who ought to know such things (iii. 10), know not whether He is from God or not, and yet He opened my eyes.' 'You' is emphatic, and perhaps is a taunting rejoinder to their '*we* know that this man is a sinner' (*v.* 24) and '*we* know that God hath spoken to Moses' (*v.* 29). The man gains courage at their evident discomfiture: moreover, his controversy with them developes and confirms his own faith. For **γάρ** see Winer, p. 559.

31. **οὐκ ἀκούει.** *Heareth not* wilful, impenitent sinners. Of course it cannot mean 'God heareth no one who hath sinned,' which would imply that God never answers the prayers of men. But the man's dictum, reasonably understood, is the plain teaching of the O.T., whence he no doubt derived it. 'The Lord is far from the wicked; but He heareth the prayer of the righteous' (Prov. xv. 29). Comp. Ps. lxvi. 18, 19; Job xxvii. 8, 9; Isai. i. 11—15. Note *οἴδαμεν*, which reproduces their own word (*vv.* 24, 29), but without the arrogant *ἡμεῖς*.

θεοσεβής. God-fearing, devout, religious: here only in N.T. The man thinks that miracles are answers to prayer: only good men can gain such answers: and only a very good man could gain such an unprecedented answer as this.

32. **ἐκ τ. αἰῶνος.** Here only: Col. i. 26 we have *ἀπὸ τῶν αἰώνων.* There is no healing of the blind in O.T.

33. **οὗτος.** He uses their pronoun without their contemptuous meaning (*vv.* 24, 29). On **παρὰ Θεοῦ** see on i. 6.

οὐδέν. Nothing like this, no miracle. For the construction see Winer, p. 382.

34. **ἐν ἁμαρτ. σύ.** Emphatic: 'In sins wast thou born altogether; thou art a born reprobate; and thou, dost thou teach us?'

ὅλος. 'Every part of thy nature (comp. xiii. 10) has been steeped in sins from thy birth.' They hold the same belief as the disciples, that sin before birth is possible, and maliciously exclude not only the alternative stated by Christ (*v.* 3) but even the one stated by the disciples (*v.* 2), that his parents might have sinned. Their passion blinds them to their inconsistency. They had contended that no miracle had been wrought; now they throw his calamity in his face as proof of his sin.

Godet points out the analogy between these Jews and modern impugners of miracles. The Jews argued: God *cannot* help a Sabbath-breaker; therefore the miracle attributed to Jesus is a fiction. The opponents of the miraculous argue: The supernatural *cannot* exist; therefore the miracles attributed to Jesus and others are fictions. In both cases the logic of reason has to yield to the logic of facts.

ἐξέβαλον. They put him forth: see on x. 4. This probably does not mean excommunication. (1) The expression is too vague. (2) There could not well have been time to get a sentence of excommunication passed. (3) The man had not incurred the threatened penalty; he had not 'confessed that He was Christ' (*v.* 22). Provoked by his sturdy adherence to his own view they ignominiously dismiss him—turn him out of doors, if (as the 'out' seems to imply) they were meeting within walls. What follows illustrates Luke vi. 22.

35. σὺ πιστ. Comp. xi. 26. 'Dost *thou*, though others blaspheme and deny, believe?' See on i. 12, viii. 30, 31. **Εὑρών**, as in i. 44, v. 14, xi. 17, xii. 14, probably implies previous seeking.

τ. υἱὸν τ. θ. Again there is much doubt about the reading. The balance of MSS. authority (including both the Sinaitic and the Vatican MSS.) is in favour of *τ. υἱ. τ. ἀνθρώπου*, which moreover is the expression that our Lord commonly uses respecting Himself in all four Gospels (see on i. 52). But the reading *τ. υἱ. τ. Θεοῦ* is very strongly supported, and is at least as old as the second century; for Tertullian, who in his work *Against Praxeas* quotes largely from this Gospel, in chap. xxii. quotes this question thus, *Tu credis in Filium Dei?* In x. 36 and xi. 4 there is no doubt about the reading, and there Christ calls himself 'the Son of God.' Moreover, this appellation seems to suit the context better, for the man had been contending that Jesus came 'from God' (*v.* 33), and the term 'Son of man' would scarcely have been intelligible to him. Lastly, a copyist, knowing that the 'Son of man' was Christ's usual mode of designating Himself, would be very likely to alter 'the Son of God' into 'the Son of man.' Neither title, however, is very frequent in St John's Gospel. For all these reasons, therefore, it is allowable to retain the common reading. But in any case we once more have evidence of the antiquity of this Gospel. If both these readings were established by the end of the second century, the original text must have been in existence long before. Corruptions take time to spring up and spread. See on i. 13, 18, iii. 6, 13.

36. ἐκεῖνος. See on *v.* 11.

καὶ τίς ἐστιν. And *who is he?* or, *Who is he* **then?** The *καὶ* intensifies the question. Winer, p. 545. Comp. *καὶ τίς ἐστί μου πλησίον;*

(Luke x. 29); *καὶ τὶς δύναται σωθῆναι*; (xviii. 26); *καὶ τὶς ὁ εὐφραίνων με*; (2 Cor. ii. 2). *Κύριε* should perhaps be rendered 'Sir,' as in iv. 11, 15, 19, 49, v. 7: see on iv. 11 and vi. 34. But the man's reverence increases, like that of the woman at the well.

ἵνα πιστ. He asks, not from curiosity, but in order to find the object of faith mentioned. He has faith, and more is given to him; he seeks and finds. Winer, p. 774.

37. **καὶ ἑώρακας.** Winer, p. 342. We are uncertain whether the first *καὶ* anticipates the second, 'Thou hast *both* seen Him,' or emphasizes the verb, 'Thou hast *even* seen Him:' the latter seems better.

ἐκεῖνος. S. John's characteristic use of *ἐκεῖνος* to reproduce a previous subject with emphasis (see on i. 18): *He that speaketh with thee is He.* Comp. iv. 26. "This spontaneous revelation to the outcast from the synagogue *finds its only parallel* in the similar revelation to the outcast from the nation" (Westcott). Not even Apostles are told so speedily.

38. **πιστ. κύριε. I believe, Lord:** the order is worth keeping. Comp. the centurion's confession (Matt. xxvii. 54). There is no need to suppose that in either case the man making the confession knew anything like the full meaning of belief in the Son of God: even Apostles were slow at learning that. The blind man had had his own uninformed idea of the Messiah, and he believed that the realisation of that idea stood before him. His faith was necessarily imperfect, a poor 'two mites;' but it was 'all that he had,' and he gave it readily, while the learned Rabbis of their abundance gave nothing. It is quite gratuitous to suppose that a special revelation was granted to him. There is no hint of this, nor can one see why so great an exception to God's usual dealings with man should have been made.

προσεκύνησεν. This shews that his idea of the Son of God includes attributes of Divinity. *Προσκυνεῖν* occurs elsewhere in this Gospel only in iv. 20—24 and xii. 20, always of the worship of God.

39. **καὶ εἶπ. ὁ Ἰ.** There is no need to make a break in the narrative and refer these words to a subsequent occasion. This is not natural. Rather it is the sight of the man prostrate at His feet, endowed now with sight both in body and soul, that moves Christ to say what follows. His words convey His own authority for finding a symbolical meaning in His miracles. They are addressed to the bystanders generally, among whom are some of the Pharisees.

εἰς κρίμα. *Κρίμα* occurs nowhere else in this Gospel. As distinct from *κρίσις*, the *act* of judging (v. 22, 24, 27, 30), it signifies the *result*, a sentence or decision (Matt. vii. 2; Mark xii. 40; Rom. ii. 2, 3, &c.). Christ came not to judge, but to save (iii. 17, viii. 15); but judgment was the inevitable result of His coming, for those who rejected Him passed sentence on themselves (iii. 19). See on i. 9 and xviii. 37. The *ἐγώ* is emphatic; I, the Light of the world (*v.* 5), I, the Son of God (*v.* 35). See on xi. 27.

οἱ μὴ βλέπ. They who are conscious of their own blindness, who know their deficiencies; like 'they that are sick' and 'sinners' in Matt. ix. 12, 13, and 'babes' in Matt. xi. 25. This man was aware of his spiritual blindness when he asked, 'Who is He then, that I may believe on Him?' *Βλέπωσιν* means **may** *see*, may pass from the darkness of which they are conscious, to light and truth.

οἱ βλέπ. They who fancy they see, who pride themselves on their superior insight and knowledge, and wish to dictate to others; like 'they that be whole,' and 'righteous' in Matt. ix. 12, 13, and 'the wise and prudent' in Matt. xi. 25. These Pharisees shewed this proud self-confidence when they declared, '*we* know that this man is a sinner,' and asked 'Dost *thou* teach *us?*'

τυφλοὶ γένωνται. **May become** *blind:* much stronger than *μὴ βλέπωσιν*. *Οἱ μὴ βλ. can* see, but *do* not; *οἱ τυφλοὶ cannot* see. These self-satisfied Pharisees must pass from fancied light into real darkness (Isa. vi. 10).

40. ἐκ τ. Φ....ὄντες. **Those** *of the P. who were with Him,* who still considered themselves in some degree His disciples.

μὴ καὶ ἡμ. **Surely we also are not blind**: comp. *v.* 27, vi. 67. Of course they understand Him to be speaking figuratively. It is strange that any should have understood their question as referring to bodily sight. They mean that they, the most enlightened among the most enlightened nation, must be among 'those who see.' 'Have we not recognised Thee as a teacher come from God (iii. 2) and listened to Thee until now? Are we also blind?'

41. εἰ τ. ἦτε. '*If ye were blind,* i.e. if ye were conscious of your spiritual darkness and yearned for the light, *ye would not have sin* (xv. 22); for either ye would find the light, or, if ye failed, the failure would not lie at your door.' Others interpret, 'If ye were really blind, and had never known the light, ye would not be responsible for rejecting it. But by your own confession ye see, and the sin of rejection abideth.' For the construction comp. v. 46, viii. 19, 42, xv. 19, xviii. 36; for **ἔχειν ἁμαρτίαν** see on xv. 22. Perhaps there is a pause after *βλέπομεν*.

ἡ ἁμαρτία ὑμ. μ. *Your sin* **abideth** (see on i. 33). 'Ye profess to see: your sin in this false profession and in your consequent rejection of Me abideth.' It was a hopeless case. They rejected Him because they did not know the truth about Him; and they would never learn the truth because they were fully persuaded that they were in possession of it. Those who confess their ignorance and contend against it (1) cease to be responsible for it, (2) have a good prospect of being freed from it. Those who deny their ignorance and contend against instruction, (1) remain responsible for their ignorance, (2) have no prospect of ever being freed from it. Comp. iii. 36.

CHAPTER X

3. **φωνεῖ** (all the best MSS.) for *καλεῖ*.

4. **πάντα** (BDLX) for *πρόβατα* (A).

5. **ἀκολουθήσουσιν** for *-σωσιν* (correction to more usual construction, comp. iv. 14; Luke x. 19).

12. **ἔστιν** for *εἰσί* (comp. *ἤκουσαν*, *v.* 8). Omit *τὰ πρόβατα ὁ δὲ μισθωτὸς φεύγει* after **σκορπίζει** with ℵBDL against A.

14. **γινώσκουσίν με τὰ ἐμά** for *γινώσκομαι ὑπὸ τῶν ἐμῶν*.

26. Omit *καθὼς εἶπον ὑμῖν* with ℵBKLM[1].

27. **ἀκούουσιν** for *ἀκούει* (grammatical correction) with ℵBLX against AD.

29. **ὅ** (ℵB[1]L) for *ὅς* (AB[2]), and **πάντων μεῖζον** for *μείζων πάντων*.

38. **πιστεύετε** (ℵBDKLU) for *πιστεύσατε*, and **γινώσκητε** for *πιστεύσητε* (to avoid apparent repetition) with BLX against A; ℵ has *πιστεύητε*.

Christ is Love

In chapters v. and vi. two miracles, the healing of the paralytic and the feeding of the 5000, formed the introduction to two discourses in which Christ is set forth as *the Source and the Support of Life*. In chapters vii. and viii. we have a discourse in which He is set forth as *the Source of Truth and Light*, and this is illustrated (ix.) by His giving physical and spiritual sight to the man born blind. In chap. x. we again have a discourse in which Christ is set forth as *Love*, under the figure of the Good Shepherd giving His life for the sheep, and this is illustrated (xi.) by the raising of Lazarus, a work of Love which costs Him His life. As already stated, the prevailing idea throughout this section (v.—xi.) is truth and love provoking contradiction and enmity. The more clearly the Messiah manifests Himself, and the more often He convinces some of His hearers of His Messiahship (vii. 40, 41, 46, 50, viii. 30, ix. 30—38, x. 21, 42, xi. 45), the more intense becomes the hostility of 'the Jews' and the more determined their intention to kill Him.

1—18. "The form of the discourse in the first half of chap. **x.** is remarkable. It resembles the Synoptic parables, but not exactly. The parable is a short narrative, which is kept wholly separate from the ideal facts which it signifies. But this discourse is not a narrative; and the figure and its application run side by side, and are interwoven with one another all through. It is an extended metaphor rather than a parable. If we are to give it an accurate name we should be obliged to fall back upon the wider term 'allegory.'

This, and the parallel passage in chap. xv., are the only instances of allegory in the Gospels. They take in the Fourth Gospel the place which parables hold with the Synoptists. The Synoptists have no allegories distinct from parables. The fourth Evangelist has no parables as a special form of allegory. What are we to infer from this? The parables certainly are original and genuine. Does it follow that the allegories are not?

(1) We notice, first, that along with the change of *form* there is a certain change of *subject*. The parables generally turn round the ground conception of the kingdom of heaven. They......do not enlarge on the relation which its King bears to the separate members...... Though the royal dignity of the Son is incidentally put forward, there is nothing which expresses so closely and directly *the personal relation of the Messiah to the community of believers*, collectively and individually, as these two 'allegories' from S. John. Their form seems in an especial manner suited to their subject-matter, which is a fixed, permanent and simple relation, not a history of successive states. The form of the allegories is at least appropriate.

(2) We notice next that even with the Synoptists the use of the parable is not rigid. All do not conform precisely to the same type. There are some, like the Pharisee and Publican, the Good Samaritan, &c., which give direct patterns for action, and are not therefore parables in the same sense in which the Barren Fig-tree, the Prodigal Son, &c. are parables..... If, then, the parable admits so much deviation on the one side, may it not also on the other?

(3) Lastly, we have to notice the parallels to this particular figure of the Good Shepherd that are found in the Synoptists. These are indeed abundant. The parable of the Lost Sheep (Luke xv. 4—7; Matt. xviii. 12, 13)...... 'I am not sent but unto the lost sheep of the house of Israel' (Matt. xv. 24)...... 'But when He saw the multitudes, He was moved with compassion on them, because they fainted, and were scattered abroad, as sheep having no shepherd' (Matt. ix. 36), which when taken with Matt. xi. 28, 29 ('Come unto Me all ye that labour,' &c.), gives almost an exact parallel to the Johannean allegory." Sanday.

1—9. The Allegory of the Door of the Fold

1. ἀμὴν ἀμήν. This double affirmation, peculiar to this Gospel (see on i. 52), never occurs at the beginning of a discourse, but either in continuation, to introduce some deep truth, or in reply. This verse is no exception. There is no break between the chapters, which should perhaps have been divided at ix. 34 or 38 rather than here. The scene continues uninterrupted from ix. 35 to x. 21, where we have a reference to the healing of the blind man. Moreover x. 6 seems to point back to ix. 41; their not understanding the allegory was evidence of self-complacent blindness. This chapter, therefore, although it contains a fresh subject, is connected with the incidents in chap. ix. and grows out of them. The connexion seems to be that the Pharisees by their conduct to the man had proved themselves bad shepherds; but he has found the Good Shepherd: they had cast him out of doors; but he has found the Door: they had put him forth to drive him away; the Good Shepherd puts His sheep forth to lead them. We are not told where these words are spoken; so that it is impossible to say whether it is probable that a sheepfold with the shepherds and their flocks was in sight. There is nothing against the supposition. Be this as it may, Jesus, who has already appropriated the types of the Brazen Serpent, the Manna, the Rock, and the Pillar of Fire (iii. 14, vi. 50, vii. 37, viii. 12) here appropriates the type of the Shepherd (Ps. xxiii.; Ezek. xxxiv.; Zech. xi.).

διὰ τῆς θύρας. Oriental sheepfolds are commonly walled or palisaded, with one door or gate. Into one of these enclosures several shepherds drive their flocks, leaving them in charge of an under-shepherd or porter, who fastens the door securely inside, and remains with the sheep all night. In the morning the shepherds come to the door, the porter opens to them, and each calls away his own sheep.

τ. αὐλὴν τ. πρ. The fold of the sheep. Comp. *ἡ θύρα τ. πρ.* (*v.* 7).

ἀλλαχόθεν. Literally, *from another quarter;* here only in N.T.

ἐκεῖνος. S. John's characteristic use: comp. i. 18, 33, v. 11, 39, vi. 57, ix. 37, xii. 48, xiv. 12, 21, 26, xv. 26.

κλέπτης...λῃστής. Everywhere in this Gospel (*vv.* 8, 10, xii. 6, xviii. 40) and in 2 Cor. xi. 26 *κλέπτης* is rightly rendered 'thief' and *λῃστής* 'robber' in A.V. But elsewhere (Matt. xxi. 13, xxvi. 55, xxvii. 38, &c. &c.) *λῃστής* is translated 'thief.' The *λῃστής* is a brigand, more formidable than the *κλέπτης*: the one uses violence and is sometimes chivalrous, the other employs cunning, and is always mean.

2. **ποιμήν ἐστιν τ. πρ.** *Is a shepherd of the sheep.* There is more than one flock in the fold, and therefore more than one shepherd to visit the fold. The Good Shepherd has not yet appeared in the allegory. The allegory indeed is twofold, or even threefold; in the first part (1—5), which is repeated (7—9), Christ is the Door of the fold; in the second part (11—18) He is the Shepherd; *v.* 10 forming a link between the two main parts.

3. **ὁ θυρωρός.** *Ostiarius.* The 'porter' is the door-keeper or gate-keeper, who fastens and opens the one door into the fold. In the allegory the fold is the Church, the Door is Christ, the sheep are the elect, the shepherds are God's ministers. What does the porter represent? Possibly nothing definite. Much harm is sometimes done by trying to make every detail of an allegory or parable significant. There must be background in every picture. But if it be insisted that the porter here is too prominent to be meaningless, it is perhaps best to understand the Holy Spirit as signified under this figure; He who grants opportunities of coming, or of bringing others, through Christ into the Kingdom of God. Comp. 1 Cor. xvi. 9; 2 Cor. ii. 12; Col. iv. 3; Acts xiv. 27; Rev. iii. 8: but in all these passages 'door' does not mean Christ, but *opportunity*.

τ. πρ....ἀκούει. All the sheep, whether belonging to his flock or not, know from his coming that they are about to be led out. *His own sheep* (first for emphasis) *he calleth by name* (Exod. xxxiii. 12, 17; Isai. xliii. 1, xlv. 3, xlix. 1; Rev. iii. 5), *and leadeth them out* to pasture. Even in this country shepherds and shepherds' dogs know each individual sheep; in the East the intimacy between shepherd and sheep is still closer. The naming of sheep is a very ancient practice: see Theocritus v. 102. *Φωνεῖ* implies more directly personal invitation (i. 49, ii. 9, iv. 16, ix. 19, 24, xi. 28, xiii. 13, xviii. 33) than *καλεῖ* (T. R.), which would express a general summons (Matt. iv. 21, xx. 8, xxii. 9, xxv. 14). The blind man had been called out from the rest, and had heard His voice.

4. ὅταν τὰ ἴδια πάντα ἐκβ. When he hath put forth all his own. 'There shall not an hoof be left behind' (Exod. x. 26). *Ἐκβάλῃ* is remarkable, as being the very word used in ix. 34, 35 of the Pharisees putting forth the man born blind: here we might have expected *ἐξάγειν* rather than *ἐκβάλλειν*. The false shepherds put forth sheep to rid themselves of trouble; the true shepherds put forth sheep to feed them. But even the true shepherds must use some violence to their sheep to 'compel them to come' (Luke xiv. 23) to the pastures. This was true at this very moment of the Messiah, who was endeavouring to bring His people out of the rigid enclosure of the Law into the free pastures of the Gospel. But there are no 'goats' in the allegory; all the flock are faithful. It is the ideal Church composed entirely of the elect. The object of the allegory being to set forth the relations of Christ to His sheep, the possibility of bad sheep is not taken into account. That side of the picture is treated in the parables of the Lost Sheep, and of the Sheep and the Goats.

ἔμπροσθεν. As soon as they are out he does not drive but leads them, as Oriental shepherds do still: and they follow, because they not only *hear* (*v.* 3) but *know* his voice. Note the change from sing. *ἀκολουθεῖ* to plur. *οἴδασιν*; Winer, p. 646.

5. ἀλλοτρίῳ δὲ οὐ μή. But *a stranger they will* **in no wise** *follow:* strong negative, as in iv. 14, 48, vi. 35, 37, viii. 12, 51, 52. The *ἀλλότριος* is anyone whom they do not know, not necessarily a thief or robber: they meet him outside the fold. There is a story of a Scotch traveller who changed clothes with a Jerusalem shepherd and tried to lead the sheep; but the sheep followed the shepherd's voice and not his clothes.

6. παροιμίαν. Allegory or similitude. The Synoptists never use *παροιμία*; S. John never uses *παραβολή*; and this should be preserved in translation. A.V. renders both words sometimes 'parable' and sometimes 'proverb.' In LXX. both are used to represent the Hebrew *mashal;* in the title to the Book of Proverbs, Prov. i. 1 and xxv. 1, *παροιμίαι*; elsewhere almost always *παραβολή*. The two words appear together in Ecclus. xxxix. 3; xlvii. 17. In A.V. we have 'parable' and 'proverb' indifferently for *mashal*. In N.T. *παροιμία* occurs only here, xvi. 25, 29, and 2 Pet. ii. 22. It means something *beside the way* (*οἶμος*); hence, according to some, a trite '*way-side* saying;' according to others, a figurative '*out-of-the-way* saying.' For *παραβολή* see on Mark iv. 2.

ἐκεῖνοι. The pronoun (vii. 45) separates them from the Teacher.

οὐκ ἔγνωσαν. Did not *recognise* the meaning. The idea that they were strangers, or even robbers, instead of shepherds to the sheep did not come home to them at all.

7. **εἶπεν οὖν.** *Jesus* therefore *said again.* Because they did not understand He went through it again, explaining the main features.

ἀμὴν ἀμ. This is *the* important point: the one Door, through which both sheep and shepherds enter, is Christ. 'Ἐγώ is very emphatic; *I* (and no other) *am the Door:* comp. 'I am the Way' (xiv. 6). For *ἐγώ εἰμι* see on vi. 35.

ἡ θ. τ. προβάτων. *The Door* for *the sheep* (*v.* 9) and also *the Door* to *the sheep* (*vv.* 1, 2). Sheep and shepherds have one and the same Door. The elect enter the Church through Christ; the ministers who would visit them must receive their commission from Christ. Jesus does not say *ἡ θ. τ. αὐλῆς*, but *ἡ θ. τ. προβάτων*. The fold has no meaning apart from the sheep.

8. **πάντες ὅσοι ἦλθον πρὸ ἐμοῦ.** These words are difficult, and some copyists seem to have tried to avoid the difficulty by omitting either *πάντες* or *πρὸ ἐμοῦ*. But the balance of authority leaves no doubt that both are genuine. Some commentators would translate *πρὸ ἐμοῦ* 'instead of Me.' But this meaning of *πρό* is not common, and perhaps occurs nowhere in N.T. Moreover 'instead of Me' ought to include the idea of 'for My advantage;' and that is impossible here. We must retain the natural and ordinary meaning of 'before Me:' and as 'before Me in *dignity*' would be obviously inappropriate, 'before Me in *time*' must be the meaning. But who are 'all that came before Me'? The patriarchs, prophets, Moses, the Baptist *cannot* be meant, either collectively or singly. 'Salvation is of the Jews' (iv. 22); 'they are they which testify of Me' (v. 39); 'if ye believed Moses, ye would believe Me' (v. 46); 'John bare witness unto the truth' (v. 33): texts like this are quite conclusive against any such Gnostic interpretation. Nor can false Messiahs be meant: it is doubtful whether any had arisen at this time. Rather it refers to the 'ravening wolves in sheep's clothing' who had been, and still were, the ruin of the nation, 'who devoured widows' houses,' who were 'full of ravening and wickedness,' who had 'taken away the key of knowledge,' and were in very truth 'thieves and robbers' (Matt. vii. 15, xxiii. 14; Luke xi. 39, 52). These 'came,' but they were not *sent.* Some of them were now present, thirsting to add bloodshed to robbery, and this denunciation of them is no stronger than several passages in the Synoptists: e.g. Matt. xxiii. 33; Luke xi. 50, 51. The tense also is in favour of this interpretation; not *were*, but '*are* thieves, and robbers.'

οὐκ ἤκουσαν. For they found no authority, no living voice in their teaching (Matt. vii. 29). Comp. 'To whom shall we go?' (vi. 68).

Hearers there were, but these were not the sheep, but blind followers, led by the blind. For the plural verb see Winer, p. 646.

9. There is a very clear reference to this verse in the Ignatian Epistles, *Philad.* ix.: *αὐτὸς ὢν θύρα τοῦ πατρός, δι' ἧς εἰσέρχονται Ἀβραὰμ κ. Ἰσαὰκ κ. Ἰακὼβ κ. οἱ προφῆται κ. οἱ ἀπόστολοι κ. ἡ ἐκκλησία.* In the message to the Philadelphian Church (Rev. iii. 8) we find *ἰδοὺ δέδωκα ἐνώπιόν σου θύραν ἀνεῳγμένην.* For other early adaptations of this image comp. Hegesippus (Eus. *H. E.* II. xxiii. 8), *τίς ἡ θύρα τοῦ Ἰησοῦ*, Hermas III. *Sim.* ix. 12, *ἡ πύλη ὁ υἱὸς τοῦ Θεοῦ ἐστί*, and Clem. Rom. I. xlviii. See on iii. 8, iv. 10, vi. 33, viii. 28, 29.

δι' ἐμοῦ. Placed first for emphasis; 'through Me and in no other way.' The main point is iterated again and again, each time with great simplicity and yet most emphatically. "The simplicity, the directness, the particularity, the emphasis of S. John's style give his writings a marvellous power, which is not perhaps felt at first. Yet his words seem to hang about the reader till he is forced to remember them. Each great truth sounds like the burden of a strain, ever falling upon the ear with a calm persistency which secures attention." Westcott, *Introduction to the Study of the Gospels*, p. 250.

ἐάν τις. *If* **anyone**: there is no limit of sex or nationality. Comp. vi. 51, viii. 51, iii. 15, xi. 25, xii. 46.

σωθήσεται. It is interesting to see how this has been expanded in the *Clementine Homilies* (III. lii.); *Ἐγώ εἰμι ἡ πύλη τῆς ζωῆς· ὁ δι' ἐμοῦ εἰσερχόμενος εἰσέρχεται εἰς τὴν ζωήν. ὡς οὐκ οὔσης ἑτέρας τῆς σώζειν δυναμένης διδασκαλίας.* See on *v.* 27 and ix. 1. These passages place the reference to the Fourth Gospel beyond a doubt. *Σωθήσεται* and *νομὴν εὑρήσει* seem to shew that this verse does not refer to the shepherds only, but to the sheep also. Although 'find pasture' may refer to the shepherd's work for the flock, yet one is inclined to think that if the words do not refer to both, they refer to the sheep only.

εἰσελεύσεται κ. ἐξ. These words also are more appropriate to the sheep than to the shepherds; but comp. Num. xxvii. 17; 1 Sam. xviii. 13; 2 Chron. i. 10. 'To go in and out' includes the ideas of security and liberty (Jer. xxxvii. 4). The phrase is a Hebraism, expressing the free activity of life, like *versari* (Deut. xxviii. 6, 19; xxxi. 2; Ps. cxxi. 8; Acts i. 21, ix. 28).

10. Just as *v.* 9 refers back to *v.* 2, so this refers back to *v.* 1. It is the same allegory more fully expounded. Note the climax; *κλέψῃ*, steal and carry off; *θύσῃ*, slaughter as if for sacrifice (LXX. in Is. xxii. 13; 1 Macc. vii. 19); *ἀπολέσῃ* utterly consume and destroy. In what follows *ζωὴν ἔχ.* is opposed to *θύσῃ κ. ἀπολέσῃ*, *περισσὸν ἔχ.* to *κλέψῃ*: instead of taking life, He gives it; instead of stealing, He gives abundance.

ἐγὼ ἦλθον. **I came** *that they* **may** *have life, and that they* **may have abundance.** *Ἐγώ* is in emphatic contrast to *ὁ κλέπτης*. This is the point of transition from the first part of the allegory to the second. The figure of the Door, as the one entrance to salvation, is dropped; and that of the Good Shepherd, as opposed to the thief, is taken up;

but this intermediate clause will apply to either figure, inclining towards the second one. In order to make the strongest possible antithesis to the thief, Christ introduces, not a shepherd, but Himself, the Chief Shepherd. The thief *takes* life; the shepherds *protect* life; the Good Shepherd *gives* it.

11—18. The Allegory of the Good Shepherd

11. ἐγώ εἰμι ὁ π. ὁ κ. See on vi. 35: *καλὸς* cannot be adequately translated: it means 'beautiful, noble, good,' as opposed to 'foul, mean, wicked.' It sums up the chief attributes of ideal perfection; comp. x. 32, ii. 10. Christ is the Perfect Shepherd, as opposed to His own imperfect ministers; He is the true Shepherd, as opposed to the false shepherds, who are hirelings or hypocrites; He is the Good Shepherd, who gives His life for the sheep, as opposed to the wicked thief who takes their lives to preserve his own. Thus in Christ is realised the ideal Shepherd of O.T. Ps. xxiii.; Isa. xl. 11; Jer. xxiii.; Ezek. xxxiv., xxxvii. 24; Zech. xi. 7. The figure sums up the relation of Jehovah to His people (Ps. lxxx. 1); and in appropriating it Jesus proclaims Himself as the representative of Jehovah. Perhaps no image has penetrated more deeply into the mind of Christendom: Christian prayers and hymns, Christian painting and statuary, and Christian literature are full of it, and have been from the earliest ages. And side by side with it is commonly found the other beautiful image of this Gospel, the Vine: the Good Shepherd and the True Vine are figures of which Christians have never wearied.

τ. ψ. αὐ. τίθησιν. Layeth down *His life.* A remarkable phrase and peculiar to S. John (*vv.* 15, 17, xiii. 37, 38, xv. 13; 1 John iii. 16), whereas *δοῦναι τ. ψ. αὐτοῦ* occurs Matt. xx. 28; Mark x. 45. 'To *lay* down' perhaps includes the notion of 'to *pay* down,' a common meaning of the word in classical Greek; if so it is exactly equivalent to the Synoptic 'to give as a *ransom*' (*λύτρον*). Others interpret, 'to lay aside' (xiii. 4), i.e. to give up voluntarily. In this country the statement 'the good shepherd lays down his life for his sheep' seems extravagant when taken apart from the application to Christ. Not so in the East, where dangers from wild beasts and armed bands of robbers are serious and constant. Gen. xiii. 5, xiv. 12, xxxi. 39, 40, xxxii. 7, 8, xxxvii. 33; Job i. 17; 1 Sam. xvii. 34, 35. **'Υπέρ**, 'on behalf of.'

12. ὁ μισθωτός. The word occurs nowhere else in N.T. excepting of the 'hired servants' of Zebedee (Mark i. 20). The Good Shepherd was introduced in contrast to the thief. Now we have another contrast to the Good Shepherd given, the *hired* shepherd, a mercenary, who tends a flock not his own for his own interests. The application is obvious; viz., to those ministers who care chiefly for the emoluments and advantages of their position, and retire when the position becomes irksome and dangerous. In one respect the hireling is worse than the thief, for he is false to his pledge and betrays a trust. He sacrifices his charge to save himself, whereas a true shepherd sacrifices himself to save his charge.

καὶ οὐκ ὢν π. *And not* a *shepherd,* as in *v.* 2.

τὸν λύκον. Any power opposed to Christ (*v.* 28).

ἀφίησιν κ.τ.λ. *Leaveth the sheep and fleeth; and the wolf snatcheth them and scattereth* (*them*); *because he is an hireling, &c.* The wolf seizes some and scatters the rest.

14—18. Further description of the True Shepherd. (1) His intimate knowledge of His sheep; (2) His readiness to die for them. This latter point recurs repeatedly as a sort of refrain, like 'I will raise him up at the last day,' in chap. vi. The passage, especially *vv.* 14, 15, is remarkable for beautiful simplicity of structure: the parallelism of Hebrew poetry is very marked. There should be no full stop at the end of *v.* 14: **I know Mine, and Mine know Me, even as the Father knoweth Me and I know the Father.** So intimate is the relation between the Good Shepherd and His sheep that it may be compared and likened (not merely *ὥσπερ*, but *καθώς*) to the relation between the Father and the Son. The same thought runs through the discourses in the latter half of the Gospel: xiv. 20, xv. 10, xvii. 8, 10, 18, 21. Note that *γίνωσκω*, not *οἶδα*, is used: it is knowledge resulting from experience and appreciation. Contrast Matt. vii. 23, 'I never knew you' (*ἔγνων*) with Luke iv. 34, 'I know Thee who Thou art' (*οἶδα*).

16. ἄλλα πρόβατα. Not the Jews in heathen lands, but Gentiles, for even among them He had sheep. The Jews had asked in derision, 'Will He go and teach the Gentiles?' (vii. 35). He declares here that among the despised heathen He has sheep. He was going to lay down His life, 'not for that nation only' (xi. 52), but that He might 'draw *all* men unto Him' (xii. 32). Of that most heathen of heathen cities, Corinth, He declared to S. Paul in a vision, 'I have much people in this city' (Acts xviii. 10; comp. xxviii. 28). The Light 'lightens *every* man' (i. 9), and not the Jews only. *Ἔχω*, not *ἕξω*, like *ἐστί μοι* in Acts xviii. 10: they are already His, given to Him (xvii. 7) by the Father. He is their Owner, but not yet their Shepherd.

ἐκ τ. αὐλῆς τ. Emphasis on *αὐλῆς* not on *ταύτης*; the Gentiles were not in any fold at all, but 'scattered abroad' (xi. 52).

ἐκεῖνα. Not *ταῦτα*: they are still remote.

δεῖ. Such is the Divine decree; see on iii. 14. It is the Father's will and the Messiah's bounden duty.

ἀγάγειν. Lead, rather than 'bring;' comp. *ἐξάγειν* (*v.* 3). Christ can lead them in their own lands. 'Neither in this mountain, nor yet at Jerusalem' (iv. 21) is the appointed place. The spiritual gathering into one (xi. 52) is not the idea conveyed here.

γενήσεται μία ποίμνη, εἷς ποιμήν. *They shall* **become** *one* **flock**, *one shepherd.* The distinction between 'be' and 'become' is worth preserving (see on ix. 27, 39), and that between 'flock' and 'fold' still more so. 'There shall become one fold' would imply that at present there are more than one: but nothing is said of any other fold. In both these instances our translators have rejected their better predecessors: Tyndale and Coverdale have 'flock,' not 'fold;' the Geneva Version has 'be made,' not 'be.' The old Latin texts have *ovile* for αὐλή and *grex* for ποίμνη; so Cyprian and (sometimes) Augustine. The Vulgate has *ovile* for both. Hence Wiclif has 'fold' for both; and this error was admitted into the Great Bible of 1539 and A.V. of 1611. One point in the Greek cannot be preserved in English, the cognate similarity between ποίμνη and ποιμήν. 'One herd, one herdsman' would involve more loss than gain. 'One flock, one flock-master' would do, if 'flock-master' were in common use. But the rendering of ποίμνη by *ovile* and 'fold' is all loss, and has led to calamitous misunderstanding by strengthening 'the wall of partition' (Eph. ii. 14), which this passage declares shall be broken down. Even O.T. Prophets seem to have had a presentiment that other nations would share in the blessings of the Messiah: Mic. iv. 2; Isa. lii. 15. The same thought appears frequently in the Synoptists; e.g. Matt. viii. 11, xiii. 24—30, xxviii. 19; Luke xiii. 29. And if S. Matthew could appreciate this side of his Master's teaching, how much more S. John, who had lived to see the success of missions to the heathen and the results of the destruction of Jerusalem. It is therefore unreasonable to urge the universalism of the Fourth Gospel as an argument against its authenticity. Here, as elsewhere in N.T., the *prior* claim of the Jews is admitted, their *exclusive* claim is denied.

17. διὰ τοῦτο. For this cause: see on v. 16, vii. 21. The Father's love for the incarnate Son is intensified by the self-sacrifice of the Son, which was a προσφορὰ κ. θυσία τῷ Θεῷ εἰς ὀσμὴν εὐωδίας (Eph. v. 2).

ἵνα π. λάβω αὐ. In order that I may *take it again.* This clause is closely connected with the preceding one, ἵνα depending upon ὅτι κ.τ.λ. Christ died *in order to* rise again; and only because Christ was to take His human life again was His death such as the Father could have approved. Had the Son returned to heaven at the Crucifixion leaving His humanity on the Cross, the salvation of mankind would not have been won, the sentence of death would not have been reversed, we should be 'yet in our sins' (1 Cor. xv. 17). Moreover, in that case He would have ceased to be the Good Shepherd: He would have become like the hireling, casting aside his duty before it was completed. The office of the True Shepherd is not finished until all mankind become His flock; and this work continues from the Resurrection to the Day of Judgment.

18. οὐδεὶς αἴρει. *No* **one** *taketh it from Me;* not even God. See on *v.* 28. Two points are insisted on; (1) that the Death is entirely voluntary: this is stated both negatively and positively: see on i. 3; (2) that both Death and Resurrection are in accordance with a commission received from the Father. Comp. 'Father, into Thy hands I commend My spirit' (Luke xxiii. 46). The precise words used by the two Apostles of Christ's death bring this out very clearly; παρέδωκεν τὸ πνεῦμα (xix. 30); ἀφῆκεν τ. πν. (Matt. xxvii. 50). The ἐξέπνευσεν of S. Mark and S. Luke is less strong; but none use the simple ἀπέθανεν. Ἐγώ is emphatic; *but* **I** *lay it down of Myself.*

ἐξουσίαν ἔχω. *I have* **right**, authority, liberty: i. 12, v. 27, xvii. 2, xix. 10. This authority is the commandment of the Father: and hence this passage in no way contradicts the usual N.T. doctrine that Christ was raised to life again by the Father. Acts ii. 24.

τ. τ. ἐντολήν. The command to die and rise again, which He 'received' at the Incarnation. Comp. iv. 34, v. 30, vi. 38.

19—21. Opposite Results of the Teaching.

19. σχίσμα πάλιν ἐγ. *There* **arose** (i. 6) *a division* (vii. 43) *again among the Jews*, as among the Pharisees about the blind man (ix. 16), and among the multitude at the Feast of Tabernacles (vii. 43). Here we see that some even of the hostile party are impressed, and doubt the correctness of their position: comp. xi. 45.

τ. λόγους τ. *These words* or discourses (*sermones*), whereas *ῥήματα* (*v.* 21) are the separate *sayings* or utterances (*verba*): *τ. λόγους* is the larger expression.

20. δαιμ. ἔχει. See last note on viii. 48 and comp. vii. 20.

τί αὐ. ἀκ. They are uneasy at the impression produced by these discourses and seek to discredit their Author,—'poisoning the wells.'

δαιμονιζ. Of one possessed with a demon. See on iii. 34.

μὴ δ. δ. Surely a demon cannot: comp. x. 40. A demon might work a miracle, like the Egyptian magicians, but not so great and so beneficent a miracle as this (comp. ix. 16). But here they stop: they declare what He *cannot* be; they do not see, or will not admit, what He *must* be.

22—38. The Discourse at the Feast of the Dedication

Again we seem to have a gap in the narrative. Between *vv.* 21—22 (but see below) there is an interval of about two months; for the Feast of Tabernacles would be about the middle of October, and that of the Dedication towards the end of December. In this interval some would place Luke x. 1—xiii. 21. If this be correct, we may connect the sending out of the Seventy both with the Feast of Tabernacles and also with John x. 16. Seventy was the traditional number of the nations of the earth: and for the nations 70 bullocks were offered at the Feast of Tabernacles—13 on the first day, 12 on the second, 11 on the third, and so on. The Seventy were sent out to gather in the nations; for they were not forbidden, as the Twelve were, to go into the way of the Gentiles or to enter any city of the Samaritans (Matt. x. 5). The Twelve were primarily for the twelve tribes; the Seventy for the Gentiles. The words 'other sheep I have which are not of this fold; them also I must lead,' must have been spoken just before the mission of the Seventy.

Dr Westcott, on the strength of the strongly attested (B L 33 and the Thebaic and Armenian Versions) *ἐγένετο τότε τὰ ἐγκ.*, **At that time** *there took place the F. of the Dedication*, would connect chaps. ix. and x. 1—21 with this later Feast rather than with Tabernacles. In this case the interval of two months must be placed between chaps. viii. and ix.

Is it possible that *τὰ ἐγκαίνια* here means the Dedication of *Solomon's* Temple, which took place at the Feast of Tabernacles (1 Kings viii. 2;

2 Chr. v. 3)? If so, there is *no* gap in the narrative. Ἐγκαίνια is used in LXX. of the Dedication of the second Temple (Ezra vi. 16), and ἐγκαινίζω is used of the first Temple (1 K. viii. 63; 2 Chr. vii. 5). At the Feast of Tabernacles some commemoration of the establishment of a permanent centre of national worship would be natural.

22. ἐγένετο δὲ τ. ἐγκ. This is the reading of ℵ A D X and the bulk of MSS., with the Syriac and some old Latin texts: the best Latin texts have *neither* τότε nor δέ: the Memphitic gives both τότε and δέ. It is possible that -το δε produced τοτε. **Now there took place** *at Jerusalem the Feast of the Dedication:* see on ii. 13. The mention of a feast of so modern and local an origin and of 'Solomon's Porch' indicate a Jewish writer familiar with Jerusalem. The vivid description (χειμών, περιεπάτει, ἐκύκλωσαν, &c) and the firm grasp of the strained situation indicate an eyewitness. The Feast of Dedication might be celebrated anywhere, and the pointed insertion of 'at Jerusalem' seems to suggest that in the interval between *v.* 21 and *v.* 22 Christ had been away from the city. It was kept in honour of the purification and restoration of the Temple (B.C. 164) after its desecration by Antiochus Epiphanes; 1 Macc. i. 20—60, iv. 36—59 (note esp. *vv.* 36 and 59); 2 Macc. x. 1—8. Another name for it was 'the Lights,' or 'Feast of Lights,' from the illuminations with which it was celebrated. Christian dedication festivals are its lineal descendants.

χειμὼν ἦν. For the asyndeton (the καί of T. R. is not genuine) comp. ὥρα ἦν ὡς ἕκτη (iv. 6, xix. 14). Perhaps χειμὼν ἦν is to be connected with what follows rather than with what precedes: *It was winter, and Jesus was walking, &c.* Certainly the words explain why He was teaching under cover, and are not a mere note of time. We are in doubt whether they refer to the winter season (2 Tim. iv. 21), or to the stormy weather (Matt. xvi. 3; Acts xxvii. 20). The latter seems preferable. (1) The Feast of Dedication always began Kisleu 25th, i.e. late in December, so that there was no *need* to add 'it was winter,' although S. John might naturally state the fact for Gentile readers. (2) ἦν δὲ νύξ (xiii. 30) is almost certainly added to symbolize the moral darkness into which the traitor went out. Perhaps here also χειμὼν ἦν is added as symbolical of the storm of doubt, passion and hostility in the midst of which Christ was teaching. See on xviii. 1.

23. ἐν τ. στ. Σ.] This was a cloister or colonnade in the Temple-Courts, apparently on the east side. Tradition said that it was a part of the original building which had survived the various destructions. No such cloister is mentioned in the account of Solomon's Temple, and perhaps the name was derived from the wall against which it was built. It is mentioned again Acts iii. 11 and v. 12 as the recognised place of worship for the first disciples. Foundations still remaining may belong to it. For **ἱερόν** see on ii. 14, 19.

24. ἐκυκλ. οὖν] The Jews therefore compassed Him about (Luke xxi. 20; Hebr. xi. 30; Rev. xx. 9) *and* **kept saying** *to Him.* For change of tense comp. iv. 27, 30. They encircled Him in an urgent manner, indicating that they were determined to have an answer. 'Therefore' means 'because of the good opportunity.'

ἕως πότε κ.τ.λ.] *How long dost Thou excite our mind*, or **hold our mind in suspense?** *If Thou art the Christ tell us with openness* (see on vii. 13). They put a point-blank question, as the Sanhedrin do at the Passion (Luke xxii. 67). Their motives for urging this were no doubt mixed, and the same motive was not predominant in each case. Some were hovering between faith and hostility and (forgetting viii. 13) fancied that an explicit declaration from Him might help them. Others asked mainly out of curiosity: He had interested them greatly, and they wanted His own account of Himself. The worst wished for a plain statement which might form material for an accusation: they wanted Him to commit Himself.

25. εἶπον...πιστεύετε. The change of tense is significant: His declaration is past; their unbelief still continues. To a few, the woman at the well, the man born blind, and the Apostles, Jesus had explicitly declared Himself to be the Messiah; to all He had implicitly declared Himself by His works and teaching.

τὰ ἔργα. See on v. 20, 36: all the details of His Messianic work. Ἐγώ is an emphatic answer to the preceding *σύ* ('If *Thou* art the Christ'), and to the following *ὑμεῖς*: *ταῦτα* also is emphatic; 'the works which *I* do...*they*...but *ye* believe not.' For this retrospective use of *οὗτος* see on iii. 32.

27, 28. Note the simple but very impressive coupling of the clauses merely by *καί* and comp. *vv.* 3, 12. The series forms a climax and seems to fall into two triplets, as A. V., rather than three pairs.

27. 'I know Mine, and Mine know Me' (*v.* 14). Winer, p. 646.

28. δίδωμι. Not δώσω. Here as in iii. 15, v. 24 and often, the gift of eternal life is regarded as already possessed by the faithful. It is not a *promise*, the *fulfilment* of which depends upon man's conduct, but a *gift*, the *retention* of which depends upon ourselves.

οὐ μὴ ἀπόλ. εἰς τ. αἰ. Literally, *Shall certainly not perish for ever:* see on viii. 51. The negative belongs to *ἀπόλωνται*, not to *εἰς τ. αἰ.*, and the meaning is, *they shall never perish*, not 'they may perish, but shall not perish *eternally*:' comp. xi. 26; Rom. viii. 38, 39.

καὶ οὐχ ἁρπ. And no one shall snatch *them.* 'No *one*' rather than 'no *man*' (as in *v.* 18) for the powers of darkness are excluded as well as human seducers. 'Snatch' rather than 'pluck,' for it is the same word as is used of the wolf in *v.* 12, and this should be preserved in translation.

This passage in no way asserts the indefectibility of the elect, and gives no countenance to ultra-predestinarian views. Christ's sheep cannot be taken from Him *against their will;* but their will is free, and they may choose to leave the flock.

χειρός. "His hand protects, bears, cherishes, leads them" (Meyer).

29. δέδωκεν. See on iii. 35 and comp. xvii. 6, 24. **That which the Father hath given Me** *is greater than all.* The unity of the Church is invincible. But the reading is doubtful: **ὃ** *δ. μ.* **μεῖζον** has the most ancient authority (B[1], old Latin, Memphitic) and agrees with vi. 39, xvii. 2: the common reading, **ὃς** *δ. μ.* **μείζων**, and **ὁ** *δεδωκὼς μ.* **μείζων** (D), are obvious corrections: that of ℵL, **ὃ** *δ. μ.* **μείζων**, is impossible: that of AB[2]X, **ὃς** *δ. μ.* **μεῖζον**, is easy and may be right; *My Father who gave them to Me is* **a greater power** *than all* (comp. Matt. xii. 6).

ἐκ τ. χ. τ. πατρός] Emphatic repetition of *πατήρ*: *ἐκ τ. χ. αὐτοῦ* would have sufficed. 'The souls of the righteous are in the hand of God, and there shall no torment touch them' (Wisd. iii. 1): comp. Deut. xxxiii. 3; Isa. xlix. 2, li. 16.

30. ἐγὼ κ. ὁ π. ἕν ἐσμεν. *I and* **the** *Father are one;* **one Substance, not one Person** (*εἷς*). Comp. xvii. 22, 23, and contrast *ἅπαντες γὰρ ὑμεῖς* **εἷς** *ἐστε ἐν χρ.* 'I.,—'are one man, one conscious agent' (Gal. iii. 28); and *τοὺς δύο κτίσῃ ἐν ἑαυτῷ εἰς* **ἕνα** *καινὸν ἄνθρωπον* (Eph. ii. 15). Christ has just implied that His hand and the Father's hand are one, which implies that He and the Father are one; and this He now asserts. They are one in power, in will, and in action: this at the very least the words must mean; the Arian interpretation of mere moral agreement is inadequate. Whether or no Unity of Substance is actually stated here, it is certainly implied, as the Jews see. They would stone Him for making Himself God, which He would not have done had He not asserted or implied that He and the Father were one in Substance, not merely in will. And Christ does not correct them, as assuredly He would have done, had their animosity arisen out of a gross misapprehension of His words. Comp. Rev. xx. 6, xxii. 3. S. Augustine is therefore right in stating that *ἐσμέν* refutes Sabellius, who denied the distinction, while *ἕν* refutes Arius, who denied the equality, between the Father and the Son. Comp. Tert. *adv. Prax.* xxii.; Hippol. *c. Noet.* vii.

31. ἐβάστ. πάλιν. They prepare to act on Lev. xxiv. 16 (comp. 1 K. xxi. 10). *Πάλιν* refers to viii. 59, where we have *ἦραν* for *ἐβάστασαν*. The latter implies more effort; 'lifted up, bore:' but we cannot be sure whether it refers to raising from the ground or to carrying from a distance. The change from *ἵνα βάλωσιν ἐπ' αὐτόν* to *ἵνα λιθάσωσιν αὐτόν*, as from *ἦραν* to *ἐβάστασαν* may indicate that this was a more deliberate attempt to carry out the law of blasphemy. S. John uses the classical *λιθάζειν* (*vv.* 32, 33, xi. 8), whereas the Synoptists use the LXX. word *λιθοβολεῖν* (Matt. xxi. 35, xxiii. 37; Luke xiii. 34). In the Acts both words occur (v. 26, vii. 58).

32. ἀπεκρίθη. Just as the Jews 'answered' His act of cleansing the Temple (ii. 18), Jesus 'answered' their act of preparing to stone: comp. v. 17. The act in each case involved an assertion.

ἔργα καλά. Works morally beautiful, noble and excellent (*v.* 14). Comp. **καλῶς** *πάντα πεποίηκε* (Mark vii. 37) and *εἶδεν ὁ Θεὸς ὅτι* **καλόν** (Gen. i. 8, 10, 12, &c.). The noble works (v. 20, 36) proceed from the Father and are manifested by the Son.

ἔδειξα. Divine works are *exhibitions* of goodness, 'signs' of something above and beyond them.

διὰ ποῖον αὐ. ἔρ. Literally, *for what kind of work among these;* i.e. 'what is the character of the work for which ye are in the act of stoning me?' It was precisely the character of the works which shewed that they were Divine, as some of them were disposed to think (*v.* 21, vii. 26). Comp. Matt. xxii. 36, where the literal meaning is, 'what *kind* of a commandment is great in the law?,' and 1 Cor. xv. 35, 'with what *kind* of body do they come?' See on xii. 33, xviii. 32, xxi. 19. The ἐμέ is emphatic, 'Me, the Representative and Interpreter of the Father.' For the present tense see Winer, p. 332.

33. περὶ κ. ἔρ. Concerning *a good work:* 'That is not the subject-matter of our charge.' Comp. viii. 46, xvi. 8; 1 John ii. 2.

καὶ ὅτι. Καί is epexegetic, explaining wherein the blasphemy consisted: it does not introduce a second charge. See on viii. 53.

34—38. Christ answers a formal charge of blasphemy by a formal argument on the other side.

34. ἔστιν γεγραμμένον. See on ii. 17.

ἐν τ. νόμῳ ὑμ. As in xii. 34, xv. 25 'the Law' is used in its widest sense for the whole of O. T. In all three places the reference is to the Psalms: comp. Rom. iii. 19; 1 Cor. xiv. 21. Ὑμῶν means, 'for which you profess to have such a regard:' comp. viii. 17.

ἐγὼ εἶπα, θεοί ἐστε. The argument is both *à fortiori* and *ad hominem*. In the Scriptures (Ps. lxxxii. 6) even unjust rulers are called 'gods' on the principle of the theocracy, that rulers are the representatives of God (comp. Ex. xxii. 8). If this is admissible without blasphemy, how much more may He call Himself 'Son of God.'

35. εἰ ἐκ. εἶ. θ. Probably, *If* it *called them gods*, viz. the Law. 'Them' is left unexplained; a Jewish audience would at once know who were meant. But how incredible that any but a Jew should think of such an argument, or put it in this brief way! These last eight verses alone are sufficient to discredit the theory that this Gospel is the work of a Greek Gnostic in the second century.

ὁ λόγος τ. θ. Practically the same as 'the Scripture;' i.e. the word of God in these passages of Scripture. The Word in the theological sense for the Son is not meant: this term appears nowhere in the narrative part of S. John's Gospel. But of course it was through the Word, not yet incarnate, that God revealed His will to His people.

οὐ δ. λυθῆναι. Literally, 'cannot be undone' or 'unloosed.' The same word is rendered 'unloose' (i. 27), 'destroy' (ii. 19; 1 John iii. 8), 'break' (v. 18 and vii. 23), 'loose' (xi. 44). i. 27 and xi. 44 are literal, of actual unbinding; the others are figurative, of dissolution or unbinding as a form of destruction. Here either metaphor, dissolution or unbinding, would be appropriate; either, 'cannot be explained away, made to mean nothing;' or, 'cannot be deprived of its binding authority.' The latter seems better. The clause depends upon 'if,' and is not parenthetical; 'if the Scripture cannot be broken.' As in ii. 22, xvii. 12, xx. 9, *ἡ γραφή* probably means a definite passage. Comp. vii. 38, 42, xiii. 18, xvii. 12, xix. 24, 28, 36, 37. Scripture as a whole is called *αἱ γραφαί*; v. 39.

36. ὃν ὁ π. ἡγ. *Of Him whom the Father* **sanctified**: in emphatic opposition to 'them unto whom the word of God came.' Men on whom God's word has conferred a fragment of delegated authority may be called 'gods' (Elohim) without scruple; He, whom the Father Himself sanctified and sent, may not be called **Son of God** (no article before 'Son') without blasphemy. By 'sanctified' is meant something analogous to the consecration of Jeremiah before his birth for the work of a Prophet (Jer. i. 5). Comp. Ecclus. xlv. 4 (Moses), xlix. 7 (Jeremiah); 1 Macc. i. 25 (the Chosen People). When the Son was sent into the world He was consecrated for the work of the Messiah, and endowed with the fulness of grace and truth (see on i. 14), the fulness of power (iii. 35), the fulness of life (v. 26). In virtue of this Divine sanctification He becomes 'the Holy One of God' (vi. 69; Luke iv. 34). See on xvii. 17, 19, the only other passages in S. John's writings where the word occurs.

ὑμεῖς λέγετε. *Ὑμεῖς*, with great emphasis; 'Do *ye*, in opposition to the Scripture, dare to say?'

37, 38. Having met their technical charge in a technical manner He now justifies the assertion of His unity with the Father by an appeal to His works. *Deum non vides, tamen Deum agnoscis ex operibus ejus* (Cicero).

37. εἰ οὐ ποιῶ. Not *εἰ* **μή**, because the negative belongs to *ποιῶ*, not to the sentence; *if I omit to do:* iii. 12, v. 47; Rev. xx. 15. Comp. Soph. *Ajax*, 1131. Winer, pp. 599, 600.

μὴ πιστ. μοι. A literal command: if His works are not those which His Father works, they *ought* not (not merely have no *need*) even to believe what He says (see on vi. 30), much less believe *on* Him (see on i. 12). Comp. v. 24, 46, viii. 31, 45, xiv. 11. His works are His Father's (ix. 3, xiv. 10).

38. τ. ἔργοις π. 'Blessed are they that have not seen and yet have believed' (xx. 29); but it is better to have the faith that comes with sight than none at all. Thus we have four stages: 1. believing the works; 2. believing Him on account of the works (xiv. 11); 3. believing on Him (viii. 30); 4. abiding in His word (viii. 31).

The true position of miracles among the Evidences of Christianity is clearly stated here and xiv. 11. They are not primary, as Paley would have it, but secondary and auxiliary. Christ's doctrine bears the evidence of its Divine origin in itself.

ἵνα γνῶτε κ. γινώσκητε. *That ye may* **come to know and continually know**; attain to knowledge and advance in knowledge in contrast to their state of suspense (*v.* 24): the aorist denotes the single act, the present the permanent growth. The apparent awkwardness of having the same verb twice in the same clause has probably caused a large number of authorities to substitute *πιστεύσητε* in the second case. But the change of tense is full of meaning, especially in reference to the Jews. Many of them attained to a momentary conviction that He was the Messiah (ii. 23, vi. 14, 15, vii. 41, viii. 30, x. 42, xi. 45); very few of them went beyond a transitory conviction (ii. 24, vi. 66, viii. 31).

κἀγὼ ἐν τ. πατρί. An instance of the solemnity and emphasis derived from repetition so frequent in this Gospel.

39—42. Opposite Results of the Discourse

39. ἐζήτουν οὖν πάλιν. Both *οὖν* and *πάλιν* are of somewhat uncertain authority: the termination of *ἐζήτουν* might cause the omission of *οὖν*. *Πάλιν* refers to vii. 30, 32, 44, and shews that *πιάσαι* (see on vii. 30) means 'arrest Him' for the Sanhedrin, not 'take Him' and stone Him.

ἐξῆλθεν ἐκ. Went forth out of. There being nothing in the text to shew that His departure was miraculous, it is safest (as in viii. 59, where also *ἐξῆλθεν ἐκ* occurs) to suppose that there was no miracle. He withdrew through the less hostile among those who encircled Him, while the others were making up their minds how to apprehend Him. The majesty of innocence suffices to protect Him, His hour not having come. They cannot snatch His sheep out of His hand (*v.* 28), but He goes forth out of their hand.

40—42. "The chapter ends with a note of place which is evidently and certainly historical. No forger would ever have thought of the periphrasis 'where John at first baptized'...'John did no miracle: but all things that John spake of this man were true.' It would be impossible to find a stronger incidental proof that the author of the Gospel had been originally a disciple of the Baptist, or at least his contemporary, and also that he is writing of things that he had heard and seen. A Gnostic, writing in Asia Minor, even though he had come into relation with disciples of John, would not have introduced the Baptist in this way. In circles that had been affected by the Baptist's teaching, and were hesitating whether they should attach themselves to Jesus, this is precisely the sort of comment that would be heard" (Sanday).

40. πάλιν π. τ. 'Ι. Referring back to i. 28. The hostility of the hierarchy being invincible and becoming more and more dangerous, Jesus retires into Peraea for quiet and safety before His Passion. This interval was between three and four months, from the latter part of December to the middle of April. Comp. Matt. xix. 1; Mark x. 1. But some portion of this time was spent at Ephraim (xi. 54) after going to Bethany in Judaea to raise Lazarus. Nothing is told us as to how much time was given to Bethany or Bethabara in Peraea, how much to Ephraim.

τὸ πρῶτον. John afterwards baptized at Aenon (iii. 23).

41. πολλοὶ ἦλθον. The harvest (iv. 35—38). The testimony of the Baptist, and perhaps the miraculous voice at Christ's Baptism, were still remembered there. Since then there had been the mission of the Seventy and Christ's own work in Galilee.

ἔλεγον. Kept saying or *used to say:* it was a common remark.

σ. ἐποίησεν οὐδέν. This is indirect evidence of the genuineness of the miracles recorded of Christ. It is urged that if Jesus had wrought no miracles, they would very possibly have been attributed to Him after His death. Let us grant this; and at the same time it must be granted that the same holds good to a very great extent of the Baptist. The enthusiasm which he awakened, as a Prophet appearing after a weary interval of four centuries, was immense. Miracles would have been eagerly believed of him, the second Elijah, and would be likely enough to be attributed to him. But more than half a century after his death we have one of his own disciples *quite incidentally* telling us that 'John did *no* sign;' and there is no rival tradition to the contrary. *All* traditions attribute miracles to Jesus.

ἐκεῖ. Last for emphasis. *There,* in contrast to Jerusalem which had rejected Him, *many believed on Him* (i. 12), not merely believed His words (*vv.* 37, 38).

CHAPTER XI

19. πολλοὶ δέ for *καὶ πολλοί* (A), and **τὴν** for *τὰς περὶ* (AC³); both on overwhelming evidence.

21. οὐκ ἂν ἀπέθανεν ὁ ἀδελφός μου for *ὁ ἀδ. μ. οὐκ ἂν ἐτεθνήκει.*

39. τετελευτηκότος for *τεθνηκότος,* with all the best MSS.

41. Omit *οὗ ἦν ὁ τεθνηκὼς κείμενος* (explanatory gloss) after **λίθον.**

45. Omit *ὁ Ἰησοῦς* after **ἐποίησεν**: comp. iv. 16, 46, vi. 14, viii. 21.

50. λογίζεσθε (ℵABDL) for *διαλογίζεσθε.* The compound is very frequent in the Synoptists.

51. ἐπροφήτευσεν for *προεφήτευσεν* (correction to usual form). In N.T. the better MSS. place the augment before the preposition (Matt. vii. 22, xi. 13, xv. 7; Mark vii. 6; Luke i. 67; Acts xix. 6): Jude 14 is possibly an exception. Winer, p. 84.

ἤμελλεν for *ἔμελλεν*: comp. iv. 47, xii. 33, xviii. 32. In vi. 71 *ἔμελλεν* is better attested: comp. *ἐδύνατο* in *v.* 37. Winer, p. 82.

54. ἔμεινεν (ℵBL), S. John's favourite word, is probably to be preferred to *διέτριβεν* (AD from iii. 22?)

57. ἐντολάς for *ἐντολήν*, with ℵBI^aM against AD.

CHAP. XI. CHRIST IS LOVE ILLUSTRATED BY A SIGN

Christ's love for His friends brings about His own death and shews the voluntariness (*v.* 8) of His death, as declared x. 18. Expressions of affection and tenderness abound in the chapter; comp. *vv.* 3, 5, 11, 15, 35, 36.

We have now reached 'the culminating point of the miraculous activity of our Lord,' and at the same time the 'crucial question' of this Gospel—the Raising of Lazarus. Various objections have been urged against it, and through it against the Fourth Gospel as a whole. The principal objections require notice. They are based (1) on the extraordinary character of the miracle itself; (2) on the silence of the Synoptists; (3) on the fact that in spite of what is narrated *vv.* 47—53, no mention is made of the miracle in the accusation of Jesus.

(1) The extraordinary character of the miracle is a difficulty of modern growth. By the writers of N. T. raising the dead was regarded as on the same level with other miracles, not as something quite apart from all others. And surely the ancient view is both more reverent and more philosophical than the modern one. Only from a purely human standpoint can one miracle be regarded as more wonderful, i.e. more difficult of performance, than another. To Omnipotence all miracles, as indeed all works, are equal: distinctions of difficult and easy as applied to the Almighty are meaningless.

(2) It is certainly surprising that the Synoptists do not mention this miracle, all the more so because S. John tells us that it was the proximate cause of Christ's arrest and condemnation. But this surprising circumstance has been exaggerated. It seems too much to say that "it must always remain a mystery why this miracle, transcending as it does all other miracles which the Lord wrought,...should have been passed over by the three earlier Evangelists." Two considerations go a long way towards explaining the mystery. (i) The Synoptical Gospels, though three in number, in the main represent only one tradition, and that *a very fragmentary tradition*. That fragmentary testimony should omit important facts is not surprising; and that out of three writers who make use of this defective evidence not one should in this important instance have supplied the deficiency, is not more than surprising. (ii) The Synoptists, until they reach the last Passover, omit almost all events in or near Jerusalem: the ministry in Galilee is their province. The omission of this raising by them is very little more strange than the omission of the other raisings by John. Each side keeps to its own scheme of narration.

To explain that the Synoptists were silent in order not to draw attention, and perhaps persecution (xii. 10, 11), on Lazarus and his sisters, whereas when S. John wrote they were dead (just as S. John alone records that it was S. Peter who cut off the high-priest's servant's ear), is not very satisfactory. There is no evidence that Lazarus and his sisters were living when the first Gospel was written, still less when S. Luke wrote. And if they were alive, were the chief priests alive, and their animosity still alive also?

(3) This last objection really tells in favour of the narrative. The hierarchy would have stood self-condemned if they had made His raising the dead a formal charge against Christ. The disciples had fled, and could not urge the miracle in His favour; and Christ Himself would not break the majestic silence which He maintained before His accusers to mention such a detail.

There are those who assume that miracles are impossible, and that no amount of evidence can render a miracle credible. This miracle is therefore dismissed, and we are to believe either that (1) Lazarus was only *apparently dead*, i.e. that Christ was an impostor and S. John a dupe or an accomplice; or that (2) the *parable* of Lazarus and Dives has been *transformed* into a miracle; or that (3) the narrative is a *myth*, or (4) an *allegory*. (1) and (2) only need to be stated: of (3) and (4) we may say with Meyer, "No narrative of the N. T. bears so completely the stamp of being the very opposite of a later invention... And what an incredible height of art in the allegorical construction of history must we ascribe to the composer!" Instead of an historical miracle we have a literary miracle of the second century. Contrast this chapter with the miracles of the Apocryphal Gospels, and it will seem impossible that both can have come from the same source. To tear out this or any other page from S. John, and retain the rest, is quite inadmissible. "The Gospel is like that sacred coat 'without seam woven from the top throughout:' it is either all real and true or all fictitious and illusory; and the latter alternative is more difficult to accept than the miracle" (Sanday).

1—33. The Prelude to the Sign

1. ἦν δέ τις ἀσθ. Once more we note the touching simplicity of the narrative. The δέ is perhaps 'but' rather than 'now': it introduces a contrast to what precedes. Christ went into Peraea for retirement, but the sickness of Lazarus interrupted it. And thus once more the Lord's repose is broken. Nicodemus breaks the quiet of the night (iii. 2); the Samaritan woman interrupts the rest beside the well (iv. 7); the importunate multitude invade the mountain solitude (vi. 5); and now His friend's death summons Him from His retreat in Peraea. In all the claims of His Father's work are paramount.

Λάζαρος. The theory that this narrative is a parable transformed into a miracle possibly represents something like the reverse of the fact. The parable of Dives and Lazarus was apparently spoken about this time, i.e. between the Feast of Dedication and the last Passover, and it may possibly have been suggested by this miracle. In no other parable does Christ introduce a proper name. Some would identify Lazarus of Bethany with the rich young ruler (Matt. xix. 16; Mark x. 17; Luke xviii. 18), and also with the young man clad in a linen cloth who followed Jesus in the Garden after the disciples had fled (Mark xiv. 51; see note there). The name Lazarus is an abbreviated Greek form of Eleazar='God is my help.' It is commonly assumed without much evidence that he was younger than his sisters: S. Luke's silence about him (x. 38, 39) agrees well with this.

Βηθανίας. A small village on the S.E. slope of the Mount of Olives, about two miles from Jerusalem (see on Matt. xxi. 9).

ἐκ τ. κώμης. Acts xxiii. 34 and Rev. ix. 18 shew that no distinction can be drawn between *ἀπό* and *ἐκ* either here or i. 45, as that *ἀπό* refers to residence and *ἐκ* to birthplace. Comp. Luke xxi. 18 with Acts xxvii. 34. But the change of preposition should be preserved in translation; **of** *Bethany*, **from** *the* **village** *of Mary*. *Κώμη* is used of Bethlehem (vii. 42), and in conjunction with *πόλις* (Luke xiii. 22). It is an elastic word; but its general meaning is 'village' rather than anything larger. Mary is here mentioned first, although apparently the younger sister (Luke x. 28), because the incident mentioned in the next verse had made her better known. They are introduced as well-known persons, like the Twelve (vi. 67), Pilate (xviii. 29), and Mary Magdalene (xix. 25). They would seem to have been people of position from the village being described as their abode (to distinguish it from the other Bethany in Peraea, to which Christ had just gone). The guests at the funeral (*vv.* 31, 45), the feast, the family burying-place (*v.* 38), and Mary's costly offering (xii. 2, 3), point in the same direction.

2. **ἦν δὲ M. ἡ ἀλείψασα. Now Mary was she** *that anointed;* or, **Now it was (the) Mary** *that anointed.* This of course does not necessarily imply that the anointing had already taken place, as those who identify Mary with the 'sinner' of Luke vii. 37 would insist: it merely implies that when S. John wrote, this fact was well known about her, as Christ had promised should be the case (Matt. xxvi. 13). S. John tells two facts omitted in the earlier Gospels; (1) that the village of Martha and Mary was Bethany, (2) that the anointing at Bethany was Mary's act. The identification of Mary of Bethany with the *ἁμαρτωλός* of Luke vii. is altogether at variance with what S. Luke and S. John tell us of her character. Nor is there any sufficient reason for identifying either of them with Mary Magdalene. Mary of Bethany, Mary of Magdala, and the 'sinner' of Luke vii. are three distinct persons.

3. **ἀπέστειλαν οὖν.** This shews that *v.* 2 ought not to be made a parenthesis; 'therefore' refers to the previous statement. Because of the intimacy, which every one who knew of the anointing would understand, the sisters sent. Note that they are not further described; S. John has said enough to tell his readers who are meant: but would not a forger have introduced them with more description?

κύριε, ἴδε ὃν φ. ἀσθ. Exquisite in its tender simplicity. The message implies a belief that Christ could cure a dangerous sickness, and no doubt (*vv.* 21, 32) would heal His friend. *Sufficit ut noveris. Non enim amas et deseris* (S. Augustine). Thus of the seven typical miracles with which S. John illustrates the Lord's ministry, the last, like the first, has its scene in the family circle. Like His Mother

(ii. 3), the sisters state the trouble, and leave the rest to Him: and here, as there, He at first seems to refuse what He afterwards grants in abundance. On ἴδε see on i. 29; on φιλεῖς *v.* 5, v. 20.

4. εἶπεν. Not ἀπεκρίθη: His words are not a mere answer to the message, but a lesson to the Apostles also.

οὐκ ἔστιν πρὸς θ. Is not to have death as its final result: for 'He Himself knew what He would do' (vi. 6). Christ foresaw both the death and the resurrection, and (as so often) uttered words which His disciples did not understand at the time, but recognised in their proper meaning after what He indicated had taken place. Comp. ii. 22, xii. 16, xxi. 23.

ἵνα δοξασθῇ. In two ways; because the miracle (1) would lead many to believe that He was the Messiah; (2) would bring about His death. Δοξάζεσθαι is a frequent expression of this Gospel for Christ's Death regarded as the mode of His return to glory (vii. 39, xii. 16, 23, xiii. 31, 32); and this glorification of the Son involves the glory of the Father (v. 23, x. 30, 38). Comp. ix. 3; in the Divine counsels the *purpose* of the man's blindness and of Lazarus' sickness is the glory of God.

We ought perhaps to connect the special meaning of 'glorified' with the first clause: 'This sickness is to have for its final issue, not the temporal death of an individual, but the eternal life of all mankind.'

It is worth noting that both the first and the last of the seven miracles of the ministry recorded by S. John are declared to be manifestations of glory (ii. 11, xi. 4, 40) and confirmations of faith (ii. 11, xi. 15).

δι' αὐτῆς, i.e. διὰ τ. ἀσθενείας, not διὰ τ. δόξης τ. Θεοῦ.

5. ἠγάπα. The loss involved here, and still more in xxi. 15—17, in translating both ἀγαπᾶν and φιλεῖν by 'love' cannot be remedied satisfactorily. Φιλεῖν (*amare*) denotes a passionate, emotional warmth, which loves and does not care to ask why; the affection which is based on natural relationship, as of parents, brothers, lovers, and the like. Ἀγαπᾶν (*diligere*) denotes a calm discriminating attachment, which loves because of the excellence of the loved object; the affection which is based on esteem, as of friends. Φιλεῖν is the stronger, but less reasoning; ἀγαπᾶν the more earnest, but less intense. The sisters naturally use the more emotional word (*v.* 3), describing their own feeling towards their brother; the Evangelist equally naturally uses the loftier and less impulsive word. The fact that the sisters are here included is not the reason for the change of expression. Both words are used of the love of the Father to the Son; φιλεῖν (v. 20), because the love is founded on relationship; ἀγαπᾶν (iii. 35, x. 17, xv. 9, xvii. 23, 24, 26), because of the character of the love.

τ. Μάρθαν κ.τ.λ. The names are probably in order of age. This and *v.* 19 confirm what is almost certain from Luke x. 38, that Martha is the elder sister. The separate mention of each of the three is touching and impressive.

6. ὡς οὖν ἤκουσεν. The connexion is a little difficult. Οὖν after the statement in *v.* 5 prepares us for a departure instead of a delay: 'He loved them; when therefore He heard......He set out immediately.' But perhaps it means that His love for them made Him delay until the time when His coming would do them most good. Or οὖν may lead on to *v.* 7, and then we must place only a semicolon at the end of *v.* 6. **When therefore He heard that he is sick, at that time indeed** *He abode two days in the place where He was; then after this He saith,* &c. The δέ after ἔπειτα, anticipated by τότε μέν, is felt, though not expressed: ἔπειτα in part supplies the place of δέ as in James iii. 17. Comp. xix. 32, Luke viii. 5, 6, where μέν is followed by a simple καί.—Μὲν...ἔπειτα and μὲν...καί are not rare in classical Greek. Winer, p. 720.

7. ἔπειτα μ. τ. See on iii. 22. The fulness of this expression emphasizes the length of the delay, so trying to the sisters, and perhaps to Jesus Himself. Winer, p. 754. But His life was a perfect fulfilment of the Preacher's rule; 'To everything there is a season, and a time to every purpose under heaven' (Eccl. iii. 1; comp. *v.* 9, ii. 4). There was a Divine plan, in conformity with which He worked.

εἰς τ. Ἰ. πάλιν. The πάλιν refers us back to x. 40. His using the general term, Judaea, instead of Bethany, leads to the disciples' reply. Judaea was associated with hostility, Bethany with love and friendship. Perhaps He wishes to prepare the disciples for the consequences of a return to Judaea.

8. Ῥαββί, νῦν κ.τ.λ. **Rabbi** (see on iv. 31) **just now** *the Jews* **were seeking** *to stone Thee* (x. 31) *and* **art Thou going** *thither again?* 'Again' is emphatic. For νῦν comp. xxi. 10.

9. οὐχὶ δώδεκα. As so often, Christ gives no direct answer to the question asked, but a general principle, involving the answer to the question. Comp. ii. 6, 19, iii. 5, 10, iv. 13, 21, vi. 32, 53, viii. 7, 25, 54, x. 25. The meaning seems to be, 'Are there not twelve working-hours in which a man may labour without fear of stumbling? I have not yet reached the end of My working-day, and so can safely continue the work I came to do. The night cometh, when I can no longer work; but it has not yet come.' Comp. ix. 4. Thus it is practically equivalent to 'Mine hour is not yet come;' it is still right for Him to work: but the figure here adopted is of wider application, and contains a moral for the disciples and all Christians as well as an application to Christ; 'Add nothing and lose nothing, but use the time that is allowed.' The expression throws no light on S. John's method of reckoning time. See on xix. 14.

προσκόπτει. Knock one's foot against; *offendere.*

τὸ φῶς τ. κ. τ. The sun: the words were spoken just before the departure, which probably took place at dawn.

10. ἐν τῇ νυκτί. Christ's night came when His hour came (xvii. 1). Then the powers of darkness prevailed (Luke xxii. 53) and His enemies became a stumbling-block in His path, bringing His work to a close (xix. 30).

τ. φῶς οὐκ ἔστιν. The light is not *in him.* This shews that the meaning has slid from the literal to the figurative. Τὸ φῶς in *v.* 9 is the physical light in the heavens; here it is the spiritual light in the heart. Comp. 1 John ii. 10, 11.

11. μετὰ τοῦτο. Perhaps indicates a pause. See on iii. 22.

Λ. ὁ φίλος ἡμ. κεκ. Lazarus, our friend, is fallen asleep. Equal in tender simplicity to the message (*v.* 3). Sleep as an image of death is common from the dawn of literature; but the Gospel has raised the expression from a figure to a fact. Paganism called death a sleep to conceal its nature; the Lord does so to reveal its nature. 'A poetic euphemism has become a gracious truth. Comp. Matt. xxvii. 52; Acts vii. 50, xiii. 36; 1 Cor. vii. 39, xi. 30, xv. 6, 18; 1 Thess. iv. 13; 2 Pet. iii. 4. The thoroughly Christian term 'cemetery' (=sleeping-place) in the sense of a place of repose for the dead comes from the same root. The exact time of Lazarus' death cannot be determined, for we do not know how long Christ took in reaching Bethany. Christ calls him '*our* friend,' as claiming the sympathy of the disciples, who had shewn unwillingness to return to Judaea.

ἵνα ἐξ. This shews that no messenger has come to announce the death. Christ sees the death as He foresees the resurrection (*v.* 4).

12. εἶπον οὖν αὐ. οἱ μ. The disciples therefore *said to Him;*— catching at any chance of escape from the dreaded journey. They accept it as quite natural that Jesus should *know* that Lazarus sleeps, and perhaps they think that He has caused the sleep. This slight touch is strong proof of their belief in His power.

εἰ κεκ., σωθήσεται. If he is fallen asleep, he shall be saved. The word *σωθήσεται* is perhaps purposely chosen as being capable of a spiritual meaning. The whole narrative is symbolical of spiritual death and resurrection; and S. John perhaps intimates that the disciples, like Caiaphas (*v.* 50), spoke more truth than they themselves knew. Of course they mean, 'He will recover.' Comp. *Ajax*, 263,

ἀλλ' εἰ πέπαυται, κάρτ' ἂν εὐτυχεῖν δοκῶ.

Their first thought probably was that Jesus meant to go and cure Lazarus; and now they think that he will recover without His going, and that therefore He need not go. The A.V. reads like an expostulation against waking Lazarus, as if it meant 'a sick man should not be disturbed': but they are too full of anxiety about *πορεύομαι* to notice *ἵνα ἐξυπνίσω αὐτόν*. It is the going, not the wakening, that perturbs them. For other instances in which the disciples grossly misunderstand Christ, see iv. 33, xiv. 5, 8, 22; Matt. xvi. 7; and comp. iii. 4, 9, iv. 11, 15, vi. 34, 52, vii. 35, viii. 22, 33, 52. This candour in declaring their own failings adds to our confidence in the veracity of the Evangelists. It is urged that the misunderstanding here is too gross to be probable: but they had not unnaturally understood Christ

Himself to have declared that Lazarus would not die (*v.* 4); this being so, they could not easily suppose that by sleep He meant death. Moreover, when men's minds are on the stretch the strangest misapprehensions become possible.

13. τ. κοιμ. τ. ὕπν. Recalling *κεκοίμηται* and *ἐξυπνίσω* in *v.* **11.**

14. τότε οὖν. Then therefore *said Jesus*. Here, as in Rom. vi. 21, A.V. makes 'then' cover both *τότε* and *οὖν*, 'then' of time, and 'then' of consequence.

παρρησίᾳ. Without metaphor: see on vii. 13.

Λαζ. ἀπέθανεν. The abruptness is startling. Contrast the aorist *ἀπέθανεν*, which indicates the *moment* of transition from life to death, with the perfect *κεκοίμηται*, which indicates the *state* of rest which has begun and continues.

15. χαίρω. Christ rejoices, not at His friend's death, but at His own absence from the scene, for the disciples' sake. Had He been there, Lazarus would not have died, and the disciples would have lost this great sign of His Messiahship.

ἵνα πιστεύσητε. S. John's favourite construction, indicating the Divine purpose: see on ix. 2, 3. Would any forger have written this? Would it not seem utterly improbable that at the close of His ministry Christ should still be working in order that Apostles might believe? Yet S. John, who heard the words, records them, and he knew from sad experience (Mark xiv. 50, xvi. 11; Luke xxiv. 11, 21) that this work was not superfluous. Just before the trial of faith which His Passion and Death would bring to them, His disciples had need of all the help and strength that He could give. See on ii. 11.

ἀλλὰ ἄγωμεν. He breaks off suddenly. *Πρὸς αὐτόν* is significant; not to the mourning sisters, but to the sleeping friend.

16. Θωμᾶς, ὁ λ. Δ. S. John thrice (xx. 24, xxi. 2) reminds his readers that Thomas is the same as he whom Gentile Christians called Didymus; just as he interprets *Μεσσίας* (iv. 25). Thomas is Hebrew, Didymus is Greek, for a twin. In all probability he was a twin, *possibly* of S. Matthew, with whom he is coupled in all three lists of the Apostles in the Gospels: in the Acts he is coupled with S. Philip. That S. Thomas received his name from Christ (as Simon was called Peter, and the sons of Zebedee Boanerges) in consequence of his character, is pure conjecture. But the coincidence between the name and his twin-mindedness (James i. 8, iv. 8) is remarkable. "In him the twins, unbelief and faith, were contending with one another for mastery, as Esau and Jacob in Rebecca's womb" (Trench). It is from S. John that we know his character: in the Synoptists and the Acts he is a mere name (see on i. 41). Not that S. John purposely sketches his character; the notices are too brief and too scattered for that. But the character shines through the lifelike narrative. He seems to have combined devotion to Christ with a tendency to see the dark side of everything. S. John's care in distinguishing him by his Gentile name adds point to the argument derived from his never distinguishing John as the Baptist (see on i. 6).

συμμαθηταῖς. The word occurs here only; perhaps it indicates that they shared his feelings. It has been remarked that S. Thomas would scarcely have taken the lead in this way had S. Peter been present, and that had S. Peter been there he would probably have appeared in the previous dialogue. If he was absent, we have an additional reason for the absence of this miracle from S. Mark's Gospel, the Gospel of S. Peter, and undoubtedly the representative of the oldest form of the Synoptic narrative.

μετ' αὐτοῦ. Of course with Christ (*v.* 8). It is strange that any should understand it of Lazarus. They could not die with him, for he was dead already, and S. Thomas knew this (*v.* 14). 'The Hope of Israel is going to certain death; there is nothing left for us but to share it.' The words fitly close a section, of which the prevailing thought is death.

17. εὗρεν, i.e. on enquiry: comp. i. 44, v. 14, ix. 35. It would seem as if Christ's miraculous power of knowing without the ordinary means of information was not in constant activity, but like His other miraculous powers was employed only on fitting occasions. It was necessary to His work that He should know of Lazarus' death; it was not necessary that He should know how long he had been buried, nor where he had been buried (*v.* 34). Comp. i. 48, iv. 18, ix. 35, xviii. 34. Thus Peter's prison-gate opens 'of its own accord;' Mary's house-door, which Rhoda could open, does not (Acts xii. 10—16).

τέσσ. ἡμ. No doubt he had been buried the day he died, as is usual in hot climates where decomposition is rapid; moreover, he had died of a malignant disease, probably a fever. Jehu ordered Jezebel to be buried a few hours after death (2 Kings ix. 34); Ananias and Sapphira were buried at once (Acts v. 6, 10). If Christ started just after Lazarus died, as seems probable, the journey had occupied four days. This fits in well with the conclusion that Bethabara or Bethany was in the north of Palestine, possibly a little south of the sea of Galilee; near Galilee it must have been (comp. i. 28, 29, 43). But on the other hand Lazarus may have died soon after Christ heard of his illness; in which case the journey occupied barely two days.

ἐν τ. μνημείῳ. *In the* **tomb**. Our translators use three different English words for *μνημεῖον*; 'grave' in this chapter, v. 28; Matt. xxvii. 52, &c.; 'tomb' Matt. viii. 28; Mark v. 2, vi. 29, &c.; 'sepulchre' of Christ's resting-place. *Τάφος*, used by S. Matthew only, is rendered 'tomb' xxiii. 29, and 'sepulchre' xxiii. 27, xxvii. 61, 64, 66, xxviii. 1. 'Tomb' being reserved for *μνημεῖον*, *τάφος* might be rendered 'sepulchre.'

18. ἦν δὲ ἡ B. *Ἦν need* not imply that when S. John wrote Bethany had been destroyed, but this is the more probable meaning; especially as no other Evangelist speaks of places in the past tense, and S. John does not always do so. The inference is that he wrote after the destruction of Jerusalem; and that what was destroyed in the siege he speaks of in the past tense; *e. g.* Bethany (here), the Garden of Gethsemane (xviii. 1), Joseph's garden (xix. 41), what was not destroyed, in the present tense; *e. g.* Bethesda (*v.* 2, where see note).

ὡς ἀπὸ σταδ. δεκαπ. A Greek stade is 18 yards less than an English furlong; but the translation is sufficiently accurate, like 'firkin' (ii. 6). This distance, therefore, was under two miles, and is mentioned to account for the many Jews who came to condole with the sisters; and also to point out the dangerous proximity into which Jesus now entered. For the ἀπό comp. xxi. 8; Rev. xiv. 20: in all three cases the preposition seems to have got out of place. We should have expected ὡς σταδίους δ. ἀπὸ Ἱεροσολύμων, as in Luke xxiv. 13. Comp. πρὸ ἓξ ἡμερῶν τοῦ πάσχα (xii. 1); and *ante diem tertium Kal. Mart.* for *tertio die ante Kal. Mart.* Or possibly the distance is looked at in the reverse way: Winer, p. 697.

19. ἐκ τῶν Ἰ. **From among** *the Jews.* 'The Jews,' as usual, are the hostile party: among the numerous acquaintances of the sisters were many of the opponents of Jesus. This visit was yet another opportunity for them to believe.

ἐλ. πρὸς τὴν Μ. κ. Μ. *Had come to M. and M.* Some good authorities support T. R. in reading πρὸς τὰς περὶ Μ. κ. Μ., 'to M. and M. *and their friends.*' Comp. οἱ περὶ τὸν Παῦλον, Paul and his companions, Acts xiii. 13.

παραμυθήσωνται. 'The empty chaff' of conventional consolation which so moved the spirit of Jesus (*v.* 33). It formed a barrier between Him and the sorrow which He alone could console. Jewish ceremonial required that many (ten at least) should come and condole. Gen. xxvii. 35; comp. 2 Sam. xii. 17; Job ii. 11. It is said that the usual period of mourning was thirty days; three of weeping, seven of lamentation, twenty of sorrow. But the instances in Scripture vary: Jacob, seventy days with an additional seven (Gen. l. 3, 10); Aaron and Moses, thirty days (Numb. xx. 29; Deut. xxxiv. 8); Saul and Judith, seven days (1 Sam. xxviii. 13; Jud. xvi. 24; comp. Ecclus. xxii. 12; 2 Esdr. v. 20). Josephus tells us that Archelaus mourned for his father seven days, and the Jews for himself, thirty days (*B. J.* II. i. 1; III. ix. 5). The Mishna prescribes seven days for near relations.

20. ἡ οὖν Μάρθα. *Martha* **therefore.** As in Luke x. 40, she takes the lead in entertaining, while Mary shrinks from it; and she was probably now engaged in some duty of this kind. As elder sister, and apparently mistress of the house (Luke x. 38), information would naturally come to her first. Without waiting to tell her sister she hurries out to meet Jesus. It is incredible that the coincidence between S. John and S. Luke as regards the characters of the sisters should be either fortuitous or designed. It is much easier to believe that both give us facts about real persons.

ἔρχεται. *Is coming;* the exact word of the message. They were perhaps still looking for His arrival, although they believed that it was now too late for Him to aid. Unwilling to mingle at once in the crowd of conventional mourners, He halts outside the village.

ἐκαθέζετο. The attitude of sorrow and meditation (Job ii. 13). She does not know of Christ's approach (*vv.* 28, 29): Martha, in discharging the duties of hospitality to fresh arrivals, would be more likely to hear of it.

21. εἰ ἦς ὧδε, κ.τ.λ. Not a reproach, however gentle (she does not say 'hadst Thou *come*'), but an expression of deep regret. This thought had naturally been often in the sisters' minds during the last four days (comp. *v.* 32). They believe that Christ could and would have healed Lazarus: their faith and hope are not yet equal to anticipating His raising him from the dead. The gradual progress of Martha's faith is very true to life, and reminds us of similar development in the woman of Samaria (iv. 19), the *βασιλικός* (iv. 53), and the man born blind (ix. 11), though she starts at a more advanced stage than they do. If all these four narratives are late fictions, we have four masterpieces of psychological study, as miraculous in the literature of the second century as would be a Gothic cathedral in the architecture of that age. For the construction comp. iv. 10, xiv. 28.

22. καὶ νῦν οἶδα. And even now (that he is dead) *I know.* She believes that had Christ been there, He could have healed Lazarus by His own power (comp. iv. 47), and that now His prayer may prevail with God to raise him from the dead. She has yet to learn that Christ's bodily presence is not necessary, and that He can raise the dead by His own power. He gradually leads her faith onwards to higher truth. *Θεός* at the end of both clauses seems to emphasize her conviction that God alone can now help them: but it may be the repetition so common in S. John's style.

αἰτήσῃ. *Αἰτεῖσθαι*, 'to ask *for oneself*' (xiv. 13, 14, xv. 7, 16, xvi. 23, 26; 1 John v. 14, 15), is a word more appropriate to merely *human* prayer, and is not used by Christ of His own prayers or by the Evangelists of Christ's prayers. She thus incidentally seems to shew her imperfect idea of His relation to God. Of His own prayers Christ uses *ἐρωτᾶν* (xiv. 16, xvi. 26, xvii. 9, 15, 20), *δεῖσθαι* (Luke xxii. 32), *προσεύχεσθαι* (Matt. xxvi. 36; Mark xiv. 32), *θέλω* (xvii. 24). The Synoptists commonly use *προσεύχεσθαι* of Christ's prayers (Matt. xxvi. 39, 42, 44; Mark xiv. 35, 39; Luke iii. 21, v. 16, vi. 12, ix. 18, 28, 29, xi. 1, xxii. 41, 44): S. John never uses the word.

23. ἀναστήσεται. He uses an ambiguous expression as an exercise of her faith. Some think that these words contain no allusion to the immediate restoration of Lazarus, and that Martha (*v.* 24) understands them rightly. More probably Christ includes the immediate restoration of Lazarus, but she does not venture to do so, and rejects the allusion to the final Resurrection as poor consolation.

24. οἶδα ὅτι ἀναστ. This conviction was probably in advance of average Jewish belief on the subject. The O.T. declarations as to a resurrection are so scanty and obscure, that the Sadducees could deny the doctrine, and the Pharisees had to resort to oral tradition to maintain it (see on Mark xii. 18; Acts xxiii. 8). But from Dan. xii. 2 and 2 Mac. vii. 9, 14, 23, 36, xii. 43, 44, a belief in a resurrection of the good as an inauguration of the Messiah's kingdom was very general. For **ἐν τ. ἐσχ. ἡμέρᾳ** see on vi. 39.

25. ἐγώ εἰμι. See on vi. 35. He draws her from her selfish grief to Himself. There is no need for Him to pray as man to God (*v.* 22); *He* (and none else) is the Resurrection and the Life. There is no need to look forward to the last day; He *is* (not 'will be') the Resurrection and the Life. Comp. xiv. 6; Col. iii. 4. In what follows, the first part shews how He is the Resurrection, the second how He is the Life. 'He that believeth in Me, **even if** he shall have died (physically), shall live (eternally). And **every one** that liveth (physically) and believeth in Me, shall never die (eternally).' The dead shall live; the living shall never die. Physical life and death are indifferent to the believer; they are but modes of existence.

26. πᾶς. There is no limitation; iii. 15, xii. 46. Comp. i. 18, iv. 14, vi. 51, viii. 51, x. 9. For *οὐ μὴ ἀπ. εἰς τ. αἰῶνα* see on viii. 51. *Πιστεύεις τοῦτο;* is a searching question suddenly put. She answers with confidence and gives the ground for her confidence.

27. ναί, κύριε. With these words she accepts Christ's declaration respecting Himself, and then states the creed which has enabled her to accept it. The change from *πιστεύω* (the natural answer) to *ἐγὼ πεπίστευκα* is remarkable: **I**, even I whom thou art questioning, **have believed**; i.e. have convinced myself and do believe; comp. vi. 69; 1 John iv. 16, v. 10. The full meaning of her confession she cannot have known: like the Apostles she shared the current imperfect views of the character and office of the Messiah. See on ix. 38.

ὁ εἰς τ. κ. ἐρχόμενος. (*Even*) **He that cometh** *into the world:* comp. vi. 14; Matt. xi. 3; Luke vii. 19; Deut. xviii. 15. She believes that as the Messiah He has the powers mentioned *vv.* 25, 26. How these will affect her own case, she does not know; but with a vague hope of comfort in store for them all she returns to the house. *Ἔρχεσθαι εἰς τ. κόσμον* is frequent in S. John (i. 9, iii. 19, vi. 14, ix. 39, xii. 46, xvi. 28, xviii. 37): as applied to Christ it includes the notion of His mission (iii. 17, x. 36, xii. 47, 49, xvii. 18). Not in the Synoptists.

28. λάθρα. Because of the presence of Christ's enemies (*vv.* 19, 31). *Λάθρα* with *εἰποῦσα,* rather than with *ἐφώνησε* (Matt. i. 19, ii. 7; Acts xvi. 37).

ὁ διδάσκαλος. i. 39, xiii. 13, 14, xx. 16, iii. 10; Mark xiv. 14. Their friendship is based on the relation between teacher and disciple. She avoids using His name for fear of being overheard.

29. ταχύ. As was natural in one so fond of sitting at His feet. Note the change from aorist to imperfect; the rising was momentary (*ἠγέρθη*), the coming continuous (*ἤρχετο*): comp. iv. 27, 30, 40, 47, 50, v. 9, vi. 1, 2, 16, 17, 66, vii. 14, 30, 31, 44, ix. 22, xx. 3.

30. ἦν ἔτι. *Was still in the place.* By remaining outside He could converse with the sisters with less fear of interruption: but the Jews, by following her, interfere with the privacy. See Winer, p. 705.

31. κλαύσῃ. Stronger than δακρύειν (*v.* 35): it means **to wail** and cry aloud, not merely shed tears (xx. 11, 13; Matt. ii. 18, xxvi. 75. It is used of Mary Magdalene (xx. 11, 13), Rachel (Matt. ii. 18), S. Peter (Mark xiv. 72), the widow at Nain (Luke vii. 13).

32. ἔπεσεν. Nothing of the kind is told of Martha (*v.* 21). Here again the difference of character between the two appears.

οὐκ ἄν μου ἀπ. The same words as those of Martha (*v.* 21); but the pronoun is here more prominent, indicating how acutely personal her loss was. No doubt the sisters had expressed this thought to one another often in the last few days. Mary's emotion is too strong for her; she can say no more than this; contrast *v.* 22. The Jews coming up prevent further conversation. For the construction comp. v. 10, xiv. 28.

33—44. The Sign

33. κλαίουσαν...κλαίοντας. The repetition emphasizes a contrast which is the key to the passage.

ἐνεβριμήσατο τ. πνεύματι. *Infremuit spiritu;* **He was angered**, or **was moved with indignation** *in the spirit.* Ἐμβριμᾶσθαι occurs five times in N.T., here, *v.* 38; Matt. ix. 30; Mark i. 43, xiv. 5 (see notes in each place). In all cases, as in classical Greek and in the LXX., it expresses not sorrow but *indignation* or severity. It means (1) literally, of animals, 'to snort, growl;' then (2) metaphorically, 'to be very angry or indignant;' (3) 'to command sternly, under threat of displeasure.' What was He angered at? Some translate '*at* His spirit,' and explain (*α*) that He was indignant at the human emotion which overcame Him: which is out of harmony with all that we know about the human nature of Christ Others, retaining '*in* His spirit,' explain (*β*) that He was indignant 'at the unbelief of the Jews and perhaps of the sisters:' but of this there is no hint in the context. Others again (*γ*) that it was 'at the sight of the momentary triumph of evil, as death,...which was here shewn under circumstances of the deepest pathos:' but we nowhere else find the Lord shewing anger at the physical consequences of sin. It seems better to fall back on the contrast pointed out in the last note. He was indignant at seeing the hypocritical and sentimental lamentations of His enemies the Jews mingling with the heartfelt lamentations of His loving friend Mary (comp. xii. 10): hypocrisy ever roused His anger.

The πνεῦμα is the seat of the religious emotions, the highest, innermost part of man's nature, the ψυχή is the seat of the natural affections and desires. Here and in xiii. 21 it is Christ's πνεῦμα that is affected, by the presence of moral evil: in xii. 27; Matt. xxvi. 38; Mark xiv. 34, it is His ψυχή that is troubled, at the thought of impending suffering: comp. x. 24.

ἐτάραξεν ἑαυτόν. *Turbavit se ipsum;* **He troubled Himself.** Not a mere periphrasis for *ἐταράχθη, turbatus est* (xiii. 21). He allowed His emotion to become evident by some external movement such as a shudder. His emotions were ever under control: when they ruffled the surface of His being (ii. 15), it was because He so willed it. *Turbaris tu nolens: turbatus est Christus quia voluit* (S. Augustine).

34. ποῦ τεθ. αὐτόν; Again He does not use His supernatural powers (*v.* 17). With *ἔρχου κ. ἴδε* contrast i. 47. On both sides "grief speaks in the fewest possible words."

35. ἐδάκρυσεν. Literally, **shed tears**: here only in N.T. See on xiii. 30. His lamentation was less violent than that of the sisters and their friends (*vv.* 31, 33). Once it is said of Him that He *wailed aloud* (*ἔκλαυσεν*, Luke xix. 41); but that was not for the loss of a friend, but for the spiritual death of the whole Jewish nation. Now He sheds tears, not because He is ignorant or doubtful of what is coming, but because He cannot but sympathize with His friends' grief. He who later shared the pains of death, here shares the sorrow for death. "It is not with a heart of stone that the dead are raised." Comp. Heb. ii. 11. For the dramatic brevity comp. v. 9, xiii. 30, xviii. 40.

36. ἔλεγον...ἐφίλει. Imperfects of continued action. As naturally as the sisters (*v.* 3) they use *φιλεῖν* rather than *ἀγαπᾶν* (*v.* 5). For Ἴδε see on i. 29.

37. τινὲς δὲ ἐξ αὐ. **But** *some of them,* in contrast to those who speak in *v.* 36, who are not unfriendly, while these sneer. The drift of this remark is 'He weeps; but why did He not come in time to save His friend? Because He knew that He could not. And if He could not, did he really open the eyes of the blind?' Or possibly, 'He weeps; but why did He not take the trouble to come in time? His tears are hypocritical.' They use the death of Lazarus as an argument to throw fresh doubt on the miracle which had so baffled them at Jerusalem; or else as evidence that His grief is feigned. Their reference to the man born blind instead of to the widow's son, or Jairus' daughter, has been used as an objection to the truth of this narrative. It is really a strong confirmation of its truth. An inventor would almost certainly have preferred more obvious parallels. But these Jews of course did not believe in those raisings of the dead: they much more naturally refer to a reputed miracle within their own experience. Moreover they are not hinting at raising the dead, but urging that if Jesus could work miracles He ought to have prevented Lazarus from dying.

38. ἐμβριμ. ἐν ἑαυτῷ. This shews that '*in* His spirit,' not '*at* His spirit,' is right in *v.* 33, to which *πάλιν* refers. Their sneering scepticism rouses His indignation afresh.

It is remarkable that this chapter, which narrates the greatest exhibition of Divine power in the ministry of Christ, contains peculiarly abundant evidence of His perfect humanity. We have His special affection for His friends (*v.* 5), His sympathy and sorrow (*v.* 35), His indignation (*vv.* 33, 38). In the rest of this Gospel, which is so full of the Divinity of Jesus, we have His humanity plainly set forth also; His weariness (iv. 6), His thirst (iv. 7, xix. 28), His love for His disciples (xx. 2), His special affection for 'His own' and for S. John (xiii. 2, 23, xix. 26, xxi. 7, 20).

μνημεῖον. See on *v.* 17. The having a private burying-place, like the large attendance of mourners and the very precious ointment (xii. 3), indicates that the family is well off. Εἰς is *unto*, not *into*.

ἐπ' αὐτῷ. *Upon it*, or *against it*. An excavation in the side of a mound or rock may be meant. What is now shewn as Lazarus' grave is an excavation in the ground with steps down to it. The modern name of Bethany, El-Azariyeh or Lazarieh, is derived from Lazarus.

39. ἄρατε τ. λίθον. Comp. τ. λίθον ἠρμένον (xx. 1) not ἀποκεκυλισμένον (Luke xxiv. 2: comp. Mark xvi. 4, Matt. xxviii. 2). The command would cause great surprise and excitement.

ἡ ἀδελφὴ τ. τετελ. Not inserted gratuitously. It was because she was his sister that she could not bear to see him or allow him to be seen disfigured by corruption. The remark comes much more naturally from the practical Martha than from the reserved and retiring Mary. There is nothing to indicate that she was mistaken; though some would have it that the miracle had begun from Lazarus' death, and that the corpse had been preserved from decomposition.

τεταρταῖος. Literally, *of the fourth day; quadriduanus*. Westcott quotes a striking Jewish tradition: "The very height of mourning is not till the third day. For three days the spirit wanders about the sepulchre, expecting if it may return into the body. But when it sees that the aspect of the face is changed, then it hovers no more, but leaves the body to itself." And "after three days the countenance is changed."

40. εἶπόν σοι. Apparently a reference to *vv.* 25, 26, and to the reply to the messenger, *v.* 4: on both occasions more may have been said than is reported. See on *v.* 4.

41. ἦραν οὖν τ. λίθον. ὁ δὲ 'Ι. ἦρεν τ. ὀφθ. They lifted therefore *the stone*. But *Jesus* lifted up *His eyes:* comp. xvii. 1.

ὅτι ἤκουσάς μου. *That Thou* didst hear *Me*. The prayer to which this refers is not recorded. He thanks the Father as a public acknowledgment that the Son can do nothing of Himself; the power which He is about to exhibit is from the Father (v. 19—26).

42. ἐγὼ δὲ ᾔδειν. But I (whatever doubts others may have had) *knew*. No one must suppose from this act of thanksgiving that there are any prayers of the Son which the Father does not hear.

διὰ τ. ὄχλον. Shewing that others were present besides 'the Jews' who had come to condole. Εἶπον, *I said* the words, εὐχαρίστω σοι κ.τ.λ. His confidence in thanking God for a result not yet apparent proved His intimacy with God.

ὅτι σύ. *That Thou,* and no one else: *σύ* is emphatic. See on xx. 21.

43. ἐκραύγασεν. The word (rare in N. T. except in this Gospel) is nowhere else used of Christ. It is elsewhere used of the shout of a multitude; xii. 13, xviii. 40, xix. 6, 12, 15. Comp. Matt. xii. 19; Acts xxii. 23. This loud cry was perhaps the result of strong emotion, or in order that the whole multitude might hear. It is natural to regard it as the direct means of the miracle, awakening the dead: though some prefer to think that 'I thank Thee' implies that Lazarus is already alive and needs only to be called forth.

44. ἐξῆλθεν. It is safest not to regard this as an additional miracle. The winding-sheet may have been loosely tied round him, or each limb may have been swathed separately: in Egyptian mummies sometimes every finger is kept distinct.

κειρίαις. The word occurs here only in N.T. Comp. Prov. vii. 16. It means the bandages which kept the sheet and the spices round the body. Nothing is said about the usual spices (xix. 40) here; and Martha's remark (*v.* 39) rather implies that there had been no embalming. If Lazarus died of a malignant disease he would be buried as quickly as possible.

ὄψις. The word occurs in N.T. only here, vii. 24, and Rev. i. 16: one of the small indications of a common authorship (see on i. 14, iv. 6, v. 2, vii. 30, [viii. 2,] xiii. 8, xv. 20, xix. 37, xx. 16).

σουδαρίῳ. The Latin *sudarium*, meaning literally 'a sweat-cloth.' It occurs xx. 7; Luke xix. 20; Acts xix. 12. Here the cloth bound under the chin to keep the lower jaw from falling is probably meant. These details shew the eyewitness.

ἄφετε αὐ. ὑπ. The expression is identical with 'let these go their way' (xviii. 8); and perhaps 'let him go his way' would be better here. Lazarus is to be allowed to retire out of the way of harmful excitement and idle curiosity. Comp. Luke vii. 15, viii. 55. On all three occasions Christ's first care is for the person raised.

The reserve of the Gospel narrative here is evidence of its truth, and is in marked contrast to the myths about others who are said to have returned from the grave. Lazarus makes no revelations as to the unseen world. The traditions about him have no historic value: but one mentioned by Trench (*Miracles*, p. 425) is worth remembering. It is said that the first question which he asked Christ after being restored to life was whether he must die again; and being told that he must, he was never more seen to smile.

45—57. Opposite results of the Sign

45. πολλοὶ οὖν κ.τ.λ. The Greek is as plain as the English of A.V. is misleading, owing to inaccuracy and bad punctuation. Ἐκ τ. Ἰουδ. means of the Jews generally; of this hostile party 'many believed;' and these 'many' were those 'who came and beheld' the miracle. *Many* **therefore** *of the Jews,* **even they who came** *to Mary and* **beheld that which He** (see on vi. 14) *did, believed on Him.* Of the

Jews who beheld, *all* believed. The reading ὃ for ἃ has the best authority though both are well supported: it is the last supreme miracle that is contemplated.

46. τινὲς δὲ ἐξ αὐτῶν. Again, of the Jews generally, rather than of those who saw and believed. With what intention they *went* away *to the Pharisees,* is not clear: possibly to convince them, or to seek an authoritative solution of their own perplexity, or as feeling that the recognised leaders of the people ought to know the whole case. Comp. v. 15, ix. 13. The bad *result* of their mission has made some too hastily conclude that their *intention* was bad.

47. συνέδριον. They summon *a meeting* of the Sanhedrin. Even the adversaries of Jesus are being converted, and something decisive must be done. The crisis unites religious opponents. The chief priests, who were mostly Sadducees, act in concert with the Pharisees; jealous ecclesiastics with religious fanatics (comp. vii. 32, 45, xviii. 3).

συνέδριον, common in the Acts and not rare in the Synoptists, occurs here only in S. John; and here only without the article, as meaning a meeting of the Sanhedrin, rather than the council itself. It is the Greek equivalent of Sanhedrin, which though plural in form is treated as a singular noun of multitude: see on Matt. xxvi. 3.

τί ποιοῦμεν; Not *τί ποιῶμεν* or *ποιήσομεν*, 'What are we to do, if anything?' But, *What are we doing?* i.e. something must be done, and we are not doing it.

οὗτος. Contemptuous: see on ix. 16.

πολλὰ π. σημεῖα. Πολλά is emphatic. It is no longer possible to question the fact of the signs. But instead of asking themselves what these signs mean, their only thought is how to prevent others from drawing the obvious conclusion. The contrast between their action and His (*ποιοῦμεν...ποιεῖ*) is probably intended by the Evangelist, if not by them.

48. ἐλεύσονται οἱ Ῥωμ. An unconscious prophecy (comp. *v.* 50, vii. 35, xix. 19) of what their own policy would produce. They do not inquire whether He is or is not the Messiah: they look solely to the consequences of admitting that He is.

ἡμῶν κ. τ. τόπον κ. τ. ἔθνος. Ἡμῶν is very emphatic and does not depend on *ἀροῦσιν*: it belongs to both substantives; *both our place and* our *nation.* 'Place' is perhaps best understood of Jerusalem, the seat of the Sanhedrin, and the abode of most of the hierarchy. Other interpretations are (1) the Temple, comp. 2 Macc. v. 19; (2) the whole land; so that the expression means 'our land and people,' which is illogical: the land may be taken from the people, or the people from the land, but how can both be taken away? (3) 'position, *raison d'être.*' In any case the sentiment is parallel to that of Demetrius and his fellow-craftsmen (Acts xix. 27). They profess to be very zealous for religion, but cannot conceal their interested motives. For *ἔθνος* of the Jews comp. *v.* 50.

49. Καϊάφας. This was a surname; *τοῦ* **λεγομένου** *Καϊάφα* Matt. xxvi. 3 (where see note on the Sanhedrin). His original name was Joseph. Caiaphas is either the Syriac form of Cephas, a 'rock,' or (according to another derivation) means 'depression.' The high-priesthood had long since ceased to descend from father to son. Pilate's predecessor, Valerius Gratus, had deposed Annas and set up in succession Ismael, Eleazar (son of Annas), Simon, and Joseph Caiaphas (son-in-law of Annas); Caiaphas held the office from A.D. 18 to 36, when he was deposed by Vitellius. Annas in spite of his deposition was still regarded as in some sense high-priest (xviii. 13; Luke iii. 2; Acts iv. 6), possibly as president of the Sanhedrin (Acts v. 21, 27, vii. 1, ix. 1, 2, xxii. 5, xxiii. 2, 4, xxiv. 1). Caiaphas is not president here, or he would not be spoken of merely as 'one of them.'

τ. ἐνιαυτοῦ ἐκείνου. This has been urged as an objection, as if the Evangelist ignorantly supposed that the high-priesthood was an annual office,—a mistake which would go far to prove that the Evangelist was not a Jew, and therefore not S. John. But 'that year' means 'that notable and fatal year.' The same expression recurs *v.* 51 and xviii. 13. Even if there were not this obvious meaning for 'that year,' the frequent changes in the office at this period would fully explain the insertion without the notion of an *annual* change being implied. There had been some twenty or thirty high-priests in S. John's lifetime.

ὑμεῖς οὐκ οἴδ. οὐδ. An inference from their asking 'What do we?' It was quite obvious what they must do. *Ὑμεῖς* is contemptuously emphatic. The resolute but unscrupulous character of the man is evident. We find similar characteristics in the Sadducean hierarchy to which he belonged (Acts iv. 17, 21, v. 17, 18). Josephus comments on the rough manners of the Sadducees even to one another: *Σαδδουκαίων δὲ καὶ πρὸς ἀλλήλους τὸ ἦθος ἀγριώτερον* (*B. J.* II. viii. 14).

50. συμφέρει ὑμῖν. *It is expedient for* **you** half-hearted Pharisees: *ὑμῖν* corresponds with the contemptuous *ὑμεῖς*, a point which is spoiled by the inferior reading *ἡμῖν*.

ἵνα εἷς ἄνθ. ἀποθ. Literally, *in order that one man should die;* S. John's favourite construction pointing to the Divine purpose: see on i. 8, iv. 34, 47, and comp. xvi. 7, vi. 29, 40, 50, ix. 2, 3, xii. 23, xiii. 34. The high-priest thus singles out the Scapegoat.

τοῦ λαοῦ. The Jews as a theocratic community; whereas **τὸ ἔθνος** (*v.* 48, xviii. 35) is the Jews as one of the nations of the earth (Luke vii. 5; Acts x. 22. *Τὰ ἔθνη* of course means the Gentiles (Acts x. 45; Rom. xi. 13, Gal. ii. 12, &c.).

51. ἀφ' ἑαυ. οὐκ εἶπ. Like Saul, Caiaphas is a prophet in spite of himself. None but a Jew would be likely to know of the old Jewish belief that the high-priest by means of the Urim and Thummim was the mouthpiece of the Divine oracle. The Urim and Thummim had been lost, and the high-priest's office had been shorn of much of its glory, but the remembrance of his prophetical gift did not become quite extinct (Hos. iii. 4); and 'in that fatal year' S. John might well believe that the gift would be restored. For ἤμελλεν see on vi. 71.

52. **οὐχ ὑπὲρ τ. ἔθνους μόνον.** S. John purposely uses the word which describes the Jews merely as one of the nations of the earth distinct from the Gentiles. We are not to understand that Caiaphas had any thought of the gracious meaning contained in his infamous advice. Balaam prophesied unwillingly, Caiaphas unconsciously.

συναγ. εἰς ἕν. *Gather together* **into** *one* (x. 16, xvii. 21). The idea of Jews scattered among Gentiles is here transferred to believers scattered among unbelievers. For ἀλλ' ἵνα see on i. 8, and for τὰ τέκνα τ. Θεοῦ, 1 John iii. 10. The Gentiles are already such potentially: they have the δύναμις, and will hereafter receive ἐξουσίαν τέκνα Θεοῦ γένεσθαι (see on i. 12).

53. **ἀπ' ἐκείνης οὖν.** *From that* (fatal) *day* **therefore**: it was in consequence of Caiaphas' suggestion that they practically, if not formally, pronounced sentence of death. The question was how to get the sentence carried out.

54. **'Ι. οὖν.** *Jesus therefore,* because He knew that in raising His friend He had signed His own death-warrant, and that He must wait until His hour was come (xiii. 1). For παρρησίᾳ see on vii. 13; for περιεπάτει, vii. 1. The time for freedom of speech and freedom of movement among them is over.

εἰς τ. χώραν ἐγγὺς τ. ἐρ. *Into* **the** *country near the wilderness,* a place of greater retirement than Peraea (x. 40). The wilderness of Judaea is probably meant. But Ephraim cannot be identified with certainty. Eusebius makes it eight miles, Jerome twenty miles, N.E. of Jerusalem: both make it the same as Ephron. If the Ephraim of 2 Chron. xiii. 19 and Josephus (*B. J.* IV. ix. 9) be meant, the wilderness would be that of Bethaven.

55. **ἦν δὲ ἐγγ. τ. π. τ. 'Ι.** **Now the passover of the Jews.** 'Of the Jews' is added with full significance: see on ii. 13 and vi. 4.

ἵνα ἁγνίσωσιν ἑαυ. (Acts xxi. 24.) Again we have evidence that the Evangelist is a Jew. No purifications are ordered by the Law as a preparation for the Passover. But to be ceremonially unclean was to be excluded (xviii. 28); hence it was customary for those who were so to go up to Jerusalem in good time, so as to be declared clean before the Feast began.

56. **ἐζήτουν οὖν.** *They sought* **therefore**: because they had come up expecting to see Him, but He remained in retirement. Note the imperfects of continued action. The restless curiosity of these country-folk, standing talking together in the Temple, whither many of them had come to bring the offerings for their purification, and where Jesus was so often to be found, is very lifelike. It is better to make two questions than to take ὅτι after δοκεῖ: *What think ye? That He will not come to the Feast?*

57. οἱ ἀρχιερεῖς κ. οἱ Φ. See on vii. 32. The verse explains why the people doubted His coming to the Feast. Note that once more the Sadducean hierarchy takes the lead. Comp. *v.* 47, xii. 10, xviii. 3, 35, xix. 6, 15, 21. In the history of the Passion the Pharisees are mentioned only once (Matt. xxvii. 62), and then, as here, after the chief priests.

ἐντολάς. This is the better reading, which has been altered to *ἐντολήν* because only one command was given: comp. our phrase 'to give orders.' We have a similar use of *ἐντολάς* in Col. iv. 10, if *ἐντολὰς* refers to *ἐὰν ἔλθῃ δέξασθε αὐτόν*. Here the plural may indicate repetition of the order.

ἵνα...πιάσωσιν. See on iv. 47, vii. 30. The decree for His arrest had been published; the sentence of death was probably kept secret. But the Babylonian Gemara preserves a tradition that "an officer for 40 days publicly proclaimed that this man, who had seduced the people by his imposture, ought to be stoned, and that any one who could say aught in his defence was to come forward and speak. But no one doing so he was hanged on the eve of the Passover."

CHAPTER XII

1. Omit *ὁ τεθνηκώς* after **Λάζαρος**, with ℵBLX against ADI[a].

2. ἀνακειμένων σύν (ℵABD) for *συνανακειμένων* (frequent in the Synoptists, not found in S. John).

7. Insert **ἵνα** after **αὐτήν** and read **τηρήσῃ** for *τετήρηκεν* (changes to escape a difficulty), with ℵBDKLQX against AI[a].

13. ἐκραύγαζον for *ἔκραζον* (from Matt. and Mark) with ℵBDLQ against A.

18. ἤκουσαν for *ἤκουσε* (correction for uniformity).

25. ἀπολλύει (ℵBL) for *ἀπολέσει* (AD).

35, 36. ὡς for *ἕως*, and **ἐν ὑμῖν** for *μεθ' ὑμῶν*.

40. ἐπώρωσεν for *πεπώρωκεν*, and **ἰάσομαι** for *ἰάσωμαι* (both corrections for uniformity): **στραφῶσιν** for *ἐπιστραφῶσι* (*ἐπιστρέψωσιν* in LXX.).

41. ὅτι for *ὅτε*: comp. *v.* 17.

47. φυλάξῃ for *πιστεύσῃ*, on overwhelming authority.

Chap. XII. The Judgment

We now enter upon the third section of the first main division of this Gospel. It may be useful to state the divisions once more. The Prologue, i. 1—18; The Ministry, i. 19—xii. 50, thus divided—(1) The Testimony, i. 19—ii. 11; (2) The Work, ii. 13—xi. 57; (3) The Judgment, xii. This third section, which now lies before us, may be subdivided thus—(α) *the Judgment of men*, 1—36; (β) *the Judgment of the Evangelist*, 37—43; (γ) *the Judgment of Christ*, 44—50.

We have not sufficient data for harmonizing this latter portion of S. John with the Synoptists. In the large gaps left by each there is plenty of room for all that is peculiar to the others. S. John's plan is precise and consistent: but once more we have a blank of undefined extent (see introductory note to chap. vi. and on vi. 1). This chapter forms at once a conclusion to the Work and Conflict and an introduction to the Passion.

1—36. The Judgment of Men

Note the dramatic contrast between the different sections of this division; the devotion of Mary and the enmity of the priests, Christ's triumph and the Pharisees' discomfiture, the Gentiles seeking the Light and the Chosen People refusing to see it.

1. ὁ οὖν 'I. The *οὖν* simply resumes the narrative from the point where it quitted Jesus, xi. 55. This is better than to make it depend on xi. 57, as if He went to Bethany to avoid His enemies. His hour is drawing near, and therefore He draws near to the appointed scene of His sufferings.

πρὸ ἓξ ἡμ. τοῦ π. The Passover began at sunset on Nisan 14: six days before this would bring us to Nisan 8, which day, Josephus states, pilgrims often chose for arriving at Jerusalem. Assuming the year to be A.D. 30, Nisan 8 would be Friday, March 31. We may suppose, therefore, that Jesus and His disciples arrived at Bethany on the Friday evening a little after the Sabbath had commenced, having performed not more than 'a Sabbath-day's journey' on the Sabbath, the bulk of the journey being over before the day of rest began. But it must be remembered that this chronology is tentative, not certain. For the construction see on xi. 18 and comp. xxi. 8 and *πρὸ δύο ἐτῶν τοῦ σεισμοῦ* (Amos i. 1): *πρὸ μιᾶς ἡμέρας τῆς Μαρδοχαικῆς ἡμέρας* (2 Macc. xv. 36). Here also the preposition seems to have been transposed; we should expect **ἓξ** *ἡμέρας πρὸ τοῦ* **π.** Perhaps S. John wishes to contrast this last week with the first; see on ii. 1.

ὃν ἤγ. ἐκ ν. 'I. This descriptive phrase may have become a common designation of Lazarus (*v.* 9): comp. *ὃν ἠγάπα ὁ* 'I. (xiii. 23, xix. 26, xxi. 7, 20).

2—8. The Devotion of Mary

2. ἐποίησαν οὖν. *They made* **therefore**; because of His great miracle just mentioned (*v.* 1) and its consequences. The banquet is a generous protest against the decree of the Sanhedrin (xi. 57). The nominative to ἐποίησαν is indefinite: if we had only this account we should suppose that the supper was in the house of Martha, Mary, and Lazarus; but S. Mark (xiv. 3) and S. Matthew (xxvi. 6) tell us that it was in the house of Simon the leper, who had possibly been healed by Christ and probably was a friend or relation of Lazarus and his sisters. Martha's serving (comp. Luke x. 40) in his house is evidence of the latter point (see the notes on S. Matthew and S. Mark).

ὁ δὲ Λάζ. κ.τ.λ. This is probably introduced to prove the reality and completeness of his restoration to life: it confirms the Synoptic accounts by indicating that Lazarus was guest rather than host.

3. λίτραν. S. John alone gives Mary's name and the amount. The pound of 12 ounces is meant. So large a quantity of a substance so costly is evidence of her overflowing love. Comp. xix. 39.

νάρδου πιστικῆς. The expression is a rare one, and occurs elsewhere only Mark xiv. 3, which S. John very likely had seen: his account has all the independence of that of an eyewitness, but may have been influenced by the Synoptic narratives. The meaning of the Greek is not certain: it may mean (1) 'genuine nard' (*πίστις*), and spikenard was often adulterated; or (2) 'drinkable, liquid nard' (*πίνω*), and unguents were sometimes drunk; or (3) 'Pistic nard,' 'Pistic' being supposed to be a local adjective. But no place from which such an adjective could come appears to be known. Of the other two explanations the first is to be preferred. The English 'spikenard' seems to recall the *nardi spicati* of the Vulgate in Mark xiv. 3: here the Vulgate has *nardi pistici*. Winer, p. 121.

πολυτίμου. Horace offers to give a cask of wine for a very small box of it; *Nardi parvus onyx eliciet cadum* (*Carm.* IV. xii. 17).

τοὺς πόδας. The two Synoptists mention only the usual (Ps. xxiii. 5) anointing of the head; S. John records the less usual act, which again is evidence of Mary's devotion. The rest of this verse is peculiar to S. John, and shews that he was present. Note the emphatic repetition of *τοὺς πόδας*. To unbind the hair in public was a disgrace to a Jewish woman; but Mary makes this sacrifice also. In **ἐκ τ. ὀσμῆς** the *ἐκ* expresses that *out of* which the filling was produced: comp. LXX. in Ps. cxxvii. 5; *ὃς πληρώσει τὴν ἐπιθυμίαν αὐτοῦ* **ἐξ** *αὐτῶν*.

4. Ἰούδας ὁ Ἰσκ. S. Mark (xiv. 4) says, quite indefinitely, *τινες*; S. Matthew (xxvi. 8), *οἱ μαθηταί*. Each probably states just what he knew; S. Mark that the remark was made; S. Matthew that it came from the group of disciples; S. John that Judas made it, and why he made it. S. John was perhaps anxious that the unworthy grumbling should be assigned to the right person. For *ὁ μέλλων αὐτὸν παρ.* see on vi. 71.

5. τριακοσίων δην. Over £20, if we reckon according to the purchasing power of the *denarius:* see on vi. 7. *Πτωχοῖς* (no article), *to poor people:* comp. *διάδος πτωχοῖς* (Luke xviii. 22).

6. γλωσσόκομον. More classical form *γλωσσοκομεῖον*, from *κομέω*. It literally means a 'case for mouthpieces' of musical instruments, and hence any portable chest. Its occurring in LXX. only of the chest into which offerings for the Temple were put (2 Chron. xxiv. 8, 10, 11) may have influenced S. John in using it of the **box** in which the funds of the little company, mainly consisting of offerings (Luke viii. 3), were kept. The word occurs in N. T. only here and xiii. 29.

ἐβάσταζεν. Either *used to carry*, or *used to carry away*, i. e. steal: comp. xx. 15. The latter is more probable: *he* **took** *what was put therein.* The *καί* after *κλέπτης ἦν* is epexegetic and introduces an explanation of the way in which he was a thief. S. Augustine, commenting on 'portabat,' which he found in the Italic Version, and which survives in the Vulgate, says "portabat an exportabat? sed ministerio portabat, furto exportabat." We have the same play in 'lift,' e.g. 'shop-*lifting;*' and in the old use of 'convey:' "To steal" ..."*Convey* the wise it call." *Merry Wives of Windsor*, I. 3. "O good! Convey?—*Conveyers* are you all." *Richard II.* IV. 1. The common meaning, 'used to carry,' gives very little sense. Of course if he carried the box he carried *τὰ βάλλομενα*, the gifts *that were being put* into it from time to time: comp. v. 7, xiii. 2, xx. 25.

7. ἄφες αὐτήν, ἵνα. *Let her alone*, **that for the day of the preparation for My burial she may preserve it**: or, more simply, *Suffer her to keep it for the day of My burial.* But *ἐνταφιασμός* (here and Mark xiv. 8 only) means the embalming and other preparations rather than the actual entombment: comp. xix. 40. The meaning is not clear: (1) Suffer her to keep what remains of it; not, however, for the poor, but for My burial, which is close at hand.' But was there any of it left? (2) 'Let her alone; (she has not sold it for the poor) that she may keep it for My burial.' (3) 'Suffer her to keep it (for she intended to do so) for the day of My burial:' i.e. do not find fault with a good intention which she has unwittingly carried out. The words are spoken from the point of view of the past, when Mary's act was still only a purpose.

8. τοὺς πτωχοὺς γὰρ κ.τ.λ. Comp. Deut. xv. 11. Every word of this verse occurs in the first two Gospels, though not quite in the same order. Here the emphasis is on 'the poor,' there on 'always.' The striking originality of the saying, and the large claim which it makes, are evidence of its origin from Him who spake as never man spake. Considering how Christ speaks of the poor elsewhere, these words may be regarded as quite beyond the reach of a writer of fiction. S. John, who gives Mary's name, omits the promise of fame as wide as Christendom. S. Matthew and S. Mark, who give the promise, do not give her name: see on ii. 19, xviii. 11.

9—11. The Hostility of the Priests

9. ὁ ὄχλος πολύς. Large caravans would be coming up for the Passover, and the news would spread quickly through the shifting crowds, who were already on the alert (xi. 55) about Jesus, and were now anxious to see Lazarus. It is the **'large multitude** of the *Jews*' who come; i.e. of Christ's usual opponents. This again (comp. xi. 45—47) excites the hierarchy to take decisive measures. See on *v.* 12. But perhaps here and in *v.* 12 *ὄχλος πολύς* is virtually a compound word, **the common people** *of the Jews*, as distinct from the leaders. Ὄχλος, in Cretan *πόλχος*, seems to be akin to *vulgus* and 'folk.'

ὃν ἤγειρεν. See on *v.* 1. These repeated references to the raising of Lazarus (xi. 45, 47, xii. 1, 9, 10, 17) greatly strengthen the historical evidence for the miracle. They are quite inconsistent with the theory either of a misunderstanding or of deliberate fraud.

10. οἱ ἀρχιερεῖς. See on vii. 32. Nothing is here said about the Pharisees (comp. xi. 47, 57), who are, however, not necessarily excluded. Both would wish to put Lazarus out of the way for the reason given in *v.* 11: but the chief priests, who were mostly Sadducees, would have an additional reason, in that Lazarus was a living refutation of their doctrine that 'there is no resurrection' (Acts xxiii. 8).

ἵνα καὶ τ. Λάζ. Whatever may be true about xi. 53, we must not suppose that this verse implies a formal sentence of death: it does not even imply a meeting of the Sanhedrin.

S. Augustine comments on the folly of the priests—as if Christ could not raise Lazarus a second time! But this ignores the 'also': the hierarchy meant to put *both* to death. Their folly consisted in failing to see, not that He could raise Lazarus again, but that He could raise Himself (ii. 19). Note that it is the unscrupulous hierarchy, who attempt this crime. Comp. xviii. 35, xix. 6, 15, 21.

11. ὑπῆγον...ἐπίστευον. The imperfects express a continual process: **were going away and believing.** It is best to leave 'going away' quite indefinite; the idea of falling away from the hierarchy lies in the context and not in the word.

The climax is approaching. Of 'the Jews' themselves many are being won over to Christ, and are ready to give Him an enthusiastic reception whenever He appears. The remainder become all the more bitter, and resolve to sweep away anyone, however innocent, who contributes to the success of Jesus.

12—18. The Enthusiasm of the People

12. τῇ ἐπαύριον. From the date given *v.* 1, consequently Nisan 9, from Saturday evening to Sunday evening, if the chronology given on *v.* 1 is correct. S. John seems distinctly to assert that the Triumphal Entry followed the supper at Bethany: S. Matthew and S. Mark both place the supper after the entry, S. Matthew without any date and probably neglecting (as often) the chronological order, S. Mark also without date, yet *apparently* implying (xiv. 1) that the supper took place two days before the Passover. But the date in Mark xiv. 1 covers only two verses and must not be carried further in contradiction to S. John's precise and consistent arrangement. S. John omits all details respecting the procuring of the young ass.

ὄχλος πολύς. Perhaps, as in *v.* 9, we should read ὁ ὄχλος πολύς, and understand the expression as one word, **the common people**. In both verses authorities are divided as to the insertion or omission of the article. But 'the common people' here are not Judaeans, but pilgrims from other parts, who have no prejudice against Jesus.

13. **τὰ βαΐα τῶν φ.** Literally, **the** *palm-branches of* **the** *palm-trees;* i.e. those which grew there, or which were commonly used at festivals. Βαΐον (here only) means a palm-branch, apparently of Coptic origin. S. Matthew (xxi. 8) has κλάδους ἀπὸ τ. δένδρων; S. Mark (xi. 8) στιβάδας ἐκ τ. δ. As often, it is S. John who is the most precise. Comp. Simon's triumphal entry into Jerusalem (1 Macc. xiii. 51). The palm-tree was regarded by the ancients as characteristic of Palestine. 'Phœnicia' (Acts xi. 19, xv. 3) is probably derived from φοῖνιξ. The tree is now comparatively rare, except in the Philistine plain: at 'Jericho, the city of palm-trees' (Deut. xxxiv. 3; 2 Chron. xxxviii. 15) there is not one. For **κραυγάζω** see on xviii. 40

Ὡσαννά. This is evidence that the writer of this Gospel knows Hebrew. See on vi. 45. In the LXX. at Ps. cxvii. 25 we have a translation of the Hebrew, σῶσον δή, 'save we pray,' not a transliteration as here. (Comp. 'Alleluia' in Rev. xix. 1, 6). This Psalm was sung both at the F. of Tabernacles and also at the Passover, and would be very familiar to the people. It is said by some to have been written for the F. of Tabernacles after the return from captivity, by others for the founding or dedicating of the second Temple. It was regarded as Messianic, and both the Psalm and the palm-branches seem to imply a welcoming of the Messiah. In what follows the better reading gives *Blessed* **is He that cometh in the name of the Lord, even the king of Israel.** The cry of the multitude was of course not always the same, and the different Evangelists give us different forms of it.

14. **εὑρών.** S. John does not repeat the well-known story of the finding: see on ix. 35. On **ἐστιν γεγραμμένον** see on ii. 17.

15. **μὴ φοβοῦ.** The quotation is freely made from Zech. ix. 9: μὴ φοβοῦ is substituted for χαῖρε σφόδρα, and the whole is abbreviated. In writing ὁ βασ. **σου** and πῶλον **ὄνου** the Evangelist seems to be translating direct from the Hebrew. The best editions of LXX. omit σου, and all have πῶλον **νέον.** Comp. i. 29, vi. 45, xix. 37. If the writer of this Gospel knew the O.T. in Hebrew, he almost certainly was a Jew.

16. **οὐκ ἔγνωσαν.** A mark of candour: see on ii. 22, xi. 12, xx. 9. After Pentecost much that had been unnoticed or obscure before was brought to their remembrance and made clear (xiv. 26). But would a Christian of the second century have invented this dulness in Apostles? Ταῦτα, with threefold emphasis, refers primarily to the placing Him on the young ass. For **ἐδοξάσθη** see on vii. 39, xi. 4. The nom. to ἐποίησαν is οἱ μαθηταί: they themselves had unwittingly helped to fulfil the prophecy (Luke xix. 29, 37, 39).

17. **ὅτε τ. Λάζ.** See on *v.* 9. *The multitude, therefore, that was with Him* **when** *He raised...were bearing witness.* See on *v.* 41. This special mention of the 'calling from the tomb' is very natural in one who was there, and remembered the *φωνῇ μεγάλῃ* (xi. 43) and the excitement which it caused; not so in a writer of fiction.

18. **τοῦτο.** Emphatic: other signs had made comparatively little impression; *this* one had convinced even His enemies. There are two multitudes, one coming with Jesus from Bethany, and one (13, 18) meeting Him from Jerusalem. The Synoptists do not notice the latter.

19. The Discomfiture of the Pharisees

19. **θεωρεῖτε.** Either (indic.) **Ye behold, or Behold ye?** or (imper.) **Behold.** The first seems best: comp. v. 39, xiv. 1, xv. 18; 1 John ii. 27, 28, 29. 'Ye see what a mistake we have made; we ought to have adopted the plan of Caiaphas long ago.'

ἴδε ὁ κόσμος. The exaggerated expression of their chagrin, which in this Divine epic is brought into strong contrast with the triumph of Jesus. Comp. a similar exaggeration from a similar cause iii. 26; '*all* men come to Him.' For *ἴδε* see on i. 29. **Ἀπῆλθεν,** *is gone* **away,** implies that Jesus' gain is the Pharisees' loss. The words are perhaps recorded as another unconscious prophecy (xi. 50, vii. 35). After this confession of helplessness the Pharisees appear no more alone; the reckless hierarchy help them on to the catastrophe.

20—33. The Desire of the Gentiles and the Voice from Heaven

20. **Ἕλληνες.** In A.V. translated 'Gentiles' vii. 35 (where see note), and 'Greeks' here. Care must be taken to distinguish in the N.T. between *Hellenes* or 'Greeks,' i.e. born Gentiles, who may or may not have become either Jewish proselytes or Christian converts, and *Hellenistae* or 'Grecians,' as our Bible renders the word, i.e. Jews who spoke Greek and not Aramaic. Neither word occurs in the Synoptists. *Ἕλληνες* are mentioned here, vii. 35, and frequently in the Acts and in S. Paul's Epistles. *Ἑλληνισταί* are mentioned only Acts vi. 1, ix. 29: in Acts xi. 20 the right reading is probably *Ἕλληνας.*

τῶν ἀναβαινόντων. *That* **were wont to go** *up to worship.* This shews that they were 'proselytes of the gate,' like the Ethiopian eunuch (Acts viii. 27): see on Matt. xxiii. 15. In this incident we have an indication of the salvation rejected by the Jews passing to the Gentiles: the scene of it was probably the Court of the Gentiles; it is peculiar to S. John, who gives no note of time.

21. **Φιλίππῳ]** Their coming to S. Philip was the result either (1) of accident; or (2) of previous acquaintance, to which the mention of his home seems to point; or (3) of his Greek name, which might attract them. See on i. 45, vi. 5, xiv. 8. In *Κύριε* they shew their respect for the disciple of such a Master (comp. iv. 11, 15, 19). Their desire to 'come and see' for themselves (θέλομεν ἰδεῖν) would at once win the sympathy of the practical Philip. See on i. 46 and xiv. 8.

22. τῷ 'Ανδρέᾳ] Another Apostle with a Greek name. They were both of Bethsaida (i. 44), and possibly these Greeks may have come from the same district. S. Philip seems to shrink from the responsibility of introducing Gentiles to the Messiah, and applies in his difficulty to the Apostle who had already distinguished himself by bringing others to Christ (i. 41, vi. 8, 9).

23. ὁ δὲ 'I. ἀποκρίνεται. He anticipates the Apostles and addresses them before they introduce the Greeks. We are left in doubt as to the result of the Greeks' request. Nothing is said to them in particular, though they may have followed and heard this address to the Apostles, which gradually shades off into soliloquy.

These men from the West at the close of Christ's life set forth the same truth as the men from the East at the beginning of it—that the Gentiles are to be gathered in. The wise men came to His cradle, these to His cross, of which their coming reminds Him; for only by His death could 'the nations' be saved.

ἐλήλυθεν ἡ ὥρα. The phrase is peculiar to S. John; vii. 30, viii. 20, xiii. 1, xvii. 1: contrast Matt. xxvi. 45; Luke xxii. 14. The verb first for emphasis (iv. 21, 23), 'it hath come—the fated hour.' See on vii. 6, xiii. 1. The **ἵνα** indicates the Divine purpose (xiii. 1, xvi. 2, 32; xi. 50); see Winer, p. 576. **Δοξασθῇ**, by His Passion and Death, through which He must pass to return to glory (vii. 39, xi. 4; i. 52).

ἀμὴν ἀμήν. i. 52. Strange as it may seem that the Messiah should die, yet this is but the course of nature: a seed cannot be glorified unless it dies. A higher form of existence is obtained only through the extinction of the lower form that preceded it. *Except* **the grain** *of wheat fall into the earth and die it abideth* **by itself** *alone.*

25. ψυχήν...ζωήν. *Ψυχή* is the life of the individual, *ζωή* life in the abstract. By a noble disregard of the former we win the latter: sacrifice of self is the highest self-preservation. See on Matt. x. 39, xvi. 25; Mark viii. 35; Luke ix. 24, xvii. 33. Most of these texts refer to different occasions, so that this solemn warning must have been often on His lips. This occasion is distinct from all the rest. *'Απολλύει* is either **destroyeth it** or **loseth it**: selfishness is self-ruin.

ὁ μισῶν. He who, if necessary, is ready to act towards his *ψυχή* as if he hated it. Neither here nor in Luke xiv. 26 must *μισεῖν* be watered down to mean 'be not too fond of:' it means that and a great deal more. For **ζωὴν αἰώνιον** see on iii. 15, 16.

26. ἐμοὶ ἀκολουθείτω. In My life of self-sacrifice: Christ Himself has set the example of hating one's life in this world. These words are perhaps addressed through the disciples to the Greeks listening close at hand. If they 'wish to see Jesus' and know Him they must count the cost first. Ἐμοί is emphatic in both clauses. Note the pronouns in what follows. *Where I am*, i.e. 'in My kingdom, which is already secured to Me:' the phrase is peculiar to this Gospel (xiv. 3, xvii. 24): Winer, p. 332. The ἐκεῖ possibly includes the *road* to the kingdom, death. On ὁ δ. ὁ ἐμός see on viii. 31.

ἐάν τις. The offer is all-embracing: vi. 51, vii. 17, 37, viii. 52, x. 9. Note the change of order. Here the verbs are emphatic, and balance one another. Such service is not humiliating but honourable. The verse is closely parallel to *v.* 25.

27. A verse of known difficulty: several meanings are admissible and none can be affirmed with certainty. The doubtful points are (1) the interrogation, whether it should come after τί εἴπω or ταύτης; (2) the meaning of διὰ τοῦτο.

ἡ ψυχή μ. τετάρακται. *My soul has been and still is troubled.* It is the ψυχή, the seat of the natural emotions and affections, that is troubled; not the πνεῦμα, as in xi. 35. But, to bring out the connexion with *vv.* 25, 26, we may render, *Now is My* **life** *troubled.* 'He that would serve Me must follow Me and be ready to hate his life; for My life has long since been tossed and torn with suffering and sorrow.'

τί εἴπω; *What* **must** *I say?* This appears to be the best punctuation; and the question expresses the difficulty of framing a prayer under the conflicting influences of fear of death and willingness to glorify His Father by dying. The result is first a prayer under the influence of fear—'save Me from this hour' (comp. 'Let this cup pass from Me,' Matt. xxvi. 39), and then a prayer under the influence of ready obedience—'Glorify Thy Name' through My sufferings. But σῶσόν με **ἐκ** means 'save me *out of*,' i.e. 'bring Me safe out of;' rather than 'save Me *from*' (σῶσόν με **ἀπό**), i.e. 'keep Me altogether away from,' as in 'deliver us *from* the evil one' (Matt. vi. 13). Note the aorist, which shews that special present deliverance, rather than perpetual preservation, is prayed for. S. John omits the Agony in the garden, which was in the Synoptists and was well known to every Christian; but he gives us here an insight into a less known truth, which is still often forgotten, that the agony was not confined to Gethsemane, but was part of Christ's whole life. Comp. Luke xii. 50. Others place the question at ταύτης, and the drift of the whole will then be, 'How can I say, Father, save Me from this hour? Nay, I came to suffer; therefore My prayer shall be, Father, glorify Thy Name.'

διὰ τοῦτο. These words are taken in two opposite senses; (1) that I might be saved out of this hour; (2) that Thy Name might be glorified by My obedience. Both make good sense. If the latter be adopted it would be better to transpose the stops, placing a full stop after 'from this hour' and a colon after 'unto this hour.'

28. ἦλθεν οὖν. *There came* **therefore**, i.e. in answer to Christ's prayer. There can be no doubt what S. John *wishes* us to understand;—that a voice was heard speaking articulate words, that some could distinguish the words, others could not, while some mistook the sounds for thunder. To make the thunder the reality, and the voice and the words mere imagination, is to substitute an arbitrary explanation for the Evangelist's plain meaning. For similar voices comp. that heard by Elijah (1 Kings xix. 12, 13); by Nebuchadnezzar (Dan. iv. 31); at Christ's Baptism (Mark i. 11) and Transfiguration (Mark ix. 7); at S. Paul's Conversion (Acts ix. 4, 7, xxii. 9), where it would seem that S. Paul alone could distinguish the words, while his companions merely heard a sound (see on Acts ix. 4); and the mixed *φωναὶ καὶ βρονταί* of the Apocalypse (iv. 5, viii. 5, xvi. 18). One of the conditions on which power to distinguish what is said depends is sympathy with the speaker.

ἐδόξασα. In all God's works from the Creation onwards, especially in the life of Christ; *δοξάσω*, in the death of Christ and its results.

30. ἀπεκρίθη. He answered their discussions about the sound, and by calling it a voice He decides conclusively against those who supposed it to be thunder. But those who recognised that it was a voice were scarcely less seriously mistaken; *their* error consisted in not recognising that the voice had a meaning for *them*. **Not for My sake hath this voice come,** *but for your sakes*, i.e. that ye might believe. Comp. xi. 42.

31. νῦν...νῦν. With prophetic certainty He speaks of the victory as already won: comp. *ὅπου* **εἰμί** (*v.* 26). *Κρίσις τ. κόσμου τ.* is the sentence passed on this world (iii. 17, v. 29) for refusing to believe. The Cross is the condemnation of those who reject it.

ὁ ἄρχων τ. κ. τ. *The* **ruler** *of this world.* This is one of the apparently Gnostic phrases which may have contributed to render this Gospel suspicious in the eyes of the Alogi (*Introduction*, Chap. II. i.): it occurs again xiv. 30, xvi. 11, and nowhere else. It was a Gnostic view that the creator and ruler of the material universe was an evil being. But in the Rabbinical writings 'prince of this world' was a common designation of Satan, as ruler of the Gentiles, in opposition to God, the Head of the Jewish theocracy. Yet just as the Messiah is the Saviour of the believing world, whether Jew or Gentile, so Satan is the ruler of the unbelieving world, whether Gentile or Jew. He 'shall be cast out' (comp. vi. 37, ix. 34, 35), by the gradual conversion of sinners, a process which will continue until the last day.

32. κἀγὼ ἐὰν ὑψωθῶ. *Ἐγώ* in emphatic opposition to *ὁ ἄρχων τ. κ. τ.* The glorified Christ, raised to heaven by means of the Cross, will rule men's hearts in the place of the devil. We need not, as in iii. 14, viii. 28, confine *ὑψωθῶ* to the Crucifixion; **ἐκ** *τῆς γῆς* seems to point to the Ascension. Yet the Cross itself, apparently so repulsive, has through Christ's death become an attraction; and this *may* be the meaning here. For the hypothetical **ἐὰν** *ὑψωθῶ* comp. *ἐὰν πορευθῶ* (xiv. 3). In both Christ is concerned not with the *time* but the ***results*** of the act; hence not 'when' but 'if.' Comp. 1 John ii. 8, iii. 2.

ἑλκύσω. Not *συρῶ* (see on vi. 44). There is no violence; the attraction is moral and not irresistible. Man's will is free, and he may refuse to be drawn. Previous to the 'lifting up' it is the Father who 'draws' men to the Son (vi. 44, 45). And in both cases *all* are drawn and taught: not only the Jews represented by the Twelve, but the Gentiles represented by the Greeks. *Πρὸς ἐμαυτόν*, *unto* **Myself**, up from the earth. The two verses (31, 32) sum up the history of the Church; the overthrow of Satan's rule, the establishment of Christ's.

33. **ποίῳ θ.** *By what* **manner** *of death* (x. 32, xviii. 32, xxi. 9). For **ἤμελλεν** see on vi. 71.

34—36. The Perplexity of the Multitude

34. **ἐκ τ. νόμου.** In its widest sense, including the Psalms and the Prophets, as in x. 34, xv. 25. Comp. Ps. lxxxix. 29, 36, cx. 4; Is. ix. 7; Ezek. xxxvii. 25, &c. The people rightly understand 'lifted up from the earth' to mean removal from the earth by death; and they argue—'Scripture says that **the** Christ (see on i. 20) will abide for ever. You claim to be the Christ, and yet *you* say that you will be lifted up and therefore *not* abide.' For **δεῖ** see on iii. 14.

οὗτος ὁ υἱ. τ. ἀν. *Οὗτος* is contemptuous (ix. 16): 'a strange Messiah this, with no power to abide!' (See i. 52.) Once more we see with how firm a hand the Evangelist has grasped the complicated situation. One moment the people are convinced by a miracle that Jesus is the Messiah, the next that it is impossible to reconcile His position with the received interpretations of Messianic prophecy. It did not occur to them to doubt the interpretations.

35. **εἶπεν οὖν αὐ. ὁ Ἰ.** *Jesus* **therefore** *said to them:* instead of answering their contemptuous question He gives them a solemn warning. *Walk* **as** *ye have the light* (*ὡς* not *ἕως*) means 'walk in a manner suitable to the fact of there being the Light *among you:* make use of the Light and work, *in order that darkness* (see on i. 5), in which no man can work, *overtake you not.*' **Καταλαμβάνειν** is used 1 Thess. v. 4 of the last day, and in LXX. of sin overtaking the sinner (Num. xxxii. 23). Some authorities have it in vi. 17 of darkness overtaking the Apostles on the lake.

36. **ὡς τ. φῶς ἔχετε.** **As** *ye have* **the** *Light* (as in *v.* 35), *believe* **on** *the Light, that ye may* **become sons** *of light.* Note the impressive repetition of *φῶς* (comp. i. 10, iii. 17, 31, xv. 19, xvii. 14), and the absence of the article before *φωτός*. In all the four preceding cases *τὸ φῶς* means Christ, as in i. 5, 7, 8, 9. The expression 'child of' or 'son of' is frequent in Hebrew to indicate very close connexion as between product and producer (see on xvii. 12): *υἱὸς εἰρήνης*, Luke x. 6; *οἱ υἱοὶ τ. αἰῶνος τούτου*, xvi. 8; *υἱοὶ βροντῆς*, Mark iii. 17. Such expressions are very frequent in the most Hebraistic of the Gospels; Matt. v. 9, viii. 12, ix. 15, xiii. 38, xxiii. 15.

ταῦτα ἐλάλησεν. He gave them no other answer, departed, and did not return. S. John is silent as to the place of retirement, which was probably Bethany (Matt. xxi. 17; Mark xi. 11; Luke xxi. 37). The one point which he would make prominent is the Christ's withdrawal from His people. Their time of probation is over. They have closed their eyes again and again to the Light; and now the Light itself is gone. *He* **was hidden** *from them.*

37—43. The Judgment of the Evangelist

S. John here sums up the results of the ministry which has just come to a close. Their comparative poverty is such that he can explain it in no other way than as an illustration of that judicial blindness which had been foretold and denounced by Isaiah. The tragic tone returns again: see on i. 5.

37. τοσαῦτα. *So many*, not 'so great' (vi. 9, xxi. 11). The Jews admitted His miracles (vii. 31, xi. 47). S. John assumes them as notorious, though he records only seven (ii. 23, iv. 45, vii. 31, xi. 47).

38. ἵνα...πληρωθῇ. Indicating the Divine purpose. Comp. xiii. 18, xv. 25, xvii. 12, xviii. 9, 32, xix. 24, 36. It is the two specially Hebraistic Gospels that most frequently remind us that Christ's life was a fulfilment of Hebrew prophecy. Comp. Matt. i. 22 (note), ii. 15, 17, iv. 14, viii. 17, xii. 17, xiii. 35, xxi. 4, xxvi. 54, 56, xxvii. 9. The quotation closely follows the LXX. Τῇ ἀκοῇ ἡμῶν is *what they heard from us* rather than *what we heard from God* (1 Thess. ii. 13): ὁ βραχίων Κυρίου means His power (Luke i. 5; Acts xiii. 17).

39. διὰ τοῦτο. For this cause: as usual (*vv.* 18, 27, v. 18, vii. 21, 22, viii. 47, x. 17) this refers to what precedes, and ὅτι following gives the reason more explicitly. For **οὐκ ἐδύναντο** see on vii. 7. It had become morally impossible for them to believe. Grace may be refused so persistently as to destroy the power of accepting it. 'I will not' leads to 'I cannot' (Rom. ix. 6—xi. 32).

40. τετύφλωκεν. The nominative is ὁ Θεός. Here the quotation follows neither the Hebrew nor the LXX. of Is. vi. 10 very closely. The nominative to ἰάσομαι is Christ. God has hardened their hearts so that Christ cannot heal them. Comp. Matt. xiii. 14, 15, where Jesus quotes this text to explain why He teaches in parables; and Acts xxviii. 26, where S. Paul quotes it to explain the rejection of his preaching by the Jews in Rome. For **ἵνα** see Winer, p. 575.

41. ὅτι εἶδεν. Because *he saw.* Here, as in *v.* 17, authorities vary between ὅτι and ὅτε, and here ὅτι is to be preferred. Christ's glory was revealed to Isaiah in a vision, and therefore he spoke of it. The glory of the Son before the Incarnation, when He was ἐν μορφῇ Θεοῦ (Phil. ii. 6), is to be understood.

42. ὅμως μέντοι. Here only in N. T. For μέντοι see on iv. 27. In spite of the judicial blindness with which God had visited them *many* **even of** *the Sanhedrin believed on Him.* We know of Joseph of Arimathea and Nicodemus. But because of the recognised champions of orthodoxy both in and outside the Sanhedrin (vii. 13, ix. 22) they continually abstained (imperf.) from making confession. Ἀποσυνάγωγος occurs in N. T. only here, ix. 22, xvi. 2.

43. τὴν δόξαν τ. ἀνθρ. *The* **glory** (*that cometh*) *from men rather than the* **glory** (*that cometh*) *from God* (see on v. 41, 44). Joseph and Nicodemus confessed their belief after the crisis of the Crucifixion. Gamaliel did not even get so far as to believe on Him.

44—50. The Judgment of Christ

The Evangelist has just summed up the results of Christ's ministry (37—43). He now corroborates that estimate by quoting Christ Himself. But as *v.* 36 seems to give us the close of the ministry, we are probably to understand that what follows was uttered on some occasion or occasions previous to *v.* 36. Perhaps it is given us as an epitome of what Christ often taught.

44. ἔκραξεν. The word implies *public* teaching (vii. 28, 37).

οὐ πιστ. εἰς ἐμέ. His belief does not end there; it must include more. This saying does not occur in the previous discourses; but in v. 36 and viii. 19 we have a similar thought. Jesus came as His Father's ambassador, and an ambassador has no meaning apart from the sovereign who sends him. Not only is it impossible to accept the one without the other, but to accept the representative is to accept *not him in his own personality* but the prince whom he personates. These words are, therefore, to be taken quite literally. Only here and xiv. 1 does S. John use πιστεύειν εἰς, so frequent of believing on Jesus, of believing on the Father.

45. ὁ θεωρῶν. *He who* **beholdeth,** *contemplateth* (vi. 40, 62, vii. 3, xiv. 17, 19, xvi. 10, 16, 17, 19, &c.).

46. ἐγὼ φῶς. *I*, with great emphasis, *am come as light* (*vv.* 35, 36, viii. 12, ix. 5). **Ἵνα**, of the Divine purpose. Till the Light comes all are in darkness (i. 5); but it is not God's will that anyone should abide in darkness. With **πᾶς** comp. i. 7, iii. 15, xi. 26: there is no limitation of race.

47. ἀκούσῃ. In a neutral sense, implying neither belief nor unbelief (Matt. vii. 24, 26; Mark iv. 15, 16). For ῥήματα see on iii. 34.

μὴ φυλάξῃ. Keep them not, i. e. fulfil them not (Luke xi. 28, xviii. 21). A few authorities omit μή, perhaps to avoid a supposed inconsistency between *vv.* 47 and 48.

48. ἔχει. Hath his judge already, without My sentencing him (iii. 18, v. 45). The hearer may refuse the word, but he cannot refuse the responsibility of having heard it. For the retrospective use of ἐκεῖνος see on i. 18, and for ἐν τ. ἐσχάτῃ ἡμέρᾳ see on vi. 39. This verse is conclusive as to the doctrine of the last judgment being contained in this Gospel.

49. ὅτι. Because. It introduces the reason why one who rejects Christ's word will be judged by His word;—because that word is manifestly Divine in origin. With ἐξ ἐμαυτοῦ, *out of Myself* as source, without commission from the Father, comp. ἀπ' ἐμαυτοῦ, v. 30, vii. 17, 28, viii. 28, 42, x. 18, xiv. 10.

αὐτός. **Himself** (and none other) **hath given** *Me commandment* (see on iii. 35, x. 18), *what I should say and how I should say it*; *εἴπω* refers to the doctrine, *λαλήσω* to the form in which it is expressed (see on viii. 43, and comp. xiv. 10, xvi. 18).

50. The Son's testimony to the Father. 'The commission which He has given Me *is* (not shall be) **eternal life**' (iii. 15, 16). **'The things therefore which** *I speak, even as the Father* **hath** *said to Me, so I speak.*'

With this the first main division of the Gospel ends. CHRIST'S REVELATION OF HIMSELF TO THE WORLD IN HIS MINISTRY is concluded. The Evangelist has set before us the TESTIMONY to the Christ, the WORK of the Christ, and the JUDGMENT respecting the work, which has ended in a conflict, and the conflict has reached a climax. We have reached the beginning of the end.

CHAPTER XIII

1. **ἦλθεν** for *ἐλήλυθεν* (from xii. 23).

2. **γινομένου** for *γενομένου*, with BLX [ℵ has *γεινομένου*] against AD. **ἵνα παραδοῖ αὐτὸν Ἰούδας Σίμωνος Ἰσκαριώτης** for *Ἰούδα Σ. Ἰσκαριώτου, ἵνα αὐτὸν παραδῷ* (correction to avoid difficulty of construction) with ℵBLMX against AD.

6. Omit *καί* before **λέγει**, and *ἐκεῖνος* before **Κύριε.**

12. **καὶ ἀνέπεσεν** for *ἀναπεσών*.

24. **καὶ λέγει αὐτῷ, Εἰπὲ τίς ἐστιν** (BCLX) for *πυθέσθαι τίς ἂν εἴη* (AD). In ℵ we have the two readings combined.

25. **ἀναπεσών** for *ἐπιπεσών* (from Luke xv. 20?).

26. **βάψω** for *βάψας*, and **καὶ δώσω αὐτῷ** for *ἐπιδώσω* (correction to avoid awkwardness). The readings vary much. **Βάψας οὖν** for *καὶ ἐμβάψας*, and **Ἰσκαριώτου** for *Ἰσκαριώτῃ* (comp. vi. 71).

38. **ἀποκρίνεται** for *ἀπεκρίθη αὐτῷ*: **φωνήσῃ** for *φωνήσει*: **ἀρνήσῃ** for *ἀπαρνήσῃ*.

We now enter upon the second main division of the Gospel. The Evangelist has given us thus far a narrative of CHRIST'S MINISTRY presented to us in a series of typical scenes (i. 18—xii. 50). He goes on to set forth the ISSUES OF CHRIST'S MINISTRY (xiii.—xx.). The last chapter (xxi.) forms the EPILOGUE, balancing the first eighteen verses (i. 1—18), which form the PROLOGUE.

The second main division of the Gospel, like the first, falls into three parts: 1. THE INNER GLORIFICATION OF CHRIST IN HIS LAST

DISCOURSES (xiii.—xvii.); 2. THE OUTER GLORIFICATION OF CHRIST IN HIS PASSION (xviii., xix.); 3. THE VICTORY COMPLETED IN THE RESURRECTION (xx.). These parts will be subdivided as we reach them. xiii. 1 is a prologue to the first part.

xiii.—xvii. THE INNER GLORIFICATION OF CHRIST IN HIS LAST DISCOURSES

1. *His love in Humiliation* (xiii. 1—30); 2. *His Love in keeping His own* (xiii. 30—xv. 27); 3. *the Promise of the Paraclete and of Christ's Return* (xvi.): 4. *Christ's Prayer for Himself, the Apostles, and all Believers* (xvii.).

CHAP. XIII. 1—30. LOVE IN HUMILIATION

This section has two parts in strong dramatic contrast: 1. the washing of the disciples' feet (2—20); 2. the self-excommunication of the traitor (21—30). As *v.* 1 forms an introduction to this part of the Gospel (xiii.—xvii.), so *vv.* 2, 3, to this section (2—20).

1. **πρὸ δὲ τ. ἑορτῆς τ. π.** Can this mean, *Now on the Feast before the Passover* (comp. xii. 1)? Nowhere else does S. John use the periphrasis 'the Feast of the Passover,' which occurs in N. T. only Luke ii. 41. The words give a date, not to εἰδώς, nor ἀγαπήσας, nor ἠγάπησεν, but to the narrative which follows. Some evening before the Passover Jesus was at supper with His disciples; and probably Thursday, the beginning of Nisan 14. But the difficult question of the Day of the Crucifixion is discussed in Appendix A.

εἰδώς. Knowing, i. e. '*because* He knew' rather than '*although* He knew.' It was precisely because He knew that He would soon return to glory that He gave this last token of self-humiliating love. For ἡ ὥρα see on ii. 4, vii. 6, xi. 9. Till His hour came His enemies could do no more than plot (vii. 30, viii. 20). The ἵνα points to the Divine purpose (xii. 23, xvi. 2, 32; xi. 50). Winer, p. 426. With μεταβῇ ἐκ τ. κ. τ., **pass over** *out of this world*, comp. μεταβέβηκεν ἐκ τ. θανάτου (v. 24; 1 John iii. 14). For ἀγαπᾶν see on xi. 5, xxi. 15.

τοὺς ἰδίους. Those whom God had given Him (xvii. 11, vi. 37, 39; Acts iv. 23, xxiv. 23), still amid the troubles of the world.

εἰς τέλος. Vulg. *in finem.* 'To the end of His life' is probably not the meaning: this would rather be μέχρι τέλους (Heb. iii. 6, 14), or ἄχρι τέλους (Heb. vi. 11; Rev. ii. 26), or ἕως τέλους (1 Cor. i. 8; 2 Cor. i. 13). A.V. renders εἰς τέλος 'unto the end,' here, Matt. x. 22, and xxiv. 13; 'continual,' Luke xviii. 5; 'to the uttermost,' 1 Thess. ii. 16. In all these passages εἰς τέλος may mean either 'at last, finally,' or 'to the uttermost, utterly.' **To the uttermost** seems preferable here. Comp. LXX. of Amos ix. 8; Ps. xvi. 11, xlix. 10, lxxiv. 3. The expression points to an even higher power of love exhibited in the Passion than that which the Christ had all along displayed.

2. δείπνου γινομένου. Neither this nor *δ. γενομένου* (Mark vi. 2) can mean 'supper being ended;' and the supper is not ended (*v.* 26). The former means 'when supper was beginning' or 'was at hand;' the latter, 'supper having begun.' If the Lord's act represents the customary washing of the guests' feet by servants before the meal, 'when supper was at hand' would be the better rendering of *δ. γινομένου*: but *ἐκ τοῦ δείπνου* in *v.* 4 seems to be against this.

τ. διαβόλου κ.τ.λ. *The devil having now put it into the heart,* **that Judas, Simon's son, Iscariot, should** *betray Him.* Whose heart? Only two answers are possible grammatically; (1) the heart of Judas, (2) the devil's own heart. The latter is incredible, if only for the reason that S. John himself has shewn that the devil had long been at work with Judas. The meaning is that of the received reading, but more awkwardly expressed. The traitor's name is given in full for greater solemnity, and comes last for emphasis. Note the position of Iscariot, confirming the view (see on vi. 71) that the word is a local epithet rather than a proper name.

3. εἰδώς. '*Because* He knew,' as in *v.* 1. For *πάντα ἔδωκεν* see on iii. 35 and comp. Eph. i. 22; Phil. ii. 9—11. Note the order; *and that it was from God He* **came forth,** *and unto God He* **is going.** "He came forth from God without leaving Him; and He goeth to God without deserting us" (S. Bernard).

4. τὰ ἱμάτια. **His upper garments** which would impede His movements. The plural includes the girdle, fastenings, &c. (xix. 23). The minuteness in *vv.* 4, 5 shews the eyewitness. Luke xxii. 27.

5. τ. νιπτῆρα. **The** *bason,* which stood there for such purposes, the large copper bason commonly found in oriental houses.

ἤρξατο νίπτειν. *Ἤρξατο* is not a mere amplification as in the other Gospels (Matt. xi. 7, xxvi. 22, 37, 74; Mark iv. 1, vi. 2, 7, 34, 55; Luke vii. 15, 24, 38, 49; &c. &c.), and in the Acts (i. 1, ii. 4, xviii. 26, &c.). The word occurs nowhere else in S. John, and here is no mere periphrasis. He began to wash, but was interrupted by the incident with S. Peter. With whom He began is not mentioned: from very early times some have conjectured Judas. Contrast the mad insolence of Caligula—*quosdam summis honoribus functos ad pedes stare succinctos linteo passus est.* Suet. *Calig.* XXVI. One is unwilling to surrender the view that this symbolical act was intended among other purposes to be a tacit rebuke to the disciples for the 'strife among them, which of them should be accounted the greatest' (Luke xxii. 24); and certainly 'I am among you as he that serveth' (*v.* 27) seems to point directly to this act. This view seems all the more probable when we remember that a similar dispute was rebuked in a similar way, viz. by symbolical action (Luke ix. 46—48). The dispute may have arisen about their places at the table, or as to who should wash the others' feet. That S. Luke places the strife *after* the supper is not fatal to this view; *he gives no note of time,* and the strife is singularly out of place there, immediately after their Master's self-humiliation and in the midst of the last farewells. We may therefore believe, in spite of S. Luke's arrangement, that the strife preceded the supper. In any case the independence of S. John's narrative is conspicuous.

6. **ἔρχεται οὖν.** *He cometh* **therefore**, i. e. in consequence of having begun to wash the feet of each in turn. The natural impression is that S. Peter's turn at any rate did not come first. But if it did, this is not much in favour of the primacy of S. Peter, which can be proved from other passages, still less of his supremacy, which cannot be proved at all. The order of his words marks the contrast between him and his Master, *Σύ μου ν. τ. π.*; *Tu mihi lavas pedes?* Strong emphasis on *σύ*: comp. *σὺ ἔρχῃ πρός με* (Matt. iii. 14).

7. **ὃ ἐγὼ π. σὺ οὐκ οἶδας.** *'Εγώ* and *σύ* are in emphatic opposition. S. Peter's question implied that he knew, while Christ did not know, what He was doing: Jesus tells him that the very reverse is the case. For **ἄρτι** see on ii. 10.

γνώσῃ δ. μ. τ. *But thou shalt come to know*, or *shalt perceive, presently*. *Μετὰ ταῦτα* (iii. 22, v. 1, 14, vi. 1, vii. 1, xix. 38) need not refer to the remote future: had this been intended we should probably have had *νῦν* and *ὕστερον* (*v.* 36) instead of *ἄρτι* and *μετὰ ταῦτα*. The promised *γινώσκειν* seems to begin *v.* 12, when Jesus explains His symbolical action, and begins with this very word, **Γινώσκετε** *τί πεποίηκα ὑμῖν*; But not till Pentecost did the Apostles fully recognise the meaning of Christ's words and acts. See on vii. 26 and viii. 55 for the converse change from *γινώσκω* to *οἶδα*.

8. **οὐ μὴ νίψῃς.** Strong negative; *Thou shalt certainly never wash my feet.* See on viii. 51, and comp. *οὐ μὴ ἔσται σοι τοῦτο* (Matt. xvi. 22). In both utterances S. Peter resents the idea of his Master being humiliated.

οὐκ ἔχεις μέρος. Comp. *ὁ ἔχων μέρος* (Rev. xx. 6). The phrase occurs nowhere else in N.T. See on *ὄψις*, xi. 44. Comp. *οὐκ ἔστι σοι μερὶς οὐδὲ κλῆρος* (Acts viii. 21; Deut. x. 9, xii. 12, xiv. 27, &c.), and *τὸ μέρος αὐτοῦ μετὰ τ. ὑποκριτῶν θήσει* (Matt. xxiv. 51). The expression is of Hebrew origin. To reject Christ's self-humiliating love, because it humiliates Him (a well-meaning but false principle), is to cut oneself off from Him. It requires much more humility to accept a benefit which is a serious loss to the giver than one which costs him nothing. In this also the surrender of self is necessary.

9. **μὴ τ. πόδας μ. μόνον.** The impetuosity which is so marked a characteristic of S. Peter in the first three Gospels (comp. especially Luke v. 8 and Matt. xvi. 22) comes out very strongly in his three utterances here. It is incredible that this should be invention; and if not, the independent authority of S. John's narrative is manifest.

10. **ὁ λελουμένος.** *He that is* **bathed** (comp. Heb. x. 22 and 2 Pet. ii. 22). *Νίπτειν* (see on ix. 7) means to wash part of the body, *λούεσθαι* to bathe the whole person. A man who has bathed does not need to bathe again when he reaches home, but only to wash the dust off his feet: then he is wholly clean. So also in the spiritual life, a

man whose moral nature has once been thoroughly purified need not think that this has been all undone if in the walk through life he contracts some stains: these must be washed away, and then he is once more wholly clean. Peter, conscious of his own imperfections, in Luke v. 8, and possibly here, rushes to the conclusion that he is utterly unclean. But his meaning here perhaps rather is; 'If having part in Thee depends on being washed by Thee, wash all Thou canst.' S. Peter excellently illustrates Christ's saying. His love for his Master proves that he had bathed; his boastfulness (*v.* 37), his attack on Malchus (xviii. 10), his d nials (25, 27), his dissimulation at Antioch (Gal. ii.), all shew how often he had need to wash his feet.

τὸν παραδιδόντα. Him that was betraying or *delivering over:* the participle marks the work as already going on (xviii. 2, 5). In Luke vi. 16 Judas is called *προδότης*, 'a traitor;' but elsewhere **παραδιδόναι**, not **προδιδόναι**, is the word used to express his crime.

οὐχὶ πάντες. The second indication of the presence of a traitor (comp. vi. 70). Apparently it did not attract much attention: each, conscious of his own faults, thought the remark only too true. The disclosure is made gradually but rapidly now (*vv.* 18, 21, 26).

12. **ἀνέπεσεν.** The word is frequent in the Gospels (nowhere else in N.T.) of reclining at meals. It always implies a *change* of position (*v.* 25, vi. 10, xxi. 20; Matt. xv. 35; Mark vi. 40; Luke xi. 37). **Γινώσκετε**, *Perceive ye?* (see on *v.* 7), directs their attention to the explanation to be given.

13. **ὁ διδάσκαλος κ. ὁ κύριος.** The ordinary titles of respect paid to a Rabbi (i. 29, xx. 16, iv. 11, 15, 19): *κύριος* is the correlative of *δοῦλος* (*v.* 16), *διδάσκαλος* of *μαθητής*. For the nominative in addresses comp. xix. 3; Matt. xi. 26; Mark v. 41; Luke viii. 54, &c. It is specially common with the imperative. Winer, p. 227.

14. **εἰ οὖν ἐγὼ ἔν. ὑμῶν τ. π.** The pronouns are emphatic and opposed. The aorist indicates the act now accomplished: comp. xv. 20, xviii. 23. But in English the perfect is more usual in such cases: *if I, therefore,* **the** *Lord and* **the** *Master,* (*have*) *washed* (see on viii. 29). Here *ὁ κύριος* stands first as the title of deeper meaning: the disciples would use it with increased meaning as their knowledge increased.

καὶ ὑμεῖς ὀφ. The custom of the 'feet-washing' on Maundy Thursday in literal fulfilment of this typical commandment is not older than the fourth century. The Lord High Almoner washed the feet of the recipients of the royal 'maundy' as late as 1731. James II. was the last English sovereign who went through the ceremony. In 1 Tim. v. 10 'washing the saints' feet' is perhaps given rather as a *type* of devoted charity than as a definite act to be required.

15. **καθὼς ἐγὼ ἐπ. ὑμῖν.** Not, '*what* I have done to you,' but '**even as** I have done:' this is the spirit in which to act—self-sacrificing humility—whether or no it be exhibited precisely in this way. Mutual service, and especially mutual cleansing, is the obligation of Christ's disciples. Comp. James v. 16.

16. οὐκ ἔστιν δοῦλος κ.τ.λ. This saying occurs four times in the Gospels, each time in a different connexion: (1) to shew that the disciples must expect no better treatment than their Master (Matt. x. 24); (2) to impress the Apostles with their responsibilities as teachers, for their disciples will be as they are (Luke vi. 40); (3) here, to teach humility (comp. Luke xxii. 27); (4) with the same purpose as in Matt. x. 24, but on another occasion (xv. 20). We infer that it was one of Christ's frequent sayings: it is introduced here with the double ἀμήν, as of special importance (i. 52). **'Απόστολος,** *one that is sent*, an apostle.

17. μακάριοί ἐστε. Blessed *are ye*, as in the Beatitudes: comp. xx. 29; Rev. i. 3, xiv. 13, &c. Knowledge must influence conduct. Εἰ introduces the general supposition, *if ye know;* ἐάν the particular condition, *provided ye do them.* Comp. Rev. ii. 5; 1 Cor. vii. 36; Gal. i. 8, 9; Acts v. 38. Winer, p. 370.

18. οὐ περὶ πάντων. There is one who knows, and does not do, and is the very reverse of blessed. *I* know the character of the Twelve whom **I chose** (vi. 70, xv. 16); the treachery of one is no surprise to Me. For the elliptical ἀλλ' ἵνα, '*but* this was done *in order that*,' so frequent in S. John, see on i. 8. Here we may supply ἐλεξάμην: *but* I chose them *in order that.* Winer, p. 398.

ἡ γραφὴ πλ. See on ii. 22 and xii. 38. The quotation is taken, but with freedom, from the Hebrew of Ps. xli. 9: for ἐπῆρεν ἐπ' ἐμὲ τ. πτέρναν αὐτοῦ both Hebrew and LXX. have 'magnified his heel against me,'. ἐμεγάλυνεν ἐπ' ἐμὲ πτερνισμόν. The metaphor here is of one lifting up his foot before kicking, but the blow is not yet given. This was the attitude of Judas at this moment. Jesus omits 'Mine own familiar friend whom I trusted.' He had not trusted Judas, and had not been deceived as the Psalmist had been: 'He knew what was in man' (ii. 25). The variations from the LXX. are still more remarkable in the first clause. S. John quotes ὁ τρώγων μετ' ἐμοῦ τὸν ἄρτον, the LXX. having ὁ ἐσθίων ἄρτους μου. We notice (1) τρώγειν, the verb used of eating Christ's Flesh and the Bread from Heaven (vi. 54, 56, 57, 58), and nowhere else in N.T. excepting Matt. xxiv. 38, instead of the much more common ἐσθίειν: (2) τὸν ἄρτον, **the** *bread*, instead of ἄρτους, *bread* or *loaves:* (3) μετ' ἐμοῦ for μου, if the reading μετ' ἐμοῦ be genuine, which is doubtful. To eat bread with a man is more than to eat his bread, which a servant might do. The variations can scarcely be accidental, and seem to point to the fact that the treachery of Judas in violating the bond of hospitality, so universally held sacred in the East, was aggravated by his having partaken of the Eucharist. That Judas did partake of the Eucharist seems to follow from Luke xxii. 19—21, but the point is one about which there is much controversy.

S. John omits the institution of the Eucharist for the same reason that he omits so much,—because it was so well known to every instructed Christian; and for such he writes.

19. ἀπ' ἄρτι. From henceforth (xiv. 7; Rev. xiv. 13): see on ii. 10. Hitherto, for Judas' sake, Jesus had been reserved about the presence of a traitor; to point him out might have deprived him of a chance of recovery. But every good influence has failed, even the Eucharist and the washing of his feet: and *from this time onward*, for the Eleven's sake, He tells them. The success of such treachery might have shaken their faith had it taken them unawares: by foretelling it He turns it into an aid to faith. Comp. xiv. 29. For *ἐγώ εἰμι* see on viii. 24, 28, 58.

20. ὁ λαμβάνων κ.τ.λ. The connexion of this saying, solemnly introduced with the double 'verily,' with what precedes is not easy to determine. The saying is one with which Christ had sent forth the Apostles in the first instance (Matt. x. 40). It is recalled at the moment when one of them is being denounced for treachery. It was natural that such an end to such a mission should send Christ's thoughts back to the beginning of it. Moreover He would warn them all from supposing that such a catastrophe either cancelled the mission or proved it to be worthless from the first. Of every one of them, even of Judas himself, the saying still held good, 'he that receiveth *whomsoever* I send, receiveth Me.' The unworthiness of the minister cannot annul the commission.

21—30. The self-excommunication of the traitor

21. ἐταράχθη τῷ πν. It is the *πνεῦμα*, the seat of the religious emotions, not the *ψυχή*, that is affected by the thought of Judas' sin (xi. 33). For the dative comp. Acts xviii. 25; Rom. xiv. 1; Eph. iv. 18, 23; Col. i. 21. Once more the reality of Christ's human nature is brought before us (xi. 33, 35, 38, xii. 27); but quite incidentally and without special point. It is the artless story of one who tells what he saw because he saw it and remembers it. The lifelike details which follow are almost irresistible evidences of truthfulness.

22. ἔβλεπον εἰς ἀλ. 'Began to inquire among themselves' (Luke xxii. 23). The other two state that all began to say to Him 'Is it I?' They neither doubt the statement, nor ask 'Is it *he?*' Each thinks it is as credible of himself as of any of the others. Judas asks, either to dissemble, or to see whether he really is known (Matt. xxvi. 25). **'Απορούμενοι** expresses bewilderment rather than doubt.

23. ἦν ἀνακείμενος...ἐν τ. κόλπῳ. It is important to distinguish between this reclining on Jesus' lap and *ἀναπέσων ἐπὶ τὸ στῆθος* in *v.* 25. The Jews had adopted the Persian, Greek, and Roman custom of reclining at meals, and had long since exchanged the original practice of standing at the Passover first for sitting and then for reclining. They reclined on the left arm and ate with the right. This is the posture of the beloved disciple indicated here, which continued throughout the meal: in *v.* 25 we have a momentary change of posture.

ὃν ἠγάπα ὁ 'I. This explains how S. John came to be nearest and to be told who was the traitor (*Introduction*, p. xxxiv.) Comp. xix. 26, xxi. 7, 20; not xx. 2. S. John was on the Lord's right. Who was next to Him on the left? Possibly Judas, who must have been very close for Christ to answer him without the others hearing.

24. **εἰπὲ τίς ἐστιν.** S. Peter thinks that the beloved disciple is sure to know. The reading of T. R., *πύθεσθαι τίς ἂν εἴη*, is wanting in authority and contains an optative, which S. John never uses.

25. **ἀναπεσὼν...ἐπὶ τὸ στῆθος.** In *v.* 23 we have the permanent posture, here a change, as in *v.* 12: **he leaning back on to Jesus' breast.** For **ἐκεῖνος** see on i. 8; for **οὕτως**, *as he was*, comp. iv. 6. "This is among the most striking of those vivid descriptive traits which distinguish the narrative of the Fourth Gospel generally, and which are especially remarkable in these last scenes of Jesus' life, where the beloved disciple was himself an eye-witness and an actor. It is therefore to be regretted that these fine touches of the picture should be blurred in our English Bibles." Lightfoot, *On Revision*, p. 73.

26. **ᾧ ἐγὼ βάψω τὸ ψ. κ. δώσω αὐτῷ. For whom I shall dip the morsel and give it to him.** The text is much confused, perhaps owing to copyists having tried to correct the awkwardness of *ᾧ* and *αὐτῷ* (comp. vi. 51, xiv. 4). *Ψώμιον* (*ψώειν*, collat. form of *ψάειν*, 'to rub') is 'a little piece broken off;' it is still the common word in Greece for bread. To give such a morsel at a meal was an ordinary mark of goodwill, somewhat analagous to taking wine with a person in modern times. Christ, therefore, as a forlorn hope, gives the traitor one more mark of affection before dismissing him. It is the last such mark: 'Friend, wherefore art thou come?' (Matt. xxvi. 50) should be 'Comrade, (do that) for which thou art come,' and is a sorrowful rebuke rather than an affectionate greeting. Whether the morsel was a piece of the unleavened bread dipped in the broth of bitter herbs depends upon whether this supper is regarded as the Paschal meal or not. The name of the traitor is once more given with solemn fulness as in *v.* 2 and vi. 71, *Judas the son of* **Simon Iscariot.**

27. **τότε εἰσῆλθεν κ.τ.λ. At that moment** *Satan entered into him.* At first Satan made suggestions to him (*v.* 2; Luke xxii. 3) and Judas listened to them; now Satan takes full possession of him. Desire had conceived and brought forth sin, and the sin full grown had engendered death (James i. 15). Jesus knew that Satan had claimed his own, and **therefore** *saith to him, That thou doest, do more quickly;* carry it out at once, even sooner than was planned (1 Tim. iii. 14), Winer, p. 304. Now that the case of Judas was hopeless, delay merely kept Jesus from His hour of victory (Matt. xxiii. 32; Luke xii. 50). He longs to be alone with the faithful Eleven. For **τάχιον** see on xx. 4.

28. **οὐδεὶς ἔγνω.** Even S. John, who now knew that Judas was the traitor, did not know that Christ's words alluded to his treachery.

29. **τινὲς γάρ.** The *γάρ* introduces a proof that they could not have understood. For **γλωσσόκομον** see on xii. 6. *Εἰς τ. ἑορτήν* agrees with *v.* 1 in shewing that this meal precedes the Passover. For *τ. πτωχοῖς* comp. xii. 5; Neh. viii. 10, 12; Gal. ii. 10. Note the change of construction from *ἀγόρασον* to *ἵνα δῷ*: comp. viii. 53, xv. 5.

30. ἐκεῖνος. Here and in *v.* 27 the pronoun marks Judas as an alien (comp. vii. 11, ix. 12, 28). *Vv.* 28, 29 are parenthetical: the Evangelist now returns to the narrative, repeating with solemnity the incident which formed the last crisis in the career of Judas. Ἐξῆλθεν εὐθύς is no evidence that the meal was not a Paschal one. The rule that 'none should go out at the door of his house until the morning' (Ex. xii. 22) had, like standing at the Passover, long since been abrogated. Judas goes out from the presence of the Christ like Cain from the presence of the Lord. *Dum vult esse praedo, fit praeda.*

ἦν δὲ νύξ. Comp. 1 Sam. xxviii. 8. The tragic brevity of this has often been remarked, and will never cease to lay hold of the imagination. It can scarcely be meant merely to tell us that at the time when Judas went out night had begun. In the Gospel in which the Messiah so often appears as the Light of the World (i. 4—9, iii. 19—21, viii. 12, ix. 5, xii. 35, 36, 46), and in which darkness almost invariably means moral darkness (i. 5, viii. 12, xii. 35, 46), a use peculiar to S. John (1 John i. 5, ii. 8, 9, 11),—we shall hardly be wrong in understanding also that Judas went forth from the Light of the World into the night in which a man cannot but stumble 'because there is no light in him' (xi. 10): see on iii. 2, x. 22, xviii. 1. Thus also Christ Himself said some two hours later, 'This is your hour, and the power of darkness' (Luke xxii. 53). For other remarks of telling brevity and abruptness comp. χειμὼν ἦν (x. 22); ἐδάκρυσεν ὁ Ἰησοῦς (xi. 35); λέγει αὐτοῖς Ἐγώ εἰμι (xviii. 5); ἦν δὲ ὁ Βαραββᾶς λῃστής (xviii. 40).

These remarks shew the impropriety of joining this sentence to the next verse; 'and it was night, therefore, when he had gone out;' a combination which is clumsy in itself and quite spoils the effect.

XIII. 31—XV. 27. Christ's Love in keeping His own

31—35. Jesus, freed from the oppressive presence of the traitor, bursts out into a declaration that the glorification of the Son of Man has begun. Judas is already beginning that series of events which will end in sending Him away from them to the Father; therefore they must continue on earth the kingdom which He has begun—the reign of Love.

This section forms the first portion of those parting words of heavenly meaning which were spoken to the faithful Eleven in the last moments before His Passion. At first the discourse takes the form of dialogue, which lasts almost to the end of chap. xiv. Then they rise from the table, and the words of Christ become more sustained, while the disciples remain silent with the exception of xvi. 17, 18, 29, 30. Then follows Christ's prayer, after which they go forth to the Garden of Gethsemane (xviii. 1).

31. ὅτε οὖν ἐξῆλθεν. Indicating that the presence of Judas had acted as a constraint, but also that he had gone of his own will: there was no casting out of the faithless disciple (ix. 34). **Νῦν**, with solemn exultation: the beginning of the end has come. For **ὁ υἱὸς τ. ἀνθ.**

see on i. 52: for the aorist **ἐδοξάσθη** see Winer, p. 345. He was glorified in finishing the work which the Father gave Him to do (xvii. 4); and thus God was glorified in Him.

32. **εἰ ὁ θ. ἐδοξ. ἐν αὐτῷ.** These words are wanting in ℵBC[1]DLX; the repetition might account for their being omitted, but they spoil the marked balance and rhythm of the clauses in *vv.* 31, 32.

καὶ ὁ θ. δοξάσει. And *God shall glorify Him*, with the glory which He had with the Father before the world was. Hence the future. The glory of completing the work of redemption is already present; that of returning to the Father will straightway follow. **Ἐν αὐτῷ** means 'in God:' as God is glorified in the Messianic work of the Son, so the Son shall be glorified in the eternal blessedness of the Father. Comp. xvii. 4, 5; Phil. ii. 9.

33. **τέκνια.** Nowhere else in the Gospels does Christ use this expression of tender affection, which springs from the thought of His orphaned disciples. S. John appears never to have forgotten it. It occurs frequently in his First Epistle (ii. 1, 12, 28, iii. 7, 18, iv. 4, v. 21), and perhaps nowhere else in the N. T. In Gal. iv. 19 the reading is doubtful. Comp. *παίδια*, xxi. 5. For **ἔτι μικρὸν** see on vii. 33, 34, viii. 21.

ζητήσετέ με. Christ does not add, as He did to the Jews, 'and shall not find Me,' still less, 'ye shall die in your sin.' Rather, 'ye shall seek Me: and though ye cannot come whither I go, yet ye shall find Me by continuing to be My disciples and loving one another.' The expression **οἱ Ἰουδαῖοι** is rare in Christ's discourses (iv. 22, xviii. 20, 36): in these cases the idea of nationality prevails over that of hostility to the Messiah.

34. **ἐντολὴν καινήν.** The commandment to love was not new, for 'thou shalt love thy neighbour as thyself' (Lev. xix. 18) was part of the Mosaic Law. But the motive is new; to love our neighbour because Christ has loved us. We have only to read the 'most excellent way' of love set forth in 1 Cor. xiii., and compare it with the measured benevolence of the Pentateuch, to see how new the commandment had become by having this motive added. *Καινὴν* not *νέαν*: *καινός* looks back, 'fresh' as opposed to 'worn out' (xix. 41; 1 John ii. 7, 8, which doubtless refers to this passage; Rev. ii. 17, iii. 12, xxi. 1—5); *νέος* looks forward, 'young' as opposed to 'aged' (Luke v. 39; 1 Cor. v. 7). Both are used Mark ii. 22, *οἶνον νέον εἰς ἀσκοὺς καινούς*, *new wine into* **fresh** *wine-skins*. Both are used of *διαθήκη*: *νέα*, Heb. xii. 24; *καινή*, Luke xxii. 20. *Ἐντολὴν διδόναι* is peculiar to S. John (xii. 49, xiv. 31; 1 John iii. 23; comp. xi. 57). *Καθὼς ἠγάπησα ὑμᾶς* belongs to the second half of the verse, being the *reason* for the fresh commandment;—**even as** *I* (*have*) *loved you*. Comp. 'If God so loved us, we ought also to love one another' (1 John iv. 11). The aorist shews that Christ's work is regarded as already completed; but the perfect is perhaps more in accordance with English idiom: see on viii. 29 and comp. xv. 9, 12.

35. ἐν τούτῳ γν. π. This is the true 'Note of the Church;' not miracles, not formularies, not numbers, but *love.* "The working of such love puts a brand upon us; for see, say the heathen, how they love one another," Tertullian, *Apol.* XXXIX. Comp. 1 John iii. 10, 14. **Ἐμοί** is emphatic; *disciples* **to Me**.

36. ποῦ ὑπάγεις; The affectionate Apostle is absorbed by the words, 'Whither I go, ye cannot come,' and he lets all the rest pass. His Lord is going away, out of his reach; he must know the meaning of that. The Lord's reply alludes probably not merely to the Apostle's death, but also to the manner of it: comp. xxi. 18, 19. But his hour has not yet come; he has a great mission to fulfil first (Matt. xvi, 18). The beautiful story of the *Domine, quo vadis?* should be remembered in connexion with this verse. See Introduction to the Epistles of S. Peter, p. 56.

37. ἄρτι. Even now, at once (ii. 10). He sees that Christ's going away means death, and with his usual impulsiveness (*v.* 9) he declares that he is ready to follow even thither at once. He mistakes strong feeling for moral strength. For **τ. ψυχήν μ. θήσω** see on x. 11.

38. λέγω σοι. In the parallel passage, Luke xxii. 34, we have *λέγω σοι,* **Πέτρε.** For the first and last time Jesus addresses the Apostle by the name which He had given him; as if to remind him that rock-like strength was not his own to boast of, but must be found in humble reliance on the Giver.

S. Luke agrees with S. John in placing the prediction of the triple denial in the supper-room: S. Matt. (xxvi. 30—35) and S. Mark (xiv. 26—30) place it on the way from the room to Gethsemane. It is possible but not probable that the prediction was repeated; though some would even make three predictions recorded by (1) S. Luke, (2) S. John, (3) S. Matt. and S. Mark. See Appendix B.

τρίς. All four accounts agree in this. S. Mark adds two details: (1) that the cock should crow *twice,* (2) that the prediction so far from checking S. Peter made him speak only the more vehemently, a particular which S. Peter's Gospel more naturally contains than the other three. S. Matthew and S. Mark both add that all the disciples joined in S. Peter's protestations. In these discourses S. Peter speaks no more.

It has been objected that fowls were not allowed in the Holy City. The statement wants authority, and of course the Romans would pay no attention to any such rule, even if it existed among the Jews.

CHAPTER XIV

4. Omit *καί* before, and **οἴδατε** after, **τὴν ὁδόν** with ℵBLQX against ADN: insertions for clearness.

10. λέγω for **λαλῶ** (correction for uniformity): and **ποιεῖ τὰ ἔργα αὐτοῦ** for *αὐτὸς π. τ. ἔργα* with ℵBD against ANQ.

16. ᾖ for μένῃ (from *v.* 17). Authorities differ as to the position of ᾖ, whether before or after **μεθ' ὑμῶν**, or after **αἰῶνα.**

19. **ζήσετε** for ζήσεσθε; comp. vi. 57; Winer, p. 105.

23. **ποιησόμεθα** (ℵBLX) for ποιήσομεν (A). The middle of ποιεῖν is comparatively rare in N.T., but here it is appropriate; Winer, p. 320.

30. Omit τούτου after **κόσμου** (insertion from xii. 31, xvi. 11).

31. **ἐντολὴν ἔδωκεν** (BLX) for ἐνετείλατο (ℵAD).

In this last great discourse (xiv.—xvii.) we find a return of the *spiral movement* noticed in the Prologue (see on i. 18). The various subjects are repeatedly presented and withdrawn in turn. Thus the Paraclete is spoken of in five different sections (xiv. 16, 17; 25, 26; xv. 26; xvi. 8—15; 23—25); the relation between the Church and the world in three (xiv. 22—24; xv. 18—25; xvi. 1—3). So also with Christ's departure and return.

Chap. XIV. Christ's love in keeping His own (continued)

1. **μὴ ταρασσέσθω ὑ. ἡ. κ.** There had been much to cause anxiety and alarm; the denouncing of the traitor, the declaration of Christ's approaching departure, the prediction of S. Peter's denial. The last as being nearest might seem to be specially indicated; but what follows shews that μὴ ταρασσέσθω refers primarily to ὅπου ἐγὼ ὑπάγω, ὑμεῖς οὐ δύνασθε ἐλθεῖν (xiii. 33). There is nothing to shew that one πιστεύετε is indicative and the other imperative. Probably both are imperative like ταρασσέσθω: comp. v. 39, xii. 19, xv. 18. In any case a full genuine belief and trust (i. 12) in God leads to a belief and trust in His Son.

2. **τῇ οἰκίᾳ τ. πατρός.** Heaven. Matt. v. 34, vi. 9. By μοναὶ πολλαί nothing is said as to mansions differing in dignity and beauty. There may be degrees of happiness hereafter, but such are neither expressed nor implied here. The abodes are many; there is room enough for all. **Μονή** occurs in N. T. only here and *v.* 23. It is derived from S. John's favourite verb μένειν (i. 33), which occurs *vv.* 10, 16, 17, 25, and 12 times in chap. xv. Μονή, therefore, is 'a place to abide in, an abode.' 'Mansion,' Scotch 'manse,' and French 'maison' are all from *manere*, the Latin form of the same root.

εἰ δὲ μή, εἶπον ἂν ὑμῖν· ὅτι π. The construction is amphibolous and may be taken in four ways. 1. *If it were not so, I would have told you;* because *I go.* This is best. Christ appeals to His fairness: would He have invited them to a place where there was not room for all? 2. 'In My Father's house are many mansions; (if it were not so, I would have told you;) *because* I go.' 3. 'Would I have said to you *that* I go?' 4. 'I would have said to you *that* I go.' The last cannot be right. Jesus had already said (xiii. 36), and says again (*v.* 3), that He is going to shew the way and prepare a place for them.

3. ἐὰν πορευθῶ. The *ἐάν* does not imply a doubt; but, as in xii. 32, it is the *result* rather than the date of the action that is emphasized; hence 'if,' not 'when.' See on xii. 26.

ἔρχομαι κ. παραλήμψομαι. The late form *λήμψομαι* occurs again Acts i. 8; we have *λάμψομαι* Hdt. IX. 108. The change from present to future is important: Christ is ever coming in various ways to His Church; but His receiving of each individual will take place once for all at death and at the last day (see on xix. 16). Christ's coming again may have various meanings and apparently not always the same one throughout these discourses; the Resurrection, or the gift of the Paraclete, or the presence of Christ in His Church, or the death of individuals, or the Second Advent at the last day. Comp. vi. 39, 40.

4. ὅπου ἐγὼ ὑπ. οἴδ. τ. ὁδόν. This seems to have been altered as in T. R. to avoid awkwardness of expression (see on vi. 51, xiii. 26). Ἐγώ is emphatic; in having experience of Him they know the way to the Father. The words are half a rebuke, implying that they ought to know more than they did know (x. 7, 9, xi. 25). Thus we say 'you know,' meaning 'you might know, if you did but take the trouble.'

5. Θωμᾶς. Nothing is to be inferred from the omission of *Δίδυμος* here (comp. xi. 16, xx. 24, xxi. 2). For his character see on xi. 16. His question here has a melancholy tone combined with some dulness of apprehension. But there is honesty of purpose in it. He owns his ignorance and asks for explanation. This great home with many abodes, is it the royal city of the conquering Messiah, who is to restore the kingdom to Israel (see on Acts i. 6); and will not that be Jerusalem? How then can He be going anywhere? *How* **do** *we know the way?* The abrupt asyndeton gives emphasis.

6. ἐγώ εἰμι. See on vi. 35. The pronoun is emphatic; I and no other: *Ego sum Via, Veritas, Vita.* S. Thomas had wished rather to know about the goal; Christ shews that for him, and therefore for us, it is more important to know the way. Hence the order; although Christ is the Truth and the Life before He is the Way. The Word is the Truth and the Life from all eternity with the Father: He becomes the Way for us by taking our nature. He is the Way to the many abodes in His Father's home, the Way to the Father Himself; and that by His doctrine and example, by His Death and Resurrection. In harmony with this passage 'the Way' soon became a recognised name for Christianity; Acts ix. 2, xix. 9, 23, xxii. 4, xxiv. 22 (comp. xxiv. 14; 2 Pet. ii. 2). But this is obscured in our version by the common inaccuracy '*this* way' or '*that* way' for '*the* Way.' (See on i. 21, 25, vi. 48.)

ἡ ἀλήθεια. Being from all eternity in the form of God, Who cannot lie (Phil. ii. 6; Heb. vi. 18), and being the representative on earth of a Sender Who is true (viii. 26). To know the Truth is also to know the Way to God, Who must be approached and worshipped in truth (iv. 23). Comp. Heb. xi. 6; 1 John v. 20.

ἡ ζωή. Comp. xi. 25. He is the Life, being one with the living Father and being sent by Him (x. 30, vi. 57). See on i. 4, vi. 50, 51, and comp. 1 John v. 12; Gal. ii. 20. Here again to know the Life is to know the Way to God. But the three thoughts must not be merged into one; 'I am the true way of life,' or 'the living way of truth.' The three, though interdependent, are distinct; and the Way is the most important to know, as Christ insists by adding *οὐδεὶς ἔρχεται π. τ. π., εἰ μὴ δι' ἐμοῦ.* Comp. *δι' αὐτοῦ ἔχομεν τὴν προσαγωγὴν πρὸς τὸν πατέρα* (Eph. ii. 18). See also Heb. x. 19—22; 1 Pet. iii. 18.

7. εἰ ἐγνώκειτέ με, κ. τ. π. μ. ἐγνώκειτε ἄν. The better reading is **ἂν ᾔδειτε**: *If ye* had learned to know *Me, ye* would know *My Father also.* The change of verb and of order are both significant. See on vii. 26, viii. 55, xiii. 7. The emphasis is on *ἐγνώκειτε* and on *πάτερα*: 'If ye had *recognised* Me, ye would know My *Father* also.' Beware of putting an emphasis on 'Me:' an enclitic cannot be emphatic.

ἀπ' ἄρτι. To be understood literally, not proleptically (comp. xiii. 19; Rev. xiv. 13). Hitherto the veil of Jewish prejudice had been on their hearts, obscuring the true meaning of Messianic prophecy and Messianic acts. But *henceforth*, after the plain declaration in *v.* 6, they *learn to know* the Father in Him. Philip's request leads to a fuller statement of *v.* 6.

Φίλιππος. For the fourth and last time S. Philip appears in this Gospel (see notes on i. 44—49, vi. 5—7, xii. 22). Thrice he is mentioned in close connexion with S. Andrew, who may have brought about his being found by Christ; twice he follows in the footsteps of S. Andrew in bringing others to Christ, and on both occasions it is specially to *see* Him that they are brought; 'Come and *see*' (i. 45); 'We would *see* Jesus' (xii. 21). Like S. Thomas he has a fondness for the practical test of personal experience; he would see for himself, and have others also see for themselves. His way of stating the difficulty about the 5000 (vi. 7) is quite in harmony with this practical turn of mind. Like S. Thomas also he seems to have been somewhat slow of apprehension, and at the same time perfectly honest in expressing the cravings which he felt. No fear of exposing himself keeps either Apostle back: and the freedom with which each speaks shews how truly Christ had 'called them friends' (xv. 15).

δεῖξον ἡμῖν. He is struck by Christ's last words, 'Ye have seen the Father,' and cannot find that they are true of himself. It is what he has been longing for in vain; it is the one thing wanting. He has heard the voice of the Father from Heaven, and it has awakened a hunger in his heart. Christ has been speaking of the Father's home with its many abodes to which He is going; and Philip longs to see for himself. And when Christ tells him that he *has* seen he unreservedly opens his mind: 'Only make that saying good, and it is enough.' He sees nothing impossible in this. There were the theophanies, which had accompanied the giving of the Law through Moses. And a greater than Moses was here.

9. τοσούτῳ χρόνῳ. Philip had been called among the first (i. 44), and yet has not learned to know the Christ. Comp. viii. 19. The Gospels are full of evidence of how little the Apostles understood of the life which they were allowed to share: and the candour with which this is confessed confirms our trust in the narratives. Not until Pentecost were their minds fully enlightened. Comp. x. 6, xii. 16; Matt. xv. 16, xvi. 8; Mark ix. 32; Luke ix. 45, xviii. 34, xxiv. 25; Acts i. 6; Heb. v. 12. Christ's question is asked in sorrowful but affectionate surprise; hence the tender repetition of the name. Had S. Philip recognised Christ, he would have seen the revelation of God in Him, and would never have asked for a vision of God such as was granted to Moses. See notes on xii. 44, 45. There is no reference to the Transfiguration, of which S. Philip had not yet been told; Matt. xvii. 9. For the dative, a doubtful reading, see Winer, p. 273.

ὁ ἑωρακὼς ἐμὲ ἑώρ. τ. πατέρα. Again there is the majesty of Divinity in the utterance. What mere man would dare to say, 'He that hath seen me hath seen God'? Comp. *v.* 30, viii. 29, 42, xv. 10.

10. οὐ πιστεύεις. S. Philip's question seemed to imply that he did not believe this truth, although Christ had taught it publicly (x. 38). What follows is stated in an argumentative form. 'That the Father is in Me is proved by the fact that My words do not originate with Myself; and this is proved by the fact that My works do not originate with Myself, but are really His.' No proof is given of this last statement: Christ's works speak for themselves; they are manifestly Divine. It matters little whether we regard the argument as *à fortiori*, the works being stronger evidence than the words; or as inclusive, the works covering and containing the words. The latter seems to agree best with viii. 28. For *τὰ ῥήματα* see on iii. 34: *λέγω* refers to the substance, λαλῶ to the form of the utterances (xii. 49, xvi. 18). On the whole statement that Christ's words and works are not His own but the Father's, comp. v. 19, 30, viii. 26—29, xii. 44: *τὰ ἔργα αὐτοῦ* are the Father's works, done and seen in the Son.

11. πιστεύετέ μοι. In English we lose the point that Jesus now turns from S. Philip and addresses all the Eleven. 'Ye have been with Me long enough to believe what I say; but if not, at any rate believe what I do. My words need no credentials: but if credentials are demanded, there are My works.' He had said the same, somewhat more severely, to the Jews (x. 37, 38, where see note); and He repeats it much more severely in reference to the Jews (xv. 22, 24). Note the progress from *πιστεύετέ* **μοι** here to *ὁ πιστεύων* **εἰς ἐμέ** in *v.* 12; the one grows out of the other.

12. κἀκεῖνος ποιήσει. Comp. vi. 57 and *vv.* 21, 26: see on i. 8, 18. 'Like Me, he shall do the works of the Father, He dwelling in him through the Son. Comp. *καθὼς ἐκεῖνός ἐστι, καὶ ἡμεῖς ἐσμεν ἐν τῷ κόσμῳ τούτῳ* (1 John iv. 17).

καὶ μείζονα τούτων. No reference to healing by means of S. Peter's shadow (Acts v. 15) or of handkerchiefs that had touched S. Paul (Acts xix. 12). Even from a human point of view no miracle wrought by an Apostle is greater than the raising of Lazarus. But from a spiritual point of view no such comparisons are admissible; to Omnipotence all works are alike. These 'greater works' refer rather to the results of Pentecost; the victory over Judaism and Paganism, two powers which for the moment were victorious over Christ (Luke xxii. 53). Christ's work was confined to Palestine and had but small success; the Apostles went everywhere, and converted thousands. The reason introduced by *ὅτι* is twofold: (1) He will have left the earth and be unable to continue these works; therefore believers must continue them for Him; (2) He will be in heaven ready to help both directly and by intercession; therefore believers will be able to continue these works and surpass them. But note that He does not say that they shall surpass His *words*. He alone has words of eternal life; never man spake as He did (vi. 68, vii. 46).

It is doubtful whether there should be a comma or a full stop at the end of this verse. Our punctuation seems the better; but to make *ὅτι* run on into the next verse makes little difference to the sense.

13. ἐν τῷ ὀνόματί μου. The phrase occurs here for the first time. Comp. xv. 16, xvi. 23, 24, 26. Anything that can rightly be asked in His name will be granted; there is no other limit. By 'in My name' is not of course meant the mere using the formula 'through Jesus Christ.' Rather, it means praying and working as Christ's representatives in the same spirit in which Christ prayed and worked,—'Not My will, but Thine be done.' Prayers for other ends than this are excluded; not that it is said that they will not be granted, but there is no promise that they will be. Comp. 2 Cor. xii. 8, 9. For **ἵνα δοξασθῇ** see on xi. 4, xii. 28, xiii. 31.

14. ἐγὼ ποιήσω. Perhaps we ought to read **τοῦτο** *ποιήσω*, **this** *will I do* (iii. 32); but the emphatic *ἐγώ* suits the context better. In *v.* 13 the prayer is regarded as addressed to the Father, but granted by the Son: in *v.* 14, if the very strongly supported *με* is genuine, the prayer is addressed to Christ. In xvi. 23 the Father with equal truth grants the prayer.

15. ἐὰν ἀγαπᾶτέ με. The connexion with what precedes is again not quite clear. Some would see it in the condition 'in My name,' which includes willing obedience to His commands. Perhaps it is rather to be referred to the opening and general drift of the chapter. 'Let not your heart be troubled at My going away. You will still be Mine, I shall still be yours, and we shall still be caring for one another. I go to prepare a place for you, you remain to continue and surpass My work on earth. And though you can no longer minister to Me in the flesh, you can prove your love for Me even more perfectly by keeping *My* commandments when I am gone.' 'My' is emphatic (see on viii. 31); not those of the Law but of the Gospel. Only in these last discourses does Christ speak of His commandments: *v.* 21, xv. 10, 12, xiii. 34.

16. κἀγὼ ἐρ. Ἐγώ is emphatic: 'you do your part on earth, and I will do Mine in heaven.' So far as there is a distinction between αἰτεῖν and ἐρωτᾷν, the latter is the less suppliant. It is always used by S. John when Christ speaks of His own prayers to the Father (xvi. 26, xvii. 9, 15, 20). Martha, less careful than the Evangelist, uses αἰτεῖν of Christ's prayers (xi. 22). But the distinction must not be pressed as if αἰτεῖν were always used of inferiors (against which Deut. x. 12; Acts xvi. 29; 1 Pet. iii. 15 are conclusive), or ἐρωτᾷν always of equals (against which Mark vii. 26; Luke iv. 38, vii. 3; John iv. 40, 47; Acts iii. 3 are equally conclusive), although the tendency is in that direction. In 1 John v. 16 both words are used. In classical Greek ἐρωτᾷν is never 'to make a request,' but always (as in i. 19, 21, 25, ix. 2, 15, 19, 21, 23, &c.) 'to ask a question:' see on xvi. 23.

παράκλητον. Advocate. Παράκλητος is used five times in N. T.—four times in this Gospel by Christ of the Holy Spirit (xiv. 16, 26, xv. 26, xvi. 7), and once in the First Epistle by S. John of Christ (ii. 1). Our translators render it 'Comforter' in the Gospel, and 'Advocate' in the Epistle. As to the meaning of the word, usage appears to be decisive. It commonly signifies 'one who is summoned to the side of another' to aid him in a court of justice, especially the 'counsel for the *defence*.' It is *passive*, not active; 'one who is summoned to plead a cause,' not 'one who exhorts, or encourages, or comforts.' A comparison of the simple word (κλητός = 'called;' Matt. xx. 16, xxii. 14; Rom. i. 1, 6, 7; 1 Cor. i. 1, 2, &c.) and the other compounds, of which only one occurs in the N. T. (ἀνέγκλητος = 'unaccused;' 1 Cor. i. 8; Col. i. 22, &c.), or a reference to the general rule about adjectives similarly formed from transitive verbs, will shew that παράκλητος must have a passive sense. Moreover, 'Advocate' is the sense which the context suggests, wherever the word is used in the Gospel: the idea of pleading, arguing, convincing, instructing, is prominent in every instance. Here the Paraclete is the 'Spirit of *truth*,' whose reasonings fall dead on the ear of the world, and are taken in only by the faithful. In *v.* 26 He is to *teach* and *remind* them. In xv. 26 He is to *bear witness* to Christ. In xvi. 7—11 He is to *convince* or *convict* the world. In short, He is represented as the Advocate, the Counsel, who suggests true reasonings to our minds and true courses for our lives, convicts our adversary the world of wrong, and pleads our cause before God our Father. He may be 'summoned to our side' to comfort as well as to plead, and in the *Te Deum* the Holy Spirit is rightly called 'the Comforter,' but that is not the function which is set forth here. To substitute 'Advocate' will not only bring out the right meaning in the Gospel, but will bring the language of the Gospel into its true relation to the language of the Epistle. 'He will give you *another* Advocate' acquires fresh meaning when we remember that S. John calls Christ our 'Advocate;' the Advocacy of Christ and the Advocacy of the Spirit mutually illustrating one another. At the same time an important coincidence between the Gospel and Epistle is preserved, one of the many which help to prove that both are by one and the same author, and therefore that evidence of the genuineness of the Epistle is also evidence of the genuineness of the Gospel. See Lightfoot, *On Revision*, pp. 50—56, from which nearly the whole of this note is taken. S. Paul, though he does not use the word, has the doctrine: in Rom. viii. 27, 34 the same language, 'to make intercession for' (*ἐντυγχάνειν ὑπέρ*), is used both of the Spirit and of Christ. Philo frequently uses *παράκλητος* of the high-priest as the advocate and intercessor for the people. He also uses it in the same sense of the Divine *Λόγος*.

εἰς τ. αἰῶνα. Their present Advocate has come to them and will leave them again; this 'other Advocate' will come and never leave them. And in Him, who is the Spirit of Christ (Rom. viii. 9), Christ will be with them also (Matt. xxviii. 20).

17. τ. πν. τ. ἀληθ. This expression confirms the rendering 'Advocate.' Truth is more closely connected with the idea of advocating a cause than with that of comforting. Comp. xv. 26, xvi. 13; 1 John v. 6. The Paraclete is the Spirit of Truth as the Bearer of the Divine revelation, bringing truth home to the hearts of men. In 1 John iv. 6 it is opposed to the 'spirit of error.' Comp. 1 Cor. ii. 12. On **κόσμος** see on i. 10.

οὐ θεωρεῖ. **Beholdeth** *Him not, neither cometh to know Him*, because the Spirit and 'the things of the Spirit' must be 'spiritually discerned' (1 Cor. ii. 14). The world may have intelligence, scientific investigation, criticism, learning; but not by these is the Spirit of Truth contemplated and recognised; rather by humility, self-investigation, faith, and love. Note the presents *γινώσκετε, μένει, ἐστίν*. The Spirit is in the Apostles already, though not in the fulness of Pentecost. Note also (in *vv.* 16, 17) the definite personality of the Spirit, distinct from the Son who promises Him and the Father who gives Him: and the three prepositions; the Advocate is *with* us for fellowship (*μετά*); abides *by our side* to defend us (*παρά*); is *in* us as a source of power to each individually (*ἐν*).

18. ὀρφανούς. Desolate, or (with Wiclif) **fatherless**, as in James i. 27, the only other place in N. T. where it occurs. 'Comfortless' gives unfair support to 'Comforter': there is no connexion between *ὀρφανός* and *παράκλητος*. The connexion is rather with *τεκνία* in xiii. 33: He will not leave His 'little children' *fatherless*.

ἔρχ. πρός. I am coming *unto you*, in the Spirit, whom I will send. The context seems to shew clearly that Christ's spiritual reunion with them through the Paraclete, and not His bodily reunion with them either through the Resurrection or through the final Return, is intended. Note the frequent and impressive asyndeton in *vv.* 17—20.

19. ἔτι μικρόν. Comp. xiii. 33, xvi. 16. They behold Him in the Paraclete, ever present with them; and they shall have that higher and eternal life over which death has no power either in Him or His followers. Christ has this life in Himself (v. 26); His followers derive it from Him (v. 21).

20. ἐν ἐκ. τ. ἡμ. Comp. xvi. 23, 26. Pentecost, and thenceforth to the end of the world. They will *come to know*, for experience will teach them, that the presence of the Spirit is the presence of Christ, and through Him of the Father. For **ὑμεῖς ἐν ἐμοί** comp. xv. 4, 5, xvii. 21, 23; 1 John iii. 24, iv. 13, 15, 16.

21. **ἔχων...τηρῶν.** Bearing them steadfastly in his mind and observing them in his life. **Ἐκεῖνος**, with great emphasis (see on i. 18); he and no else.

ἐμφανίσω. Once more, as in vii. 17, willing obedience is set forth as the road to spiritual enlightenment. *Ἐμφανίζειν* (here only in S. John) is stronger than *φανεροῦν*.

22. **Ἰούδας.** Excluding the genealogies of Christ we have six persons of this name in N. T. 1. This Judas, who was the *son* of a certain James (Luke vi. 16; Acts i. 13): he is commonly identified with Lebbaeus or Thaddaeus (see on Matt. x. 3). 2. Judas Iscariot. 3. The brother of Jesus Christ, and of James, Joses, and Simon (Matt. xiii. 55; Mark vi. 3). 4. Judas, surnamed Barsabas (Acts xv. 22, 27, 32). 5. Judas of Galilee (Acts v. 37). 6. Judas of Damascus (Acts ix. 11). Of these six the third is probably the author of the Epistle; so that this remark is the only thing recorded in the N. T. of Judas the Apostle as distinct from the other Apostles. Nor is anything really known of him from other sources.

τί γέγονεν. What is come to pass; what has happened to determine Thee to so strange a course? *Ἐμφανίσω* rouses S. Judas just as *ἑωράκατε* (*v.* 7) roused S. Philip. Both go wrong from the same cause, inability to see the spiritual meaning of Christ's words; but they go wrong in different ways. Philip wishes for a vision of the Father, a Theophany, a suitable inauguration of the Messiah's kingdom. Judas supposes with the rest of his countrymen that the manifestation of the Messiah means a bodily appearance in glory before the whole world, to judge the Gentile and restore the kingdom to the Jews. Once more we have the Jewish point of view given with convincing precision. Comp. vii. 4.

23. **ἀπεκρίθη.** The answer is given, as so often in our Lord's replies, not directly, but by repeating and developing the statement which elicited the question. Comp. iii. 5—8, iv. 14, vi. 44—51, 53—58, &c. The condition of receiving the revelation is loving obedience; those who have it not cannot receive it. This shews that the revelation cannot be universal, cannot be shared by those who hate and disobey (xv. 18).

ἐλευσόμεθα. For the plural comp. x. 30; it is a distinct claim to Divinity: for **μονήν** see on *v.* 2. The thought of God dwelling among His people was familiar to every Jew (Ex. xxv. 8, xxix. 45; Zech. ii. 10; &c.). There is a thought far beyond that,—God dwelling in the heart of the individual; and later Jewish philosophy had attained to this also. But the united indwelling of the Father and the Son by means of the Spirit is purely Christian.

24. **οὐκ ἔστιν ἐμός.** Quite literally; comp. xii. 44. This explains why Christ cannot manifest Himself to the world: it rejects God's

word. On **πέμψαντος** see on i. 33. Perhaps there is a pause after *v.* 24: with *v.* 25 the discourse takes a fresh departure, returning to the subject of the Paraclete.

25. ταῦτα. First for emphasis in opposition to *πάντα* in *v.* 26: 'Thus much I tell you now; the Advocate shall tell you all.'

26. ἅγιον. This epithet is given to the Spirit thrice in this Gospel; i. 33, xx. 22, and here: in vii. 39 *ἅγιον* is an insertion. It is not frequent in any Gospel but the third; 5 times in S. Matt., 4 in S. Mark, 12 in S. Luke. S. Luke seems fond of the expression, which he uses some 40 times in the Acts; rarely using *Πνεῦμα* without *ἅγιον*. Here only does S. John give the full phrase: in i. 33 and xx. 22 there is no article.

ἐν τ. ὀν. μ. As My representative, taking My place and continuing My work: see on *v.* 13 and comp. xvi. 13, 14. The mission of the Paraclete in reference to the glorified Redeemer is analogous to that of the Messiah in reference to the Father. And His two functions are connected: He teaches new truths, 'things to come,' things which they 'cannot bear now,' in recalling the old; and He brings the old to their remembrance in teaching the new. He recalls not merely the words of Christ, a particular in which this Gospel is a striking fulfilment of the promise, but also the meaning of them, which the Apostles often failed to see at the time: comp. ii. 22, xii. 16; Luke ix. 45, xviii. 34, xxiv. 8. "It is on the fulfilment of this promise to the Apostles, that their sufficiency as Witnesses of all that the Lord did and taught, and consequently the *authenticity of the Gospel narrative*, is grounded" (Alford).

27. εἰρήνην ἀφ. This is probably a solemn adaptation of the conventional form of taking leave in the East: comp. 'Go in peace,' Judg. xviii. 6; 1 Sam. i. 17, xx. 42, xxix. 7; 2 Kings v. 19; Mark v. 34, &c. See notes on James ii. 16 and 1 Pet. v. 14. The Apostle of the Gentiles perhaps purposely substitutes in his Epistles '*Grace* be with you all' for the traditional Jewish 'Peace.' **Τὴν ἐμήν** is emphatic (viii. 31): this is no mere conventional wish.

οὐ καθώς. It seems best to understand 'as' literally of the world's *manner* of giving, not of its *gifts*, as if 'as' were equivalent to 'what.' The world gives from interested motives, because it has received or hopes to receive as much again (Luke vi. 33, 34); it gives to friends and withholds from enemies (Matt. v. 43); it gives what costs it nothing or what it cannot keep, as in the case of legacies; it pretends to give that which is not its own, especially when it says 'Peace, peace,' when there is no peace (Jer. vi. 14). The manner of Christ's giving is the very opposite of this. He gives what is His own, what He might have kept, what has cost Him a life of suffering and a cruel death to bestow, what is open to friend and foe alike, who have nothing of their own to give in return. With **μὴ ταρασσέσθω** comp. *v.* 1. It shews that the peace is internal peace of mind, not external freedom from hostility. **Δειλιᾶν, to be fearful,** frequent in LXX., occurs here only in N. T.

28. ἐχάρητε ἄν. *Ye would* **have rejoiced that I am going.** Comp. the construction in iv. 10, xi. 21, 32. Winer, p. 381. Their affection is somewhat selfish: they ought to rejoice at His gain rather than mourn over their own loss. And His gain is mankind's gain.

ὅτι ὁ πατήρ. Because the *Father is greater than I.* Therefore Christ's going to Him was gain. This was a favourite text with the Arians, as implying the inferiority of the Son. There is a real sense in which even in the Godhead the Son is subordinate to the Father: this is involved in the Eternal Generation and in the Son's being the Agent by whom the Father works in the creation and preservation of all things. Again, there is the sense in which the ascended and glorified Christ is 'inferior to the Father as touching His manhood.' Lastly, there is the sense in which Jesus on earth was inferior to His Father in Heaven. Of the three this last meaning seems to suit the context best, as shewing most clearly how His going to the Father would be a gain, and that not only to Himself but to the Apostles; for at the right hand of the Father, who is greater than Himself, He will have more power to advance His kingdom. See notes on 1 Cor. xv. 27, 28; Mark xiii. 32, [xvi. 19].

29. πιστεύσητε. Comp. xiii. 19 and see on i. 7. By foretelling the trouble Jesus turns a stumblingblock into an aid to faith.

30. οὐκέτι. No longer *will I speak much with you* (comp. xv. 15), *for the* **ruler** *of* **the** *world* **is coming** (see on xii. 31). The powers of darkness are at work in Judas and his employers; and yet there is nothing in Jesus over which Satan has control. His yielding to the attack is voluntary, in loving obedience to the Father. For the import of this confident appeal to His own sinlessnes, **in Me he hath nothing,** see on *v.* 9, viii. 29, 46, xv. 10.

31. ἀλλ' ἵνα. See on i. 8. *But* (Satan cometh) *in order that.* Some would omit the full stop at *ποιῶ* and make *ἵνα* depend on *ἐγείρεσθε*: 'But that the world may know that I love the Father, and that as the Father commanded Me so I do, arise, let us go hence.' There is a want of solemnity, if not a savour of 'theatrical effect,' in this arrangement. Moreover it is less in harmony with S. John's style, especially in these discourses. The more simple construction is the more probable. But comp. Matt. ix. 6.

ἄγωμεν. 'Let us go and meet the power before which I am willing in accordance with God's will to fall.'

We are probably to understand that they rise from table and prepare to depart, but that the contents of the next three chapters are spoken before they leave the room (comp. xviii. 1). Others suppose that the room is left now and that the next two chapters are discourses on the way towards Gethsemane, chap. xvii. being spoken at some halting-place, possibly the Temple. See introductory note to chap. xvii.

CHAPTER XV

4 and 6. **μένῃ, μένητε, μένῃ** for *μείνῃ, μείνητε, μείνῃ*.

6. **τὸ** should probably be inserted before **πῦρ** with ℵAB: omitted as less usual; comp. Matt. iii. 10, vii. 19; Luke iii. 9.

7. **αἰτήσασθε** for *αἰτήσεσθε* (influenced by *γενήσεται*).

11. **ᾖ** for *μείνῃ* (influenced by *v.* 10).

22 and 24. **εἴχοσαν** for *εἶχον* (more usual form).

The general subject still continues from xiii. 31—CHRIST'S LOVE IN KEEPING HIS OWN. This is still further set forth in this chapter in three main aspects: 1. *Their union with Him*, illustrated by the allegory of the Vine (1—11); 2. *Their union with one another in Him* (12—17); 3. *The hatred of the world to both Him and them* (18—25).

CHAP. XV. 1—11. THE UNION OF THE DISCIPLES WITH CHRIST. THE ALLEGORY OF THE VINE

The allegory of the Vine is similar in kind to that of the Door and of the Good Shepherd in chap. x. (see introductory note there): this sets forth union from within, the other union from without.

ἡ ἄμπ. ἡ ἀληθινή. For **Ἐγώ εἰμι** see on vi. 35. Christ is the true, genuine, ideal, perfect Vine, as He is the perfect Witness (Rev. iii. 14), the perfect Bread (vi. 32), and the perfect Light (see on i. 9). Whether the allegory was suggested by anything external,—vineyards, or the vine of the Temple visible in the moonlight, a vine creeping in at the window, or the 'fruit of the vine' (Matt. xxvi. 29) on the table which they had just left,—it is impossible to say. Of these the last is far the most probable, as referring to the Eucharist just instituted as a special means of union with Him and with one another. But the allegory may easily have been chosen for its own merits and its O.T. associations (Ps. lxxx. 8—19; Is. v. 1—7; Jer. ii. 21; &c.) without any suggestion from without. The vine was a national emblem under the Maccabees and appears on their coins.

ὁ γεωργός. The Owner of the soil Who tends His Vine Himself and establishes the relation between the Vine and the branches. There is therefore a good deal of difference between the form of this allegory and the parable of the Vineyard (Mark xii. 1) or that of the Fruitless Fig-tree (Luke xiii. 6). *Γεωργός* occurs nowhere else in the Gospels except of the wicked husbandmen in the parable of the Vineyard.

2. **κλῆμα.** Occurs here only (*vv.* 2—6) in N.T. In classical Greek it is specially used of the vine. *Κλάδος* (Matt. xiii. 32, xxi. 8, xxiv. 32; Mark iv. 32, xiii. 28; Luke xiii. 9; Rom. xi. 16—21) is the smaller branch of any tree. So that *κλῆμα* itself, independently of the context, fixes the meaning of the allegory. Every *vine*-branch, every one who is by origin a Christian, if he continues such by origin only, and bears no fruit, is cut off. The allegory takes no account of the branches of other trees: neither Jews nor heathen are included. These could not be called *κλήματα ἐν ἐμοί*. Note the *casus pendens* in both clauses. Comp. vi. 39, vii. 38; 1 John ii. 24, 27; Rev. ii. 26, iii. 12, 21.

καθαίρει. *He* **cleanseth** *it.* Mark the connexion with *καθαροί* in *v.* 3. The play between *αἴρει* and *καθαίρει* is perhaps intentional; but cannot be reproduced in English. *Καθαίρειν* means freeing from excrescences and useless shoots which are a drain on the branch for nothing. The Eleven are now to be cleansed by suffering.

3. **ἤδη ὑμεῖς κ.** **Already** *are ye clean* **because** *of the word.* Distinguish *διά* with the accusative from *διά* with the genitive. A.V. confounds the two here and Matt. xv. 3, 6. Ὁ *λόγος* is the whole teaching of Christ, not any particular discourse (xiv. 23). *Ἤδη* assures the disciples that the chief part of their cleansing is accomplished: in the language of xiii. 10, they are *λελουμένοι*. *Ὑμεῖς* is emphatic: many more will become *καθαροί* hereafter.

4. **κἀγὼ ἐν ὑμῖν.** This may be taken either as a promise ('and then I will abide in you'), or as the other side of the command ('take care that I abide in you'). The latter is better. The freedom of man's will is such that on his action depends that of Christ. The branches of the spiritual Vine have this mysterious power, that they can cut *themselves* off, as Judas had done. Nature does something and grace more; but grace may be rejected. The expression **ἀφ' ἑαυτοῦ**, *from itself*, as the source of its own productiveness, is peculiar to S. John (v. 19, vii. 18, xi. 51, xvi. 13).

5. The text of the allegory is repeated and enlarged. That the disciples are the branches has been implied but not stated. Note the irregular construction and comp. v. 44.

ὅτι χωρὶς ἐμοῦ. **Because apart from Me** (i. 3; Eph. ii. 12). Christians cannot live as such if severed from Christ. Nothing is here said about those who are not Christians; but there is a sense in which the words are true of them also.

6. **ἐβλήθη ἔξω.** *Is cast out* of the vineyard. The vineyard is a further enlargement of the idea. The aorist shews the inevitable nature of the consequence: he is already cast out and withered by the very fact of not abiding in Christ. Winer, p. 345. These words were spoken in spring, the time for pruning vines. Heaps of burning twigs may have been in sight. This part of the picture looks forward to the day of judgment. Meanwhile the cast-out branch may be grafted in again (Rom. xi. 23) and the dead branch may be raised to life again (v. 21, 25). With **συνάγουσιν, they** *gather*, comp. *αἰτοῦσιν*, Luke xii. 20: the nominative is quite indefinite. **Αὐτά** refers to *τὰ κλήματα* implied in *ἐάν τις*.

7. **ὃ ἐὰν θέλ. αἰτ.** **Ask whatsoever** *ye will.* Both in its comprehensiveness and in its limitation the promise is similar to that in xiv. 13, 14. One who abides in Christ and has His **sayings** (iii. 34) abiding in him cannot ask amiss: His words inspire and guide prayer.

8. ἐν τούτῳ. Looks back to *vv.* 5 and 7 or perhaps forward to *ἵνα*; comp. iv. 37, xvi. 30; 1 John iv. 17. The aorist **ἐδοξάσθη** is similar to those in *v.* 6. The Father is already glorified in the union between Christ and His disciples. He is glorified whenever the occasion arises. For **ἵνα** see on i. 8: *that ye may bear much fruit and* **become** *My disciples*, or *disciples to Me*. Even Apostles may *become* still more truly disciples to Christ. A well-supported reading (*γενήσεσθε*) gives **ye shall become.**

9. καθὼς ἠγ. Authorities differ as to whether we should place a comma or a colon at *ἠγάπησα*: either, **Even as** *the Father hath loved Me* **and** *I have loved you*, **abide** *in My love;* or, **Even as** *the Father hath loved Me*, **I also** *have loved you* (xvii. 18, xx. 21): **abide** *in My love*. The latter is better as keeping in due prominence the main statement, that the love of Christ for His disciples is analogous to that of the Father for the Son. The aorists may be translated as such, the love being regarded as a completed whole, always perfect in itself. But perhaps this is just one of those cases where the Greek aorist is best translated by the English perfect: see on viii. 29. *Ἐν τ. ἀγ. τ. ἐμῇ* may mean either *My love* or *the love of Me*. The former is more natural and better suited to the context, which speaks of His love to them as similar to the Father's towards Him; but the latter need not be excluded. See on viii. 31.

10. καθὼς ἐγώ. This being a subordinate sentence, the tremendous import of it is liable to pass unnoticed. Looking back over a life of thirty years Jesus says, *I have kept the Father's commandments.* Would the best man that ever lived, if only a man, dare to say this? See on viii. 29, 46, xiv. 9, 30. Between the disciple and Christ, as between Christ and the Father, obedience proves love and secures love in return.

11. The verse forms a conclusion to the allegory of the Vine: comp. v. 17, xiv. 25, xvi. 25, 33. For **ἡ χ. ἡ ἐμή** see on viii. 31: *that the joy that is Mine may be in you* means the joy which Christ experienced through consciousness of His fellowship with the Father, and which supported Him in His sufferings, may be in His disciples and support them in theirs. Here first, on the eve of His Passion, does Jesus speak of His joy. For **ἡ χ. ὑμ. πλ.** see on iii. 29. Human happiness can reach no higher than to share that joy which Christ ever felt in being loved by His Father and doing His will.

12—17. THE UNION OF THE DISCIPLES WITH ONE ANOTHER IN CHRIST

12. ἡ ἐντ. ἡ ἐμή. See on iii. 29. In *v.* 10 He said that to keep His commandments was the way to abide in His love. He now reminds them what His commandment is (see on xiii. 34). It includes all others. A day or two before this Christ had been teaching that all the Law and the Prophets hang on the two great commands, 'love God with all thy heart' and 'love thy neighbour as thyself' (Matt. xxii. 37—40). S. John teaches us that the second really implies the first (1 John iv. 20). For **ἵνα** see on i. 8 and comp. xi. 57, xiii. 34, xv. 17.

13. This verse and the next three are an expansion of *καθὼς ἠγάπησα ὑμᾶς*. The standard of Christian love is the love of Christ for His disciples: that is the ideal to be aimed at. For **τ. ψυχὴν αὐ. θῇ** see on x. 11. Needless difficulty has been made about **ὑπὲρ τ. φίλων αὐ.**, as if it contradicted Rom. v. 6—8. Christ here says that the greatest love that any one can shew towards his friends is to die for them. S. Paul says that such cases of self-sacrifice for good men occur; but they are very rare. Christ, however, surpassed them, for He died not only for His friends but for His enemies, not only for the good but for sinners. There is no contradiction. Nor is there any emphasis on 'friends;' as if to suffer for friends were higher than to suffer for strangers or enemies. The order of the Greek words throws the emphasis on 'life:' it is the unique character of the thing sacrificed that proves the love. Christ says 'for His friends' because He is addressing His friends.

14. **ὑμεῖς φίλοι.** *Ὑμεῖς* is emphatic: 'and when I say "friends" I mean you.' This shews that 'friends' was used simply because He was speaking to Apostles.

15. **οὐκέτι.** **No longer** *do I call you servants* (see on viii. 34 and comp. xiv. 30. He had implied that they were His servants xii. 26 and stated it xiii. 13—16. The two relationships do not exclude one another. He had called them *φίλοι* before this (Luke xii. 4); and they did not cease to be His *δοῦλοι* after this (Rom. i. 10; 2 Pet. i. 1; Rev. i. 1).

ὑμᾶς δὲ εἴρ. *But* **you have I called** *friends;* **because** *all things that I* **heard** *from My Father I* **made known to** *you:* as they were able to bear it (xvi. 12). After Pentecost they would be able to bear much more. Thus he who wills to do his will as a servant shall know of the doctrine as a friend (vii. 17).

16. **οὐχ ὑμεῖς.** **Not ye chose** *Me, but I* **chose** *you.* *Ὑμεῖς* and *ἐγώ* are emphatic. *Ἐκλέγειν* refers to their election to be Apostles (vi. 70, xiii. 18; Acts i. 2); therefore the aorist as referring to a definite act in the past should be preserved. So also **ἔθηκα, I appointed** *you*, i.e. assigned you to a definite post, as in 2 Tim. i. 11; Heb. i. 2. This is better than 'I ordained,' as A. V. here and 1 Tim. ii. 7, 'ordain' having become a technical term in ecclesiastical language. Comp. Acts xiii. 47, xx. 28; 1 Cor. xii. 28. The repetition of *ὑμεῖς* throughout the verse emphasizes the personal responsibility of the Apostles.

ὑπάγητε. See on i. 7: *that ye should go and* **bear** *fruit.* *Ὑπάγητε* must not be insisted on too strongly as if it referred to the missionary journeys of the Apostles. On the other hand it is more than a mere auxiliary or expletive: it implies the active carrying out of the idea expressed by the verb with which it is coupled (comp. Luke x. 37; Matt. xiii. 44, xviii. 15, xix. 21), and perhaps also separation from their Master (Matt. xx. 4, 7). The missionary work of gathering in souls is not specially indicated here: the 'fruit' is rather the holiness of their own lives and good works of all kinds. The second **ἵνα** is partly coordinate with, partly dependent on, the first: comp. the double **ἵνα** xiii. 34 and see on *v.* 7. Several ancient commentators take *δῶ* as the first person in harmony with xiv. 13. The three passages, xiv. 13, xv. 7 and 16 should be compared.

17. ταῦτα. The verse sums up what precedes and prepares for a new departure (comp. *v.* 11, xiv. 25, xvi. 1, 25, 33), *ταῦτα* referring to what has been said about being one with Him and with one another. For **ἵνα** see on i. 8 and comp. *v.* 12, xi. 57, xiii. 34. The idea of *purpose* is probably to be included.

Note the solemn effect produced by prolonged asyndeton. In *vv.* 1—17 there is not a single connective particle. A Greek uninfluenced by Hebrew would be very unlikely to write thus. See on i. 6.

18—25. The Hatred of the World to both Him and them

In strong contrast to the love and union between Christ and His disciples and among the disciples themselves is the hatred of the world to Him and them. He gives them these thoughts to console them in encountering this hatred of the world. (1) It hated Him first: in this trial also He has shewn them the way. (2) The hatred of the world proves that they are not of the world. (3) They are sharing their Master's lot, whether the world rejects or accepts their preaching. (4) They will suffer this hatred not only with Him, but for His sake. All this tends to shew that the very hatred of the world intensifies their union with Him.

18. γινώσκετε] Either *ye know*, or *know ye, that it* **hath** *hated Me.* As in xiv. 1, the imperative seems preferable to the indicative: in *v.* 27 and v. 39 the context throws the balance the other way.

μεμίσηκεν expresses what has been and still is the case. **Πρῶτον ὑμῶν** is similar to *πρῶτός μου* (see on i. 15); *first of you, first in regard to you.* To avoid the unusual construction some good authorities omit *ὑμῶν*. Comp. 1 John iii. 13.

19. τὸ ἴδιον. *Its own.* In vii. 7 He told His brethren, who did not believe on Him, that the world could not hate them. This shews why. In their unbelief it still found something of its own (1 John iv. 5). The selfishness of the world's love is thus indicated. It loves not so much them, as that in them which is to its own advantage: hence the lower word *φιλεῖν* rather than *ἀγαπᾷν* (contrast *v.* 17); it is mere natural liking. With the solemn repetition of **κόσμος** comp. iii. 17, 31, xii. 36, xvii. 14. For the construction comp. v. 46, viii. 19, 42, ix. 41, xviii. 36 and contrast iv. 10, xi. 21, xiv. 28. For **διὰ τοῦτο** see on vii. 21, 22.

20. μνημονεύετε. See note on xiii. 16: of the passages noticed there Matt. x. 24 is similar in meaning to this. Christ may here be alluding to the occasion recorded in Matt. x. 24. On the blessedness of sharing the lot of Christ comp. 1 Pet. iv. 12, 13.

εἰ ἐμὲ ἐδ. *If they* **persecuted** *Me...if they* **kept** (xiii. 14, xviii. 23) *My* word. *Τηρεῖν* must not be rendered 'watch, lay wait for' in a hostile sense: the two halves of the sentence are opposed, not parallel. *Τὸν λ.* or *τοὺς λ. τηρεῖν* is peculiar to S. John (viii. 51, 52, 55, xiv. 23, 24, xvii. 6) always in the sense of the parallel phrase *τὰς ἐντολὰς τ.* (xiv. 15, 21, xv. 10). Both phrases link the Gospel with the First Epistle (ii. 3, 4, 5, iii. 22, 24, v. 2, 3), and these two with the Apocalypse (iii. 8, 10, xii. 17, xiv. 12, xxii 7, 9). Comp. John ix. 16; Rev. i. 3, ii. 26, iii. 3, and see on John vii. 30, 37, xi. 44, xix. 37, xx. 16. These passages shew that *τηρεῖν* cannot be taken in a hostile sense. The meaning of the verse as a whole is that both in failure and in success they will share His lot.

21. ἀλλά. *But* be of good cheer, it is *διὰ τὸ ὄνομά μου.* This thought is to turn their suffering into joy: Acts v. 41, xxi. 13; 2 Cor. xii. 10; Gal. vi. 14; Phil. ii. 17, 18; 1 Pet. iv, 14. With **οὐκ οἴδασιν** comp. vii. 28, xvi. 3, xvii. 25. They not merely did not know that God had sent Jesus; they did not know God Himself, for their idea of Him was radically wrong. And this ignorance is moral; it has its root in hatred of good: it is not the intellectual darkness of the heathen.

22. εἰ μὴ...ἐλάλησα. He had spoken as man had never spoken before (vii. 16), in words sufficient to tell unprejudiced minds Who He was. Their hatred was a sin against light: without the light there would have been no sin. **Ἔχειν ἁμαρτίαν** is peculiar to S. John (*v.* 24, ix. 41, xix. 11; 1 John i. 8): *they* **would not have** *sin* (xix. 11; Rom. vii. 7). **Πρόφασιν** is **excuse** rather than 'cloke.' The notion is not of hiding, but of excusing what cannot be hid: 'colour' (Acts xxvii. 30) is better than 'cloke' (1 Thess. ii. 5).

νῦν δέ here and in *v.* 24 introduces a sharp contrast: the two verses exhibit the parallelism so frequent in S. John. For **περὶ** *τῆς ἁμ.* comp. viii. 46, xvi. 8.

24. τὰ ἔργα. If they did not perceive that His words were Divine, they might at least have recognised His works as such (x. 38, xiv. 11, v. 36). Here again their sin was against light: they admitted the works (xi. 47) as such that none other did (ix. 32), and like Philip they had seen, without recognising, the Father (xiv. 9, 10).

25. τ. νόμῳ. In the wide sense for the O. T. as a whole (x. 34, xii. 34; Rom. iii. 19). The passage may be from Ps. lxix. 4 or xxxv. 19: there are similar passages cix. 3 and cxix. 161. That their hatred is gratuitous is again inexcusable.

26. ἐγὼ πέμψω. Ἐγώ is an emphatic claim to Divinity. Here it is the Son who sends the **Advocate** from the Father (see on i. 6). In xiv. 16 the Father sends in answer to the Son's prayer. In xiv. 26 the Father sends in the Son's name. These are three ways of expressing that the mission of the Paraclete is the act both of the Father and of the Son, Who are one. See on i. 33. For **τ. πν. τ. ἀληθ.** see on xiv. 17.

ὃ π. τ. πατρὸς ἐκπορεύεται. It seems best to take this much discussed clause as simply yet another way of expressing the fact of the *mission* of the Paraclete. If the Paraclete is sent by the Son from the Father, and by the Father in the Son's name and at the Son's request, then the Paraclete 'proceedeth from the Father.' If this be correct, then this statement refers to the *office* and not to the *Person* of the Holy Spirit, and has no bearing either way on the great question between the Eastern and Western Churches, the *Filioque* added in the West to the Nicene Creed. The word used here for 'proceed' is the same as that used in the Creed of Nicea, and the Easterns quote these words of Christ Himself as being against not merely *the insertion of the clause* 'and the Son' into the Creed (which all admit to have been made irregularly), but against the *truth* of the statement that the Spirit, not only in His temporal mission, but in His Person, from all eternity proceeds from both the Father and the Son. On the whole question see Pearson *On the Creed*, Art. viii.; *Reunion Conference at Bonn*, 1875, pp. 9—85, Rivingtons; Pusey *On the Clause "and the Son,"* a Letter to Dr Liddon, Parker, 1876. Ἐκπορεύεσθαι occurs in this Gospel only here and v. 29, but is frequent in the other Gospels and in Revelation (Matt. iii. 5, iv. 4, xv. 11, 18; Mark vii. 15, 18, 20, 21, 23; Luke iv. 22, 37; Rev. i. 16, iv. 5, &c.), and there seems to be nothing in the word itself to limit it to the Eternal Procession. On the other hand the *παρά* is strongly in favour of the reference being to the mission. Comp. xvi. 27, xvii. 8. In the Creeds *ἐκ* is the preposition invariably used of the Eternal Procession, *τὸ* **ἐκ** *τ. πατρὸς ἐκπορευόμενον*: and "the Greek Fathers who apply this passage to the eternal Procession instinctively substitute *ἐκ* for *παρά*" (Westcott). For **ἐκεῖνος** see on i. 18; *He* in contrast to the world which hates and rejects Christ. Christ has the witness of the Spirit of truth, and this has the authority of the Father: it is impossible to have higher testimony than this.

27. καὶ ὑμ. δὲ μ. Nay, ye also bear witness, or **Nay, bear ye also witness** (Winer, p. 53): but the conjunctions are against *μαρτυρεῖτε* being imperative; comp. 3 John 12 and see on *v.* 18 and viii. 16. The testimony of the disciples is partly the same as that of the Spirit, partly not. It is the same, so far as it depends on the illumination of the Spirit, who was to bring all things to their remembrance and lead them into all truth. This would not be true in its fulness until Pentecost. It is not the same, so far as it depends upon the Apostles' own personal experience of Christ and His work; and this is marked by the emphatic *ὑμεῖς*. This is the case at once; the experience is already there; and hence the present tense. Comp. Acts v. 32, where the Apostles clearly set forth the twofold nature of their testimony, and Acts xv. 28, where there is a parallel distinction of the two factors.

ἀπ' ἀρχῆς. Comp. 1 John ii. 7, 24, iii. 11 and especially iii. 8, where as here we have the present: Winer, p. 334. The context must decide the meaning (see on i. 1, vi. 64): here the beginning of Christ's ministry is clearly meant. They could bear witness as to what they themselves had seen and heard (Luke i. 2; Acts i. 22). See on xvi. 4.

CHAPTER XVI

3. After **ποιήσουσιν** omit *ὑμῖν* (inserted from *vv.* 1 and 4).

7. For **οὐκ ἐλεύσεται** some of the best authorities have *οὐ μὴ ἔλθῃ*.

13. For **εἰς τ. ἀλήθειαν π.** ℵDL have *ἐν τῇ ἀλ. π.*, perhaps because *ἐν* after *ὁδηγεῖν* is more common in LXX. **ἀκούσει** for *ἂν ἀκούσῃ*, with BDEHY: ℵL have *ἀκούει*.

14, 15, 24. **λήμψεται** for *λήψεται*: Winer, p. 53.

16. After **ὄψεσθέ με** omit *ὅτι ἐγὼ ὑπάγω πρὸς τὸν πατέρα* (inserted from *v.* 17) with ℵBDL against A.

17. After **ὅτι** omit *ἐγώ* (inserted from xiv. 12).

20. Before **λυπηθήσεσθε** omit *δέ* (inserted to point a contrast with **ὁ κόσμος χαρήσεται**).

22. **ἀρεῖ** for *αἴρει*: both are strongly supported.

23. **δώσει ὑμῖν** before **ἐν τῷ ὀνόματί μου.**

25. Before **ἔρχεται** omit *ἀλλ'*, and read **ἀπαγγελῶ** for *ἀναγγελῶ* (from *vv.* 13, 14, 15).

27. **παρὰ τ. Θεοῦ** (ℵAC[3]) perhaps comes from xiii. 3: *π. τ. πατρός* (BC[1]DLX) seems preferable.

28. **ἐκ τ. πατρός** (BC[1]LX) for *παρὰ τ. π.* (ℵAC[2]) from *v.* 17.

29. Before **παρρησίᾳ** insert **ἐν** (overlooked after **νῦν** or omitted in harmony with S. John's usage; see on vii. 13).

32. Before **ἐλήλυθεν** omit *νῦν* (inserted from iv. 23, v. 25).

We are still in the first part of the second main division of the Gospel, THE INNER GLORIFICATION OF CHRIST IN HIS LAST DISCOURSES (xiii.—xvii.). We now enter upon the third division of this first part (see introductory note to chap. xiii.).

THE PROMISE OF THE PARACLETE AND OF CHRIST'S RETURN

As has been remarked already, the subjects are not kept distinct; they cross and interlace, like the strands in a rope. But the following divisions may conduce to clearness; 1. *The World and the Paraclete* (1—11); 2. *The Disciples and the Paraclete* (12—15); 3. *The Sorrow of Christ's Departure turned into Joy by His Return* (16—24); 4. *Summary and Conclusion of the Discourses* (25—33).

1—11. THE WORLD AND THE PARACLETE

1. **ταῦτα.** These discourses generally, especially the last section, about the world's hatred of Him and them: see on xv. 11, 17.

σκανδαλισθῆτε. The verb combines the notions of 'trip up' and 'entrap.' *Σκάνδαλον* is a later form of *σκανδάληθρον* (Aristoph. *Ach.*

687), which is the *bait-stick* in a trap, to touch which makes the trap close. Σκάνδαλον hence comes to mean any snare set to catch or trip up. The metaphor occurs often in LXX. and in S. Matt. and S. Mark, thrice in S. Luke, and twice in S. John (vi. 61: comp. 1 John ii. 10). The fanatical hatred of the Jews might make Jewish Apostles stumble at the truth.

2. **ἀποσυναγώγους.** See on ix. 32. The **ἀλλά** introduces a gradation, as in 2 Cor. vii. 11: **Nay, there cometh an hour.** 'You may think excommunication a strong measure, *but* they will go greater lengths than this.' In **ἵνα** the Divine purpose again seems indicated (xii. 23, xiii. 1); 'an hour for every one that killeth you to think,' *ut omnis...arbitretur*. In **πᾶς** the universality of the delusion appears: Jew and Gentile alike will put down Christians as blasphemers and atheists and the perpetrators of every crime. The history of religious persecution is the fulfilment of this prophecy: comp. Acts viii. 1, ix. 1. **Λατρείαν** expresses a *religious* service (Rom. ix. 4; Heb. ix. 1, 6); **προσφέρειν** the offering of *sacrifice* (Heb. v. 1, viii. 3, ix. 7): **offereth service to God.**

3. **οὐκ ἔγνωσαν. Did not recognise,** implying that they had the opportunity of knowing. They failed to see that God is Love, and that Jesus came to bring in, not to shut out; to save, not to destroy. The very names 'Father' (here used with special point) and 'Jesus' might have taught them better things.

4. **ἀλλά.** *But,* to return (to *v.* 1), *these things* **have I spoken** *to you* (*vv.* 1, 4, 6 must be rendered alike), *that when* **their hour** (the hour appointed for these things; *v.* 2) *is come, ye may remember* **them, how that** *I told you.* **'Εγώ** is emphatic, 'I Myself, the object of your faith.'

ἐξ ἀρχῆς. Here and vi. 64 only: it expresses consequence and continuity, whereas ἀπ' ἀρχῆς (xv. 27) expresses simple departure. *And these things* **I told you not from** *the beginning.* There is no inconsistency between this statement and passages like Matt. x. 16—39, xxiv. 9; Luke vi. 22: ταῦτα covers not only the prediction of persecutions, but the *explanation* of them, and the promise of the Paraclete, &c. All this was new. While He was with them to explain and exhort, they did not need these truths.

5. **ὑπάγω πρός. I go away unto:** the notion is that of withdrawal (see on *v.* 7). Hitherto He has been with them to protect them and to be the main object of attack: soon *they* will have to bear the brunt without Him. This is all that they feel at present,—how His departure affects themselves, not how it affects Him. And yet this latter point is all important even as regards themselves, for He is going in order to send the Paraclete. As to **Ποῦ ὑπάγεις,** as far as words go S. Peter had asked this very question (xiii. 36) and S. Thomas had suggested it (xiv. 5); but altogether in a different spirit from what is meant here. They were looking only at their own loss instead of at His gain. Sorrow has so filled their hearts that there is no room for thoughts of His glory and their future consolation.

7. ἐγὼ τ. ἀλ. λ. 'I who know, and who have never misled you:' comp. xiv. 2. For **ἵνα** comp. xi. 50. Note the different words for 'go' in *vv.* 5, 7: in *ὑπάγω* the primary idea is *withdrawal*, **I go away**; in *ἀπέρχομαι*, *separation*, **I depart**; in *πορεύομαι*, *progress to a goal*, **I go my way**. For **παράκλητος** see on xiv. 16. Jesus as *Man* must possess the Spirit, before He can impart the Spirit to men: it is in virtue of His glorified Manhood that He sends the Advocate.

8. The threefold office of the Advocate towards those who do not believe, but may yet be won over. **And He, when He is come, will convict** *the world* **concerning** *sin, and* **concerning** *righteousness, and* **concerning** *judgment*. 'Convict' is better than 'convince,' much better than 'reprove:' it means forcing a man to condemn himself after a scrutiny in the court of conscience (see on iii. 20). This rendering gives additional point to the rendering 'Advocate' for Paraclete. To convince and convict is a large part of the duty of an advocate. He must vindicate and prove the truth; and whoever, after such proof, rejects the truth, does so with responsibility in proportion to the interests involved. *Ἁμαρτίας*, *δικαιοσύνης* and *κρίσεως*, not having the article, are left quite indefinite. The conviction about each may bring either salvation or condemnation, but it must bring one or the other. Comp. Acts ii. 37, iv. 1—4, v. 33, &c.

9. ἁμαρτίας. This must come first: the work of the Spirit begins with convicting man of having rebelled against God. And the source of sin is unbelief; formerly, unbelief in God, now unbelief in His Ambassador. Not that the sin is limited to unbelief, but this is the beginning of it: 'Because' does not explain 'sin,' but 'will convict.' The Spirit, by bringing the fact of unbelief home to the hearts of men, shews what the nature of sin is.

10. δικαιοσύνης. The word occurs here only in this Gospel; but comp. 1 John ii. 29, iii. 7, 10; Rev. xix. 11. Righteousness is the keeping of the law, and is the natural result of faith; so much so that faith is reckoned as if it were righteousness (Rom. iv. 3—9) so certain is this result regarded. Here *δικαιοσύνη* is used not in the lower sense of keeping prescribed ordinances (Matt. iii. 15), but in the highest and widest sense of keeping the law of God; internal as well as external obedience. The lower sense was almost the only sense both to Jew and Gentile (Matt. v. 20). The Spirit, having convinced man that sin is much more than a breaking of certain ordinances, viz. a rejection of God and His Christ, goes on to convince him that righteousness is much more than a keeping of certain ordinances. As before, *ὅτι* explains *ἐλέγξει*, not *δικαιοσύνης*. The pattern life of Christ being completed, the Spirit makes known to man the nature of that life, and thus shews what the nature of righteousness is. Sin being resistance to God's will, righteousness is perfect harmony with it. For **θεωρεῖτε, behold**, comp. *v.* 16, vi. 40, 62, vii. 3, xiv. 19, &c. Jesus here shews His sympathy with His disciples: in speaking of His return to glory, He does not forget the sorrow which they feel and expect always to feel. Contrast Acts ii. 46.

11. ὁ ἄρχων. *The* **ruler** *of this world* **hath been** *judged* (see on xii. 31 and xiv. 30). As the world has had its own false views about sin and righteousness, so also it has had its own false standards of judgment. The Advocate convicts the world of its error in this point also. The world might think that 'the power of darkness' conquered at Gethsemane and Calvary, but the Resurrection and Ascension proved that what looked like victory was most signal defeat: instead of conquering Satan was judged. This result is so certain that from the point of view of the Spirit's coming it is spoken of as already accomplished.

12—15. The Disciples and the Paraclete

The Paraclete not only convicts and convinces the world, He also enlightens the Apostles respecting Christ and thereby glorifies Him, for to make Christ known is to glorify Him. These verses are very important as shewing the authority of the Apostles' teaching: it is not their own, but it is the truth of Christ revea'ed by the Spirit.

12. πολλὰ...λέγειν. They are His friends (xv. 15), and there is nothing which He wishes to keep back from them; He would give them His entire confidence. But it would be useless to tell them what they cannot understand; cruel to impart knowledge which would only crush them. **Ἄρτι** is emphatic (see on *v.* 31): at Pentecost they will receive both understanding and strength to know even that 'which passeth knowledge' (Eph. iii. 19).

13. ὁδηγήσει. He will be your guide into this new country. Christ is the Way and the Truth. The Spirit of Truth (see on xiv. 17) leads men into the Way and thus *into all* **the** *Truth.* Comp. *ὑμεῖς δ' ἐμοῦ ἀκούσεσθε πᾶσαν τὴν ἀλ.* Plato *Apol.* 17. But He does not compel, does not carry: they may refuse to follow; and if they follow they must exert themselves. Contrast Matt. xv. 14; Acts viii. 31.

ἀφ' ἑαυτοῦ. See on v. 19, xv. 4. The Spirit, like the Son, cannot speak what proceeds from Himself as distinct from what proceeds from the Father, the Source of all Divine energy. This is the security for infallibility: Satan, who speaks out of his own resources, is consequently a liar (viii. 44).

Note the threefold *ἀναγγελεῖ ὑμῖν.* **He shall declare to you the things that are coming** (comp. *ὁ ἐρχόμενος*): among *τὰ ἐρχόμενα* we may place the constitution of the Church and all those truths which Christian experience would teach.

14. ἐκεῖνος ἐμέ. Both pronouns are emphatic; 'Me shall that Spirit glorify.' Just as the Son glorifies the Father by revealing Him (i. 18, xvii. 4) both in word and work, so does the Spirit glorify the Son by revealing Him. In both cases to reveal is necessarily to glorify: the more the Truth is known, the more it is loved and adored. **Λήμψεται** here and *λαμβάνει* in *v.* 15 must be rendered alike, and by **take** rather than 'receive;' it implies that the recipient is not wholly passive: comp. x. 17, xii. 48, xx. 22.

16—24. The Sorrow of Christ's Departure turned into Joy by His Return

16. θεωρεῖτε. Ye behold, as in *vv.* 10 and 17. Mark the difference between this and the more general word ὄψεσθε. When His bodily presence was withdrawn, their view of Him was enlarged: no longer after the flesh, He is seen and known by faith.

17. καὶ ὅτι. They refer to what was said in *v.* 10: there ὅτι is 'because,' here it probably is 'that,' to introduce what follows. They are perplexed about not beholding and yet seeing, and about His departure to the Father. For **ἐκ τῶν** see on xxi. 10.

19. ἔγνω. Perceived or *recognised:* see on ii. 25. We are perhaps to understand from γινώσκειν being used rather than εἰδέναι that it was by His natural powers of observation that He perceived this. Where these sufficed we may believe that His supernatural power of reading men's thoughts was not used: comp. v. 6, vi. 15. In translation mark the difference between μετ' ἀλλήλων, *one with another*, πρὸς ἀλλήλους (*v.* 17, iv. 33), *one to another*, and πρὸς ἑαυτούς (vii. 35, xii. 19), *among themselves:* **Concerning this do ye enquire one with another.**

20. We have two contrasts; between the Apostles (ὑμεῖς last to emphasize the contrast) and ὁ κόσμος: and between their present sorrow and their future joy. **Κλαύσετε** (xi. 33, xx. 11) and **θρηνήσετε** (Luke vii. 32, xxiii. 27) express the outward manifestation of grief: **λυπηθήσεσθε** expresses the feeling. The world will rejoice at being rid of One whose life was a reproach to it and whose teaching condemned it. Their sorrow shall not merely be followed by joy, but shall *become* joy. The loss of Christ's bodily presence shall be first a sorrow and then a joy. Γίνεσθαι εἰς is used of the rejected stone becoming the head of the corner (Matt. xxi. 42; Acts iv. 11), of the mustard sprout becoming a tree (Luke xiii. 19), of the first man Adam becoming a living soul (1 Cor. xv. 45). See on i. 52.

21. ἡ γυνή. The article is generic; this is the general law: comp. ὁ δοῦλος (xv. 15). The metaphor is frequent in O. T. Isai. xxi. 3, xxvi. 17, lxvi. 7; Hos. xiii. 13; Mic. iv. 9. See on Mark xiii. 8. Note the articles in what follows; *the* child, *the* anguish, *the* joy,—always to be found in such a case. But the joy effaces the anguish, because a human being (ἄνθρωπος), the noblest of God's creatures, is born. Μόχθου γὰρ οὐδεὶς τοῦ παρελθόντος λόγος.

22. καὶ ὑμεῖς. *And ye therefore now*, or *Ye also therefore now.* As in childbirth, the disciples' suffering was the necessary condition of their joy. This suffering took a new form in the work of converting souls (Gal. iv. 19). In *vv.* 16, 17, 19 we had ὄψεσθέ με: here we have the other side of the same truth, ὄψομαι ὑμας. In Gal. iv. 9 we have both sides.

23. ἐκείνῃ. Not the forty days of His bodily presence after the Resurrection, but the many days of His spiritual presence after Pentecost. Comp. *v.* 26 and xiv. 20.

οὐκ ἐρωτ. *Ask no question* (*v.* 19), or *Make no petition* (see on xiv. 16). The former is better. When they are illuminated by the Spirit there will be no room for such questions as 'What is this little while? How can we know the way? Whither goest Thou? How is it that Thou wilt manifest Thyself unto us and not unto the world?' His going to the Father will gain for them (1) perfect knowledge. **Αἰτήσητε** must mean 'pray,' not 'question.' Note that the answer (according to the better reading), as well as the prayer (xiv. 13, xv. 16), is in Christ's name; and all such prayers will be answered. His return to the Father will gain for them (2) perfect response to prayer.

24. αἰτεῖτε. *Go on asking* (present imperative; v. 14, [viii. 11,] xx. 17: contrast Matt. vii. 7; Mark vi. 22) *that your joy may be* **fulfilled**, may become complete and remain so (see on iii. 29). His return to the Father will gain for them (3) perfect joy.

25—33. Summary and conclusion of these Discourses

25. ταῦτα. As in *v.* 1 there is some uncertainty as to how much is included. Some refer 'these things' to *vv.* 19—24; others to xv. 1—xvi. 24. Perhaps even the latter is too narrow; the words can apply to all Christ's teaching, of which there was much which the multitudes were not allowed (Matt. xiii. 11) and the Apostles were not able (ii. 22) to understand at the time. For **παροιμίαις** see on x. 6, and for **παρρησίᾳ** on vii. 13. **'Απαγγελῶ**, the better reading, looks to the maker of the announcement, *ἀναγγελῶ* to the recipients of it.

26. With the perfect knowledge just promised they will discern what may be asked in His name (see on xiv. 13): *cognitio parit orationem.* The **οὐ λέγω** does not mean 'I need not say, for of course I shall do so;' which does not harmonize with *v.* 27. The meaning rather is, that so long as through the power of the Advocate they have direct communion with the Father in Christ's name, there is no need to speak of Christ's intercession. But this communion may be interrupted by sin, and then Christ becomes their Advocate (1 John ii. 1; Rom. viii. 34). Note the emphatic *ἐγώ*. On *ἐρωτᾶν* see on xiv. 6.

27. αὐτός. Without My intercession; vi. 6. We might have expected *ἀγαπᾷ* for *φιλεῖ* here (see on xi. 5): but it is a *Father's* love, flowing spontaneously from a *natural relationship* as distinct from discriminating friendship. It is their love for the Son which wins the Father's love (xiv. 21, 23). The two pronouns, **ὑμεῖς ἐμέ**, are in emphatic contact. The two perfects signify what has been and still continues. No argument can be drawn from the order of the verbs as to love preceding faith: *πεφιλήκατε* naturally comes first on account of *φιλεῖ* just preceding. 'Love begets love' is true both between man and man and between God and man. 'Faith begets faith' cannot have any meaning between God and man. For *π. τ.* Θεοῦ we should probably read *π. τ.* **πατρός** (xv. 26). It was because they recognised Him as the Son sent from the Father, and not merely as a man sent from God (i. 6), that they won the Father's love.

28. Note the change from **παρὰ τ. π.** to **ἐκ τ. π.** In *v.* 27 'I came *forth* from' refers to the temporal mission of Christ from the Father (xvii. 8); here 'I came *out* from' includes the Eternal Generation of the Son (viii. 42). This verse would almost form a creed. The Son, of one Substance with the Father, was born into the world, suffered, and returned to the Father.

29. ἴδε νῦν ἐν παρ. See on i. 29 and vii. 4, 13.

30. οἴδαμεν ὅτι οἶδας. *We* **know** *that Thou knowest* (comp. 2 Cor. xii. 2, 3, where the A.V. is similarly capricious). Christ had spoken in the future tense (*v.* 25): they speak in the present. They feel that His gracious promise is already coming true. He had shewn them that He had read their hearts (*v.* 19); like Nathanael (i. 50) and the Samaritan woman (iv. 29, 39), and S. Thomas (xx. 28), they conclude that He knows all.

ἐν τούτῳ. Herein: see on iv. 37. His all-embracing knowledge is that *in* which their faith has root. The **ὅτι** is probably 'that,' not 'because,' as the context and S. John's usage shew: xiii. 35; 1 John ii. 3, 5, iii. 19, 24, v. 2. The disciples' **ἀπὸ Θεοῦ** implies a less intimate union between the Father and Jesus than either *παρὰ τ. π.* (*v.* 27) or *ἐκ τ. π.* (*v.* 28). Their views of Christ are still very imperfect.

31. ἄρτι πιστεύετε; The words are only half a question: comp. i. 51, xx. 29. The belief of which they are conscious is no illusion, but it is far more defective than they in their momentary enthusiasm suppose. *Ἄρτι* means 'at this stage of your course:' contrast *νῦν* (*vv.* 29, 30) and see on ii. 10.

32. ἵνα σκορπ. See on *v.* 2. This part of the allegory of the sheepfold will be illustrated even in the shepherds themselves (x. 12). Comp. *Πατάξω τ. ποιμένα, καὶ διασκορπισθήσονται τ. πρόβατα* (Matt. xxvi. 31). With **εἰς τ. ἴδια** comp. i. 11, xix. 27: 'to his own home, property, or pursuits.' **Ἀφῆτε** depends upon *ἵνα*; **may** *be scattered and* **may** *leave:* all this is part of the Divine plan. They must be taught their weakness, and this foretelling of it is, as it were, pardon granted by anticipation.

καὶ οὐκ εἰμί. *And yet I am not.* The 'yet' is implied, as so often in S. John, in the collocation of the sentences: i. 10, 11, iii. 19, 32, vi. 70, vii. 4, 26, viii. 20, ix. 20. As a rule it is best to leave S. John's simple conjunctions to tell their own meaning.

ὁ πατὴρ μετ' ἐμοῦ. The Divine background (as it seems to us) of Christ's life was to Him a *Presence* of which He was always conscious (viii. 29), with the awful exception of Matt. xxvii. 46.

33. εἰρήνην. The purpose of all these farewell discourses (*ταῦτα*) is *that they* **may** *have peace.* His ministry ends, as His life began, with this message: *ἐπὶ γῆς εἰρήνη* (Luke ii. 14).

θλῖψιν ἔχετε. Ye have anguish: not 'shall have;' the anguish (*v.* 21) has already begun.

ἐγώ. With great emphasis. At the very moment when He is face to face with treachery, and disgrace, and death, Christ triumphantly claims the victory. Comp. 1 John ii. 13, 14, v. 4. In His victory His followers conquer also.

CHAPTER XVII

1. **ἐπάρας** for *ἐπῆρε*. Omit *καί* before **εἶπεν** and before **ὁ υἱός**, and omit *σου* after **ὁ υἱός**.

3. **γινώσκουσιν** (ADGLYΔΛ) for *γινώσκωσι*: but *γινώσκωσιν* (ℵBC) is probably right.

4. **τελειώσας** (ℵABCL) for *ἐτελείωσα* (D).

11, 12. **ᾧ** for *οὕς*: *οὕς* in *v.* 12 caused the omission of **καί** before **ἐφύλαξα**, a colon being placed at *σου*.

16. **οὐκ εἰμί** before **ἐκ τ. κ.** (ℵABCD). The converse arrangement (E) is an imitation of the preceding clause.

19. **ὦσιν** before **καὶ αὐτοί**: comp. *v.* 16.

20. **πιστευόντων** (ℵABCD[1]) for *πιστευσόντων* (alteration to what seemed more in harmony with facts).

21. After **ἐν ἡμῖν** omit *ἕν* (an insertion from the first clause: comp. *vv.* 11, 22). Confusion between the clauses makes several patristic quotations ambiguous; but the insertion is strongly supported.

22. Omit *ἐσμεν* at the end of the verse with ℵ[1]BDL against Aℵ[3].

24. **Πατήρ, ὅ** for *Πάτερ, οὕς* (an obvious correction).

The Prayer of the Great High Priest

The prayer which follows the last discourse is unique in the Gospels. The other Evangelists, especially S. Luke, mention the fact of Christ praying (Matt. xiv. 23; Mark i. 35; Luke iii. 21, v. 16, vi. 12, ix. 18, &c.), and give some words of His prayer at Gethsemane; but here the substance of a long act of devotion is preserved. S. John never mentions the fact of Christ praying, but in xii. 27 he perhaps gives us a few words of prayer, and in xi. 41 a thanksgiving which implies previous prayer. There is an approach to the first portion of this prayer in the thanksgiving in Matt. xi. 25, 26.

This Oratio Summi Sacerdotis falls naturally into three portions; 1. *for Himself* (1—5); 2. *for the disciples* (6—19); 3. *for the whole Church* (20—26), the last two verses forming a summary, in which the relations of Christ to the Father and to His own, and of His own to both Father and Son are gathered up. The leading thought throughout is *the glory of God* in the work of Christ and in those who continue it.

The prayer was spoken aloud (*v.* 1), and thus was not only a prayer, but a source of comfort to those who heard it (*v.* 13), and by its preservation a means of faith and life to all (xx. 31). He had taught by action (xiii.) and by discourse (xiv.—xvi.); now He teaches by prayer. No doubt it was spoken in Aramaic, and we have here also, as in the discourses, no means of determining how far the Greek version preserves the very words, how far only the substance, of what was spoken. We must take it reverently as it has been given to us, and we shall find abundant reason for believing that on the one hand it quite transcends even the beloved disciple's powers of invention; on the other that there is nothing in it to make us doubt that this report of it is from his pen. "It is urged that the triumphant elevation of this prayer is inconsistent with the Synoptic account of the Agony. But the liability to fluctuations of feeling and emotion is inherent in humanity, and was assumed with His manhood by Him Who was perfect man" (Sanday). "All human experience bears witness in common life to the naturalness of abrupt transitions from joy to sadness in the contemplation of a supreme trial. The absolute insight and foresight of Christ makes such an alteration even more intelligible. He could see, as man cannot do, both the completeness of His triumph and the suffering through which it was to be gained" (Westcott). The three characteristics of the Gospel, simplicity, subtlety, and sublimity, reach a climax here. Bengel calls this chapter the simplest in language, the profoundest in meaning, in the whole Bible. All is natural, for it is a son speaking to a father; all is supernatural, for the Son is the Lord from heaven.

The *place* where these words were spoken is not stated. If the view taken above (xiv. 31) is correct, they were spoken in the upper room, after the company had risen from supper, in the pause before starting for the Mount of Olives (xviii. 1). Westcott thinks that "the upper chamber was certainly left after xiv. 31," and that as "it is inconceivable that chap. xvii. should have been spoken anywhere except under circumstances suited to its unapproachable solemnity," these would best be found in the Temple Courts. Here was the great Golden Vine, to suggest the allegory of the Vine (xvi. 1—11), and "nowhere could the outlines of the future spiritual Church be more fitly drawn than in the sanctuary of the old Church." It is perhaps slightly against this attractive suggestion, that surroundings so rich in meaning would probably have been pointed out by a writer so full of feeling for dramatic contrasts and harmonies as the writer of this Divine Epic (comp. iii. 2, iv. 6, xx. 22, xiii. 30, xviii. 1, 3, 5, 28, 40, xix. 23—27, 31—42).

1—5. The Prayer for Himself

The Son was sent to give to men eternal life, which consists in the knowledge of God. This work the Son has completed to the glory of the Father, and therefore prays to be glorified by the Father.

1. ἐπάρας. As before the raising of Lazarus (xi. 41), Jesus looks heavenwards in calm confidence as to the issue (xvi. 33). The attitude is in marked contrast to His falling on His face in the garden (Matt.

xxvi. 39). *Els τ. οὐρ.* does not prove that He was in the open air: comp. Acts vii. 55; Luke xviii. 13.

πάτερ. This is His claim to be heard: the prayer throughout is the prayer of a son. Comp. 'Abba, Father' in Mark xiv. 36, and see Lightfoot on Gal. iv. 6. For **ἡ ὥρα** see on ii. 4 and xii. 23. S. John loves to mark each great crisis in Christ's life: this is the last.

δόξασον. By His return to glory (*v.* 5); so that His human nature might share the Divine attributes, and thus glorify the Father by continuing with higher powers in heaven the work which He has completed on earth. Comp. Phil. ii. 9—11. The tone from the first is one of triumph.

2. **καθὼς ἔδωκας.** **Even** *as thou* **gavest** (iii. 35) *Him* **authority** (i. 12) *over all flesh.* The authority was given once for all (v. 27), and is the reason for the petition in *v.* 1. **Πᾶσα σάρξ** is a Hebraism not used elsewhere in this Gospel. Comp. Matt. xxiv. 22; Luke iii. 6; Acts ii. 17; Rom. iii. 20, &c. Fallen man, man in his frailty, is specially meant; but the Second Adam has dominion also over 'all sheep and oxen, yea, and the beasts of the field, the fowl of the air, and the fish of the sea.' Ps. viii. 7, 8. In the following texts 'all flesh' includes the brute creation; Gen. vi. 19, vii. 15, 16, 21, viii. 17, ix. 11, 15, 16, 17; Ps. cxxxvi. 25; Jer. xxxii. 27, xlv. 5. Once more, therefore, Jewish exclusiveness is condemned. The Messiah is King of 'all flesh,' not of the Jews only. For the *casus pendens* comp. vi. 39, vii. 38, xv. 2. Note the change from neut. sing. to masc. plur. in what follows: *in order that* **all that** *Thou hast given Him, He should give* **to them** *eternal life.* Believers are given to Christ as a united whole; they earn eternal life as individuals: comp. *v.* 24, i. 11, vi. 37.

3. **αὕτη δέ.** *But* **the** *life eternal* (just mentioned) *is this:* 'is' not 'will be' (see on iii. 36, v. 24, vi. 47, 54); and 'is this' means 'this is what it consists in' (iii. 19, xv. 12). The truth of man's religion depends on his conception of God. For *ἵνα* after *οὗτος* comp. vi. 29, 39, 49, 50, xv. 12; 1 John iii. 11, 23, v. 3; 2 John 6.

ἵνα γινώσκουσιν. The present indicative after *ἵνα* is surprising, but not very rare in late Greek: comp. 1 Cor. iv. 6; Gal. iv. 17: Winer, p. 362. The future is comparatively common; Gal. ii. 4. There is no need to give *ἵνα* a *local* as distinct from a *final* meaning in such constructions; 'where' or 'in which case' instead of 'in order that.' The meaning is rather 'that ye may continue to recognise, as you do now.' But *γινώσκουσιν*, though adopted by Tischendorf and Tregelles, is rejected by Westcott and Hort, who retain *γινώσκωσιν* with Alford and the Revisers. (Westcott and Hort adopt *δώσει* for *δώσῃ* in *v.* 2.) It is the *appropriation* of the knowledge that is emphasized: hence *γινώσκειν*, not *εἰδέναι.* Comp. Wisd. xv. 3. For **ἀληθινόν** see on i. 9, iv. 23: 'the only true God' is directed against the many false, spurious gods of the heathen. This portion of the truth *the Gentiles* signally failed to recognise.

ὃν ἀπ. Ἰ. Χρ. Him whom thou didst send (see on i. 33),—**Jesus Christ**; or, *Jesus* **as** *Christ*. This portion of the truth *the Jews* failed to recognise. But the words are not without difficulty, even when we insert the 'as;' and the run of the Greek words is rather against the insertion of 'as.' If 'Christ' were a predicate and not part of the proper name we should expect 'Jesus, whom Thou didst send, as Christ.' Probably in this verse we have the *substance* and not the exact words of Christ's utterance. That He should use the name 'Jesus' here is perhaps improbable; that He should anticipate the use of 'Jesus Christ' as a proper name is very improbable; and the expression 'the true God' is not used elsewhere by Christ and is used by S. John (1 John v. 20). We conclude, therefore, that the *wording* here is the Evangelist's, perhaps abbreviated from the actual words.

4. ἐδόξασα. I glorified *Thee on the earth*, **having perfected.** In confident anticipation Christ looks back from the point when all shall be accomplished, and speaks of the whole work of redemption as one act. The A.V. is very capricious throughout this chapter, rendering aorists as perfects and perfects as aorists. Comp. *vv.* 6, 8, 18, 21, 22, 23, 25, 26. For **δέδωκας** see on iii. 35: Christ did not choose His work for Himself. The **ἵνα** indicates God's purpose in giving it.

5. This and *v.* 4 are parallels: 'I Thee glorified on earth; glorify Me Thou in heaven;' the pronouns being placed side by side for emphasis. **Καὶ νῦν** means 'now that all is completed;' and **παρὰ σεαυτῷ** 'side by side with Thee, in fellowship with Thee.' The imperfect, **εἶχον**, implies continual possession. The following great truths are contained in these two verses; (1) that the Son is in Person distinct from the Father; (2) that the Son, existing in glory with the Father from all eternity, working in obedience to the Father on earth, existing in glory with the Father now, is in Person one and the same.

6—19. The Prayer for His Disciples

6—8. The basis of the intercession;—they have received the revelation given to them. The intercession itself begins *v.* 9.

6. ἐφανέρωσα. See on i. 31. The manifestation was not made indiscriminately, but to persons fitted to receive it. Sometimes the Father is said to 'give' or 'draw' men to Christ (*v.* 24, vi. 37, 44, 65, x. 29, xviii. 9); sometimes Christ is said to 'choose' them (vi. 70, xv. 16): but it is always in their power to refuse; there is no compulsion (i. 11, 12, iii. 18, 19, xii. 47, 48). For **τετήρηκαν** see on viii. 51: the notion is that of intent watching. For **τὸν λόγον** and **τὰ ῥήματα** (*v.* 8) see on iii. 34.

7. ἔγνωκαν. *They have recognised* and therefore **know** (v. 42, vi. 69, viii. 52, 55, xiv. 9) that the whole of Christ's work of redemption in word and act was in its origin and still is (*εἰσίν*) of God.

8. ἔγνωσαν...ἐπίστευσαν. They *recognised* that His mission was Divine (see on xvi. 28): they *believed* that He was sent as the Messiah. They had proof of the one; the other was a matter of faith.

9—19. The intercession for the disciples based on their need.

9. 'For them who have believed I, who have laboured to bring them to this belief, am praying; for the world I am not praying.' Ἐγώ, *αὐτῶν* and *κόσμου* are emphatic. **Περί** indicates the subject of the petition: for **ἐρωτῶ** see on xiv. 16. Of course this does not mean that Christ never prays for unbelievers; *v.* 23 and Luke xxiii. 34 prove the contrary: but it is for the chosen few, in return for their allegiance, that He is praying now. He could not pray for unbelievers that they should be *kept* (*v.* 11) and *sanctified* (*v.* 17), but that they should be converted and forgiven.

10. τὰ ἐμά. *All* **things** *that are Mine are Thine and Thine are Mine.* This does not refer to persons only; it continues and also amplifies *ὅτι σοί εἰσιν*. The double mode of statement insists on the perfect union between the Father and the Son: what follows shews the perfect union between Christ and believers. Christ is glorified in them as the vine in its branches and fruit: they are the vehicles and monuments of the glory (1 Thess. ii. 20). **Δεδόξασμαι,** 'I have been and still am glorified.'

11—16. In *vv.* 6—8 the disciples' acceptance of Christ is given as the basis of intercession for them: here another reason is added,—their need of help during Christ's absence. This plea is first stated in all simplicity, and then repeated at intervals in the petition. Note the simple and solemn coupling of the clauses.

11. πάτερ ἅγιε. The expression occurs here only; but comp. Rev. vi. 10; 1 John ii. 20 and *v.* 25. The epithet agrees with the prayer **ἁγίασον** *αὐτούς* (*v.* 17), *ἵνα ὦσιν καὶ αὐτοὶ* **ἡγιασμένοι** (*v.* 19). God has given His name (see on i. 12) to Christ to reveal to His disciples; and Christ here prays that they may be kept true to that revelation of the Divine character. And **even as** (*καθώς*) the Father and Son are one in the possession of the Divine nature, so the disciples are to be kept one by the knowledge of it. Comp. Rev. ii. 17, xxii. 4.

12. ἐτήρουν. The imperfect expresses Christ's continual watching. Ἐγώ is emphatic: '*I* kept them while I was with them; but now do Thou keep them.' Mark the change to **ἐφύλαξα, I guarded:** this is the protection which is the *result* of the watching.

ὁ υἱὸς τ. ἀπωλείας. The phrase occurs twice in N.T.; here of Judas, and 2 Thess. ii. 3 of the 'man of sin.' See on xii. 36 and comp. *τέκνα ἀπωλείας* (Is. lvii. 4), *υἱὸς θανάτου* (2 Sam. xii. 5). The connexion between *ἀπώλετο* and *ἀπωλείας* cannot easily be shewn in English. Ἡ *γραφή* refers to Ps. xli. 9: see on x. 35, xiii. 18, xii. 38.

13. νῦν δέ. But *now.* Hitherto He has been with them to guard them, but now He is going away: and He is praying thus aloud in order that His words may comfort them when they remember that before He went He consigned them to His Father's keeping. Comp. xi. 42. For **τ. χαρὰν τ. ἐμήν** see on viii. 31.

14. ἐγὼ δέδ. *I,* in emphatic opposition to the world, *have given them the revelation of Thee; and the world* **hated** *them.* The aorist expresses the single act of hate in contrast to the gift which they continue to possess. These are the two results of discipleship; Christ's protection with the gift of God's word and the world's hate.

15. ἐκ τ. πονηροῦ. *From the* **evil one**: comp. 1 John ii. 13, 14, iii. 12, and especially v. 18, 19. The world and the Gospel are regarded as in ceaseless opposition in S. John's writings, and the evil one is 'the ruler of this world' (xii. 31, xvi. 11). Just as Christ is that *in* which His disciples live and move, so the evil one is that *out of* which (*ἐκ*) He prays that they may be kept. Believers are *ἐν τῷ ἀληθινῷ, ἐν τῷ υἱῷ αὐτοῦ Ἰησοῦ Χριστῷ* (1 John v. 20): but the world *ἐν τῷ πονηρῷ κεῖται*. In 1 John iv. 4 we have the opposite mode of statement; Christ is in believers and the evil one is in the world. All these passages seem to shew that *τοῦ πονηροῦ* must be masculine.

16. What was stated in *v.* 14 as the reason for the world's hate is repeated as the introduction to a new petition for not merely protection but sanctification.

17. ἁγίασον. *Sanctify* or **consecrate.** It expresses God's destination of them for their work and His endowment of them with the powers necessary for their work. The word is used of God's consecration of Jeremiah, Moses, and the Chosen People (Jer. i. 5; Ecclus. xlix. 7, xlv. 4; 2 Macc. i. 25). This prayer has been called "the Prayer of Consecration." The Truth *in* which they are consecrated is the whole Christian revelation, the new environment in which believers are placed for their sanctification; just as a sickly wild plant is strengthened and changed by being transplanted into a garden. For **ὁ λόγος ὁ σός** see on viii. 31: God's revelation as a whole is meant, not any single utterance or collection of utterances: see on iii. 34.

19. Christ does for Himself that which He prays the Father to do for His disciples. In x. 36 He speaks of Himself as consecrated by the Father; set apart for a sacred purpose. But only thus far is the consecration of Christ and of His disciples the same. In them it also implied redemption and cleansing from sin; and in this sense *ἁγιάζω* is frequently connected with *καθαρίζω* (2 Cor. vii. 1; Eph. v. 26; 2 Tim. ii. 21; Heb. ix. 13). The radical meaning of the word is not separation, as is sometimes stated, but holiness, which involves separation, viz. the being set apart *for God*. In O. T. consecration is a *ritual* act; in N. T. a *spiritual* act, the consecration of the heart and will to God. **Ἐν ἀληθείᾳ,** *in truth* and reality, not in mere name, is different from **ἐν τῇ** *ἀληθείᾳ in* **the** *Truth* (see on *v.* 17). As a Priest consecrated by the Father (x. 36) He consecrates Himself as a Sacrifice (Eph. v. 2), and thereby obtains a real internal consecration for them through the Paraclete (xvi. 7).

20—26. The Prayer for the whole Church

Christ having prayed first for the *Author* of salvation, and then for the *instruments* of the work, now prays for the *objects* of it. The limitation stated in *v.* 9 is at an end: through the Church He prays for the whole race of mankind (*v.* 21).

20. πιστευόντων. Present: the future body of believers is regarded by anticipation as already in existence: the Apostles are an earnest of the Church that is to be. The order emphasizes the fact that those who believe on Christ believe through the Apostles' word.

21. ἓν ὦσιν. This is the purpose rather than the purport of the prayer: Christ prays for blessings for His Church with this end in view—that all may be one.

καθώς depends on the second ἵνα, not on the first (comp. xiii. 34): the unity of believers is even as the unity of the Father with the Son (x. 30); not a mere moral unity of disposition, but a vital unity, in which the members share the life of one and the same organism (Rom. xii. 4, 5). Mere agreement in opinion and aim would not convert the world; whereas the eternal unity of believers will produce such external results ('see how these Christians love one another'), that the world will believe that God sent their Master. Christian unity and love (Matt. vii. 12; Luke vi. 31; 1 Cor. xiii.) is a moral miracle, a conquest of the resisting will of man, and therefore more convincing than a physical miracle, which is a conquest of unresisting matter. Hence the quarrels of Christians are a perpetual stumbling-block to the world.

The parallel between this verse and 1 John i. 3 is remarkable. If *ἀπαγγέλλομεν* refers to the Gospel and not to the Epistle, as is probable, then S. John wrote his Gospel in order that this prayer of Christ might be fulfilled.

22—24. Having prayed for them with a view to their unity, Jesus passes to His final petition, a share in His glory for His disciples. In leading up to this He states what He Himself has done for them: **κἀγώ** is emphatic.

22. δέδωκας. See on iii. 35. The meaning of this gift of *δόξα* is clear from *v.* 24; the glory of the ascended and glorified Christ in which believers are His *συνκληρονόμοι* (see on Rom. viii. 17). In full assurance of victory (xvi. 33), Jesus speaks of this glory as already given back to Him (*v.* 5) and shared with His followers.

23. The basis of the unity of believers is their union with Christ and through Him with the Father: in this way they are *perfected* **into** *one*, completed and made one. It is in the unity that the completeness consists. For **τελειοῦσθαι** comp. 1 John ii. 5, iv. 12, 17, 18; for **εἰς ἕν** comp. xi. 52 (1 John v. 8).

γινώσκῃ. Come to know, recognise (*v.* 3) gradually and in time. This is the second effect of the unity of Christians, more perfect than the first. The first (*v.* 21) was that the world is induced to *believe* that God sent Christ; the second is that the world comes to *know* that God sent Christ, and moreover that He loved the world even as He loved Christ. The **σύ** and **ἐμέ** in what follows are emphatic.

24. πατήρ. Comp. *vv.* 1, 5, 11, 25, xi. 41, xii. 27. The relationship is the ground of appeal; He knows that His 'will' is one with His Father's. The position of **ὃ δέδωκάς μοι** (see on *v.* 2) is remarkable: the fact of the gift is another ground of appeal.

θέλω. The expression, as used here by Christ, is unique: but comp. xxi. 22; Matt. viii. 3, xxiii. 37, xxvi. 39; Luke xii. 49. It is His last will and testament, which the Christ on the eve of His death here deposits in the Father's hands. For **τ. δόξαν τ. ἐμήν** see on viii. 31: it is not the glory of the Word, the Eternal Son, which was His in His equality with the Father, but the glory of Christ, the Incarnate Son, with which the risen and ascended Jesus was endowed. In sure confidence Christ speaks of this as already given, and wills that all believers may behold and share it. Thus two gifts of the Father to the Son meet and complete one another: those whom He has given behold the glory that He has given. See on xii. 24.

καταβολῆς κόσμου. Christ thrice uses this expression; here, Luke xi. 50; Matt. xxv. 34. Two of those who heard it reproduce it (1 Pet. i. 20; Rev. xiii. 8, xvii. 8). Comp. Eph. i. 4; Heb. iv. 3, ix. 26, xi. 11.

25, 26. SUMMARY

25. πατὴρ δίκαιε. The epithet (comp. *v.* 11) harmonizes with the appeal to the *justice* of God which follows, which is based on a simple statement of the facts. The world knew not God; Christ knew Him; the disciples knew that Christ was sent by Him. 'Shall not the Judge of all the earth do right?' **Καί** before *ὁ κόσμος* may be rendered 'indeed:' 'it is true the world knew Thee not, but yet, &c.'

26. ἐγνώρισα. Shew in translation that the verb is cognate with *ἔγνων* in *v.* 25; **made known.** In both cases the aorist should be kept in English. Christ knows the Father and makes known His name, i.e. His attributes and will (see on i. 12), to the disciples. This imparting of knowledge is already accomplished in part,—'I made known' (comp. xv. 15); but the knowledge and the love which imparts it being alike inexhaustible, there is room for perpetual instruction throughout all time, especially after the Paraclete has been given,—'I will make known' (comp. xiv. 26, xvi. 13). With the double accusative, **ἣν ἠγάπησάς με** comp. vii. 24; Rev. xvi. 9; Eph. ii. 4: this love is to rule in their hearts as a guiding principle, without which they cannot receive the knowledge here promised; 'he that loveth not, knoweth not God (1 John iv. 8).

κἀγὼ ἐν αὐτοῖς. These last words of Christ's mediatorial Prayer are the thread which runs through all these farewell discourses. He is going away and yet abides with them. His bodily presence passes away, His spiritual presence remains for ever; not seen with the eye without, but felt as life and strength within. Having known Christ after the flesh, now they know Him so no more; they are in Christ, a new creation (2 Cor. v. 16, 17).

CHAPTER XVIII

1. τῶν Κέδρων (ℵ[3]BCLX Origen) is to be preferred to *τοῦ Κέδρου* (ℵ[1]D) or *τοῦ Κεδρών* (ASΔ). Both *τῶν Κέδρων* and *τοῦ Κεδρών* occur in LXX. as various readings (2 S. xv. 23; 1 K. ii. 37, xv. 13; 2 K. xxiii. 6, 12): Josephus uses *Κεδρῶνος* as the genitive of *Κεδρών* (*A. J.* VIII. i. 5). We infer that both names were current, the Hebrew having given birth to a Greek name of different meaning but similar sound.

4. ἐξῆλθεν καὶ λέγει (BC[1]D Origen) for *ἐξελθὼν εἶπεν* (ℵAC[3]).

10. ὠτάριον (ℵBC[1]LX) for *ὠτίον* (AC[3]D from Matt. xxvi. 51?).

14. ἀποθανεῖν (ℵBC[1]DLX) for *ἀπολέσθαι* (AC[3]).

16. ὁ γνωστὸς τοῦ ἀρχιερέως (BC[1]L) for *ὃς ἦν γνωστὸς τῷ ἀρχιερεῖ* (ℵAC[2] from *v.* 15).

21. ἐρωτᾷς; ἐρώτησον (ℵBC[1]LX) for *ἐπερωτᾷς; ἐπερερώτησον* (*v.* 7).

29. Insert **ἔξω** (ℵBC[1]LX) after **Πιλάτος: φησίν** (ℵBC[1]LX) for *εἶπεν* (AC[3] correction to harmonize with **ἐξῆλθεν**).

30. κακὸν ποιῶν (ℵ[3]BL) for *κακοποιός* (AC[3] for simplification; the word perhaps comes from 1 Pet. ii. 12, 14, iii. 16, iv. 15).

We enter now upon the second part of the second main division of the Gospel. The Evangelist having given us the INNER GLORIFICATION OF CHRIST IN HIS LAST DISCOURSES (xiii.—xvii.), now sets forth HIS OUTER GLORIFICATION IN HIS PASSION AND DEATH (xviii., xix.). This part, like the former (see Introduction to chap. xiii.), may be divided into four sections. 1. *The Betrayal* (xviii. 1—11); 2. *The Jewish Trials* (12—27); 3. *The Roman Trial* (xviii. 28—xix. 16); 4. *The Death and Burial* (17—42).

Dr Westcott (*Speaker's Commentary*, N. T., Vol. II. p. 249) observes; "1. It is a superficial and inadequate treatment of his narrative to regard it as a historical supplement of the other narratives, or of the current oral narrative on which they are based......*The record is independent and complete in itself.* It is a whole, and like the rest of the Gospel an interpretation of the inner meaning of the history which it contains.

"Thus in the history of the Passion three thoughts among others rise into clear prominence:

(1) *The voluntariness of Christ's sufferings;* xviii. 4, 8, 11, 36; xix. 28, 30.

(2) *The fulfilment of a divine plan in Christ's sufferings;* xviii. 4, 9, 11, xix. 11, 24, 28, 36, 37.

(3) *The Majesty which shines through Christ's sufferings;* xviii. 6, 20—23 (comp. Luke xxii. 53), 37, xix. 11, 26, 27, 30.

"The narrative in this sense becomes a commentary on earlier words which point to the end; (1) x. 17, 18; (2) xiii. 1; (3) xiii. 31.

"2. In several places the full meaning of S. John's narrative is first obtained by the help of words or incidents preserved by the synoptists. *His narrative assumes facts found in them:* e.g. xviii. 11, 33, 40, xix. 41.

"3. The main incidents recorded by more than one of the other Evangelists which are *omitted by S. John* are: (by *all three*) the agony, traitor's kiss, mockery as prophet, council at daybreak, impressment of Simon, reproaches of the spectators, darkness, confession of the centurion; (by *S. Matthew and S. Mark*) the desertion by all, examination before the Sanhedrin at night, false witness, adjuration, great Confession, mockery after condemnation, cry from Ps. xxii., rending of the veil.

"Other incidents omitted by S. John are recorded by single Evangelists: (*S. Matthew*) power over the hosts of heaven, Pilate's wife's message, Pilate's hand-washing, self-condemnation of the Jews, earthquake; (*S. Mark*) flight of the young man, Pilate's question as to the death of Christ; (*S. Luke*) examination before Herod, lamentation of the women, three 'words' from the Cross (xxiii. 34, 43, 46), repentance of one of the robbers.

"4. The main incidents *peculiar to S. John* are: the words of power at the arrest, examination before Annas, first conference of the Jews with Pilate and Pilate's private examination, first mockery and *Ecce Homo*, Pilate's maintenance of his words, the last charge (xix. 25—27), the thirst, piercing of the side, ministry of Nicodemus.

"5. In the narrative of incidents recorded elsewhere *S. John constantly adds details*, often minute and yet most significant: e.g. xviii. 1, 2, 10, 11, 12, 15, 16, 26, 28, xix. 14, 17, 41. See the notes.

"6. In the midst of great differences of detail *the Synoptists and S. John offer many impressive resemblances* as to the spirit and character of the proceedings: e.g. (1) the activity of the 'High Priests' (i.e. the Sadducaean hierarchy) as distinguished from the Pharisees; (2) the course of the accusation—civil charge, religious charge, personal influence; (3) the silence of the Lord in His public accusations, with the significant exception, Matt. xxvi. 64; (4) the tone of mockery; (5) the character of Pilate."

1—11. The Betrayal

1. ἐξῆλθεν. From the upper room. The word is used of leaving the room, Matt. xxii. 39; Mark xiv. 26; Luke xxii. 39. Those who suppose that the room is left at xiv. 31 (perhaps for the Temple), interpret this of the departure from the city.

τῶν Κέδρων. Of the Cedars, rather than *τοῦ Κεδρών, of the Kedron.* Kedron or Kidron = 'black,' and is commonly referred to the dark colour of the water or to the gloom of the ravine. But it might refer to the black green of the cedars, and thus both names would be united. **χειμαρροῦς** or *φάραγξ* (Josephus uses both words) indicates the *ravine* rather than the water: even in winter the stream

is small. This detail of Jesus crossing the 'Wady' of the Kidron is given by S. John only; but he gives no hint of a reference to the flight of David from Absalom and Ahithophel (2 S. xv. 23). If we are to seek a reason for his noting the fact, we may find it in his characteristic symbolism: *ἐκ* **χειμάρρου** *ἐν ὁδῷ πίεται* (Ps. cx. 7); **χείμαρρον** *διῆλθεν ἡ ψυχή* (Ps. cxxiv. 4). This gloomy ravine with its dusky waters is a figure of the affliction through which the Messiah is passing. See on iii. 2, x. 22, xiii. 30.

κῆπος. *Garden* or *orchard.* Gethsemane means 'oil-press,' and olives probably abounded there. The very ancient olive-trees still existing on the traditional site were probably put there by pilgrims who replanted the spot after its devastation at the siege of Jerusalem. S. John gives no hint of a comparison between the two gardens, Eden and Gethsemane, which commentators from Cyril to Isaac Williams have traced. See on Mark i. 13 for another comparison.

2. ὁ παραδιδούς. *Who* **was betraying**; he was at that moment at work: his knowing the place disproves the sneer of Celsus, that Jesus went thither to hide and escape. Origen (*Cels.* II. x.) appeals to *vv.* 4, 5 as shewing that He deliberately surrendered Himself. **Συνήχθη** (literally, **assembled**) suggests that they met for a definite purpose, such as teaching or devotion. The owner must have known of these frequent gatherings and may have been a disciple.

3. ὁ οὖν Ἰ. *Judas* **therefore.** It was because he knew that Jesus often went thither that he came hither to take Him. The details which follow are minute and accurate as of an eyewitness.

τὴν σπεῖραν. The *band of* **soldiers**: this is one part of the company; Roman soldiers sent to prevent 'an uproar' among the thousands of pilgrims assembled for the Passover (see on Matt. xxvi. 5). **Σπεῖρα** seems elsewhere in N.T. to mean 'cohort,' the tenth of a legion (Matt. xxvii. 27; Mark xv. 16; Acts x. 1, xxi. 31, xxvii. 1), and with this Polybius (XI. xxi. 1; [xxiii. 1]) agrees. But Polybius sometimes (VI. xxiv. 5, xv. ix. 7, III. cxiii. 3) appears to use *σπεῖρα* for 'maniple,' the third part of a cohort and about 200 men. In any case only a portion of the cohort which formed the garrison of the fortress of Antonia can here be meant: but that the arrest of Jesus was expected to produce a crisis is shewn by the presence of the *chief* officer of the cohort (*v.* 12). The Jewish hierarchy had no doubt communicated with Pilate, and his being ready to try the case at so early an hour as 5 A.M. may be accounted for in this way.

ἐκ τ. ἀρχ. κ. τ. Φ. From the Sanhedrin (see on vii. 32, 45, xi. 47). These *ὑπηρέται* may have been either officers of justice appointed by the Sanhedrin, or a portion of the Levitical temple-police: that some of the latter were present is clear from Luke xxii. 4, 52. This is a second part of the company. S. Luke (xxii. 52) tells us that some of the chief priests themselves were there also. Thus there were (1) Roman soldiers, (2) Jewish officials, (3) chief priests. The **φανοί** and **λαμπάδες** were the common equipment for night duty, not rendered useless by the Paschal full moon. Dark woods or buildings might need searching. *Φανός* occurs here only in N.T. Both A.V. and R.V. vary between 'torch,' 'light,' and 'lamp' for *λαμπάς* (Matt. xxv. 1—8; Acts xx. 8; Rev. iv. 5, viii. 10). Torches were fed with oil carried in a vessel for the purpose, and perhaps 'torch' would be best everywhere for *λαμπάς*, leaving 'lamp' for the translation of *λύχνος* (v. 35; Matt. v. 15, vi. 22; Luke viii. 16, &c.). There is a suppressed irony in the details of this verse: 'all this force against one; against one who intended no resistance; against One who with one word (*v.* 6; Matt. xxvi. 53) could have swept them all away.'

4. ἐξῆλθεν. From what? (1) from the shade into the light; (2) from the circle of disciples; (3) from the depth of the garden; (4) from the garden itself. It is impossible to say which of these is right; the last is not contradicted by *v.* 26. The kiss of Judas is by some placed here, by others after *v.* 8. While 'His hour was not yet come' (vii. 30, viii. 20), He had withdrawn from danger (viii. 59, xi. 54, xii. 36); now He goes forth to meet it. He who had avoided notoriety (v. 13) and royalty (vi. 15), goes forth to welcome death. His question may have had two objects; to withdraw attention from His disciples (*v.* 8), and to make His captors realise what they were doing.

5. 'Ι. τ. Ναζωραῖον. *Jesus* **the Nazarene** (Matt. ii. 23), a rather more contemptuous expression than 'Jesus of Nazareth' (i. 46; Acts x. 38; comp. Matt. xxi. 11). 'The Nazarene' in a contemptuous sense occurs xix. 19; Matt. xxvi. 71; Mark xiv. 67. It is sometimes used in a neutral sense (Mark x. 47; Luke xviii. 37, xxiv. 19). Later on the contempt of Jews and heathen became the glory of Christians (Acts ii. 22, iii. 6, iv. 10, vi. 14).

ἐγώ εἰμι. These words to Jewish ears were the name of Jehovah. We have had the same expression several times in this Gospel (iv. 26), vi. 20, viii. 24, 28, 58, xiii. 1 (see notes). Judas, if not the chief priests, must have noticed the significant words. There is nothing in the narrative to shew that either the whole company were miraculously blinded (Luke xxiv. 16), or that Judas in particular was blinded or paralysed. Even those who knew Him well might fail to recognise Him at once by night and with the traces of the Agony fresh upon Him.

εἱστήκει...ὁ παραδιδούς. *Judas,* **who was betraying Him** (*v.* 2) **was standing** *with them.* This tragic detail is stamped on the Evangelist's memory: that one dark figure standing as the chief representative of the *ἐξουσία τοῦ σκότους*. S. John has been accused of personal hatred towards Judas; but he alone of the four Evangelists omits the traitor's kiss. For *εἱστήκει v.* 16, comp. i. 35, vii. 35, xix. 25, xx. 11.

6. ὡς οὖν εἶπεν. When therefore He said; intimating that what followed was the immediate consequence of His words. They fell backwards, recoiling from the majesty of goodness, not forwards in adoration of it. Whether their falling was the natural effect of guilt meeting with absolute innocence, or a supernatural effect wrought by Christ's will, is a question which we have not the means of determining.

Moreover, the distinction may be an unreal one. Is it not His will that guilt should quail before innocence? The result in this case proved both to the disciples and to His foes that His surrender was entirely voluntary (x. 18). Once before, the majesty of His words had overwhelmed those who had come to arrest Him (vii. 46); and it would have been so now, had not He willed to be taken. Comp. Matt. xxvi. 53, where the expression '*legions* of angels' may have reference to the fragment of a legion that had come to superintend His capture.

7. **πάλιν οὖν.** *Again* **therefore.** Their first onset had been baffled: He Himself gives them another opening. They repeat the terms of their warrant; they have been sent to arrest 'Jesus the Nazarene.'

8. **ἄφετε τούτους ὑπάγειν.** He is no hireling (x. 12); His first thought is for the sheep. At first Jesus had gone forward (*v.* 4) from His company, as Judas, to give the kiss, from his. Judas has fallen back on his followers, while the disciples gather round Christ. Thus the two bands and two leaders confront one another.

9. **οὓς δεδ. μ., οὐκ ἀπ.** *Of those whom Thou* **hast given** *Me, I* **lost** *not one.* The reference is to xvii. 12, and is a strong confirmation of the historical truth of chap. xvii. If the prayer were the composition of the Evangelist to set forth in an ideal form Christ's mental condition at the time, this reference to a definite portion of it would be most unnatural. The change from 'not one of them perished' to 'I lost of them not one' brings out the protective intervention of Christ.

It does not follow, because S. John gives this interpretation of Christ's words, that therefore they have no other. This was a first fulfilment, within an hour or two of their utterance, an earnest of a larger fulfilment in the future. The meaning here must not be limited to bodily preservation. Had they been captured, apostasy might have been the result, as was actually the case with S. Peter.

10. **Σ. οὖν Π.** *Simon Peter* **therefore**; because he 'saw what would follow' (Luke xxii. 49). The position of *οὖν* is remarkable, as if *Πέτρος* had been added as an after-thought, possibly in allusion to the significance of the name. All four Evangelists mention this act of violence; S. John alone gives the names. While S. Peter was alive it was only prudent not to mention his name; and probably S. John was the only one who knew (*v.* 15) the servant's name. This impetuous boldness of *ὁ θερμὸς Πέτρος* illustrates his impetuous words xiii. 37 and Mark viii. 32. The sword was probably one of the two produced in misunderstanding of Christ's words at the end of the supper (Luke xxiii. 38). To carry arms on a feast-day was forbidden; so that we have here some indication that the Last Supper was not the Passover. No doubt Malchus had been prominent in the attack on Jesus; hence **τὸν** *τ. ἀρχ. δοῦλον*, which does not mean that only one servant was there (*v.* 26). Or *τὸν δ.* may mean 'the servant of whom you have so often heard.' S. Peter had aimed at his head. S. Luke also mentions that it was the ***right*** ear that was cut, and he alone mentions the healing, under cover of which S. Peter probably escaped.

11. βάλε. See on v. 7. S. John alone gives the words about the cup: the Synoptists alone (Matt. xxvi. 39, &c.) give the prayer to which they obviously refer. Thus the two accounts confirm one another. Comp. ii. 19, xii. 8; and for the metaphor Ps. lxxv. 8, lx. 3; Job xxi. 20; Rev. xiv. 10, xvi. 19. S. Matthew gives another reason for sheathing; 'all they that take the sword shall perish with the sword' (xxvi. 52). "Any zeal is proper for religion but the zeal of the sword and the zeal of anger" (Jeremy Taylor). For **οὐ μή** interrogative comp. Ruth iii. 1; *οὐ μὴ εὕρω σοι ἀνάπαυσιν*; See on iv. 48.

12—27. The Jewish or Ecclesiastical Trials

12—27. Much space is given in all four Gospels to the Jewish and Roman trials, space apparently disproportionate to the brief account of the Crucifixion. But the two trials illustrate the two great elements of Christ's Messiahship. By the Sanhedrin He was condemned as claiming to be the *Son of God*, by Pilate as claiming to be the *King of the Jews*. The Crucifixion would be unintelligible if we did not clearly understand *Who* was crucified, and *why*.

12. ἡ οὖν σπ. Therefore *the band;* because of S. Peter's violent attempt at rescue. The **χιλίαρχος** is the tribune of the Roman cohort. His presence with the detachment shews that the hierarchy had prepared the Romans for serious resistance. Peter's violence confirms these representations. Jesus the Nazarene is a dangerous character who incites His followers to rebellion; He must be secured and bound. And the incident in *v.* 6 would suggest great caution, as in dealing with a powerful magician.

13. πρὸς Ἄνναν πρῶτον. The *πρῶτον* shews that S. John is aware of the subsequent examination before Caiaphas given by the Synoptists. Whether Annas was 'chief' of the priests (2 Kings xxv. 18), or president, or vice-president, of the Sanhedrin, we have no information. Certainly he was one of the most influential members of the hierarchy, as is shewn by his securing the high-priesthood for no less than five of his sons as well as for his son-in-law Caiaphas, after he had been deposed himself. He held office A.D. 7—14, his son Eleazar A.D. 16, Joseph Caiaphas A.D. 18—36; after Caiaphas four sons of Annas held the office, the last of whom, another Annas (A.D. 62), put to death S. James, the first bishop of Jerusalem. The high-priests at this time were often mere nominees of the civil power, and were changed with a rapidity which must have scandalized serious Jews. There were probably five or six deposed high-priests in the Sanhedrin which tried our Lord (see on xi. 49 and Luke iii. 2). Other forms of the name Annas are Ananias, Ananus, and Hanan.

ἦν γὰρ πενθ. And therefore Caiaphas would be sure to respect the results of a preliminary examination conducted by him. Possibly the chief priests thought that Annas was a safer man than Caiaphas. This examination before Annas is given us by S. John only, who tacitly corrects the impression that the examination before Caiaphas was the only one.

14. συμφέρει. See on xi. 50—52. S. John intimates that a trial conducted under such auspices could have but one issue.

15. ἠκολούθει. *Was following;* the descriptive imperfect. Some good authorities (ℵ[3] C) insert ὁ before ἄλλος, but the balance is decidedly against it. There is no very strong reason for rejecting the almost universal opinion that this ἄλλος μαθητής is S. John himself. It agrees with his habitual reserve about himself (i. 40, xiii. 23—25, xix. 26, xx. 2—8, xxi. 20—24); with his being often found with S. Peter (Luke xxii. 8; Acts iii. 1, iv. 13, viii. 14); and with his knowledge of the high-priest's servant's name (*v.* 10). Yet the opinion is not a certainty; the facts just mentioned would fit his brother S. James almost equally well; and the fact of S. John's elsewhere designating himself as the μαθητὴς ὃν ἠγάπα ὁ Ἰησοῦς is slightly against the opinion. But on the other hand that designation would have no point here; the unnamed disciple is not receiving any mark of favour from Jesus. See *Introduction*, p. xxxiv.

γνωστὸς τ. ἀρχ. Comp. Luke ii. 44, xxiii. 49. The nature of the acquaintance is not explained: in connexion with it we may remember the tradition that S. John himself wore the high-priestly badge in later life; p. xvii. Τῷ ἀρχ. is probably Caiaphas (*vv.* 13, 24): deposed high-priests were thus designated sometimes (Luke iii. 2; Acts iv. 6), but never by S. John. Possibly Annas lived in his son-in-law's official residence; but if not, there is nothing improbable in his conducting a preliminary examination there. The **αὐλή** (x. 1, 16) is the **court** or open space in the centre or in front of the house (Luke xxii. 55): **ἔξω** (*v.* 16) agrees better with an interior court.

16. εἱστήκει. Was standing; descriptive imperfect, as in *vv.* 5, 15, 18. The details again indicate an eyewitness. Female doorkeepers were common among the Jews: LXX. in 2 Sam. iv. 6; Rhoda, Acts xii. 13; Josephus, *Ant.* VII. ii. 1.

17. μὴ καὶ σύ. Art thou also (shewing that she knew his companion to be a disciple), or, *surely thou also art not.* See on iv. 29 and comp. iv. 33, vi. 67, vii. 47, ix. 40; where, as here, the μή anticipates a *negative* answer. S. Peter's denial is thus put into his mouth. **Τούτου** and the turn of the sentence are contemptuous; ix. 16, 24, xi. 47. S. John had hurried on to the room where Christ was being examined; as at the Cross (xix. 26) he kept close to his Master; and in neither case was molested. S. Peter, who 'followed afar off' (Luke xxii. 54) and that rather out of curiosity 'to see the end' (Matt. xxvi. 58) than out of love, encountered temptation and fell.

18. εἱστήκ. δὲ οἱ δ. Now *the servants and* **the** *officers* **were standing** ...*and* **were warming** *themselves.* The tribune (*v.* 12) has withdrawn his men, having completed the arrest. Only the officials of the Sanhedrin remain, joined now by the household servants of the high-priest. **Ἀνθρακιά** means charcoal in a brazier, πρὸς τὸ φῶς of which S. Peter stood and sat, pretending to be indifferent, but restlessly changing his posture (Luke xxii. 56): comp. xxi. 9; Ecclus. xi. 32. Cold nights in

April are exceptional but not uncommon in Palestine, and Jerusalem stands high.

μετ' αὐτῶν. Peter also is with the Lord's enemies, making himself comfortable in this night of cold. *Otia pulvinar Satanae.*

19. ὁ οὖν ἀρχ. The *οὖν* connects what follows with *vv.* 13, 14. Again we are in doubt as to who is meant by the high-priest (see on *v.* 15), but it will be safest to consider that Caiaphas is meant throughout. Neither hypothesis is free from difficulty. If the high-priest here is Caiaphas, the difficulty is to explain *v.* 24 (see note there). But we may suppose that while Annas is conducting the examination Caiaphas enters and takes part in it. It was hoped that some evidence might be obtained which would be of service in the formal trial that was to follow.

20. ἐγώ. With strong emphasis. He answers no questions about His disciples, but bears the brunt alone. Moreover He seems to contrast His openness with the secrecy of His enemies: for **παρρησίᾳ** see on vii. 13, and for **ἐν συναγωγῇ** on vi. 59. 'I always taught in public places, where all the Jews come together. I am not the head of a secret society; nor am I ashamed of My doctrine.' Comp. Matt. x. 27 *Veritas nihil erubescit praeter abscondi* (Tertullian).

21. ἴδε οὗτοι. As if implying that they were present and ought to be examined. Witnesses for the defence were heard first. *Οὗτοι* cannot mean S. Peter and S. John: S. Peter is still outside by the fire. For *ἴδε* see on i. 29.

22. ῥάπισμα. Elsewhere only xix. 3 and Mark xiv. 65. Literally, 'a blow with a *rod*,' and *δέρεις* (*v.* 23) agrees with this. But *ῥάπισμα* is also used for 'a blow with the open hand:' comp. *ῥαπίζειν*, Matt. v. 39. In later Greek this meaning prevailed, perhaps exclusively. Christ's conduct here shews how Matt. v. 39 is to be understood: personal retaliation is forbidden, but not calm protest and rebuke.

23. εἰ κ. ἐλάλησα. *If I* **spake** *evil* is perhaps better than *If I have spoken evil.* Like *ἐλάλησα* in *v.* 20 and *εἶπον* in *v.* 21, this seems to refer to Christ's teaching, about which He is being examined, rather than to His reply to the high-priest. For the construction comp. xiii. 14, xv. 20.

24. ἀπέστ. οὖν. The *οὖν* (see critical note) shews that the remark is not an afterthought. Because the preliminary examination before Annas produced a *primâ facie* case, but nothing conclusive, *Annas* **therefore** *sent Him* for formal trial to Caiaphas, who had apparently been present during the previous examination and had taken part in it (*v.* 19). Hence there is no need to discuss whether *ἀπέστειλεν* may be equivalent to a pluperfect: comp. Matt. xxvi. 48, xiv. 3, 4.

Christ had been bound at His arrest (*v.* 12) to prevent escape. During the examination He would be unbound as possibly innocent. He is now bound again. Apparently He was unbound a second time before the Sanhedrin, and then bound afresh to be taken to Pilate (Matt. xxvii. 2).

25. The narrative is resumed from *v.* 18: **But** *Simon Peter* **was standing and warming** *himself*. Dramatic contrast: the Lord stands bound; His disciple stands and warms himself. A look of distress on his face, when his Master appears bound as a criminal, and perhaps with the mark of the blow (*v.* 22) on His face, provokes (*οὖν*) the exclamation, *Surely thou also art not one of His disciples:* see on *v.* 17.

26. συγγενής. How natural that an acquaintance of the high-priest (*v.* 15) known to his portress (*v.* 16) should know this fact also as well as Malchus' name (*v.* 10). This confirms the ordinary view that the 'other disciple' (*v.* 15) is the Evangelist himself. This third accusation and denial was, as S. Luke tell us, about an hour after the second; so that our Lord must have 'turned and looked upon Peter' either from a room looking into the court, or as He was being led to receive the formal sentence of the Sanhedrin after the trial before Caiaphas, not as He was being taken from Annas to Caiaphas. The *ἐγώ* is emphatic; 'with my own eyes:' the man speaks with bitterness and assurance. Comp. *διϊσχυρίζετο λέγων* (Luke xxii. 59).

27. πάλιν οὖν. *Again* **therefore**, because he had denied before and yet another denial had become necessary. S. John, like S. Luke, omits the oaths and curses (Mark xiv. 71; Matt. xxvi. 73). We may believe that S. Peter himself through S. Mark was the first to include this aggravation of his guilt in the current tradition.

ἀλέκτωρ ἐφ. **A** *cock crew.* In none of the Gospels is there the definite article which our translation inserts. This was the second crowing (Mark xiv. 72). A difficulty has been made here because the Talmud says that fowls, which scratch in dunghills, are unclean. But (1) the Talmud is inconsistent on this point with itself; (2) not all Jews would be so scrupulous as to keep no fowls in Jerusalem; (3) certainly the Romans would care nothing about such scruples.

Just as the Evangelist implies (*v.* 11), without mentioning, the Agony in the garden, so he implies (xxi. 15), without mentioning, the repentance of S. Peter. The question has been raised, why he narrates S. Peter's fall, which had been thrice told already. There is no need to seek far-fetched explanations, as that "there might be contained in it some great principle or prophetic history, and perhaps both: some great principle to be developed in the future history of the Church, or of S. Peter's Church." Rather, it is part of S. John's own experience which falls naturally into the scope and plan of his Gospel, setting forth on the one side the Divinity of Christ, on the other the glorification of His manhood through suffering. Christ's foreknowledge of the fall of His chief Apostle (xiii. 38) illustrated both: it was evidence of His Divinity (comp. ii. 24, 25), and it intensified His suffering. S. John, therefore, gives both the prophecy and the fulfilment. It has been noticed that it is "S. Peter's friend S. John, who seems to mention most what may lessen the fault of his brother apostle;" that servants and officers were about him; that in the second case he was pressed by more than one; and that on the last occasion a kinsman of Malchus was among his accusers, which may greatly have increased Peter's terror. Moreover, this instance of human frailty in one so exalted (an instance which the life of the great Exemplar Himself *could* not afford), is given us with fourfold emphasis, that none may presume and none despair.

On the difficulties connected with the four accounts of S. Peter's denials see Appendix B.

28—XIX. 16. The Roman or Civil Trial

As already stated, S. John omits both the examination before Caiaphas and the Sanhedrin at an irregular time and place, at midnight and at 'the Booths' (Matt. xxvi. 57—68; Mark xiv. 53—65), and also the formal meeting of the Sanhedrin after daybreak in the proper place (Matt. xxvii. 1; Mark xv. 1; Luke xxii. 66—71), at which Jesus was sentenced to death. He proceeds to narrate what the Synoptists omit, the conference between Pilate and the Jews (*vv.* 28—32) and two private examinations of Jesus by Pilate (*vv.* 33—38 and xix. 8—11). Here also we seem to have the evidence of an eyewitness. We know that S. John followed his Lord into the high-priest's palace (*v.* 15), and stood by the Cross (xix. 26); it is therefore probable enough that he followed into the Procurator's court.

28. ἄγουσιν οὖν. They lead therefore (*v.* 3). S. John assumes that his readers know the result of Jesus being taken to Caiaphas (*v.* 24): He had been condemned to death; and now His enemies (there is no need to name them) take Him to the Roman governor to get the sentence executed.

ἀπὸ τ. K. *From* **the house of** *Caiaphas.* Comp. Mark v. 35; Acts xvi. 40.

τὸ πραιτώριον. The palace, Pilate's house, the *praetorium.* Our translators have varied their rendering of it capriciously: Matt. xxvii. 17, 'common hall,' with 'governor's house' in the margin; Mark xv. 16, 'Praetorium;' John xviii. 33 and xix. 9, 'judgment-hall.' Yet the meaning must be the same in all these passages. Comp. Acts xxiii. 35, 'judgment-hall;' Phil. i. 13, 'the palace.' The meaning of *praetorium* varies according to the context. The word is of military origin; (1) 'the general's tent' or 'head-quarters.' Hence, in the provinces, (2) 'the governor's residence,' the meaning in Acts xxiii. 35: in a sort of metaphorical sense, (3) a 'mansion' or 'palace' (Juvenal I. 75): at Rome, (4) 'the praetorian guard,' the probable meaning in Phil. i. 13. Of these leading significations the second is probably right here and throughout the Gospels; *the official residence of the Procurator.* Where Pilate resided in Jerusalem is not quite certain. We know that 'Herod's Praetorium,' a magnificent building on the western hill of Jerusalem, was used by Roman governors somewhat later (Philo, *Leg. ad Gaium*, p. 1034). But it is perhaps more likely that Pilate occupied part of the fortress Antonia, on the supposed site of which a chamber with a column in it has recently been discovered, which it is thought may possibly be the scene of the scourging.

S. John's narrative alternates between the *outside* and *inside* of the Praetorium. *Outside;* 28—32, 38—40, xix. 4—7, 12—16. *Inside;* 33—37, xix. 1—3, 8—11.

28—32. *Outside the Praetorium;* the Jews claim the execution of the Sanhedrin's sentence of death, and Pilate refuses it.

πρωΐ. This is rendered 'morning' Matt. xvi. 3; Mark i. 35, xi. 20, xiii. 35, xv. 1; the last passage being partly parallel to this. In Mark xiii. 35 the word stands for the fourth watch (see on Mark vi. 48), which lasted from 3.0 to 6.0 A.M. A Roman court might be held directly after sunrise; and as Pilate had probably been informed that an important case was to be brought before him, delay in which might cause serious disturbance, there is nothing improbable in his being ready to open his court between 4.0 and 5.0 A.M. The hierarchy were in a difficulty. Jesus could not safely be arrested by daylight, and the Sanhedrin could not legally pronounce sentence of death by night: hence they had had to wait till dawn to condemn Him. Now another regulation hampers them: a day must intervene between sentence and execution. This they shuffled out of by going at once to Pilate. Of course if he undertook the execution, he must fix the time; and their representations would secure his ordering immediate execution. Thus they shifted the breach of the law from themselves to him.

As in the life of our Lord as a whole, so also in this last week and last day of it, the exact sequence and time of the events cannot be ascertained with certainty. Chronology is not what the Evangelists aim at giving us. For a tentative arrangement of the chief events of the Passion see Appendix C.

αὐτοί. The "most characteristic trait of a religious and godless nation ever put on record" (Maurice). *They themselves* (in contrast to their Victim, whom they sent in under a Roman guard) *entered not into the palace, that they might not be defiled* by entering a house possibly polluted by heathen abominations and certainly not cleansed from leaven (Ex. xii. 15). But Jewish zeal had taught the Romans that idols could not be tolerated in the Holy City.

ἵνα φάγωσιν τὸ π. It is evident that S. John does not regard the Last Supper as a Paschal meal. Comp. xiii. 1, 29. It is equally evident that the synoptic narratives convey the impression that the Last Supper was the ordinary Jewish Passover (Matt. xxvi, 17, 18, 19; Mark xiv. 14, 16; Luke xxii. 7, 8, 11, 13, 15). Whatever be the right solution, the independence of the author of the Fourth Gospel is manifest. Would anyone counterfeiting an Apostle venture thus to contradict what seemed to have such strong Apostolic authority? Would he not expect that a glaring discrepancy on so important a point would prove fatal to his pretensions? Assume that S. John is simply recording his own vivid recollections, whether or no we suppose him to be correcting the impression produced by the Synoptists, and *this* difficulty at any rate is avoided. S. John's narrative is too precise and consistent to be explained away. On the difficulty as regards the Synoptists see Appendix A; see also Excursus V at the end of Dr Farrar's *S. Luke*.

29. ἐξῆλθεν οὖν ὁ Π. ἔξω. Because they would not enter, therefore *Pilate went out to them.* The emphatic position of ἐξῆλθεν and the addition of ἔξω seem to call attention to this Roman concession to Jewish religiousness. The Evangelist assumes that his readers know who Pilate is, just as he assumes that they know the Twelve, Martha and Mary, and Mary Magdalene (vi. 67, xi. 1, xix. 25).

τίνα κατηγορίαν. No doubt Pilate knew, but in accordance with strict procedure he demands a formal indictment.

κακὸν ποιῶν. An evil-doer: distinguish from *κακοῦργος* (Luke xxiii. 32). The Jews are taken aback at Pilate's evident intention of trying the case himself. They had expected him merely to carry out their sentence, and had not come provided with any definite accusation. Blasphemy, for which they had condemned Him (Matt. xxvi. 65, 66), might be no crime with Pilate (comp. Acts xviii. 16). Hence the vagueness of their first charge. Later on (xix. 7) they throw in the charge of blasphemy; but they rely mainly on three distinct charges, which being political, Pilate must hear; (1) seditious agitation, (2) forbidding to give tribute to Caesar, (3) assuming the title, 'King of the Jews' (Luke xxiii. 3).

31. εἶπεν οὖν αὐτοῖς ὁ Π. Because of their vague accusation. If they will not make a specific charge, he will not deal with the case. Pilate, impressed probably by his wife's dream (Matt. xxvii. 19) tries in various ways to avoid sentencing Jesus to death. (1) He would have the Jews deal with the case themselves; (2) he sends Jesus to Herod; (3) he proposes to release Him in honour of the Feast; (4) he will scourge Him and let Him go. Roman governors were not commonly so scrupulous, and Pilate was not above the average: a vague superstitious dread was perhaps his strongest motive. Thrice in the course of these attempts does he pronounce Jesus innocent (*v.* 39, xix. 4, 6). Note the emphatic and somewhat contemptuous *ὑμεῖς* and *ὑμῶν*; *Take Him yourselves and according to your law judge Him.* Pilate disdains to interfere in Jewish religious disputes.

οὐκ ἔξεστιν. These words are to be taken quite literally, and without any addition, such as 'at the Passover' or 'by crucifixion,' or 'for high treason.' The question whether the Sanhedrin had or had not the right to inflict capital punishment at this time is a vexed one. On the one hand we have (1) this verse; (2) the statement of the Talmud that 40 years before the destruction of Jerusalem the Jews lost this power; (3) the evidence of Josephus (*Ant.* xx. ix. 1; comp. XVIII. i. 1; XVI. ii. 4, and VI.) that the high-priest could not summon a judicial court of the Sanhedrin without the Procurator's leave; (4) the analogy of Roman law. To this it is replied (Döllinger, *First Age of the Church*, Appendix II.); (1) that the Jews quibbled in order to cause Jesus to be crucified at the Feast instead of stoned after all the people had dispersed; and Pilate would not have insulted the Jews from the tribunal by telling them to put Jesus to death, if they had no power to do so; (2) that the Talmud is in error, for the Roman dominion began 60 years before the destruction of Jerusalem; (3) that Josephus (xx. ix. 1) shews that the Jews *had* this power: Ananus is accused to Albinus not for *putting people to death*, but for *holding a court* without leave: had the former been criminal it would have been mentioned; (4) that the analogy of Roman law proves nothing, for cities and countries subject to Rome often retained their autonomy: and there are the cases of S. Stephen, those for whose death S. Paul voted (Acts xxvi. 10), and the Apostles, whom the Sanhedrin wished to put to death (Acts v. 33); and Gamaliel in dissuading the council never hints that to inflict death will bring trouble upon themselves. To this it may be replied again; (1) that Pilate would have exposed a quibble had there been one, and his dignity as judge was evidently not above shewing ironical contempt for the plaintiffs; (2) that the Talmud may be wrong about the date and right about the fact; possibly it is right about both; (3) to mention the holding of a court by Ananus was enough to secure the interference of Albinus, and more may have been said than Josephus reports; (4) autonomy in the case of subject states was the exception; therefore the burden of proof rests with those who assert it of the Jews. S. Stephen's death and the other cases (comp. John v. 18, vii. 1, 25, viii. 3, 59; Acts xxi. 31) only prove that the Jews sometimes ventured on acts of judicial rigour and violence of which the Romans took little notice. Besides we do not know that in all these cases the Sanhedrin proposed to do more than to *sentence* to death, trusting to the Romans to execute the sentence, as here. Pilate's whole action, and his express statement xix. 10, seem to imply that he alone has the power to inflict death.

ποίῳ θανάτῳ. *By what* manner of *death* (xii. 33, xxi. 19; comp. x. 32; Matt. xxi. 23, xxii. 36; Luke vi. 32, xxiv. 19). Had the Sanhedrin executed Him as a blasphemer or a false prophet, He would have been stoned. The Jews had other forms of capital punishment (see on [viii. 5]), but not crucifixion; and by them He could not have been *lifted up* (viii. 28) like the Brazen Serpent (iii. 14).

33—37. *Inside the Praetorium;* Jesus is privately examined by Pilate, and makes *τὴν καλὴν ὁμολογίαν* (1 Tim. vi. 13).

33. Because of the importunity of the Jews (*οὖν*) Pilate is obliged to investigate further; and being only Procurator, although *cum potestate*, has no Quaestor, but conducts the examination himself. Probably the Roman guards had already brought Jesus inside the Praetorium: Pilate now calls Him before the judgment-seat. What follows implies that He had not heard the previous conversation with the Jews.

σὺ εἶ ὁ β. τ. 'I. In all four Gospels these are Pilate's first words to Jesus, and S. Luke (xxiii. 2) gives the Jewish accusation which suggested them; 'saying that He Himself is Christ a king.' In all four *Σύ* is emphatic. The appearance of Jesus is in such contrast to royalty that Pilate speaks with surprise (comp. iv. 12, viii. 53): his meaning is either 'Dost *Thou* claim to be King?' or, 'Art *Thou* the so-called King?' The civil title, 'the King of the Jews,' first appears in the mouth of the wise men (Matt. ii. 1), next in the mouth of Pilate: contrast the theocratic title, 'the K. of Israel' (i. 50).

34. Note the solemn brevity of the introductions to *vv.* 34, 35, 36. Jesus demands that the responsibility of making this charge against Him be laid on the right persons. Moreover the meaning of the charge, and therefore the truth of it, would depend on the person making it. In Pilate's sense He was not King; in another sense He was. Note that He *asks* for information; see on xi. 17, 34.

35. 'Is it likely that I, a Roman governor, have any interest in Jewish questions? Am *I* likely to call Thee King? It was Thine *own* nation (double article; see next note) that delivered Thee to me. What made them do it?'

36. ἡ β. ἡ ἐμή. This emphatic form, 'the kingdom that is Mine' (see on viii. 31) prevails throughout the verse. **Ὑπηρέται** must be rendered 'servants,' not 'officers,' although there is doubtless an allusion to the officials of the hierarchy (*vv.* 3, 12, 18, 22, vii. 32, 45, 46; Matt. v. 25). In Luke i. 2 and 1 Cor. iv. 1, the only places in Gospels and Epistles in which the word is used of Christians, it is rendered 'ministers,' both in A.V. and R.V. 'Officers' would here suggest military officers. 'The kingdom that is really Mine does not derive its origin (ἐκ) from this world (iv. 22, viii. 23, xv. 19, xvii. 14, 16, x. 16): if from this world sprang My kingdom, then would the servants that are really Mine be striving' (Luke xiii. 24; 1 Cor. ix. 25). For the construction see on v. 46, and for **τοῖς Ἰουδαίοις** see on xiii. 33.

νῦν δέ. The meaning of νῦν is clear from the context; 'as it is, as the case really stands:' comp. viii. 40, ix. 41, xv. 22, 24. It does not mean 'My kingdom is not of this world *now*, but shall be so hereafter;' as if Christ were promising a millennium.

37. οὐκοῦν. Here only in N.T. Combined with the position of σύ it gives a tone of scorn to the question, which is half an exclamation: 'So then, *Thou* art a *King!*' We might write οὔκουν and render, 'Art Thou not then a King?' or, 'Thou art not then a King.' But οὐκοῦν is simpler and is preferred by most editors. See Winer, p. 643.

σὺ λέγεις ὅτι. The rendering, *Thou sayest* (*well*), *because*, is much less natural than *Thou sayest that.* Christ leaves the royal title which Pilate misunderstands and explains the nature of His kingdom—the realm of truth.

εἰς τοῦτο. To this end have I been born *and* **to this end am I come** *into the world.* To be a King, He became incarnate; to be a King, He entered the world: and this in order to witness to the truth. The second εἰς τοῦτο does not, any more than the first, refer exclusively to what follows; both refer partly to what precedes, partly (1 John iii. 8) to what follows. The perfects express a past act continuing in the present; Christ has come and remains in the world. **Ἐγώ** is very emphatic; in this respect Christ stands alone among men. **Ἔρχεσθαι εἰς τ. κόσμον** is frequent in S. John (i. 9, ix. 39, xi. 27, xvi. 28). Applied to Christ it includes the notions of His mission and of His pre-existence: but Pilate would not see this.

ἵνα μαρτ. τῇ ἀλ. This is the Divine purpose of His royal power: not merely 'witness the truth,' i.e. give a testimony that is true, but bear witness to the objective reality of the Truth: again, not merely 'bear witness *of*,' i.e. respecting the Truth (i. 7, 15, ii. 25, v. 31—39, viii. 13—18, &c.), but 'bear witness *to*,' i.e. in support and defence of the Truth (v. 33). Both these expressions, 'witness' and 'truth,' have been seen to be very frequent in S. John (see especially chaps. i. iii. v. viii. *passim*). We have them combined here, as in v. 33. This is the object of Christ's sovereignty,—to bear witness to the Truth. It is characteristic of the Gospel that it claims to be 'the Truth.' "This title of the Gospel is not found in the Synoptists, Acts, or Apocalypse; but it occurs in the Catholic Epistles (James i. 19; 1 Pet. i. 22; 2 Pet. ii. 2) and in S. Paul (2 Thess. ii. 12; 2 Cor. xiii. 8; Eph. i. 13, &c.). It is specially characteristic of the Gospel and Epistles of S. John." Westcott, *Introduction to S. John*, p. xliv.

ὁ ὢν ἐκ τ. ἀλ. That has his root in the Truth, so as to draw the power of his life from it: comp. *v.* 36, iii. 31, viii. 47, and especially 1 John ii. 21, iii. 19. "It is of great interest to compare this confession before Pilate with the corresponding confession before the high priest (Matt. xxvi. 64). The one addressed to the Jews is in the language of prophecy, the other addressed to a Roman appeals to the universal testimony of conscience. The one speaks of a future manifestation of glory, the other of a present manifestation of truth......... It is obvious how completely they answer severally to the circumstances of the two occasions." Westcott, *in loco.*

38. τί ἐστιν ἀλήθεια; Pilate does not ask about '*the* Truth,' but truth in any particular case. His question does not indicate any serious wish to know what truth really is, nor yet the despairing scepticism of a baffled thinker; nor, on the other hand, is it uttered in a light spirit of 'jesting' (as Bacon thought). Rather it is the half-pitying, half-impatient, question of a practical man of the world, whose experience of life has convinced him that truth is a dream of enthusiasts, and that a kingdom in which truth is to be supreme is as visionary as that of the Stoics. He has heard enough to convince him that the accused is no dangerous incendiary, and he abruptly closes the investigation with a question, which to his mind cuts at the root of the Prisoner's aspirations. "It was a good question; but Pilate's haste lost him the answer": he asked it and went out. *Quid est Veritas? Vir est qui adest* (Anagram attributed to Charles I.). Here probably we must insert the sending to Herod Antipas, who had come from Tiberias, as Pilate from Caesarea, on account of the Feast, the one to win popularity, the other to keep order (Luke xxiii. 6—12).

38—40. *Outside the Praetorium;* Pilate pronounces Him innocent and offers to release Him for the Feast: the Jews prefer Barabbas.

38. τ. Ἰουδαίους. Apparently this means the mob and not the hierarchy. Pilate hoped that only a minority were moving against Jesus; by an appeal to the majority he might be able to acquit Him without incurring odium. By pronouncing Him legally innocent he would gain this majority; by proposing to release Him on account of the Feast rather than of His innocence he would avoid insulting the Sanhedrin, who had already pronounced Him guilty. From S. Mark (xv. 8, 11) it would appear that *some* of the multitude hoped to deliver Jesus on the plea of the Feast and took the initiative in reminding Pilate of the custom, but were controlled by the priests and made to clamour for Barabbas.

ἐγώ...αἰτίαν. 'Whatever you fanatics may do, **I** *find no* **ground of accusation** *in Him:*' comp. xix. 6. *Αἰτία* means 'legal ground for prosecution, crime' (Matt. xxvii. 37; Mark xv. 26; Acts xiii. 28, xxviii. 18).

39. συνήθεια. Nothing is known of this custom beyond what the Gospels tell us. It may have been a memorial of the deliverance from Egypt. But prisoners were sometimes released at Rome at certain festivals, and it would be quite in harmony with the conciliatory policy of Rome to honour native festivals in this way in the case of subject nations. In Luke xxiii. 17 the custom is said to be an obligation, *ἀνάγκην εἶχεν*: but the verse is of very doubtful genuineness. For *ἵνα* comp. xi. 57, xv. 12. **'Εν τ. πάσχα** is no evidence that the Passover had been already celebrated: the prisoner would naturally be released in time to share in the Paschal meal. The Synoptists use the less definite expression, *κατὰ ἑορτήν* (Matt. xxvii. 15; Mark xv. 6). For the construction **βούλεσθε ἀπολύσω** comp. *θέλεις συλλέξωμεν, ποῦ θέλεις ἑτοιμάσωμεν* (Matt. xiii. 28, xxvi. 17; Luke xxii. 9), where in each case the fut. ind. is found as a various reading, perhaps from the LXX. (Heb. viii. 5). Matt. xx. 32, xxvii. 17, 21; Mark x. 51, xv. 9, 12; Luke xviii. 41, like this, are ambiguous; but the aor. subj. is much more intelligible (though not as a kind of deliberative subjunctive; comp. 1 Cor. iii. 21) than the fut. ind. Luke ix. 54 *must* be aor. subj. Comp. *βούλει φράσω*, Arist. *Eq.* 36. The subj. intensifies the demand: *would ye have me release*.

40. ἐκραύγασαν. *They* **cried out therefore** *again: πάντες* is of very doubtful authority. S. John has mentioned no previous shout, but, as usual, assumes that his readers know the main facts. Pilate declared Jesus innocent both before and after sending Him to Herod, and in both cases this provoked an outcry (Luke xxiii. 4—7, 14—21): S. John in narrating the later clamour implies the earlier. *Κραυγάζω* expresses a loud cry, and (excepting Matt. xii. 19; Acts xxii. 23) occurs only in S. John (xi. 43, xii. 13, xix. 6, 12, 15).

τ. Βαραββᾶν. *Bar-Abbas*, son of Abba (father): the derivation *Bar-rabban*, son of a Rabbi, seems fanciful. The innocent Son of the Father is rejected for the blood-stained son of a father. The name has the article, although *S. John* has not mentioned him before. *The Jews who speak* had mentioned him before. In Matt. xxvii. 16 and 17 some inferior authorities give '*Jesus* Barabbas' as his name, and Pilate asks 'Which do ye wish that I release to you, Jesus

Barabbas, or Jesus Who is called Christ?' The reading is remarkable, but it is supported by no good MS.

ἦν δὲ ὁ Β. λῃστής. For the tragic brevity of this remark comp. *ἐδάκρυσεν ὁ Ἰησοῦς* (xi. 35) and *ἦν δὲ νύξ* (xiii. 30). The *λῃστής* as distinct from the *κλέπτης* (x. 1) is the man of violence, the bandit or brigand, more dangerous to persons than to property. In the case of Barabbas we know from S. Mark and S. Luke that he had been guilty of insurrection and consequent bloodshed rather than of stealing; and this was very likely the case also with the two robbers crucified with Jesus. Thus by a strange irony of fate the hierarchy obtain the release of a man guilty of the very political crime with which they charged Christ,—sedition. The people no doubt had some sympathy with the insurrectionary movement of Barabbas, and on this the priests worked. Barabbas had done, just what Jesus had refused to do, take the lead against the Romans. "They laid information against Jesus before the Roman government as a dangerous character; their real complaint against him was precisely this, that He was not dangerous. Pilate executed Him on the ground that His kingdom was of this world; the Jews procured His execution precisely because it was not." *Ecce Homo*, p. 27.

CHAPTER XIX

3. Insert **καὶ ἤρχοντο πρὸς αὐτόν** before **καὶ ἔλεγον** with ℵBLUXΛ against A (homoeoteleuton; omission from *αὐτόν* to *αὐτόν*).

4. **καὶ ἐξῆλθεν** (ℵABKLX) for *ἐξῆλθεν οὖν* (Δ).

7. After **τὸν νόμον** omit *ἡμῶν* (obvious amplification) with ℵBLΔ against A.

12. Authorities vary much between **ἐκραύγαζον**, *ἐκραύγασαν*, and *ἔκραζον*.

13. **τῶν λόγων τούτων** (ℵAB) for *τοῦτον τὸν λόγον* (from *v.* 8).

17. After **Ἰησοῦν** omit *καὶ ἀπήγαγον* (perhaps from Matt. xxvii. 31). **Αὐτῷ τὸν σταυρόν** (BLX) for *τ. στ. αὐτοῦ* (E): there are other variations.

20. **Ῥωμαϊστί** before **Ἑλληνιστί** with ℵBLX against AI[a].

26, 27. **ἴδε** (S. John's usual form) for *ἰδού*, with ℵB and others against A.

29. **σπόγγον οὖν μεστὸν τοῦ ὄξους** (ℵBLX) for *οἱ δὲ πλήσαντες σπόγγον ὄξους καὶ* (A), a combination with Matt. xxvii. 48 and Mark xv. 36, which caused *οὖν* to be transferred to the previous clause,—*σκεῦος οὖν ἔκειτο*.

38. Before and after **Ἰωσήφ** omit *ὁ* (usual in mentioning a well-known person).

39. **αὐτόν** for *τὸν Ἰησοῦν* (correction for clearness).

1—3. *Inside the Praetorium;* the scourging and mockery by the soldiers.

1. τότε οὖν. Because the attempt to release Him in honour of the Feast had failed, Pilate tries whether the severe and degrading punishment of scourging will not satisfy the Jews. In Pilate's hands the boasted justice of Roman Law ends in the policy "What evil did He do? I found no cause of death in Him: I will *therefore* chastise Him and let Him go" (Luke xxiii. 22). Scourging was part of Roman capital punishment, and had we only the first two Gospels we might suppose that the scourging was inflicted immediately before the crucifixion: but this is not stated, and S. John, combined with S. Luke, makes it clear that scourging was inflicted as a separate punishment in the hope that it would suffice. The supposition of a second scourging as part of the execution is unnecessary and improbable. Pilate, sick of the bloody work and angry at being forced to commit a judicial murder, would not have allowed it; and it may be doubted whether any human frame could survive a Roman scourging twice in one day. One infliction was sometimes fatal; *ille flagellis ad mortem caesus*, Hor. *S.* I. ii. 41. Comp. '*horribile flagellum*,' *S.* I. iii. 119.

2. οἱ στρατιῶται. Herod and his troops (Luke xxiii. 11) had set an example which the Roman soldiers were ready enough to follow. Pilate countenances the brutality as aiding his own plan of satisfying Jewish hatred with something less than death. The soldiers had inflicted the scourging; for Pilate, being only Procurator, would have no lictors. They crown Him in mockery of royalty rather than of victory, as what follows shews. The plant used was probably the thorny *nâbk*, *lycium spinosum*, with flexible branches and leaves like ivy, abundant round about Jerusalem.

ἱμ. πορφυροῦν. S. Mark has *πορφύραν*, S. Matthew *χλαμύδα κοκκίνην*. Purple with the ancients was a vague term for rich bright colour, crimson as well as violet. The robe was a military *chlamys* or *paludamentum*, representing a royal robe. That in which Herod mocked Jesus was probably white: 1 Macc. viii. 14, x. 20, 62. The soldiers act in derision of the detested Jews generally, who could probably see all this from the outside, rather than of Jesus in particular. The whole is a caricature of Jewish expectations of a national king.

ἤρχοντο πρ. αὐ. This graphic touch is omitted by the Synoptists and by some authorities here. We see each soldier coming up (imperfect) to offer his mock homage. As in xviii. 22, **ῥάπισμα** is probably a blow with the hand rather than with a rod. Comp. Is. l. 6, I gave my back, *εἰς μάστιγας*, and my cheek, *εἰς ῥαπίσματα*. The Old Latin adds *in faciem*. The blow is the mock gift brought by the person doing homage.

4—7. *Outside the Praetorium;* Pilate's appeal, 'Behold *the Man;*' the Jews' rejoinder, 'He made Himself *Son of God.*'

4. ἄγω. On the previous occasion (xviii. 38) Pilate left Jesus within, while he pronounced Him innocent. Note the absence of *ἐγώ* and the change of order.

5. **φορῶν.** Not *φέρων*; *wearing*, not merely 'bearing.' The cro. n and the robe are now His permanent dress. The Evangelist repeats the details (*v.* 2) as of a picture deeply imprinted in his memory: whether or no he entered the Praetorium, he no doubt witnessed the *Ecce Homo*.

ἰδοὺ ὁ ἄνθρωπος. In pity rather than contempt. Pilate appeals to their humanity: surely the most bitter among them will now be satisfied, or at least the more compassionate will control the rest. No one can think that this Man is dangerous, or needs further punishment. When this appeal fails, Pilate's pity turns to bitterness (*v.* 14).

6. **οἱ ἀρχ. κ. οἱ ὑπ.** Repeat the article as in xi. 47. The leaders take the initiative, to prevent any expression of compassion on the part of the crowd. The sight of 'the Man' maddens rather than softens them. For **κραυγάζω** see on xviii. 40.

σταύρ. σταύρ. Crucify, crucify. The imperative without an accusative better expresses the cry which was to give the cue to the multitude. According to all four Gospels the demand for *crucifixion* was not made until after the offer to release Jesus for the Feast.

λαβ. αὐ. ὑμεῖς. *Take Him* **yourselves**, as in xviii. 31. We may admit that it ought to have been beneath the dignity of a Roman judge to taunt the people with a suggestion which they dared not follow; but there is nothing so improbable in it as to compel us to believe that the Jews *had* the power of inflicting capital punishment (see on xviii. 31). Pilate is goaded into an exhibition of feeling unworthy of his office. The **ἐγώ** again (xviii. 38) contrasts his verdict with that of the Jews.

7. **νόμον.** They refer to Lev. xxiv. 16. The Jews answer Pilate's taunt by a plea hitherto kept in the background. He may think lightly of the seditious conduct of Jesus, but as a Procurator he is bound by Roman precedent to pay respect to the law of subject nationalities. He has challenged them to take the law into their own hands; let him hear what their law is. Pilate had said 'Behold *the Man!*' The Jews retort, 'He made Himself *Son of God*.' They answer his appeal to their compassion by an appeal to his fears. See on viii. 53.

8—11. *Inside the Praetorium;* Christ's origin is asked and not told; the origin of authority is told unasked.

8. **τ. τ. λόγον. This word**: it is no mere 'saying' (*ῥῆμα*); like the word of Caiaphas, it has more meaning than the speakers know. It intensifies Pilate's disquietude. The message from his wife and the awe which Christ's presence was probably inspiring had already in some degree affected him. This mysterious claim still further excites his fears. Was it the offspring of a divinity that he had so infamously handled? Comp. Matt. xxvii. 54.

9. **πραιτώριον.** See on xviii. 28. **Πόθεν εἶ σύ;** is a vague question which might apply to Christ's dwelling-place, already known to Pilate

(Luke xxiii. 6); he hoped for an answer as to His *origin*. Would the Prisoner repeat this mysterious claim, or explain it? But Pilate could not have understood the answer; and what had it to do with the merits of the case? No answer is given. Comp. Matt. xxvii. 12—14 and Christ's own precept, Matt. vii. 6.

10. Baffled and still in doubt as to the relations between himself and his Prisoner he takes refuge in a domineering tone of assumed confidence. *To* **me** *speakest Thou not?* Whatever He might do before His countrymen, it was folly to refuse to answer the Roman governor. For **ἐξουσίαν**, *authority*, see on i. 12 and comp. v. 27, x. 18, xvii. 2: note the emphatic repetition.

11. **οὐκ εἶχες.** Comp. xv. 20. This is Christ's last word to Pilate; a declaration of the supremacy of God, and a protest against the claim of any human potentate to be irresponsible. The Accused has become the judge's Judge. Even Pilate could understand **ἄνωθεν**: had Jesus said *παρὰ τοῦ πατρός μου*, he would have remained uninstructed. The point is not, that Pilate is an instrument ordained for the carrying out of God's purposes (Acts ii. 23); he was such, but that is not the meaning here. Rather, that the possession and exercise of all authority is the gift of God; iii. 27; Rom. xiii. 1—7 (see notes there). To interpret 'from above' of the higher tribunal of the Sanhedrin is quite inadequate. Comp. iii. 3, 7, 31; James i. 17, iii. 15, 17, where the same adverb is used: see notes in each place. It is **for this cause** (see on i. 31), because Pilate's authority over Jesus is the result of a Divine commission, whereas that of His enemies was usurped, that their sin is greater than His. Moreover, they might have known Who He was.

ὁ παραδούς. The addition of **σοι** (contrast xiii. 11, xviii. 2, 5) shews that Caiaphas, the representative of the Sanhedrin and of the nation, and not Judas, is meant: comp. xviii. 35. Judas had delivered Jesus to the Sanhedrin, not to Pilate. For **ἔχειν ἁμαρτίαν** see on xv. 22.

12—16. *Outside the Praetorium.* The power from above controlled from below pronounces public sentence of death on the Innocent.

12. **ἐκ τούτου.** **Upon this**; see on vi. 66. The imperfect expresses continued efforts. Indirect means, as the release in honour of the Feast, the appeal to compassion, and taunts, have failed; Pilate now makes more direct efforts. We are not told what they were; but the Evangelist shews by the unwillingness of Pilate how great was the guilt of 'the Jews.'

ἐὰν τ. ἀπολύσῃς. *If thou* **release** *this man*: *ἀπολῦσαι* and *ἀπολύσῃς* must be translated alike. The Jews once more shift their tactics and from the ecclesiastical charge (*v.* 7) go back to the political, which they now back up by an appeal to Pilate's own political interests. They know their man: it is not a love of justice, but personal feeling which moves him to seek to release Jesus; and they will overcome one personal feeling by another still stronger. Pilate's unexplained interest in Jesus and supercilious contempt for His accusers must give way before a fear for his own position and possibly even his life. Whether or no there was any such honorary title as *Amicus Caesaris*, like our 'Queen's Counsel,' it is unlikely that the Jews allude to it here: they simply mean 'loyal to Caesar.' For **ἑαυτὸν ποιῶν** see on viii. 53.

ἀντιλέγει τ. K. **Setteth himself** *against Caesar; ipso facto* declares himself a rebel: thus the rebellion of Korah is called *ἀντιλογία* (Jude 11). For a Roman governor to protect such a person would be high treason (*majestas*). The Jews scarcely knew how powerful their weapon was. Pilate's patron Sejanus (executed A.D. 31) was losing his hold over Tiberius, even if he had not already fallen. Pilate had already thrice nearly driven the Jews to revolt, and his character therefore would not stand high with an Emperor who justly prided himself on the good government of the provinces. Above all, the terrible *Lex Majestatis* was by this time worked in such a way that prosecution under it was almost certain death. *Atrocissime exercebat leges majestatis* (Suetonius).

13. Pilate's mind seems to have been made up at once: without replying he prepares to pass sentence. The fatal moment has come, and as in the case of the arrest (xviii. 1—4) the Evangelist gives minute particulars.

ἤγαγεν ἔξω. Sentence must be pronounced in public. Thus we find that Pilate, in giving judgment about the standards, which had been brought into Jerusalem, has his tribunal in the great circus at Caesarea, and Florus erects his in front of the palace (Josephus, *B. J.* II. ix. 3, xiv. 8).

ἐκάθισεν may be either transitive, as in 1 Cor. vi. 4; Eph. i. 20, or intransitive, as in Matt. xix. 28, xxv. 31. If it is transitive here, the meaning will be, 'placed him on a seat,' as an illustration of his mocking exclamation, 'Behold your King!'—i.e. 'There He sits enthroned!' But [viii. 2;] xii. 14; Rev. iii. 21, xx. 4, the only places where S. John uses the word, and Acts xii. 21, xxv. 6, 17, where we have the same phrase as here, are against the transitive meaning in this place. The absence of the article before **βήματος** perhaps indicates that the *Bema* was a temporary and not the usual one; everywhere else in N. T. *βῆμα* has the article. With the pregnant use of **εἰς** comp. xx. 19, (xxi. 4).

Λιθόστρωτον. Josephus (*Ant.* v. v. 2) says that the Temple-Mount, on part of which the fortress of Antonia stood, was covered with a tesselated pavement. This fact and the Aramaic name tend to shew that the portable mosaic which Imperators sometimes carried about for their tribunals is not meant here. But *Gab Baitha* is no equivalent of *Λιθόστρωτον*, though it indicates the same place: it means 'the ridge of the House,' i.e. the Temple-Mound. For **Ἑβραϊστί** see on v. 2.

14. ἦν δὲ π. τ. π., ὥρα ἦν ὡς ἕκτη. In two abrupt sentences S. John calls special attention to the day and hour; *now it was the eve of the Passover: it was about the sixth hour.* It is difficult to believe that he can be utterly mistaken about both. The question of the day is discussed in Appendix A; the question as to the hour remains.

We have seen already (i. 39, iv. 6, 52, xi. 9), that whatever view we may take of the *balance* of probability in each case, there is nothing thus far which is conclusively in favour of the antecedently improbable view, that S. John reckons the hours of the day as we do, from midnight to noon and noon to midnight.

The modern method is sometimes spoken of as the *Roman* method. This is misleading, as it seems to imply that the Romans counted their hours as we do. If this were so, it would not surprise us so much to find that S. John, living away from Palestine and in the capital of a Roman province, had adopted the Roman reckoning. *But the Romans and Greeks, as well as the Jews, counted their hours from sunrise.* Martial, who goes through the day hour by hour (IV. viii.), places the Roman method beyond a doubt. The difference between the Romans and the Jews was not as to the *mode of counting the hours*, but as to the *limits of each individual day*. The Jews placed the boundary at sunset, the Romans (as we do) at midnight. (Pliny, *Nat. Hist.* II. lxxvii.) The 'this day' of Pilate's wife (Matt. xxvii. 19) proves nothing; it would fit either the Roman or the Jewish method; and some suppose her to have been a proselyte. In this particular S. John *does* seem to have adopted the Roman method; for (xx. 19) he speaks of the evening of Easter Day as 'the *same* day at evening' (comp. Luke xxiv. 29, 33). This must be admitted as against the explanation that 'yesterday' in iv. 54 was spoken before midnight and refers to the time before sunset: but the servants may have met their master after midnight.

Yet there is some evidence of a custom of reckoning from midnight in Asia Minor. Polycarp was martyred 'at the eighth hour' (*Mart. Pol.* XXI.), Pionius at 'the tenth hour' (*Acta Mart.* p. 137); both at Smyrna. Such exhibitions commonly took place in the morning (Philo ii. 529); so that 8.0 and 10.0 A.M. are more probable than 2.0 and 4.0 P.M.

McClellan adds another argument. "The phraseology of our present passage is unique in the Gospels. The *hour* is mentioned *in conjunction with the day*. To cite the words of St Augustine, but with the correct rendering of *Paraskeuê*, 'S. John does not say, *It was about the sixth hour of the day*, nor merely, *It was about the sixth hour*, but *It was the* FRIDAY *of the Passover; it was about the* SIXTH *hour.*' Hence in the straightforward sense of the words, the sixth hour that he means is the *sixth hour of the Friday;* and so it is rendered in the Thebaic Version. But *Friday* in S. John is the name of the whole *Roman civil day*, and the *Roman civil days* are reckoned from *midnight.*" *New Test.* I. p. 742.

This solution may therefore be adopted, not as certain, but as less unsatisfactory than the conjecture of a false reading either here or in Mark xv. 25, or the various forced interpretations which have been given of S. John's words. The reading τρίτη in some MSS. here is evidently a harmonizing correction. If, however, the mode of reckoning in both Gospels be the same, the preference in point of accuracy must be given to the Evangelist who stood by the cross.

ἴδε ὁ βας. ὑμῶν. Like the title on the cross, these words are spoken in bitter irony. This Man in His mock insignia is a fit sovereign for the miserable Jews. Perhaps Pilate would also taunt them with their own glorification of Him on Palm Sunday. To the Christian the words are another unconscious prophecy.

15. ἐκεῖνοι. The pronoun indicates their opposition. The four aorists are all appropriate: *ἐκραύγασαν, they shouted out* once for all; while the three aorists imperative shew their impatience to have their will. **Σταυρώσω** is either *Shall I* or *Must I.* Note the emphatic position of *τ. βασ. ὑμῶν*: 'Must I crucify your *King?*' Pilate begins (xviii. 33) and ends with the same idea, the one dangerous item in the indictment, the claim of Jesus to be King of the Jews. This explains the length at which S. John describes the scenes with Pilate: see introductory note on xviii. 12—27.

οἱ ἀρχιερεῖς. This depth of degradation is reserved for them. "The official organs of the theocracy themselves proclaim that they have abandoned the faith by which the nation had lived." Sooner than acknowledge that Jesus is the Messiah they proclaim that a heathen Emperor is their King. And their baseness is at once followed by Pilate's: sooner than meet a dangerous charge he condemns the Innocent to death. To rid themselves of Jesus they commit political suicide; to free himself from danger he commits a judicial murder.

16. τότε οὖν π. In none of the Gospels does it appear that Pilate pronounced sentence *on* Jesus; he perhaps purposely avoided doing so. But in delivering Him over to the priests he does not allow them to act for themselves: 'he delivered Him to them that *He might be crucified*' by Roman soldiers; not that they might crucify Him themselves.

17—42. The Death and Burial

For what is peculiar to S. John's narrative in this section see the introductory note to chap. xviii. Besides this, the title on the cross, the Jews' criticism of it, and the conduct of the four soldiers, are given with more exactness by S. John than by the Synoptists.

The section falls into four double parts, all four of which contain a marked dramatic contrast, such as S. John loves to point out (see on *vv.* 18 and 30):—

(1) *The Crucifixion and the title on the cross* (17—22).
(2) *The four enemies and the four friends* (23—27).
(3) *The two words*, 'I thirst,' 'It is finished' (28—30).
(4) *The hostile and the friendly petitions* (31—42).

17—22. The Crucifixion and the Title on the Cross

17. παρέλαβον οὖν. *They took Jesus therefore*, or *they received*, as in i. 11, xiv. 3. The verb means 'to accept what is offered, receive from the hands of another.' A comparison of the three texts is instructive. The eternal Son is given by the Father, comes to His own inheritance, and His own people received Him not (i. 11). The Incarnate Son is given up by Pilate to His own people, and they received Him to crucify Him (xix. 16). The glorified Son comes again to His own people, to receive them unto Himself (xiv. 3).

βαστ. αὐτῷ τ. στ. ἐξῆλθεν. *Bearing the cross* **for Himself** *went forth.* S. John omits the help which Simon the Cyrenian was soon compelled to render, as also (what seems to be implied by Mark xv. 22) that at last they were obliged to carry Jesus Himself. Comp. the Lesson for Good Friday morning, Gen. xxii., especially *v.* 6. "The place of public execution appears to have been situated north of the city. It was outside the gate (Heb. xiii. 12) and yet 'nigh unto the city' (*v.* 20). In the Mishna it is placed outside the city by a reference to Lev. xxiv. 14. It is said to have been 'two men high' (Sanh. vi. 1). The Jews still point out the site at the cliff, north of the Damascus gate, where is a cave now called 'Jeremiah's Grotto.' This site has therefore some claim to be considered as that of the Crucifixion. It was within 200 yards of the wall of Agrippa, but was certainly outside the ancient city. It was also close to the gardens and the tombs of the old city, which stretch northwards from the cliff; and it was close to the main north road, in a conspicuous position, such as might naturally be selected for a place of public execution." Conder, *Handbook to the Bible*, pp. 356, 7. **Κρανίου τόπον** refers to the shape of the ground. To leave skulls unburied would violate Jewish law; and this would require *κρανίων τόπον*. For **Ἑβραϊστί** see on v. 2.

18. μέσον δὲ τ. Ἰ. Dramatic contrast; the Christ between two criminals. It is the place of honour mockingly given to Him as King. The two were robbers or bandits, as S. Matthew and S. Mark call them, probably guilty of the same crimes as Barabbas. In the *Acta Pilati* they are named Dysmas and Gestas. Jesus suffers with them under a similar charge of sedition. Whether this was mere convenience, or a device of the Romans to insult the Jews, is uncertain. The latter is probable. *Omnium par poena, sed dispar causa* (S. Augustine). The whole of humanity was represented there: the sinless Saviour, the saved penitent, the condemned impenitent.

19. καὶ τίτλον. *A title* **also**: the meaning of the *καί* is not clear; perhaps it looks back to *v.* 16, or to *μέσον τ. Ἰησοῦν*, as being Pilate's doing: he placed Jesus between two criminals, and *also* insulted the Jews by a mocking inscription. Τίτλος is *titulus* Graecized. It was common to put on the cross the name and crime of the person executed, after making him carry the inscription round his neck to the place of execution. S. Matthew (xxvii. 37) has *τ. αἰτίαν αὐτοῦ*, S. Mark (xv. 26) *ἡ ἐπιγραφὴ τ. αἰτίας αὐτοῦ*, S. Luke (xxiii. 38) *ἐπιγραφή*. For **ἦν γεγραμ., there was written**, see on ii. 17. The title is given differently in all four Gospels, and possibly varied in the three languages. Its object was to insult the Jews, not Jesus: all variations contain the offensive words "The King of the Jews."

20. ἐγγύς. S. John's exact topographical knowledge appears again here. Pictures of the Crucifixion mislead in placing the city a mile or two off in the background. Τῆς πόλεως with ἐγγύς (xi. 18), not after ὁ τόπος: 'the place of the city was near' is scarcely sense.

Ἑβρ., Ῥωμ., Ἑλλ. This is the order in the better authorities. The national and official languages would naturally be placed before Greek,—and for different reasons either Hebrew or Latin might be placed first. In Luke xxiii. 38 the order is Greek, Latin, Hebrew; but the clause is of very doubtful authority. In any case the three representative languages of the world at that time, the languages of religion, of empire, and of intellect, were employed. Thus did they 'tell it out among the heathen that the Lord is king,' or (according to a remarkable reading of the LXX. in Ps. xcvi. 10) 'that the Lord reigned from the tree.'

21. οἱ ἀρχ. τ. Ἰουδ. Now that they have wrung what they wanted out of Pilate they see that in granting it he has insulted them publicly before the thousands present at the Passover, and in a way not easy to resent. The addition 'of the Jews' is remarkable, and it occurs nowhere else in N. T. It probably refers to the title: these 'chief priests *of the Jews*' objected to His being called 'the King *of the Jews*.'

22. Pilate's answer illustrates the mixture of obstinacy and relentlessness, which Philo says was characteristic of him. His own interests are not at stake, so he will have his way: where he had anything to fear or to gain he could be supple enough. A shrewd, practical man of the world, with all a Roman official's contemptuous impartiality and severity, and all the disbelief in truth and disinterestedness which the age had taught him, he seems to have been one of the many with whom self-interest is stronger than their convictions, and who can walk uprightly when to do so is easy, but fail in the presence of serious difficulty and danger.

23—27. The four Enemies and the four Friends

23. τὰ ἱμάτια. The upper garment, girdle, sandals, &c. The ἱμάτιον was large enough to be worth dividing. By the law *De bonis damnatorum* the clothes of executed criminals were the perquisite of the soldiers on duty. The **τέσσερα** shews accurate knowledge: a quaternion has charge of the prisoner, as in Acts xii. 4; but there the prisoner has to be kept a long time, so four quaternions mount guard in turn, one for each watch. Here there was probably a quaternion to each cross. The danger of a popular outbreak (xviii. 3) is at an end, and a small force suffices.

ἄραφος. Josephus (*Ant.* III. vii. 4) tells us that the high-priest's tunic was seamless, whereas in other cases this garment was commonly made of two pieces. Possibly S. John regards it as a symbol of Christ's Priesthood. The χιτών was a shirt, reaching from the neck to the knees or ancles. "It is noted by one of the Fathers, that Christ's coat indeed had no seam, but the Church's vesture was 'of divers colours;' whereupon he saith, *In veste varietas sit, scissura non sit:* they be two things, unity and uniformity" (Bacon, *Essay* III.).

24. λάχωμεν. This use of *λαγχάνω* is rare, if not unique. Its proper meaning is 'to *obtain* by lot' (Luke i. 9; Acts i. 17; 1 Pet. i. 1).

ἵνα ἡ γραφή. See on ii. 22 and xii. 38. It was in order that the Divine purpose, already declared by the Psalmist, might be accomplished, that this twofold assignment of Christ's garments took place. S. John quotes the LXX. verbatim, although there the difference, which both he and the original Hebrew mark between the upper and under garment, is obliterated. It is from this passage that the reference to Ps. xxii. 18 has been inserted in Matt. xxvii. 35; none of the Synoptists refer to the Psalm. By **οἱ μὲν οὖν στρ. τ. ἐπ.** S. John emphasizes the fact that this prophecy was most literally fulfilled by men who were utterly ignorant of it.

25. εἱστήκ. δέ. But *there* **were standing.** The *δέ* answers to the previous *μέν*, and these two particles mark the contrast between the two groups. On the one hand, the four plundering soldiers with the centurion; on the other, the four ministering women with the beloved disciple. It is not improbable that the women had provided (Matt. xvii. 55; Luke viii. 2, 3) the very clothing which the soldiers had taken away.

ἡ ἀδ. τ. μ. αὐ., M. ἡ. τ. K. We are left in doubt whether we here have two women or one, whether altogether there are four women or three. The former is much the more probable alternative. (1) It avoids the very improbable supposition of two sisters having the same name. (2) S. John is fond of *parallel* expressions; 'His mother and His mother's sister, Mary of Clopas and Mary Magdalene' are two pairs set one against the other. (3) S. Mark (xv. 40) mentions Mary Magdalene, Mary the mother of James the Less, and Salome. Mary Magdalene is common to both narratives, 'Mary the mother of James the Less' is the same as 'Mary of Clopas:' the natural inference is that Salome is the same as 'His mother's sister.' If this is correct, (4) S. John's silence about the name of 'His mother's sister' is explained: she was his own mother, and he is habitually reserved about all closely connected with himself. We have seen already that he never mentions either his own name, or his brother's, or the Virgin's. (5) The very ancient Peshito or Syriac Version adopts this view by inserting 'and' before 'Mary the (wife) of Clopas.' **Ἡ τοῦ Κλωπᾶ** may mean *the daughter, mother*, or even *sister of Clopas;* but *the wife* is more probable: comp. *ἐκ τῆς τοῦ Οὐρίου* (Matt. i. 6); *τὴν Σμικυθίωνος* (Arist. *Eccles.* 46); *Verania Pisonis* (Plin. *Ep.* II. 20). There is no reason for identifying Clopas here with Cleopas in Luke xxiv. 18: Clopas is Aramaic, Cleopas is Greek. The spelling Cleop*h*as is a mistake derived from Latin MSS. All Greek authorities have Cleopas. If 'wife' is rightly inserted, and she is the mother of James the Less, Clopas is the same as Alphaeus (Matt. x. 3; comp. xxvii. 56). It is said that Clopas and Alphaeus may be different forms of the same Aramaic name. For **Μαρία ἡ Μαγδ.** see on vi. 67; Matt. xxvii. 56; Luke viii. 2.

26. ὃν ἠγάπα. See on xiii. 23: it is no mere periphrasis to avoid naming him, still less a boastful insertion. It explains why Jesus committed him to His Mother and His Mother to him.

γύναι, ἴδε ὁ υἱός σου. See on ii. 4. The act is one of filial care for the soul-pierced Mother (Luke ii. 35), who perhaps was thus spared the agony of seeing her Son die. If S. John took her home at once, this accounts for his omitting the third and fourth Words (Appendix C), which would be uttered during his absence. He who had just asked God's forgiveness for His murderers and promised Paradise to His fellow-sufferer, now gives another son to His Mother, another mother to His friend. If S. John was the Virgin's nephew, and if Christ's 'brethren' were the sons of Joseph by a former marriage, the fact that Christ committed His Mother to her nephew and His own beloved disciple rather than to her step-sons requires no explanation. Even if His 'brethren' were the sons of Joseph and Mary, their not believing on Him (vii. 5) would account for their being set aside; and we have no evidence that they believed till after the Resurrection (Acts i. 14).

εἰς τὰ ἴδια. See on i. 11 and xvi. 32. Although the commendation was double, each being given to the other, yet (as was natural) S. John assumes the care of Mary rather than she of him. This shews the untenability of the view that not only S. John, but in him all the Apostles, were committed by Christ to the guardianship of Mary. That S. John was known to the high-priest (xviii. 15) and that his family had hired servants (Mark i. 20) would seem to imply that he was a man of some position and substance.

28—30. The two words from the cross, 'I Thirst,' 'It is Finished.'

28. μετὰ τοῦτο εἰδώς. See on *v.* 38, iii. 22, xiii. 1. The identity between **τετέλεσται** here and in *v.* 30 must be preserved in translation; **are now finished.** The construction that follows is amphibolous. In order to avoid the apparent contradiction between all things being already finished and something still remaining to be accomplished, many critics make **ἵνα τελειωθῇ** depend upon *τετέλεσται.* But this is awkward. It is better to connect *ἵνα τελ.* with *λέγει*, especially as Ps. lxix. speaks so plainly of the thirst. The seeming contradiction disappears when we consider that the thirst had been felt before it was expressed. All things were finished, including the thirst; but Jesus alone knew this. *In order that the Scripture might be* **accomplished** and *made perfect*, it was necessary that He should make known His thirst. "He could have borne His drought: He could not bear the Scripture not fulfilled" (Bishop Hall). *Τελειόω* in this sense is remarkable and very unusual.

29. S. John's exact knowledge appears again. The Synoptists do not mention the **σκεῦος**, but he had stood beside it. The **ὄξος** was either the *posca* or sour wine for the soldiers during their long watch, or something prepared for the sufferers. The sponge and the stalk of hyssop being ready at hand is in favour of tne latter. Criminals sometimes lived a day or two on the cross. Vinegar is degenerate wine, and may symbolize the fallen nature of those who offered it. *Hyssop* cannot be identified with certainty. The caper-plant, which is as likely as any, has stalks which run to two or three feet, and this would suffice. It is not probable that Christ's feet were on a level with the spectators' heads, as pictures represent: this would have involved needless trouble and expense. Moreover the mockery of the soldiers recorded by S. Luke (see on xxiii. 36) is more intelligible if we suppose that they could almost put a vessel to His lips. S. John alone mentions the hyssop; another mark of exact knowledge. Did he see in it a coincidence with Exod. xii. 22?

περιθέντες προσήνεγκαν. Very graphic; *περιθ.* expresses the placing of the sponge round the stalk (Matt. xxi. 33, xxvii. 28, 48), *προσήν.* the offering (xvi. 2) and applying (Mark x. 13) to His lips. The actors and their motive are left doubtful. Probably they were soldiers and acted in compassion rather than in mockery; or in compassion under cover of mockery (Mark xv. 36; Ps. lxix. 22).

30. ἔλαβεν. He had refused the stupefying draught (Matt. xxvii. 34; Mark xv. 23), which would have clouded His faculties: He accepts what will revive them for the effort of a willing surrender of His life.

τετέλεσται. Just as the thirst was there before he expressed it, so the consciousness that His work was finished was there (*v.* 28) before He declared it. The Messiah's work of redemption was accomplished; His Father's commandment had been obeyed; types and prophecies had been fulfilled; His life had been lived, and His teaching completed; His last earthly tie had been severed (*vv.* 26, 27); and the end had come. The final 'wages of sin' alone remained to be paid.

κλίνας τ. κεφαλήν. Another detail peculiar to the Evangelist who witnessed it.

παρέδωκεν τ. πν. The two Apostles mark with special clearness that the Messiah's death was entirely voluntary. S. Matthew says, 'He *let go* His spirit' (*ἀφῆκεν*); S. John, 'He *gave up* His spirit.' None of the four says 'He died.' The other two have *ἐξέπνευσεν*; and S. Luke shews clearly that the surrender of life was a willing one by giving the words of surrender, 'Father, into Thy hands I commend My spirit.'—'No one taketh it from Me, but I lay it down of Myself.' It was the one thing which Christ claimed to do 'of Himself' (x. 18). Contrast v. 30, vii. 28, viii. 28, 42. Thus the spirit which He surrendered, and the water and the blood (*v.* 34), bear witness to his Messiahship.

For 'the seven words from the cross' see Appendix C and notes on Luke xxiii. 34; Mark xv. 34; Matt. xxvii. 48. Between the two words recorded in these verses (28—30) there is again a marked contrast. 'I thirst' is an expression of suffering; the only one during the Passion. 'It is finished' is a cry of triumph; and the 'therefore' in *v.* 30 shews how the expression of suffering led on to the cry of triumph. S. John omits the 'loud voice' which all the Synoptists give as immediately preceding Christ's death. It proved that His end was voluntary and not the necessary result of exhaustion. *Quis ita dormit quando voluerit, sicut Jesus mortuus est quando voluit? Quis ita vestem ponit quando voluerit, sicut se carne exuit quando voluit? Quis ita cum voluerit abit, quomodo cum voluit obiit?* (S. Augustine).

31—42. The Petition of the Jews and the Petition of Joseph

31. As in xviii. 28, the Jews shew themselves to be among those 'who strain out a gnat and swallow a camel.' In the midst of deliberate judicial murder they are scrupulous about ceremonial observances. The **οὖν**, as in *v.* 23, probably does not refer to what immediately precedes: it looks back to *vv.* 20, 21. The Jews still continue their relentless hostility. They do not know whether any one of the three sufferers is dead or not; their request shews that; so that 'therefore' cannot mean in consequence of Jesus' death. In order to save the Sabbath, and perhaps also to inflict still further suffering, they ask Pilate for this terrible addition to the punishment of crucifixion. Certainly the lesson 'I will have mercy and not sacrifice,' of which Christ had twice reminded them, and once in connexion with the Sabbath (Matt. xii. 7, ix. 13), had taken no hold on them.

παρασκευή. The *eve* of the Sabbath; and the Sabbath on this occasion coincided with the 15th Nisan, the first day of the Passover. This first day ranked as a Sabbath (Exod. xii. 16: Lev. xxiii. 7); so that the day was doubly holy. Comp. vii. 37.

κατεαγῶσιν. The *σκελοκοπία* or *crurifragium*, like crucifixion, was a punishment commonly reserved for slaves. The two were sometimes combined, as here. Lactantius (IV. xxvi.) says, 'His executioners did not think it necessary to break His bones, *as was their prevailing custom;*' which seems to imply that to Jewish crucifixions this horror was commonly added, perhaps to hasten death. For even without a Sabbath to make matters more urgent, corpses ought to be removed before nightfall (Deut. xxi. 23); whereas the Roman custom was to leave them to putrefy on the cross, like our obsolete custom of hanging in chains. The plural verb (contrast *μείνῃ* just before) emphasizes the separate acts: comp. *ἃ ἐπερίσσευσαν* (vi. 13). Winer, p. 645.

34. **ἔνυξεν.** *Pricked* or **stabbed**, a milder word than *ἐξεκέντησαν* (*v.* 37). All ancient Versions mark the difference between the two verbs. The Vulgate (*aperuit*) and Philox. Syriac indicate a reading *ἤνοιξεν*. The object of the *νύττειν* was to make sure that He was dead. The word occurs here only in N. T.

αἷμα κ. ὕδωρ. There has been very much discussion as to the *physical* cause of Christ's death; and those who investigate this try to frame an hypothesis which will at the same time account for the effusion of blood and water. Two or three such hypotheses have been put forward. But it may be doubted whether they are not altogether out of place. It has been seen (*v.* 30) how the Evangelists insist on the fact that the Lord's death was a voluntary surrender of life, not a result forced upon Him. Of course it may be that the voluntariness consisted in welcoming causes which must prove fatal. But it is more simple to believe that He delivered up His life before natural causes became fatal. 'No one,' neither Jew nor Roman, 'took it from Him' by any means whatever: He lays it down 'of Himself' (x. 18). And if we decline to investigate the physical cause of the Lord's death, we need not ask for a physical explanation of what is recorded here. S. John assures us that he saw it with his own eyes, and he records it that we may believe: i.e. he regards it as a 'sign' that the corpse was no ordinary one, but a Body that even in death was Divine.

We can scarcely be wrong in supposing that the blood and watei are symbolical. The order confirms this. Blood symbolizes the work of redemption which had just been completed by His death; and water symbolizes the 'birth from above,' with its cleansing from sin, which was the result of His death, and is the means by which we appropriate it. Thus the great Sacraments are represented. Some Fathers see in the double effusion the two baptisms, of blood (in martyrdom) and of water. Others see the Church, the Spouse of Christ, issuing in the Sacraments from the side of the sleeping Second Adam, as Eve from the side of the first Adam.

35. ὁ ἑωρακὼς κ.τ.λ. *He that* **hath seen hath borne witness** *and his* **witness** *is true* (comp. i. 19, 32, 34, viii. 13, 14, xii. 17). The use of the perfect participle rather than the aorist is evidence that the writer himself is the person who saw. If he were appealing to the witness of another person he would almost certainly have written, as the A. V., 'he that *saw.*' The inference that the author is the person who saw becomes still more clear if we omit the centre of the verse, which is somewhat parenthetical: '*He that hath seen hath borne witness, in order that ye also may believe.*' The natural sense of this statement is that the narrator is appealing to his own experience. Thus the Apostolic authorship of the Gospel is again confirmed. (See Westcott, *Introduction*, p. xxvii.) **'Αληθινή** means not simply truthful, but genuine, perfect: it fulfils the conditions of sufficient evidence. (See on i. 9 and comp. viii. 16, vii. 28.) On the other hand **ἀληθῆ** means **things that are true**. There is no tautology, as in the A. V. S. John first says that his evidence is adequate; he then adds that the contents of it are true. Testimony may be sufficient (e.g. of a competent eyewitness) but false: or it may be insufficient (e.g. of half-witted child) but true. S. John declares that his testimony is both sufficient and true.

ἵνα καὶ ὑμεῖς π. *That ye* **also may** *believe;* as well as the witness who saw for himself.

Why does S. John attest thus earnestly the trustworthiness of his narrative at this particular point? Four reasons may be assigned. This incident tended to shew (1) the reality of Christ's *humanity* against Docetic views; and these verses therefore are evidence against the theory that the Fourth Gospel is the work of a Docetic Gnostic (see on i. 14, vi. 21, vii. 10): (2) the reality of Christ's *Divinity*, against Ebionite views; while His human form was no mere phantom, but flesh and blood, yet He was not therefore a mere man, but the Son of God: (3) the reality of Christ's *death*, and therefore of His *Resurrection*, against Jewish insinuations of trickery (comp. Matt. xxviii.

13—15); (4) the clear and unexpected fulfilment of two Messianic prophecies.

36. ἐγένετο. Came to pass. Note that S. John uses the aorist, where S. Matthew, writing nearer to the events, uses *γέγονεν*. 'Hath come to pass' implies that the event is not very remote; Matt. i. 22, xxi. 4, xxvi. 56. The **γάρ** depends on *πιστεύσητε*. Belief is supported by Scripture; *for* the two surprising events, Christ's escaping the *crurifragium* and yet having His side pierced, were evidently preordained in the Divine counsels. The first **γραφή** (ii. 22, xii. 38) is Exod. xii. 46. For **συντρίβειν** comp. Matt. xii. 20; Mark v. 4, xiv. 3; Rev. ii. 27. Thus He who at the opening of this Gospel was proclaimed as the Lamb of God (i. 29, 36), at the close of it is declared to be the true Paschal Lamb. The Paschal Lamb, as dedicated to God, was protected by the Law from rough treatment and common uses. Its bones must not be broken; its remains must be burned. Once more we have evidence that S. John's consistent and precise view is, that *the death of Christ coincided with the killing of the Paschal Lamb*. And this seems also to have been S. Paul's view (see on 1 Cor. v. 7).

37. ὄψονται. All present, especially the Jews. The whole world was represented there. **Ἐκκεντᾶν**, 'to pierce deeply,' occurs nowhere else in N.T. excepting Rev. i. 7, and forms a connexion worth noting between the Gospel and the Apocalypse (see on i. 14, iv. 6, vii. 30, viii. 2, xi. 44, xiii. 8, xv. 20, xx. 16); all the more so because S. John here agrees with the present Masoretic Hebrew text and in every word differs from the LXX. The LXX. softens down *ἐξεκέντησαν* (which seemed a strange expression to use of men's treatment of Jehovah) into *κατωρχήσαντο* ('insulted'). See on vi. 45, xii. 13, 15, where there is further evidence of the Evangelist having independent knowledge of Hebrew. With the construction *εἰς ὄν* comp. vi. 29, xvii. 9.

38. μετὰ δὲ ταῦτα. But *after* these things. The *δέ* marks a contrast between the hostile petition of the Jews and the friendly petition of Joseph. *Ταῦτα* as distinct from *τοῦτο* shews that no one event is singled out with which what follows is connected: the sequence is indefinite (iii. 22). Contrast *v.* 28: there the sequence is direct and definite (ii. 12, xi. 7, 11). For Joseph of Arimathaea see on Matt. xxvii. 57; Mark xv. 43; Luke xxiii. 50. The Synoptists tell us that he was rich, a member of the Sanhedrin, a good and just man who had not consented to the Sanhedrin's counsel and crime, one who (like Simeon and Anna) waited for the kingdom of God, and had become a disciple of Christ. **Διὰ τ. φόβον** forms a coincidence with S. Mark, who says of him (xv. 43) that '*having summoned courage* (*τολμήσας*) he went in unto Pilate,' implying that like Nicodemus he was naturally timid. Joseph probably went to Pilate as soon as he knew that Jesus was dead: the vague 'after these things' need not mean that he did not act till after the piercing of the side. With **ἦρεν τ. σῶμα** comp. Matt. xiv. 12; Acts viii. 2.

39. Another coincidence. Nicodemus also was a member of the Sanhedrin (iii. 1), and his acquaintance with Joseph is thus explained. But it is S. Mark who tells us that Joseph was one of the Sanhedrin, S. John who brings him in contact with Nicodemus. It would seem as if Joseph's unusual courage had inspired Nicodemus also. Thus Jesus by being lifted up is already drawing men unto Him. These Jewish aristocrats first confess Him in the hour of His deepest degradation. **Τὸ πρῶτον** is either at the beginning of Christ's ministry, or the first time He came to Jesus. The meaning of the Brazen Serpent, of which he heard then (iii. 14), is becoming plain to him now.

μίγμα. This may be a correction of *ἕλιγμα* (אB), **a roll.** Myrrh-gum (Matt. ii. 11) and pounded aloe-wood (here only) are both aromatic: 'All thy garments are myrrh and aloes' (Ps. xlv. 8). The quantity is royal (2 Chron. xvi. 14), but not improbable, and reminds us of Mary's profusion (xii. 3). It is a rich man's proof of devotion, and possibly of remorse for a timidity which now seemed irremediable: his courage had come too late.

40. ἔδησαν αὐτὸ ὀθ. Bound *it in linen* **cloths.** The *ὀθόνια* (see on Luke xxiv. 12) seem to be the bandages, whereas the *σινδών* (Matt. xxvii. 59; Mark xv. 46; Luke xxiii. 53) is a large sheet (Mark xiv. 51) to envelope the whole. **Καθὼς ἔθος ἐ. τ. 'Ι.** distinguishes Jewish from other modes of embalming. The Egyptians had three methods, but in all cases removed part of the intestines and steeped the body in nitre (Herod. II. 86 ff.) **'Ενταφιάζειν** occurs elsewhere only Matt. xxvi. 12: *ἐνταφιασμός* occurs xii. 7; Mark xiv. 8: in LXX. (Gen. l. 2) it is used for the embalming of Jacob.

41. κῆπος. S. John alone mentions it, as he alone mentions the other garden (xviii. 1). It probably belonged to Joseph, for the tomb was his (Matt. xxvii. 60). This shews that Joseph, though of Arimathaea, had settled in Jerusalem. For **καινόν** see on xiii. 34. S. Matthew also says that it was new, S. Luke that never man had yet lain in it. S. John states the fact both ways with great emphasis. It is another royal honour. Not even in its contact with the grave did 'His flesh see corruption.' Comp. the colt, *whereon no man ever yet sat* (Luke xix. 30).

42. The burial was hastily performed: after the great Sabbath they intended to make a more solemn and complete burial. The fact of his having a tomb of his own close to Golgotha had perhaps suggested to Joseph the thought of going to Pilate. For the addition **τῶν 'Ιουδαίων** see on ii. 13, xi. 55: it suggests a time when there was already a *Christian* 'Preparation.' The order of the words, with the pathetic ending, should be preserved. *There therefore, because of the Jews' Preparation* (*for the tomb was nigh at hand*), **laid they Jesus.**

CHAPTER XX

11. **τῷ μνημείῳ** for *τὸ μνημεῖον* with AB against KUX.

16. Before **Ῥαββουνί** insert **Ἑβραϊστί** with ℵBDLXΔ against A (omitted as unnecessary).

19. Before **σαββάτων** omit *τῶν* (from *v.* 1), and before **διό.** omit *συνηγμένοι* (explanatory gloss).

20. After **ἔδειξεν** omit *αὐτοῖς*: **αὐτοῖς** for *αὐτοῦ*.

29. After **με** omit Θωμᾶ with ℵABCD.

We enter now upon the third and last part of the second main division of the Gospel. The Evangelist having set before us the INNER GLORIFICATION OF CHRIST IN HIS LAST DISCOURSE (xiii.—xvii.), and HIS OUTER GLORIFICATION IN HIS PASSION AND DEATH (xviii., xix.), now gives us his record of THE RESURRECTION AND THREEFOLD MANIFESTATION OF CHRIST (xx.).

The chapter falls naturally into five sections. 1. *The first Evidence of the Resurrection* (1—10). 2. *The Manifestation to Mary Magdalene* (11—18). 3. *The Manifestation to the Ten and others* (19—23). 4. *The Manifestation to S. Thomas and others* (24—29). 5. *The Conclusion and Purpose of the Gospel* (30, 31).

S. John's Gospel preserves its character to the end. Like the rest of his narrative, the account of the Resurrection is not intended as a complete record;—it is avowedly the very reverse of complete (*v.* 30);—but a series of typical scenes selected as embodiments of spiritual truth. Here also, as in the rest of the narrative, we have individual characters marked with singular distinctness. The traits which distinguish S. Peter, S. John, S. Thomas, and the Magdalene in this chapter are clear and completely in harmony with what is told of the four elsewhere.

Of the incidents omitted by S. John many are given in the other Gospels or by S. Paul. *S. Matthew and S. Mark;* the angel's message to the two Marys and Salome. *S. Matthew and* [*S. Mark*]; the farewell charge and promise. *S. Luke and* [*S. Mark*]; the manifestation to two disciples not Apostles. *S. Matthew;* the earthquake, angel's descent to remove the stone, soldiers' terror and report to the priests, device of the Sanhedrin, manifestation on the mountain in Galilee (comp. 1 Cor. xv. 6). [*S. Mark*]; the reproach for unbelief. *S. Luke;* the manifestation to S. Peter (comp. 1 Cor. xv. 5), conversation on the road to Emmaus, proof that He is not a spirit, manifestation before the Ascension (comp. Acts i. 6—9). *S. Paul;* manifestations to the *Twelve*, to S. James, and to S. Paul himself (1 Cor. xv. 6—8).

To these incidents S. John adds, besides the contents of chap. xxi., the gift of the power of absolution, and the manifestation on the second Lord's Day, when S. Thomas was present.

It may be freely admitted that the difficulty of harmonizing the different accounts of the Resurrection is very great. As so often in the Gospel narrative, we have not the knowledge required for piecing together the fragmentary accounts that have been granted to us. To this extent it may be allowed that the evidence for the Resurrection is not what we should antecedently have desired.

But it is no paradox to say that for this very reason, as well as for other reasons, the evidence is sufficient. Impostors would have made the evidence more harmonious. The difficulty arises from independent witnesses telling their own tale, not caring in their consciousness of its truth to make it clearly agree with what had been told elsewhere. The writer of the Fourth Gospel must have known of some, if not all, of the Synoptic accounts; but he writes freely and firmly from his own independent experience and information. All the Gospels agree in the following very important particulars;

1. The Resurrection itself is left undescribed. Like all beginnings, whether in history or nature, it is hidden from view.

2. The manifestations were granted to disciples only, but to disciples wholly unexpectant of a Resurrection. The theory that they were visions resulting from enthusiastic expectations, is against all the evidence.

3. They were received with doubt and hesitation at first.

4. Mere reports were rejected.

5. The manifestations were granted to all kinds of witnesses, both male and female, both individuals and companies.

6. The result was a conviction, which nothing ever shook, that 'the Lord had risen indeed' and been present with them.

All four accounts also agree in some of the details;

1. The evidence begins with the visit of women to the sepulchre in the early morning.

2. The first sign was the removal of the stone.

3. Angels were seen before the Lord was seen.

(See Westcott, *Speaker's Commentary*, II. pp. 287, 8.

1—10. The first Evidence of the Resurrection

1. τ. σαββ. Τὰ *σάββατα* may mean either *the Sabbath*, on the analogy of names of festivals, *τὰ ἐγκαίνια*, *τὰ παναθήναια*, &c., or *the week*, as the interval between two Sabbaths: here literally, *on day one of the week* (Luke xxiv. 1). S. John has not mentioned the stone; but he speaks of it as known, **τὸν** *λίθον*. S. Mark notes the placing of it, S. Matthew the sealing: all four note the displacement: **ἠρμένον ἐκ, lifted out of.**

2. Concluding that the body must be gone, *she runneth* **therefore** to S. Peter. He is still chief of the Apostles, and as such is consulted first, in spite of his fall. The repetition of **πρός** implies that he was not living with S. John, though (*v.* 3) near him. We are in doubt whether **ὃν ἐφίλει** applies to him as well as to 'the other disciple.' The special phrase for S. John is **ὃν ἠγάπα** (xiii. 22).

ἦραν. She makes no attempt to determine whether friends or foes have done it (comp. Luke xii. 20): **οἴδαμεν** agrees with the Synoptists' account, that other women came also. She left them to go to the Apostles.

3. The change from the single act, **ἐξῆλθεν,** to that which lasted some time, **ἤρχοντο,** is marked by change of tense; see on xi. 29.

4. ἔτρεχον...προέδ. τάχ. τ. Π. Literally, *began to run...ran on before, more quickly than Peter: τάχ. τ.* Π. being epexegetic. The more usual form *θᾶσσον* does not occur in N. T. (xiii. 27; 1 Tim. iii. 14; Heb. xiii. 19, 23). S. John ran more quickly as being much younger. Would a second century writer have thought of this in inventing a story? And how simply does S. John give us the process of conviction through which his mind passed: the dull unbelief beforehand, the eager wonder in running, the timidity and awe on arriving, the birth of faith in the tomb. This is true psychology free from all self-consciousness.

5. παρακύψας. The word occurs again *v.* 11 and Luke xxiv. in a literal sense, of 'bending down to look carefully at;' in a figurative sense 1 Pet. i. 12; James i. 25 (see notes). In Ecclus. xiv. 23 it is used of the earnest searcher after wisdom; in xxi. 23 of the rude prying of a fool. **Βλέπει** is *seeth* at a glance, as distinct from *θεωρεῖ* (*v.* 6).

6. Both Apostles act characteristically. S. John remains without in awe and meditation: S. Peter with his natural impulsiveness goes in at once. He takes a complete survey (**θεωρεῖ**), and hence sees the **σουδάριον** (xi. 44), which S. John in his short look had not observed. How natural is the *αὐτοῦ* (*v.* 7): the writer is absorbed in his subject and feels no need to mention the name. The details (so meagre in Luke xxiv. 12) here tell of the eyewitness: he even remembers that the napkin was folded.

8. καὶ ἐπίστευσεν. See on i. 7. More difficulty has perhaps been made about this than is necessary. 'Believed what?' is asked. That Jesus was risen. The whole context implies it; and comp. *v.* 25. The careful arrangement of the grave-clothes proved that the body had not been taken away in haste as by a foe: and friends would scarcely have removed them at all. It is thoroughly natural that S. John speaks only of himself, saying nothing of S. Peter. He is full of the impression which the empty and orderly tomb made upon his own mind; and it is to this that *vv.* 1—7 lead up, just as the whole Gospel leads up to *v.* 29. S. Luke (xxiv. 12—of doubtful genuineness) speaks only of S. Peter's wonder, neither affirming nor denying his belief.

9. οὐδέπω. Not even yet. S. John's belief in the Resurrection was as yet based only on what he had seen in the sepulchre. He had nothing derived from prophecy to help him. The candour of the

Evangelists is again shewn very strongly in the simple avowal that the love of Apostles failed to grasp and remember what the enmity of the priests understood and treasured up. Even with Christ to expound Scripture to them, the prophecies about His Passion and Resurrection had remained a sealed book to them (Luke xxiv. 25—27). For **δεῖ** comp. iii. 14, xii. 34; Matt. xvi. 21, xxvi. 54; Mark viii. 31; Luke ix. 22, xvii. 25, xxii. 37, xxiv. 7, 26, 44. The Divine determination meets us throughout Christ's life on earth, and is pointed out with frequency towards the close of it. Comp. Eph. iii. 11.

10. ἀπῆλθον...πρὸς αὐτούς. The reading is doubtful: *αὑτοὺς* =*ἑαυτούς* is best. Comp. *ἀπῆλθον καθ' ἑαυτούς* (1 Sam. xxvi. 12).

11—18. THE MANIFESTATION TO MARY MAGDALENE

11—18. It has been noticed that the three manifestations in this Chapter correspond to the three divisions of the Prayer in Chap. xvii. Here we see Jesus Himself; in the second, Jesus in relation to His disciples; in the third, Jesus in relation to all who have not seen and yet have believed.

11. Μαρία δέ. She had returned to the sepulchre after the hurrying Apostles. Mark xvi. 9 states definitely, what we gather from this section, that the risen Lord's first appearance was to Mary Magdalene: the details of the meeting are given by S. John alone. She **continued standing** (xviii. 5, 16, 18, xix. 25) after the other two had gone.

12. ἀγγέλους. Here only do angels appear in S. John's narrative. Comp. i. 52, xii. 29, [v. 4]. An appearance of angels to women occurs in all the accounts of the Resurrection. We are ignorant of the laws which determine such appearances; the two Apostles had seen nothing. For **ἐν λευκοῖς** comp. Rev. iii. 4: in Rev. iii. 5, iv. 4, *ἱματίοις* is added.

13. τ. κύριόν μου...οἶδα. In *v.* 2 it was *τ. κύριον* and *οἴδαμεν.* In speaking to Apostles she includes other believers; in speaking to strangers she represents the relationship and the loss as personal. These words express the burden of her thoughts since she first saw that the stone had been removed. She is so full of it that she has no thought of the strangeness of this appearance in the tomb. We may reasonably suppose that the Evangelist obtained his information from Mary herself. "The extreme simplicity of the narrative reflects something of the solemn majesty of the scene. The sentences follow without any connecting particles till *v.* 19. Comp. c. xv." (Westcott).

14. ἐστράφη. Perhaps she becomes in some way conscious of another Presence. But Christ's Risen Body is so changed as not to be recognised at once even by those who had known Him well. It has new powers and a new majesty. Comp. xxi. 4; Luke xxiv. 16, 37; Matt. xxviii. 17; [Mark xvi. 12].

15. κηπουρός. Because He was there at that early hour. The omission of His name is again (*v.* 7) very natural: she is so full of her loss that she assumes that others know all about it. **Σύ** is emphatic;

'Thou, and not some enemy.' For **ἐβάστασας** see on xii. 6. In her loving devotion she does not measure her strength: *κἀγὼ αὐτὸν ἀρῶ.* Note that it is *τ. κύριον* (*v.* 2), *τ. κ. μου* (*v.* 13), *αὐτόν* thrice (*v.* 15); never *τ. σῶμα* or *τ. νεκρόν*. His lifeless form to her is still Himself.

16. Μαριάμ. The term of general address, *Γύναι*, awoke no echo in her heart; the sign of personal knowledge and sympathy comes home to her at once. Thus 'He calleth His own sheep *by name*' (x. 3). The addition of **Ἑβραϊστί** is of importance as indicating the language spoken between Christ and His disciples. S. John thinks it well to remind Greek readers that Greek was not the language used. Comp. Acts xxii. 2, xxvi. 14, and see on v. 2. The form **Ῥαββουνί** or **Ῥαββουνεί** occurs also in Mark x. 51, but has been obliterated in A.V. It is said to be Galilean, and if so natural in a woman of Magdala. Would any but a Jew of Palestine have preserved this? Its literal meaning is 'my Master,' but the pronominal portion of the word had lost almost all meaning: comp. '*Mon*sieur.' S. John's translation shews that as yet her belief is very imperfect: she uses a mere human title.

17. μή μ. ἅπτου. This is a passage of well-known difficulty. At first sight the reason given for refraining from touching would seem to be more suitable to a permission to touch. Comp. iv. 44. It is perhaps needless to enquire whether the **γάρ** refers to the whole of what follows or only to the first sentence, 'I am not yet ascended to the Father.' In either case the meaning would be, that the Ascension has not yet taken place, although it soon will do so, whereas Mary's action assumes that it has taken place. If *γάρ* refers to the first clause only, then the emphasis is thrown on Mary's mistake; if *γάρ* refers to the whole of what is said, then the emphasis is thrown on the promise that what Mary craves shall be granted in a higher way to both her and others very soon. The translation 'touch Me not' is inadequate and gives a false impression. *Ἅπτεσθαι* does not mean to 'touch' and 'handle' with a view to seeing whether His body was real; this Christ not only allowed but enjoined (*v.* 27; Luke xxiv. 39; comp. 1 John i. 1): rather it means to 'hold on to' and 'cling to.' Moreover it is the present (not aorist) imperative; and the full meaning will therefore be, '*Do not continue holding Me*,' or simply, **hold Me not.** The old and often interrupted earthly intercourse is over; the new and continuous intercourse with the Ascended Lord has not yet begun: but that Presence will be granted soon, and there will be no need of straining eyes and clinging hands to realise it. (For a large collection of various interpretations see Meyer.) The reading **πρὸς τ. πατέρα** (without *μου*) agrees better with **πρ. τ. ἀδ. μου.** The general relationship applying both to Him and them is stated first, and then it is pointedly distinguished in its application to Him and to them.

ἀναβαίνω. I am ascending. The change has already begun: earth is His home no longer. In Luke xxiv. 44 Jesus says, 'These are My words which I spake unto you, *while I was yet with you.*' Mary's error consisted in supposing that Jesus was again with her under the old conditions. He *is with* them no longer after the flesh: He only *appears to* them. Soon He will *be in* them as the glorified Christ. The present interval is one of transition. But He remains perfect Man: He still speaks of '*My* God.' Comp. Rev. iii. 12. Thus also S. Paul and S. Peter speak of 'the *God* and Father of our Lord Jesus Christ.' Comp. Eph. i. 3; 2 Cor. xi. 31; 1 Peter i. 3; and see on Rom. xv. 6; 2 Cor. i. 3, where the expression is blurred in the A.V.

18. ἔρχεται...ἀγγέλλουσα. The more usual form is *ἐλθοῦσα ἀγγέλλει*; xi. 17, xvi. 8. Comp. xx. 6. She becomes an Apostle to the Apostles.

Thus as Mary's love seems to have been the first to manifest itself (*v.* 1), so the first Manifestation of the Risen Lord is granted to her. It confirms our trust in the Gospel narratives to find this stated. A writer of a fictitious account would almost certainly have represented the first appearance as being to the Virgin, or to S. Peter, the chief of the Apostles, or to S. John, the beloved disciple, or to the chosen three. But these are all passed over, and this honour is given to her, who had once been possessed by seven devils, to Mary of Magdala, 'for she loved much.' A late and worthless tradition does assign the first appearance to the Virgin; but so completely has Christ's earthly relationship to her been severed (xix. 26, 27), that henceforth she appears only among the other believers (Acts i. 14).

19—23. The Manifestation to the Ten and others

19. οὔσης οὖν ὀψ. Note the great precision of the expression. **When therefore it was evening on that day, the first of the week**: that memorable day, the 'day of days.' Comp. i. 39, v. 9, xi. 49, xviii. 13, where 'that' has a similar meaning. Evidently the hour is late; the disciples have returned from Emmaus (Luke xxiv. 23), and it was evening when they left Emmaus. At least it must be long after sunset, when the second day of the week, according to the Jewish reckoning, would begin. And S. John speaks of it as still part of the first day. This is a point in favour of S. John's using the modern method in counting the hours: it has a special bearing on the explanation of 'the seventh hour' in iv. 52. See notes there and on xix. 14.

τ. θυρῶν κεκλ. This is mentioned both here and *v.* 26 to shew that the appearance was miraculous. After the Resurrection Christ's human form, though still real and corporeal (Luke xxiv. 39), is not subject to the ordinary conditions of material bodies. It is *ἐν ἀφθαρσίᾳ, ἐν δόξῃ, ἐν δυνάμει, πνευματικόν* (1 Cor. xv. 42—44). Before the Resurrection He was visible, unless He willed it otherwise; after the Resurrection it would seem that He was invisible, unless He willed it otherwise. Comp. Luke xxiv. 31. **Οἱ μαθηταί** includes more than the Apostles, as is clear from Luke xxiv. 33. It was natural that the small community of believers should come together, to discuss the reported appearances of the Lord, as well as for mutual comfort and support under the (prevailing) *fear of the Jews* (comp. vii. 13). The Sanhedrin might go on to attack Jesus' disciples; all the more so now that rumours of His being alive were spreading.

ἦλθεν ὁ Ἰ. It is futile to discuss how; that the doors were miraculously opened, as in S. Peter's release from prison, is neither stated nor implied. For **εἰς** after **ἔστη** comp. xix. 13, (xxi. 4). His greeting is the ordinary greeting intensified. For this very simple form of it comp. Judg. vi. 23; 1 Chron. xii. 18. His last word to them in their sorrow before His Passion (xvi. 33), His first word to them in their terror (Luke xxiv. 37) at His return, is 'Peace.' Possibly the place was the same; the large upper room where they had last been all together.

20. καὶ τ. πλευράν. S. Luke, who does not mention the piercing of the side, has *καὶ τ.* **πόδας** (xxiv. 39:—*v.* 40, the exact parallel of this, is of very doubtful genuineness). **Τὸν κύριον** (not *αὐτόν*) is important: till then they had seen a form, but like Mary of Magdala and the two at Emmaus, they knew not whose it was. Thus their sorrow is turned into joy (xvi. 20).

21. εἶπεν οὖν. He *said* **therefore:** because now they were able to receive it. Their alarm was dispelled and they knew that He was the Lord. He repeats His message of 'Peace.' For **ἀπέσταλκεν** and **πέμπω** see on i. 33. Christ's mission is henceforth to be carried on by His disciples. He is *ὁ ἀπόστολος* (Heb. iii. 1), even as they are *ἀπόστολοι*. The close correspondence between the two missions is shewn by **καθώς, even as** (xvii. 18). Note the present tense, *I am sending;* their mission has already begun (xvii. 9); and the first part of it was to be the proclamation of the truth just brought home to themselves—the Resurrection (Acts i. 22, ii. 32, iv. 2, 33, &c.).

22. ἐνεφύσησεν. The very same verb (here only in N. T.) is used by the LXX. in Gen. ii. 7 (Wisdom xv. 11) of breathing life into Adam. This Gospel of the new Creation looks back at its close, as at its beginning (i. 1), to the first Creation.

We are probably to regard the breath here not merely as the emblem of the Spirit (iii. 8), but as the *means* by which the Spirit was imparted to them. 'Receive ye,' combined with the action of breathing, implies this. This is all the more clear in the Greek, because *πνεῦμα* means both 'breath' and 'spirit,' a point which cannot be preserved in English; but at least 'Spirit' is better than 'Ghost.' We have here, therefore, an anticipation and earnest of Pentecost; just as Christ's bodily return from the grave and temporary manifestation to them was an anticipation of His spiritual return and abiding Presence with them 'even unto the end of the world.' *Verus homo, qui spirare, verus Deus, qui Spiritum potuit donare* (S. Anselm).

λάβετε. Take ye, implying that the recipient may welcome or reject the gift: he is not a mere passive receptacle. It is the very word used for '*Take*' (Matt. xxvi. 26; Mark xiv. 22; Luke xxii. 17) in the account of the institution of the Eucharist; which somewhat confirms the view that here, as there, there is an outward sign and vehicle of an inward spiritual grace. The expression still more plainly implies that some gift was offered and bestowed then and there: it is wresting plain language to make 'Take ye' a mere promise. There was therefore a Paschal as distinct from a Pentecostal gift of the Holy Spirit, the one preparatory to the other. It should be noticed that **πνεῦμα ἅγιον** is without the article, and this seems to imply that the gift is not made in all its fulness. See on xiv. 26, where both substantive and adjective have the article.

23. ἄν τινων ἀφῆτε. Comp. ἄφες in the Lord's Prayer. This power accompanies the gift of the Spirit just conferred. It must be noticed (1) that it is given to the whole company present; not to the Apostles alone. Of the Apostles one was absent, and there were others present who were not Apostles: no hint is given that this power is confined to the Ten. The commission *in the first instance* is to the community as a whole, not to the Ministry alone. Of course this does not imply that all present were raised to the rank of Apostles; which would contradict the plain narrative of the Acts; nor that the commission could not be delegated to the Ministry; which would contradict the history of the Church.

It follows from this (2) that the power being conferred on the community and never revoked, the power continues so long as the community continues. While the Christian Church lasts it has the power of remitting and retaining along with the power of spiritual discernment which is part of the gift of the Spirit. That is, it has the power to declare the conditions on which forgiveness is granted and the fact that it has or has not been granted.

It should be noted (3) that the expression throughout is plural on both sides. As it is the community rather than individuals that is invested with the power, so it is classes of men rather than individuals on whom it is exercised. *God* deals with mankind not in the mass but with personal love and knowledge soul by soul. His *Church* in fulfilling its mission from Him, while keeping this ideal in view, is compelled for the most part to minister to men in groups and classes. The plural here seems to indicate not what must always be or ought to be the case, but what generally is.

ἀφέωνται...κεκράτηνται. The force of the perfect is—'are *ipso facto* remitted'—'are *ipso facto* retained.' But ἀφέωνται is not a secure reading: ἀφίενται is strongly supported; and there are other variations. When the community under the guidance of the Spirit has spoken, the result is complete. The meaning of **κρατῆτε** is 'hold fast,' so that they do not depart from the sinner. The word occurs here only in this Gospel. In Revelation it is used of 'holding fast doctrine,' &c. (ii. 14, 15, 25, iii. 11; comp. 2 Thess. ii. 15).

24—29. The Manifestation to S. Thomas and others. Peculiar to S. John

24. Θωμᾶς...οὐκ ἦν μετ' αὐτῶν. His melancholy temperament (see on xi. 16) might dispose him to solitude and to put no trust in the rumours of Christ's Resurrection if they reached him on Easter Day. And afterwards his despondency is too great to be removed by the repeated (ἔλεγον) testimony even of eyewitnesses. He has but one reply (εἶπεν); and the test which he selects has various points of contact with the surroundings. The wounds had been the cause of his despair; it is they that must reassure him. The print of them would prove beyond all doubt that it was indeed his Lord that had returned to him. Moreover, the Ten had no doubt told him of their own terror and hesitation, and how Jesus had invited them to 'handle Him and see' in order to convince themselves. This would suggest a similar mode of proof to S. Thomas.

25. βάλω...βάλω. In both places, **put**: see on v. 7. The negation is in the strongest form, **οὐ μὴ πιστ.**, *I will* **in no wise** *believe;* and the condition is stated without hope: not, '*If* I see, I *will* believe,' but, '*Except* I see, I will *not*.' This obstinacy appears also in the repetitions in the asseveration. **Τόπον** for the second **τύπον** is an early corruption. It is asked, as in *v.* 8, 'Believe what?' The answer is the same with even more certainty; that Jesus was risen.

26. ἡμ. ὀκτώ. Including both extremes, according to the Jewish method. This is therefore the Sunday following Easter Day. We are not to understand that the disciples had not met together during the interval, but that there is no appearance of Jesus to record. They are left to ponder over what they have seen. The first step is here taken towards establishing 'the Lord's Day' as the Christian weekly festival. The Passover is over, so that the meeting of the disciples has nothing to do with that. It is not clear why they had not already started for Galilee as commanded (Mark xvi. 7; Matt. xxviii. 7). Perhaps the obstinacy of S. Thomas had detained them. **Πάλιν** and **ἔσω** shew that the place is the same: the time of day is not given.

27. Jesus at once shews S. Thomas that He knows the test which he had demanded. The reproduction of his very words helps to bring home the grossness of the demand. Note **γίνου**: **become.** He is at the point where faith and unbelief part company: his suspense of judgment has been neither the one nor the other. It is not worth while to strain after a literal reproduction in English of the verbal contradiction between **ἄπιστος** and **πιστός**, as 'unbelieving' and 'believing' or 'faithless' and 'faithful.'

28. Not merely the sight of Jesus but the conviction of His omniscience overwhelms S. Thomas, as it did Nathanael (i. 50), and the Samaritan woman (iv. 29). His faith rises with a bound to its full height in the cry of adoration, with which the Gospel closes.

ὁ κύριός μ. κ. ὁ θεός μ. For the nominatives comp. xix. 3; Matt. xi. 26; Luke viii. 54, xii. 32. Most unnatural is the Unitarian view, that these words are an expression of astonishment addressed *to God.* Against this are (1) the plain and conclusive *εἶπεν* **αὐτῷ**; (2) *ὁ κύριός μου*, which is manifestly addressed to Christ (comp. *v.* 13); (3) the fact that this confession of faith forms a climax and conclusion to the whole Gospel. The words are rightly considered as an impassioned declaration on the part of a devoted but (in the better sense of the term) sceptical Apostle of his conviction, not merely that his Risen Lord stood before him, but that this Lord was also his God. And it must be noted that Christ does not correct His Apostle for this avowal, any more than He corrected the Jews for supposing that He claimed to be ἴσον τῷ Θεῷ (v. 18); rather He accepts and approves this confession of belief in His Divinity.

29. **ἑώρακας.** See on i. 18. This seems to shew that sight without touch sufficed. **Πεπίστευκας** (xi. 27) is half question, half exclamation: comp. i. 51, xvi. 31. The change from perfects to aorists should be noted: *Blessed are they who* **saw** *not and* (*yet*) **believed.** There were already disciples who believed without having seen the Risen Lord; and from a point of view in the future Jesus sees many more such.

This last great declaration of blessedness is a Beatitude which is the special property of the countless number of believers who have never seen Christ in the flesh. Just as it is possible for every Christian to become equal in blessedness to Christ's Mother and brethren by obedience (Matt. xii. 49, 50), so it is possible for them to transcend the blessedness of Apostles by faith. All the Apostles, like S. Thomas, had seen before they believed: even S. John's faith did not shew itself until he had had evidence (*v.* 8). S. Thomas had the opportunity of believing without seeing, but rejected it. The same opportunity is granted to all believers now.

Thus this wonderful Gospel begins and ends with the same article of faith. 'The Word was God,'—'the Word became flesh,' is the Evangelist's solemn confession of a belief which had been proved and deepened by the experience of more than half a century. From this he starts, and patiently traces out for us the main points in the evidence out of which that belief had grown. This done, he shews us the power of the evidence first over himself (*v.* 8), and then over one who was needlessly wary of being influenced by insufficient testimony. The result in the one case is silent conviction, in the other the instantaneous confession, at once the result of questioning and the victory over it, 'My Lord and my God.' Thomas has 'died with Him' and risen again.

30, 31. The Conclusion and Purpose of the Gospel

πολλὰ μ. οὖν κ. ἄλλα σ. *Many* **and** *other* **signs, therefore** (as might be expected from those which *have* been recorded in this book). The context shews that **σημεῖα** must not be limited to proofs of the Resurrection. S. John is glancing back over his whole work, **τὸ βιβλίον τοῦτον**, and the *σημεῖα* are miracles generally: comp. xii. 37. Πολλὰ *κ.* ἄλλα points the same way; the signs of the Resurrection were few and similar. Μὲν anticipates δέ in *v.* 31, and οὖν marks the transition: comp. Mark xvi. 19, 20; Phil. ii. 23, 24. Winer, p. 556. With **ἐνώπιον τ. μαθητῶν** comp. xvi. 26, Acts i. 21, 22.

31. **ταῦτα δέ.** *But these* (*signs*). On the one hand there were many unrecorded; *but* on the other hand some have been recorded. And these are all *signs:* every act has been significant. It was not S. John's purpose to write a complete 'Life of Christ;' it was not his purpose to write a 'Life' at all. Rather he would narrate just those

facts respecting Jesus which would produce a saving faith in Him as the Messiah and the Son of God. S. John's work is 'a Gospel and not a biography': most imperfect as a biography, it is 'complete as a Gospel.'

ἵνα πιστεύητε. That those who read this record may be convinced of two things,—identical in the Divine counsels, identical in fact, but separate in the thoughts of men,—(1) *that Jesus*, the well-known Teacher and true man, *is the Christ*, the long looked for Messiah and Deliverer of Israel, the fulfiller of type and prophecy; (2) that He is also *the Son of God*, the Divine Word and true God. Were He not the latter He could not be the former, although men have failed to see this. Some had been looking for a mere Prophet and Wonder-worker,—a second Moses or a second Elijah; others had been looking for an earthly King and Conqueror,—a second David or a second Solomon. These views were all far short of the truth, and too often obscured and hindered the truth. Jesus, the Lord's Anointed, must be and is—not only very man but very God: 1 John iv. 14, 15. This truth is worth having for its own sake; but, as S. John's experience had taught him, to possess it is to possess eternal life: 1 John v. 13, a passage which seems to shew that the object of the Epistle is similar to that of the Gospel as here set forth. See on iii. 36. For **ἐν τῷ ὀνόματι αὐτοῦ** see on i. 12. The conclusion of the Gospel is an echo of the beginning (i. 4, 12); and it once more gives a flat contradiction to Gnostic teaching. (1) Jesus is no mere man to whom a divine being was for a time united, but the Messiah and very God. (2) Eternal life is to be obtained, not by intellectual enlightenment, but by faith in the name of Jesus. Comp. Acts iv. 10; 1 Cor. vi. 11.

It is quite manifest that this was in the first instance intended as the end of the Gospel. The conflict between belief and unbelief recorded in it reaches a climax in the confession of S. Thomas and the Beatitude which follows: the work appears to be complete; and the Evangelist abruptly but deliberately brings it to a close. What follows is an afterthought, added by S. John's own hand, as the style and language sufficiently indicate, but not part of the original plan. There is nothing to shew how long an interval elapsed before the addition was made, nor whether the Gospel was ever published without it. The absence of evidence as to this latter point favours the view that the Gospel was not given to the world until after the appendix was written.

CHAPTER XXI

3. **ἐνέβησαν** for **ἀνέβησαν**. Omit *εὐθύς* after **πλοῖον.**

6. **ἴσχυον** (ℵBCDLΔ) for *ἴσχυσαν* (AP to suit **ἔβαλον**).

11. **εἰς τὴν γῆν** (ℵABCLPXΔ) for *ἐπὶ τῆς γῆς* (E). After **ἀνέβη** we should probably insert *οὖν* with ℵBCLX against ADP.

15, 16, 17. Ἰωάνου (ℵBC¹DL) for Ἰωνᾶ (AC² from Matt. xvi. 17).

16, 17. προβάτια for *πρόβατα*: in *v.* 16 the balance of evidence against *πρόβατα* is less strong than in *v.* 17.

17. πάντα before **σύ,** with ℵBC¹D against AC³.

21. After **τοῦτον** insert **οὖν**, with ℵBCD against A.

23. οὗτος before **ὁ λόγος**, with ℵBCD against A.

25. ἅ (ℵBC¹X) for *ὅσα* (AC²D). At the end omit Ἀμήν, with ℵABD against E. See *Hermathena* No. 19, 1893.

The Epilogue or Appendix

This Epilogue to a certain extent balances the Prologue, the main body of the Gospel in two great divisions lying in between them; but with this difference, that the Prologue is part of the original plan of the Gospel, whereas the Epilogue is not. It is evident that when the Evangelist wrote xx. 30, he had no intention of narrating any more 'signs.' The reason for adding this appendix can be conjectured with something like certainty: the Evangelist wished to give a full and exact account of Christ's words respecting himself, about which there had been serious misunderstanding. In order to make the meaning of Christ's saying as clear as possible, S. John narrates in detail the circumstances which led to its being spoken.

Twenty-five distinct marks tending to shew that chap. xxi. is by S. John are pointed out in the notes and counted up by figures in square brackets, thus [1]. Besides these points it should be noticed that S. John's characteristic *οὖν* occurs seven times (*vv.* 5, 6, 7, 9, 15, 21, 23) in 23 verses.

The whole of the chapter is peculiar to S. John's Gospel. It falls into four parts. 1. *The Manifestation to the Seven and the Miraculous Draught of Fishes* (1—14). 2. *The Commission to S. Peter and the Prediction as to his Death* (15—19). 3. *The Misunderstood Saying respecting the Evangelist* (20—23). 4. *Concluding Notes* (24, 25).

1—14. The Manifestation to the Seven and the Miraculous Draught of Fishes

1. μετὰ ταῦτα. This vague expression (see on iii. 22) suits an afterthought which has no direct connexion with what precedes. **Ἐφανέρωσεν, manifested** (see on ii. 11) is one of S. John's expressions [1]: so also is the construction *ἐφ.* **ἑαυτόν**; vii. 4, xi. 33, 55, xiii. 4; 1 John iii. 3; Rev. vi. 15, viii. 6, xix. 7: see also note on viii. 53 [2]. **Πάλιν**, as *v.* 14 shews, points back to the manifestation to S. Thomas and the rest (xx. 26).

ἐπὶ τ. θ. τ. Τιβεριάδος. By *the sea of Tiberias.* Contrast vi. 19; Rev. v. 13. S. John alone (see on vi. 1) uses this name for the lake [3]. The departure to Galilee is commanded Matt. xxviii. 7; Mark

xvi. 7. S. John does not relate the command, but gives its result (see on ii. 19, xviii. 11). S. Matthew gives only the appearances in Galilee, S. Luke and [S. Mark] only those in Jerusalem. S. John gives some of both.

The repetition of **ἐφανέρωσεν** is quite in S. John's style [4]. **Οὕτως** gives a tone of solemnity to what is coming.

2. Probably all seven disciples belonged to the neighbourhood; we know this of four of them. For **Θωμᾶς** see on xi. 16, xiv. 5, xx. 24; all particulars about him are given by S. John [5]. S. John alone mentions Nathanael [6]; see on i. 46. The descriptive addition, **ὁ ἀπὸ Κανᾶ τ. Γ.**, occurs here only: see on ii. 1. If one of **οἱ τ. Ζεβεδαίου** were not the writer, they would have been placed first after S. Peter, instead of last of those named [7]. The omission of their personal names is in harmony with S. John's reserve about all that is closely connected with himself [8]. The **ἄλλοι δύο** are probably not Apostles; otherwise, why are the names not given?

3. S. Peter, as so often, takes the lead: and again we have precise and vivid details, as from an eyewitness. In the interval of waiting for definite instructions the disciples support themselves by their old employment, probably at Capernaum or Bethsaida. Night was the best time for fishing (Luke v. 5); and the **ἐκείνῃ** may indicate that this failure was exceptional: or it may mean 'in *that memorable* night' (xi. 49, 51, xix. 27, 31, xx. 19).

ἐπίασαν οὐδέν. Failure at first is the common lot of Christ's fishers. His Presence again causing success after failure might enforce the lesson that apart from Him they could do nothing (xv. 5). Πιάζειν occurs six times in this Gospel besides here, and also Rev. xix. 20: elsewhere only Acts iii. 7, xii. 4; 2 Cor. xi. 32 [9]. The asyndeta, λέγει, λέγουσιν, ἐξῆλθον, are in S. John's style [10]: xviii. 34—36.

4. ἐπὶ τὸν αἰγ. Pregnant construction; 'He came *to* and stood *on* the beach.' Comp. i. 32, 33, iii. 36 (xix. 13, xx. 19); Matt. iii. 2. **Μέντοι, howbeit** or **nevertheless**, implies that their not knowing was surprising: *μέντοι*, besides here, occurs four times in S. John (iv. 27, vii. 13, xii. 42, xx. 5); elsewhere three times [11]. For **οὐκ ᾔδεισαν** see on xx. 14.

5. παιδία. Perhaps a mere term of friendly address, like our 'young people' (1 John ii. 14, 18); less affectionate than *τεκνία* (xiii. 33; 1 John ii. 1, 12, 28, iii. 7, 18, iv. 4, v. 21), which implies the filial relationship. Thus Jesus addressed the Magdalene as *Γύναι* before He called her by name (xx. 15, 16). **Προσφάγιον** occurs here only: it seems to mean anything eaten with bread, especially fish: comp. *ὄψον*, *ὀψάριον* (vi. 9). Possibly it means no more than 'something to eat:' but it may also mean 'fish;' and **ἔχειν** in fishing and fowling is used in the sense of 'to catch.' Perhaps we should translate **Have ye taken any fish?** This agrees with the context better than enquiries about food. A negative answer is anticipated: comp. iv. 29, vii. 31, viii. 22, xviii. 35.

6. There is no need to seek symbolical meanings for the right and left side. The difference is not between right and left, but between working with and without Divine guidance.

7. The characteristics of the two Apostles are again delicately yet clearly given (xx. 2—9): S. John is the first to apprehend; S. Peter the first to act, and with impulsive energy [12]. Perhaps S. Peter's haste to reach his Lord and S. John's abiding in the boat to finish the fishing is meant to symbolize the early martyrdom foretold to the one (*v.* 18) and the indefinite abiding suggested of the other (*v.* 22).

ὁ κύρ. ἐστιν. For the third and last time S. John speaks in his own narrative: comp. i. 38, xiii. 25. The interval in time and thought between 'Rabbi, where abidest thou?' and 'It is the Lord!' sums up the contents of the Gospel.

ἐπενδύτης (here only in N.T.) is neither the *ἱμάτιον* nor the *χιτών*, but the workman's 'frock' or 'blouse,' which he gathered round him "with instinctive reverence for the presence of his Master" (Westcott). **Γυμνός** need not mean more than 'stripped' of the upper garment. "No one but an eyewitness would have thought of the touch in *v.* 7, which *exactly inverts* the natural action of one about to swim, and yet is quite accounted for by the circumstances" (Sanday).

8. τ. πλοιαρίῳ. *In the boat*, or *by means of the boat*. As in vi. 17—24, *πλοῖον* and *πλοιάριον* are both used; we are not sure whether with or without a difference of meaning. This mixture of the two words is not found in the Synoptists: excepting Mark iii. 9, *πλοιάριον* is peculiar to S. John [13]. **Ἀπό**, in measuring distance, occurs only in S. John's writings (xi. 18; Rev. xiv. 20) [14]: 200 cubits would be about 100 yards.

9. ἀνθρακιάν. See on xviii. 18: the word occurs only there and here in N. T. [15]; moreover **κεῖσθαι** is more frequent in S. John's writings than elsewhere. We are uncertain whether **ὀψάριον** and **ἄρτον** are generic or not, *fish* and *bread*, or **a fish** and **a loaf**: *ὀψάριον* occurs only in S. John (vi. 9, 11) in N. T. [16].

10. There is again (see on *v.* 3) a solemn simplicity in the narrative; *vv.* 10—14 open in each case without connecting particles: comp. xv. *passim* and xx. 13—19 [17].

ἀπὸ τ. ὀψ. We have **ἐκ** *τῶν* as a nominative i. 24, vii. 40, xvi. 17; Rev. xi. 9; and as an accusative, 2 John 4; Rev. ii. 10: here we have **ἀπὸ** *τῶν* as an accusative. Comp. *ἐξ αὐτοῦ*, vi. 39. This elliptical form is frequent in S. John, elsewhere rare [18]. Comp. Luke xi. 49, xxi. 16. **Ὧν** (attraction) **ἐπιάσατε νῦν**, *which* **ye caught just now**: the aorist is worth keeping. For *νῦν* comp. xi. 8; '*Just now* the Jews were seeking to stone Thee.' As their success in fishing depended partly on the Lord's guidance, partly on their own efforts, so their refreshment comes partly from Him and partly from themselves.

11. ἀνέβη. The meaning probably is 'went on board' the vessel, now in shallow water. The details in this verse are strong evidence of the writer having been an eyewitness: he had helped to count these 'great fishes' and gives the number, not because there is anything mystical in it, but because he remembers it; just as he remembers and states the six large water-pots (ii. 6), the five loaves and two fishes, the 5000 men and the 12 baskets (vi. 9—13).

The points of contrast between this Draught of Fishes and the similar miracle at the beginning of Christ's ministry are so numerous and so striking, that it is difficult to resist the conclusion that the spiritual meaning, which from very early times has been deduced from them, is divinely intended. Symbolical interpretations of Scripture are of three kinds: (1) Fanciful and illegitimate. These are simply misleading: they force into plain statements meanings wholly unreal if not false; as when the 153 fishes are made to symbolize Gentiles, Jews, and the Trinity. (2) Fanciful but legitimate. These are harmless, and may be edifying: they use a plain statement to inculcate a spiritual lesson, although there is no evidence that such lesson is intended; as when the miracle at Cana is made to symbolize the substitution of the Gospel for the Law, or the intermittent spring at Bethesda, to mean the meagreness of Judaism in contrast to the fulness of Christ. (3) Legitimate and divinely intended. In these cases the spiritual meaning is either pointed out for us in Scripture (Luke v. 10), or is so strikingly in harmony with the narrative, that it seems reasonable to accept it as purposely included in it. Of course it requires both spiritual and intellectual power to determine to which class a particular interpretation belongs; but in the present instance we may safely assign the symbolism to the third class.

The main points are these. The two Miraculous Draughts represent the Church Militant and the Church Triumphant. The one gathers together an untold multitude of both good and bad in the troubled waters of this world. Its net is rent with schisms and its Ark seems like to sink. The other gathers a definite number of elect, and though they be many contains them all, taking them not on the stormy ocean but on the eternal shore of peace.

12. ἀριστήσατε. Not the afternoon or evening *δεῖπνον* (xii. 2, xiii. 2), but the morning *ἄριστον*, which could be rejected *before* going to one's day's work (Matt. xxii. 4), is intended: see on Luke xi. 37. Here the Apostles listen to the invitation with mingled perplexity, awe, and conviction. They know that He is the Lord, but feel that He is changed, and reverence restrains them from curious questions (comp. iv. 27). Thus the writer shews knowledge of the inmost feelings of Apostles: ii. 11, 17, 22, iv. 27, 33, vi. 21, ix. 2, xx. 20 [19].

13. They are afraid to approach, so He comes to them; and gives them the bread and the fish which were by the fire when they landed. It is futile to ask how it was provided; but from His invariable practice before His Resurrection we may suppose that He did not create it. It is a gift from the Lord to His disciples.

14. τοῦτο ἤδη τρίτον. Comp. ii. 11, iv. 54. The remark in all three cases guards against a possible misunderstanding of the Synoptic narrative [20]. We have a similar construction 2 Pet. iii. 1.

The two previous manifestations are probably those related xx. 19—23, 26—29, that to the Magdalene not being counted, as not granted to *the disciples:* but we have not sufficient knowledge to arrange the different appearances in chronological order. See on Luke xxiv. 49.

15—19. The Commission to S. Peter and Prediction as to his Death

15—19. There had been an appearance to S. Peter alone (Luke xxiv. 34; 1 Cor. xv. 5), and it was then, we may believe, that he was absolved. His conduct here (*v.* 7) is not that of one in doubt as to his relation to his Master. But he has not yet been reinstated as chief of the Apostles. This takes place now. He received his Apostleship after the first Miraculous Draught; he receives it back again after the second.

15. Note that the writer speaks of 'Simon Peter,' but represents the Lord as calling him 'Simon son of John.' This is in harmony not only with the rest of this Gospel, but with the Gospels as a whole. Although Jesus gave Simon the name of Peter, yet, with one remarkable exception (see on Luke xxii. 34), He never addresses him as Peter, but always as Simon. Matt. xvi. 17, xvii. 25; Mark xiv. 37; Luke xxii. 31. The Synoptists generally call him Simon, sometimes adding his surname. S. John always gives both names, excepting in i. 41, where the surname just about to be given would be obviously out of place. Contrast in this chapter *vv.* 2, 3, 7, 11 with 16, 17. Should we find this minute difference observed, if the writer were any other than S. John? [20]. This being the general usage of our Lord, there is no reason to suppose that His calling him Simon rather than Peter on this occasion is a reproach, as implying that by denying his Master he had forfeited the name of Peter. That S. John should add the surname with much greater frequency than the Synoptists is natural. At the time when S. John wrote the surname had become the more familiar of the two. S. Paul never calls him Simon, but uses the Aramaic form of the surname, Cephas.

Note also that Jesus uses **ἀγαπᾷς** twice, and the third time **φιλεῖς** (*v.* 17), whereas S. Peter in all three answers says **φιλῶ**. The change is not accidental; and once more we have evidence of the accuracy of the writer: he preserves distinctions which were actually made. S. Peter's preference for *φιλῶ* is doubly intelligible: (1) it is the less exalted word; he is sure of the natural affection which it expresses; he will say nothing about the higher love implied in *ἀγαπῶ*; (2) it is the warmer word; there is a calm discrimination implied in *ἀγαπῶ* which to him seems cold. In the third question Christ takes him at his own standard; he adopts S. Peter's own word, and thus presses the question more home.

πλέον τούτων. *More than these*, thy companions, love Me. The Greek is as ambiguous as A.V. and R.V., but there cannot be much doubt as to the meaning: 'more than thou lovest these things' gives a very inadequate signification to the question. At this stage in S. Peter's career Christ would not be likely to ask him whether he preferred his boat and nets to Himself. S. Peter had professed to be ready to die for his Master (xiii. 37) and had declared that though *all* the rest might deny Him, *he* would never do so (Matt. xxvi. 33). Jesus recalls this boast by asking him whether he *now* professes to have more loyalty and devotion than the rest.

σὺ οἶδας ὅτι φ. σε. Not only does he change *ἀγαπῶ* to *φιλῶ*, but he says nothing about 'more than these:' he will not venture any more to compare himself with others. Moreover he makes no professions as to the future; experience has taught him that the present is all that he can be sure of. Σύ is emphatic. This time he will trust the Lord's knowledge of him rather than his own estimate of himself. Can all these delicate touches be artistic fictions?

βόσκε τ. ἀ. μ. Not only is he not degraded on account of his fall, he receives a fresh charge and commission. The work of the fisher gives place to that of the shepherd: the souls that have been brought together and won need to be fed and tended. This S. Peter must do.

16. Jesus drops *πλέον τούτων*, which the humbled Apostle had shrunk from answering, but retains His own word *ἀγαπᾷς*. With **πάλιν δεύτερον** comp. iv. 54 and *πάλιν ἐκ δευτέρου* (Acts x. 15), *πάλιν ἄνωθεν* (Gal. iv. 9), *rursus denuo*. Winer, p. 755.

ποίμ. τ. προβάτιά μ. Tend, or *shepherd, My sheep*. *Βόσκειν* is 'to supply with food,' as of the herd of swine (Matt. viii. 30, 33; Mark v. 11, 14; Luke viii. 32, 34; xv. 15; the only other passages where it occurs in N. T.): *ποιμαίνειν* is 'to be shepherd to:' literally Luke xvii. 7; 1 Cor. ix. 7; figuratively Matt. ii. 6; Acts xx. 28; 1 Pet. v. 2. Comp. Jude 12; Rev. ii. 27, vii. 17, xii. 5, xix. 15. It implies more of guidance than *βόσκειν* does. The lambs, which can go no distance, scarcely require guidance; their chief need is food. The sheep require both.

17. τρίτον. He had denied thrice, and must thrice affirm his love. This time Jesus makes a further concession: He not only ceases to urge the 'more than these,' but He adopts S. Peter's own word *φιλεῖν*. The Apostle had rejected Christ's standard and taken one of his own, about which he could be more sure; and Christ now questions the Apostle's own standard. This is why 'Peter was grieved' so much; not merely at the threefold question recalling his threefold denial, not merely at his devotion being questioned more than once, but that the humble form of love which he had professed, and that without boastful comparison with others, and without rash promises about the future, should seem to be doubted by his Lord.

σὺ οἶδας· σὺ γινώσκεις. Once more (vii. 27, viii. 55, xiii. 7, xiv. 7) we have a sudden change between *οἶδα* and *γινώσκω*: *οἶδας* refers to Christ's supernatural intuition; *γινώσκεις* to His experience and discernment; *Thou recognisest*, **seest**, *that I love Thee*. See on ii. 25.

β. τ. προβάτιά μ. One is tempted to think that *ἀρνία*, *προβάτια*, *πρόβατα*, supported by S. Augustine's *agnos*, *oviculas*, *oves*, and apparently by the old Syriac, is right: but the balance of evidence is against it. If *πρόβατα* is admissible, it must (on the external evidence) come second, not third. But in any case there is a climax: leading the sheep is more difficult work than feeding the lambs; and feeding the sheep is the most difficult of all. To find healthful *στερεὰ τροφή* for *τέλειοι* Christians tasks the shepherd's powers more than finding *γάλα* for *νήπιοι* (Heb. v. 13).

S. Peter seems to recall this charge in his First Epistle (v. 2, 3), a passage which in the plainest terms condemns the policy of those who on the strength of this charge have claimed to rule as his successors over the whole of Christ's flock.

18, 19. This high charge will involve suffering and even death. In spite of his boastfulness and consequent fall the honour which he once too rashly claimed (xiii. 37) will after all be granted to him.

18. ἀμὴν ἀμήν. This peculiarity of S. John's Gospel (see on i. 52) is preserved in the appendix to it [21]. **Νεώτερος, younger** than thou art now. The middle instead of **ἐζώννυες σεαυτόν** would have been correct, as in Acts xii. 8; but then the contrast between *σεαυτόν* and *ἄλλος* would have been lost: *ἐζώννυσο* is 'thou didst *gird* (thyself);' *ἐζώννυες σεαυτόν* is 'thou didst gird *thyself*.'

ἐκτενεῖς τ. χ. Either for help, or in submission to the enforced girding to which the condemned are subjected. **Ὅπου οὐ θ.** means to death: not that S. Peter will be unwilling to die for his Lord, but that death, and especially a criminal's death, is what men naturally shrink from. The expression would be a strange one if *ἄλλος* means God, and the reference is to His equipping the Apostle for an unwelcome (!) career. And what in that case can *ὅταν γηράσῃς* mean?

The common interpretation that 'stretch forth thy hands' refers to the attitude in crucifixion, and 'gird thee' to binding to the cross, is precarious, on account of the order of the clauses, the taking to execution being mentioned after the execution. But it is not impossible; for the order of this group of clauses may be determined by the previous group, and the order there is the natural one. The girding naturally precedes the walking in the first half; therefore 'gird' precedes 'carry' in the second half, and 'stretch forth thy hands' is connected with 'gird' rather than 'carry' and therefore is coupled with 'gird.' Or again 'carry thee &c.' may possibly refer to the setting up of the cross after the sufferer was bound to it: in this way all runs smoothly.

19. ποίῳ θανάτῳ. *By* **what manner** *of death.* This comment is quite in S. John's style: comp. xii. 33, xviii. 32 [22]. It will depend on the interpretation of *v.* 18 whether we understand this to mean crucifixion or simply martyrdom. That S. Peter was crucified at Rome rests on sufficient evidence, beginning with Tertullian (*Scorp.* xv.); and that he requested to be crucified head downwards is stated by Eusebius (*H. E.* III. i. 2) on the authority of Origen.

ἀκολούθει μοι. Certainly the literal meaning cannot be excluded. It is plain from *ἐπιστραφείς* that S. Peter understood the command literally, and began to follow, then turned and saw S. John following. The correspondence between *ἀκολούθει* and *ἀκολουθοῦντα* cannot be fortuitous. But the act is another instance of the symbolism which runs through the whole of this Gospel [23]: comp. iii. 1, x. 22, xiii. 30, xviii. 1. Thus the command is *also* to be understood, as elsewhere in the Gospels, *figuratively*, the precise shade of meaning being determined by the context: comp. i. 43; Matt. viii. 22, ix. 9, xix. 21. Here there is probably a reference to *ἀκολουθήσεις δὲ ὕστερον* (xiii. 36); and *ἀκολουθεῖν* includes following to a martyr's death, and perhaps death by crucifixion.

20—23. The Misunderstood Saying respecting the Evangelist

20. The details are those of an eyewitness. With *ἐπιστραφεὶς* comp. xx. 14, 16. For **ὃν ἠγάπα ὁ Ἰ.** and **ἀνέπεσεν** see on xiii. 23, 25.

21. **οὗτος δὲ τί;** Literally, **but** *this man, what?* Not so much, 'what shall he *do?*' as 'what about him?' What is the lot in store for Thy and my friend? The question arises from sympathy and the natural wish that he and his habitual companion should be treated alike. An awful but glorious future has been promised to S. Peter; what is in store for S. John? Hence the *οὖν*. As usual, S. Peter acts on the first impulse; and we once more see the intimacy between these two Apostles [24]: comp. xiii. 6—9, 24, xviii. 15, xx. 1, 6.

22. **ἐὰν αὐ. θ. μέν.** Christ died and rose again that He might become the Lord and Master both of the dead and the living (Rom. xiii. 9). He speaks here in full consciousness of this sovereignty. For the use of *θέλω* by Christ comp. xvii. 24; Matt. viii. 3 (and parallels), xxvi. 39. While *θέλω* asserts the Divine authority, *ἐάν* keeps the decision secret. *Μένειν* should be rendered *that he* **abide**; it is S. John's favourite word which we have had so often, and this important link with the rest of the Gospel must not be lost [25]: see on i. 33. S. Peter's lot was to suffer, S. John's to wait. For 'abide' in the sense of remain in life comp. xii. 34; Phil. i. 25; 1 Cor. xv. 6. **Ἕως ἔρχομαι** is literally *while I am coming*. The words express rather the *interval* of waiting than the *end* of it. Comp. ix. 4; Mark vi. 45; 1 Tim. iv. 13. This at once seems to shew that it is unnecessary to enquire whether Pentecost, or the destruction of Jerusalem, or the apocalyptic visions recorded in the Revelation, or a natural death, or the Second Advent, is meant by Christ's 'coming' in this verse. He is not giving an answer but refusing one. The reply is purposely hypothetical and perhaps purposely indefinite. But inasmuch as the longer the interval covered by the words, the greater the indefiniteness, the Second Advent is to be preferred as an interpretation, if a distinct meaning is given to the 'coming.' This agrees with **τί πρός σε;** which is evidently a rebuke. There is a sense in which 'Am I my brother's keeper?' is a safeguard against curiosity and presumption rather than a shirking of responsibility. **Σύ** and **αὐτόν** are emphatic and opposed: 'whatever I may will respecting *him*, *thou* must follow Me. This is what concerns thee.'

23. **ἐξῆλθεν.** **There went forth therefore this word unto the brethren, That disciple dieth not.** Comp. Luke vii. 17. *Οἱ ἀδελφοί* for believers generally, common in the Acts (ix. 30, xi. 1, 29, xv. 1, 3,

22, 23, &c.), is not found elsewhere in the Gospels: but we see the way prepared for it in the Lord's words to Mary Magdalene (xx. 17), to the disciples (Matt. xxiii. 8), and to S. Peter (Luke xxii. 32). The mistake points to a time when Christians generally expected that the Second Advent would take place in their own time; and the correction of the mistake points to a time when the Apostle was still living. If this chapter was added by another hand after the Apostle's death it would have been natural to mention his death, as the simplest and most complete answer to the misunderstanding. The cautious character of the answer given, merely pointing out the hypothetical form of Christ's language, without pretending to explain it, shews that the question had not yet been solved in fact. Thus we are once more forced back within the first century for the date of this Gospel. Godet is inclined to believe that in some mysterious way the hypothesis is a fact; and that, as the primeval Church has its Enoch, and the Jewish Church its Elijah, so the Christian Church may have its S. John, preserved in special connexion with its progress to the very end.

24, 25. Concluding Notes

Again the question of authorship confronts us. Are these last two verses by the writer of the rest of the chapter? Are they both by the same hand? The *external* evidence, as in the case of the preceding verses, is in favour of their being both by the same hand, and by the writer of the first twenty-three verses, and therefore S. John. No MS. or version is extant without *v.* 24, and all except the Sinaitic have *v.* 25 also; nor is there any evidence that a copy was ever in existence lacking either this last chapter or *v.* 24.

The *internal* evidence is the other way. The natural impression produced by *v.* 24 is that it is not the writer of the Gospel who here bears witness to his own work, but a plurality of persons who testify to the trustworthiness of the Evangelist's narrative. So that we possibly have in this verse a note added by the Ephesian elders before the publication of the Gospel. The change to the singular in *v.* 25 would seem to imply that this verse is an addition by a third hand of a remark which the writer may have heard from S. John.

But the internal evidence is not conclusive, and the impression naturally produced by the wording of the verses need not be the right one. The aged Apostle in bringing his work a second time (xx. 30, 31) to a conclusion may have included that inmost circle of disciples (to whom he had frequently *told* his narrative by word of mouth) among those who were able to guarantee his accuracy. With a glance of affectionate confidence round the group of devoted hearers, he adds their testimony to his own, and gives them a share in bearing witness to the truth of the Gospel. But this is less simple than the other hypothesis.

24. τούτων...ταῦτα. It is more natural to understand 'these things' as referring to the whole Gospel and not to the appendix only. The Johannean phraseology is here of little weight as regards authorship: the Ephesian elders would naturally follow xix. 35. The change from present (*μαρτυρῶν*) to aorist (*γράψας*) indicates that the witness continues, the writing took place once for all. S. Chrysostom's proposal to read *οἶδα μέν* for **οἴδαμεν** is quite inadmissible: but it does not follow from *οἶδεν* in xix. 35 that S. John would not write *οἴδαμεν* here. It would have been out of place in the middle of his narrative to add the testimony of the Ephesian elders to his own as to details which he saw with his own eyes at the foot of the cross. But it is not unnatural that at the close of his Gospel he should claim them as joint witnesses to the fidelity with which he has committed to writing this last instalment of evangelical and apostolic traditions. Comp. 1 John v. 18, 19, 20, 15, iii. 14, i. 1; 3 John 12.

25. If this verse is an addition by an unknown hand it appears to be almost contemporary. The wording seems to imply that it would still be possible to write a great deal: additional materials still abound. Ἐάν with the subjunctive states an objective possibility with the prospect of a decision: Winer, p. 366. Late in the second century this possibility had ceased.

οἶμαι. The word occurs in N.T. Phil. i. 17; James i. 7 only. We should expect **μηδέ** after it: and Origen (*Philoc.* xv.) has **ὡς** *ἄρα* **μηδὲ** *κόσμον οἶμαι χωρεῖν*. The first person singular is very unlike S. John. The bold hyperbole which follows, and which may be a saying of S. John's added by one who heard it, expresses the yearnings of Christendom throughout all ages. The attempts which century after century continue to be made to write the 'Life of Christ' seem to prove that even the fragments that have come down to us of that 'Life' have been found in their many-sidedness and profundity to be practically inexhaustible. After all that the piety and learning of eighteen hundred years have accomplished, Christians remain still unsatisfied, still unconvinced that the most has been made of the very fragmentary account of about a tenth portion of the Lord's life on earth. What would be needed to make even this tenth complete? What, therefore, to complete the whole?

APPENDICES

APPENDIX A. THE DAY OF THE CRUCIFIXION

It can scarcely be doubted that if we had only the Fourth Gospel no question would have arisen as to the date of the Last Supper and of the Crucifixion. S. John's statements are as usual so clear and precise, and at the same time so entirely consistent, that obscurity arises only when attempts are made to force his plain language into harmony with the statements of the Synoptists which appear to contradict his as regards the day of the *month*. All four Gospels agree as to the day of the *week*.

S. John gives five distinct intimations of the date.

1. **Πρὸ** *δὲ τῆς ἑορτῆς τοῦ πάσχα* (xiii. 1); which shews that the feet-washing and discourses at the Last Supper preceded the Passover.

2. *Ἀγόρασον ὧν χρείαν ἔχομεν* **εἰς τὴν ἑορτήν** (xiii. 29); which shews that the Last Supper was not the Passover.

3. *Ἦν δὲ* **πρωΐ·** *καὶ οὐκ εἰσῆλθον εἰς τὸ πραιτώριον, ἵνα μὴ μιανθῶσιν ἀλλ'* **ἵνα φάγωσιν τὸ πάσχα** (xviii. 28); which proves that *early* on the day of the Crucifixion the Jews who delivered the Lord to Pilate had not yet eaten the Passover.

4. *Ἦν δὲ* **παρασκευὴ τοῦ πάσχα,** *ὥρα ἦν ὡς ἕκτη* (xix. 14); which shews that these Jews had not postponed eating the Passover because of urgent business: the Passover had not yet begun.

5. *Οἱ οὖν Ἰουδαῖοι, ἐπεὶ* **παρασκευὴ** *ἦν ἵνα μὴ μείνῃ ἐπὶ τοῦ σταυροῦ τὰ σώματα ἐν τῷ σαββάτῳ, ἦν γὰρ* **μεγάλη** *ἡ ἡμέρα ἐκείνου τοῦ σαββάτου, κ.τ.λ.* (xix. 31). Here *παρασκευή* may mean either Friday, the preparation for the Sabbath, or Nisan 14, the preparation for the Passover. The statement that that Sabbath was a *μεγάλη ἡμέρα* most naturally means that the Sabbath in that week coincided with the first day of the Feast: so that the day of the Crucifixion was 'the Preparation' for *both* the Sabbath and the Feast.

It is evident, therefore, that **S. John places the Crucifixion on the Preparation or Eve of the Passover**, i.e. on Nisan 14, on the afternoon of which the Paschal Lamb was slain; and that he makes the Passover begin at sunset that same day. Consequently *the Last Supper cannot have been the Paschal meal.*

It is from the Synoptists that we inevitably derive the impression that the Last Supper *was* the Paschal meal (Matt. xxvi. 2, 17, 18, 19;

Mark xiv. 14—16; Luke xxii. 7, 11, 13, 15). Whatever method of explanation be adopted, it is the impression derived from the Synoptists that must be modified, not that derived from S. John. Their statements refer rather to the *nature* of the Last Supper, his cover the whole field from the Supper to the taking down from the cross, giving clear marks of *time* all along. No doubt they are correct in stating that the Last Supper had *in some sense* the character of a Paschal meal; but it is quite evident from S. John that the Last Supper was not the Passover in the ordinary Jewish sense. And this conclusion is confirmed:—

1. *By the Synoptists themselves.* They state that the priests and their officials went to arrest Jesus immediately after the Last Supper (Luke xxii. 52). Would this have been possible while the whole nation was at the Paschal meal? Could Simon have been coming out of the country (Mark xv. 21) on such a Sabbatical day as Nisan 15? Could Joseph have bought a winding-sheet (xv. 46) on such a day? Would the women have postponed the full embalming of the body *on account of the Sabbath* (Luke xxiii. 56), if the day of the entombment was already a Sabbatical day? Moreover it was *on the evening between Nisan* 13 *and* 14 that people went to draw water with which to make the unleavened bread for the Feast. Might not the "man bearing a pitcher of water" (Mark xiv. 13), who provided the large upper-room for the Last Supper, be bringing water for this purpose? Comp. Ὁ καιρός μου ἐγγύς ἐστιν· πρὸς σὲ ποιῶ τὸ πάσχα (Matt. xxvi. 18). What logical connexion have these two sentences, if they do not mean that Jesus was obliged to keep the Passover *before* the time?

2. *By S. Paul.* In speaking of the Resurrection he says **ἀπαρχὴ Χριστός** (1 Cor. xv. 23). The sheaf which was the *ἀπαρχή* or first-fruits of the harvest was gathered on Nisan 16. If Jesus died on Nisan 14, His Resurrection exactly corresponded with this *ἀπαρχή*.

3. *By Christian tradition.* Clement of Alexandria says expressly that the Last Supper took place Nisan 13, and that "our Saviour suffered on the following day; for He was Himself the true Passover." And the fact that the whole Church for eight centuries always used *leavened* bread at the Eucharist, and that the Eastern Church continues to do so to this day, points to a tradition that the meal at which the Eucharist was instituted was not the Paschal meal.

4. *By Jewish tradition.* The execution of Jesus is noticed in two passages in the Talmud. In the one He is said to have been hung, in the other to have been stoned: but both agree in placing the execution *on the eve of the Passover*.

Jews, to whom the Gospel was to be preached first, might have found a serious stumbling-block in the fact that He who was proclaimed as the Paschal Lamb partook of the Paschal Feast and was slain afterwards. Whereas S. John makes it clear to them, that on the very day and at the very hour when the Paschal lambs had to be slain, the True Lamb was sacrificed on the Cross. (See note on Matt. xxvi. 17 and Excursus V. in Dr Farrar's *S. Luke*.)

APPENDIX B. S. PETER'S DENIALS

The difficulties which attend all attempts at forming a Harmony of the Gospels are commonly supposed to reach something like a climax here. Very few events are narrated at such length by all four Evangelists; and in no case is the narrative so carefully divided by them into distinct portions as in the case of S. Peter's threefold denial of his Master. Here therefore we have an exceptionally good opportunity of comparing the Evangelists with one another piece by piece; and the result is supposed to be damaging to them. A careful comparison of the four accounts will establish one fact beyond the reach of reasonable dispute;—that, whatever may be the relation between the narratives of S. Matthew and S. Mark, those of S. Luke and S. John are independent both of the first two Gospels and of one another. So that we have at least three independent accounts.

It would be an instructive exercise for the student to do for himself what Canon Westcott has done for him (Additional Note on John xviii: comp. Alford on Matt. xxvi. 69), and tabulate the four accounts, comparing not merely verse with verse but clause with clause.

His first impression of great discrepancy between the accounts will convince him of the independence of at least three of them. And a further consideration will probably lead him to see that this independence and consequent difference are the result of fearless truthfulness. Each Evangelist, conscious of his own fidelity, tells the story in his own way without caring to correct his account by that of others. In the midst of the differences of details there is quite enough substantial agreement to lead us to the conclusion that each narrative would be found to be accurate if we were acquainted with all the circumstances. All four Evangelists tell us that *three denials were predicted* (Matt. xxvi. 34; Mark xiv. 30; Luke xxii. 34; John xiii. 38) and all four *give three denials* (Matt. xxvi. 70, 72, 74; Mark xiv. 68, 70, 71; Luke xxii. 57, 58, 60; John xviii. 17, 25, 27).

The *apparent discrepancy with regard to the prediction* is that S. Luke and S. John place it during the Supper, S. Mark and S. Matthew during the walk to Gethsemane. But the words of the first two Evangelists do not quite necessarily mean that the prediction was made precisely where they mention it. Yet, if the more natural conclusion be adopted, that they do mean to place the prediction on the road to Gethsemane; then, either the prediction was repeated, or they have placed it out of the actual chronological sequence. As already remarked elsewhere, chronology is not what the Evangelists care to give us.

The *numerous differences of detail with regard to the three denials*, especially the second and third, will sink into very small proportions if we consider that the attack of the maid which provoked the first denial, about which the four accounts are very harmonious, led to a series of attacks gathered into two groups, with intervals during which S. Peter was left unmolested. Each Evangelist gives us salient points in these groups of attacks and denials. As to the particular words put into the mouth of S. Peter and his assailants, it is quite unnecessary to suppose that they are intended to give us more than *the substance* of what was said (see Introductory Note to chap. iii.). Let us remember S. Augustine's wise and moderate words respecting the differences of detail in the narratives of the storm on the lake. "There is no need to enquire which of these exclamations was really uttered. For whether they uttered some one of these three, or other words which none of the Evangelists have recorded, yet conveying the same sense, *what does it matter?*" *De Cons. Ev.* II. xxiv. 55.

APPENDIX C

ORDER OF THE CHIEF EVENTS OF THE PASSION

This part of the Gospel narrative is like the main portion of it in this, that the exact sequence of events cannot in all cases be determined with certainty, and that the precise date of events can in no case be determined with certainty. But for the sake of clearness of view it is well to have a tentative scheme; bearing in mind that, like a plan drawn from description instead of from sight, while it helps us to understand and realise the description, it must be defective and may here and there be misleading.

Thursday after 6.0 P.M. (Nisan 14)	The Last Supper and Last Discourses.
11 P.M.	The Agony.
Midnight	The Betrayal.
Friday 1 A.M.	Conveyance to the high-priest's house.
2 A.M.	Examination before Annas.
3 A.M.	Examination before Caiaphas at an informal meeting of the Sanhedrin.
4.30 A.M.	Condemnation to death at a formal meeting of the Sanhedrin.
5 A.M.	First Examination before Pilate.
5.30 A.M.	Examination before Herod.
6 A.M.	Second Examination before Pilate.
	The Scourging and first Mockery by Pilate's soldiers.
6.30 A.M.	Pilate gives sentence of Crucifixion.
	Second Mockery by Pilate's soldiers.
9 A.M.	The Crucifixion.
	First Word. '*Father, forgive them, &c.*'
	Second Word. '*Woman, behold thy son.*' '*Behold thy mother.*'
	Third Word. '*To-day shalt thou be, &c.*'
Noon to 3 P.M.	The Darkness.
	Fourth Word. '*My God, My God, &c.*'
	Fifth Word. '*I thirst.*'
	Sixth Word. '*It is finished.*'

(Nisan 14)	3 P.M.	Seventh Word. '*Father, into Thy hands I commend My spirit.*'
		The Centurion's Confession.
		The Piercing of the Side.
	3 to 5 P.M.	Slaughter of the Paschal lambs.
	5 P.M.	The Burial.
	6 P.M.	The Sabbath begins.
(Nisan 15)		The Passover.
Saturday		The Great Day of the Feast.
		Jesus in the Grave.

APPENDIX D

SUMMARY OF THE EXTERNAL EVIDENCE RESPECTING THE PARAGRAPH VII. 53—VIII. 11

(1) The paragraph is absent from every known *Greek MS.* earlier than the *eighth* century, except the Western and eccentric D. A and C are defective here, but in the missing leaves there cannot have been room for the paragraph. In L and Δ (eighth and ninth cent.) there are spaces, shewing that the transcribers knew of its existence, but did not find it in their copies. (2) In the whole range of *Greek patristic literature* of the first nine centuries there is no trace of any knowledge of it, excepting a reference to it in the Apostolic Constitutions (ii. 24) as an authority for the reception of penitents; but without any indication of the book from which it is quoted. (3) In *Oriental Versions* it is found only in inferior MSS., excepting the Ethiopic and the Jerusalem Syriac. (4) The silence of Tertullian in his *De Pudicitiâ* and of Cyprian in *Ep.* LV. (which treats of the admission of adulterous persons to penitence) and the evidence of MSS. shew that it was absent from the *earliest Latin texts*.

Thus it is absent from the oldest representatives of every kind of evidence; Greek MSS., Versions, and Fathers both Greek and Latin.

With regard to the authorities which contain or support the section several points must be noted. (1) D is notorious for insertions and additions, such as Matt. xx. 29 and Luke vi. 5. But nowhere else has it an insertion so considerable. Jerome's statement that this paragraph is found '*in evangelio secundum Johannem in multis et Graecis et Latinis codicibus*' implies that in the *majority* of MSS. it is *not* found. In many of the extant MSS. which contain the passage it is marked as dubious. (2) The date of the text of the Apostolic Constitutions is uncertain, and we cannot tell whether the reference is to the Gospel narrative or to tradition. The earliest Greek commentator who notices the section, Euthymius Zygadenus in the twelfth century, marks it as probably an interpolation. (3) The MS. of the Jerusalem

Syriac lectionary is not older than the eleventh century. (4) The early Latin copies, like D, admitted interpolations very freely. Jerome, on the authority of some Greek MSS., retained it in the Vulgate. Ambrose and Augustine treated it as authentic. Later Latin writers naturally followed the authority of these great names.

We conclude "that the Section first came into S. John's Gospel as an insertion in a comparatively late Western text, having originally belonged to an extraneous independent source......that the Section was little adopted in texts other than Western till some unknown time between the fourth or fifth and the eighth centuries, when it was received into some influential Constantinopolitan text" (Westcott and Hort). Having found its way into most of the late Greek MSS. and into almost all the Latin texts, it was allowed by Erasmus to remain in its usual place, and hence became established in the *Textus Receptus.*

APPENDIX E

Εἰς τὸν αἰῶνα and Ζωὴ αἰώνιος.

Both these expressions are of frequent occurrence in S. John's Gospel: the former of them is best rendered 'for ever,' and the second, 'eternal life.'

The literal meaning of *εἰς τὸν αἰῶνα* (vi. 51, 58, viii. 35, xii. 34, xiv. 16; 1 John ii. 17; 2 John 2) is 'unto the age.' The expression is of Jewish origin. The Jews were accustomed to divide time into two periods, the time preceding the coming of the Messiah, and the age of the Messiah. The latter was spoken of as 'the Age,' the age *κατ' ἐξοχήν*, the age to which the hopes of all Israel looked forward: it was '*the* Age,' *ὁ αἰών*, just as the Messiah Himself was 'the Coming One,' *ὁ ἐρχόμενος* (vi. 14, xi. 27; Matt. xi. 3; Luke vii. 19, 20). The Apostles and the Early Christian Church adopted the same language with an important change of meaning. They knew that the Messiah had come, and that 'the Age' in the Jewish sense of the term had already begun: but they once more transferred 'the Age' to the unknown and possibly remote future. 'The Age' for them meant the period which would be inaugurated by the *Return* of the Messiah rather than by His First Coming: it represented, therefore, the period of Christ's Second Coming, when all His enemies shall be put under His feet, and 'He shall deliver up the kingdom to God, even the Father' (1 Cor. xv. 24). Hence, *εἰς τὸν αἰῶνα* means 'unto the age' of the Kingdom of God. *Literally*, therefore, the expression states no more than that there is to be duration to the end of the world; for this world ends when 'the Age' begins. But the expression seems to imply a good deal more than this. It appears to have behind it the understood belief, that whatever is allowed to see the Kingdom of God will continue to endure in that kingdom; and as that kingdom is to have no end, so enduring εἰς τὸν αἰῶνα includes, though it does not express, enduring, not merely until the end of this world, ἡ συντέλεια τοῦ αἰῶνος [τούτου] (Matt. xiii. 40, 49, xxiv. 3, xxviii. 20), but '*for ever.*'

Similarly, ζωὴ αἰώνιος means life that is suitable to 'the Age,' the life of those who share in the Kingdom of God. Like εἰς τὸν αἰῶνα, it does not express, but it probably implies, the notion of endlessness: and we have a word in English which does much the same, and which is therefore the best rendering to give of αἰώνιος, viz. 'eternal.' 'Everlasting,' which in A.V. is frequently used to translate αἰώνιος (iii. 16, 36, iv. 14, v. 24, vi. 27, 40, 47, xii. 50; Matt. xviii. 8, &c.) expresses the notion of endlessness and nothing more: it expresses, therefore, just that idea which αἰώνιος probably implies, but does not directly state. Whereas 'eternal' is almost exactly the word we require. Eternity is the negation of time, that which to higher intelligences than ours takes the place of time, and will do so to our glorified intelligences when time has ceased to be. But when we have said that eternity is not time, we have said all that intelligibly and with certainty can be said about it. All our experience and thought involve the condition of time; and to endeavour to imagine a state of things from which time is absent is to attempt an impossibility. When we banish time from thought, we cease to think. Time, then, is the condition of life in this world; eternity is the condition of life in the world to come: and therefore ζωὴ αἰώνιος, the life of 'the Age,' the life of the world to come, is best expressed in English by the words '*eternal life.*' This eternal life, S. John assures us again and again (iii. 36, v. 24, vi. 47, 54, xvii. 3), can be *possessed* in this world, but it can only be *understood* in the world to come (1 John iii. 2).

It is worth remarking that S. John applies the term αἰώνιος to nothing but 'life,' and that for this aeonian life the word is always ζωή and never βίος. Βίος does not occur in S. John's Gospel at all, and only twice in the First Epistle;—in the phrases ἡ ἀλαζονεία τοῦ βίου (ii. 16), 'the vainglory of life,' i.e. arrogancy and ostentation exhibited in the manner of living, and ὁ βίος τοῦ κόσμου (iii. 17), 'the world's means of life,' i.e. the goods of this world. In Aristotle and Greek philosophy generally βίος is higher than ζωή: βίος is the life peculiar to man as a moral being; ζωή is the vital principle which he shares with brutes and vegetables. In N.T. ζωή is higher than βίος: βίος is, as before, the life or livelihood of man; but ζωή is the vital principle which he shares with God. Contrast βίος in Luke viii. 14, 43, xv. 12, 30; 1 Tim. ii. 2; 2 Tim. ii. 4, &c. with ζωή in John i. 4, iii. 36, v. 24, 26, 29, 40, &c., &c. Βίος occurs less than a dozen times in the whole of the N.T., whereas ζωή occurs upwards of a hundred times: ζωή is the very sum and substance of the Gospel. 'The life eternal is this, that they should know Thee the only true God, and Him whom Thou didst send, even Jesus Christ' (xvii. 3).

APPENDIX F

On some points of Geography

It seems to be quite certain that the attractive reconciliation of the two readings, Βηθανίᾳ and Βηθαβαρᾷ, derived from Lieutenant Conder's conjectures, and suggested in the note on i. 28, must be abandoned. And, what is of much more serious moment, it is becoming clear that Lieutenant Conder's identifications, when they depend upon philological theories, must be received with the utmost caution. It is true that the Arabs call Batanaea, the Βαταναία of Josephus, Băthănia; changing the Aramaic 't', corresponding to the Hebrew 'sh' in Bashan, to 'th', by a well-known phonetic relation between these three dialects. But a Jewish writer would not adopt a pure Arabic form, which is therefore impossible in a Gospel written by a Jew. And even if this point could be conceded there would remain the further improbability that the Arabic 'ă' in *Băthănîya* should be represented by η in Βηθανία. Bethania is a compound of Bêth, and some place on the Jordan. It might possibly mean 'boat-house'; and this would coincide pretty closely with Bethabara, which means 'ford-house' or 'ferry-house.'

In any map of Jerusalem there must of necessity be either serious omissions, or insertions which are more or less conjectural. In the present map the traditional name of Zion has been retained for the Western Hill, and also the name of Hippicus for the great Herodian tower which still stands close to the Jaffa Gate. Recent measurements, however, have shewn that of the three Herodian towers, Hippicus, Phasael, and Mariamne, the existing tower, often called the Tower of David, may be Phasael rather than Hippicus. The name, Tower of David, is mediaeval, and is a perpetuation of the error of Josephus, who supposed that the fortress of David belonged to the Upper City, and that the Western Hill had always been part of Jerusalem.

Again, the position of the Acra is much disputed. In the map it is not intended to affirm the special conjecture of Warren and Conder, but merely to retain, until something better is fully established, their present view. There is, however, good reason for doubting its correctness. On this and other topographical questions see the very interesting article on Jerusalem in the *Encycl. Britan.* (xiii. p. 641) by Professor Robertson Smith, to whom the writer of this Appendix is much indebted.

INDICES

I. GENERAL

Abraham seeing Christ's day, meaning of, 201
Abraham's seed, supposed privileges of, 70, 120, 193, 196
abstract for concrete, 176
adultery, the woman taken in, 181—186; internal evidence as to authenticity of the passage, 181; external evidence, 362
Aenon, 108
Agony, the, implied but not narrated by S. John, 257, 313
Ahithophel and Absalom, 307
Alexander the Great and the Samaritans, 118
Alford on Christ's dismissal of the adulteress, 186; on the basis of the authenticity of the Gospel narrative, 281
allegories in S. John, 215, 283
Alogi, rejection of the Fourth Gospel by, xxiii
Alphaeus, or Clopas, 169, 330
Ambrose's mistaken charge against the Arians, 102
analysis of the Gospel, brief, xl; in detail, lxi—lxiv
anathema, Jewish forms of, 208
Andrew, character of, 84, 148, 256
angels, 88; appear once only in S. John's narrative, 340
Annas, his office and influence, 310; examination of Jesus before him peculiar to S. John, 310
Anselm on the gift of the Spirit, 343
antithetic parallelism, 65, 71, 77
aorist and imperfect, 89, 122, 127, 241
aorist and perfect, 192, 210, 237, 285, 346
aorist imperative, 257, 327
Apocalypse, relation of the Fourth Gospel to the, xxxiii; similarities between the two, 71, 80, 82, 115, 175, 183, 255, 265, 288, 319, 335
Apocryphal Gospels, miracles of the Child Jesus in, 92
aposiopesis, 163
Apostles' defects stated without reserve, 92, 97, 122, 124, 236, 254, 274, 276, 280, 303, 313, 345
Apostolic Fathers, witness of, to the Fourth Gospel, xxi, xxii
appearances of Jesus after the Resurrection sufficiently attested, 338
Arianism condemned, 136, 226
Aristophanes quoted, 290, 330
Aristotle on the invisibility of God, 75
Arrian quoted, 127
article, force of the, 106, 140, 179, 197, 256, 259, 294

article, absence of the, 87, 162, 205, 251, 259, 292, 313, 325, 344, 350
article repeated, very frequent in S. John, 116, 117, 193
article with Ἱεροσόλυμα peculiar to S. John, 89
assimilation a frequent cause of corruption of the text, lvii, lviii, 89, 113, 130, 145, 167, 183, 203
attempts to proclaim Jesus king, 150, 254
attempts to arrest Jesus, 175, 179, 249
attempts to stone Jesus, 202, 226
attraction, 191, 350
Ascension, the, implied but not narrated by S. John, 104, 105, 163, 258, 341
asyndeton, 67, 74, 111, 224, 274, 340
augment, triple, 203
Augustine, on S. John's living in the grave, xviii; on sacred solitude, 134; on selfishness in religion, 154; on the paragraph respecting the adulteress, 181, 186; on ἕν ἐσμεν, 226; on the voluntariness of Christ's death, 332; on differences in the Gospels, 361; quoted, 121, 124, 136, 148, 157, 166, 168, 191, 243, 328

Bacon, Lord, on Pilate's question, 319; on the rending of His garment, 329
Baptism, the, implied but not narrated by S. John, xlix
Baptism, of John, 108; of Jesus, 108, 113, 114
Baptism, Christian, referred to in the Fourth Gospel, 102, 334
Baptist, the, his connexion with the Evangelist, xiv. 83; his threefold testimony, 76—83; crisis in his ministry, 76; argument from his being called simply 'John' by the Evangelist, xxxii, 67
Barabbas, 320, 321, 328
Barnabas, Epistle of, its witness to the Fourth Gospel, xxi
Bartholomew, reasons for identifying him with Nathanael, 86; *see* Nathanael
barley loaves, 149
Basilides, xxii
baskets, significant distinction of, 149
Bernard on Christ's coming and departure, 264
Bethabara, a false reading, 79
Bethany, two places of this name, xxxii
Bethesda, an uncertain reading, 131
Bethsaida, two places of this name, xxxii, 86, 147
blasphemy, the Lord accused of, 136, 202, 226
blind, man born, 204; his progressive faith, 207; his confession of faith, 211
brethren of the Lord, various theories respecting, 93, 168, 331; cannot be the sons of Alphaeus, 94, 169
bride, figure of the Church, 109

Caesar's friend, 325
Caesar, setting oneself against, 325
Caesarea, Pilate's head-quarters, 319, 325
Caiaphas, his office, character, and prophecy, 247, 248
Calvary, its position, 328
Cana, two places of this name, xxxii; nature of the miracle at, 91, 93
Capernaum, the modern *Tell-Hûm*, 93, 163; argument from the mention of a brief visit to, 93
capital punishment, whether al-

lowed to the Jews by the Romans, 184, 316
Cardinal Newman, on the discourses in S. John's Gospel, 100
casus pendens, 157, 178, 284, 299
centurion's servant different from the nobleman's son, 128, 129
Cerinthus, the Fourth Gospel attributed to, xxiii
change of gender, 69, 157, 299
changes of tense, 122, 127, 133, 155, 225, 241
characteristics of the Fourth Gospel, xli—xlix, 66, 68—70, 81, 82, 88, 99
chief priests, mostly Sadducees, 175, 176, 246; their baseness, 327
Christology of S. John and of the Synoptists, 139
chronology of the Fourth Gospel consistent but often undefined, xxx, l, 108, 124, 131, 145, 146, 167, 223
Chrysostom, 90, 201, 357
Church, first beginning of the, 83; Christ's prayer for, 302—304; powers granted to the, 344
Circumcision prior to the Sabbath, 173
cleansing of the Temple in S. John distinct from that in the Synoptists, 96
Clement of Alexandria quoted, xli, 359, xxii, xxxvi
Clementine Homilies, 204, 219
Clementine Recognitions, 68
climax, 69, 354
cloths, 245, 336, 339
Clopas or Alphaeus, 330
cocks not excluded from Jerusalem, 313
codices, principal, which contain the Fourth Gospel, lv; relations between, lvi, lvii
coincidences between S. Paul and S. John, 69, 70, 279, 359; between the Synoptists and S. John, xlix, liii, 149, 306, 338, 359· between the Fourth Gospel and Revelation, xxxiii, 71, 80, 82, 115, 175, 183, 255, 265, 288, 319, 335
Commandment, Christ's new, 271; its comprehensiveness, 285
Communion of Saints, the, scriptural, 201
Conder, on Bethany, 79; on Calvary, 328
connexion of thought in S. John sometimes obscure, 141, 191
Court of the Women, 187, 189
corruption of the text, *see* false readings, glosses, &c.
cross, size of the, 332; title on the, 328
crown of thorns, 322
crurifragium, 333
cup of suffering, coincidence with the Synoptists respecting, 310

date of the Gospel, xxxvi, 131, 238, 239
darkness, in a figurative sense, for moral darkness, peculiar to S. John, 66, 270
David's flight probably not alluded to in xviii. 1, 307
death, punishment of, whether allowed to the Jews by the Romans, 184, 316
Dedication, Feast of, 223, 224; its mention evidence that the Evangelist is a Jew, xxviii
delegated authority of Christ, 81
demon, *see* devil
denials, S. Peter's, 311; why narrated by S. John, 313; difficulties respecting, 360
descent of the Spirit, its effects, 81
destruction of Jerusalem, the Fourth Gospel written after the, xxxvi, 131, 238, 239
devil, personal existence of the, 197; his influence over Judas, 264, 269, 166

devil or demon, Christ accused of being possessed by a, 207, 199, 223
difficult passages, 126, 190, 195, 197, 218, 257, 341
disciples' imperfections candidly admitted, 92, 97, 122, 124, 236, 254, 274, 276, 280, 308, 313, 345
discourses in the Fourth Gospel contrasted with those in the Synoptic Gospels, li, 99, 100
Divine Generation of Christ, 196, 296
Divinity plainly claimed by Jesus, 192, 198, 276, 280, 285, 288
Docetism utterly foreign to the Fourth Gospel, 71, 116, 152, 170, 334
Döllinger quoted, xxiv, 316
door of the fold, allegory of the, 215, 218
dove visible at the Baptism, 81

Ecce Homo quoted, 321
East, turning to the, a very ancient custom, 187
Elijah, argument from the Baptist's denial that he is, 78
epexegetic clauses common in S. John, 70, 74, 339
Ephesus, the abode of S. John, xvi, xvii; the place where he wrote his Gospel, xxxv, 68; the elders of, the probable authors of xxi. 24, 356
Ephraim, a town called, 248
Epilogue, an afterthought, 348
Epiphanius, on Ebion, xvii; on the Alogi, xxiii
Epistle, First of S. John, its relation to the Gospel, liv, 303; coincidences between it and the Gospel, 68, 72, 80, 81, 82, 105, 278
eternal life the present possession of believers, 112, 138, 159, 161, 299, 364; the phrase a favourite one with S. John, 105
Eucharist, implied in the discourse on the Bread of Life, 153, 154, 160, 267; the institution omitted by S. John, xlix, 267, 283; symbolized at the Crucifixion, 334
Evangelists, concurrence of all four, liii, 88, 145, 306, 338, 360
evening, S. John's method of reckoning the, 128, 342
evenings, the two Jewish, 151
examination of Jesus before Annas peculiar to S. John, 310
excommunication, Jewish, 180, 208, 211; the lot of Christians, 291; external evidence of the authenticity of the Gospel, xx—xxiv

faith, gradual progress in, 119, 129, 207, 240, 339
faith in Jesus Christ, the test of a child of God, 70; the beginning and end of the Fourth Gospel, 346, 347, xxxviii; without sight, 346
false readings, their evidence to the date of the Gospel, 70, 71, 75, 102, 104, 211
feast, the unnamed in v. 1, probably not a Passover, 131
feasts, Jewish, S. John has exact knowledge of, xxvii; groups his narrative round, 94
fickleness of the multitude, *see* multitude
five thousand, the feeding of the, superiority of S. John's account of, 148
forger of a gospel confronted by insuperable difficulties, xxv, xxvi
four thousand, coincidences in the feeding of the, 149
fourth commandment, the stronghold of Jewish religiousness, 133
fragments, argument from the command to gather up the, 149

funeral customs among the Jews, 238, 239, 245, 336
futile questions, 91, 149, 161, 350, 351

Gabbatha, or Gab Baitha, not a mosaic pavement, but the Temple-Mound, 328
Galileans, characteristics of, xii; ill repute of, 86, 179, 181
Galilee, mixed population in, xiii; prophets from, 181; Christ's ministry in, 167
gaps in S. John's narrative, l, 145, 146, 167, 223, 337
garments, 264, 322, 329
Gemara, the Babylonian, quoted, 249
Generation, Divine, of the Son, 196, 296
genitive after superlative, 73, 287
Gentiles, the, seek Christ, 255; are to be sought through the dispersed Jews, 177; are Christ's sheep, 221; are sons of God, 70; are sharers in the Atonement, 80; the Dispersion among the, 176
Gerizim, temple on Mount, 119
Gethsemane, anticipation of, 257
glosses intruded into the text, lviii, 98, 111, 130, 144, 182, 184, 185, 203, 230, 337
Gnostic demonology, 197, 198
Gnostics, the witness of, to the Fourth Gospel, xxv
Gnosticism excluded from the Fourth Gospel, xxiv, 71, 104, 120, 152, 227, 229, 334, 347
Godet quoted, 86, 91, 108, 178, 211
Golgotha, or place of a skull, 328
Gospel, Fourth, not a biography, xxxvii, 145, 346
grace before meat, 149
grave, 238; of Lazarus, 244; of Christ, 336, 339
Greek names among the Apostles, 255, 256
Greeks, *see* Gentiles
guards at the cross, 329

Hall, Bishop, quoted, 331
Hebrew elements in this Gospel; *see* Jewish
Hebrew, evidence that the author of the Fourth Gospel knew, xxix, 158, 254, 267, 335
Hegesippus quoted, 219
Hermas quoted, 219
Herod Antipas, 126, 319
Herod's Praetorium, 314
Herod's sycophancy, 147
Herod's Temple, 97
high-priest, supposed to have prophetic gifts, 247; doubt as to who is meant by the, 311, 312; the disciple known to the, 311, 313
high-priests, rapid changes among the, 247, 310
Holy Spirit, 82, 281, 344
homoeoteleuton, 321
Horace quoted, 251, 322
hyssop, 332

Ignatian Epistles, their evidence to the Fourth Gospel, xxi, 117, 156; quoted, 103, 163, 192, 219
imperative or indicative, doubt as to which is intended, 142, 255, 273, 287, 289
imperative, aorist, 257, 357; present, 134, 186, 341
imperfect, of continued action, 135, 151, 152, 322; descriptive, 177, 184, 229, 268, 311, 313
imperfect and aorist, 89, 122, 127, 241
indirectness of Christ's answers, 235
interpolations, 132, 181, 362; *see* glosses
Ionic form, 89
Irenaeus, his evidence to the Fourth Gospel, xxii, xxxviii; quoted, xvii, 202; his evidence

to the duration of Christ's ministry, li

Jacob, references to the history of, 87, 88; well of, 115, 118

James, brother of S. John, xi; not mentioned by name in this Gospel, 90; possibly the unnamed disciple who was known to the high-priest, 311

Jeremiah, expected to return to life, 78; specially consecrated, 223

Jeremy Taylor on religious zeal, 310

Jerome, on S. John's last days, xviii; on the origin of the Fourth Gospel, xxxvi; on the brethren of the Lord, 94; on Sychar, 115; on the paragraph respecting the adulteress, 182, 362; on Christ's writing on the ground, 185; on Ephraim, 248

Jerusalem, two forms of the name, 77; with the article peculiar to S. John, 89; destroyed before S. John wrote, xxxvi, 131, 238; his minute knowledge of its topography, xvi, xxix

Jesus:

(i) *The Ministry.*

Baptist's testimony to Him, 73, 79; disciples' testimony to Him, 83, 84; turns water into wine at Cana, 89; pays a brief visit to Capernaum, 93; cleanses the Temple the first time, 94; discourses with Nicodemus, 99; and with the woman at the well, 116; converts many Samaritans, 125; heals the royal official's son, 127; and a paralytic at Bethesda, 131; reasons with the Jews about the Son as the Source of Life, 135; feeds five thousand, 146; walks on the water, 151; reasons with the Jews about the Son as the support of Life, 154; with the Twelve about desertion of Him, 165; with His brethren about manifesting Himself, 167; with the Jews at the Feast of Tabernacles, 170; is marked for arrest, 175; [rescues the woman taken in adultery, 183;] claims to be God, 192, 198, 202; heals a man born blind, 205; and reveals Himself to him, 212; delivers the Allegories of the Fold and of the Good Shepherd, 215, 220; reasons with the Jews at the Feast of the Dedication, 223; retires into Peraea, 229; returns to Bethany and raises Lazarus from the dead, 238, 244; is marked for death by Caiaphas, 247; retires to the borders of the desert, 248; returns and is anointed by Mary of Bethany, 250; enters Jerusalem in triumph, 254; is sought by Gentile proselytes, 256; receives the testimony of a voice from heaven, 257; retires from public teaching, 260

(ii) *The Issues of the Ministry.*

washes His disciples' feet, 263; rebukes Peter, 265; points out the traitor, 269; delivers His new commandment, 271; foretells Peter's denials, 272; answers Thomas, 274; Philip, 275; Judas not Iscariot, 280; delivers the allegory of the Vine, 283; promises to send the Paraclete and to return, 290; prays for Himself, 298; for His disciples, 300; for all believers, 302; is arrested in the garden, 307; examined before Annas, 310; denied by Peter, 313; examined by

Pilate, 317; mocked, sentenced and crucified, 322; dies and is buried, 332; manifests Himself after His resurrection to Mary of Magdala, 340; to the ten Apostles, 342; to Thomas, 344; to seven disciples at the sea of Tiberias, 348; gives the second miraculous draught of fishes, 350; gives Peter his last commission and foretells his death, 352; rebukes his curiosity about the Evangelist, 355

Jewish elements in the Fourth Gospel, xxvii, xxix, xliv, xlviii, 89, 203, 229

Jews, S. John's view of them, 77

John, the Baptist; the Evangelist's manner of naming him, xxxii, 67; his connexion with the Evangelist, xiv, 83; his testimony, 76—83; not the Light but the Lamp, 68, 140; the friend of the Bridegroom, 109; his baptism, 108; his last utterance minatory, 112; not a worker of miracles; importance of this statement, 230

John, the Evangelist; his parentage, xi; his nationality, xii, xiii; his connexion with the Baptist, xiv, 83; his fiery zeal, xv, xvii; gives a home to the Blessed Virgin, xv, 331; life at Ephesus, xvi, xvii, xlix; traditions about him, xviii; his chief characteristics, xviii, xix; probably the unnamed disciple in i. 35, 83; and in xviii. 15, 311; certainly 'the disciple whom Jesus loved,' xxxi, xxxiv, 268; in his Gospel speaks only thrice, xxxiv

John, the father of Peter, 85, 352

Jordan, ford of, at Bethany, 79; its associations, 79

Joseph, husband of the Blessed Virgin, 89

Joseph of Arimathea, 335; his connexion with Nicodemus, 336

Josephus, on the date of Herod's Temple, 97; on the removal of Israel at the captivity, 118; on the Jews' love of liberty, 193; on a stoning in the Temple, 202; on the rudeness of the Sadducees, 247; on Ephraim, 248; on the tesselated pavement, 325; on the high-priest's tunic, 329; his language about the Kedron, 305, 306; about the sea of Galilee, 146

Judas; six persons so named in N.T., 280

Judas Iscariot; his name and character, 166; murmurs at Mary of Bethany, 251; receives the sop and goes out into the night, 269, 270; helps to arrest Jesus, 308

Judas not Iscariot; the nature of his question, 280

Judas of Galilee, rising of, xiii

Justin Martyr; knew the Fourth Gospel, xxii; seems to quote it twice, 78, 101; twice states that Jesus healed those who were diseased from birth, 204

Kedron, ravine of the; doubt as to the reading, 305; meaning of the name, 306; significance of Christ's crossing the ravine, 307

kingdom, nature of Christ's, 101, 150, 318

Lactantius on the *crurifragium*, 333

Last Day; the phrase peculiar to S. John, 157

Lazarus, objections to the raising of, 231, 232; identifications of, 232; conspired against, 253

Levites, argument from the mention of, 77

Liddon, on the discourse with Nicodemus, 103
Life, 65, 256, 275; eternal, 105, 106
Light, of Christ, 66, 187, 205, 259; of the Baptist, 140, 308
Lightfoot, Bishop, on the witness of the Ignatian Epistles to the Fourth Gospel, xxi; on πλήρωμα, 73; on the Shechinah, 71; on the vivid descriptive traits in this Gospel, 269; on the meaning of Paraclete, 279; on ὁ Χριστός, 74
Litotes, or understatement, 106, 157, 195
living water, meaning of, 117
Lord or Sir, 117, 156, 212
Love, the Fourth Gospel the Gospel of, xix, liv, 214, 271, 285
Lucretius quoted, 86
Luther on futile questions, 161

Magdalene; *see* Mary Magdalene
Majestas, Pilate's fear of being accused to Tiberius of, 325
Malchus, mentioned by name by S. John alone, 309, 313
Manasseh, founder of the rival worship on Gerizim, 119
Marcion's rejection of the Fourth Gospel, xxiii
marriage, Christ gives His sanction to, 93; symbolical of His relation to His Church, 109
Martha of Bethany, probably the eldest of the family, 234, 239; coincidence between S. John and S. Luke respecting her, liii, 239; her progressive faith, 240
Mary Magdalene, introduced as a person well known, 165; at the Cross, 330; at the sepulchre, 338; manifestation to her, 340; nature of the rebuke to her, 341
Mary of Clopas, probably the wife of Clopas and mother of James the less, 330
Mary of Bethany, different from the 'sinner' of Luke vii. 37 and from Mary Magdalene, 233; coincidence between S. John and S. Luke respecting her, liii, 239; her devotion, 251; coincidence respecting her name and promised fame, 252
Mary, the Blessed Virgin, never named by S. John, 90; rebuked for interference at Cana, 90; her relationship to the brethren of the Lord, 93, 168; to S. John, xi, 330; no special manifestation to her after the Resurrection, 342; her death, whether at Jerusalem or Ephesus, xvi
Maurice, F. D., quoted, 65, 315
McClellan, on Christ's writing on the ground, 184; on the hour of the Crucifixion, 326
measures, of quantity, 91; of distance, 239, 350
Messiah, Jewish ideas respecting, well known to the Evangelist, xxvii, 78, 87, 89, 150, 174, 179, 259; Samaritan ideas respecting, 114, 122
Meyer, on the last words of the Baptist, 110; on the discourse on the Bread of Life, 166; on the Jewish hierarchy, 170; on the gift of the Spirit, 179; on the raising of Lazarus, 232
ministry, duration of Christ's, l, li, 202
miracles in N.T., their character, 92, 93; in the Fourth Gospel, symbolical, xliii, xliv, 92, 129, and spontaneous, 132; culminate in the raising of Lazarus, 231; confined to the ministry, 98; not attributed to John the Baptist, 230
mission, of Jesus, 81, 106, 124, 141, 172, 175, 228, 300; of the Paraclete, 281, 288, 289, 292; of the Baptist, 67, 81, 199; of the disciples, 81, 268, 302, 343

money, changers of, 95; sums of, 148, 251
Moses, the actual giver, neither of the Law, 74; nor of the manna, 155; testifies to the Christ, 86, 144; and against the Jews, 144, 173; contrasted with Christ, 155, 210
Mount Gerizim, temple on, 119
Mount of Olives, not mentioned by S. John, 183
Mount of the Temple, 325
multitude, fickleness of the, 150, 155, 163, 167, 179, 188, 190, 193, 225, 243, 245, 259
Muratorian Fragment, xxii, xxxv

Nathanael, possibly the same as Bartholomew, 86; his character, 87
Nazarene, 308
Nazareth, evil repute of, 86
Neapolis, or Sychem, 115
new commandment, 271
Newman, Cardinal, on the discourses in S. John's Gospel, 100
Nicodemus, mentioned by S. John only, 100; his character, 100, 180, 335; coincidence between S. John and S. Mark respecting him, 336
nobleman's son distinct from the centurion's servant, 128, 129
nominative indefinite, 284
nominativus pendens, 157, 178, 299

objections, S. John's manner of treating, 86, 179
Olives, Mount of, *see* Mount
optative mood rare in N.T., 67
orally, the Fourth Gospel delivered at first, xxxvi, liv, 356
Origen, mainly responsible for the reading Bethabara in i. 28, 79; on the Jewish lie respecting Christ's birth, 196; on Christ's voluntary surrender, 307; on the crucifixion of S. Peter, 354

Papias, knew the First Epistle of S. John, xxii; a possible source of the paragraph about the adulteress, 182
parables, not found in the Fourth Gospel, 215; principles of interpretation of, 104, 216
Paraclete, threefold office of, 292; mission of, 281, 288, 289
parallelism in the Fourth Gospel, xlviii, 156, 190, 288; *see* antithetic
paralytic at Bethesda, 132
Passion, prominent thoughts in S. John's narrative of the, 305; reason for the space allotted to the trials in the, 310; probable order of events in the, 361
Passover, customs at the, 268, 269, 270, 320, 359; the first in Christ's ministry, 94; the second, 147; the last, 263; the unnamed Feast in v. 1 not the Passover, 130, 131; the Last Supper not the Passover, 358, 359
Paul, coincidences between S. John and S., 69, 70, 279, 359
pendens, casus, see *casus*
Pentecost anticipated, 343
perfect and aorist, *see* aorist
perfect with present meaning, 73, 143
Peter, brought to Jesus by his brother Andrew and named by Jesus, 84, 85; his impetuosity, 265, 272, 309, 339, 350, 355; his intimacy with S. John, xiii, 269, 311, 339, 355; his primacy fully recognised by S. John, xxxiv; his confessions, 165; his denials, 360; his repentance implied but not narrated by S. John, 352; argument from the method of naming him in xxi, 352; Christ's last commission to

him and prediction of his death, 353, 354
Pharisees, the only Jewish sect named by S. John, 78; their position, 76, 78, 100, 180, 207, 246; are led by the Sadducean hierarchy in the persecution of Jesus, 249
Philip, found by Jesus, 85; consulted by Him, 147, 148; rebuked by Him, 276; his character, 256, 275
Philo, his doctrine of the Logos compared with S. John's, 63, 64, 71; on Herod's Praetorium, 314; on the character of Pilate, 329
Pilate, introduced as well known to the reader, 316; his residence, 319, 325; his first words to Jesus, 317; his attempts to avoid putting Jesus to death, 316; his famous question, 319; his policy, 322; his conflicting fears, 324, 325; his character, 329; his recall to Rome, li
Plautus quoted, 191
Pliny quoted, 335
Plutarch quoted, 184
Polybius' use of σπεῖρα for maniple, 307
Polycarp's evidence to the First Epistle of S. John, xxii; fallacious argument from his controversy with Anicetus, xxxiv, xxxv
Polycrates on S. John's sacerdotal dress, xvii
Porphyry's charge against Jesus, 170
Praetorium, 314
Prayer of the Great High Priest, where spoken, 298
predestinarianism not countenanced in the Fourth Gospel, 166, 204, 225
pregnant construction, 81, 87, 112, 325, 343, 349
preposition apparently transposed, 239, 250, 350
priests, 77; mostly Sadducees, yet combine with the Pharisees against Jesus, 180, 246, 249
primacy of S. Peter, *see* Peter
Procession of the Holy Spirit, 289
Prophet, the, 78, 150, 179, 241
Prophets, the, as a division of Scripture, 159
Procurator, Pilate as, has no Quaestor to conduct the examination, 317; nor lictors to inflict the scourging, 322
prophecies fulfilled in Christ, 86, 95, 144, 179, 254, 259, 317, 330, 331, 335
psychological consistency in S. John's narrative, 100, 115, 119, 127, 128, 207, 237, 240, 244, 265, 275, 309, 339, 344, 345
punctuation, differences of, 65, 173, 208, 235, 248, 257, 270, 277, 296
purification, ceremonial, 91, 109, 248
Purim, Feast of, 131
purple robe, 322
purpose, constructions implying, frequent in S. John, xlvii, 68, 124, 125, 127, 201, 204, 247, 256
purpose of the Gospel, xxxvii, liv, 303, 346, 347

Rabbi, meaning of, 83; not to be rendered 'Master,' 123
Rabbinical sayings and traditions, 78, 122, 134, 174, 180, 184, 244
Rabboni, a Galilean form, 341
readings, important differences of, lvii, 66, 70, 71, 75, 79, 130, 160, 170, 211, 269, 305, 312, 348
remission of sins by the Church, 344
repetition, characteristic of S. John, xlvi, 106, 162, 219, 259, 286
reserve about all connected with

himself characteristic of S. John, 84, 90, 311, 330, 349
resurrection, spiritual, 137, 138; actual, 139; of the wicked, 140; of Lazarus, 231; of Christ, 338; Jewish belief respecting, 240
Revelation, *see* Apocalypse
robber or bandit, 95, 216, 321; S. John and the robber, xvii

Sabbath, the attitude of Jesus towards the, 133; yields to Circumcision and therefore to charity, 173; miracles wrought on the, 207
Sadducees, not mentioned by S. John, 78; combine with the Pharisees against Jesus, 249
Salome, mother of S. John, probably the sister of the Blessed Virgin, 330
Samaria, 116
Samaritan, Jesus called a, 199
Samaritans, 114; their origin, 117; their relations to the Jews, 116, 120; their religion, 120; their idea of the Messiah, 122; their readiness to believe in Jesus, 125
Sanhedrin, its attitude towards the Baptist, 76; towards Jesus, 175, 180, 246; had lost the power to inflict capital punishment, 184, 316; takes part in the arrest of Jesus, 307; in a difficulty respecting His execution, 315; ex-high-priests among its members, 310; S. John's formula for the, 207; its place of meeting, 189
Satan, *see* devil
scourging, inflicted only once on Jesus, 322; with what object, 316, 322, 323
Sebaste, or Samaria, 116, 147
Seneca quoted, 106
sepulchre, 238
serpent, argument from the mention of the, 104
signs, miracles to S. John are, 92, 212
Siloam, identified with *Birket Silwân*, 206; the pouring of the water from, 177
Simon, S. John's usage in applying this name to S. Peter, 352
Solomon's Porch, 224
Son of Man, use of the phrase in the O. T. and in the Gospels, 88
spiral movement, in the Prologue, 75; in the last discourses, 273
style of S. John, xlvi—xlviii, 219
subjunctive, after a past tense, 67; after verbs of wishing, 320
Suetonius quoted, 264, 325
superscription or title, of the Gospel, 61; on the cross, 328
Supper, at Bethany, 251; the Last, 264; its character, 359
Sychar, probably not Sychem, 115
symbolical interpretations of Scripture, authorised by Christ, 212; to be made with caution, 351
symbolism a characteristic of the Fourth Gospel, xliii, 100, 206, 224, 270, 307
synagogue at Capernaum, existing ruins of, 163
Synoptic Gospels, their relation to the Fourth, xlix—liii, 145, 306, 337

Tabernacles, Feast of, 168; special ceremonies at the, 177, 187
table, mode of reclining at, 268
Talmud, on thanksgiving, 149; on Elijah's return, 78; on the execution of Jesus, 249, 359; on the uncleanness of fowls, 313; on capital punishment, 316
Targums, their use of the periphrasis 'Word of God,' 63
Tatian; his testimony to the Fourth Gospel, 65, 66

Temple; traffic in the Court of the Gentiles, 94; date of building, 97; treasury in the Court of the Women, 189; Christ's public teaching there, 171, 186, 225; Solomon's Porch, 224

Tertullian, gives three renderings of Λόγος, 62; witnesses to very early differences of reading, 70, 211; to the crucifixion of S. Peter at Rome, 354; to the story of S. John at Latin Gate, xvii; to the true 'Note of the Church,' 272; quoted, 312

Thaddaeus, or Judas, 280

Theophilus of Antioch, xxii

Thomas, name and character of, 237, 238, 274, 363; compared with Philip, 275; nature of his scepticism, 345, 346; his confession the conclusion of the Gospel, 339, 346

thorns, crown of, 322

Tiberias, not mentioned by the Synoptists, 146, 348; because a new town, 147; a centre of education, xiii; various names for the sea of, 146

Tiberius; chronology of his reign in connexion with Christ's ministry, li; Pilate's fear of him, 325

title, *see* superscription

tomb, 238, 339

tragic brevity in S. John, 270, 321

tragic tone in S. John, 66, 69, 104, 106, 111, 142, 156

Transfiguration, not recorded by S. John, xxiii; nor alluded to in v. 37, 141

transmigration of souls, 204

treasury in the Court of the Women, 189

Trench, Archbishop, on the character of S. Thomas, 237; on a tradition respecting Lazarus, 245

trial of Jesus, why given at such length in the Gospels, 310; the ecclesiastical, 310—313; the civil, 314—327

triple augment, 203

triumphal entry into Jerusalem, date of the, 253; Messianic in its externals, 254; two multitudes at, 255

Truth, Jesus is the, 274; the Gospel is the, 319

Twelve, the, spoken of as well known, 165

typical characters in the Fourth Gospel, xliii, 129

typical miracles, xliii, 351

Uncial manuscripts, table of, lv; their relations to one another, lvi

Unitarianism condemned, 136, 226, 345

Vedas quoted, 65

Versions, table of ancient, lvi

vine, allegory of, how suggested, 283

vinegar, 331

Virgil quoted, 158

voice in the wilderness, 78

voices from heaven, 258

washing the disciples' feet, 264

washing the saints' feet, 266

water, the living, 117; from Siloam, 177

water, Christ walking on the, 151

Way, Jesus is the, 274, 275; Christianity is the, 274

Westcott, on the relation between the Fourth Gospel and the Synoptists, liii; on the discourse on the Bread of Life, 153; on S. John's style, 219; on the scene of, xvii, 298; on the narratives of the Passion and of the Resurrection, 305, 338

Westcott and Hort on the number of doubtful readings in N.T., lviii; on the paragraph respecting the adulteress, 363

wine, amount of water turned into, 91; objections answered, 93
women prominent in S. John's narrative, xliii, 330
words from the cross, 361, 362

Xenophon quoted, 103

II. GREEK

ἀγαπᾶν, 105, 137, 234, 352
ἁγιάζειν, 228, 302
ἀδελφοί, οἱ, 355
αἵματα, 70
αἴρειν, 80, 222
αἰτεῖν, 278, 295
αἰτεῖσθαι, 240
αἰτία, 320
αἰῶνα, εἰς τὸν, 200, 363
αἰώνιος, 105, 106, 363
ἀκολούθει μοι, 85
ἀληθινός, 68, 121, 155
ἀλλ' ἵνα, 68
Ἄλογοι, xxiii
ἀμὴν ἀμήν, 88
ἀνά, distributive, 91
ἀναβλέπειν, 207
ἀνακεῖσθαι, 268
ἀναμάρτητος, 185
ἀναπίπτω, 269
ἄνδρες and ἄνθρωποι, οἱ, 149, 123
ἀντί, 74
ἀντιλέγειν, 325
ἀντλεῖν, 91
ἄνωθεν, 101, 110
ἀπαρχή, 359
ἀπείθειν, 112
ἀπό of distance, apparently transposed, 239, 350
ἀποκρίνεσθαι, 135
ἀποστέλλειν, 67, 81
ἀποσυνάγωγος, 208
ἀπὸ τῶν used substantively, 350
ἀριστᾶν, 351
ἄρτι, 92, 296
ἀρχή, 62
ἀρχήν, τὴν, 190
ἀρχιερεῖς, 175
ἀρχιτρίκλινος, 91
ἄρχομαι, 264
ἄρχων, 100
ἄρχων, ὁ τοῦ κόσμου τούτου, 258
αὐλή and ποίμνη, 221
ἀφ' ἑαυτοῦ, 137, 293
ἀφῆκεν, 114, 123, 192

βαΐα, 254
βάλλειν, 133, 345
βαπτίζειν, 79, 82
βασιλικός, 126
βαστάζειν, 226, 252
βῆμα, 325
βόσκειν, 353
βραχίων Κυρίου, 260
βρῶμα and βρῶσις, 126

γαζοφυλακίον, 189
γεγραμμένον ἐστίν, 95
γεωργός, 283
γίνεσθαι and εἶναι, 62, 65, 67
γίνεσθαι εἰς, 294
γινώσκειν, 69, 98, 174, 200, 201, 228
γλωσσόκομον, 252
γογγύζειν, 158, 175
γραμματεῖς, 183
γραφή, ἡ, 97

δαιμόνιον, 199
δακρύειν, 243
δέδωκεν, 112
δηνάριον, 148, 251
διὰ τοῦτο, 135, 173
διασπορά, 176, 177
δικαιοσύνη, 292
δόξα, 72, 142, 143
δὸς δόξαν τῷ Θεῷ, 209

δύναμις, 69, 92

Εβραϊστί, 132, 341
ἐγκαίνια, 224
Ἐγώ εἰμι, 151, 156, 190, 308
ἔθνος, 247, 248
εἰ with the aorist, 117; with the imperfect, 144
εἰδέναι and γινώσκειν, 98
εἶναι and γίνεσθαι, 62, 65, 67
εἶναι ἐκ, 110
εἰς τέλος, 263
εἰς τὸν αἰῶνα, 200, 363
ἐκ, different forces of, 102, 109, 110, 111, 116, 164, 257
ἐκ τούτου, 164, 324
ἐκ τῶν used substantively, 78, 179, 350
ἐκβάλλειν, 211
ἐκεῖνος, S. John's use of, 67, 75, 134, 206, 212, 216
ἐκκεντᾶν, 335
ἐκπορεύεσθαι, 288, 289
ἐλέγχειν, 107, 292
ἐλήλυθεν ἡ ὥρα, 256
ἑλκύειν, 158, 259
Ἕλληνες, 117, 255
ἐμβλέπειν, 83
ἐμβριμᾶσθαι, 242
ἐμφανίζειν, 282
ἐμφυσᾶν, 343
ἐν, different forces of, 97, 107, 189
ἐν τῷ ὀνόματί μου, 277, 281
ἐνταφιασμός, 252
ἐξηγεῖσθαι, 75
ἐξουσία, 69, 222
ἐπάρατος, 180
ἐπίγεια and ἐπουράνια, 104
ἐρωτᾶν, 240, 278, 295
ἐσχατη ἡμέρα, ἡ, 157
εὐχαριστεῖν, 149
ἔχειν μέρος, 265
ἕως, 205, 355

ζάω, 145
ζωή, 65, 256, 275
ζωὴ αἰώνιος, 105, 106, 363

ἡμέρα, ἡ ἐσχάτη, 157

θεᾶσθαι, 72
θέλειν, 151, 165, 171, 197, 304
θεοσεβής, 210
θεωρεῖν, 147, 157
θυρωρός, 216

ἴδε and ἰδού, 80
ἴδια, τὰ, 69
ἱερόν and ναός, 94, 96
Ἱεροσόλυμα and Ἱερουσαλήμ, 77
ἱμάτια, τὰ, 264, 329
ἵνα, xlvii, 124, 127, 201, 204
ἵνα with the indicative, 299
Ἰουδαῖοι, οἱ, 77
Ἰσκαριώτης, 166
Ἰσραήλ, 104

καθίζειν, 325
καί intensive, 211
Καϊάφας, 247
καινός and νέος, 271
καιρός, 169
καλεῖν, 217
καλός, 220, 226
καλῶς, 198
κατακρίνειν, 186
καταλαμβάνειν, 66
κειρίαι, 245
κερματιστής, 94
Κηφᾶς, 85
κλαίειν, 242, 294
κλέπτης and λῃστής, 216, 321
κλῆμα, 283
κοιμᾶσθαι, 236
κολλυβιστής, 95
κομψότερον ἔχειν, 127
κόσμον, ἔρχεσθαι εἰς τὸν, 241
κόσμος, 69, 169
κόφινος, 149
κράβαττος, 133
κράζειν, 73, 174, 261
κραυγάζειν, 245
κρίμα, 212
κρίνειν and κρίσις, 106, 139, 140, 187
κύριε, 117, 156, 212

λαλεῖν, 111, 191
λαλία and λόγος, 125, 196
λαμπάς, 307, 308

λαός and ἔθνος, 247
Λιθόστρωτον, 325
λόγος, 111, 125, 163, 196
Λόγος, ὁ, 62
λούεσθαι, 265
λύειν, 135, 227
λύχνος, 140, 308

μακάριος, 267
μαρτυρία, 67, 82
μεθύσκεσθαι, 92
μέλλειν, 127, 166
μέν without δέ, 235
μένειν, 81
μέντοι, 122
μέρος ἔχειν, 265
Μεσσίας, 85, 122
μετὰ ταῦτα, 108, 265
μετὰ τοῦτο, 108
μετρητής, 91
μή interrogative, 123, 311
μή and οὐ, 164
μισθωτός, 220
μνημεῖον, 238
μονή, 273
μονογενής, 72

ν ἐφελκυστικόν, 61
Ναζωραῖος, 308
ναός, 94, 96, 97
νέος and καινός, 271
νίπτω, 206
νόμος, ὁ, 227, 259, 288
νύμφη, 109
νύττειν, 333

ὁδός, ὁ, 274
ὀθόνια, 336
οἶδα, 98
ὄνομα, 70, 277, 281
ὄντως, 194
ὄξος, 331
ὄρθρου, 183
ὀρφανός, 279
οὖν, xlvii, 109, 159, 184, 309, 312, 313
οὗτος, S. John's use of, 64, 100, 111, 172
οὗτος as predicate, 106, 159, 299
οὗτος contemptuous, 109, 158, 171, 177, 207, 259
ὄφις, 104
ὀψάριον, 149
ὀψία, 151
ὄψις, 174, 245

παιδάριον, 148
παιδία, 349
παιδίον and παῖς, 127
πάντα and τὰ πάντα, 65
παρά, 67
παραδίδωμι, 266, 307
παράκλητος, 278
παρακύπτειν, 339
παραλαμβάνειν, 69
παρασκευή, 326, 333, 358
παροιμία, 217
παῤῥησίᾳ, 171
πᾶσα σάρξ, 299
Πατήρ, ὁ, 120
πέμπειν, 81
πέταλον, xvii
πηγή, 115
πιστεύειν, 67, 138, 155
πιστεύειν εἰς, 70
πιστικός, 251
πλανᾶσθαι, 180
πλήρωμα, 73
πνεῦμα, 103, 178, 242, 268
Πνεῦμα Ἅγιον, 82, 281, 344
ποιεῖν, 106
ποιεῖν ἑαυτόν, 201
ποιεῖν τὴν ἀλήθειαν, 107
ποιεῖσθαι, 273
ποιμαίνειν, 353
ποίμνη and αὐλή, 222
ποῖος, 227, 259, 317
πονηρός, ὁ, 302
πονηρός and φαῦλος, 106
πραιτώριον, 314
πράσσειν and ποιεῖν, 106
πρό apparently transposed, 250, 263
προβατική, 131
προσεύχεσθαι, 240
προσκυνεῖν, 212
προσφάγιον, 349
προσφέρειν, 291
προφήτης, 119, 208

προφήτης, ὁ, 78, 150, 179
προφῆται, οἱ, 159
πρῶτον ὑμῶν, 287
πρῶτός μου, 73

Ραββί, 83, 123
ῥάπισμα, 312, 322
ῥήματα, 111
Ῥωμαϊστί, 329

σάββατα, τὰ, 338
σάρξ, 71, 160, 161, 164, 299
σημεῖον, 92
σκανδαλίζειν, 290
σκελοκοπία, 333
σκηνοπηγία, 168
σκηνοῦν, 71
σκληρός, 163
σκοτία, 66
σουδάριον, 245, 339
σπεῖρα, 307
στήκειν, lvii, 197
συνάγεσθαι, 307
συνέδριον, 246
σφραγίζειν, 111
σχίσμα, 179
σώζειν ἐκ, 257

τάχιον, 339
τέκνα Θεοῦ, 69
τέκνια, 271
τελειοῦν, 124
τέρατα, 92
τεταρταῖος, 244
τηρεῖν, 200, 288
τί ἐμοὶ καὶ σοί; 90
Τιβεριάς, 146
τιθέναι, 220
τίτλος, 328
τρώγειν, 161

ὕδατος, ἐξ, 102
ὑδρία, 91, 123
υἱὸς, 127, 259
υἱὸς τοῦ ἀνθρώπου, ὁ, 88, 139
υἱὸς τῆς ἀπωλείας, ὁ, 301
υἱὸς τοῦ Θεοῦ, ὁ, 82
ὑψωθῆναι, 105, 258

φαίνειν, 66
φανεροῦν, 80, 92, 348
φανός, 307
φαῦλος, 106
φίλος τοῦ Καίσαρος, 325
φιλεῖν, 137, 234, 352
φοίνιξ, 254
φρέαρ, 115
φυλάσσειν, 200, 261
φωνεῖν, 217
φωνή, 78, 141
φῶς, 68, 187, 205, 259

χαίρω, 201
χάρις, 72
χειμαρροῦς, 306, 307
χειμών, 224
χιτών, 329
Χριστός, ὁ, 74, 179
χωρεῖν, 194

ψυχή, 242, 256, 257
ψυχὴν τιθέναι, 220
ψώμιον, 269

ὥρα, 84, 91, 127, 175, 256, 325
Ὡσαννά, 254

Thornapple Commentaries

Alexander, Joseph Addison
The Gospel According to Mark
The Gospel According to Matthew

Bernard, J. H.
The Pastoral Epistles

Henderson, Ebenezer
The Twelve Minor Prophets

Hodge, Charles
A Commentary on the Epistle to the Ephesians
An Exposition of the First Epistle to the Corinthians
An Exposition of the Second Epistle to the Corinthians

Kelly, J. N. D.
A Commentary on the Epistles of Peter and Jude
A Commentary on the Pastoral Epistles

Lightfoot, J. B.
Notes on Epistles of St. Paul

Maier, Walter A.
The Book of Nahum

McNeile, Alan Hugh
The Gospel According to St. Matthew

Moule, H. C. G.
The Epistle to the Philippians

Plummer, Alfred
The Epistles of St. John
The Gospel According to St. John

Selwyn, Edward Gordon
The First Epistle of St. Peter

Shedd, William G. T.
Commentary on Romans

Taylor, Vincent
The Gospel According to St. Mark

Westcott, Brooke Foss
The Gospel According to St. John

Baker Book House, Box 6287, Grand Rapids, Michigan 49506